Growth and Welfare in Advanced Capitalist Economies

Growth and Welfare in Advanced Capitalist Economies

How Have Growth Regimes Evolved?

Edited by
ANKE HASSEL
BRUNO PALIER

OXFORD
UNIVERSITY PRESS

OXFORD
UNIVERSITY PRESS

Great Clarendon Street, Oxford, OX2 6DP,
United Kingdom

Oxford University Press is a department of the University of Oxford.
It furthers the University's objective of excellence in research, scholarship,
and education by publishing worldwide. Oxford is a registered trade mark of
Oxford University Press in the UK and in certain other countries

First Edition published in 2021

Published in the United States of America by Oxford University Press
198 Madison Avenue, New York, NY 10016, United States of America

British Library Cataloguing in Publication Data
Data available

Library of Congress Control Number: 2020942133

ISBN 978–0–19–886617–6

DOI: 10.1093/oso/9780198866176.001.0001

Preface

This book is the product of a long journey of conversations and discussions over the last eight years about the transformation of the welfare state and the tools to analyze it. It started with a series of seminars in France on "croissance et protection sociale" (growth and social protection), organized by Bruno Palier, Nathalie Morel, and Bruno Amable, launched in 2012 with the aim of better connecting economic and social policies, with the support of the French Ministry of Social Affairs.[1] Based on this, the two of us decided to work on an integrated research project that we launched in 2014.

We observe that welfare states of rich industrialized countries develop in very different ways despite common challenges of deindustrialization, financialization, and the rise of the knowledge economy. This observation is not new but a core result of decades of research in comparative political economy. However, the theoretical toolbox for understanding the diversity of welfare and economic systems has not advanced accordingly. Rather the opposite: On the one hand, work based on the concept of the Varieties of Capitalism (VoC) that flourished in the first decade of the 21st century has come to a standstill. On the other hand, new approaches on financialization and the knowledge economy do not embrace enough institutional diversity.

When we started our journey, two important new developments were yet to emerge in comparative political economy. First, the book on *The Politics of Advanced Capitalism* by Beramendi et al. (2015) argued in favor of looking at welfare state developments from the perspective of electoral groups and potential coalitions that underpin party manifestos. In their theory of constrained partisanship, Beramendi et al. propose that different welfare states produce legacies which shape the feasibility sets of parties to pursue new policies. The cleavage of different policies is divided between consumption and investment. This distinction is also key for our understanding when we analyze different social policy reforms. Like Beramendi et al., we aim to explain why governments of some countries pursue investment-based policies and others focus on consumption.

Second, Baccaro and Pontusson (2016) started a new research agenda on the different demand drivers for growth in different countries. Their starting point is post-Keynesian economics and the observation that export-led growth has

[1] Results have been published in Palier, B. and R. Roussel 2016. Stratégies de croissance, emploi et protection sociale. Special issue of the *Revue Française des Affaires sociales*, vol. 1.

fundamentally different implications for wages and distribution than wage-led growth.

Both contributions have been important sources for this book. Our approach focuses on growth strategies as incremental government decisions in favor or against certain policies in the realm of welfare systems. We argue that the welfare state is at the core of growth regimes of national political economies because social policies affect both the demand and the supply side of the economy. For instance, welfare payments affect the activation of long-term unemployed and sustain domestic demand. Education policies shape the skill set of a society and—if provided by the public sector—present a big pool of public sector jobs and thereby demand. Growth regimes, however, are long-term institutional arrangements that specialize in particular economic activities.

Whereas Beramendi et al. (2015) focus on the demand for policies through electoral coalitions and Baccaro and Pontusson (2016) look at the drivers for growth, we combine both perspectives, while keeping the institutional perspective dear to the French Regulation school or Variety of Capitalism, and argue that governments have to mediate between both arenas of electoral politics and growth regimes. The rise of the knowledge economy, as a culmination of the decline of manufacturing, an increase of a diversity of different kinds of service sector activities, and the shift towards service-based innovation, presents governments with a different set of options. These options, we argue, are embedded in different kinds of growth regimes.

The book is grounded in the broad literature of comparative political economy as it has evolved over the last thirty years, starting with Esping-Andersen's *Three Worlds of Welfare Capitalism* (1990). It aims to present a perspective on how to integrate a completely new kind of economy, the knowledge economy, into these theories. It takes financialization and digitalization as a process of reorganization of economies that need the support of government policies. In that sense, it goes beyond a demand-side perspective that Baccaro and Pontusson but also Beramendi et al. provide. Despite the long gestation of the book, we think that we are only at the beginning of understanding new paradigms of the knowledge economy.

We started the project in December 2014 with an initial conference in Paris, which was generously funded by the German Thyssen Foundation and the French Agence Nationale de la Recherche (through its LABEX Sciences Po-LIEPP, Laboratory for Interdisciplinary Evaluation of Public Policies (ANR-11-LABX-0091, ANR-11-IDEX-0005-02)). We had a second meeting one year later, also in Paris, funded by the same organizations. The participants and discussants of these conferences encouraged us to go ahead, and we would like to thank all those present, namely Sonja Avlijaš, Lucio Baccaro, Robert Boyer, Moo-Kwon Chung, Jon Erik Dølvik, María González Menéndez, Ana M. Guillén, Peter A. Hall, Abby Innes, Jette Steen Knudsen, Christian Lyhne Ibsen, Cathie Jo Martin,

Daniel Mügge, Marek Naczyk, George Pagoulatos, Georg Picot, Herman Mark Schwartz, David Soskice, Kathleen Thelen, Chloé Touzet, Christos Triantopoulos, and Anne Wren.

Since then, we have held numerous meetings and made many conference presentations at CES, SASE, Espanet, WZB, the Hertie School, Nuffield College, EUI Florence as well as other workshops. We would like to thank all those who made useful comments to us, without being able to mention them all. During this journey, we also brought on board new project partners such as Tom Chevalier, Alison Johnston, Aidan Regan, Alexander Reisenbichler, and Fritz Scharpf. We had planned in the beginning a comprehensive volume with a number of country case chapters. As the project grew bigger, we took the decision to divide the volume into two separate books. The second book on country cases is now in preparation.

We would like to thank again our contributors for both their strong commitment and their unwavering patience in this journey exploring the evolution of growth regimes in advanced capitalist economies. Also, we benefited tremendously from a lot of support on the way from many people. We would like to thank Licia Bobzien, Joshua Cova, Lukas Jerg, Regina List, Claudia Müller, Julia Seefeld, Felix Sieker, Amanda Slater, and Ivan Tubio Sanles.

Finally, the book also progressed during a time which was professionally challenging for both of us. We both directed research centers that underwent turbulent developments over the last six years. Given the circumstances, it was not always easy to stay on course with the project. Navigating these rough waters demanded a lot from our families. We owe our partners more than gratitude and want to express our love to Hugh Williamson and Nathalie Morel.

Anke Hassel
Bruno Palier

Berlin and Paris
March 2020

Financing acknowledgement: This work is supported by a public grant overseen by the French National Research Agency (ANR) as part of the "Investissements d'Avenir" program LIEPP (ANR-11-LABX-0091, ANR-11-IDEX-0005-02) and by a grant of the Thyssen Foundation.

Contents

PART III: GROWTH STRATEGIES AND WELFARE REFORMS

List of Figures

List of Tables

List of Contributors

Sonja Avlijaš is a Political Economist and Marie Sklodowska-Curie Fellow at Belgrade University's Faculty of Economics. She is also associate research fellow at the Laboratory for Interdisciplinary Evaluation of Public Policies (LIEPP) at Sciences Po. Paris and the 2020 Wayne Vuchinich Fellow at Stanford University. Dr Avlijaš completed her post-doctoral fellowship between 2016 and 2018 at LIEPP-Sciences Po, and she holds a PhD from the London School of Economics and Political Science (LSE). Her research focuses on how the experience of post-socialist transition in Eastern Europe can help us to understand the evolution of capitalist political economies in the era of globalization.

Lucio Baccaro is Director of the Max Planck Institute for the Study of Societies in Cologne. His research focuses on the political economy of labor markets and growth models, and, more recently, on the politics of macroeconomic policy. He has published *Trajectories of Neoliberal Transformation* (with Chris Howell, CUP 2017).

Tom Chevalier is a CNRS Researcher in political science at the research center Arènes. He works on young people in a comparative perspective. Within comparative political economy, he has written on the ways European welfare states structure the transition to adulthood, looking at social protection, education, and active labor market policies. He also works on youth poverty and young people's political attitudes.

Peter A. Hall is Krupp Foundation Professor of European Studies at the Minda de Gunzburg Center for European Studies of Harvard University. Among his publications are edited volumes on *Social Resilience in the Neoliberal Era* (with M. Lamont, 2013), *Successful Societies* (with M. Lamont, 2010), *Changing France* (with P. Culpepper and B. Palier, 2007), *Varieties of Capitalism* (with D. Soskice, 2001) and *The Political Power of Economic Ideas* (1989) as well as *Governing the Economy* (1986) and more than a hundred articles on comparative political economy, politics, and public policy-making in Europe.

Anke Hassel is Professor of Public Policy at the Hertie School. From 2016 to 2019 she was the Scientific Director of the WSI at the Hans Böckler Foundation. Her research focus is on the labor market regulation, social partnership, and comparative political economy of developed industrial nations. She has served as expert in various committees on economic and labor policy of the German Federal Government. Her latest publication is a special issue of the *Journal of European Public Policy* entitled "The Political Economy of Pension Financialisation: Public Policy Responses to the Crisis" (with Tobias Wiß). She has published in the *British Journal of Industrial Relations, European Journal of Industrial Relations, Journal of European Public Policy, Governance, German Politics*, among others.

Alison Johnston is an Associate Professor of Political Science and Public Policy at Oregon State University. Her recent book *From Convergence to Crisis: Labor Markets and the*

Instability of the Euro (published by Cornell University Press) examines how wage-setting institutions interact with European monetary integration in exposing countries to debt crisis. Her current research focuses on the political economy of housing and sovereign credit ratings. She has recently co-edited special issues for *West European Politics* (on the politics of housing, with Paulette Kurzer) and *New Political Economy* (on the compatibility of capitalist diversity within the European Union, with Aidan Regan). Her work has appeared in *Comparative Political Studies, Comparative Politics, Politics & Society, Journal of European Public Policy*, and the *Journal of Common Market Studies*, among other outlets.

Cathie Jo Martin is Professor of Political Science at Boston University, former President of the Comparative Politics Section of the American Political Science Association, and former Chair of the Council for European Studies. Martin's current book project uses machine learning applied to large corpora of British and Danish literature to understand the deep cultural roots of education reform. Her book with Duane Swank, *The Political Construction of Business Interests* (CUP, 2012) received the APSA Politics and History book award. Martin has published several other books and many articles in the *American Political Science Review, World Politics, British Journal of Political Science, Comparative Political Studies, Socio-Economic Review, Governance, Business History Review, Regulation and Governance, Politics and Society*, and *Polity*, among others. Martin has held fellowships at the Radcliffe Institute for Advanced Study, the Russell Sage Foundation, the National Endowment for the Humanities, the German Marshall fund, and the University of Copenhagen.

Bruno Palier is CNRS Research Director at Sciences Po, Centre d'études européennes et de politique comparée. Trained in social science, he has a PhD in Political Science. He works on the comparative political economy of welfare state reforms. He has been Director of LIEPP (Laboratory for Interdisciplinary Evaluation of Public Policies) between 2014 and 2020, and the Scientific Coordinator of a European Network of excellence RECWOWE between 2007 and 2011 (Reconciling Work and Welfare, involving thirty European research institutions or universities, and 190 researchers from 19 European countries). He has published numerous articles on welfare reforms in France and in Europe. His last book publication is *Welfare Democracies and Party Politics* (co-edited with Philip Manow and Hanna Schwander, Oxford University Press).

Georg Picot is Professor in Comparative Politics at the University of Bergen. His research interests are in comparative political economy, comparative welfare state research, and labor market policy. He obtained his PhD in political science at the University of Milan and held positions at the universities of Heidelberg, Oxford, and Manchester. He has published in journals such as the *British Journal of Political Science, Comparative Political Studies, Journal of European Public Policy, Journal of European Social Policy*, and *Socio-Economic Review*. His book *Politics of Segmentation: Party Competition and Social Protection* was published in 2012 by Routledge. Recently, Georg Picot was awarded a Young Research Talents Grant from the Research Council of Norway for his project on the politics of wage regulation and low-wage employment.

Jonas Pontusson is Professor of Comparative Politics at the University of Geneva. He is currently engaged in two streams of research, one on the politics of growth models and the other on political inequality in liberal democracies. The latter research is supported by a five-year Advanced Grant from the European Research Council.

Alexander Reisenbichler is Assistant Professor of Political Science at the University of Toronto. His research specializes in comparative political economy, with a particular focus on the politics of housing, labor, and financial markets in Western Europe and the United States. His articles have appeared in *Politics & Society*, the *Review of International Political Economy*, *West European Politics*, *Foreign Affairs*, and several other outlets.

Fritz W. Scharpf is Emeritus Director of the Max Planck Institute for the Study of Societies. His areas of interest include the organizational problems and decision processes in governments at all levels; the political economy of inflation and unemployment; and comparative political economy of the welfare state. In 2000, Scharpf was awarded the Johan Skytte Prize in Political Science.

Kathleen Thelen is Ford Professor of Political Science at MIT and a permanent external member of the Max Planck Institute in Cologne, Germany. Her most recent books include *Varieties of Liberalization and the New Politics of Social Solidarity* (Cambridge University Press, 2014) and *Advances in Comparative Historical Analysis*, co-edited with James Mahoney (Cambridge University Press, 2015). She has recently completed a book, co-edited with Jacob Hacker, Alexander Hertel-Fernandez, and Paul Pierson, on the American political economy in comparative perspective.

Anne Wren is a Political Economist who has researched extensively on the political and distributional impact of deindustrialization, and the political economy of globalized and services-based societies. She previously (2006 to 2011) directed a Marie Curie Excellence Team, funded by the European Commission, at Trinity College Dublin on "Political Responses to Economic Change: De-Industrialization, Globalization and Service Sector Development." Her publications on this topic include *The Political Economy of the Service Transition* (Ed., Oxford University Press 2013); 'Employment, Equality, and Budgetary Restraint: The Trilemma of the Service Economy', *World Politics*, 50/4 (1998); and 'The end of the consensus? Labour market developments and the politics of retrenchment', *Socio-Economic Review* (April 2014).

PART I

THE EVOLUTION OF GROWTH REGIMES AND STRATEGIES

1

Tracking the Transformation of Growth Regimes in Advanced Capitalist Economies

Anke Hassel and Bruno Palier

1. Introduction

Since the late 1990s, the literature in the fields of comparative political economy and welfare state research has become accustomed to standard typologies of advanced industrialized countries.[1] A whole generation of scholars of comparative political economy has analyzed the workings of liberal versus coordinated market economies, based on the basic distinction between degrees of coordination within economies (Hall and Soskice 2001). In the field of welfare state research, the seminal book by Gøsta Esping-Andersen (1990) on the three worlds of welfare capitalism has provided a similarly elegant classification of three different types of welfare regimes. These contributions have been immensely important for the understanding of modern economies.

However, the key concepts were mainly based on an era which is known as the "Trente Glorieuses," the thirty prosperous years following World War II. This era was characterized by a continuous level of high growth in gross domestic product (GDP) (4% on average in the Organisation for Economic Co-operation and Development (OECD) countries) and a low rate of unemployment (below 2% for most OECD countries). In all OECD countries, growth and job creation were based on vast productivity gains in mass production in manufacturing industries and on mass consumption, which were at the core of "Fordism" (Boyer 1990). This spectacular period of continuous growth and job creation was associated with the rapid expansion of the welfare state. Social spending increased fivefold between 1945 and the late 1970s in the OECD countries (Flora 1986). The development of the welfare state enabled a redistribution of the increasing wealth, but it also contributed to growth by supporting citizens' consumption and by enhancing workers' productivity through educational, training, and health policies.

[1] We would like to thank Sonja Avlijaš for her research assistance. This chapter received many comments during various presentations and seminars, and we are grateful to all commentators for their helpful insights. This volume is the result of research conducted since 2014 and has been supported by a public grant overseen by the French National Research Agency (ANR) as part of the "Investissements d'Avenir" program at LIEPP (ANR-11-LABX-0091, ANR-11-IDEX-0005–02).

Anke Hassel and Bruno Palier, *Tracking the Transformation of Growth Regimes in Advanced Capitalist Economies*
In: *Growth and Welfare in Advanced Capitalist Economies: How Have Growth Regimes Evolved?* Edited by: Anke Hassel and Bruno Palier, Oxford University Press (2021). © Oxford University Press. DOI: 10.1093/oso/9780198866176.003.0001

Since the mid-1970s, however, in most OECD countries average growth rates have been lower and average unemployment levels higher than during the Trente Glorieuses. Unemployment levels have increased since the early 1970s by 5–10 percentage point and have more or less hovered between 5 and 15% since the 1980s in the OECD. Moreover, the share of atypical employment in the overall OECD workforce (part-time and fixed-term combined) has grown from around 10% to country-specific levels of 25–35% (Emmenegger et al. 2012).

It has now become increasingly clear that advanced industrialized countries have undergone major economic restructuring since the 1970s. The internationalization and globalization of production, as well as the diffusion of information and communication technologies (ICT), have posed enormous challenges to mature industrialized countries. Deindustrialization is associated with job losses and declining growth rates and is having a strong, negative impact on the sustainability of welfare states (Pierson 1996).

During the process of restructuring, countries' socio-economic systems have changed. The Netherlands, once viewed as a classic coordinated market economy and traditionally a conservative welfare state, today has the biggest private system of pension funds in the Western world (measured as percentage of GDP). Sweden, a coordinated market economy known for its generous and egalitarian welfare system, has experienced rapidly rising levels of inequality, in particular among household incomes. On the other hand, countries classified as liberal market economies, such as the United Kingdom, Australia, and New Zealand, have higher minimum wages (measured as a percentage of average hourly pay) than Germany, Belgium, and the Netherlands (Schulten and Lübker 2019), which are traditionally classified as coordinated market economies. In Western Europe, Germany is the country with the largest low-pay segment as of 2019 and has had the biggest increase in working poor since the late 1990s (Spannagel et al. 2017). The established wisdom that divided the advanced industrialized world into two camps of socially balanced, Continental European economies versus unequal, Anglo-Saxon economies should be revisited. Also, welfare systems today function and redistribute differently compared to forty years ago because they have been the object of many reforms since the 1990s.

The aim of this book is threefold: first, to further our understanding of how political economies have transformed since the 1970s; second, to analyze the contribution of governments to these changes by looking at their growth strategies; and third, to highlight and analyze the role of the reforms of welfare systems in this transformation. In a nutshell, this book aims to map and understand the evolution of growth regimes in the advanced capitalist countries of the OECD.

The rich research tradition in comparative political economy on the importance of patterns between the structures of the economy, economic policies, employment policies, skill formation schemes, and social protection systems is the starting point of our analysis. We situate ourselves in the French school tradition of "regulation" (Boyer 1979; Théret 1997), the varieties of capitalism (VoC) approach (Crouch and Streeck 1997; Hall and Soskice 2001; Estevez-Abe et al. 2001; Iversen and Soskice 2015), and the welfare capitalism literature (Esping-Andersen 1990; Ebbinghaus and Manow 2004). These contributions to the literature, which will be discussed below, are the foundation for understanding the interconnection between economic development and the welfare systems in advanced industrialized countries. However, as noted earlier, these approaches were deeply rooted in the Fordist era of economic development. We now need to update and expand them to analyze recent developments of economic restructuring, where national political economies face financialization and the knowledge economy (we return to the details of these trends and the ways countries have been facing them in section 4).

It is by looking in detail at how various governments have tried to boost job creation through growth (as in GDP per capita) that this book contributes to understanding the transformation of advanced political economies. For this we have gathered prominent scholars of comparative political economy who provide their own views on these transformations and how to analyze them. The chapters in this book provide a number of distinct analyses of how economies and welfare systems have been adapted to the common challenges of post-industrialization, financialization, and the knowledge economy. They show that, despite the global interconnectedness of modern economies, national trajectories of growth and policy-making remain distinct.

In section 4.5 of this chapter, we identify five main growth regimes in contemporary advanced capitalist economies: three export-led growth regimes and two domestic demand-based growth regimes. As shown in the concluding chapter of this volume, these five growth regimes are supported by specific growth strategies based on particular welfare reforms: export of high-quality manufacturing (to be associated with dualization of welfare); export of dynamic services (to be associated with social investment); foreign direct investment (FDI)-financed export-led growth (to be associated with fiscal and social attractiveness); domestic consumption driven by financialization (to be associated with the commodification of welfare); and domestic consumption driven by wages and welfare (to be associated with social protectionism). Under European Union (EU) pressure, this last strategy turned into rather a "competitiveness through impoverishment" one. These strategies are not mutually exclusive but, in many cases, there is a dominant strategy which policy-makers rely on in the decision-making process (see Avlijaš et al., this volume).

The variety of answers to the challenge of the knowledge economy is a testimony to the persistence of different growth and welfare regimes even among the advanced industrialized countries, as the VoC and the welfare regime literature have argued. But there has been immense transformation of these regimes. This book shows that, by tracing the implementation of the various growth strategies followed by governments and particularly their welfare system reforms, we can understand how growth regimes have changed and what they have become.

By way of introduction to the various chapters, we prepare the common ground for understanding the evolution of advanced political economies in the remaining parts of this chapter. We start by recalling the main questions, approaches, and current debate on the dynamics of capitalist development in the comparative political economy literature. In a second step, we revisit the terms of the various approaches considered, present our framework of analysis, and explain why we choose to speak of growth regimes and growth strategies. Third, we present the main economic challenges that capitalist economies have been confronted with (i.e., financialization and the rise of the knowledge economy) and underline the fact that, despite common challenges, the economies have remained distinct. As explained below, the existence of a variety of growth regimes in advanced capitalist economies opens the general question of how to understand these different developments, a task undertaken by the various chapters of this book. We summarize the main contributions of those chapters in the final section of this chapter. In the conclusion of this volume, we and our colleague Sonja Avlijaš rely on these contributions to propose our own view on how growth regimes have evolved.

2. The Dynamics of Capitalist Development

In the 1990s, there was a period of convergence in the theory and research of various strands of the comparative political economy literature (Crouch and Streeck 1997; Hall and Soskice 2001; Amable 2003; for a summary of the different approaches see Box 1.1). The institutional configurations of national political economies were seen as the main category of distinction between countries with a strong emphasis on the interdependence (or "institutional complementarities") between the mode of corporate finance, innovation, and the use of human resources within firms that compete on international markets. Non-liberal forms of market economies displayed a number of features that were in stark contrast to liberal English-speaking countries, such as the concentrated ownership of firms, plant-level cooperation between workers and managers, higher levels of and more specific skills in core industries, and pathways of specialization in different technologies and industries. These theories also underlined that core aspects of the welfare systems, such as the provision of skills and social protection, became a major feature of economic organization and development (Estevez-Abe et al. 2001; Amable 2003). Such literature focused merely on providing the most relevant and parsimonious depiction of the various types of capitalist economies.

Box 1.1. Different Approaches to Comparative Political Economy

The Regulation School: The Regulation School analyzes patterns of production, consumption, and distribution through the lens of capital accumulation over time. It is based on an analysis of the Fordist production regime in which mass production was combined with sharing the value added with workers at full capacity and full employment (Boyer 2000).

Varieties of Capitalism (VoC): The VoC theory (Hall and Soskice 2001) states that there are several ways to organize the economy and create growth. It assumes that leading firms in national political economies are governed by sets of institutions that affect their strategic behavior when making business decisions. Firms need to employ labor, capital, and technology in order to produce for markets. The way the labor market, capital market, and transfer of technology are governed is, therefore, crucial for firms. The theory argues that some countries govern these relationships via coordination, while others rely on market mechanisms. The VoC theory does not make assumptions about growth trajectories but maintains that it is essential for these institutions to be complementary. It is essentially a supply-oriented model for explaining the different behavior of firms.

Welfare Capitalism: Esping-Andersen's *Three Worlds of Welfare Capitalism* analyzes the three main types of welfare regimes (liberal, social-democratic and conservative-corporatist) and their role in stimulating economic prosperity. It focuses on the degree of decommodification of labor through the welfare state and the underlying politics shaping the welfare state (Esping-Andersen 1990).

As we are reminded in Peter Hall's chapter (this volume), advanced capitalist economies have gone through three consecutive historical sequences since World War II: Fordism, the era of liberalization, and the era of knowledge-based growth. The two last periods have seen tremendous changes for growth regimes. We come back here to the main arguments raised in the comparative political economy literature on these two last periods.

2.1 Neoliberalism and Liberalization of Capitalist Political Economies

The dynamics of capitalist development have always challenged the notion of stable models. In comparison to feudal and pre-modern economies, capitalist market economies are based on expansion, growth, and increasing marketization

(Streeck 2016). The economic development of the last 150 years does not suggest that anything in capitalist development is static or fixed. The task is, therefore, to develop an understanding of the relationship between institutional configurations of national economies which—as defined in the VoC literature—are conceived as mechanisms of stability and equilibrium, with various exogenous and endogenous dynamics of change.

National institutions of the post-war period, such as labor market regulation, collective bargaining, tight capital market regulation, and social policies, were part of the social order that allowed market economies to develop. They are the social foundation on which market transactions can take place. But they are bound to the historic period when they were politically imposed. There is no reason to assume that they will survive or remain effective if the political forces that brought them there cease to be strong and prominent. In other words, if regulations and institutions are not guarded and enforced by social and political actors, the rules governing capitalist markets will not be sustained. As firms and financial market actors have started to abandon those rules and turned towards rule-breaking (through tax havens and profit-shifting), the rules might eventually break down. The transformation, undermining, and perhaps even destruction of these rules are discussed in the literature around the notion of liberalization imposed by neoliberal ideas and interests.

The most radical proponent of a theory of capitalism as a process of unlimited market expansion is Wolfgang Streeck. Drawing on Schumpeter (1975 [1942]), he argues that change is inherent in capitalism. While Schumpeter refers to changes in consumer taste, products, and industrial organization and does not suggest a particular direction of change, Streeck argues that change in contemporary capitalism is directed towards liberalization, as market actors redefine the rules in order to expand the market and their market share. This induces a bias towards privatization in the social order of societies, which ultimately leads to a contestation between entrepreneurs, who aim to destroy social rules, and political actors, who aim to maintain social order (Streeck 2009: 246). When economic actors, investors, and firms pursue liberalization, a Polanyian social countermovement is needed to impose social obligations on them. If a social countermovement is not in sight, capitalism will ultimately destroy the social fabric it feeds off and, therefore, die (Streeck 2016).

A counterargument on the survival of capitalism is presented by Iversen and Soskice (2019), who also assume that political forces are necessary in order to enforce constraints on market actors for the sake of general prosperity and growth. In contrast to Streeck, who argues that political actors are weak, Iversen and Soskice propose that the middle classes, whose living standards depend on functioning economies, expect political parties to employ the right economic tools for economic development, such as enforcing competition and restraining monopoly rents. They claim that the democratic process that appoints governments in the interest of the majority of the electorate, who are assumed to have a strong interest in growth, protects market economies from their own destruction when facing challenges such as the transition to the knowledge economy and the threat of populist movements. They echo the increasingly important emphasis on electoral politics in the study of comparative political economy, as in Bermendi et al. (2015).

Many accounts in the comparative political economy literature are posited in between these two radical propositions and have more nuanced arguments regarding the dynamics of capitalist development and the role of national institutions. The authors in this edited volume have taken varying positions on the continuum between the potentially destructive forces of radical liberalization highlighted by Streeck and the nuanced process of stability and change outlined by Iversen and Soskice.

Some parts of the literature have embraced the trend towards liberalization as a key characteristic of economic development since the 1980s, sometimes attributing to neoliberalism the capacity to impose convergence towards one distinct political economy. For instance, Baccaro and Howell (2011: 551) have argued that a "common imperative of liberalization, is changing the landscape of European industrial relations along a similar trajectory." The weakness of collective actors to impose rules on the labor market is driven by deindustrialization and economic restructuring (Baccaro and Howell 2011). Beginning in the mid-1970s, many governments embraced financial liberalization, reforming capital markets and corporate governance regulations (Cioffi and Höpner 2006; Culpepper 2011). Since the mid-1990s, advanced political economies have started to display rather strong evidence of transformative change, in particular in Continental European, non-liberal market economies. Labor market regulation was loosened, unemployment benefits were cut, and activation policies introduced more market mechanisms and less protection. Neoliberalism has been frequently blamed and identified as a driver for change towards liberalization.

But rather than uniform processes of liberalization, Thelen (2014) has identified different types of trajectories in different countries, which vary particularly with regard to the effects on social cohesion and solidarity. Thelen points out that the Nordic countries employed a much more solidaristic pattern of liberalization compared to Germany or France, where liberalization led to deep segmentation between insiders and outsiders (Martin and Thelen 2007; Palier and Thelen 2010; Hassel 2014; Thelen 2014). In effect, the literature on liberalization has shown that market economies are changing, but in terms that, rather than converging toward a single political economy, leave them different from each other, despite the liberalizing reforms in many countries (Hall and Thelen 2008). Firms adjust to regulatory change, but are still bound by other institutions in the economy in which they are situated. There is no clear and unifying path towards liberalization. What is missing in this literature, however, is the analysis of the role of finance capitalism in driving these changes, as we will develop further in section 4.

2.2 Entering the Knowledge-Based Economy

While most of the literature in comparative political economy remains centered on liberalization and neoliberalism and neglects the impact of the turn towards services and knowledge-based capitalism, the comparative welfare state literature features many analyses of deindustrialization and the development of the knowledge-based economy. The knowledge economy relies more on intellectual capabilities than on physical inputs or natural resources and is characterized by a higher pace of technical and scientific advance (Powell and Snellman 2004). Here again, it has become clear that, while deindustrialization has hit all industrialized economies—although at varying speeds—the implications are country-specific.

There is a strong argument that deindustrialization reinforces the importance of the welfare state and has made social protection more important rather than less (Iversen and Cusack 2000). By the same token, how the transition towards the knowledge economy actually takes place depends, at least in part, on the type of coordination in the economy and welfare state institutions. Wren (2013) has shown that liberal, social-democratic, and Christian-democratic welfare states have taken different paths towards the service economy, in particular with regard to their underlying educational systems. As high-productivity service sectors require certain skill sets, the institutions of the welfare state become important for facilitating the transition. Zysman et al. (2010) argue similarly that the rise of ICT and the knowledge economy has had particular implications for national economies. They found that social policies and educational and labor market regulation have provided crucial institutional and regulatory preconditions for making the transition fruitful and compatible with social cohesion.

Deindustrialization and the challenges of the service economy are also the starting point of analyses of electoral and policy changes in advanced industrialized countries. Beramendi et al. (2015) analyze changes in the occupational composition of the electorate of such countries and identify different policy preferences vis-à-vis the welfare state. The massive increase of high-skilled service sector jobs and the decline of low-skilled manufacturing jobs have changed the electoral landscape that policy-makers face. Important policy trade-offs emerge, particularly with regard to what they call "consumptive" versus "investive" policies. Old-style, low-skilled, manufacturing workers prefer consumption over investment, while the new educated middle class (service sector workers and professionals) have the opposite preference. Also, different electoral groups see the state's role as intervenor differently (Beramendi et al. 2015). According to this perspective, countries can be classified into types according to the strengths and composition of groups in the labor market. The grouping resembles that of Esping-Andersen, with Southern Europe as a separate group. Beramendi et al. (2015) assume that policy responses, particularly with regard to welfare state policies, are more or less likely depending on these compositions and the coalitions they enable. Their types describe the new policy space under deindustrialization and predict the most likely policy outcomes.

2.3 Tracing National Trajectories of Growth Regimes

The chapters in our volume help trace and analyze the various trajectories followed by different existing growth regimes and welfare systems as they have been affected by and adjusted to the changes brought about by the historical sequences of liberalization and deindustrialization. They demonstrate that liberalization and neoliberal policies have indeed been pursued by many governments and have transformed existing national regimes. However, the chapters do not subscribe to the perspective that the political struggle to rein in economic power has been lost nor that capitalism is dying. The control of democratic governments over business and, in particular, financial markets has become more of an imperative in the new economic climate as financialization and the political power of financial market actors have risen. Even ten years after the financial crisis of 2008, governments have to deal with the fallout through the regulation of banks and tax havens, as well as dealing with higher levels of public debt. The chapters also show that, despite a general trend towards deindustrialization, some countries continued to rely on the manufacturing industry for their growth, while others shifted towards dynamic services.

In the process of economic restructuring, governments often pursue different policies that are sometimes contradictory and serve different constituencies. Contestation over policy responses drives and shapes the development of these economies until a new path is found. In these processes of transformation, national growth regimes are, however, still relevant for analysis, as policy-making is overwhelmingly national and, for EU countries, only partly European.

Many chapters show that the perspectives focusing on the different ways nations have organized their economy (such as those provided by VoC or the Regulation School) continue to provide relevant insights into understanding the evolution of political economies, even in a global setting. We contend that the "VoC" and "regulation" frameworks must be applied, not as coherent and static economic regimes, *but as contested political space*, where institutions work best if they are complementary. In order to understand the dynamics of change, our volume adds to these traditional perspectives (and does not seek to substitute them), taking into account the demand drivers for growth, as well as the role of electoral demand in the contestation and recomposition of existing institutions.

While the patterns of adjustment vary, the degree of freedom for governments is limited. Financialization, deindustrialization, and the knowledge economy pose challenges to all economies. How some governments have managed to turn these challenges into opportunities is not random, but comes out of their institutional toolbox, which is made up of the existing growth regimes and welfare systems, as discussed in the next section.

3. Growth, Regimes, and Strategies

In this section, we review the various concepts used in comparative political economy to analyze the way economies are organized and introduce our understanding of "growth regimes" and "growth strategies" that will be used by the authors in this volume (see Box 1.2 for a summary). We also highlight the role that welfare systems play in the functioning of growth regimes.

Box 1.2. The Terminology

Growth models: The discussion on post-Fordist growth models (Baccaro and Pontusson 2016) is based on post-Keynesian, Kaleckian macroeconomics. As Baccaro and Pontusson explain in their chapter, the approach relies partly on the three-equation model by Carlin and Soskice in Keynesian economics, which combines aggregate demand, the equilibrium rate of unemployment, and the balance of payments. It argues that in the Fordist period all economic growth was wage-led. When the Fordist growth model came to an end, countries specialized in either domestic demand-led growth (through credit or public spending), export-led growth, or balanced growth (domestic demand and exports). The use of growth models has brought back examination of the role of aggregate demand for macroeconomic development and provided new insight into the post-Fordist transformations of political economies.

Growth regimes: We define a growth regime, in its broadest term, as a mode of governance for the economy. There are three key components of growth regimes: the engine of growth, i.e., the sectors that contribute to wealth creation, job creation, and productivity gains (manufacturing sector, finance, high-tech, agriculture…); the five institutions governing the economy (see Amable 2003; and section 3.2 in this chapter); and the main components of aggregate demand (private consumption, private investment, public spending, and net exports). Our growth regime approach combines the insights of VoC theory and the growth model arguments. Besides the importance of market product regulations and the modes of financing the economy, it underlines the prominent role of welfare institutions (educational system, labor markets rules, and social insurance/social policy) in shaping economic activities.

Growth strategies: Governments are concerned with job creation and economic growth for electoral reasons. To this aim, they pursue growth strategies, which refer to a (relatively coherent) series of decisions and reforms, taken by either governments or producers' groups (economic and social actors) in order to boost growth and stimulate job creation in a specific nation, and the rationale for these decisions (on this, see also Hall, this volume). Over a mid-range period of time, growth strategies follow an observable, coherent, and systematic pattern. They involve policy changes and adaptations in different policy fields that affect the demand and supply sides of an economy, including structural and welfare reforms. Since it often means reforming some of the main institutions of a growth regime, implementing a growth strategy can contribute to changing the existing growth regime over time.

Comparative political economy helps understand the various ways to organize the economy. The literature, however, proposes different dimensions to be taken into account for this classification. While VoC focused on the supply side, the French Regulation School argued, especially when they analyzed the "Fordist" growth regime, that the interaction between the demand and supply sides is key (Boyer 1979). Moreover, as the recent literature on growth models argues, the demand side and its composition matter too, and governments need to balance both sides of the economy in order to provide prosperity (Baccaro and Pontusson 2016 and this volume). We thus propose that, in order to capture the main differences between various political economies, we need to combine (and not substitute) an understanding of how the supply side of the economy adjusts to existing and changing institutions with an analysis of how aggregate demand is driving economic growth. In the following, we argue in favor of a comprehensive approach that emphasizes the relationship between the supply and demand sides. This is particularly important when focusing on growth regimes and the role played by welfare institutions in them. The institutions and policies of welfare systems play important roles in balancing both sides of the economy. The welfare state offers key instruments to governments, which they employ to shape and pursue what we call their growth strategies. However, different policies correspond to different growth strategies, which in turn impacts overall economic and social performance.

Since the onset of the era of low growth that started in the late 1970s in advanced economies, governments have tried to stimulate growth in various ways that interact with the structural changes in capitalism, including financialization and the knowledge economy. Their policies were shaped by existing institutional arrangements, as have been identified in the comparative political economy literature. However, these policies very often mean reforming existing economic and social institutions. The policies aimed at boosting growth have thus, in return, contributed to changing these existing institutions. Hence, growth regimes have evolved since the 1980s, and the differences between institutional regimes today appear even more diverse than the basic distinction between the liberal and coordinated market economies identified in the 1980s (Hall and Soskice 2001). It is today more complicated than ever to cluster advanced economies into only two groups.

3.1 Demand and Supply—the Two Sides of Growth

There is currently a lively debate amongst political economists on the best way to qualify and analyze the different ways in which economies are organized.[2] The VoC literature focuses on the production side (supply side) of the economy and its institutional configuration (Hall and Soskice 2001), while others argue that the consumption side (demand side) and its composition are most important (Baccaro and Pontusson 2016 and this volume). We contend that what matters most is understanding how supply and demand interact in order to forge a specific growth regime (see also Boyer 1990).

Focusing on the supply side and firms' behavior, the VoC literature provides a very stylized, but quite compelling, distinction between two types of economies that, at least implicitly, correspond to two different growth regimes. Varieties come from the different institutional arrangements in which firms operate. Firms adjust to their institutional environment in order to develop specific competitive advantages. Hall and Soskice (2001) point to the main institutional structures that condition corporate strategies: the financial system and corporate governance, the internal structure of firms, industrial relations, the education and training system, and the institutions organizing inter-company relations. As they argue:

> The firms located within any political economy face a set of coordinating institutions whose character is not fully under their control. These institutions offer firms a particular set of opportunities; and companies can be expected to gravitate towards strategies that take advantage of these opportunities. In short, there are important respects in which strategy follows structure. For this reason, our approach predicts systematic differences in corporate strategy across nations, and differences that parallel the overarching institutional structures of the political economy. (Hall and Soskice 2001: 15)

[2] See, for instance, the debate via commentaries in *Politics and Society* (issue 44, number 2) around Baccaro and Pontusson (2016).

We take from this approach that institutions and the interdependence of institutions matter in shaping firm strategies and comparative advantages. We follow their assumption by stating that that these institutional arrangements structure constraints and opportunities also for governments and shape governments' strategies, decisions, and policies.

Hall and Soskice (2001) distinguish between two main institutional arrangements that shape two main types of capitalism. Coordinated market economies (CMEs) are characterized by a multiplicity of coordinating and deliberating institutions. CMEs are based on non-market mechanisms, such as organizational interaction and long-term relationships in industry and employment. Workers and firms invest in specific skills, which are insured by welfare state policies, such as unemployment insurance or old-age insurance (Estevez-Abe et al. 2001). CMEs have specialized in manufacturing industries that produce for world markets and tend to have trade surpluses. They benefit from prudent monetary and fiscal policy and put strong emphasis on wage control, in order not to endanger their competitive position (Iversen and Soskice 2012). The Nordic and Continental European countries are both classified as CMEs.

In liberal market economies (LMEs), by contrast, economic relations are governed by market mechanisms. LMEs are based on deregulated markets, general skills, and a universal, but minimalist, welfare state. They tend to have trade deficits and specialize in radical innovation as well as financial services. Their approach towards monetary and fiscal policy is more accommodating, as prudent policies will not help to control wages. In LMEs, corporate financing is dominated by the stock market, wage levels are determined by individual productivity, and workers have an interest in acquiring general skills, in order to have flexibility in an industry at the mercy of economic cycles and technological revolutions.

However, more detailed analyses invite us to differentiate among these two families. In addition to the finer distinctions between Nordic and Continental CMEs (Thelen 2014), one needs to provide a nuanced understanding of the mixed market economies (MMEs) of Southern Europe and France (Molina and Rhodes 2007; Beramendi et al. 2015) and the Visegrád countries of Eastern Europe (Nölke and Vliegenhardt 2009; Bohle and Greskovits 2012).

Integrating the insights of the Regulation School and the comparative welfare state literature with the VoC account, Bruno Amable distinguished five types of capitalism (Amable 2003).[3] Like other comparative political economists, he also considers that institutions shape economic relations, but he proposes a new definition of these institutions, in order to better understand the differences between (the five) types of capitalism. He shows that between various types of capitalism, institutions differ in the areas of product market competition, labor

[3] Neoliberal or market-based capitalism, Continental European capitalism, social-democratic capitalism, Mediterranean capitalism, and Asian capitalism.

market and labor relations, social protection, education systems, and financial systems (Amable 2003).

On the other side, the "growth model" literature, in particular Baccaro and Pontusson (2016), propose to re-emphasize the role demand plays in economic growth. They offer "to distinguish three different alternatives to the traditional Fordist model of wage-led growth: consumption-led growth financed by credit, investment-led growth and export-led growth" (2016: 186). They focus on what they consider to be the two main models: the consumption-led and the export-led growth models, with four possible cases: Germany, relying exclusively on exports; the UK, driven by domestic demand (financed by credit); Sweden, as a combination of consumption and export; and Italy, where neither exports nor consumption seem to work. In their discussion of Baccaro and Pontusson's paper, Hope and Soskice (2016) agree that one should distinguish between export-led and demand-led growth models, but they argue that this just confirms VoC, in the sense that LMEs are usually domestic consumption-led, whereas CMEs rely more on exports. We can indeed notice that CMEs are more oriented towards export-led growth (we document this later in this chapter). In LMEs, private consumption remains comparatively high, while in a CME like Germany, it is comparatively low (Hassel 2017).

Export-led growth is associated with a regime in which economic relationships are negotiated and controlled by economic players (employers and unions), who have coordinated interaction, especially with regard to wage-setting and training. In many CMEs, wage-setting is the central object of negotiation. High levels of centralization and the coordination of wage-setting help to contain wage pressure and, therefore, control the real exchange rate. They also contribute to a compressed wage structure, which gives incentives to train the low-skilled and asks the high-skilled to forego higher wages. Wage moderation allows for higher investment. All these elements are conducive to the competitiveness of exports. Fiscal and monetary policies are rather restrictive, due to the high share of exposed sectors in the economy (Hall and Soskice 2001; Scharpf, this volume). By contrast, LMEs have a tendency to rely more on domestic demand for their growth, which can be associated with a regime where dynamic services, and especially the financial sector, play a bigger role (and allow access to consumption through credit, see Crouch 2009 and 2013).

The focus on aggregate demand by the "growth model" literature is a necessary complement to the previous literature focusing on the supply side of the economy and does not seem to contradict its classification of the economies, but rather enriches it. However, once again, a mere binary distinction (here the role of exports versus domestic demand in stimulating growth), while elegant in its simplicity, overlooks the stark differences between economies, such as the United States and France, on the one hand (both recognized as domestic, demand-led growth models), and Sweden and Germany, on the other (both belonging to the realm of export-led growth models). These countries differ significantly on other accounts, such as their level of financialization, ICT use, private debt, the capacity to use currency devaluation, as well as their levels of inequality, and ultimately their rates of economic growth and employment. As acknowledged by Baccaro and Pontusson (2016), we need to further the analysis of the variety of domestic demand-led and export-led growth models, their origins, and implications.

In order to do so, we need more details and understanding of the nature of exports, as well as the nature of domestic demand. Different types of export-led growth models have developed, based on the export of manufacturing goods versus dynamic services, as well as the various degrees to which these exports are price-sensitive or based on quality and innovation. Also, on the side of domestic demand, it is important to distinguish between different types of domestic consumption-led growth, depending on the drivers of demand, which can be dominated by wage increases or be financed by private debt or by public spending on social benefits.

Instead of juxtaposing the demand-focused growth model perspective of Baccaro and Pontusson with the more supply-side VoC perspective of Hall and Soskice, we propose an augmented synthesis with our own approach in terms of "growth regimes." Adopting a growth regimes perspective allows us to gather the insights of both perspectives and provide a more detailed and differentiated account of existing regimes, while also examining the evolution of growth regimes.

3.2 Growth Regimes

A ***growth regime,*** *in its broadest sense, is* ***a mode of governance of the economy.*** *It encompasses the institutional, policy, and organizational frameworks that shape the specialization of firms and the consumption and saving patterns of the population, as well as the use of technology and work organization. A growth regime can be based on a particular type of innovation, the evolution of a particular high-value-added industry, the use of fiscal and monetary policy, and policy instruments that affect the employment rate and human capital. The (welfare) state is an important component of growth regimes for economic management.*

Growth regimes, therefore, not only include all the components of the neoclassical model of growth, in particular labor, capital, and technology, and the specification of aggregate production functions, but, moreover, they give them a particular framework. While neoclassical growth theory has become more sophisticated in specifying particular aspects of the production function, such as consumer behavior, it is generally not interested in the institutional and policy configurations, either between countries or across time, beyond a very general view on institutions such as property rights (Acemoglu and Johnson 2005). The inclusion of a variety of institutions, sectors, and policies (including social protection policies) distinguishes different types of growth regimes. In order to emphasize the interaction and complementarity between the various components of each institutional configuration, we use the notion of regime and "growth regime" rather than "growth model." We use the terminology of "growth model" when we refer to the literature focusing on the demand side of the economy.

We consider that there are three main important aspects of growth regimes:

- **The engine of growth** as the sectors that contribute to wealth creation, job creation, and productivity gains: i.e. agriculture, manufacturing, services (high/low value-added services), finance, housing, knowledge-based activities, and ICT.
- **The institutions organizing the economy**: 1. the modes of financing the economy and corporate governance; 2. product market regulation (including industrial policies, subsidies, state ownership); 3. industrial relations, modes and rules of wage-setting, labor market rules and organizations; 4. skill-formation systems (education and vocational training); 5. social protection policies (social insurance, social investment, and social assistance).[4]
- **The main components of aggregate demand**: private consumption (household and firms), private investment, public spending (consumption and investment), and net exports (Baccaro and Pontusson 2016).

Our understanding of growth regimes is comprehensive and embraces both the demand side and the supply side of the economy (Figure 1.1). It assumes that socio-economic institutions, as established in the comparative political economy literature, shape the key dynamics of growth. As is demonstrated by many chapters in this volume, these institutions inform both the supply and demand sides. For instance, wage-bargaining institutions, on the one hand, support the skill-formation system, as centralized wage-bargaining provides wage limits for skilled labor. In tandem with different kinds of training institutions, welfare systems and wage-bargaining institutions prop up particular skill patterns and, thereby, form a skills regime (Chevalier, this volume). At the same time, wage-bargaining institutions determine the wage structure in an economy, which, in turn, affects the demand side (Baccaro and Pontusson; Johnston, this volume). Higher wage increases, as well as lower levels of wage inequality, should prompt higher levels of domestic demand. Similarly, equity-based corporate finance and fluid capital markets facilitate financialization, which impacts the demand side by creating credit (Reisenbichler, this volume). On the other hand, the fluidity and availability of corporate finance also interact with opportunities for radical innovation on the supply side (Wren, this volume).

[4] We elaborate here on the five institutions already identified by Amable (2003).

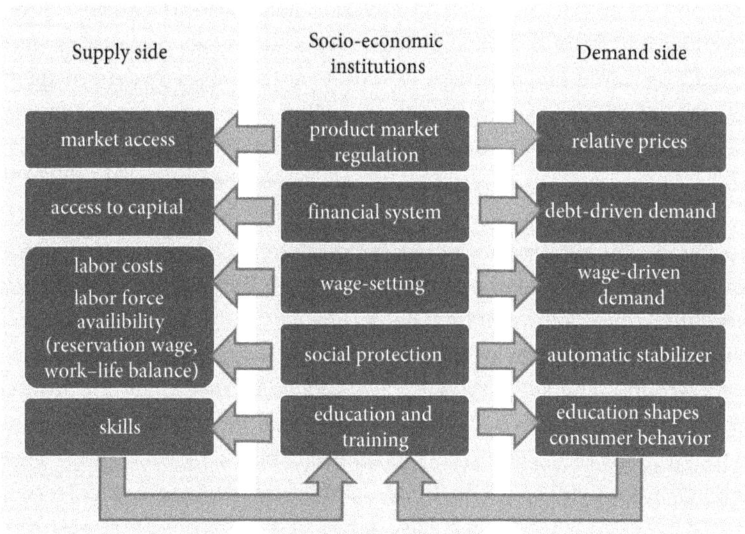

Figure 1.1 The institutional foundations of growth regimes
Note: We would like to thank Georg Picot for helpful suggestions improving this graph.

In a specific growth regime, the interaction between the supply and the demand sides of the economy are influenced by the same economic institutions. These institutions also prompt economic actors to specialize in particular kinds of economic activities and political actors to attempt to support and reinforce these specializations with their economic policies. In section 4.5 of this chapter, we identify five main growth regimes in contemporary advanced capitalist countries.

3.3 Growth and Welfare Regimes

Few welfare state researchers have tried to connect welfare regimes to the varieties of capitalism and growth regimes.[5] This might partly be because very often social policies are perceived as an attempt to compensate for the most negative impacts of capitalism, and thus one rarely analyzed their connection to, and their positive interaction with, the economy (Iversen and Soskice 2015). Iversen and Soskice (2015: 82) remind us that

[5] Martin Schröder (2009, 2013) is an exception. He shows that there is one constant in the literature and in the data that he correlates: all LMEs have a liberal welfare regime. He also points out that CMEs either have a conservative, corporatist welfare state or a social-democratic one. Schröder speaks of "cultural affinities" that link welfare and growth regimes, but he overlooks the economic relations between the two and the way welfare institutions interact with economic activities and growth regimes. For a very interesting discussion of the incompatibilities between "worlds" (of welfare) and "varieties" (of capitalism), see Schelkle (2012).

> social protection (including job protection, unemployment benefits, income protection, and a host of related policies, such as active labor market programs and industry subsidies) encourages workers to acquire skills that are co-specific to employers, which in turn enhances the ability of firms to compete in international markets. Central features of the welfare state are thus linked to the economy in a manner that creates beneficial complementarities.

More generally, the welfare state occupies a prominent place in the VoC literature. Coordinated and liberal market economies are not defined but underwritten by important functions of the welfare state. As noted earlier, CMEs are based on non-market mechanisms, such as long-term relationships between employer and employee groups. The skills in which workers and firms invest are insured by welfare state policies, such as unemployment insurance. In LMEs, by contrast, economic relations are governed by market mechanisms, by which wage levels are determined by individual productivity. LMEs tend to feature a universal, but minimalist, welfare state. Workers have access to social protection, such as health insurance, mainly through their job contract.

Bruno Amable is certainly the one who underlined most clearly the role of welfare policies in the functioning of growth regimes. As noted earlier, in his definition of the institutions organizing the economy, he distinguishes the areas of product market competition, financial system, labor market and labor relations, education systems, and social protection (Amable 2003). As he demonstrated, for each type of political economy, the functioning of and differences in the skill-formation systems and the way the labor market and the welfare systems are organized are crucial.

Taken together, these sets of institutions (educational system, labor market rules, and social protection) are key elements of what the comparative welfare state literature would call "welfare regimes." Comparative research has shown that these three key elements often (but not always) systematically complement each other, and thus work as a system to form a "regime" (Esping-Andersen (1990) speaks of different "welfare regimes" to characterize his three worlds of welfare capitalism). For instance, centralized wage-setting institutions go hand in hand with more comprehensive social protection systems and often focus on mid-level (specific) skills, whereas decentralized wage-setting and a low-regulated labor market go hand in hand with educational systems that provide general skills (with little involvement from both the state and employers) and residual social policies.

Education, labor market regulation, social insurances, and other social policies thus contribute to both the supply and the demand sides of the economy (see Figure 1.1). In this sense, the welfare regime is an integral part of growth regimes. On the demand side, these elements provide certain sources of demand (assistance benefits, unemployment benefits, old-age pensions, etc.), act as automatic stabilizers, and can also provide a minimum reservation wage. On the supply side, they can contribute to increasing productivity and increasing employment through specific employment policies and/or education policies. Welfare systems provide different types of skills that are employed in different production regimes (Streeck 1991; Estevez-Abe et al. 2001). Unemployment insurance and other social insurance, associated with specific employment statuses, protect skill acquisition. In the last chapter of this volume, Avlijaš et al. detail the various configurations to be currently found between growth regimes and welfare regimes in Europe.

The interplay between the supply and demand sides of a national economy remains the key variable in the political toolbox of governments when attempting to stimulate economic growth. The chapters in this volume provide analyses of the dynamics of policy-making in the context of different growth regimes when facing new challenges. Governments can choose to spend to increase demand or to improve the supply side by enhancing skills or markets. When governments employ policy tools to adjust both sides, they encounter trade-offs, decisions regarding priorities, and calculations of political costs. In the end, governments choose a combination of supply and demand policies. Besides political and electoral factors, the choice of instruments is also shaped by the institutional environment of the economy and, particularly, by the dominant economic sectors in a country.

3.4 Growth Strategies

As the world is changing, we need to improve comparative political economy theories to help us understand how the various ways of organizing the economy are changing. Our volume shows that growth regimes have indeed changed over time and that these changes are largely due to reforms implemented by governments and collective economic and social actors, such as employers' representatives and trade unions ("producer groups" in the political economy literature).

The series of decisions taken by governments are not random. They define a specific way to stimulate growth and job creation. They are taken in particular institutional and economic contexts and reflect specific political compromises. Taken together, they form a more or less coherent set of (economic and social) goals and (economic and social) policies that we call "growth strategies." ***By growth strategy, we refer to a (relatively coherent) series of decisions and reforms, taken by either governments or producers' groups (economic and social actors) in order to boost growth and stimulate job creation in a specific nation, and the rationale for these decisions.*** Governments develop either explicit or implicit growth strategies. Speaking of strategies does not mean that governments know what the consequences of their actions are, but that they have some intention, that they follow a general aim to boost employment and growth, and that there is (some) coherence in a series of economic and social policy decisions.

To give examples of what we mean by "growth strategies," one can refer to the most explicit ones, like those formulated by international organizations. In 1993, the famous World Bank (1994) report on "averting the old age crisis" presented its new pension model and the reforms leading to it as a growth strategy.[6] One could also refer to the "Jobs Strategy" developed by the OECD (1994) during the 1990s: the aim was to promote (liberalizing) labor market reforms in order to boost job creation.

At the EU level, in 2000, the Lisbon Strategy was explicitly presented as a "growth strategy." It aimed to make the European Union "the most competitive and dynamic knowledge-based economy in the world, capable of sustainable economic growth with more and better jobs and greater social cohesion" (EU European Council 2000). The details of this strategy include many different aspects from investment in research and development to the modernization of social protection systems. Adopted in 2010, the following "Europe 2020 strategy" focused on "smart, sustainable and inclusive growth," including specific social policies and reforms. Within these strategies, a diagnosis of the structural changes in the economy (such as the shift towards a knowledge-based economy) and in societies (such as aging or the entry of women into the labor market) is put forward, and then prescriptions on what governments should do to reorient their economies and favor growth and job creation are presented (all these ideas correspond to what Peter Hall calls a specific "economic gestalt" in his chapter in this volume). When following these strategies, governments are supposed to reform some of the institutions that are constitutive of a growth regime and thus have the potential to transform the existing one. All the strategies referred to above imply important reforms in the labor market, education, training, and social policies.

While international organizations explicitly use the terminology of "growth strategy," national governments are less explicit. Presenting and analyzing the national logic of action, the manner in which various economic factors are agreed upon to find a specific way to boost growth and jobs, and the coherence of the policies and reforms implemented is more a task undertaken by social scientists. We assume that, when looking at economic and social reforms implemented in a country, one can detect a strategy, i.e., "a pattern in the stream of decisions" to refer here to Henry Mintzberg's approach to strategy (Mintzberg 1979: 582). As suggested by Fritz Scharpf to us, some countries may have differentiated

[6] The full title of the report is: *Averting the Old Age Crisis: Policies to Protect the Old and Promote Growth* (World Bank 1994), the argument being that switching from PAYGO pension systems to fully funded schemes would both preserve future pensioners from the negative impact of demographic imbalances and create funds that would attract and increase investments in the economy.

strategic capacities. Sweden and France may have been able to proactively design growth strategies (at least in the post-war era), while others have developed their growth strategies through an evolutionary process of coordination through mutual adaptation. Our notion of growth strategy assumes less an ex ante strategic planning capacity than the progressive (and post hoc) discovery of what Mintzberg calls an emergent strategy.[7]

As shown by the contributions to this volume, the policy fields and reforms differ from one country to another (in content and in timing). These differences reveal a certain level of internal consistency and coherence within individual countries that might be construed as strategy. The internal consistency partly derives from the diagnosis of the problem to be solved and partly in the proposed solutions. Most of the coherence in the policies adopted in order to solve the identified problem comes, however, from the specific national growth and welfare regimes, since they structure the decisions taken and the strategies adopted in a specific country. These solutions to revive growth and stimulate job creation are shaped by the existing growth and welfare regimes. When adjusting to new contexts, these reforms can, however, contribute to progressively reshaping and transforming existing growth regimes.

Even in contexts where "strategies" are not explicit, governments have developed standardized responses to economic threats that correspond to their own economic specialization and regime. The reactions by governments to the economic recession following the financial crisis illustrate this point. For instance, the German government responded to the financial crisis by immediately protecting the economy's manufacturing base through short-shift working arrangements and a "cash-for-clunkers" program. In the UK, all attempts to rein in financial services industries (especially at the EU level) have been scrutinized as to whether and to what extent they might endanger the competitive advantage of the City of London. These governmental responses to the financial crisis reveal an underlying economic growth strategy.

These examples of (more or less) short-term government strategies to protect the economic base of national political economies are embedded in broader institutional settings that define the production and welfare regime of a country. As is illustrated in this volume, there are many government decisions that follow the same pattern of protecting/enhancing/renewing the existing growth regime.

[7] As Mintzberg reminds us, the ancient Greeks used the notion of strategy to describe the art of the army general, and strategy is often associated with strategic planning. Through his empirical observation of firms' strategy-making, Mintzberg however proposes an approach to strategy that inspired our own approach, meaning not a plan for action, but a pattern in action in a series of decisions. As Mintzberg states: "Ask almost anyone what strategy is, and they will define it as a plan of some sort, an explicit guide to future behavior. Then ask them what strategy a competitor or a government or even they themselves have actually pursued. Chances are they will describe consistency in past behavior—a pattern in action over time. Not 'planning', nor 'expression of intention', but 'patterns in action'" (Mintzberg 1987: 67–8).

These decisions and policy reforms are influenced by the dominant production regime and profile—i.e., manufacturing or finance, export-oriented or domestic demand, etc.—and have implications for the reforms of the welfare state. In other words, a country dominated by financial services has a different approach to welfare reform than a country dominated by manufacturing.

Obviously, the production regime is not the only factor at play. Electoral rules, political institutions, political parties, and external events matter as well (Beramendi et al. 2015; Hall, this volume). Policy-makers can adopt growth strategies that are not necessarily in line with the growth regime for reasons such as party ideology or values or with the aim of developing a new growth regime. There is also reverse causality: political institutions have shaped production regimes, as Iversen and Soskice have argued (2009). However, we assume that growth and welfare regimes play an important role in these strategies. This is partly because the preference of the dominant sector informs policy-makers as to what the priorities of economic and social policies should be (see also Iversen and Soskice 2018; Baccaro and Pontusson, this volume).

Business groups in the dominant sector(s) have privileged access to governments and to media reporting about the economic situation. The interests of the business community might be in conflict with government priorities, and we do not assume that business will always have the upper hand. But we do expect government policy-making to take into account the demands of the dominant business community and their strategies to cope with economic and welfare state restructuring. Depending on the kind of dominant business community, we presume a variety of business preferences for welfare state reforms. These preferences are analyzed in details by Cathie Jo Martin in this volume. In many cases, these preferences may be supported by workers in key industries. As workers and their representatives are aware of the relevance of the industry and are usually the beneficiaries of the economic specialization process, they might support the business community in their political demands for government policies. Cross-class coalitions are, therefore, sector- or country-specific and, by and large, focused on or coming from the economy's dominant sector (for the importance of producers' coalitions in shaping growth strategies, see Thelen in this volume).

Growth strategies most often involve significant welfare reform. International organizations regularly suggest reforms of the welfare state to reach economic and employment objectives. The EU, OECD, and World Bank emphasize the necessity of reforming education and skill-formation systems, advocating structural reforms of labor markets, wage-bargaining, and social protection systems in the name of boosting growth and creating more jobs. The EU's competitiveness strategy, developed after the great recession, associates economic policy orientations (austerity, growth through cost competitiveness, and export capacities) with welfare reforms (cuts in welfare spending, as well as the "structural reforms" of labor markets, pensions, and healthcare systems) (Heins and De la Porte 2015).

At the national level, welfare states have been, and continue to be, reformed in the name of job creation and growth. Since the 1990s, especially in Europe, many of the policy reforms implemented by governments concerned mostly the welfare system in a broad sense: changes in wage policies, in labor market regulation, in employment policies, in educational and training policies, and in social policies. The neoliberal governments of Thatcher and Major in the UK were famous for their privatization policies (which partly included pension schemes), but also for having liberalized the labor market and increased pressure and conditionality on unemployed persons. Nordic countries implemented labor market and pension reforms in the early 1990s. Gerhard Schröder gained his reputation through his labor market and unemployment insurance reforms in Germany in the early 2000s. Emmanuel Macron is accumulating reforms in France's welfare domain (labor market deregulation, training, unemployment benefits, and pensions). As shown in the final chapter of this volume, these reforms are quite different in the different growth strategies.

One possible reason that these labor market, skill formation, and social policy domains are so prominent in governments' agendas, when they want to boost growth and create jobs, is that these fields are still under the jurisdiction of national governments. By contrast, the management of other economic policy fields that constitute the specific growth regime, such as product market regulation, financial rules, and monetary policy, are being increasingly overtaken by supranational bodies because of liberalization, globalization, and/or the independence of central banks. This situation holds particularly in the EU and the Eurozone area (see both Scharpf and Johnston in this volume).

4. Challenges to Growth Regimes

As noted at the outset of this chapter, average GDP growth rates have been lower and average unemployment levels higher for most OECD countries since the mid-1970s (Emmenegger et al. 2012). At the same time, advanced industrialized countries have been confronted with the globalization of production, financialization, as well as the diffusion of ICT. The future of manufacturing as the basis of national wealth and well-paid employment is in question, if not in peril (Zysman and Breznitz 2013; Wren 2013). One can easily imagine that the shift towards the service economy means pressure for change in growth regimes. In this section, we go beyond the state of the literature on liberalization and deindustrialization presented earlier by analyzing both the key challenges to and opportunities for growth regimes and their transformation since the 1980s.

Instead of focusing merely on the losses implied by liberalization (deregulation and privatization) and deindustrialization (loss of jobs and demise of industrial institutions and relations), we try to understand how growth regimes evolved in this context, finding that financialization and the ICT revolution presented both problems and solutions by providing new engines for growth. We thus identify the main differences in orientation taken by growth regimes when they confronted these challenges. This allows us to identify five types of growth regimes existing today amongst the cases analyzed in this volume. It is this variety, and how countries got there, that will be the object of explanation in the remaining chapters.

4.1 The Rise of the Service Economy

The comparative political economy literature generally agrees that the late 1970s are marked by the end of Fordism. Deindustrialization has meant that manufacturing has lost its importance as the key source of economic growth and job creation. The emerging service economies in the rich countries of the OECD are shaping economic development and prosperity, but are still not well understood.

Early contributions (Iversen and Wren 1998; Scharpf 2000) assumed that the Baumol disease—the weakness of productivity gains in the service economy—would present trade-offs for modern welfare states. Since productivity gains in the service sector are comparatively small, jobs in the service economy would become relatively more expensive and would eventually not be provided by the market. Policy-makers would face the trilemma of having to either accept lower wages and increasing wage inequality, spend increasing amounts on the public sector, or accept high levels of joblessness and low employment in the service sector (Iversen and Wren 1998).

Others have challenged this traditional position on low productivity gains in the service economy. Zysman and Breznitz (2013) emphasize the digital revolution in the service sector and show how it contributes to the fragmentation of value chains. ICT-based services, as in the health, retailing, and education sectors, can overcome productivity gaps and deliver more and better services at a lower cost (see also Wren 2013). The development of digital technologies might transform the very nature of work and welfare systems (Colin and Palier 2015).

There is reason to believe that both perspectives are partially true. Wages in personal services have been comparatively low and stagnant. Governments in many countries have tolerated rising wage inequality in order to facilitate employment growth in the service economy; many have implemented policies aimed at decreasing the cost of low-skilled labor, including, contrary to Iversen and Wren's expectation, the Continental European countries (Palier 2010). The issue of creating a low-wage sector in order to facilitate employment was taken seriously by policy-makers and has guided those policies. At the same time, there are many examples of the integration of ICT-based services in the global value chain. Retailing has been revolutionized by online services, and the health sector has seen massive productivity gains by delivering diagnostics through outsourcing to low-cost countries. The ICT-based knowledge economy shows one way out of the low productivity trap of the service economy, as Wren (2013) has suggested, and confirms in her chapter in this volume.

Since the 1990s, the move towards the service economy has posed strong challenges to the welfare state (Esping-Andersen 1999). A context of low growth means fewer resources in increasingly inegalitarian societies. The welfare state seems trapped in "permanent austerity" (Pierson 2001), having to confront aging, unemployment, precariousness, and a series of new social risks, such as single parenthood, the need to reconcile work and family life, lack of continuous careers, more precarious forms of contracts, and workers possessing low or obsolete skills (Bonoli 2005).

If the literature is now clear that there have been various ways to adjust to this post-industrial context, we still need to identify systematically how various growth and welfare regimes evolved in different countries in this new context. Countries have tried to seize opportunities to replace manufacturing as the main engine of growth in different ways. Two new domains can broadly be identified as likely to bring back growth: finance and knowledge/ICT-based economic activities. In the following sections we discuss these new engines of growth and which role they play in the various growth regimes.

4.2 Finance as a New Engine of Growth—How Far Have Various Countries Gone Through Financialization?

The Fordist growth regime was largely wage-led (Baccaro and Pontusson 2016). To what extent has it been replaced by a "finance-led" or wealth-based accumulation regime (Boyer 2000)? In the comparative political economy literature, the financialization of the global economy has been relatively neglected, despite its increasing importance and the severe effects of the global financial crisis on the real economy.[8] The literature is more extensive in sociology and geography than in comparative political economy, and also covers the effects of the financialization of the corporate sector, which has shifted its profit strategies from the real economy to the financial sector. However, as economists frequently point out, there is no financial economy without the real economy. We will not pursue the wider discussion on financialization (see van Treeck 2009; van der Zwan 2014). Here we just use the main insights from the financialization literature to feed our thinking on the transformation of growth regimes.

[8] Exceptions are Boyer (2000), Krippner (2011), Streeck (2014), and various contributions on the financial crisis, such as Bermeo and Pontusson (2012) and Woll (2015).

One strand of the financialization literature claims that the slowing of economic growth since the early 1970s has prompted governments to use the financial sector to avoid distributional social conflicts. Empirically, we can see a steady rise in financialization, while growth rates have dwindled in the OECD. Greta Krippner (2005; 2011) argues that policy-makers in the US turned to financial markets when growth slowed in order to avoid the difficult choice of social priorities. In the process, policy-makers eliminated limits to credit access in order to enable consumers to maintain their living standards. The access to credit thereby served a function similar to inflation during the 1970s, since consumer debt blurs winners and losers during economic stagnation. Similarly, Wolfgang Streeck (2014) assumes that the turn towards increasing public debt was fueled by the lower growth rates of the 1970s. Both see increasing credit and debt rates as a compensation mechanism for lower growth rates.

Another strand of the literature suggests that financialization can also be perceived as a growth regime in itself (Boyer 2000). Financialization contributes to, and is an expression of, the wealth of households and thereby can become an important influence on the consumption of durable goods and houses. Financialization, therefore, can potentially have overall expansionary effects on the economy (Boyer 2000). Boyer does not argue, as some of the other financialization literature does, that the provision of credit replaces social policy, and thereby feeds both the financial services industries and the poor. Rather, he suggests that financialization is an expression of the use of credit and a decline of savings among the upper-middle classes. The main effect comes from a decline in savings rates and increasing private indebtedness. In this view, financialization is driven by consumer behavior, which embraces both consumer debt and financial instruments to invest for private financial gains. It spurs the increase of asset management services, as well as mortgages and other bank products, while at the same time stimulating domestic demand.

The expansion of the financial services sector has three distinct functions for political economies.[9] First, it stimulates demand, either because consumers can borrow against their house if mortgages are readily available (as in the US) or because liberalization of mortgage-lending increases demand, house prices, and wealth (see also Reisenbichler, this volume). Second, financial centers provide well-paid jobs and attract investors. Both create additional economic activities and, thereby, domestic demand. And finally, financialization helps to spur the supply side by fostering investments in the knowledge economy either directly, through digitalized financial services, or indirectly, through the provision of non-standardized financial support and insurance, which are not available without the support of new financial products. All three functions combined suggest that

[9] We are grateful to David Soskice for this insight.

economies with stronger financial services are more driven by domestic demand and more closely related to a highly productive service economy (as confirmed by our data below).

The prime example for financialization as an expression of wealth, and a driver of financialization more generally, is the housing sector. The housing sector is also arguably the single most important area that links the financial world to the real economy. A large part of the increasing financialization of modern economies is rooted in the housing market in several ways. First, the majority of bank lending is mortgage-based, and banks, as well as asset management firms, benefit from rising mortgage levels (Jordà, Schularick, and Taylor 2016). Second, the housing market is an important transmission channel for monetary policy. Interest rate changes affect the housing market first and foremost, and, thereby, indirectly have an impact on house price developments. The extent to which house prices respond to interest rates determines the effectiveness of monetary policy.[10] Third, rising house prices add to the wealth effect of financialization, as higher house prices contribute to the wealth of homeowners directly or allow them to use their houses as collateral (see Reisenbichler, this volume). Fourth, pension retrenchment and pension privatization has increased the importance of homeownership for the middle class as a source of retirement income. This, in turn, has effects on the political preferences of homeowners on social policy issues. Funded pensions spur financialization not only directly, through the assets of pension funds, but also indirectly, through the increased pressure on the housing market (Hassel et al. 2019).

Finally, there is a link between financialization and the trade balance, in particular with emerging and developing economies, but also between advanced industrialized countries. While emerging economies, in particular in Asia, accumulated foreign currency reserves and, thereby, fueled the financial markets in countries with trade deficits, advanced countries with a current account surplus also added to financialization in countries with deficits (van Treeck 2009).

In order to analyze the degree of financialization of advanced capitalist economies, we gathered data on households saving rates, house prices, the share of private pension funds and the rate of home ownership, and the current account, as shown in Table 1.1. This allows us to cluster countries according to different degrees and dimensions of financialization.

The most financialized countries are those which have a low savings rate (below 5%), high house price inflation (more than 100% since 1980), high shares of pension funds (more than 50% of GDP), and a current account deficit. Using these

[10] "If the financial accelerator hypothesis is correct, changes in home values may affect household borrowing and spending by somewhat more than suggested by the conventional wealth effect because changes in homeowners' net worth also affect their external finance premiums and thus their costs of credit" (Bernanke 2007).

Table 1.1 Indicators of financialization

	Household savings rates	Real house prices		Current account	Pension funds (autonomous)	Home ownership
	Average	Index based in 2010		Average	Assets (% of GDP)	Percentage of households that own their homes
	1995–2007	1980	2000	2000–7	2000–7	2017 (except when specified)
Australia	2.39	34.5	54.17	–4.77	78.69	67.00*
Austria	10.76		92.65	0.66	4.27	55.00
Belgium	10.87	55.1	62.08	3.58	4.47	72.70
Canada		48.3	57.79	1.00	54.34	67.60*
Czech Republic	6.19			–3.82	3.46	78.5
Denmark	–2.52	61.8	73.74	2.01	30.19	62.4
Finland		46.9	75.12	5.52	60.86	71.4
France	10.41	51.7	55.68	1.06	0.03	64.4
Germany	9.99	124.6	113.67	1.98	3.91	51.4
Greece	–3.44		74.64	–6.79	0.00	73.3
Hungary	7.07			–7.12	7.14	85.3
Ireland	0.12	42.8	81.44	–1.02	43.09	69.50
Italy	10.36	62.7	72.67	–0.44	2.63	72.40
Japan	5.40	103.5	130.84	3.14	10.76	61.70
South Korea			77.04	2.95	1.98	57.7
Netherlands	7.85	54.3	82.34	4.95	111.09	69.4
New Zealand	–2.75	32.8	59.02	–4.30	12.57	64.80**
Norway		38.2	62.20		6.34	81.50
Poland	6.54			–3.83	7.16	84.2
Portugal	3.18		119.60	–8.59	11.77	74.70
Slovak Republic				–6.87	0.94	90.10
Slovenia				–1.55	1.22	75.60
Spain	4.12	31.1	55.97	–4.47	6.74	77.10

Sweden	5.56	62.6	54.46	5.55	8.10	65.20
Switzerland	14.78	85.6	79.45	10.34	105.24	38.00
United Kingdom	2.85	33.5	60.98	−1.84	69.89	65.00
United States	4.82	77.1	90.36	−4.08	72.57	64.40***

Notes: Data mainly cover the period before the financial crisis in order to illustrate the long-term trend. Home ownership rates are quite stable.

*2016; **2013; ***2018

Sources: Household savings rates: OECD National Accounts; Real house prices: OECD Analytical House Price database; Current Account: OECD National Accounts; Pension funds: OECD Funded Pensions Indicators; Home Ownership: European Mortgage Federation Hypostat 2019, US Census. https://www.census.gov/housing/hvs/files/qtr319/hown319.png, Canada census, New Zealand census https://tradingeconomics.com for South Korea and Japan, https://www.aihw.gov.au/reports/australias-welfare/home-ownership-and-housing-tenure, Swiss Federal Statistic Office. https://www.bfs.admin.ch/bfs/en/home/statistics/construction-housing/dwellings/housing-conditions/tenants-owners.html

indicators based on data prior to the financial crisis, we can identify four more or less distinct groups:

(1) All English-speaking countries (identified as LMEs in the VoC literature and domestic, demand-led growth models by Baccaro and Pontusson) are in the group of most financialized countries (though Canada shows a positive current account balance and Ireland and New Zealand less than a 50% share of pension funds).
(2) At the other end of the spectrum, the least financialized countries with a high savings rate of more than 9%, low house price inflation and pension funds, and a positive current account are Austria and Germany, but also Korea and Japan (though low savings rate). Switzerland follows closely (but for a high share of pension funds as share of GDP), as well as France and Belgium (but for a relatively high degree of house price inflation).
(3) Among the exporting countries with a positive trade balance, the Nordic countries and the Netherlands are the most financialized: all of them have substantial house price inflation of almost 100% in 20 years; the Netherlands and Finland have high shares of pension funds; Norway has the Sovereign Wealth Fund that replaces the role of pension funds; Denmark has negative savings rates, while the others (for which there are data) have moderate ones.
(4) The remaining group of countries consists of Southern and Eastern European countries, which have less of a wealth effect to begin with and show a mixed pattern. All of them have a low share of pension funds. Spain and Greece have the lowest savings rates and the highest house price inflation and are, therefore, the closest to a financialized growth regime. Italy also shows signs of house price inflation, but has a high savings rate.

Financialization has a number of direct effects on and policy implications for growth regimes. For one, highly financialized countries have bigger employment segments in dynamic services (financial services, but also business services). These services, which rely heavily on ICT specialists, will compete with the manufacturing sector over graduates, and financial services might start to dominate the graduate market (see Figure 1.2).

Furthermore, highly financialized countries also see a shift in the wage structure favoring the financial services industries and thus reinforcing the trend towards increasing income inequalities. Indeed, they have already seen an increase in wage dispersion at the high end of the wage structure. A comparison between Germany and Sweden shows the extent to which financial services gained relatively higher wages in Sweden compared to Germany (see Thelen; Baccaro and Pontusson in this volume).

With regards to (welfare) policy strategies, countries with a more financialized growth regime are more prone to private funding and the private organization of

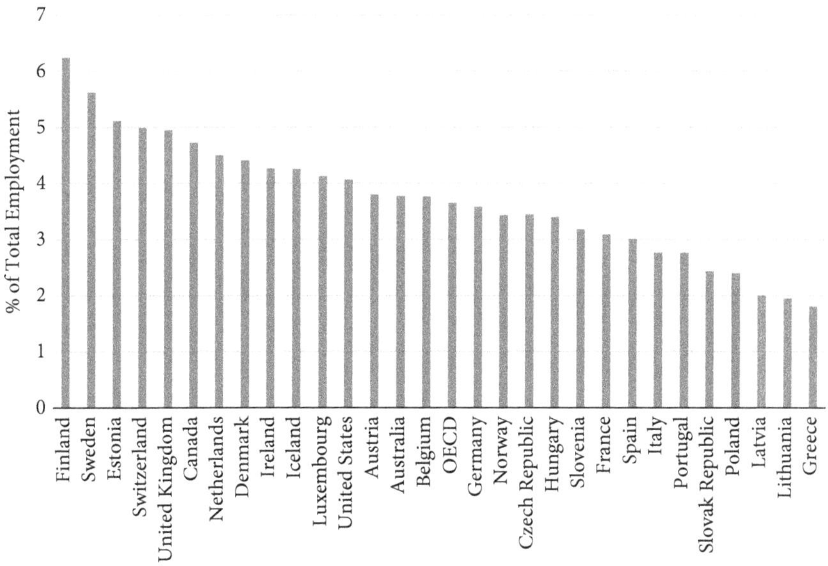

Figure 1.2 Employment of ICT specialists across the economy, 2016, as share of total employment

Source: OECD (2017), Digital Economy Outlook, p. 182. Based on Figure 4.22, Employment of ICT specialists across the economy, 2016.

social and infrastructure services, as the financial services industries supply models and expertise for this (see Thelen in this volume for Swedish and Dutch examples; Avlijaš et al. in this volume more generally). In those countries which pursue a more financial growth strategy, we see private funding for infrastructure, but also moves towards private, fully-funded pension schemes, as well as private education services (Chevalier, this volume).

Finally, more financialized growth regimes also pursue more radical innovation paths in ICT. To start with, the financial services industry itself is highly technologically advanced. According to Wren (2013; and this volume), the financial intermediation sector is the sector with the highest ICT intensity. Furthermore, high levels of financialization allow for venture capital for hi-tech firms through pension and mutual funds. There is, therefore, a close link between financialization and the ICT sector, as we discuss in section 4.3.

4.3 Innovation, Digitalization, and the Knowledge-Based Economy

Despite the profound impact of ICT on the economy since the 1990s and the resulting changes in peoples' lives, the effects of digitalization and the knowledge-based economy on the political economies of the advanced world are even less researched and discussed in the comparative political economy literature than the role of financialization. There is very little research by political economy researchers into the role and meaning of ICT for either growth regimes or the welfare state.[11]

ICT has fundamentally changed value creation in rich countries. The low end of manufacturing has, in many cases, been relocated to developing countries, while firms have started to create new higher-value-added products in manufacturing and services through newly developed ICT. ICT transforms the nature of work and organization, as well as the monetization of work. Beginning with the introduction of computer-aided manufacturing and design (CAD) and robots in production processes during the 1980s, the 2010s have seen a rapid proliferation of a new kind of information technology–based innovation.

This innovation has come in different forms:

- In manufacturing, ICT has enabled complex, cross-national global value chains, based on a process of decomposition (regional specialization) and recomposition (reintegration of development and production). Production has been outsourced, but also reintegrated, depending on whether specific parts of production are seen as strategically important.
- ICT-based dynamic services, such as those in telecommunications, and financial and business services, have been fast-growing employment segments in advanced, industrialized countries (Wren 2013; and this volume). In the richest countries of the OECD, employment levels in dynamic services are now higher than in traditional manufacturing sectors.
- The role of ICT in non-dynamic services, such as retail, transport, and hotels, is also ever more visible. Cloud computing enables the creation of both new workplaces and new markets for work. It changes the way paid work is organized through cyber-platforms, ranging from oDesk, Amazon Mechanical Turk, Uber, Airbnb, and TaskRabbit to YouTube, Udemy, and Amazon self-publishing (Zysman and Kenney 2014).
- The integration of platforms in mature production processes in manufacturing and in services through web services and cloud computing changes value creation (Rahman and Thelen 2019).

In contrast to earlier processes of innovation, diffuse spans of technology and organizational disruption are short and global (Rahman and Thelen 2019). Independent of the regulatory and institutional setting, the dynamic but destabilizing

[11] See, for the few exceptions, Zysman and Breznitz (2012) and Colin and Palier (2015). Wren (2013, and this volume) discusses the role of ICT for dynamic services. On the specific role of digital platforms, see Rahman and Thelen (2019).

effects of digitalization and the importance of the knowledge economy are enormous. Some economists assume that increasing automation will eliminate a large part of semi-skilled, routine-based occupations (Brynjolfsson and McAfee 2014; Frey and Osborne 2013; for a reassessment of these predictions, see Arntz et al. 2016). This development has been forecasted by theories of task-biased technological change, which assumes a polarization of the workforce. They argue that ICT technology is a substitute for workers with mid-range skills, but is likely to complement the skills of those with tertiary education (Autor et al. 2003; Goos et al. 2009). Some studies in sociology assessing changes in employment structures have supported this view (Oesch and Rodriguez Menés 2011). However, technological change itself cannot explain all the transformations, since more detailed analyses of polarization in the labor market have shown different patterns (Fernandez-Macias and Hurley 2016; Peugny 2019). It is argued in this volume's final chapter that these variations have to be linked to the variety of growth strategies.

These new patterns of value creation and innovation contribute to the transformation of growth regimes and changes in the welfare and labor market regulation of modern societies in several ways. They feed in particular into the existing mix of export-based and/or financialized growth regimes and shape them further towards specialization in either manufacturing exports (such as in Germany), high-tech services exports (such as Sweden), and financial and ICT services (such as the UK and the US).

As mentioned earlier, financialization had an impact on the ICT revolution since the development of financial capital contributed to boosting investment and ICT-based jobs. Correlating data on employment in ICT with pension fund assets as a proxy indicator for financialization gives a first indication that the more financialized countries are also those which have the highest employment share in ICT. As Figure 1.3 shows, all countries with pension fund assets higher than 20% of GDP also have higher levels of ICT employment than countries with low or no pension fund assets. Sweden is the only country with rather low pension fund assets but high shares of employment in ICT. In addition to high financialization, another driver for this development is the higher levels of university graduates with more general skills in these countries (see both Wren and Chevalier in this volume).

On the whole, different countries have tackled the issues of financialization and digitalization in different ways. Some countries have transformed their growth regimes around ICT innovation in combination with financialization. Other countries have focused on export and refrained from engaging in financialization. In section 4.4 we put this in the framework of the growth model literature in order to illustrate the new dynamics of growth regimes as a synthesis of domestic demand versus exports in combination with new sources of growth. This provides us with a basic mapping of the transformed growth regimes of advanced capitalist economies in the 21st century (post-financial crisis).

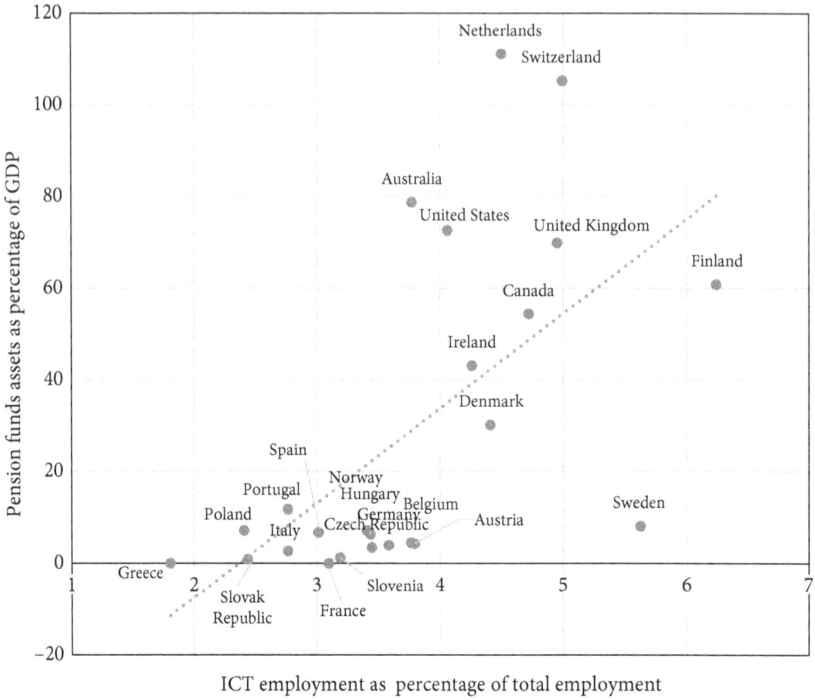

Figure 1.3 ICT employment as percentage of total employment, 2016, and pension fund (autonomous) assets (% of GDP, 2000–7)

Source: See Figure 1.1 on ICT employment and Table 1.1 on pension fund assets.

4.4 Export and Demand-Driven Growth in the Twenty-First Century

The policy response to the financial crisis and to the subsequent Eurozone crisis has triggered fierce debates among economists on both sides of the Atlantic about policy measures to combat stagnation and weak growth. US macroeconomists insist on demand deficiency as a major part of the problem and suggest stronger economic stimuli as the answer. Policy-makers in Europe, however, have largely opted for austerity policies, hoping for supply-side economic restructuring. Underlying this debate is, however, the question of what is seen as the engine of growth and job creation in national economies.

As discussed in the current comparative political economy debate and by Baccaro and Pontusson, Picot, and Scharpf (among others) in this volume, there can be two main types of driver of economic growth: foreign demand (exports) or domestic demand (household and government consumption). In Table 1.2 we divide the countries into exporters and consumers in 2016.

Table 1.2 Export share in GDP of OECD countries (2016)

Consumers	Percentage of exports in GDP	Exporters	Percentage of exports in GDP
Australia	21.2	Austria	52.5
Canada	31.5	Belgium	79.4
Finland	34.8	Czech Republic	79.6
France	30.2	Denmark	53.4
Greece	30.1	Estonia	77.5
Italy	29.6	Germany	46.0
Japan	16.3	Hungary	87.2
New Zealand	26.4	Ireland	120.8
Spain	33.1	Korea	40.1
United Kingdom	28.4	Luxembourg	213.0
United States	11.9	Netherlands	79.5
		Poland	52.2
		Portugal	40.2
		Slovak Republic	93.7
		Slovenia	78.0
		Sweden	43.3
		Switzerland	65.7

Note: Exporters are open economies with an export share of around and above 40% of GDP. Consumers are more closed economies. Latest available data. https://data.oecd.org/trade/trade-in-goods-and-services.htm#indicator-chart (accessed January 29, 2020).

Source: OECD.

During the Fordist era, economies benefitted from advances in productivity and more technological upgrading on the supply side that allowed for a wage increase, but there were already differences between countries favoring more domestic demand or more exports.[12] Since the early 1970s, most countries have compensated for lower growth rates through higher public spending (Streeck 2014; see Picot, this volume). Today, the source for domestic demand has diversified even more. Demand stimulus to the domestic economy stems from raising household incomes either through wages, social benefits, public deficits, or the capacity to access credit (see Picot, this volume). As financial services are a key component of consumption, new financial products stimulate domestic demand.

However, countries can (also or alternatively) privilege the export of goods in order to maintain high-value-added employment by producing for world markets. Export can thus temporarily protect the manufacturing industry from deindustrialization (Dauth et al. 2017). But countries can also specialize in high-value-added, high-skill services to boost export, as is demonstrated by Wren in this volume. Export-led growth regimes specialize especially in export commodities

[12] Germany was already focused on wage moderation and supporting its exporting industry in the 1950s (Höpner 2019), and the Nordic countries, as many other small countries, relied on exports to boost growth and wages (Katzenstein 1985).

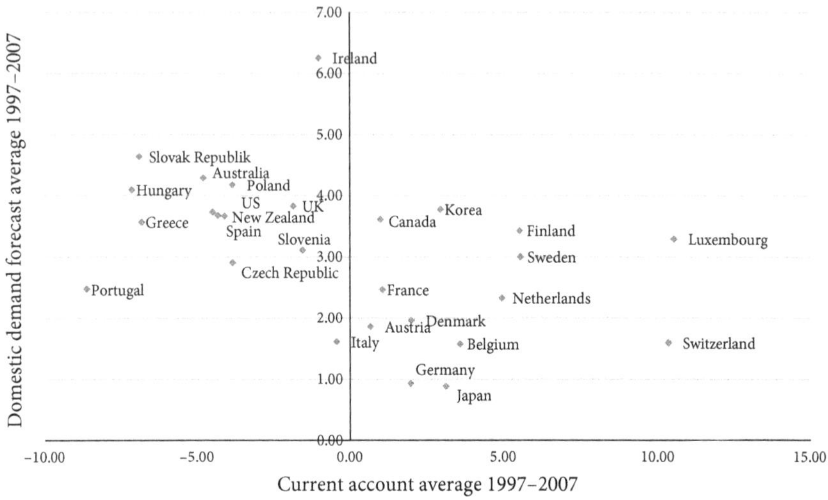

Figure 1.4 Current account balance, 1997–2007 and change in domestic demand, 1997–2007 (%)

Source: OECD Statistics, Key Short-term Economic Indicators; Domestic demand forecast.

that may require different types of skills and social protection. In all these cases, the value-added in exposed sectors is higher than it would be if the country focused on domestic markets. Thus, manufacturing and other exposed sectors are privileged over other protected sectors.

As discussed by Baccaro and Pontusson in this volume, it is not clear to what extent both strategies can co-exist. Theoretically, domestic consumption-led growth regimes do not undermine export-led growth as long as higher labor costs do not endanger competitiveness.[13] Empirically, there seems to be a trade-off between export-led and domestic consumption-led growth (see Figure 1.4 and Picot, this volume). Figure 1.4 indicates that the more positive a country current account is, the less it sees its domestic demand increase. This was at least the case during the period before the financial crisis.[14] Furthermore, as analyzed by Scharpf in this volume, the export-led growth model is currently imposed on all countries of the Eurozone, including those which had a domestic demand-led growth regime (see also Hall 2018; Iversen and Soskice 2018).

[13] Baccaro and Pontusson (2016) argue that the Fordist growth regime is, in principle, domestic demand-led (wage-led in their terminology). Only extreme versions of export-led growth, which are dependent on price-sensitive manufacturing exports, might turn against demand in order to control labor costs and the real exchange rate.

[14] After 2008 and the start of the financial crisis the correlation between change in domestic demand and current account turns positive (until 2016), as domestic demand-led countries experience austerity and export-driven economies temporarily stimulate domestic demand (see Baccaro and Pontusson, this volume).

4.5 The Five Growth Regimes of Contemporary Advanced Capitalist Economies

If one distinguishes between those economies that rely on exports as a source of growth and those that do not (see Table 1.2), we see a clear pattern. All English-speaking liberal market economies (in the VoC terminology), except Ireland, and most Southern European economies (including France) are largely domestic demand-led economies, whereas both Nordic and Continental as well as Eastern European economies are nearly all export-focused. We are here able to broaden the scope of Baccaro and Pontusson's growth models approach beyond the four countries that have been the focus of their work.

However, if we look closely at the different components of growth regimes as we have defined them in section 3.2 (i.e., the various engines of growth, the institutions organizing the economy, and the main component of aggregate demand), on the basis of the information gathered in Tables 1.1 and 1.2 and Figure 1.4 and summarized in Table 1.3, we can distinguish five different configurations: three types of export-led growth regimes and two types of domestic demand-led ones.

Among the export-focused countries, we can identify three subgroups:

- Countries which combine an export focus with strong domestic demand, such as all but one of the Nordic economies (Denmark is an exception as far as demand is concerned), Luxembourg, and the Netherlands (this is what Baccaro and Pontusson call "balanced growth models"). They are progressively shifting from the manufacturing industry to dynamic services as the key driver of growth, benefiting from financialization to feed the growth of ICT-based service sectors. They have also developed low-pay private services.
- Countries where export of manufacturing goods is the main driver of growth, with low growth in domestic demand (below 2%) before the financial crisis, such as Germany, but also Austria, Belgium, and Switzerland. These countries rely heavily on the competitive position of companies in high-quality manufacturing and often use the most refined mechanisms of diversified quality production (Streeck 1991) to protect this position. They primarily benefit from high growth rates in emerging economies that satisfy their demand for machinery and high-end consumer goods.
- Countries with increasing shares of exports, but negative current accounts and relatively high rates of domestic demand, such as those in Central and Eastern Europe. Like the subgroup that includes Germany and Austria, these countries follow a manufacturing, export-oriented strategy (Bohle and Greskovits 2012; Picot, this volume). They are heavily integrated into German-based production networks and depend even more on low prices (hence low wages and low welfare). They (together with Ireland) are also highly dependent on foreign direct investment (Bohle and Regan forthcoming).

Table 1.3 Characteristics of the five growth regimes

	Dynamic services export-led growth regime	**High-quality manufacturing export-led growth regime**	**FDI-financed export-led growth regime**	**Finance-based domestic demand-led growth regimes**	**Publicly financed domestic demand-led growth regime**
Demand drivers of growth	Export	Export	Export	Domestic consumption	Domestic consumption
Current account	Surplus	Surplus	Mixed	Deficit	Deficit
Financialization	High	Low	Low	High	Low
Knowledge economy (ICT)	High	Medium	Low	High	Low
Education system	Inclusive high-level	Inclusive mid-level	Inclusive mid-level	Elitist	Elitist
Social protection	Social investment	Social insurance	Social insurance	Private insurance and investment	Social insurance
Wage-setting	Coordinated	Coordinated	Deregulated	Deregulated	Regulated

Source: Rows 1-3 are based on Table 1.1; row 4 is based on Figure 1.2, row 5 is based on Chevalier (this volume), row 6 on Palier and Hay (2017), and row 7 on Visser (2019) ICTWSS database on wage-setting.

We can also identify two subgroups among the countries relying foremost on domestic consumption and demand-led growth:

- Countries with a high level of domestic consumption, a high degree of financialization, and also high development of ICT (all the English-speaking LMEs of the VoC but one: Ireland). As restructuring is more rapid, and fluctuations more pronounced, these economies saw deindustrialization earlier, and more deeply, than the coordinated market economies of Northern Europe. For example, the decline of British manufacturing already took place in the 1960s, when British companies could no longer deliver high-quality products at a reasonable price due to higher levels of industrial conflict, lower investment in training and quality, and difficulties in implementing wage moderation. Colin Crouch (2009) has convincingly shown how easy access to credit and a vibrant housing market have been key to consumption-based growth in the UK and the US since the 1980s.
- Countries with a high level of domestic consumption but relatively low level of financialization and ICT development (mostly the countries of Southern Europe, including France). This is due to relatively easy access to cheap credit (especially after the introduction of the euro) and generous "consumption-oriented" social insurance (Beramendi et al. 2015). In Southern Europe, labor market institutions appear to be centralized, and corporate finance is closer to the model typical of the CMEs. However, these regulations and institutions do not deliver the same collective goods as in typical CMEs (Molina and Rhodes 2007; Hassel 2014). Because their coordination depends on the intervention of the (welfare) state, governments have pursued a more active, consumption-led growth policy and let wages and social spending rise (see also Höpner and Lutter 2014). Therefore, this type of country generally has a lower export orientation.

As explained above, the domestic-demand regimes can connect well with financialization, which has an expanding effect on the economy through higher consumption due to wealth effects (Boyer 2000). Wealth effects are primarily created by house price inflation. But, as we have shown in Table1.1 and in Figure1.3, financialization itself, through its capacity to finance start-ups and new economic activities, can also facilitate the development of new, high-end sectors, based on ICT, that can lead to national consumption as well as to exports (Uber or Amazon rely on the national consumption of services, but are global companies) (see Wren, this volume). Domestic demand can thus be fueled by financialization, which, in turn, is driven by the housing market, pension privatization, and low savings rates. The current account deficit also drives financialization, as it attracts foreign financial assets, which in turn expand financial services in countries with trade deficits.

By contrast, as indicated partly in Figure 1.4, a high share of exports and a current account surplus are often correlated with comparatively lower rates of increase in domestic demand. As a result, we generally see a complementary relationship between countries' trade deficits and surpluses (Iversen and Soskice 2013). Still, financialization has also occurred in some countries with an export-based growth regime. In particular, the Nordic countries and the Netherlands have combined domestic demand policies via financialization with an export strategy (see Baccaro and Pontusson; Thelen, this volume). However, another possibility for stimulating domestic demand is to rely on private and public debt that supports wage increases and/or consumption-oriented social benefits, as is typical in Southern Europe.

As far as ICT is concerned, all advanced countries are affected by the ICT revolution and embrace investment in ICT. Nevertheless, investment in ICT is higher in countries with higher levels of financialization. This potentially puts the Continental European countries apart from the Nordic countries (including the Netherlands), which have higher rates of domestic demand, financialization, and ICT investment compared to the German-speaking coordinated market economies (see Figures 1.2 and 1.3; Wren, this volume).

Southern European countries have embraced financialization to some extent, as home ownership rates are high and house prices have become inflated. It is, however, less related to ICT innovation, but is a primarily domestic, consumption-driven regime. Data on Eastern Europe regarding financialization and ICT are very limited. They have low levels of financialization but high levels of home ownership, which might trigger faster financialization in the future.

In Table 1.3, we summarize the main traits of the five identified growth regimes, including those we have highlighted in this section (i.e. the demand driver of growth, the current account situation, the degree of financialization, and the development of the knowledge economy) as well as those related to the labor market, education, and welfare systems. The table is heuristic in nature with empirical observations clustering to ideal types rather than defined characterizations. As demonstrated in the rest of the volume, the different growth regimes show a number of characteristics that are particularly relevant for understanding the specific growth strategies developed by different countries. The concluding chapter of the book comes back to these five growth regimes to analyze more specifically the growth strategies that can be associated with them, and more specifically the distinct labor market, education, and welfare state reforms they pursued (Avlijaš et al., this volume).

5. Plan of the Book

This volume is divided into three parts. The first part, chapters 1–5, further explores the general evolution of growth strategies and growth regimes. The second part comprises chapters 6–8 and analyzes the politics of various growth strategies and their changes over time in specific countries. The last part, covering chapters 9–12, focuses on the connection between growth strategies and welfare reforms.

In the first part, four chapters focus on how growth strategies and regimes have developed over time, one (Hall) from the post-war to the contemporary period and two (Baccaro and Pontusson, Picot) on the years since the 2008 financial crisis. This part also provides a look at changes at the EU level, showing how the export-led regime has been imposed on all Eurozone countries (Scharpf). It confirms that growth regimes have changed tremendously since Fordism. While Hall's chapter traces the general evolution of government growth strategies over six decades, the three other chapters allow for a precise understanding of the developments of growth regimes since the 2008 financial crisis.

Chapter 2 by Peter Hall analyses the growth strategies pursued by governments in the developed democracies over the decades since World War II. It identifies three main periods: the era of modernization, the era of liberalization and the era of knowledge-based growth. The first runs from 1950 to about 1975, the second from 1980 to the late 1990s, and the third from 2000 to the present. It charts the relationship between developments in the political economy and changes in the realm of electoral politics. Using the examples of the UK, France, Sweden, and Germany, the chapter shows how growth strategies shifted across these three eras in response to secular developments in the international economy that altered the terms on which growth could be secured and shifts in what might be termed the "economic gestalt" of each era, namely, how economic problems are perceived as well as changes to the cleavage structures of the electoral arena which alter the terms on which coalitions of support for specific policies can be assembled. Although the chapter does not address them in depth, it acknowledges the importance of a parallel set of changes in the realm of producer group politics which alter the influence of particular groups, the kinds of policies they seek, and the levels of cooperation on which governments can count to operate growth strategies.

Chapter 3 by Lucio Baccaro and Jonas Pontusson mobilizes their "growth models" approach to analyze how the governments of Sweden, Germany, the UK, and Italy responded to the Great Recession. The patterns of economic growth in its wake shows that the growth models that were adopted in the previous period have so far been remarkably resilient. Sweden is the only case for which a significant shift in the drivers of economic growth is visible: household consumption played a more important role in 2010–14 than in 2001–7 and, conversely, net exports played a less important role. In Germany, net exports became the main driver of demand over the period 1994–2007, due to the combination of domestic demand repression, institutionalized wage moderation, and the single currency. In the UK, by contrast, a demand boost was engineered by easing the conditions for access to credit, while accepting a systematic deterioration of the current account. Prior to the Great Recession, the Swedish case stood between those of Germany and the UK: stimulated by higher wage growth than in Germany and also by easing access to credit, domestic demand and exports both contributed to GDP growth. This balanced growth pattern was accompanied by the diversification of Swedish exports, with manufacturing playing a less prominent role than in the past. Finally, Italian stagnation before and after the Great Recession has been the result of extremely difficult external circumstances (particularly the decreased attractiveness of Italian exports as a result of increased international competition) combined with inappropriate policy choices, especially the choice to accept an overvalued exchange rate through membership in the single currency (Eurozone).

Chapter 4 by Georg Picot maps the variety of growth models across developed countries since 1995. It focuses on three broad potential sources of additional economic demand: public deficits, private deficits, and trade surpluses. The empirical section uses fuzzy-set ideal-type analysis to identify the combinations in which advanced economies used these three "demand boosters" in three subperiods between 1995 and 2016. The results show that most economies used at least one of these three ways of generating extra demand to tackle the era of low growth. The chapter shows that, over the period under scrutiny, in Continental and Nordic Europe as well as in East Asia, current account surpluses are the main way of boosting economic growth by profiting from demand abroad. By contrast, Southern and Eastern Europe as well as English-speaking countries tend to boost economic demand through domestic deficits, in Southern and Eastern Europe more strongly through public deficits and in English-speaking countries more strongly through private deficits. While some countries have changed their growth strategies after the global financial and economic crisis, the abovementioned pattern holds broadly both before and after the crisis. Therefore, most countries build their economic recovery by and large on the same demand boosters as before the crisis. Looking at the performances of each model, the chapter shows that the finance-led growth model fares best in terms of economic growth and has the highest private spending on education. The export-led model performs best in terms of job creation and, for the Nordic countries, in public investment in education. The state-led model is associated with the lowest growth and lowest levels of employment.

Finally, chapter 5 by Fritz Scharpf focuses on the interaction and evolution of growth regimes within the Eurozone. It shows that the deep divide between countries in the Eurozone can be explained as a consequence of the structural diversity in growth regimes among Northern and Southern economies and of an asymmetrical euro regime that must try to enforce the structural convergence of their political economies. The chapter emphasizes that the structural differences of Northern and Southern political economies include two dimensions: institutional differences in the capacity of unions to achieve voluntary wage restraint and differences in the relative size of the exposed and sheltered sectors (i.e., whether the economy is export-led or domestic demand-led). Northern economies (Germany, Austria, the Netherlands, Belgium, Finland, and Ireland) are structurally defined by the combination of a large export sector with an institutional capacity for wage restraint. Southern economies (Greece, Spain, and Portugal, but also Italy and France) combine a large domestic sector with industrial relations systems that tend to generate wage inflation. The chapter analyzes the impact of the current euro regime, which attempts to enforce the structural convergence of Eurozone economies through austerity and supply-side reforms and thus imposes one main growth strategy on everyone (the export-led one). It concludes by pointing out that the economic success of enforced convergence is still in doubt, whereas its political sustainability is undermined by a persistent lack of democratic legitimacy.

In the *second part* of the book, three chapters engage with the political economy of growth strategies in Europe. They trace the process of economic and social policy change in specific European countries since the 1990s, including since the financial crisis. The chapters focus on the politics of growth strategies, and on the complementarities between various sectors' growth strategies. They allow identification of the role played by actors and by institutions in the framing and transformation of growth strategies. They emphasize the importance of welfare regimes and institutions in the shaping and evolution of growth strategies. Kathleen Thelen underlines the role played by producers' groups in the decision-making process leading to specific growth strategies and their reorientation over time, while Cathie Jo Martin analyzes the variety of employers' preferences in terms of growth strategies in different growth regimes. Anne Wren focuses on the complementarities between low- and high-skill services growth strategies. Each of these chapters show how the implementation of various growth strategies can progressively transform the very growth regime of a country.

Kathleen Thelen's chapter 6 proposes an understanding of how growth regimes can change through the implementation of different growth strategies. It examines the role of producers' groups (unions, employers, and trade associations) in defending and/or (re-)defining national growth regimes through a comparison of three countries identified by VoC as coordinated market economies: Germany, the Netherlands, and Sweden. The chapter shows that differences in the structure of organized interests in the three countries produced divergent trajectories of change in industrial relations, education and training, and labor market policy. As a result, the three countries evolved differently. In Germany, intense cross-class cooperation within industry has sustained a growth strategy based on labor market and social protection dualization that has allowed the country's traditional strength in high-quality manufacturing to be shored up. By contrast, the Netherlands explicitly abandoned the heavily manufacturing-based growth regime in the 1980s that it had embraced in the

1950s and 1960s in favor of a move (back) to its traditional strengths in trade and business services. In this case, wholly new groups progressively emerged, groups whose interests were then increasingly reflected across all three arenas—industrial relations, the labor market, and education policy. In Sweden, union strength in low-end services prevented a German-style dualization and pushed firms upmarket, a move that also contributed to enhancing the power (on the union side) of white-collar interests, while also (on the employer side) giving rise to vocal new actors (particularly the employers and trade associations for the Swedish service sector). These developments contributed to a move of the Swedish growth regime into higher-end, more knowledge-intensive segments of manufacturing and services.

Cathie Jo Martin's chapter 7 explores how employers form preferences for social policies, participate in reform coalitions, and gain collective capacities to influence government. It starts by exploring the welfare state preferences of diverse producer coalitions, identifying the interest of business in six different sectors (from high-quality manufacturing to low-pay services through to highly-skilled services) and show how they pursue different avenues for growth. These include the alternative growth strategies articulated in earlier chapters: growth through the export of manufacturing goods, growth through exports of dynamic services, demand-led growth relying on public Keynesian fiscal policies, and demand-led growth relying on private Keynesian policies to foster easy credit and household debt. It then discusses cases in which policies seem to deviate from these predicted positions. Finally, the chapter explores how industrial relations organizations contribute to firms' preferences, coalitions, and their capacities for economic adjustment. It shows that macro-corporatist peak business associations expose employers to arguments about social contributions to economic growth, overcome limits to collective action, enforce compliance with negotiated regulations, and cede significant influence over policy outcomes to business. Furthermore, high levels of coordination also augment capacities for economic correction at points in which older growth strategies become less viable.

Anne Wren's chapter 8 focuses on the role of skill formation, wage-setting, and public service provision in shaping national growth strategies in a post-industrial context, taking the cases of Germany, Sweden, and the UK as detailed examples. It helps to understand the interactions between the supply and demand sides of the economy. In particular it highlights the role played by skills policy in shaping patterns of specialization in high-productivity, traded sectors, which are important engines of growth even in "consumption-led" regimes. It shows that Sweden's ability to compete in less price-sensitive, high-end services (and manufacturing) markets rests on the availability of a workforce with high levels of tertiary skills. In contrast, Germany's reliance on more traditional manufacturing sectors is rooted in its well-established system of firm-based vocational training and its limited tertiary education sector. In the UK, the expansion of domestic demand has, in part, been debt-driven, although it has also, as in the Swedish case, been facilitated by rising real wages. While domestic demand has contributed more to growth in relative terms in the UK than in Sweden, nevertheless a key driver of rising real wages in the UK has also been productivity growth and the expansion of trade in high-end, ICT-intensive services. The chapter confirms that welfare state policies (including the protection of relative wages, public service provision, and, above all, strategies of skill formation) are critical to the outcomes observed in the context of deindustrialization and technological change. It concludes that the development of sustainable strategies for growth and employment creation in a context of deindustrialization and of revolutionary changes in ICT rely on the creation of a capacity to expand into ICT-intensive, high-value-added sectors, and especially in dynamic services sectors.

The third part of this volume consists of chapters 9–12. These four chapters delve into the evolution of welfare regimes and their contribution to growth regime changes. Chapters in this part focus on welfare reforms (i.e., changes in labor market policies and reforms of the education system and social policies) within growth strategies and the feedback effect of their implementation on growth regimes. The first three chapters focus on specific aspects of welfare reforms and how they are connected to specific growth strategies: wage formation, housing policies, and education and youth policies. The last chapter identifies five main growth strategies implemented in Europe and analyzes the connections between these and five main types of welfare state reforms. These chapters connecting growth strategies and welfare reforms contribute to our understanding of the process of transformation of growth and welfare regimes.

Chapter 9 by Alison Johnston demonstrates a clear connection between growth regimes and labor market policies, especially wage policies. It analyzes the impact of wage restraint on different growth models. It questions the supply-side, comparative capitalism research (VoC especially) assumption that wage moderation—facilitated through highly-coordinated wage-setting institutions—always produces beneficial growth outcomes. This supposition stems from the logic that restrained unit labor cost growth causes firms to increase employment and output. However, through its demand-side perspective, the growth model literature questions the virtues of wage moderation, because the restraint of wages can be detrimental to growth via its suppression of domestic consumption. The chapter empirically tests under what conditions wage moderation produces beneficial growth outcomes. Using a first-difference, distributive lag panel analysis of eighteen OECD countries during the period 1970–2015, its findings largely resonate with predictions within the growth model literature. In the presence of wage restraint, countries with larger export shares and highly-coordinated wage-setting institutions realize higher growth and lower unemployment than countries with smaller export shares and uncoordinated wage-setting institutions. In contrast, wage inflation produces better growth outcomes for countries with uncoordinated wage-setting, relative to those with highly-coordinated wage-setting institutions. These results suggest that wage restraint is not a winning strategy for all growth regimes. Rather, wage moderation is associated with better growth (and employment) outcomes only for countries with export-facing growth strategies.

In chapter 10, Alexander Reisenbichler explores the interlinkages between housing finance, the welfare state, and growth regimes and how these links shape how policy-makers utilize housing finance policies as growth strategies. The chapter shows that demand-led economies relying on credit and consumption, such as the US and the UK, have complementary "financialized" growth strategies in the housing finance area. These include policies to stimulate demand, credit, and growth in the wider economy. In contrast, countries based on exports and manufacturing, such as Germany, have complementary growth strategies in the housing sector to secure cost competitiveness. These include conservative housing finance policies designed to restrain demand and dynamic housing markets, so as to keep down the cost of living, wages, and price developments. Export-oriented economies specializing in high-tech manufacturing and dynamic services, such as the Nordic economies, might be characterized as intermediate cases, where dynamic housing finance markets neither reinforce nor contradict their growth regimes. As high-tech firms are less concerned with securing wage competitiveness or restraining credit and consumption, these countries can adopt "financialized" housing policies as part of a larger strategy to liberalize financial markets and boost private wealth. To illustrate these arguments, the chapter discusses housing finance policies as growth strategies in the US and Germany since the late 1970s. In the US, policy-makers have employed "financializing" housing policies as growth strategies in pursuit of stimulating demand, credit, and consumption. By contrast, German policy-makers have adopted structural reforms that scaled down public support for housing finance, with the goal of balancing budgets, reviving competitiveness, and reducing distortions that channel investments away from production. Focusing on housing finance confirms that states are often active drivers of growth in key sectors of advanced economies.

Tom Chevalier's chapter 11 focuses on education, labor market policies, and welfare policies for young people in France, Germany, Sweden, and the UK. It underlines the coherence between specific growth strategies and the way socio-economic institutions structure the entry into adulthood, leading to a specific "youth welfare citizenship regime." The four types of "youth welfare citizenship regimes" presented (*denied*, *monitored*, *second-class*, and *enabling*) correspond to four growth strategies presented in this volume (the FDI-led strategy is not analyzed in this chapter). In the UK, the growth of high-skill services, such as finance, requires the expansion of higher education, which is possible only if there is an individualization of social citizenship. Young people are required to rely on loans for their study, which is in line with the financialization strategy. In the UK, to fight youth unemployment, the flexibilization of the labor market, the lowering of youth labor cost as well as incentives reinforcement have been fostered. In contrast, the "manufacturing-based, export-led" strategy of Germany translates into "monitored" citizenship. It stems from a (specific) skilled labor force that is possible thanks to its encompassing economic citizenship and the importance given to apprenticeship and vocational training. However, as it focuses on the manufacturing industry, it is less important to develop higher education for all, hence no need to individualize social citizenship. According to this strategy, vocational education and training is the main policy implemented in order to keep youth unemployment low. Third, the "enabling" citizenship strategy reflects the "export of dynamic services" strategy present in Sweden. It also stems from a (general) skilled labor force, so the economic citizenship is also encompassing, but fosters higher education rather than vocational training because of the importance of dynamic services. Accordingly, the fight against youth unemployment has led to the development of youth guarantee programs for the low-skilled. Fourth, the publicly-supported domestic-demand strategy relates to the "denied" citizenship. France is an example of this "denied" citizenship type. The selective economic citizenship reflects demand-led growth, as the overall economy is not competitive enough on international markets, lacking an overall skilled labor force. On the one hand, policy-makers try to lower youth labor costs. On the other hand, the elitist education system, without a good-quality apprenticeship system, echoes a polarized economy, where the leading firms are the former *champions nationaux*. Yet, the recent expansion of services has required the expansion of higher education. Individualization has, therefore, happened at the margin through the "conversion" of housing benefits. To fight youth unemployment, there has been a hesitation between the creation of atypical jobs and the launch of a youth guarantee program.

Finally, chapter 12, contributed by Sonja Avlijaš and us as co-authors, analyzes welfare state reforms since the 1990s and how they are connected to the identified growth strategies. It shows how five main growth strategies connect to five different types of welfare state reforms and how crucial welfare reforms in the country cases had economic strategies as their driving force. The chapter starts by identifying these five growth strategies according to the engine of growth chosen and the type of welfare reform: export of dynamic services; export of high-quality manufacturing products; FDI-financed exports; domestic consumption driven by financialization; and domestic consumption driven by wages and welfare spending (which has transformed into "competitiveness through impoverishment" under pressure from the EU). Then it shows that these five growth strategies can be associated with five types of welfare state reform: dualization of welfare, social investment, fiscal and social attractiveness, commodification of welfare, and social protectionism. The detailed account of the cases of the UK, Germany, Sweden, Denmark, Baltic and Visegrád Eastern European countries, Italy, France, and other Southern European countries analyzes the actual connections between growth strategies and welfare reforms. The cases analyses reveal that these strategies are not mutually exclusive and that more than one strategy might be pursued in a country. The chapter contributes to an understanding of how growth regimes change, thanks to its analyses of the transformative feedback effect that the implementation of growth strategies has on the growth regimes. The chapter concludes with the politics of growth strategies and welfare state reforms and the respective roles of producers' coalitions and electoral politics.

References

Acemoglu, D., and Johnson, S. 2005. "Unbundling Institutions." *Journal of Political Economy* 113(5): 949–95.

Amable, B. 2003. *The Diversity of Modern Capitalism* (1st edition). Oxford; New York: Oxford University Press.

Arntz, M., Gregory, T., and Zierahn, U. 2016. The risk of automation for jobs in OECD countries: A comparative analysis. *OECD Social, Employment, and Migration Working Papers*, 189, 0_1.

Autor, D. H., Levy, F., and Murnane, R. J. 2003. "The Skill Content of Recent Technological Change: An Empirical Exploration." *The Quarterly Journal of Economics* 118(4): 1279–33. https://doi.org/10.1162/003355303322552801

Baccaro, L., and Howell, C. 2011. "A Common Neoliberal Trajectory: The Transformation of Industrial Relations in Advanced Capitalism." *Politics and Society* 39(4): 521–63. https://doi.org/10.1177/0032329211420082

Baccaro, L., and Pontusson, J. 2016. "Rethinking Comparative Political Economy: The Growth Model Perspective." *Politics and Society* 44(2): 175–207.

Beramendi, P., Häusermann, S. Kitschelt, H., and Kriesi. H. 2015. "Introduction: The Politics of Advanced Capitalism." In *The Politics of Advanced Capitalism*, edited by P. Beramendi, S. Häusermann, H. Kitschelt, and H. Kriesi. Cambridge, UK; New York: Cambridge University Press, 1–64.

Bermeo, N., and Pontusson, J. (eds.). 2012. *Coping with Crisis: Government Reactions to the Great Recession*. New York: Russell Sage Foundation.

Bernanke, Ben S. 2007. Speech at The Credit Channel of Monetary Policy in the Twenty-first Century conference, Federal Reserve Bank of Atlanta, Atlanta, Georgia, June 15, 2007.

Bohle, D., and Greskovits, B. 2012. *Capitalist Diversity on Europe's Periphery*. Ithaca, New York: Cornell University Press.

Bohle, D., and Regan, A. forthcoming. "Business Power, Quiet Politics and State Elites. Explaining the Continuity of Foreign Direct Investment (FDI) Growth Models." Forthcoming in *Politics and Society*.

Bonoli, G. 2005. "The Politics of the New Social Policies: Providing Coverage Against New Social Risks in Mature Welfare States." *Policy & Politics* 33(3): 431–49.

Boyer, R. 1979. "Crise Actuelle (la): une mise en perspective historique. Quelques réflexions à partir d'une analyse du capitalisme Français en longue période." *Critiques de l'Économie Politique*, nouvelle série (7–8): 3–113.

Boyer, R. 1990. *The Regulation School. A Critical Introduction*. New York: Columbia University Press.

Boyer, R. 2000. "Is a Finance-Led Growth Regime a Viable Alternative to Fordism? a Preliminary Analysis." *Economy and Society* 29(1): 111–45. https://doi.org/10.1080/030851400360587

Brynjolfsson, E., and McAfee, A. 2014. *The Second Machine Age: Work, Progress, and Prosperity in a Time of Brilliant Technologies* (1st edition). New York: W. W. Norton and Company.

Cioffi, J. W., and Höpner, M. 2006. "The Political Paradox of Finance Capitalism: Interests, Preferences, and Center-Left Party Politics in Corporate Governance Reform." *Politics & Society* 34(4): 463–502. https://doi.org/10.1177/0032329206293642

Colin, N. and Palier, B. 2015. "The Next Safety Net: Social Policy for a Digital Age." *Foreign Affairs* (July/August): 29–33.

Crouch, C. 2009. "Privatised Keynesianism: An Unacknowledged Policy Regime." *The British Journal of Politics and International Relations* 11(3): 382–99. https://doi.org/10.1111/j.1467-856X.2009.00377.x

Crouch, C. 2013. *Making Capitalism Fit For Society*. Cambridge: Polity Press.

Crouch, C., and Streeck, W. (eds.). 1997. *Political Economy of Modern Capitalism. Mapping Convergence and Diversity*. London: Sage.

Culpepper, P. 2011. *Quiet Politics and Business Power: Corporate Control in Europe and Japan*. Cambridge: Cambridge University Press.

Dauth, W., Findeisen, S., and Suedekum, J. 2017. "Trade and Manufacturing Jobs in Germany." *American Economic Review* 107(5): 337–42.

Ebbinghaus, B., and Manow, P. (eds.). 2004. *Comparing Welfare Capitalism: Social Policy and Political Economy in Europe, Japan and the USA*. London, New York: Routledge.

Emmenegger, P., Häusermann, S., Palier, B., and Seeleib-Kaiser, M. 2012. "How We Grow Unequal." In *The Age of Dualization: The Changing Face of Inequality in Deindustrializing Societies*, edited by P. Emmenegger, S. Häusermann, B. Palier, and M. Seeleib-Kaiser. Oxford; New York: Oxford University Press, 3–26.

Esping-Andersen, G. 1990. *The Three Worlds of Welfare Capitalism*. Princeton, N.J: Princeton University Press.

Esping-Andersen, G. 1999. *Social Foundations of Postindustrial Economies*. Oxford: Oxford University Press.

Estevez-Abe, M., Iversen, T., and Soskice, D. 2001. "Social Protection and the Formation of Skills: A Reinterpretation of the Welfare State." In *Varieties of*

Capitalism: The Institutional Foundations of Comparative Advantage, edited by P. Hall and D. Soskice. Oxford: Oxford University Press, 145–83.

EU European Council. 2000. Presidency Conclusions. Lisbon European Council 23 and 24 March 2000, https://www.consilium.europa.eu/ueDocs/cms_Data/docs/pressData/en/ec/00100-r1.en0.htm.

Fernández-Macías, E., and Hurley, J. 2016. "Routine-Biased Technical Change and Job Polarization in Europe." *Socio-Economic Review* 15(3): 563–85.

Flora, P. 1986. *Growth to Limits: The Western European Welfare States Since World War II*. Berlin; New York: de Gruyter.

Frey, C. B., and Osborne, M. A. 2013. *The Future of Employment: How Susceptible Are Jobs to Computerisation*. Oxford: University of Oxford.

Goos, M., Manning, A., and Salomons, A. 2009. "Job Polarization in Europe." *American Economic Review* 99(2): 58–63.

Hall, P. A. 2018. "Varieties of Capitalism in light of the Euro Crisis." *Journal of European Public Policy* 25(1): 7–30.

Hall, P. A., and Soskice, D. 2001. "An Introduction to Varieties of Capitalism." In *Varieties of Capitalism: The Institutional Foundations of Comparative Advantage*, edited by P. A. Hall and D. Soskice. Oxford; New York: Oxford University Press, 1–62.

Hall, P. A., and Thelen, K. 2008. "Institutional Change in Varieties of Capitalism." *Socio-Economic Review* 7: 7–34.

Hassel, A. 2014. "The Paradox of Liberalization—Understanding Dualism and the Recovery of the German Political Economy." *British Journal of Industrial Relations* 52(1): 57–81. https://doi.org/10.1111/j.1467-8543.2012.00913.x

Hassel, A. 2017. "No Way to Escape Imbalances in the Eurozone? Three Sources for Germany's Export Dependency: Industrial Relations, Social Insurance and Fiscal Federalism." *German Politics* 26(3): 360–79.

Hassel, A., Wiss, T., and Naczyk, M. 2019. "The Political Economy of Pension Financialisation: Public Policy Responses to the Crisis." *Journal of European Public Policy* 26(4): 483–500.

Heins, E., and de la Porte, C. 2015. "The Sovereign Debt Crisis, the EU and Welfare State Reform." *Comparative European Politics* 13(1): 1–7.

Hope, D., and Soskice, D. 2016. "Growth Models, Varieties of Capitalism, and Macroeconomics." *Politics and Society* 44(2): 209–26. https://doi.org/10.1177/0032329216638054

Höpner, M. 2019. The German Undervaluation Regime Under Bretton Woods: How Germany Became the Nightmare of the World Economy. MPIfG Discussion Paper, No. 19/1, Max Planck Institute for the Study of Societies, Cologne.

Höpner, M., and Lutter, M. 2014. One Currency and Many Modes of Wage Formation. Why the Eurozone Is Too Heterogeneous for the Euro. MPIfG Discussion Paper 14/14.

Iversen, T., and Cusack, T. R. 2000. "The Causes of Welfare State Expansion: Deindustrialization or Globalization?" *World Politics* 52(3): 313–49.

Iversen, T., and Soskice, D. 2009. "Distribution and Redistribution: The Shadow of the Nineteenth Century." *World Politics* 61(3): 438–86. https://doi.org/10.1017/S004388710900015X

Iversen, T., and Soskice, D. 2012. "Modern Capitalism and the Advanced Nation State: Understanding the Causes of the Crisis." In *Coping with Crisis: Government Reactions to the Great Recession*, edited by N. Bermeo and J. Pontussen. New York: Russell Sage Foundation, 35–64.

Iversen, T., and Soskice, D. 2013. "A Political-Institutional Model of Real Exchange Rates, Competitiveness, and the Division of Labor." In *The Political Economy of the Service Transition*, edited by A. Wren. Oxford: Oxford University Press, 73–106.

Iversen, T., and Soskice, D. 2015. "Politics for Markets." *Journal of European Social Policy* 25(1): 76–93.

Iversen, T., and Soskice, D. 2018. "A Structural-Institutional Explanation of the Eurozone crisis." In *Welfare Democracies and Party Politics: Explaining Electoral Dynamics in Times of Changing Welfare Capitalism*, edited by P. Manow, B. Palier, and H. Schwander. Oxford: Oxford University Press, 257–80.

Iversen, T., and Soskice, D. 2019. *Democracy and Prosperity Reinventing Capitalism through a Turbulent Century.* Princeton: Princeton University Press.

Iversen, T., and Wren, A. 1998. "Equality, Employment, and Budgetary Restraint: The Trilemma of the Service Economy." *World Politics* 50(4): 507–46. https://doi.org/10.1017/S0043887100007358

Jordà, Ò., Schularick, M., and Taylor, A. M. 2016. "The Great Mortgaging: Housing Finance, Crises and Business Cycles." *Economic Policy* 31(85): 107–52. https://doi.org/10.1093/epolic/eiv017

Katzenstein, P. J. 1985. *Small States in World Markets: Industrial Policy in Europe.* Ithaca, New York: Cornell University Press.

Krippner, G. R. 2005. "The Financialization of the American Economy." *Socio-Economic Review* 3: 173–208.

Krippner, G. R. 2011. *Capitalizing on Crisis.* Cambridge, MA: Harvard University Press.

Martin, C. J., and Thelen, K. 2007. "The State and Coordinated Capitalism: Contributions of the Public Sector to Social Solidarity in Postindustrial Societies." *World Politics* 60(1): 1–36.

Mintzberg, H. 1979. "Editorial." *Administrative Science Quarterly* 24(4): 582–9.

Mintzberg, H. 1987. "Crafting Strategy." *Harvard Business Review* 65 (July–August 1987): 66–75.

Molina, O., and Rhodes, M. 2007. "The Political Economy of Adjustment in Mixed Market Economies: A Study of Spain and Italy." In *Beyond Varieties of Capitalism: Conflict, Contradictions, and Complementarities in the European Economy*, edited by B. Hancké, M. Rhodes, and M. Thatcher. Oxford: Oxford University Press.

Nölke, A., and Vliegenthart, A. 2009. "Enlarging the Varieties of Capitalism: The Emergence of Dependent Market Economies in East Central Europe." *World Politics* 61(4): 670. https://doi.org/10.1017/S0043887109990098

OECD Statistics, Key Short-term Economic Indicators; Domestic demand forecast. https://stats.oecd.org/Index.aspx?DataSetCode=KEI

OECD. 1994. *The OECD Jobs Strategy: Pushing Ahead with the Strategy*. Paris: OECD Publishing, Paris. Retrieved from https://www.oecd.org/els/emp/boostingjobsandincomestheoecdjobsstrategy.htm (accessed January 24, 2020).

OECD. 2017. *OECD Digital Economy Outlook 2017*. Paris: OECD Publishing. Retrieved from https://doi.org/10.1787/9789264276284-en (accessed July 24, 2020).

Oesch, D., and Rodríguez Menés, J. 2011. "Upgrading or Polarization? Occupational Change in Britain, Germany, Spain and Switzerland, 1990–2008." *Socio-Economic Review* 9(3): 503–31. https://doi.org/10.1093/ser/mwq029

Palier, B. and Hay, C. 2017. "The Reconfiguration of the Welfare State in Europe: Paying its Way in an Age of Austerity." In *Reconfiguring European States in Crisis*, edited by D. King and P. Le Galès. Oxford: Oxford University Press, 331–50.

Palier, B., and Thelen, K. 2010. "Institutionalizing Dualism: Complementarities and Change in France and Germany." *Politics & Society* 38(1): 119–48.

Palier, B. 2010. "The Dualizations of the French Welfare System." In *A Long Goodbye to Bismarck*, edited by B. Palier. Amsterdam: Amsterdam University Press, 73–99.

Peugny, C. 2019. "The Decline in Middle-Skilled Employment in 12 European Countries: New Evidence for Job Polarisation." *Research and Politics* (January–March): 1–7. https://doi.org/10.1177/2053168018823131

Pierson, P. 1996. "The New Politics of the Welfare State." *World Politics* 48(2): 143–79. https://doi:10.1353/wp.1996.0004

Pierson, P. 2001. *New Politics of the Welfare State*. Oxford: Oxford University Press.

Powell, W. W., and Snellman, K. 2004. "The Knowledge Economy." *Annual Review of Sociology* 30(1): 199–20

Rahman, K. S., and K. Thelen. 2019. "The Rise of the Platform Business Model and the Transformation of Twenty-First-Century Capitalism." *Politics & Society* 47(2): 177–204.

Scharpf, F. W. 2000. "The Viability of Advanced Welfare States in the International Economy: Vulnerabilities and Options." *Journal of European Public Policy* 7(2): 190–28. https://doi.org/10.1080/135017600343160

Schelkle, W. 2012. "Collapsing Worlds and Varieties of Welfare Capitalism: In Search of a New Political Economy of Welfare." *LEQS Paper* (54).

Schröder, M. 2009. "Integrating Welfare and Production Typologies: How Refinements of the Varieties of Capitalism Approach call for a Combination of Welfare Typologies." *Journal of Social Policy* 38(1): 19–43. https://doi.org/10.1017/S0047279408002535

Schröder, M. 2013. *Integrating Varieties of Capitalism and Welfare State Research. A Unified Typology of Capitalisms*. Basingstoke: Palgrave Macmillan.

Schulten, T., and Lübker, M. 2019. "WSI-Mindestlohnbericht 2019: Zeit für kräftige Lohnzuwächse und eine europäische Mindestlohnpolitik." *WSI Mitteilungen* 79(2): 133–41.

Schumpeter, J. A. (1975) [1942]. *Capitalism, Socialism and Democracy* (2nd edition). Floyd, Virginia: Impact Books.

Spannagel, Dorothee, Seikel, D., Schulze-Buschoff, K., and Baumann, H. 2017. Aktivierungspolitik und Erwerbsarmut. *WSI Report*, 36.

Streeck, W. 1991. "On the Institutional Conditions of Diversified Quality Production." In *Beyond Keynesianism: The Socio-Economics of Production and Employment*, edited by E. Matzner and W. Streeck. London: Edward Elgar, 21–61.

Streeck, W. 2009. *Re-Forming Capitalism: Institutional Change in the German Political Economy*. Oxford: Oxford University Press.

Streeck, W. 2014. *Buying Time: The Delayed Crisis of Democratic Capitalism*. Brooklyn, NY: Verso.

Streeck, W. 2016. *How Will Capitalism End? Essays on a Failing System*. London: Verso.

Thelen, K. 2014. *Varieties of Liberalization and the New Politics of Social Solidarity*. Cambridge; New York, N.Y.: Cambridge University Press.

Théret, B. 1997. "Méthodologie des comparaisons internationales, approches de l'effet sociétal et de la régulation: fondements pour une lecture structuraliste des systèmes nationaux de protection sociale." *L'Année de la régulation* 1: 163–228.

Van der Zwan, N. 2014. "Making Sense of Financialization." *Socio-Economic Review* 12(1): 99–129. https://doi.org/10.1093/ser/mwt020

Van Treeck, T. 2009. "The Political Economy Debate on "Financialization"—A Macroeconomic Perspective—." *Review of International Political Economy* 16(5): 907–44. https://doi.org/10.1080/09692290802492158

Visser, J. 2019. *ICTWSS Database*. Version 6.1. Amsterdam: Amsterdam Institute for Advanced Labour Studies (AIAS), University of Amsterdam. November 2019.

Woll, C. 2015. Politics in the Interest of Capital: A Not-So-Organized Combat. *MaxPo Discussion Paper* 15(2).

World Bank. 1994. *Averting the Old Age Crisis: Policies to Protect the Old and Promote Growth* (A World Bank Policy Research Report). Oxford: Oxford University Press.

Wren, A. 2013. "Introduction: The Political Economy of Post-Industrial Societies." In *The Political Economy of the Service Transition*, edited by A. Wren. Oxford: Oxford University Press, 1–99.

Zysman, J., and Breznitz, D. 2012. "Double Bind: Governing the Economy in an ICT Era." *Governance* 25: 129–50. https://doi.org/10.1111/j.1468-0491.2011.01556.x

Zysman, J., and Breznitz, D. 2013. "Introduction: Facing the Double Bind: Maintaining a Healthy and Wealthy Economy in the 21st Century." In *The Third Globalization: Can Wealthy Nations Stay Rich in the Twenty-First Century?*, edited by D. Breznitz and J. Zysman (1st edition). New York: Oxford University Press.

Zysman, J., Feldman, S., Murray, J., Nielsen, N.C., and Kushida, K. 2010. Services with Everything: The Digital Transformation of Services. Economic Sinkhole to Productivity Driver. *BRIE Working Paper 187a.*

Zysman, J., and Kenney, M. 2014. Sustainable Growth and Work in the Era of Cloud and Big Data: Will Escaping the Commodity Trap Be our Undoing? or Where Will Work Come from in the Era of the Cloud and Big Data? Presented at the Berkeley Roundtable on the International Economy. *BRIE Working Paper* 2014–6.

2

How Growth Strategies Evolve in the Developed Democracies

Peter A. Hall

Every country has a growth regime, understood as the ensemble of means, both technological and institutional, used to generate economic growth. These regimes turn on how the organization of the political economy conditions the behavior of firms, workers, and consumers. But equally intrinsic to these regimes are the economic and social policies that governments devise to foster economic growth, which constitute what I will call the "growth strategy" of a country (see Hassel and Palier in this volume).[1] These strategies have changed dramatically over the past sixty years. How should changes in these growth strategies be characterized and explained? The objective of this chapter is to describe the growth strategies pursued by governments in the developed democracies over the decades since World War II and to advance our understanding of how they change. Important national variations in such strategies also deserve attention (see other chapters and particularly Avlijaš et al. in this volume), but my focus here is on change over time and thus on broad commonalities across countries.

This analysis is framed by two alternative perspectives, each with real value but serious limitations. The first is a view central to mainstream economics that sees changes in economic policy as direct responses to developments in the economy, such as technological change and the globalization of production. Such processes play an important role in my analysis, but these perspectives often fail to capture how the policy response to such developments is mediated by politics. A second approach analyzes recent changes in policy as the reflection of a gathering crisis of capitalism, driven by the efforts of states to meet the functional requirements of accumulation and legitimation (Streeck 2014; Crouch 2011; O'Connor 1979. Cf. Sewell 2008). These panoramic views of capitalism illuminate many features of its movement, but their abstract functionalism often understates the role played by politics in the processes whereby developed political economies change.

By contrast, I am especially interested in how to understand the relationship between developments in the economy and developments in politics—a longstanding

[1] Although this term reflects the broad coherence of these policy regimes, it is not meant to imply that the process whereby they are enacted is entirely strategic.

Peter A. Hall, *How Growth Strategies Evolve in the Developed Democracies* In: *Growth and Welfare in Advanced Capitalist Economies: How Have Growth Regimes Evolved?* Edited by: Anke Hassel and Bruno Palier, Oxford University Press (2021).
 DOI: 10.1093/oso/9780198866176.003.0002

puzzle somewhat neglected in comparative political economy.[2] I outline my approach to the problem and follow with sections tracing the evolution of growth strategies in the developed democracies through three eras defined by evolving sets of economic and political challenges. Brief discussions of four cases—Britain, France, Sweden, and Germany—illustrate the account, and I close with some remarks about the reach and limits of the analysis.

1. The Approach

To delineate the post-war growth strategies of the developed democracies, I distinguish three periods, which can be labeled: an era of modernization, running from 1950 to about 1974, an era of liberalization, stretching from 1980 to about 2000, and an era of movement toward knowledge-based growth from the late 1990s to the present. Each is defined by the character of prevailing economic and political challenges. Because the pace of developments varies across countries, the borders of these periods are fuzzy and they overlap on some dimensions.

To understand how and why growth strategies changed across these eras, we need to take four sets of factors into account. The first are secular developments in the domestic and international economies. Those matter. But policy is never an unmediated response to such developments because economic trends must be identified and their significance interpreted—a process involving the promulgation and revision of economic doctrines. Thus, the second factor entails shifts is what I will call the "economic gestalt" of each era, namely, how the problems of the political economy are perceived by economists and the general public.

Even when there is agreement on the problems, however, choices must be made about how to address them and political support for those choices mobilized. Economic policy-making is always coalition-building (Thelen 2004; Hall and Thelen 2009). Thus, the third set of factors conditioning changes in growth strategies are developments in the electoral arena that shift the terms on which coalitions of support for specific policies can be assembled; and the fourth is a set of parallel changes in the realm of producer group politics which alter the influence of groups, the policies they seek, and the capacities of producer groups to cooperate in the operation of a growth strategy.

Although the economic gestalt of a given era is anchored in prevailing economic conditions, several components go into its construction. Especially central here are immediately preceding events. Governance is an "eventful" process: politicians and officials react to what their nation has just experienced and

[2] Although there are multiple works on producer group politics, relatively few address the relationship between developments in electoral politics and the political economy. For a few exceptions, see: Kitschelt *et al.* 1999; Iversen and Soskice 2009, 2015: Beramendi et al. 2015.

prevailing interpretations of that (Sewell 2005; Hall 2005, 2013). Obvious failures of policy set in motion a search for alternatives, while conspicuous successes provide templates for the future course of policy (Hall 1993; Culpepper 2009; Dobbin 1997). In this process, economic doctrines loom large, since they are the lens through which officials interpret the economy and popular versions of these doctrines can capture the imagination of producer groups and the electorate (McNamara 1998; Fourcade 2009). However, there are political elements to these popular versions, since they are used to mobilize consent for policies; and the case governments make to electorates always has a moral as well as technical basis. In this respect, changes in growth strategies are not simply technical adjustments but components of a wider movement in normative orders.

Democratic governments seek growth because their continued electoral success depends on it; and this electoral constraint enhances the influence of popular economic doctrines, as governments seek to show that they are "competent" by implementing policies in line with these doctrines (Lindblom 1977; Iversen and Soskice 2015). Governments also choose economic and social policies with distributive effects that will appeal to groups they hope to attract to their electoral coalitions. However, the terms on which such coalitions can be formed shift over time with changes in the composition and preferences of the electorate. From this perspective, the most important feature of electoral politics is the structure of political cleavages, a term I use here to specify the issues most salient to electoral politics and the alignment of social groups along them. Cleavage structures evolve in response to changes in the size and socioeconomic position of specific social groups, which are affected in turn by economic developments, and in response to changes in the appeals mounted by political parties (Cf. Iversen 1999; Evans and Tilley 2012).

Producer group politics conditions the formulation and implementation of growth strategies in two ways. Within the broad constraints of electoral competition, governments respond to the detailed demands of producer groups (Culpepper 2011). Social democratic governments are more likely to pursue policies supported by trade unions, while conservative parties are usually more attentive to business interests. In many cases, economic policy is a response to cross-class coalitions of producer groups (Swenson 2002). Second, the capacity of governments to operate some kinds of growth strategies depends on cooperation from trade unions and employer associations. The types of policies producer groups seek change over time, as firms alter strategies to cope with secular changes in the economy; and the coordinating capacities of producer groups shift when new economic circumstances generate divisions among their membership (Thelen and Van Winjbergen 2003; Martin and Swank 2012).

In the following sections, I consider how changes in economic challenges, the economic gestalt, and electoral politics have conditioned movements in growth strategies among the developed democracies, with brief references to producer group politics which deserves a more extended treatment than this chapter allows (See Thelen in this volume, Martin in this volume).

2. The Era of Modernization, 1950–75

In the aftermath of World War II, the western democracies faced a distinctive set of economic challenges. For many, the most pressing problem was how to rebuild an industrial infrastructure heavily damaged by the war. As international trade was restored under the aegis of the GATT and the 1958 Treaty of Rome, securing a competitive position in international markets also became a national goal (Servan-Schreiber 1969). Both challenges were defined by the central role manufacturing still played in these economies. Whether organized along Fordist lines, as in the United States, France, and Britain, or by methods of "diversified quality production" in Germany and Italy, manufacturing remained the motor for economic growth (Boyer 1990; Piore and Sabel 1984; Streeck 1991; Herrigel 2000). The key issues were how to expand manufacturing and how to make it more efficient.

2.1 The Economic Gestalt

Within a decade after the war, these challenges were being interpreted through an economic gestalt that emphasized the importance of "modernizing" the economy and assigned considerable responsibility for doing so to governments. The French focused on the inefficiencies of an economy dominated by "Malthusian" competition among overly small firms, while the British began to worry about economic decline (Landes 1949; Elbaum and Lazonick 1985; Shonfield 1958). By the end of the 1950s when Sputnik was launched, even the Americans worried that they were losing a technological race with the Soviet Union. The approaches taken toward modernization varied across countries, but all endorsed an active role for government, whether in the form of economic planning in France, Britain, and Japan, increased public investment in education, research, and infrastructure in the US, or the public–private partnerships established in Sweden and Germany (Cohen 1977; Leruez 1975; Block 2011; Johnson 1982; Ziegler 1997).

Support for these approaches could be found in the most prominent economic doctrines of the day. At the heart of many was the contention of John Maynard Keynes that governments can promote growth via the management of aggregate demand—popularized after the war by scholars such as Paul Samuelson, whose textbook sold more than 4 million copies in forty-one languages (Johnson 1971; Hall 1989). Keynesian views were codified in econometric models that became a staple of policy analysis and adapted to support distinctive national strategies, such as industrial planning in France and the Rehn-Meidner model in Sweden.

Within the wider universe of political discourse, there was general acceptance of the "mixed economy"—a phrase used to describe growth strategies in which the state and private sector both played active roles (Stilwell 2006).

2.2 Growth Strategies

The underlying structure of the economy influenced the growth strategies of this era. Because manufacturing was still a large component of the economy, productivity could often be increased by moving labor from agriculture into manufacturing where Fordist methods of production rendered semi-skilled workers more productive (Crafts and Toniolo 1996). Within industry itself, the dominant approach to improving productivity was to increase the size of companies and the volume of production in order to seek economies of scale, often based on technology imported from the US and encouraged by the expansion of trade.

To achieve industrial scale, many governments channeled investment toward industry through state-owned enterprises, systems of industrial planning and publicly owned banks. These were strategies seen as appropriate for modernizing states. Since firms were likely to invest on a large scale only if they could be assured a steady demand for their products, many governments also adopted some form of countercyclical demand management (Boyer 1990). Although his fiscal prescriptions were greeted with varying degrees of enthusiasm across countries, Keynes' contention that governments had a responsibility for actively managing the economy became widely accepted (Hall 1989).

Faced with the demobilization of millions of military personnel, post-war governments were also deeply concerned about how to secure full employment, albeit construed largely in terms of a male breadwinner model (Beveridge 1942). Creating employment was seen as a matter of sustaining demand for national products, but there was variation in how countries achieved that. The governments of the US and Britain sought to sustain domestic demand through countercyclical fiscal policies, while France relied on a high minimum wage, and other countries, such as Germany and Sweden, devoted more attention to sustaining demand for exports by holding down the exchange rate and limiting the growth of unit labor costs via coordinated wage bargaining.

In general, the growth strategies of this era were marked by relatively high levels of state activism, as governments sought to rebuild infrastructure, channel investment into industry or construct neocorporatist systems of industrial coordination. However, there were significant national variations, reflecting national differences in the complexion of economic challenges and the economic gestalt.

Britain entered the era of modernization with a burst of state intervention. Elected on a tidal wave of demands for a break with interwar policies, a post-war Labour government nationalized leading firms in key industries, including the

Bank of England, established a National Health Service, and imposed wage and price controls (Beer 1969). Succeeding Conservative governments accepted many features of this mixed economy and tried a tepid form of economic planning with the establishment of a National Economic Development Corporation in 1962 (Leruez 1975). Promising to "reforge Britain in the white heat of the scientific revolution," a Labour government elected in 1964 initiated ambitious plans to reorganize the manufacturing base under the direction of a Ministry for Economic Affairs and Industrial Reconstruction Corporation (Hall 1986). However, most of these attempts foundered on the limited institutional capacities of an arm's length state and the difficulties of securing cooperation from fragmented trade unions and business interests.

Thus, the British approach to securing full employment eventually turned on efforts to sustain domestic demand via countercyclical macroeconomic policies. But an insistence on maintaining the exchange rate to protect the value of overseas balances of sterling, on which the standing of Britain's financial sector in the City of London was thought to depend, meant that efforts at expansion usually ended prematurely in balance of payments crises, contributing little to growth (Brittan 1971; Hansen 1968). Partly as a result, at 2.6 percent per annum, British rates of growth in this period were well below those of its neighbors.

The French growth strategy during this era entailed more assertive intervention. It was built around a system of indicative economic planning, in which public officials developed priorities for investment in consultation with representatives from business and (sometimes) labor, and then used the government's influence over large state-owned banks to channel funds to the sectors deemed most central to growth (Cohen 1977; cf. McArthur and Scott 1969; Zysman 1977, 1983). Increases in productivity were achieved by funneling finance only to the most efficient firms; and exports were promoted through support for firms thought to be "national champions" on world markets, while domestic demand was sustained by active macroeconomic policies and a statutory minimum wage to which 40 percent of French wages were eventually tied. The system was inflationary—as the French President Valéry Giscard d'Estaing once said "*la planification, c'est l'inflation*"—but French governments devalued the exchange rate periodically to offset the effect of inflation on exports (Lord 1973: 182).

The growth strategies pursued by Sweden and Germany stand in contrast to intermittent intervention in Britain and sustained intervention in France. Although both governments were active in this period, their objective was to develop growth strategies built on neocorporatist coordination among producer groups rather than on state intervention; and each cultivated coordinating capacities among their producer groups that privileged export-led growth over the expansion of domestic demand.

With the *Saltsjöbaden* accords of 1938, Sweden had already developed a system of wage bargaining coordinated at the peak level, and its post-war growth policies took advantage of these strategic capacities (Martin 1979; Pontusson 1992). Often labeled the Rehn-Meidner model after two economists influential in its design, the Swedish approach rested on three pillars. The first was solidaristic wage bargaining. Wage increases across most sectors of the economy were determined by peak-level negotiations between labor and employers' confederations, but this meant that the wages of low-paid workers would rise faster in percentage terms than those of higher-paid workers. By consolidating a coalition between skilled and semi-skilled labor, this solidaristic approach served the political purposes of a dominant social democratic party, and in economic terms it increased productivity by pressing firms dependent on low-wage labor to become more efficient or go out of business. Because this strategy entailed lay-offs, the second pillar of the model was an active labor market policy, featuring generous public support for job search and retraining. The third pillar specified a relatively austere macroeconomic stance to maintain pressure on firms to become more efficient. Market competition was used to rationalize the economy, but the state played key roles by providing active labor market policy, a suitable macroeconomic stance and implicit guarantees that the profits generated by wage restraint would go to investment (Przeworski and Wallerstein 1982; Eichengreen 1996).

Exploiting regional and sectoral capacities for collaboration that survived the war, West Germany also built a growth strategy centered on coordination in the private economy—between workers and employers, among firms, and between firms and banks. In the industrial relations arena, coordination on wages, working conditions, and vocational training was underpinned by a balance of power between trade unions and employers, enhanced by codetermination legislation that established influential works councils in larger firms (Thelen 1991; Streeck 1994). Along with vocational training schemes managed by employers and trade unions, built around apprenticeships conferring high levels of industry-specific skills, these arrangements gave German manufacturers formidable capacities for the continuous innovation that promoted exports (Hall and Soskice 2001). Flows of investment into industry were orchestrated by a few universal banks which also held shares in firms and by networks of savings banks sponsored by regional governments (Shonfield 1969; Deeg 1999).

These high levels of private-sector coordination were made possible by legislation—in the form of framework policies delegating decisions to specified producer groups in classic neocorporatist fashion (Schmitter and Lehmbruch 1979; Katzenstein 1987). Built on an economic gestalt marked by reaction against the Third Reich, the German government's stance was less interventionist than those of its neighbors and underpinned by ordo-liberal doctrines that were popularized by the Christian Democratic Party, which dominated German governments for twenty years after the war. Those doctrines held that the center of economic dynamism should lie in the private sector, while the state's role was to make rules ensuring that economic behavior was orderly and social groups protected from the most adverse effects of market competition (Sally 2007). However, the resulting "social market economy" was far from a system of laissez-faire capitalism. At the regional level, it nurtured systems of diversified quality production heavily dependent on regulations ensuring that actors provided high levels of collective goods (Streeck 1991; Herrigel 2000).

The macroeconomic complement to these arrangements was a restrained fiscal stance, guaranteed by a powerful Bundesbank, independent of political control and focused on inflation. The Bundesbank threatened monetary retaliation if wage bargains exceeded its norms or fiscal policy became too expansionary (Hall 1994; Hall and Franzese 1998; Carlin and Soskice 2009). The result was a strategy oriented toward export-led growth. Wage bargaining was led by *IG Metall*, the powerful metalworking union central to the export sector; and the Bundesbank held the exchange rate at undervalued levels until the 1970s when continued efforts to do so threatened to import inflation (Kreile 1978). As a result, Germany became one of the most successful manufacturing exporters in the world.

2.3 Electoral Politics

Although the economic gestalt of the "mixed economy" built on contemporary interpretations of economic challenges during the 1950s and 1960s provided the template for the growth strategies of this era, much of the impetus for their adoption came from electoral politics, which had a distinctive character in this era. In advanced democracies, the most prominent electoral cleavage at this time was a class cleavage, dividing manual and lower-level non-manual workers from a middle class composed of white-collar employees in supervisory, professional, or managerial positions (Manza et al. 1995). This cleavage was based on material interests and a distinctive identity politics. Many people in this era saw politics in class terms—as a terrain in which parties representing the "working-class" were arrayed against those representing a "middle-class"—and political parties campaigned in precisely those terms. This cleavage was most prominent in Western Europe. On one side of it were Social Democratic and Communist parties claiming to speak for the working class and committed to using the full levers of state power, including central planning and large-scale nationalization of enterprises, to achieve full employment. On the other side were Conservative, Liberal, and Christian Democratic parties more representative of the middle class and committed to securing prosperity through free enterprise.

The centrality of this cleavage affected economic policy-making in two ways. Because the policy debate between Social Democratic and Conservative parties turned on issues of state intervention, those issues became the fulcrum for electoral competition. Political parties interested in attaining office were forced to find middle ground on these issues in order to draw votes from their opponents while retaining their core constituents. Out of this conflict, the growth strategies of the mixed economy emerged as a political compromise—just interventionist enough to attract support from the center-left but rooted enough in market competition to win support from center-right voters. In Britain, Keynesian doctrines of demand management were an ideal vehicle for this compromise because they offered a formula for securing full employment without large-scale nationalization (cf. Offe 1983). In France, indicative economic planning played a similar role, while in Germany consensus emerged on a market economy that was sufficiently "social" to offer trade unions considerable influence over wages, working conditions, social insurance, and vocational training.

In the face of these electoral incentives, the Social Democratic parties of Europe gradually dropped their insistence on nationalization and embraced the mixed economy at landmark party conferences from Bad Godesberg to Blackpool, while Conservative and Christian Democratic parties gradually accepted active economic management and elements of industrial intervention as viable strategies for managing a free market economy (Crosland 1956; Przeworski and Sprague 1986). Modernizing the economy became a valence issue and, as Figure 2.1

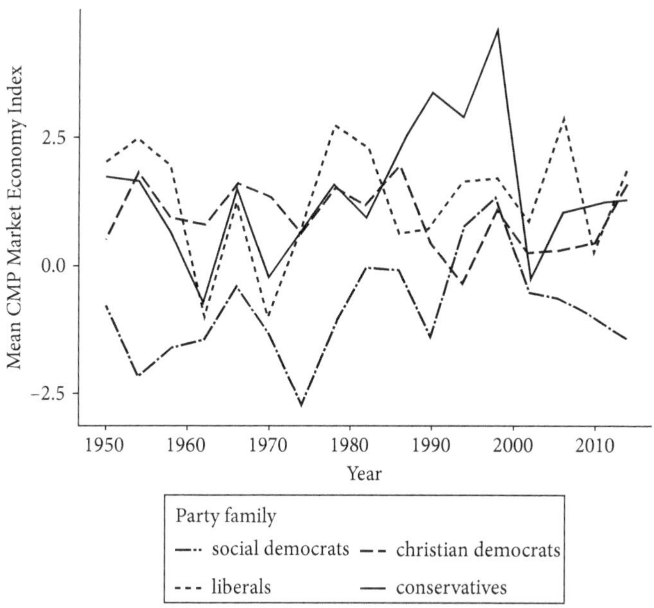

Figure 2.1 Support for "free markets" in the platforms of European political parties, 1957–2015

Note: Party positions on the "free market economy" index of Lowe et al. (2011) indicating the prevalence in party platforms of support for a free market economy and market incentives as opposed to more direct government control of the economy, nationalization, or other Marxist goals. Higher values indicate more support for free market positions. The countries included are: Austria, Belgium, Denmark, Finland, France, Germany, Greece, Ireland, Italy, Netherlands, Norway, Portugal, Spain, Sweden, United Kingdom.

Source: Comparative Manifesto Project database.

indicates, the result was a convergence in party platforms during the 1950s and early 1960s on the policies of the mixed economy, whose social corollary was a set of pension, unemployment and health insurance policies that laid the groundwork for contemporary welfare states.

Of course, the policies of each nation were inflected by the relative power there of the political left and right, rooted in electoral rules and the presence of ancillary cleavages (Manow 2009). In Sweden, a growth strategy centered on solidaristic wage bargaining owed much to Social Democratic dominance, while an influential Christian Democratic Party built Germany's social market economy. But it is striking how many countries converged on the growth strategies of a mixed economy. Government intervention could be as extensive in polities dominated by the center-right, such as Italy and France, as in those dominated by the center-left, such as Sweden and Denmark.[3]

3. The Era of Liberalization, 1980–2000

The era of modernization reached its economic apogee and political perigee in the middle of the 1970s, when three decades of rapid growth ended with simultaneous increases in unemployment and inflation. In most developed democracies, subsequent growth rates were to be barely half those of preceding years, and three developments that had been gathering force for some time profoundly altered the economic challenges facing governments after 1980. These included a shift in the locus of employment from manufacturing to services, rising competition from developing economies made possible by more open global trade, and the growth of international finance.

Employment in the service sector had been rising in the OECD countries since the 1950s but, by the early 1980s, governments began to realize that, if they wanted to create jobs, these would have to be in services (Wren 2013; Iversen and Cusack 2000). The roots of this shift lay in secular economic developments. As incomes rose and the prices of manufactures fell, consumers could devote more income to services. As advances in containerization and information technology, as well as new trade agreements, made it more feasible to situate plants in the developing world, manufacturing jobs moved away from the developed democracies (Wood 1994; Keohane and Milner 1996; Rodrik 1997; Palley 2018). And, as supply chains became more global and international competition more intense, wage bargaining came under new pressures. At the same time, rapid growth in international

[3] In the United States, government intervention increased earlier, during the 1930s when the class cleavage was at its height, but, cross-cut by regional and racial divisions, that cleavage was weaker than in Europe during the 1950s and 1960s and government intervention was correspondingly more limited, although far from negligible. Cf. Block 2011.

financial markets, beginning with the Eurodollar markets, changed the terms on which firms could raise finance. By the middle of the 1980s, larger portions of capital investment were going to come from foreign rather than domestic sources (Berger and Dore 1996).

As governments came to appreciate the scale of these developments, they gradually adapted their growth strategies to cope with them. However, the immediate impetus for a change was the failure of existing policies to cope with simultaneous increases in inflation and unemployment during the 1970s. The triggers for this stagflation were sharp increases in the price of oil and other commodities; but its basis lay in increases in the world money supply following the collapse of the Bretton Woods monetary system in 1971 and endogenous developments within the prior growth strategy which was undermined by its very success (Keohane 1978; Ferguson et al. 2010.). Post-war governments had strengthened collective bargaining regimes in order to ensure that wages were bargained peacefully and the fruits of growth widely shared. As a decade of full employment strengthened trade unions, however, they began to secure wage settlements that firms could accommodate only by raising prices, which led to inflationary wage-price spirals. In effect, the failure of social institutions established during the previous era to regulate distributive conflict fueled the inflation of the 1970s (Crouch and Pizzorno 1978; Goldthorpe 1978; Glyn and Sutcliffe 1972).

In the face of this stagflation, existing growth strategies proved largely impotent. Keynesian policies designed to address unemployment had no antidote for inflation; and efforts to revive ailing industries with further subsidies yielded few results (Berger 1981; Hall 1993). Devising a new growth strategy took time, however, because governments react to new challenges incrementally, making ad hoc efforts to adjust their existing strategies before experimenting with new ones. Mistaking structural shifts in the economy for cyclical fluctuations, many governments initially responded with more generous social assistance—on the premise that they could pay for that assistance when high rates of growth returned. When those rates of growth did not return, social expenditure as a percentage of GDP soared and governments began to run endemic deficits.

The result was a political climacteric for the mixed economy. Electorates threw out virtually every government in office during the late 1970s. The political crisis was most acute in liberal market economies, such as Britain and the US, where faltering efforts to deploy statutory incomes policies led many people to question the legitimacy of state intervention (Crozier et al. 1974). Not surprisingly, these countries were pioneers in the movement to reduce the role of the state in the economy. Where effective systems of wage coordination managed to contain inflation at lower cost in terms of unemployment, as in Sweden and Germany, the reaction against state intervention was more muted (Lindberg and Maier 1985; Goldthorpe 1984). But, as rates of unemployment continued to rise, politicians in all countries sought new ways to reduce it. While the British and Americans worried about national decline, Europeans became anxious about "Eurosclerosis" (Giersch 1985; Krieger 1986).

3.1 The Economic Gestalt

Accordingly, the new economic gestalt that emerged in the 1980s was a reaction against the apparent failure of interventionist policies during the 1970s. In the wake of that failure, policy-makers moved toward the view that markets allocate resources more efficiently than governments. The watchword of a new era of liberalization became "market competition." If growth had previously been said to turn on management of the demand side, it was now said to depend on reforms to the supply side of the economy, where privatization replaced nationalization as a key instrument, and industrial subsidies designed to make firms more competitive were replaced by manpower policies designed to make labor markets more efficient.

The academic rationale for this new gestalt lay in the growing popularity of a "new classical economics" which discounted governments' capacities to manage the economy and presented deregulatory reforms as the best route to economic growth. Although parallel ideas had been advanced since the 1960s, the rational expectations perspectives that underpinned this new economics gained adherents during the 1980s. They argued that there is a "natural" level of unemployment reducible only by reforms to labor markets, that efforts to manage demand usually end in failure, and that monetary policy has few durable effects on the real economy, thereby making it desirable to render central banks independent of the political authorities (Stein 1981; Stockman 1986; Dornbusch 1990; McNamara 1998). The influence of these doctrines lay to some extent in their political appeal. Faced with rising unemployment, politicians who had been happy to take credit for two decades of full employment welcomed doctrines that attributed unemployment to the operation of labor markets rather than to the government's management of the economy.

As the 1980s wore on, market-oriented thinking seeped into ever more spheres of social life. Market competition came to be seen as the "natural" way to organize human endeavor. Governments inserted competition into their own operations, shifting from the view that they had a responsibility to provide "citizens" with "public services" toward the perspective that, like market actors, they should deliver goods more efficiently to citizens now seen as "consumers" (Hall 2015). Firms that once felt responsibilities to stakeholders as well as shareholders began to attach overriding importance to increasing the value of their shares, especially in liberal market economies; and the practices of monitoring via measurement associated with effective market competition crept into many social organizations

(Lazonick and O'Sullivan 2000; Gomory and Sylla 2013; Espeland and Sauder 2007). The counterpart to this economic liberalism was a new personal liberalism: the criteria for judging people's worth began to turn on their possession of the attributes necessary for successful market competition (Boltanski and Chiapello 2007; Hall and Lamont 2009; Centeno and Cohen 2012). In short, the economic gestalt of the era of liberalization rested on a deep ideological foundation permeating many spheres of social life.

3.2 Growth Strategies

The focus of growth strategies in this era was on the liberalization of markets, albeit at different paces across countries and sectors. The Single European Act of 1986 that created a single market in goods and services turned the European Commission into a powerful agent for market liberalization (Jabko 2006; see also Moravcsik 1998). At the national level, parallel initiatives were taken to privatize state-owned enterprise, contract out public services, and alter regulations so as to promote more competition in markets ranging from air transport to telecommunications (Riddell 1991; Thatcher 1999). The pioneers were Margaret Thatcher and Ronald Reagan who took office on the eve of the 1980s but many governments followed suit throughout the 1990s (Krieger 1986).

In the name of improving productivity, Reagan and Thatcher attacked the influence of trade unions, notably by breaking the American air controllers' strike of 1981 and the British miners' strike of 1984–85. Many European governments could not manage coordinated market economies without robust unions but, under pressure from firms seeking the flexibility to meet more intense international competition, they presided over changes in collective bargaining that shifted influence over wages and working conditions from the peak or sectoral level to the firm and plant levels (Pontusson and Swenson 1996; Lallement 2006).

Government efforts to expand employment moved from the demand-side to reforms on the supply side of the economy, including the deregulation of labor markets via the promotion of temporary contracts and part-time employment. Many of these steps were motivated by the need to create jobs in the service sector—to which there seemed to be only two routes (Iversen and Wren 1998; Scharpf 2000). One was to expand public employment in education, healthcare, and social services—a path taken by several Nordic countries as early as the 1970s (Esping-Andersen 1990). The other was to create jobs in private services, including restaurants, tourism, retailing, and domestic service, typically at low wages, on the premise that there was not much scope for productivity increases in these jobs. This path entailed keeping minimum wages low, encouraging part-time work, and restricting social benefits to lower the reservation wage, a strategy pursued most aggressively in the Anglo-American democracies.

Some countries hesitated to go down either path. Thus, the governments of France, Germany and the Netherlands initially responded to rising unemployment with measures to reduce the numbers of people seeking work, through early retirement programs, generous disability benefits, and social policies that made it difficult for women to pursue paid employment. However, when it became apparent that a smaller labor force would depress rates of growth, these governments shifted gears to promote part-time employment. In France and Germany, secondary labor markets dominated by precarious low-wage employment were built alongside primary labor markets offering relatively secure jobs; and the Netherlands vastly expanded part-time employment, albeit with provisions offering more job security and social benefits to part-time workers (Palier and Thelen 2010; Thelen 2014).

Policy-makers also took new approaches to securing capital investment. Most efforts to channel funds directly to industry ended, and state-owned enterprises were privatized, partly to make it more feasible for them to draw on international capital markets. After 1979, the OECD governments gradually eliminated exchange controls and many governments strengthened protections for minority shareholders or loosened their rules on foreign ownership in order to encourage inflows of foreign direct investment (Culpepper 2005). Indeed, some countries built entire growth strategies around foreign direct investment, based on light-touch regulation and low rates of corporate taxation. Ireland was one of the first to take this approach followed by several East European nations in the early 1990s (Regan 2014; Nölke and Vliegenthart 2009). Although some governments, such as those of the US and Britain, continued to rely on domestic demand to stimulate investment, all countries looked increasingly toward international sources for capital (Rajan 2010).

Of course, there were national variations in the nature of these growth strategies and the pace at which they were implemented. The new strategies came first and most forcefully in Britain, where splits within the opposition and the popularity of a Falklands War provided electoral insulation for successive Conservative governments (Gamble 1994; Sandbrook 2010). These governments privatized national enterprises, bringing windfalls to government coffers, and took steps to increase competition within public transport, water supply, telecommunications, health and energy (Riddell 1991). The premise was that more intense competition would increase productivity, while sales of public housing and shares in privatized enterprises would create new groups of property owners more likely to vote for the Conservative party. With a series of industrial relations acts, Thatcher succeeded in reducing the influence of the unions, whose strength fell further with a decline in manufacturing accelerated by a high exchange rate that was propped up by North Sea oil and gas. In the decades after 1979, trade union membership fell from a half to less than a quarter of the British workforce.

Although manufacturing employment declined, Britain was well-placed to create low-wage jobs in retailing, tourism and personal services as well as high wage jobs in its large financial sector. The low benefit levels in Britain's liberal welfare state held down the reservation wage (Esping-Andersen 1990). As international flows of funds increased, the government shook up the City of London with a "big bang" of reforms designed to consolidate its position as a leading financial center and allow its firms to exploit new financial instruments (Busch 2008). In both Britain and the US, regulatory changes to commercial and consumer credit markets encouraged firms and households to increase their levels of debt, thereby propping up domestic demand despite stagnating median incomes (Rajan 2010; Krippner 2011). To some degree, access to credit became a substitute for countercyclical economic policy in countries whose growth strategies still depended on domestic demand; and in the wake of these developments expanding financial sectors secured huge profits (Baccaro and Pontusson 2016).

The growth strategy of France also changed over this period, albeit with a slight delay. When a political backlash against the failures of the 1970s brought a Socialist-Communist coalition to power for the first time during the Fifth Republic, in 1981, the initial strategy of President François Mitterrand was to intensify intervention—via a *politique de filières* designed to substitute public investment for declining levels of private investment (Hall 1986). However, with the prospect of another devaluation that would take France out of the European monetary system, Mitterrand abandoned this growth strategy in 1983 in favor of a new one based on four pillars. French capital markets were deregulated so as to encourage inflows of foreign investment, by eliminating the state's stakes in privatized enterprises and facilitating mergers and acquisitions (Culpepper 2005). Second, the government passed a series of laws, ostensibly aimed at improving worker representation, which made it easier for firms to set wages at plant rather than sectoral levels (Lallement 2006). These were complementary measures: the wage flexibility firms gained improved their capacities to cope with the rising threat of hostile takeovers (Goyer 2012). The third pillar was strong French support for the creation of a single European market on the premise that more intense competition would force French firms to become more efficient. Finally, the government abandoned its policy of periodic depreciation in favor of maintaining a high exchange rate backed by a more austere fiscal stance. By forcing French firms to compete in more open European markets under a high exchange rate, this strategy of "competitive deflation" was meant to induce them to rationalize and move toward higher value-added production.

French governments never assembled an electoral coalition behind these policies. They were initiated by a Socialist government elected on an entirely different platform and continued by a center-right government whose only open advocate for neoliberalism was a marginal figure. Many of the responsibilities for liberalizing the French economy were delegated to the European Commission, an approach that allowed French political leaders to rail against liberalization while endorsing it behind closed doors in Brussels (Hall 2006). The effects of the strategy were mixed: although it pushed some firms toward higher-valued-added production, French rates of unemployment hovered around double digits into the 1990s (Hancké 2002; Fitoussi et al. 1993).

In Sweden, the Rehn-Meidner model foundered during the 1970s, when rising rates of unemployment induced the government to mount more expansionary macroeconomic policies and subsidize industries in distress. The Social Democratic party was voted out of office in 1976 for the first time in the post-war period. However, decisions taken during the late 1960s helped Sweden cope with one of the principal economic challenge of the era, namely the shift of employment to services. While other countries, such as Germany and France, addressed the labor shortages of the 1960s by importing foreign workers, Swedish governments resolved it by drawing women into the labor force, often as public employees delivering an expanding set of health, educational and social services. Although this approach segmented the labor market by gender, it had generated well-paid jobs in services without creating a low-wage service sector and consolidated the electoral coalition of the Social Democrats (Esping-Andersen 1990; Iversen and Wren 1998).

During the 1980s, however, the growing power of public-sector trade unions threatened the capacity of the export sector to lead the coordination of wages. As employers and unions in metalworking sought more flexibility to set wages in response to global competition, peak-level bargaining collapsed (Pontusson and Swenson 1996; Iversen 1999). Wage coordination was reestablished at the sectoral level during the 1990s but in terms that left individual firms with more flexibility to set wages. Thus, Sweden saw some decentralization of wage bargaining, but one that did not entirely eliminate the strategic capacities of Swedish producer groups.

In other respects, however, Swedish governments struggled to find an effective growth strategy. To shore up investment and its political coalition, a Social Democratic government established wage-earner funds that were to invest a portion of enterprise profits on behalf of employees (Pontusson 1992). When this step antagonized employers without reviving investment, however, Swedish governments resorted to expansionary macroeconomic policies that threatened wage coordination; and they liberalized financial markets to attract foreign investment. The result was an asset boom whose collapse in the early 1990s left Sweden with a deep economic crisis.

By contrast, the German growth strategy was robust enough to survive the economic turmoil of the 1970s largely unscathed. After a few outbursts of industrial conflict when profits rose unexpectedly following bargaining rounds that had restrained wages, an effective system of coordinated wage bargaining managed to reduce inflation at modest cost in terms of unemployment; and, during the early 1980s, West Germany looked like an economic success story (Kreile 1978;

Cameron 1984). Partly for this reason, the liberalizing moves taken by German governments in these years were more limited than in many other countries, despite Chancellor Helmut Kohl's promise to preside over a *Wende*.

Liberalization was most pronounced in corporate finance and industrial relations. The growing importance of international finance disorganized the long-standing system whereby large German firms secured capital via close relationships with a few key banks. To operate effectively in expanding international financial markets, the large universal banks realized that they would have to free up the funds they previously held in German shares. Accordingly, they pushed for a series of legislative acts between 1990 and 2002 that allowed them to do so, and German firms turned increasingly to international markets for funding (Deeg 2010). Despite concerns that these steps would force firms to privilege shareholders over stakeholders, many German companies found patient sources of international capital from institutional investors looking for long-term returns (Goyer 2012); and German parliamentarians watered down European legislation to limit the prospect of hostile takeovers that might have forced firms to become more attentive to the price of their shares (Callaghan and Höpner 2005). Meanwhile, the close relationships between regional banks and companies in the *Mittelstand* remained largely intact, leaving the German corporate sector with a stakeholder orientation and considerable coordinating capacities.

For German industrial relations the era proved more disruptive. As international competition intensified, many firms sought more flexibility to adjust wages and working times to changing market conditions. Rifts opened up between large firms with the wherewithal to cede higher wage increases or tolerate strikes and smaller firms lacking such margins for maneuver, especially in the Eastern Länder that joined a reunified Germany in 1990 (Thelen and Winjbergen 2003). As a result, many companies dropped out of employers' associations; and trade unions began to accept agreements ceding more control over wages and working conditions to firm-level negotiations, where works councils played a greater role. Some see these developments as a major shift in the growth regime, but German producer groups retained considerable strategic capacities and the contrast with wage-setting in liberal market economies remained striking (cf. Streeck 2009).

By comparison, although successful at manufacturing, Germany did not find a formula for creating jobs in services. Christian Democratic governments were opposed to increasing public employment, while proposals to expand low-wage services evoked the ire of the trade unions and threatened the egalitarian wage structures underpinning the cross-class coalitions of the CDU and SPD. Therefore, despite stagnating employment, successive governments temporized by promoting early retirement on the premise that this would open up jobs and maintaining regulatory regimes, such as the short school day, that kept women out of the workforce. Only later would German governments take major steps to build service-sector employment on the back of a low-wage labor market.

3.3 Electoral Politics

Once again, there is a political side to the story. In some instances, liberalizing initiatives were pressed on governments by business interests seeking more flexibility to respond to international competition (Prasad 2006; Hacker and Pierson 2010). In others, they were initiated by policy-makers and their economic advisors, convinced by the failures of the 1970s that there were no alternative routes to growth (Gamble 1994; Woll 2008; Mudge 2018). But, apart from initial support for Thatcher's break with the past and passing enthusiasm for the Single European Act of 1986, liberalizing initiatives were rarely popular with electorates. They carried many adverse effects—reducing job security, social benefits, and income equality. Thus the puzzle is: why would governments dependent on electorates adopt such measures? What kind of political conditions made such reversals of policy possible?

In large measure, the answer turns on shifts in electoral cleavages. The decline of the class cleavage and growing salience of a values cleavage cross-cutting it reorganized the electoral space of the developed democracies, leaving the electorate more ideologically fragmented (Dalton et al. 1984, Clark and Lipset 2001). This fragmentation gave rise to a permissive electoral dynamics in which durable electoral coalitions in favor of neoliberal policies were rarely formed but the potential for effective opposition to them was preempted, allowing governments to pursue new growth strategies.[4]

By the early 1980s, the salience of the class cleavage had been declining for more than a decade. Fewer people in the developed democracies were voting along class lines and political debate was less likely to be couched in class terms (Manza et al. 1995; Evans and Tilly 2017). The roots of this decline lay in three sets of developments at least partly endogenous to the prior growth regime. Thirty years of prosperity under that regime had improved the living standards of ordinary workers enough to mitigate the sense of grievance that once animated class-centric political debates (Lipset 1964). The shift of employment from manufacturing to services decimated cohesive working-class communities and blurred the social divisions once separating white- and blue-collar workers. The social programs of the welfare state built under the preceding regime reduced the material insecurity central to working-class mobilization; and, once the welfare state was in place, social democratic parties lost the distinctive political mission around which they had mobilized working-class voters.

The 1980s also saw the rising salience of a new cleavage based largely on cultural values, sometimes labeled a right-authoritarian/left-libertarian divide (Kitschelt 1997). On one side of it were voters embracing the post-materialist

[4] For an alternative argument that notes support for neoliberal initiatives among some middle-class voters and thus electoral incentives to implement them in some contexts, see Ellis 1998.

values that became prominent in the early 1980s, linked to new social movements focused on the environment, gender equality and human rights. On the other side were voters attached to more traditional values, concerned about material security, immigration and the protection of national culture. New Green and radical right parties speaking to each side of this divide became more prominent political actors in Europe during the 1980s and 1990s. To some extent, this cleavage was also endogenous to the previous growth regime. Three decades of prosperity weaned generations that grew up in affluence away from the material anxieties of their parents and drew them toward a search for personal fulfillment that found expression in the liberation politics of the 1960s and the new social movements of the 1980s (Beer 1982; Inglehart 1990).

The rising salience of this values cleavage set in motion a dynamic that would affect the growth strategies adopted by governments in several ways. Social democratic parties embraced left-libertarian values in order to attract support from middle-class voters whose affluence inclined them toward such values. By 1990, social democratic parties in Europe were securing more votes from the middle class than from the working class, largely on values issues (Gingrich and Häusermann 2015: 58). Because they enjoyed strong market positions, however, many of those middle-class voters benefited from liberalizing reforms. That provided center-left parties with incentives to accept some elements of market liberalization; and, as Figure 2.1 indicates, they did so during the 1980s and 1990s. Convergence toward market-oriented policies in this era was based largely on the movement of center-left parties. The "Third Way" of Tony Blair was as consequential as the neoliberal policies of Margaret Thatcher.

In tandem with their increasing dependence on middle-class votes, social democratic parties also began to deemphasis class-based political appeals; and working-class voters saw fewer reasons to support parties whose economic platforms had converged to the right, thereby further eroding the salience of the class cleavage (Iversen 2006; Mudge 2011; Evans and Tilley 2012). Moreover, as their economic positions became increasingly similar, parties of the center-left and center-right began to rely more heavily on values issues to render their electoral appeals distinctive (see Figure 2.2); and, for similar reasons, values became more important to voter's decisions about which party to support.[5] But working-class voters were more likely than middle-class voters to hold right-authoritarian views. Thus, the salience of values issues drove a wedge through the electoral coalitions of social democratic parties, alienating working-class constituents whom those parties might otherwise have mobilized in opposition to neoliberal reform. By the end of the 1990s, substantial portions of the European working class were voting

[5] Spatial electoral analysis predicts that issues on which the parties are more distinctive will weigh more heavily in the voting decisions of citizens who care about such issues. Cf. Rabinowitz and Macdonald 1989.

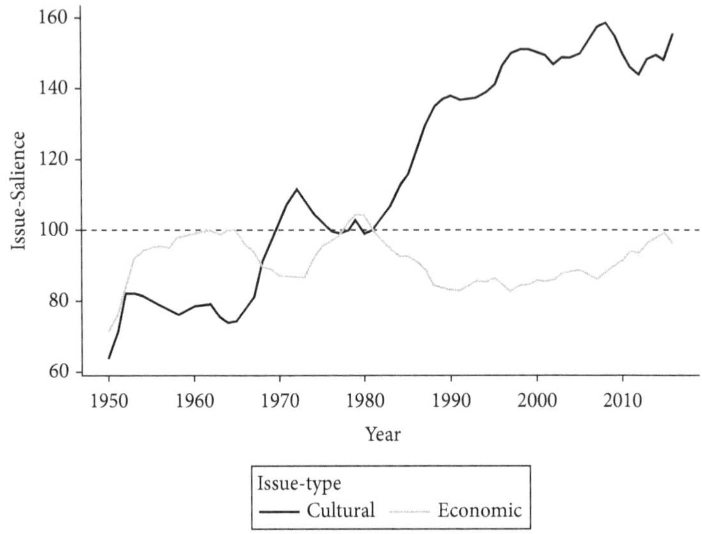

Figure 2.2 The relative prominence of economic and cultural issues in the party manifestos of western democracies

Note: Proportion of references to each kind of issue in party manifestos weighted by party vote share in the most recent election for each country, indexed to 1980 levels.

Based on the CMP categories, references to the following are classified as cultural/values issues: Environmental protection (501); Culture (502); Social Justice (503); National way of life (601); National way of life negative (602); Traditional morality (603); Traditional morality (604); Multiculturalism (607); Multiculturalism negative (608). The following are classified as economic issues: Free market economy (401); Incentives (402); Market regulation (403); Protectionism (406); Protectionism negative (407); Economic goals (408); Demand management (409); Economic growth (410); Controlled economy (412); Economic orthodoxy (414); Marxist analysis (415). Countries included: Australia, Austria, Belgium, Canada, Denmark, Finland, France, Germany, Greece, Iceland, Ireland, Italy, Luxembourg, Netherlands, Norway, Portugal, Spain, Sweden, Switzerland, US, UK.

Source: Comparative Party Manifesto database.

instead for parties of the radical right. The result was a permissive electoral dynamic in which public support for liberalizing reforms was only intermittent but effective opposition to them largely absent from the arena of party competition.

4. An Era of Knowledge-Based Growth, 2000–

By the end of the 1990s, the economic challenges facing the developed democracies were shifting again, presaging a new era of knowledge-based growth that continues to the present day. As usual, there was cross-national variation in the timing and pace of change. However, the inception of this era dates to the late 1990s when two developments advanced enough to transform the global economy. The first was a revolution in information and communications technology (ICT) which altered business practices across sectors, as productivity became increasingly dependent on its diffusion. The patenting rate began to grow exponentially during the 1990s, and productivity growth in the US leapt ahead of Europe for the first time in several decades, as American firms became the first to deploy the new technologies (Powell and Snellman 2004; van Ark et al. 2008; Brynjolfsson and McAfee 2014). The second was a large-scale shift of manufacturing toward emerging economies, accompanied by the rise of global value chains as firms began to off-shore more elements of their production (Antràs et al. 2006; Milberg and Winkler 2013; Dicken 2015). An increase in the volumes of foreign direct investment going toward the developing economies and the entry of China into the World Trade Organization in 2000 signaled these changes.

In the wake of these developments, the employment challenges facing governments began to shift. In many developed democracies, occupational structures polarized, as technology and offshoring displaced routine jobs in manufacturing and services, while high-skill positions and sometimes low-skill positions that could not readily be automated continued to grow at the two ends of the income distribution (Autor and Dorn 2013; Oesch and Menes 2010). Employment in business services expanded more rapidly as the new technology made it easier for firms to outsource services; and economic growth now turned less on how many products a nation shipped than on the proportion of their value-added it supplied (Berger 2005; Wren 2013; Tassey 2014). Thus, for the developed countries, the employment challenge of the 2000s was no longer simply how to create jobs in services but how to cultivate the skills required for the growing numbers of high-skill positions in a knowledge economy and how to shift production toward high value-added links in global supply chains.

Changes in financial markets also created new challenges for governments. At their heart was a series of innovations in financial instruments, made feasible by ICT, which outpaced the efforts of governments to regulate them. The central development was the proliferation of financial derivatives, namely securities whose value is tied to the value of other securities, following the invention of credit default swaps in the mid-1990s. In theory, derivatives could diffuse risk among counterparties, thereby allowing enterprises to operate at higher leverage ratios. In reality, the effect was to expand the levels of debt held by the financial, corporate, and household sectors, to increase the interdependence of financial enterprises, and thereby raise by an order of magnitude the systemic risks present in national financial systems (Glick and Lansing 2010). The share of profits going to the financial sector grew, notably in the international financial centers of the US and Britain; but, even in smaller nations such as Spain, Ireland, Iceland, and the Netherlands, governments faced the problem of coping with asset booms fostered by looser finance. With the inception of European monetary union in 1999, financial interdependence across the member states increased. but their governments had to address economic shocks without the national monetary instruments once used for these purposes.

4.1 The Economic Gestalt

Although techno-optimists and pessimists are still debating the implications, the idea that developed countries were becoming "knowledge economies" became increasingly influential among policy-makers and the public during the 1990s (cf. Brynjolfsson and McAfee 2014; Gordon 2016). Affirming an emerging consensus, the OECD published a 1996 report which declared that "Knowledge is now recognised as the driver of productivity and economic growth, leading to a new focus on the role of information, technology and learning in economic performance" and, in 2000, the members states of the European Union signed onto a Lisbon Strategy aimed at making the EU "the most competitive and dynamic knowledge-based economy in the world" (OECD 1996: 3; European Union 2000). By the turn of the new century, the "knowledge economy" was a feature of common parlance.

Several currents in economic thought influenced this perspective. During the 1990s, economists devoted increasing attention to theories of endogenous growth which viewed economic growth as a function of technological changes that were conditioned by public policy; and they began to ponder to the labor-market effects of skill-biased technological change (Katz and Murphy 1992; Krueger 1993; Autor and Dorn 2013; Oesch 2013; Lucas 1988; Romer 1990; Grossman and Helpman 1993; Aghion and Howitt 2008). Building on Becker's pioneering work about human capital, many economists explored the relationship between economic growth and education, while scholars of innovation gained influence within the EU (Becker 1964; Goldin and Katz 2008; Heckman and Masterov 2007; Freeman and Soele 1997; Dosi et al. 1990; Lundvall 1992). This emphasis on the importance of human capital to the knowledge economy encouraged policy-makers to reconceptualize social policy as an effort to make its beneficiaries more productive; and such views were soon joined to neoliberal views about the value of "workfare" via the premise that effective integration into the labor market required work experience.

The result was a profound shift in how many policy-makers came to see social policy (Jenson and Saint-Martin 2003; Morel et al. 2012; Hemerijck 2013). In the eyes of many policymakers, the notion of "social investment" replaced "social protection" as the objective of the welfare state. They no longer saw social benefits primarily as the reward for a lifetime of work, insurance against market adversity, or a means for addressing social disadvantage. Instead, policy was to be aimed at delivering future economic returns to individuals and society. That implied targeting more resources on the young than the old and promoting "activation"—namely, measures designed to push people at the margins of the labor market into paid work. In some cases, this was to be done by enhancing their skills. In others, it was accomplished by attaching work requirements to the receipt of social benefits.

In 1994 observers could note that "a 'social investment' model is replacing the 'social security' paradigm inherited from the sixties," and by 1997 the OECD was endorsing the movement from a social expenditure to a social investment model. In an influential 1998 book on *The Third Way*, Anthony Giddens contended that "welfare states" which protected people from the adverse effects of market competition should be replaced by "social investment states" whose objective would be to prepare people for market competition (Myles and Street 1994: 7; OECD 1997; Giddens 1998). In short, social policy was reconceptualized as a vehicle for economic growth rather than a salve for its distributive failures.

4.2 Growth Strategies

In contrast to the 1970s. when countries were pushed toward new policies by dramatic economic failures, the challenges of the information age crept up on governments, and many have been slow to respond to them. As a result, various features of neoliberal growth strategies still remain in place; movement toward new strategies for a knowledge economy has been sporadic; and there is significant cross-national variation in the pace of change. However, by the late 1990s, a broad consensus had emerged that prosperity now depended on finding ways to promote innovation, diffuse ICT, and increase the human capital embodied in the workforce. One of the most widespread results was a substantial increase in the resources governments devoted to education, reflected in rising rates of tertiary education across the OECD.

In line with social investment perspectives, the efforts of governments to increase employment have put more emphasis on pushing people into the labor force. Many governments have reduced the duration for which unemployment benefits are available and made their receipt contingent on active job search or retraining. The initiatives of the Clinton administration to turn "welfare" into "workfare," and parallel moves by the Blair government in Britain, exemplify this dimension of the new policy regime. In Continental Europe, such measures have been supplemented by active labor market policies (ALMP) that devote more resources to improving skills and drawing people into the workforce. These policies can take several forms (Bonoli 2005). One approach provides more resources for those searching for jobs, as in Germany, Denmark and Sweden. Another focuses on training the unemployed, while a third approach pursued in France supplies subsidies to firms to hire the young or long-term unemployed on the premise that job experience confers the contacts and skills necessary to secure permanent employment. Many European countries have been spending close to one percent of GDP on such programs (Morel et al. 2012). In this context, family policy has also assumed a new importance. To draw more women into the workforce, governments have made more generous provisions for parental leave and daycare; and there is increasing interest in early childhood development, seen as a form of social investment, based on evidence that occupational achievement is closely related to the quality of a child's early years (Heckman and Masterov 2007).

In the realm of financial markets, governments have shown a high tolerance for new financial instruments and higher leverage ratios, including a substantial expansion of household debt. The American government repealed the Glass-Steagall Act in 1999, thereby allowing banks to engage in riskier financial operations; and governments accommodated asset booms buoying constructions in Ireland, Spain, the Netherlands, Britain, the US, and several parts of Eastern Europe. Of course, accumulating risk culminated in the global financial crisis of 2008–9; and financial policy since then has included efforts to reduce systemic risk by raising the capital requirements for financial firms. At the same time, many governments took steps to ensure venture capital for start-ups (Breznitz 2007; Ornston 2012). The French authorities seeded several venture capital firms and made it easier for entrepreneurs to start small enterprises, while Swedish governments moved regional development funds into new pools of venture capital (Trumbull 2004; Schnyder 2012; Stevens 2012).

Once again, national strategies reflect both commonalities and variations. Under the 1997 Blair government, the British pursued "third way" policies that put a heavy emphasis on improving the nation's human capital. Within months of taking office, Blair set a goal of sending 50 percent of the relevant age cohort to university and dramatically increased spending on education. At the other end of the labor market, he implemented a "Fair Deal" program providing more support for job searches but requiring recipients of social benefits to engage in active job search or training. Social benefits for single mothers were increased with a view to enhancing early child development. Britain could depend on the competitive product markets of a liberal market economy to diffuse ICT, and it fared well in the early years of knowledge-based growth. ICT currently contributes more to value-added in Britain than in most European countries and exports in business services grew rapidly in the first decade of the twenty-first century (Timmer et al. 2011).

French governments also emphasized education as the route to higher rates of growth, initially by mandating two years of training after the *baccalauréat* for all young people and then by increasing funding for higher education (Culpepper 2003). In France, the minimum wage is an entrenched feature of the labor market and a totem of the national commitment to maintaining purchasing power. Therefore, rather than lower it in order to give the unemployed a foothold in the labor market, successive governments chose to subsidize the social contribution paid on new hires by employers and employees, funded via a series of special taxes on incomes. By the early 2000s, these subsidies totaled almost €6 billion a year; and social spending rose from 24 to 28 percent of GDP between 1990 and

2005 (Carbonnier et al. 2014). However, by subsidizing low-wage jobs, these programs inhibited firms from moving toward higher-valued added forms of production; and French investment in research and development languished well below OECD norms into the early 2000s (Palier 2012). The French economy remains unusually dependent on a few national champions in energy, armaments and aerospace, whose sales are often as much a diplomatic as an economic achievement (Cohen 1977).

Growth strategies in Sweden have changed more than in most countries. In the wake of the 1992 economic collapse, Sweden entered the era of knowledge-based growth convinced that prosperity required a new growth strategy. The result was a new set of policies often facilitated by the concerted action of organized producer groups (Ornston 2013). Between 1990 and 2000, public investment on education grew from 5 to 7 percent of GDP; and two programs of continuing education, focused on the skills required by ICT, enrolled almost 10 percent of the adult population between 1997 and 2000. Urged on by the government, firms doubled their investment in research and development; and, with the agreement of producer groups, the government shifted tax advantages from large corporations to start-ups and diverted regional development funds to venture capital. By 2003 the value of private equity funds in Sweden was close to American levels at 26 percent of GDP. The share of high-technology products in Swedish manufactures also rose from 10 percent to 17 percent between 1980 and 2007, while the low-technology share dropped from 34 to 23 percent. Important clusters for high-tech production have grown up around several Swedish cities; and the contribution of ICT to Swedish value-added is among the highest in the OECD (Schnyder 2012; van Ark et al. 2008).

However, Swedish efforts to manage the labor market have not been as successful. Levels of social investment remain high and public services remain an important source of employment, even though the delivery of many services has been privatized. But divisions between white and blue-collar trade unions have hampered efforts to reform the vocational training system; and recent governments have struggled to integrate large numbers of immigrants into the labor market (Thelen 2014; Dolvik et al. 2015). Sweden may soon have to tolerate the growth of a secondary labor market, although it has recently generated some of the highest rates of growth in the OECD.

Germany's efforts to cope with the revolution in ICT have centered on the manufacturing sector and also been facilitated by the capacities of its producer groups for strategic coordination. German governments were slow to increase enrollments in tertiary education, partly because industry depends heavily on vocational training; but that training has gradually been upgraded to accommodate the growing role of ICT in production, and college enrollments are now rising (Busemeyer 2015). As firms began to contract out more operations, Germany also developed a significant presence in business services, an important adjunct to its manufacturing strengths; and its industries have been adept at taking advantage of global value chains, notably after the fall of communism in 1990 when German firms developed extensive supply chains in Eastern Europe.

On social investment, however, the country has been a laggard. Facing endemic unemployment problems after reunification, German governments introduced a series of measures to make temporary labor contracts, agency employment and part-time work more feasible. The most prominent steps in this direction came in 2002–3 when a coalition government of the SPD and Greens under Gerhard Schröder implemented the recommendations of the Hartz commission. In order to push people into work, these measures reduced the duration of unemployment benefits and expanded part-time "mini-jobs" whose occupants could earn up to 400 euros a month with few taxes or social charges on their earnings but correspondingly few social benefits. By 2010, about 7 million people held marginal jobs, many of them women (Hassel 2014).

These steps took levels of female and total employment in Germany toward European averages, but at the cost of creating a large secondary labor market of precarious employment alongside more secure positions in manufacturing (Thelen 2014; Hassel 2006). Focused on activation, the measures entailed only modest levels of social investment, mainly in the form of more extensive aid for job searches, and they did little to increase the skills of the workforce. Nevertheless, intensifying competition for the votes of women has inspired some other forms of social investment, such as the 2006 von der Leyen reforms to expand daycare facilities and extend paternity leave.

In this context, much of Germany's otherwise considerable economic success after 2000 is attributable to the effectiveness with which coordinated wage bargaining held down unit labor costs to offset the losses in competitiveness that followed reunification (Carlin and Soskice 2009; Dustmann et al. 2014). The effect was to shift a growth strategy that had been relatively balanced between reliance on domestic demand and exports toward one exceptionally dependent on exports. For a decade after 2000, real wages barely increased and restrictive fiscal policies compressed domestic demand. Public investment stagnated as budgets were cut; and levels of private investment initially suffered from high real interest rates linked to the strict monetary policies of the new European central bank (ECB). Since wages were barely rising, German firms faced few incentives to engage in labor-saving investment and increases in productivity have remained low. Although wage increases picked up after 2015, the result is now an on-going debate about the need for higher public investment.

4.3 Electoral Politics

Once again, the movement toward new growth strategies has been influenced by movements in voter preferences and party alignments in the electoral arena—conditioned by economic developments during the previous era. Rising rates of female labor force participation, promoted by the growth strategies of the era of liberalization, have been especially important.[6] As women have entered the labor force, their political preferences have changed. For much of the post-war years, women were a mainstay of Christian Democratic parties—more religiously observant than men and widely seen as a conservative force in politics. By the 1990s, however, working women had become strong supporters of subsidized childcare, parental leave, and programs for early childhood development as well as other steps to expand educational opportunities. Those who work part-time tend to favor the active labor market policies that expanded such positions (Morgan 2013; Marx and Picot 2013). Thus, women have become a powerful force pushing for policies of social investment and competition for their votes a major factor behind the expansion of such policies. In the first instance, social democratic parties were the beneficiaries of this development, as increasing numbers of women shifted their allegiance to them. By the 2000s, however, Christian Democratic parties were also bidding for women's votes, with policies such as the von der Leyen reforms (Seeleib-Kaiser et al. 2008).

Shifts in the occupational structure that have increased the number of sociocultural professionals, working in education, healthcare, and business services, have also added to electoral pressures for social investment. People in those occupations now form 15 to 20 percent of the electorate in most developed democracies; and, perhaps because their work entails high levels of interpersonal interaction, support for spending on education and daycare is higher among this group than among the industrial working class (Kitschelt and Rehm 2014; Gingrich and Häusermann 2015; Marx and Picot 2013; Beramendi et al. 2015). Thus, mainstream parties of the center-right and left have sought to build electoral coalitions of working women and sociocultural professionals by advocating policies of social investment.

However, the electoral conditions of the past two decades have not been entirely auspicious for growth strategies oriented to a knowledge economy. In many countries, longstanding voter allegiances have eroded, as the distinctiveness of the economic platforms of center-right and center-left parties has declined, and divisions on cultural issues have driven wedges through the electoral coalitions of mainstream parties.[7] As a result, the share of the electorate those parties attract has declined, party systems have become more fragmented, and partisan competition is increasingly based on assembling ad hoc coalitions behind the platforms of the day (Mair 2013).

In this context, if large segments of the electorate embrace the economic gestalt of knowledge-based growth, it may be possible for governments to pursue such

[6] By 2000, for instance, more women than men were members of British trade unions.

[7] The United States, where partisan identities loom large amidst a polarization of the electorate, is a notable exception to this trend.

strategies. Some analysts are optimistic about this possibility on the grounds that parties will be able to form coalitions between sociocultural professionals and others who benefit from knowledge-based growth along with aspirational voters who may not benefit directly from the relevant policies but believe they enhance the prospects of their children (Iversen and Soskice 2019). Such coalitions are more likely to be feasible in countries with relatively advanced economies, such as those of northern Europe, than in countries where small businesses and low-skill workers comprise more of the electorate, as in many parts of Southern Europe (Beramendi et al. 2015).

However, recent economic developments have also given rise to a new electoral cleavage, separating those who expect to benefit from an internationally interdependent knowledge economy and those who see themselves as losing from it (Kriesi et al. 2008; Hooghe and Marks 2018). As global outsourcing and skill-biased technological change eliminate well-paid routine jobs and accompanying policies render many other positions less secure, close to a fifth of voters in western electorates have come to see themselves as losers in this new economy. The result is an "integration cleavage" rooted in differences in material interest but rendered more powerful by the fact that those on one side of it tend to embrace post-materialist values, while those on the other side often hold more traditional views. The key characteristic separating the two sides is the experience of tertiary education, which confers both job prospects in the new knowledge economy and more cosmopolitan values. Because knowledge-based growth tends to concentrate prosperity in urban clusters and move good jobs away from small cities or rural areas, there is also a regional dimension to this cleavage whose network effects enhance its electoral salience (Moretti 2012).

On one side of this cleavage, many voters, often from the working class, have been drawn away from parties of the center-right and center-left, seen as defenders of the status quo, toward new parties on the right and left ends of the political spectrum. The rise of these radical parties will not necessarily prevent governments from assembling majorities for knowledge-based growth strategies. But, in countries with electoral systems based on proportional representation, assembling governing coalitions has become more difficult; and, in majoritarian systems, parallel discontents have intensified factional infighting within the major parties. As a result, it has become more difficult for governments to adopt initiatives that advance the knowledge economy but might disadvantage others. At best, these political developments are delaying the formulation of forceful responses to the economic challenges of this era, as parties on the radical right argue for social protection, often in the form of trade protection, rather than social investment. At worst, unless new ways are found to provide decent jobs for people with lower qualifications in an era of knowledge-based growth, populist candidates hostile to global economic integration and more devoted to social consumption than social investment may come to power. Amidst the occupational turbulence caused by a new technological revolution, the prospect that quasi-permanent minorities may be left out of prosperity threatens continuing political turbulence (See Gidron and Hall 2019).

5. Conclusion

Although the quest for economic growth has been a constant of the post-war years, the growth strategies of the developed democracies have changed dramatically over that time. In an era of modernization, governments circumscribed the operation of markets via assertive state intervention, as in France and Britain, or via the development of dense networks of rules to govern coordination by producer groups, as in Sweden and Germany. The social policies of this period laid the ground for contemporary welfare states, as governments gave priority to ensuring that markets were embedded within broader social orders. During a subsequent era of liberalization, growth strategies rolled back these measures and increased competition in markets for labor, capital, and goods. Governments embraced privatization, the contracting-out of public services, more intense market competition, and more decentralized wage bargaining. During the current era of knowledge-based growth, growth strategies have shifted again toward efforts to promote new technology, venture capital, and social investment in the skills of the workforce.

Each of these growth strategies was a response to secular developments in the economy. However, that response was mediated by shifts in the gestalt through which economic events are interpreted and by developments in the electoral arenas where coalitions for growth strategies are assembled. Economic policymaking entails coalition-building among both producer groups and electorates. I have focused here on coalition-building in the electoral arena where the coalitions that can be assembled are conditioned by political cleavages that shift over time, often as a result of developments under the previous growth regime. Thus, the economic policies of the era of modernization were advanced by electoral competition dominated by a class cleavage, while the decline of that cleavage and the rise of a cross-cutting values cleavage provided a permissive electoral context for the growth strategies of an era of liberalization. In the contemporary era of knowledge-based growth, the success of new strategies will depend once again on the capacities of governments to assemble new coalitions; but they do so in an electoral space that is increasingly fragmented and marked by the rise of an incipient integration cleavage that calls into question the fairness of the knowledge economy.

Any survey of this sort necessarily leaves out some pieces of the puzzle. I have not discussed the important issues of sustainability raised by this quest for growth, and I have said little about the important role that producer-groups play in the evolution of growth strategies.[8] My focus has been on common changes over time rather than on divergence across nations, and closer inspection would reveal national adjustment trajectories, rooted in the institutional features defining distinctive varieties of capitalism. However, I hope that this analysis is revealing, not only about the extent to which the growth strategies of the developed democracies have changed since World War II, but also about and how economics and politics combine to yield those changes.

Acknowledgments

I am grateful to Noam Gidron and Georgie Evans for efficient research assistance, to Peter Gourevitch, Deborah Mabbett, Dani Rodrik, Waltraud Schelkle, and Rosemary Taylor for comments on earlier versions of this chapter, and to Princeton University and the Russell Sage Foundation for financial support while the research was done.

References

Aghion, P. and Howett, P. 2008. *The Economics of Growth*. Cambridge, MA: MIT Press.

Antràs, P., Garicano, L., and Rossi-Hansberg, E. 2006. "Offshoring in a Knowledge Economy." *Quarterly Journal of Economics* 121(1): 31–77.

Autor, D. H. and Dorn, D. 2013. "A Theory of Low-Skill Jobs and the Polarization of the U.S. Labor Market." *American Economic Review* 103(5): 1553–97.

Baccaro, L. and Pontusson J. 2016. Rethinking Comparative Political Economy: The Growth Model Perspective. *Politics & Society* 44(2): 175–207.

Becker, G. S. 1964. *Human Capital*. New York: Columbia University Press.

Beer, S. H. 1969. *Modern British Politics*. New York: Norton.

Beer, S. H. 1982. *Britain Against Itself: The Political Contradictions of Collectivism*. New York: Norton.

Beramendi, P., Häusermann, S., Kitschelt H., and Kriesi, H. P. eds. 2015. *The Politics of Advanced Capitalism*. New York: Cambridge University Press.

Berger, S. 1981. "Lame Ducks and National Champions: Industrial Policy in the Fifth Republic." In *The Fifth Republic at Twenty*, edited by E. Andrews and S. Hoffmann. Albany: SUNY Press, 292–10.

Berger, S. 2005. *How We Compete*. New York: Broadway Business.

[8] On sustainability, see Hirsch 1978; OECD 2001 and, for insightful treatments of producer group politics, see: Hacker and Pierson 2010; Culpepper 2011; Thelen 2014, Thelen in this volume, Martin in this volume.

Berger, S. and Dore, R. 1996. *National Diversity and Global Capitalism*. Ithaca: Cornell University Press.

Beveridge, W. 1942. *Social Insurance and Allied Services*. London: HMSO.

Block, F. 2011. *State of Innovation: The US Government's Role in Technology Development*. New York: Paradigm.

Boltanski, L. and Chiapello, E. 2007. *The New Spirit of Capitalism*. London: Verso.

Bonoli, G. 2005. The Political Economy of Active Labor Market Policy. *Politics & Society* 37 (4): 435–57.

Boyer, R. 1990. *The Regulation School: A Critical Introduction*. New York: Columbia University Press.

Breznitz, D. 2007. *Innovation and the State: Political Strategies for Growth in Israel, Taiwan and Ireland*. New Haven: Yale University Press.

Brittan, S. 1971. *Steering the Economy*. Harmondsworth: Penguin.

Brynjolfsson, E. and McAfee, A. 2014. *The Second Machine Age*. New York: Norton.

Busch, A. 2008. *Banking Regulation and Globalization*. Oxford: Oxford University Press.

Busemeyer, M. 2015. *Skills and Inequality: Partisan Politics and the Political Economy of Education Reforms in Western Welfare States*. New York: Cambridge University Press.

Callaghan, H. and Höpner, M. 2005. "European Integration and the Clash of Capitalisms: Political Cleavages over Takeover Liberalization." *Comparative European Politics* 3(3): 307–32.

Cameron, D. 1984. "Social Democracy, Corporatism, Labor Quiescence and the Representation of Economic Interest in Advanced Capitalist Society." In *Order and Conflict in Contemporary Capitalism*, edited by J. Goldthorpe. Oxford: Oxford University Press.

Carbonnier, C., Palier, B. and Zemour, M. 2014. Tax Cuts or Social Investment: Evaluating the Opportunity Costs of the French Employment Strategy. LIEFF Working Paper, Sciences Po, Paris.

Carlin, W. and Soskice, D. 2009. "German Economic Performance: Disentangling the Role of Supply-Side Reforms, Macroeconomic Policy and Coordinated Economy Institutions." *Socio-Economic Review* 7(1): 69–99.

Centeno, M. A. and Cohen, J. N. 2012. "The Arc of Neoliberalism." *Annual Review of Sociology* 38: 317–40.

Clark, T. N. and Lipset, S. M., eds. 2001. *The Breakdown of Class Politics: A Debate on Post-Industrial Stratification*. Baltimore: Johns Hopkins University Press.

Cohen, S. S. 1977. *Modern Capitalist Planning: the French Model*. Berkeley: University of California Press.

Crafts, N. and Toniolo, G. eds. 1996. *Economic Growth in Europe since 1945*. Cambridge: Cambridge University Press.

Crosland, C. A. R. 1956. *The Future of Socialism*. London: Jonathan Cape.

Crouch, C. 2011. *The Strange Non-Death of Neoliberalism*. Cambridge: Polity Press.

Crouch, C. and Pizzorno, A. eds. 1978. *The Resurgence of Class Conflict in Western Europe*. London: Macmillan.

Crozier, M., Huntington, S.P. and Watanuki, J. 1974. *The Crisis of Democracies*. New York: New York University Press.

Culpepper, P. D. 2003. *Creating Cooperation: How States Develop Human Capital in Europe*. Ithaca: Cornell University Press.

Culpepper, P. D. 2005. "Institutional Change in Contemporary Capitalism: Coordinated Financial Systems since 1990." *World Politics* 57(2): 173–99.

Culpepper, P. D. 2009. "The Politics of Common Knowledge: Ideas and Institutional Change in Wage Bargaining." *International Organization* 62(1): 1–33.

Culpepper, P. D. 2011. *Quiet Politics and Business Power: Corporate Power in Europe and Japan*. New York: Cambridge University Press.

Dalton, R. J., Flanagan, S. C. and Beck, P. A. eds. 1984. *Electoral Change in Advanced Industrial Democracies: Realignment or Dealignment*? Princeton: Princeton University Press.

Deeg, R. 1999. *Finance Capitalism Unveiled: Banks and the German Political Economy*. Ann Arbor: University of Michigan Press.

Deeg, R. 2010. "Industry and Finance in Germany since Reunification." *German Politics and Society* 28(2): 116–29.

Dicken, P. 2015. *Global Shift: Mapping the Changing Contours of the World Economy*. Seventh Ed. London: Guilford.

Dobbin, F. 1997. *Forging Industrial Policy: The United States, Britain and France in the Railway Age*. New York: Cambridge University Press.

Dolvik, J. E., Goul Andersen, J. and Variainen, J. 2015. "The Nordic Social Models in Turbulent Times: Consolidation and Flexible Adaptation." In *European Social Models from Crisis to Crisis*, edited by J. E. Dolvik and A. Martin. Oxford: Oxford University Press, 246–86.

Dornbusch, R. 1990. "The New Classical Economics and Stabilization Policy." *American Economic Review* 80(2): 143–7.

Dosi, G., Pavitt, K. and Soele, L. 1990. *The Economics of Technical Innovation and International Trade*. Turin: LEM Books.

Dustmann, C., Fitzenberger, B., Schönberg, U. and Spitz-Oener, A. 2014. "From Sick Man of Europe to Economic Superstar: Germany's Resurgent Economy." *Journal of Economic Perspectives* 28(1): 167–88.

Eichengreen, B. 1996. "Institutions and Economic Growth: Europe after World War II." In *Economic Growth in Europe since 1945*, edited by N. Crafts and G. Toniolo. Cambridge: Cambridge University Press, 38–72.

Elbaum, B. and Lazonick, W. eds. 1985. *The Decline of the British Economy*. New York: Oxford University Press.

Ellis, J. 1998. *Voting for Markets or Marketing for Votes? The Politics of Neoliberal Economic Reform.* Doctoral Dissertation, Department of Government, Harvard University.

Espeland, W. N. and Sauder, M. 2007. "Rankings and Reactivity: How Public Measures Recreate Social Worlds." *American Journal of Sociology* 113(1): 1–40.

Esping-Andersen, G. 1990. *Three Worlds of Welfare Capitalism.* Princeton: Princeton University Press.

European Union. 2000. Presidency Conclusions, Lisbon European Council 23–4 March http://www.consilium.europa.eu/en/uedocs/cms_data/docs/pressdata/en/ec/00100-r1.en0.htm

Evans, G. and Tilley, J. 2012. "How Parties Shape Class Politics: Explaining the Decline of the Class Basis of Party Support." *British Journal of Political Science* 41(1): 137–61.

Evans, G. and Tilley, J. 2017. *The New Politics of Class.* Oxford: Oxford University Press.

Ferguson, N., Maier, C.S., Manela, E. and Sargent, D. J. (eds.). 2010. *The Shock of the Global: The 1970s in Perspective.* Cambridge, MA.: Harvard University Press.

Fitoussi, J. P. *et al.* 1993. *Competitive Disinflation: The Mark and Budgetary Politics in Europe.* Oxford: Oxford University Press.

Fourcade, M. 2009. *Economists and Societies: Discipline and Profession in the United States, Britain and France, 1890s–1990s.* Princeton: Princeton University Press.

Freeman, C. and Soele, L. 1997. *The Economics of Industrial Innovation.* London: Pinter.

Gamble, A. 1994. *The Free Economy and the Strong State: The Politics of Thatcherism.* 2nd ed. Houndsmills: Palgrave Macmillan.

Giddens, A. 1998. *The Third Way: The Renewal of Social Democracy.* Cambridge: Polity.

Gidron, N. and Hall, P. A. 2019. Populism as a Problem of Social Integration. *Comparative Political Studies.* https://doi-org.ezp-prod1.hul.harvard.edu/10.1177/00104140(19879947

Giersch, H. 1985. Eurosclerosis. Diskussionbeiträge 112. Kiel Institute for the World Economy.

Gingrich, J. and Häusermann, S. 2015. "The Decline of the Working-Class Vote, the Reconfiguration of the Welfare Support Coalition and Consequences for the Welfare State." *Journal of European Social Policy* 25(1): 50–75.

Glick, R. and Lansing, K. J. 2010. Global Household Leverage, House Prices and Consumption, Federal Reserve Bank of San Francisco Economic Letter. (January 11).

Glyn, A. and Sutcliffe, B. 1972. *British Capitalism, Workers and the Profits Squeeze.* Harmondsworth: Penguin.

Goldin, C. and Katz, L. F. 2008. *The Race between Education and Technology.* Cambridge, Ma.: Belknap Press.

Goldthorpe, J. H. 1978. "The Current Inflation: Towards a Sociological Account." In *The Political Economy of Inflation*, edited by F. Hirsch and J. H. Goldthorpe. London: Martin Robertson, 187–14.

Goldthorpe, J. H. ed. 1984. *Order and Conflict in Contemporary Capitalism*. New York: Oxford University Press.

Gomory, R. and Sylla. R. 2013. "The American Corporation." *Daedalus* 142(2): 102–18.

Gordon, R. J. 2016. *The Rise and Fall of American Growth*. Princeton: Princeton University Press.

Goyer, M. 2012. *Contingent Capital: Short-Term Investors and the Evolution of Corporate Governance in France and Germany*. Oxford: Oxford University Press.

Grossman, G. and Helpman, E. 1993. *Innovation and Growth in the Global Economy*. Cambridge Ma: MIT Press.

Hacker, J. and Pierson, P. 2010. *Winner Take All Politics* New York: Simon and Schuster.

Hall, P. A. 1986. *Governing the Economy*. Oxford: Polity Press.

Hall, P. A. ed. 1989. *The Political Power of Economic Ideas*. Princeton: Princeton University Press.

Hall, P. A. 1993. "Policy Paradigms, Social Learning and the State: The Case of Economic Policy-Making in Britain." *Comparative Politics* 25(3): 275–96.

Hall, P. A. 1994. "Central Bank Independence and Coordinated Wage Bargaining: Their Interaction in Germany and Europe." *German Politics and Society* (Winter): 1–23.

Hall, P. A. 2005. "Preference Formation as a Political Process: The Case of Monetary Union in Europe." In *Preferences and Situations: Perspectives from Rational Choice and Historical Institutionalism*, edited by I. Katznelson and B. Weingast. New York: Russell Sage Foundation, 129–60.

Hall, P. A. 2006. "The Politics of Social Change in France." In *Changing France: The Politics that Markets Make*, edited by P. Culpepper, P. A. Hall and B. Palier. London: Palgrave Macmillan, 1–26.

Hall, P. A. 2013. "The Political Origins of our Economic Discontents." In *Politics in the New Hard Times*, edited by M. Kahler and D. Lake. Ithaca: Cornell University Press, 129–49.

Hall, P. A. 2015. "The Changing Role of the State in Liberal Market Economies." In *The Oxford Handbook of Transformations of the State*, edited by S. Leibfried et al. Oxford: Oxford University Press, 426–44.

Hall, P. A. and Franzese, Jr, R. 1998. "Mixed Signals: Central Bank Independence, Coordinated Wage Bargaining, and European Monetary Union." *International Organization* 52(3): 505–35

Hall P. A. and Lamont, M. eds. 2009. *Social Resilience in the Neoliberal Era*. New York: Cambridge University Press.

Hall, P. A. and Soskice, D. eds. 2001. *Varieties of Capitalism: The Institutional Foundations of Comparative Advantage*. Oxford: Oxford University Press.

Hall, P. A. and Thelen, K. 2009. "Institutional Change in Varieties of Capitalism." *Socio-Economic Review* 7(1): 7–34

Hancké, B. 2002. *Large Firms and Institutional Change: Industrial Renewal and Economic Restructuring in France.* Oxford: Oxford University Press.

Hansen, B. 1968. *Fiscal Policy in Seven Countries 1955-(1965).* Paris: OECD.

Hassel, A. 2006. *Wage Setting, Social Pacts and the Euro.* Amsterdam: Amsterdam University Press.

Hassel, A. 2014. "The Paradox of Liberalization: Understanding Dualism and the Recovery of he German Economy." *British Journal of Industrial Relations* 52(1): 57–81.

Heckman, J. J. and Masterov, D. V. 2007. "The Productivity Argument for Investing in Young Children." *Applied Economic Perspectives and Policy* 29(3): 446–93.

Hemerijck, A. 2013. *Changing Welfare States.* Oxford: Oxford University Press.

Herrigel, G. 2000. *Industrial Constructions: The Sources of German Industrial Power.* New York: Cambridge University Press.

Hirsch, F. 1978. *Social Limits to Growth.* 2nd ed. London: Routledge.

Hooghe, L. and Marks, G. 2018. "Cleavage Theory Meets Europe's Crises: Lipset, Rokkan, and the Transnational Cleavage." *Journal of European Public Policy* 25(1): 109–35.

Inglehart, R. 1990. *Culture Shift.* Princeton: Princeton University Press.

Iversen, T. 1999. *Contested Economic Institutions.* New York: Cambridge University Press.

Iversen, T. 2006. "Class Politics is Dead! Long Live Class Politics! A Political Economy Perspective on the New Partisan Politics." *APSA-CP Newsletter* 17(2): 1–6.

Iversen, T. and Cusack, T. 2000. "The Causes of Welfare State Expansion: Deindustrialization or Globalization." *World Politics* 52(3): 313–49.

Iversen, T. and Soskice, D. 2009. "Distribution and Redistribution: The Shadow of the Nineteenth Century." *World Politics* 61(3): 438–86.

Iversen, T. and Soskice, D. 2015. "Democratic Limits to Redistribution: Inclusionary versus Exclusionary Coalitions in the Knowledge Economy." *World Politics* 67(2): 185–25.

Iversen, T. and Soskice, D. 2019. *Democracy and Prosperity: Reinventing Capitalism through a Turbulent Century.* New York: Oxford University Press.

Iversen, T. and Wren, A. 1998. "Equality, Employment and Budgetary Restraint." *World Politics* 50(2): 507–46.

Jabko, N. 2006. *Playing the Market: A Political Strategy for Uniting Europe, 1985–2005.* Ithaca: Cornell University Press.

Jenson, J. and Saint-Martin. D. 2003. "New Routes to Social Cohesion? Citizenship and the Social Investment State." *The Canadian Journal of Sociology* 28(1): 77–99.

Johnson, C. 1982. *MITI and the Japanese Miracle.* Stanford: Stanford University Press.

Johnson, H. 1971. "The Keynesian Revolution and the Monetarist Counter-Revolution." *American Economic Review* 61(2): 1–14.

Katz, L. F. and Murphy, K. M. 1992. "Changes in Relative Wages, 1963–87: Supply and Demand Factors." *Quarterly Journal of Economics* 107(1): 35–78.

Katzenstein, P. 1987. *Policy and Politics in Germany: The Growth of a Semi-Sovereign State*. Philadelphia: Temple University Press.

Keohane, R. O. 1978. "Economics, Inflation and the Role of the State: Political Implications of the McCracken Report." *World Politics* 31(1): 108–28.

Keohane, R. and Milner, H. eds. 1996. *Internationalization and Domestic Politics*. New York: Cambridge University Press.

Kitschelt, H. 1997. *The Radical Right in Western Europe*. Ann Arbor: University of Michigan Press.

Kitschelt, H., Lange, P. Marks. G. and Stephens, J. eds. 1999. *Continuity and Change in Contemporary Capitalism*. New York: Cambridge University Press.

Kitschelt, H. and Rehm, P. 2014. "Occupations as Sites of Preference Formation." *Comparative Political Studies* 47(12): 1670–06.

Kreile, Michael. 1978. "West Germany: Dynamics of Change." In *Between Power and Plenty*, edited by Peter Katzenstein. Madison: University of Wisconsin Press: 191–24.

Krieger, J. 1986. *Reagan, Thatcher and the Politics of Decline*. New York: Oxford University Press.

Kriesi, H. P., Grande, E., Lachat, R., Dolezal, M., Bornschier, S. and Frey, T. eds. 2008. *West European Politics in the Age of Globalization*. Cambridge: Cambridge University Press.

Krippner, G. 2011. *Capitalizing on Crisis*. Cambridge, MA: Harvard University Press.

Krueger, A. B. 1993. "How Computers Have Changed the Wage Structure: Evidence from Microdata, 1984–89." *Quarterly Journal of Economics* 108(1): 33–60.

Lallement, M. 2006. "New Patterns of Industrial Relations and Political Action since the 1980s." In *Changing France*, edited by P. Culpepper, P. A. Hall and B. Palier. Houndmills: Palgrave Macmillan, 50–79.

Landes, D. 1949. "French Entrepreneurship and Industrial Growth in the 19th Century." *Journal of Economic History* 9(1): 45–61.

Lazonick, W. and O'Sullivan, M. 2000. "Maximizing Shareholder Value: A New Ideology for Corporate Governance." *Economy and Society* 29(1): 13–35.

Leruez, J. 1975. *Economic Planning and Politics in Britain*. London: Martin Robertson.

Lindberg, L. M. and Maier, C. S. eds. 1985. *The Politics of Inflation and Economic Stagnation*. Washington: Brookings Institution.

Lindblom, C. 1977. *Politics and Markets: The World's Political Economic Systems*. New York: Basic.

Lipset, S. M. 1964. "The Changing Class Structure and Contemporary European Politics." *Daedalus* 93(1): 271–03.

Lord, G. 1973. *The French Budgetary Process.* Berkeley CA: University of California Press.

Lowe, W., Benoit, K., Mikhaylov, S. and Laver, M. 2011. "Scaling Policy Preferences from Coded Political Texts," *Legislative Studies Quarterly* 36(1): 123–55.

Lucas, R. E. 1988. "On the Mechanics of Economic Development." *Journal of Monetary Economics* 22(1): 3–42.

Lundvall, B. A. ed. 1992. *National Systems of Innovation.* London: Pinter.

Mair, P. 2013. *Ruling the Void: The Hollowing of Western Democracy.* London: Verso.

Manow, P. 2009. "Electoral Rules, class coalitions and welfare state regimes—or how to explain Esping-Andersen with Stein Rokkan," *Socio-Economic Review* 7(1): 101–21.

Manza, J., Hout, M. and Brooks, C. 1995. "Class Voting in Capitalist Democracies since World War II: Dealignment, Realignment or Trendless Fluctuation?" *Annual Review of Sociology* 21: 137–62.

Martin, A. 1979. "The Dynamics of Change in a Keynesian Political Economy: The Swedish Case and its Implications." In *State and Economy in Contemporary Capitalism*, edited by C. Crouch. London: Croom Helm.

Martin, C. J. and Swank, D. 2012. *The Political Construction of Business Interests.* New York: Cambridge University Press.

Marx, P. and Picot, G. 2013. "The Party Preferences of Atypical Workers in Germany." *European Journal of Social Policy* 23(2): 164–78.

McArthur, J. and Scott, B. 1969. *Industrial Planning in France.* Boston: Harvard Business School.

McNamara, K. 1998. *The Currency of Ideas.* Ithaca: Cornell University Press.

Milberg, W. and Winkler, D. 2013. *Outsourcing Economics: Global Value Chains in Capitalist Development.* New York: Cambridge University Press.

Moravcsik, A. 1998. *The Choice for Europe.* Ithaca: Cornell University Press.

Morel, N., Palier, B. and Palme, J. eds. 2012. *Towards a Social Investment Welfare State: Ideas, Policies and Challenges.* London: Policy Press.

Moretti, E. 2012. *The New Geography of Jobs.* New York: Houghton Mifflin Harcourt.

Morgan, K. J. 2013. "Path Shifting of the Welfare State: Electoral Competition and the Expansion of Work-Family Policies in Western Europe." *World Politics* 65(1): 73–115.

Mudge, S. 2011. "What's Left of Leftism: Neoliberal Politics in Western Party Systems 1945–2008." *Social Science History* 35(3): 337–80.

Mudge, S. 2018. *Leftism Reinvented: Western Parties from Socialism to Neoliberalism.* Cambridge MA: Harvard University Press.

Myles, John and Debra Street. 1994. "Should the Economic Life Course be Redesigned?" Working Paper Series, Pepper Institute on Aging and Public Policy, Florida State University.

Nölke, A. and Vliegenthart, A. 2009. "Enlarging the Varieties of Capitalism: The Emergence of Dependent Market Economies in East Central Europe." *World Politics* 61(4): 670–702.

O'Connor, J. 1979. *The Fiscal Crisis of the State*. New Brunswick NJ: Transaction.

Oesch, D. 2013. *Occupational Change in Europe: How Technology & Education Transform the Job Structure*. Oxford: Oxford University Press.

Oesch, D. and Rodriguez Menés, J. 2010. "Upgrading or Polarization: Occupational Change in Britain, Germany, Spain and Switzerland. 1990–2008." *Socio-Economic Review* 9(3): 503–31.

Offe, C. 1983. "Competitive Party Democracy and the Keynesian Welfare State: Factors of Stability and Disorganization." *Policy Sciences* 15: 225–46.

Organisation for Economic Cooperation and Development. 1996. *The Knowledge-Based Economy*. Paris: OECD.

Organisation for Economic Cooperation and Development. 1997. *Societal Cohesion and the Globalising Economy*. Paris: OECD.

Organisation for Economic Cooperation and Development. 2001. *Sustainable Development: Critical Issues*. Paris: OECD.

Ornston, D. 2012. *When Small States Make Big Leaps: Institutional Innovation and High Tech Competition in Western Europe*. Ithaca: Cornell University Press.

Ornston, D. 2013. "Creative Corporatism: The Politics of High-Technology Competition in Nordic Europe." *Comparative Political Studies* 46(6): 702–29.

Palier, B. 2012. Construire un Avenir de Qualité pour Tous et Toutes. Terra Nova Note 1/3, Paris.

Palier, B. and Thelen, K. 2010. "Institutionalizing Dualism: Complementarities and Change in France and Germany." *Politics & Society* 38(1): 119–48.

Palley, T. 2018. "Three Globalizations, Not Two: Rethinking the History and Economics of Trade and Globalization." *European Journal of Economics and Economic Policy* 2: 174–92.

Piore, M. and Sabel. C. 1984. *The Second Industrial Divide*. New York: Basic Books.

Pontusson, J. 1992. *The Limits of Social Democracy: Investment Politics in Sweden*. Ithaca: Cornell University Press.

Pontusson, J. and Swenson, P. 1996. "Labor Markets, Production Strategies, and Wage Bargaining Institutions: The Swedish Employer Offensive in Comparative Perspective." *Comparative Political Studies* 29(3): 223–50.

Powell, W. W. and Snellman, K. 2004. "The Knowledge Economy." *Annual Review of Sociology* 30: 199–20.

Prasad, M. 2006. *The Politics of Free Markets*. Chicago: University of Chicago Press.

Przeworski, A. and Sprague, J. 1986. *Paper Stones: A History of Electoral Socialism.* Chicago: University of Chicago Press.

Przeworski, A. and Wallerstein, M. 1982. "The Structure of Class Conflict in Democratic Capitalist Societies." *American Political Science Review* 76(2): 215–38.

Rabinowitz, G. and Macdonald, S. E. 1989. "A Directional Theory of Issue Voting." *American Political Science Review* 83(1): 93–121.

Rajan, R. 2010. *Fault Lines: How Hidden Fractures Still Threaten the World Economy.* Princeton: Princeton University Press.

Regan, A. 2014. *The Rise and Fall of Irish Social Partnership.* Doctoral Thesis. University College Dublin.

Riddell, P. 1991. *The Thatcher Era and its Legacy.* Oxford: Basil Blackwell.

Rodrik, D. 1997. *Has Globalization Gone Too Far?* Washington: Institute for International Economics.

Romer, P. M. 1990. "Endogenous Technological Change." *Journal of Political Economy* 98(5): S71–102.

Sally, R. 2007. "The Social Market and Liberal Order: Theory and Policy Implications." *Government and Opposition* 29(4): 461–76.

Sandbrook, D. 2010. *State of Emergency: The Way We Were. Britain. 1970–1974.* London: Allen Lane.

Scharpf, F. 2000. "Economic Changes, Vulnerabilities and Institutional Capabilities." In *Welfare and Work in the Open Economy: From Vulnerability to Competitiveness,* edited by F. Scharpf and V. Schmidt. Oxford: Oxford University Press, 21–124.

Schmitter, P. and Lehmbruch, G. eds. 1979. *Trends toward Corporatist Intermediation.* Beverly Hills: Sage.

Schnyder, G. 2012. "Like a Phoenix from the Ashes? Reassessing the Transformation of the Swedish Political Economy since the 1970s." *Journal of European Public Policy* 19(8): 1126–45.

Seeleib-Kaiser, M, van Dyuk, S. and Roggenkamp, M. 2008. *Party Politics and Social Welfare: Comparing Christian and Social Democracy in Austria, Germany and the Netherlands.* Cheltenham: Edward Elgar.

Servan-Schreiber, J. J. 1969. *The American Challenge.* New York: Avon.

Sewell, W. H. 2005. *Logics of History: Social Theory and Social Transformation.* Chicago: University of Chicago Press.

Sewell, W. H. 2008. "The Temporalities of Capitalism." *Socio-Economic Review* 6(3): 517–37.

Shonfield, A. 1958. *British Economic Policy since the War.* London: Penguin.

Shonfield, A. 1969. *Modern Capitalism.* Oxford: Oxford University Press.

Stein, J. L. 1981. "Monetarist, Keynesian and New Classical Economics." *American Economic Review* 71(2): 139–44.

Stevens, H. 2012. "La Régime de l'Auto-Entrepreneur: Une Alternative Désirable au Salariat?" *Savoir/agir*. 21 (September): 21–8.

Stilwell, F. 2006. *Political Economy: The Contest of Ideas*. 2nd ed. Oxford: Oxford University Press.

Stockman, D. 1986. *The Triumph of Politics: Why the Reagan Revolution Failed*. New York: Harper and Row.

Streeck, W. 1991. "On the Institutional Conditions for Diversified Quality Production." In *Beyond Keynesianism*, edited by E. Matzner and W. Streeck. Aldershot: Elgar, 21–61.

Streeck, W. 1994. "Pay Restraint without Incomes Policy: Institutionalized Monetarism and Industrial Unionism in Germany" In *The Return of Incomes Policy*, edited by R. Dore, R. Boyer and Z. Mars. London: Pinter, 118–30.

Streeck, W. 2009. *Re-Forming Capitalism: Institutional Change in the German Political Economy*. Oxford: Oxford University Press.

Streeck, W. 2014. *Buying Time: The Delayed Crisis of Democratic Capitalism*. London: Verso.

Swenson, P. 2002. *Capitalists against Markets*. NY: Oxford University Press.

Tassey, G. 2014. "Competing in Advanced Manufacturing: The Need for Improved Growth Models and Policies." *Journal of Economic Perspectives* 28(1): 27–48.

Thatcher, M. 1999. *The Politics of Telecommunications*. Oxford: Oxford University Press.

Thelen, K. 1991. *Union of Parts: Labor Politics in Postwar Germany*. Ithaca: Cornell University Press.

Thelen, K. 2004. *How Institutions Evolve*. New York: Cambridge University Press.

Thelen, K. 2014. *Varieties of Liberalization and the New Politics of Social Solidarity*. New York: Cambridge University Press.

Thelen, K. and van Wijnbergen, C. 2003. "The Paradox of Gobalization: Labor Relations in Germany and Beyond." *Comparative Political Studies* 36(8): 859–80.

Timmer, M. P., Inklaar, R., O'Mahony, M. and van Ark, B. 2011. "Productivity and Economic Growth in Europe: A Comparative Industry Perspective." *International Productivity Monitor* 21: 3–23.

Trumbull, G. 2004. *Silicon and the State: French Innovation Policy in the Internet Age*. Washington: Brookings Institution.

Van Ark, B., O'Mahony, M. and Timmer, M. P. 2008. "The Productivity Gap between Europe and the United States: Trends and Causes." *Journal of Economic Perspectives* 22(1): 25–44.

Wood, A. 1994. *North-South Trade, Employment and Inequality: Changing Fortunes in a Skill-Driven World*. Oxford: Oxford University Press.

Woll, C. 2008. *Firm Interests: How Governments Shape Business Lobbying on Global Trade*. Ithaca: Cornell University Press.

Wren, A. ed. 2013. *The Political Economy of the Services Transition*. Oxford: Oxford University Press.

Ziegler, N. J. 1997. *Governing Ideas: Strategies for Innovation in France and Germany*. Ithaca: Cornell University Press.

Zysman, J. 1977. *Political Strategies for Industrial Order: State, Market and Industry in France*. Berkeley: University of California Press.

Zysman, J. 1983. *Governments, Markets and Growth: Financial Systems and the Politics of Industrial Change*. Ithaca: Cornell University Press.

3

European Growth Models Before and After the Great Recession

Lucio Baccaro and Jonas Pontusson

This chapter is part of our ongoing effort to develop a new approach to comparative political economy centered on the notion of "growth models." Baccaro and Pontusson (2016) spelled out why comparative political economy needs to go beyond "Varieties of Capitalism" and other analytical paradigms that treat supply-side institutions as the main source of cross-national variation among advanced capitalist political economies, and pay more attention to the politics of aggregate demand. Drawing on post-Keynesian macroeconomics, our previous work sketched elements of a new analytical framework in which the level and composition of aggregate demand played a key role (to the detriment of "supply-side" institutions), and illustrated how that framework might be put to use by looking at divergent patterns of economic growth in Germany, Italy, Sweden, and the UK over the period 1994–2007.

The current chapter contributes to the further development of the growth model framework by beginning to tackle the relationship between growth models and macroeconomic policy and by extending the analysis to the early post-crisis period (2010–14). Focusing on Germany, Italy, Sweden, and the UK (as in Baccaro and Pontusson 2016), we identify four ideal typical "growth regimes" (in the sense of Hassel and Palier's definition in Chapter 1). In Germany, net exports became over this period the main driver of demand thanks to the combination of domestic demand repression, institutionalized wage moderation, and the European single currency, which ensured an undervalued real exchange rate.[1] In the UK, a demand boost was engineered by easing the conditions for access to credit, while accepting a systematic deterioration of the current account. The Swedish case stands in between the other two: unlike the German case, there was no wage repression and domestic demand was stimulated by both higher wage growth and easier access

[1] Differently from Avlijaš, Palier, and Hassel (this volume), we do not think that Germany was always an export-led growth model. Until reunification, the coordinated bargaining system ensured that real wages grew in line with national labor productivity in both the manufacturing and the service sector, and thus contributed to feed domestic demand. Even then, the export sector was very important as a locus of innovation and productivity improvement for the German economy (see Baccaro and Pontusson 2016; Baccaro and Benassi 2017).

Lucio Baccaro and Jonas Pontusson, *European Growth Models Before and After the Great Recession* In: *Growth and Welfare in Advanced Capitalist Economies: How Have Growth Regimes Evolved?* Edited by: Anke Hassel and Bruno Palier, Oxford University Press (2021). © Oxford University Press. DOI: 10.1093/oso/9780198866176.003.0003

to credit. The presence of a dual driver was made possible by the greater diversification of the production and export structure in Sweden, which in turn was linked to the declining prominence of manufacturing and the rise of high-end services. Finally, the Italian case is a case of stagnation, which emerged from the combination of extremely difficult background conditions (such as high public debt and the decreased attractiveness of Italian exports, due to increased international competition), and the choice to accept an overvalued exchange rate through membership in the single European currency.

Our empirical analysis remains descriptive and limited to the four countries featured in Baccaro and Pontusson (2016), but we extend it to cover the period after the Great Recession. Skipping our critique of supply-side-institutionalist approaches to comparative political economy (see Pontusson and Baccaro 2020 as well as Baccaro and Pontusson 2016), the chapter is organized as follows. We begin by providing a stylized account of the crisis of wage-led growth and then set out how the post-Fordist alternatives exemplified by our four country cases might be conceptualized within a standard macroeconomic framework. Turning to empirics, we rehearse the evidence on pre-crisis growth trajectories and then assess how the Great Recession affected these trajectories. Against this background, we consider cross-national differences in macroeconomic policy responses to the crisis and, finally, analyze the evolution of the sectoral composition of employment and value-added over the period 1994–2014.

1. The Crisis of Wage-Led Growth

In Baccaro and Pontusson (2016), we argued that export-led growth epitomized by the recent trajectory of Germany, consumption-led growth epitomized by the UK, and the balancing of export-led growth with growth of household consumption in the case of Sweden, represented three different responses to the crisis of wage-led Fordist growth, while Italy's stagnation was a consequence of the inability to find a viable post-Fordist growth driver.

In sketching the basic features of the wage-led model and its post-Fordist successors, we relied on Regulation School and on post-Keynesian economics, particularly of the neo-Kaleckian kind (Boyer 1990; Boyer 2015; Lavoie and Stockhammer 2013; Storm and Naastepad 2012). In a wage-led growth model, growth is pushed by real wage gains, specifically by the tendency (at the margin) of real wages to increase faster than productivity, which implies an increase in the wage share of GDP. Since it is generally the case that when labor income increases, controlling for labor productivity, a lower proportion of income is saved and a greater proportion spent, a real wage increase has at the margin an expansionary effect on GDP in a wage-led growth model because it stimulates household consumption. Furthermore, if investments respond positively to the prospect of expanding demand and are not too sensitive to the profit share, they will be stimulated too. At the same time, an increase in the wage share (equivalent to an increase in real unit labor costs) will likely produce a loss of competitiveness and a decline of net exports. However, if the economy is sufficiently closed, or if net exports are not strongly sensitive to price competitiveness,[2] the recessionary impact associated with the decline of net external demand will be more than compensated by the expansionary effect on other components of aggregate demand (consumption and investments).

Econometric analyses suggest that all four countries examined in this chapter—Germany, Italy, Sweden, and the UK—were wage-led for most of the post-war period (see Onaran and Obst 2015 and the literature cited therein, also Onaran and Galanis 2014). Although it is difficult to identify a clear turning point, the facilitating conditions ensuring the viability of wage-led growth began to unravel with the internationalization of the economy. While wage moderation has a deflationary impulse in wage-led economies, with the rise of international trade the effect may turn around. As trade openness increases, wage moderation stimulates net exports and thus has an expansionary effect, which may counterbalance the depressing impact on domestic demand. At some point, when the export sector becomes sufficiently large, the growth model may switch from wage-led to export-led (Bhaduri and Marglin 1990).

In addition, the lifting of restrictions on capital movements rendered investments more sensitive to the rate of profit. Attempts at financial repression—i.e. remunerating capital at a lower rate than the rate prevailing in international markets—became unfeasible as they would unleash capital flight. By the early 1990s, restrictions of capital movements were eliminated everywhere and capital markets were fully liberalized (Chwieroth 2010; Frieden 2006), thus removing another facilitating conditions for wage-led growth.

Finally, the generalized transition to inflation-targeting central banks further undermined the viability of a growth model based on real wage growth (Storm and Naastepad 2012). Post-Keynesian macroeconomics tends to underestimate the inflationary consequence of demand expansion since it assumes that there is idle capacity in the economy, and that faced with increasing demand firms will respond by increasing supply rather than prices (Lavoie 2014). In reality, wage-led growth was marred by an endemic inflation problem, which in turn was the manifestation of underlying distributive conflict. Unions stepped up demands for nominal wage increases, but firms in oligopolistic markets protected their margins by raising prices. Monetary policy accommodation helped produce a wage-price spiral (Armstrong, Glyn and Harrison 1991).

[2] Specifically, if the Marshall-Lerner condition does not hold; see Carlin and Soskice 2015: 385–6.

With the transition to central bank independence, reigning in inflation became the overarching goal of macroeconomic policy. Independent central banks use interest rates to reduce demand every time wage bargaining produce wage settlements which central banks deem incompatible with their estimates of equilibrium output, corresponding to the "non-accelerating inflation unemployment rate" (NAIRU). NAIRU-based macroeconomics assumes that equilibrium output and employment are determined by supply-side forces in the labor market. Specifically, institutional rigidities increase the NAIRU and the corresponding equilibrium level of output (by pushing up the workers' reservation wage) (Carlin and Soskice 2015; Storm and Naastepad 2012), while the reduction of rigidities or institutionalized wage moderation through centralized or coordinated collective bargaining has the opposite effect. If workers and unions insist on demanding a real wage incompatible with the employers' mark-up expectations, ever faster inflation ensues (because the Phillips curve is vertical in the long run). To preempt inflation acceleration, the central bank intervenes to depress aggregate demand by increasing the interest rate. This pushes up unemployment and moderate the unions' nominal wage demands.

In a standard New Keynesian framework, aggregate demand has no impact on productivity. Instead, in a post-Keynesian framework there are feedback effects between demand-stimulating wage growth and the production potential of the economy. For example, Storm and Naastepad (2012) argue that an expanding demand favors economies of scale and stimulates investments. Investments, in turn, incorporate the latest generation of technical change. Furthermore, they argue that wage increases or the introduction of labor market protections affect labor productivity positively by stimulating capital deepening (i.e. the substitution of relatively expensive labor with relatively cheaper capital), and by eliciting loyalty and workers' cooperation.[3] In other words, in post-Keynesian macro models aggregate demand generates (at least partially) its own aggregate supply. When unions seek to alter the functional distribution of income in their favor, they set in motion a series of mechanisms (investment stimulation, productivity growth) which also increase the denominator of the wage share ratio, i.e. GDP. The level of inflation may be higher as a result, but in post-Keynesian macro there is no infinitely accelerating inflation as predicted by NAIRU-models.

We would argue that NAIRU-based macroeconomics has had "performative" effects, i.e. it has contributed to bring about the reality it aimed to analyze.[4] Before the crisis, central banks around the world fully bought into the NAIRU framework (Carlin and Soskice 2015). This means that they would raise interest rates and

[3] This mechanism is also emphasized by the literature on efficiency wages, see Akerlof (1982), Shapiro and Stiglitz (1984).

[4] On performativity, see MacKenzie, Muniesa, and Siu (2007); on the performativity of central banks, see Holmes (2019).

unemployment every time they saw signs of inflationary wage settlements, particularly when their mandate solely emphasized price stability (as in the case of the Bundesbank before and the ECB later). This made wage militancy for all purposes self-defeating, and unions (German unions before anybody else) eventually learned that wage moderation was the most effective strategy (Scharpf 1991; Streeck 1994). For wage-led growth model, this shift posed a problem of potentially insufficient demand, and spurred the search for alternative ("post-Fordist") drivers of growth. Interestingly, according to the pre-crisis consensus, the central bank should not try to deflate an asset bubble (such as a house price bubble), since asset prices are much less sluggish than wages and other prices, and therefore better regulated by market forces (Goodfriend 2007; Woodford 2003).

2. Post-Fordist Growth Models: A Framework

In this section, we provide a stylized reconstruction of the post-Fordist trajectories of our four countries. Our point of departure is that once any positive feedback effect from the labor market to the productive potential of the economy has been preempted by the central bank, the macroeconomy can be described by three sets of relationships (Carlin and Soskice 2015; Temin and Vines 2014: Ch. 8).[5] The first relationship, known as Aggregate Demand (AD) curve, expresses a positive link between real exchange rate devaluation and output and vice versa. As domestic prices (expressed in foreign currency) grow more slowly than the price of trade competitors, the competitiveness of the country exports augments (i.e. the real exchange rate depreciates), and this increases exports and reduces imports.[6] It is assumed that in a world of perfect capital mobility the domestic real interest rate cannot deviate from the real interest rate determined by global markets, and that any deviation is immediately compensated by forward-looking financial markets through nominal exchange rate adjustment (i.e. appreciation if the domestic interest rate exceeds the world interest rate, depreciation otherwise). In brief, the AD curve depicts the combinations of real exchange rate and output which obtain when the interest rate is equal to the international rate.

The second relationship, known as the Equilibrium Rate of Unemployment (ERU) curve, represents the set of combinations between real exchange rate and output, which keep inflation constant. It captures the labor market equilibrium and has the opposite sign from the AD curve: as the real exchange rate depreciates, output shrinks; vice versa, as the real exchange rate appreciates, output expands.

[5] In this section, we use a three-equation, new Keynesian framework (Carlin and Soskice 2015), as opposed to a post-Keynesian framework. Our purpose is to illustrate how ideas about growth models are compatible with different theoretical perspectives.

[6] This assumes that the Marshall-Lerner condition holds.

The intuition behind this relationship is that as the real exchange rate appreciates, the price of imports goes down and it is thus possible to pay workers a higher real consumption wage (nominal wage normalized by the consumer price index which includes the price of imports) while preserving the profit margins of firms and keeping inflation stable; vice versa for a real exchange rate depreciation.

The third relationship, known as the Balance of Trade curve (BT), expresses, like the AD curve, a positive link between real exchange rate devaluation and output, but differently from the AD curve, each point of BT curve is associated with balanced trade, i.e. with exports equal to imports. One noticeable feature of the BT curve is that its slope is greater than the AD curve's.[7] Essentially, when the economy expands as a result of a real exchange devaluation, the expansion is not sufficient to generate the level of imports needed to bring the trade account back to balance. This implies that for given values of real exchange rate devaluation, the level of output associated with balanced trade is, all other things being equal, greater than the corresponding level of output on the aggregated demand curve, i.e. the economy could grow faster, for example by increasing government expenditures, while remaining in external balance. Whether or not it decides to do so is a matter for growth strategy, as argued in this volume.

Figure 3.1 provides a graphic representation of the AD-ERU-BT relationships. The point of intersection of the three curves is one in which the economy is

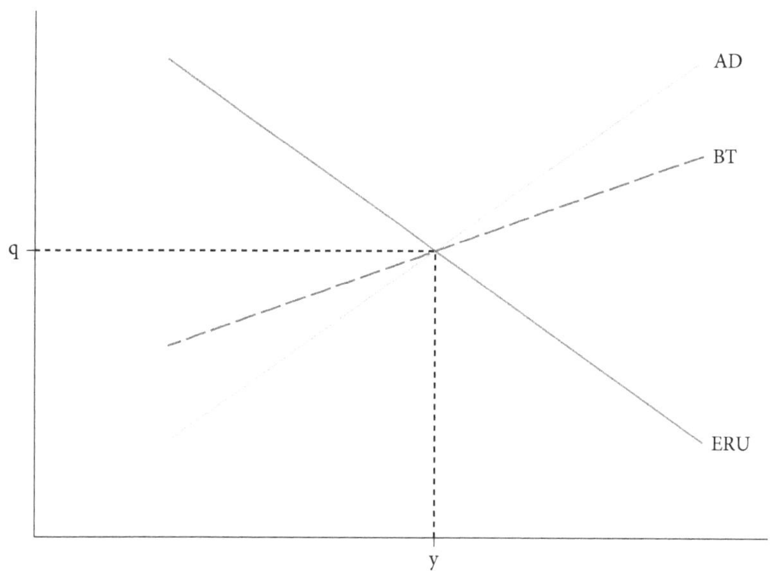

Figure 3.1 The AD-BT-ERU diagram

Note: Higher values of q imply real exchange rate devaluation; higher values of y imply higher output.

[7] For an extended explication, see Carlin and Soskice 2015: 371–3.

simultaneously in internal and external equilibrium and inflation is constant. When values are to the right of the ERU curve, aggregate demand is too high for price stability: workers will step up their wage demands threatening a wage-price spiral and forcing the central bank to intervene to raise interest rates and reduce aggregate demand and employment to levels compatible with price stability.

The three curves provide a useful framework to understand the problem involved in finding a suitable alternative to wage-led growth. As argued above, in a world of inflation-targeting independent central bank, trying to alter the functional distribution of income (i.e. to obtain a higher real wage for a given level of labor productivity) is inane: fearing the beginning of a wage-price spiral, the central bank will responds by forcing a return to the ERU curve by reducing demand and increasing unemployment.

In these circumstances, any viable growth strategy has to dodge the central bank's punishment, and to do so it has to be perceived as non-inflationary by the central bank. Since independent central banks, while targeting inflation, do not monitor developments in competitiveness and the external account (at least until the Great Recession and the euro crisis), the new level of equilibrium output may well be associated with a trade surplus (in which case the new equilibrium will be on the part of the AD curve above the BT curve) or a trade deficit (in which case it will be below the BT curve) (Carlin and Soskice 2015, Iversen and Soskice 2012).

The German export-led growth model can be seen as an attempt to promote growth by pushing out the NAIRU/ERU curve through wage moderation (see Figure 3.2). Wage moderation leads to real exchange rate devaluation, which stimulates external demand. The devaluation is magnified by Germany's membership in the Eurozone, which allows the nominal exchange rate applied to Germany to be lower than a solely German nominal exchange rate would be (as the euro's exchange rate depends on the general conditions of the currency area, including the Southern countries). The economy moves up the AD curve to a higher equilibrium output. As shown in Figure 3.2, the economy ends up above the BT curve, in trade surplus. In theory, it could expand output and employment further while keeping inflationary expectations in check and inflation at target, but this would lead to an appreciation of the real exchange rate, and would have negative repercussions for a real exchange rate sensitive sector like manufacturing.

To understand why a country like Germany may refuse to rebalance, the politics of the export-led growth model needs to be considered. The burden of wage moderation is unequally distributed across sectors. While German manufacturing wages grew in line with labor productivity, at least until 2005, service sector wages remained flat (Baccaro and Benassi 2016). It may be argued that manufacturing wages cannot decline too much below productivity in order not to compromise the collaborative relationships between managers and core workers—arguably a key determinant of German manufacturing success. There is also some

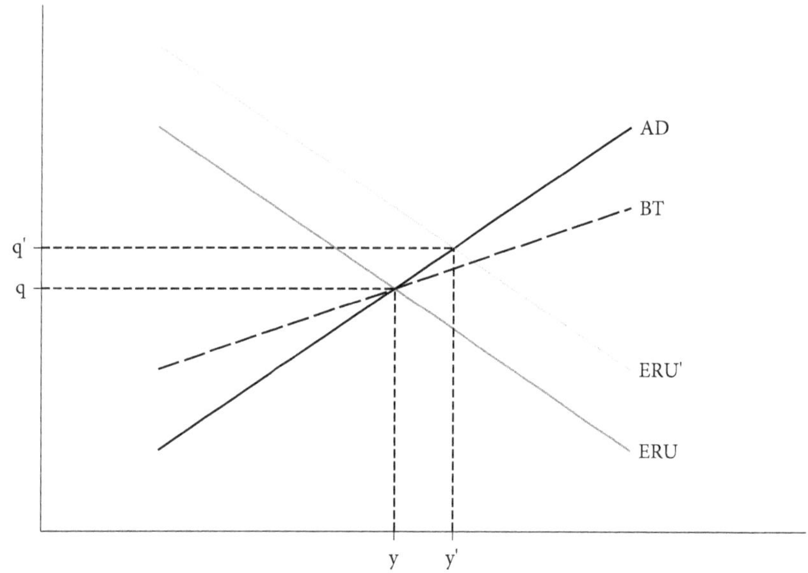

Figure 3.2 The German growth model in AD-BT-ERU diagram
Note: Higher values of q imply real exchange rate devaluation; higher values of y imply higher output.

evidence that German net exports have become more sensitive to price differences over time (Baccaro and Benassi 2016). Faster growth, e.g. through a more expansionary fiscal policy, would strengthen the labor market conditions of service sector workers and undermine wage moderation, which depends heavily on wage restraint in "non-exposed" sectors (Johnston, Hancké, and Pant 2014). Furthermore, if exports are strongly price sensitive, they are likely to shrink as a result of the real exchange rate appreciation resulting from higher internal demand. All in all, expanding the economy to balance the trade account would weaken the manufacturing sector and strengthen the domestic sector. If policy-makers regard the manufacturing sector as the country's main source of productivity and innovation, their reluctance to rebalance becomes understandable.

The Swedish growth trajectory is different from the German one. The Swedish service sector is much better organized than the German one (Pontusson 2013), and this rules out wage repression, while the large public sector improves the job prospects of service workers (Martin and Thelen 2007). In the account we sketched in Baccaro and Pontusson (2016), the Swedish economy was seen as seeking to strengthen the non-price competitiveness of its exports by moving out of manufacturing into ICT and high value-added services. In terms of the AD-BT-ERU diagram depicted in Figure 3.3, this corresponds to a shift of both the AD curve and the BT curve to the right through the autonomous component of foreign demand, which does not depend on relative prices. In other words,

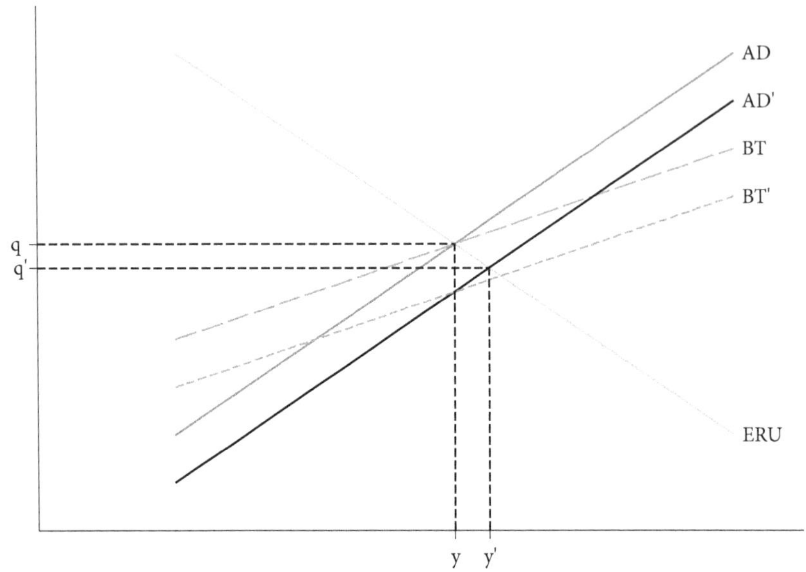

Figure 3.3 The Swedish growth model in AD-BT-ERU diagram
Note: Higher values of q imply real exchange rate devaluation; higher values of y imply higher output.

because Swedish exports become more attractive, internal and external balance are compatible with a stronger real exchange rate (which moves from q to q'). Figure 3.3 shows that while the economy grows from y to y', it remains in trade surplus and thus could expand faster by reaching the point of intersection between the ERU curve and the BT′ curve. Furthermore, if one accepts the post-Keynesian argument about expanding demand feeding into productivity gains, the ERU curve may even have shifted out, thus contributing to increasing equilibrium output even further.

In reality, the Swedish trajectory is more complicated than implied by this stylized account. As discussed later in the paper, aggregate demand was also stimulated by facilitating household access to debt, both before and after the financial crisis.

The British growth model of the pre-crisis period is analyzed in Figure 3.4. The AD-BT-ERU framework suggests that key for the British consumption-led model is an increase in the autonomous domestic component of aggregate demand resulting from a relaxation of criteria for access to credit. This shifts the AD out, leading to higher equilibrium output and an appreciated real exchange rate. Since the BT curve stays put (the positive shock is only to the domestic component of demand), there is a trade deficit. As argued by Baccaro and Pontusson (2016), the presence of a large and highly liquid financial center like the City of London contributes to attracting the foreign capital needed to finance the current account

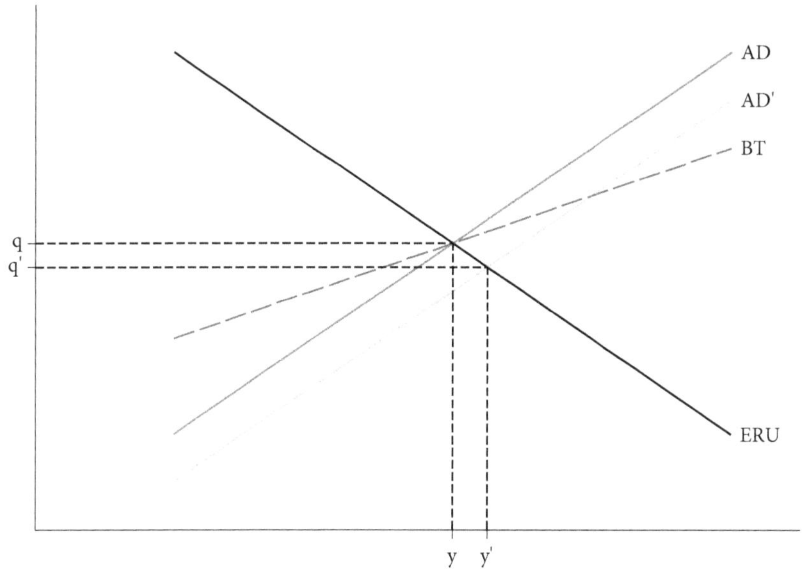

Figure 3.4 The UK growth model in AD-BT-ERU diagram
Note: Higher values of q imply real exchange rate devaluation; higher values of y imply higher output.

deficit, thus making the deficit sustainable at least for some time. One may wonder why the demand shock does not produce inflation. Carlin and Soskice (2015: 202) provide an answer. "The measures of inflation targeted by central banks do not typically include house prices directly... The elements of housing costs included do not influence the overall price indices that enter the inflation target to a high degree." In other words, the central bank does not pay a lot of attention to housing prices provided general inflation, and particularly wage inflation, remain subdued. The weakness of trade unions and collective bargaining contribute to keeping wage settlements in check. Nonetheless, the stimulation of domestic consumption creates favorable conditions for low and medium-skilled service workers. In fact, British service sector wages grow faster than the German (and Italian) ones until 2007 (Baccaro and Pontusson 2016).

The Italian case can be conceived of as a case of decline in equilibrium output, and as the specular opposite to the Swedish case (Figure 3.5). Arguable, there has been a decline in the attractiveness of Italian exports in international markets as a result of higher competition from low-cost producers, especially Chinese exporters, operating in the same markets as Italian firms (Faini and Sapir 2005). This has led to an upward shift of both the AD and BT curves in the AD-BT-ERU diagram. Maintaining the same level of output now requires a weaker real exchange rate. Figure 3.5 shows a new equilibrium below the new BT' curve, indicating a trade deficit. A demand boost (e.g. easier access to credit

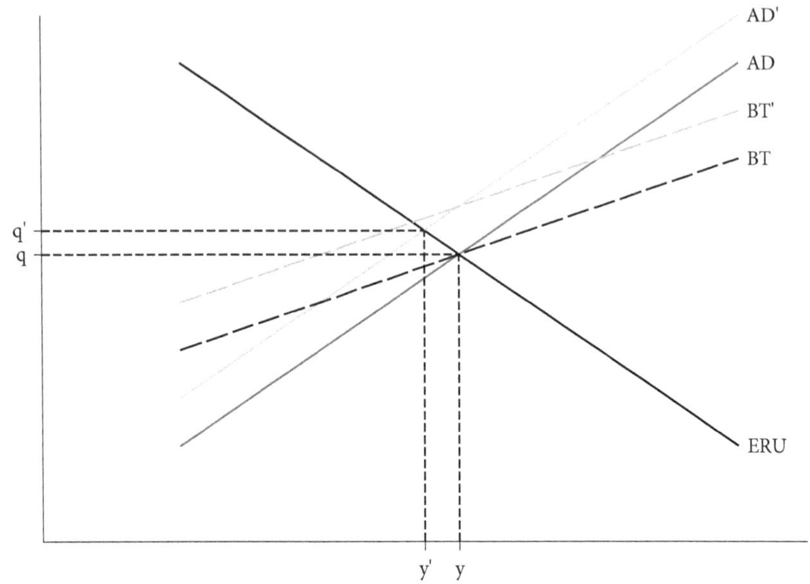

Figure 3.5 The Italian growth model in AD-BT-ERU diagram
Note: Higher values of q imply real exchange rate devaluation; higher values of y imply higher output.

or expansionary fiscal policy) would increase output but at the price of a further deterioration of the external position. In any case, fiscal expansion is precluded by the fiscal rules of the Eurozone. Furthermore, international bond markets have doubts about the solvency of the Italian government, and therefore ask (since the beginning of the European sovereign debt crisis) for hefty risk premia on Italian bonds, thus contributing to depressing aggregate demand further through higher real interest rates.

In these conditions, two responses are conceivable for the Italian economic authorities. First, they could engineer a nominal exchange rate devaluation. Given the depressed conditions of the economy, this is likely to turn into a real exchange rate devaluation and to boost external demand (Dornbusch 1996). However, this response is ruled out by membership in the Eurozone. The other policy move for this economy would be to try and shift out the ERU curve through labor market liberalization and institutionalized wage restraint, i.e. through a cut in real wages. This is exactly what the European authorities have been trying to accomplish in the aftermath of the sovereign debt crisis through austerity policies, without much success in Italy or elsewhere. It seems that notwithstanding high levels of unemployment, nominal wage and price reductions are difficult to achieve because wages and prices are "downwardly rigid." Furthermore, according to post-Keynesian theory, the depression of aggregate demand has a negative impact on labor productivity (through the mechanisms discussed above), shifting the

ERU curve in and further reducing equilibrium output. In other words, the Italian economy may be facing a choice between two unpalatable alternatives: either to leave the Eurozone or to stay in the euro and implement (further) draconian liberalization reforms. Both alternatives have clear downside risks, and there is no guarantee that either one will succeed in relaunching a stagnating economy.

3. Post-Fordist Growth Models: Illustrative Evidence

In this section we present some macro-evidence about the four countries before the Great Recession. Our goal is to illustrate the plausibility of the framework introduced in the previous section or to identify inconsistencies.

The period between 1994 and 2007 can be characterized as the most sustained growth period that the advanced capitalist economies have experienced since the end of *trentes glorieuses*. In real terms, GDP in the OECD area as a whole grew at an annual rate of 2.8% over these fourteen years. With annual growth rates of 3.3%, the UK and Swedish economies outperformed the OECD average while the German and Italian economies, growing at 1.8% and 1.7% respectively, lagged behind the OECD average. The contrast between the UK and Sweden, on the one hand, and Germany and Italy, on the other, clearly has to do with Eurozone membership. As many scholars have noted, the launch of the euro was accompanied by the adoption of restrictive macroeconomic policies, depressing growth rates in Germany, Italy and other countries that opted to join the Eurozone. However, the Eurozone can hardly be considered an exogenous variable: the choice of whether or not to join the Eurozone must be seen as part and parcel of choosing among different post-Fordist growth models.

For our four illustrative cases, Table 3.1 shows the annual growth of exports and household consumption over the period 1994–2007. In all four countries, exports grew faster than household consumption, but the ratio of export growth to consumption growth varied greatly. In Germany and Sweden alike, exports grew

Table 3.1 Annual growth rates of exports and household consumption, 1994–2007

	GDP	(A)	(B)	A/B
		exports	household consumption	
Germany	1.7	7.7	0.9	8.6
Italy	1.6	4.2	1.6	2.7
Sweden	3.3	7.3	2.7	2.7
UK	3.3	5.2	3.6	1.4
OECD	2.8		2.9	

Note: Annualized quarterly change in logged variables (volume series).

Source: OECD Quarterly National Accounts.

at an annual rate of more than 7%. Germany stands out as the country in which exports grew fastest and household consumption grew slowest, suggesting that the German "export miracle" was, in this period, achieved by containing household consumption. Yet, Sweden experienced robust growth of household consumption along with strong growth of exports. A critical question emerges, could Germany also have achieved more balanced growth and, if so, why did Germany miss this opportunity?

Taking into account the share of exports in GDP, the UK stands out in Table 3.1 as the clearest case of consumption-led growth. While exports grew faster than household consumption, consumption growth exceeded GDP growth in the UK. Italy, like Sweden, might be characterized as a case of balanced growth, but stagnation is surely the outstanding characteristic of the Italian experience. Despite slower consumption growth, Italian exports grew more slowly than Swedish or UK exports.

In Sweden and the UK alike, the strong growth of household consumption was accompanied by growing household indebtedness. In Sweden, average household debt rose from ca. 90% of net disposable income in 1995 to ca. 160% in 2007. Starting at ca. 110%, average British household debt had reached nearly 180% by the start of the financial crisis. In marked contrast, average German household debt hovered around 100%, rising slightly in the second half of the 1990s and falling after 2000 while Italian household debt rose from about 40% to 80% of net disposable income over the period 1994–2007.

Financial deregulation and relatively expansionary macroeconomic policies—in particular, low interest rates—must feature prominently in any account of the rise of credit-financed consumption in Sweden and the UK. However, it also deserves to be noted that the wage share (and average wage growth) held up much better in Sweden and the UK than in Germany and Italy from the mid-1990s onwards (see Figure 3.6). The rise of top income shares in the UK and, to a lesser extent, Sweden must be taken into account in this context, but income inequality also rose in Germany over this period. Indeed, the 50:10 earnings ratio and the incidence of low-wage employment rose sharply in Germany while these measures of low-end earnings inequality held up reasonably well in both Sweden and the UK (see Baccaro and Pontusson 2016). Crudely put, consumption-led growth creates labor market conditions favorable to low-skilled and poorly paid workers.

Our interpretation of the German case it that the combination of macroeconomic policies depressing domestic consumption and dualizing labor-market reforms served to decouple earnings developments in the export-oriented sectors and low-end private services, and that falling relative wages in low-end private services boosted the competitiveness of German exports. Why, then, didn't domestic consumption growth and relative earnings more favorable to workers in low-end private services inhibit Swedish export growth? The answer to this question, we believe, has to do with the fact that information technology and

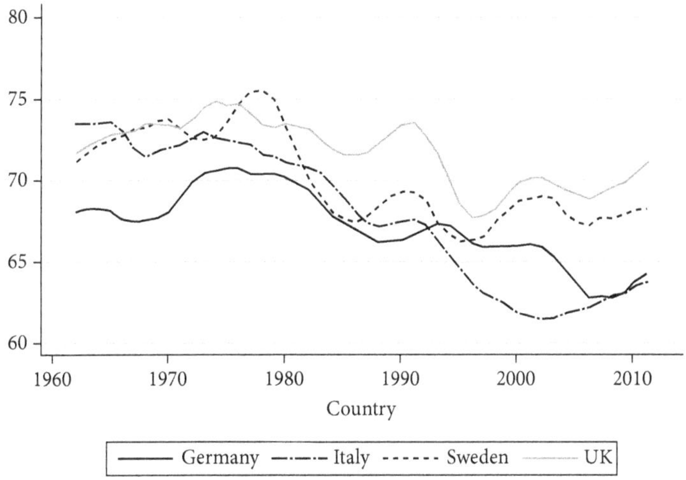

Figure 3.6 Labour compensation in percent of GDP ("wage share"), five-year moving averages, 1960–2012
Source: AMECO Database.

tradeable services played a key role in Sweden's export-led recovery from the crisis of the early 1990s. To a much greater extent, engineering and chemicals have retained their dominance as Germany's main export sectors. While high-end services—finance in particular—are, of course, also a key component of UK exports, Italy's main export sectors are similar to Germany's, though its exports are undoubtedly less sophisticated. Econometric evidence presented in Baccaro and Pontusson (2016) as well as later in this chapter suggest that German and Italian exports were considerably more sensitive to real exchange-rate fluctuations (measured either by consumer prices or unit labor costs) than UK or Swedish in the period 1994–2007 and afterwards.

Did German policy-makers decide to join the Eurozone, repress domestic consumption and introduce dualizing labor-market (and welfare-state) reforms because they recognized that domestic costs had become a problem for German exports? Or did these policy changes and institutional reforms, introduced for other reasons, incentivize German exporters to pursue more cost-based strategies? We are inclined towards the latter interpretation, but we shall not attempt to resolve this conundrum here. Instead, we turn now to explore the impact of the crisis on the growth models that we have briefly sketched above.

4. The Impact of the Crisis

Figure 3.7 tracks the evolution of real GDP over the period 2000–14. Italy, Sweden, and the UK, but not Germany, experienced negative growth in 2008.

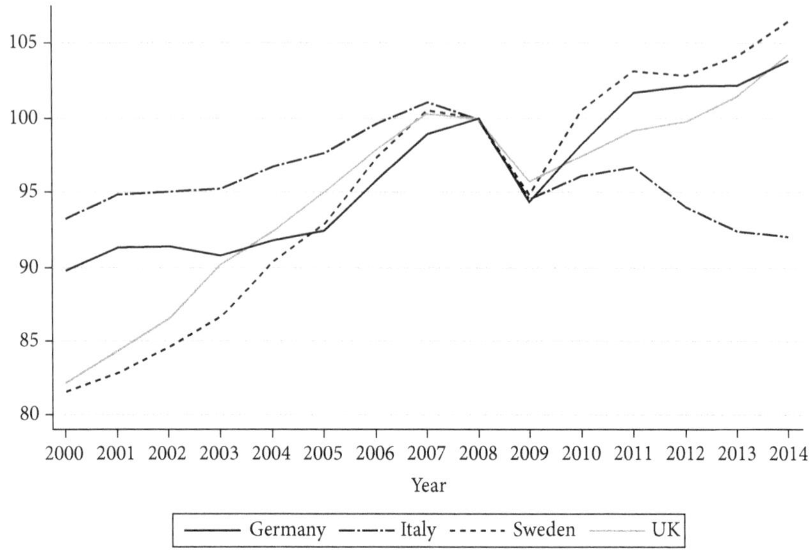

Figure 3.7 Real GDP (2008 = 100), 2000–14
Source: Eurostat.

In 2009, GDP contracted by about 5% in all four countries. With GDP returning to its 2008 level already by end of 2010, Sweden recovered most rapidly from this dramatic shock. By the 2011, German GDP had surpassed the 2008 level, and by the end of 2013, the UK economy had also recovered by this standard. The Italian story is, of course, entirely different: following a slight recovery in 2010–11, the Italian economy contracted further in 2012–14. Another noteworthy feature of Figure 3.7 is that the growth rate of the German economy since 2010 has been quite similar to the growth rate in 2000–7 (about 1% per year), while UK and Swedish growth since 2010 has been much more sluggish than it was in the period leading up to the crisis.

As shown in Figure 3.6, the crises of the 1970s and early 1990s triggered sharp declines in the wage share in all four countries. The Great Recession stands out as quite exceptional in this respect. In percent of the GDP, the wage share actually increased in all four countries over the period 2008–14. This partly reflects the fact that labor productivity fell more sharply than real (production) wages in all four countries between 2008 and 2009. Connected to that, the Great Recession appears to have been less "unemployment-intensive" than the recessions of the 1970s and early 1990s. By historic standards, we would have expected such a sharp contraction of GDP to trigger bigger increases in unemployment than what we observe over the period 2008–12. The decline in labor productivity probably contributed to attenuate the employment effects of the recession. Related to this, it deserves to be noted, as shown in Table 3.2, that in Germany, Italy and Sweden pre-fisc

Table 3.2 Change in Gini coefficients for working-age households

	1990–95		2007–12	
	pre-fisc	post-fisc	pre-fisc	post-fisc
Germany	0.035	0.017	0.003	−0.001
Italy	0.063	0.05	0.022	0.025
Sweden	0.05	0.011	0.003	0.034
UK	0.021	−0.013	0.025	−0.011

Note: For the early 1990s, UK figures refer to 1990–94, Italian and Swedish figures to 1991–95.
For the Great Recession, pre-fisc UK figures refer to 2007–10, pre-fisc Swedish figures to 2008–12.
Source: Calculations based on data from the Luxembourg Income Study and European Union Statistics on Income and Living Conditions reported in Pontusson and Weisstanner (2018).

income inequality among working-age households increased more during the crisis of the early 1990s than it did in the the Great Recession (while taxes and transfers apparently did less to compensate for rising inequality).[8] For our present purposes, the important point is that labor-market dynamics during and immediately following the Great Recession have been relatively favorable to household consumption growth.

Using the same methodology as in Baccaro and Pontusson (2016), Table 3.3 displays the results of a growth decomposition exercise that aims to quantify the extent to which annual growth of GDP is driven by different components of aggregate demand. The annual growth of each component (Component[t]/Component[t−1]−1]) is multiplied by the component's share of GDP (Component[t−1]/GDP[t−1]). Interested in the medium-term impact of the crisis, we ignore what happened in 2008–9 and report results for two periods: 2001–7 and 2010–14.[9]

[8] As the figures in Table 3.2 indicate, disposable income inequality has grown sharply in Sweden, but this is due almost entirely to the effects of taxes and transfers.

[9] Subtracting the value added of imports solely from exports, and not from the other demand components as well, exaggerates the contribution of domestic demand and downplays the contribution of exports. A better assessment of the growth contribution of different components of aggregate demand should take into account the direct and indirect uses of imports for private final consumption purposes, government consumption, investment, and exports, as opposed to simply subtracting them from exports. Following the approach of Bussière et al. (2013) and Auboin and Borino (2017), Baccaro and Pontusson (2020) perform import-adjusted decomposition using Input–Output data. The results are broadly in line with those reported here. (1) Italy remains a clear case of stagnation, both before and after the crisis. (2) Germany remains a case of export-led growth in the pre-crisis period. It seems to have slightly rebalanced (in comparative perspective) in the post-crisis period, even in the post-crisis period the contribution of exports remains much greater than the contribution of consumption. (3) With the new operationalization, Sweden looks more like a case of export-led growth in the pre-crisis period, but the contribution of (import-adjusted) consumption is larger than in Germany and Sweden shifts decisively towards consumption and domestic demand-led growth. (4) The UK is a consumption-led economy both before and after the crisis. With the new data, the contribution of British exports to pre-crisis growth seems a bit larger than in the previous analysis.

Table 3.3 Demand contributions to annual GDP growth in Germany, Italy, Sweden, and UK (yearly averages in percentage)

country	period	GDP	consumption	investment	government	exports	imports	net trade
Germany	2001–7	1.41	0.30	0.04	0.12	2.50	−1.55	0.96
Germany	2010–14	1.95	0.62	0.55	0.19	2.53	−1.92	0.61
Italy	2001–7	1.17	0.54	0.46	0.23	0.78	−0.89	−0.11
Italy	2010–14	−0.52	−0.62	−0.79	−0.15	1.10	−0.17	0.93
Sweden	2001–7	3.04	1.14	0.97	0.20	2.25	−1.59	0.66
Sweden	2010–14	2.39	1.02	0.83	0.29	2.00	−2.11	−0.11
UK	2001–7	2.90	2.11	0.44	0.62	1.14	−1.47	−0.33
UK	2010–14	1.74	0.73	0.65	0.16	0.83	−0.99	−0.16

Source: AMECO.

Over the period 2001–7, net trade contributed more than any other demand component to German growth. All other components, and specifically household consumption, played a negligible role. During the crisis years of 2008–9, international trade contracted sharply and the contribution of trade to German growth turned negative. German growth in 2010–14 relied less on exports, and more on household consumption and capital accumulation than it did prior to the Great Recession. In this sense, the crisis can be said to have rebalanced the German model. Nonetheless, the German current account surplus remains very high, which indicates that the country could grow faster by expanding domestic demand. The trade surplus never went below 4% of GDP during the crisis and exceeded the 2007 level by 2012.

British growth in 2001–7 was largely pulled by household consumption and to a more limited extent by government consumption. The contribution of net exports was negative. In 2008–9, household consumption declined sharply, and net trade became positive. Since 2010, the UK has slowly moved back towards consumption-led growth, though with a more important contribution by gross capital formation (despite the housing market correction) and a smaller trade deficit. But consumption growth has clearly been much more sluggish than it was in the period prior to the Great Recession. The stagnation of wages in Britain after the crisis (discussed later in the paper) is also to blame for the sluggish consumption growth. As Figure 3.8 indicates, the crisis triggered a reduction of credit-financed consumption in the British case.

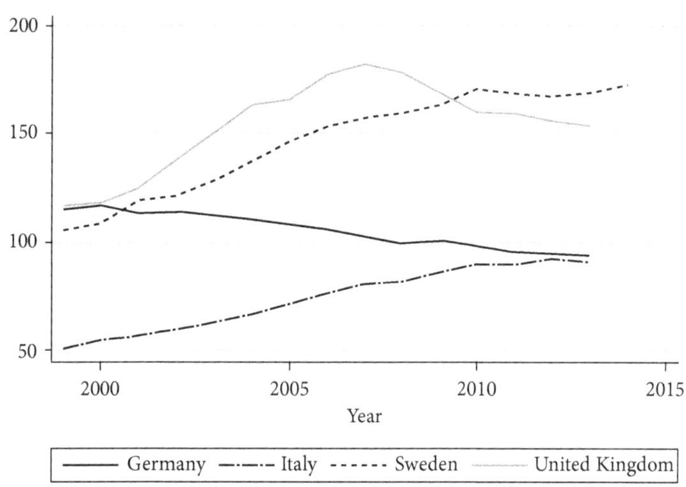

Figure 3.8 Debt of households and non-profit institutions serving households (NPISHs) as percentage of net disposable income, 1998–2014

Source: OECD.

Sweden's healthy pace of growth in 2001–7 was not only depended on buoyant domestic demand (household consumption and investments especially, with an increase in the housing share of investment), but also on trade surpluses (see Table 3.3). In the post-crisis period, growth was somewhat faster than in other countries but entirely pulled by the domestic components: household consumption and government consumption and, to a limited extent, gross capital formation. Over the five years 2010–14, the contribution of net trade to GDP turned negative. Contrary to what one might have expected, the crisis seems to have pushed the Swedish model in the direction of greater consumption-led growth rather than export-led growth. In marked contrast to the UK, household indebtedness has continued to rise (see Figure 3.8), raising questions about the long-term sustainability of this shift.

Finally, with regard to the Italian case, most of the country's anemic growth in 2001–7 was due to household consumption and capital accumulation (Table 3.3). The contribution of net trade was negative. Things changed in the aftermath of the crisis: pressured by the sovereign debt crisis, the Italian economy responded by compressing domestic demand in order to stimulate export-led growth. However, the small size of the export sector (26% of GDP at constant prices in 2008 compared with Germany's 4%) meant that export-led growth was unable to compensate for the decline in domestic demand.

Returning to the question of the price-sensitivity of exports, Table 3.4 presents the results of replicating our previous regression analysis with data for 2000–13. Over this period, we observe that German, Italian, and especially Swedish exports were highly sensitive to world demand growth. The drop of exports in 2009, net of other determinants, led to an export decline in the order of 10–11% for Germany and Italy (statistically significant) and 6% for Sweden and the UK (not significantly different from zero). Most importantly, the results with 2000–13 data indicate that German and Italian exports are significantly sensitive to changes in the real effective exchange rate while Swedish and UK exports are not. Indeed, the effect of the REER on the volume of German and Italian exports is bigger with 2000–13 data than with 1994–2007 data.[10]

Table 3.5 in turn explores the effects of the crisis for export dependence and the composition of exports, measured in terms of goods and services. Comparing averages for 2010–13 with averages for 2004–7, the German, Italian, and British economies have become more export dependent, while the Swedish economy has become less export dependent. As a percentage of total exports, services have increased in Germany as well as Sweden and the UK, while they have not increased in Italy. There is no evidence that Germany has caught up with Sweden with regard

[10] The results presented in Table 3.4 are based on real effective exchange rates measured in terms of unit labor costs. The results are very similar with consumer price indices as the basis for measuring REERs.

Table 3.4 Impact of change in REER on volume export growth (2000–13): ULC-based

Variables	(1)	(2)	(3)	(4)
	Germany	Italy	Sweden	UK
REER	-0.788***	-0.779***	-0.0205	0.0873
	(0.193)	(0.178)	(0.207)	(0.238)
World growth	1.946***	2.554***	3.217***	1.472
	(0.549)	(0.546)	(0.658)	(1.085)
Year 2009	-9.232***	-11.63***	-6.529	-6.095
	(2.911)	(3.095)	(3.718)	(5.623)
Constant	-1.995	-6.241**	-8.499**	-2.179
	(2.316)	(2.435)	(2.807)	(4.717)
Observations	14	14	14	14
R-squared	0.941	0.947	0.903	0.596
Durbin test	n.s.	n.s.	n.s.	n.s.

Note: *** $p<0.01$, ** $p<0.05$, * $p<0.1$. Standard errors in parentheses
Source: Own elaborations on data from Eurostat and IMF's World Economic Outlook.

Table 3.5 Export dependence and the composition of exports

	Percentage of GDP				services in percentage of total exports	
	goods	goods	services	services		
	2004–7	2010–13	2004–7	2010–13	2004–7	2010–13
Germany	35.4	38.8	6.1	7.8	14.7	16.7
Italy	21	23.4	5.1	5.1	19.5	17.9
Sweden	33.9	31	12	13.4	26.1	30.2
UK	15.9	18.4	9.4	11.9	37.2	39.3

Source: Eurostat.

to service exports. For reasons that we intend to explore in future research, Swedish export services would appear to be more sensitive to economic growth abroad than UK export services (see Table 3.4).

5. Policy Responses to the Crisis

In this section, we explore policy responses during the Great Recession and its aftermath and their relevance for the adjustment of the growth models. We examine monetary and fiscal policies as well as exchange rate policies, as these are the main policy tools governments deployed in response to the contraction of the economy. Setting aside bailouts of financial institutions, industrial policy interventions have been rare, at least by comparison to the 1970s and early 1980s (Pontusson and Raess 2012). In the next section, we discuss wage trends and shifts in the sectoral composition of these economies.

With respect to welfare provisions and labor-market regulation, governments in Germany, Sweden and the UK have not taken any major new initiatives. As Pontusson and Raess (2012) have argued, this itself represents an important contrast with the 1970s, when governments responded to rising unemployment by enacting new employment protection provisions and by increasing the coverage and generosity of unemployment compensation. The story of the Great Recession is instead, at least in Germany and Sweden, a story of governments resisting pressures to retreat from liberalizing or dualizing reforms introduced in the decade before the onset of the crisis.

As shown in Figure 3.9, all four countries responded to the collapse of aggregate demand in 2008–9 by sharply reducing short-term interest rates. Over the two years of the Great Recession, the short-term rate was cut by 3.4% in Germany and Italy, by 3.8% in Sweden, and by 4.3% in the UK. In response to a sharp decline of the exchange rate and signs of rising inflation, the Swedish Central Bank increased the short-term interest rate in 2011. Short-term Eurozone interest rates also increased in 2011, but this policy correction proved short-lived as it became clear that the recovery was less robust than expected. By 2014, short-term interest rates in all four countries were close to the "zero lower bound"—the level at which it is no longer possible to stimulate aggregate demand through traditional monetary policy. Following the US Fed, the Bank of England engaged in a series of

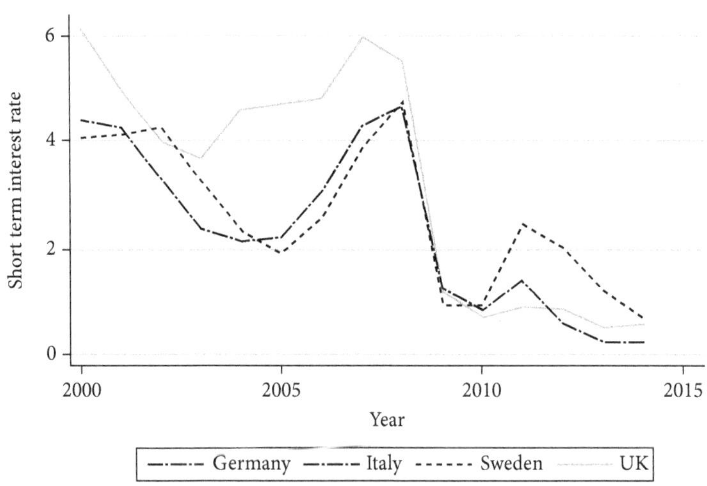

Figure 3.9 Short-term interest rates, 2000–14

Note: The short-term interest rate is the three-month interbank rate, which is targeted by the ECB for all countries in the Eurozone and hence the same for Germany and Italy.

Source: OECD.

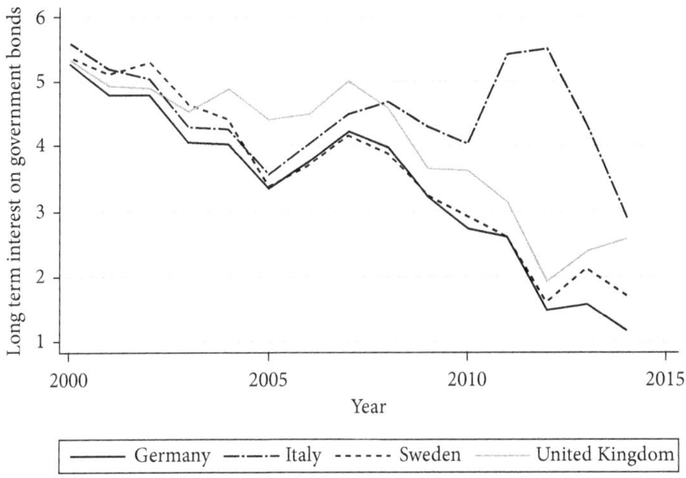

Figure 3.10 Long-term interest rates on government bonds, 2000–14
Source: OECD.

"quantitative easing" programs from March 2009 onwards and, in 2015, the ECB and the Swedish Central Bank both followed suit with their own quantitative easing programs.

Reported in Figure 3.10, long-term interest rates on government bonds also fell in Germany, Sweden, and the UK between 2008 and 2012, but they increased in Italy over the same period. Uncertain about the continued viability of the common currency, international financial markets began to demand higher risk premia on the sovereign bonds of peripheral Eurozone countries, including Italy, thus further compromising their economic prospects (Armingeon and Baccaro 2012). The panic stopped after Mario Draghi's "whatever it takes" speech of July 2012, in which he vouched to act as a lender of last resort for embattled peripheral governments. Since 2012, long-term interest rates on Italian government bonds have fallen (but still remain above nominal growth rates, thus imparting an inertial tendency for the Italian public debt to grow).

Setting Italy side, monetary policy and the evolution of interest rates have been similar across countries since the onset of the crisis. By contrast, we observe significant cross-national variation in fiscal policy responses to the crisis (see also Raess and Pontusson 2015). Table 3.6 shows year-on-year changes in the cyclically adjusted primary government balance, measured in percent of potential GDP. Positive values represent a discretionary fiscal stimulus of demand, i.e., discretionary spending increasing faster (or falling slower) than discretionary revenues. These figures show that the British Labour government of Gordon Brown responded more quickly to the Great Recession than Continental governments and engaged in a massive fiscal stimulus in 2007–9 (corresponding to 4.78% of potential GDP). All four governments engaged in fiscal stimulus in 2008.

The Swedish government retreated from fiscal stimulus in 2009, but again stimulated domestic demand by fiscal means in 2010, as did the German government. Italy and the UK embarked on multi-year budget consolidation in 2010, with Germany following suit in 2011. In the period since the end of the Great Recession, Sweden stands out as the one country with an expansionary fiscal policy stance. Summing over the period since the onset of the crisis (2007 for the UK, 2008 for the other countries), the cumulative fiscal stimulus in Sweden amounted to 2.74% of GDP by the end of 2014, as compared to 1.45% for the UK, -0.04% for Germany, and a mind-boggling -3.4% for Italy.

Table 3.6 Fiscal stimulus

	2007	2008	2009	2010	2011	2012	2013	2014
Germany	−0.86	**0.05**	**0.71**	**0.96**	−1	−0.66	−0.04	−0.06
Italy	−0.98	**0.73**	1	−1.11	−0.19	−2.84	−0.26	−0.43
Sweden	−0.49	**0.45**	−0.23	**1.11**	**0.37**	**0.53**	**0.11**	**0.33**
UK	**0.5**	**1.14**	**3.14**	−1.32	−1.64	**0.54**	−0.9	−0.01

Note: The table shows inverted year-on-year changes in the cyclically adjusted primary government balance as percentage of potential GDP. Bolded (positive) values represent moves towards government deficit (or bigger deficit)

Source: OECD Economic Outlook statistics.

Table 3.7 in turn reports on changes in government revenues and taxes (percentage of GDP) over 2006–10 and 2010–14. In Germany and Italy, the fiscal stimulus undertaken in the first phase of the crisis was all about increased spending. By contrast, the UK and Sweden alike relied on tax cuts as well as spending increases to stimulate demand in this phase. While the Italian government has relied entirely on tax increases to consolidate its overall budget position since 2010, the German and British governments have deployed a combination of tax increases and spending cuts, with spending cuts being more important in Germany than the UK. Sweden's heavy reliance on tax cuts to stimulate domestic demand over the entire period 2008–14 provides at least some insight into the

Table 3.7 Change in government revenues and disbursements (GDP percentage points)

	revenues		disbursements	
	2006–10	**2010–14**	**2006–9**	**2010–14**
Germany	0.18	1.29	2.71	-3.43
Italy	1.67	2.42	2.34	1.21
Sweden	-1.43	-1.11	0.79	0.74
UK	-2.6	3.02	5.56	-4.3

Source: OECD Economic Outlook statistics.

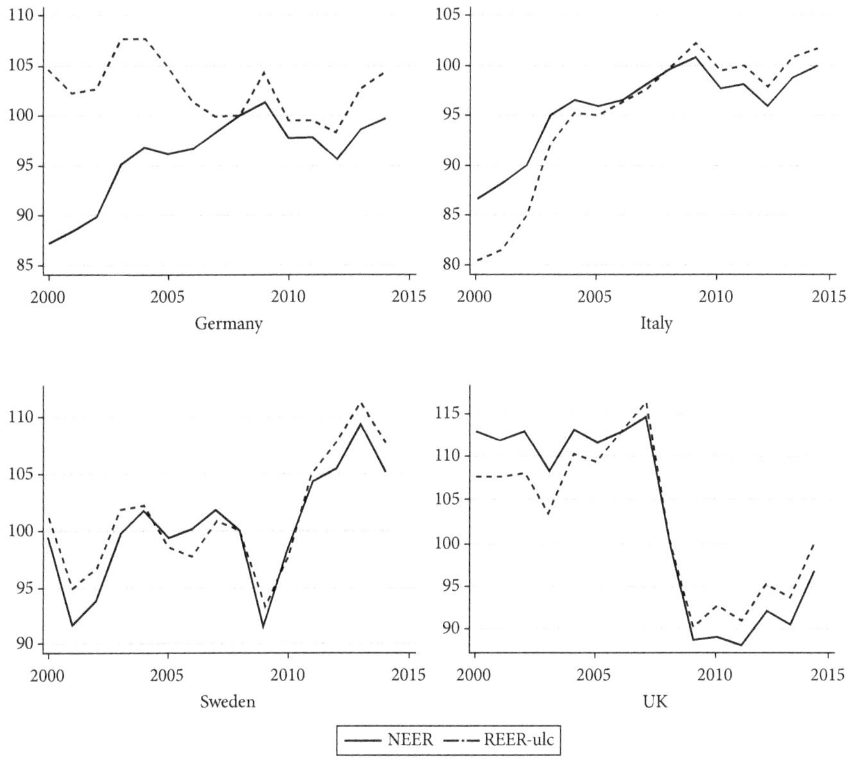

Figure 3.11 Nominal and real (ULC-based) effective exchange rates (2008 = 100), 2000–14

Source: Eurostat.

Swedish puzzle: while Sweden has engaged in more fiscal stimulus, it has also experienced a larger increase in disposable income inequality than the other three countries covered by our analysis (see Table 3.2).

Unlike Germany and Italy, where the real exchange rate did not decline much in 2008–9, the British pound and the Swedish krona depreciated sharply in nominal and real terms during the Great Recession (Figure 3.11). However, the Swedish krona appreciated quickly as the economy began to recover in 2010, pre-empting an export-led recovery based on an improvement in cost competitiveness.

6. Wage and Sectoral Trends

In order to appreciate the impact of real exchange rates on living standards it is helpful to compare the price index based on consumer prices (CPI), which includes the price of imports, with the deflator of GDP, which only includes domestically produces goods and services, excluding imports. If the CPI grows more slowly than the GDP deflator, real consumption wage of workers is growing even though the real production wage (nominal wage deflated with the GDP deflator) may not be growing, thanks to real exchange rate appreciation, i.e. cheaper imports. According to the AD-ERU-BT framework presented above, the resulting real wage increase is not inflationary and is thus compatible with higher equilibrium output and employment (in the sense that an inflation-targeting central bank will see no need to intervene to deflate the economy).

Figure 3.12 reports the CPI and GDP deflator for the four countries between 1994 and 2016. While the two series move more or less in lockstep in Italy and the UK (specifically: producer prices tend to grow faster than consumer prices in the 2000s in both countries, but the trends invert after the crisis), Germany and Sweden move in opposite directions from one another: German producer prices grow more slowly than consumer prices throughout the period, a sign of real exchange rate depreciation. The opposite happens in Sweden, where particularly after the crisis a gap opens between producer prices (which continue to rise) and consumer prices (which remain flat).

Based on OECD STAN data, Figure 3.13 compares consumption and production wages (nominal wages deflated with the consumer price index and the GDP deflator, respectively) between 1994 and 2015 for five industries: total economy,

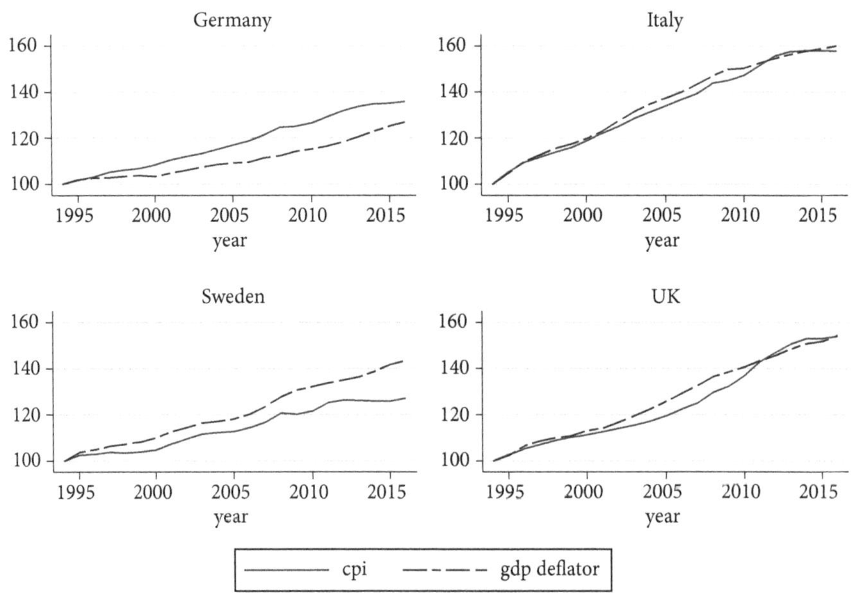

Figure 3.12 Consumer price indices and GDP deflators, 1994–2016
Source: OECD.

manufacturing, construction, food and accommodation, and finance and insurance. For comparison purposes, the graphs also report the trend of labor productivity for the total economy (defined as value-added at constant prices per hour worked). The sectors are chosen to ensure variation in average worker skills: high skills (finance and insurance); medium-high skills (manufacturing), medium-low skills (construction), and low skills (food and accommodation).

German consumption wages grow more slowly than production wages as a consequence of real exchange rate depreciation. To the extent that they are unable to substitute imports with domestically produced goods and services, German workers become poorer as a result. Overall, German production wages have grown more slowly than productivity—which has translated into a decline of the wage share. However, the gap between real wages and productivity has been shrinking after the crisis, which is another sign of rebalancing of the German growth model. Of the various industries, only the production wages of manufacturing workers and finance workers have—almost—kept pace with labor productivity. By contrast, the consumption wage gains of food and accommodation workers have been negative until 2014, and those of construction workers have been negative until 2008. Overall, the wage trends confirm that the German growth model has relied on wage compression, especially of low-skilled workers, even though low-skilled workers have been catching up a bit after the crisis.

Wage trends have been very different in Sweden. In this country consumption wages have been higher than production wages as a result of real exchange rate appreciation. While overall production wages have grown more slowly than productivity before the crisis, they have exceeded productivity afterwards, thus leading to a loss of competitiveness. The intersectoral distribution of wage increases is also very different from Germany, and the wages of low-skilled accommodation and food workers have increased at almost the same rate as manufacturing wages. These trends confirm that the Swedish growth model is characterized by much greater real wage growth than the German one, and that Swedish wage growth is less inegalitarian than the German one. After the crisis, however, wage growth may have begun to erode the cost competitiveness of Swedish exports, tilting the growth model towards consumption-led.

In the British case, real wages (both consumption and production-based) have grown faster than productivity until 2014. The wage rates of accommodation and food workers have stagnated relative to other categories of workers, although (unlike in Germany) even for these workers there have been real wage gains relative to the mid-1990s. The real wages of workers in the finance and insurance sector have grown much faster than average until 2007 and then have declined. Perhaps the most notable British trend is the stagnation of both real wages and productivity from 2007 on. Average consumption wages have declined in real terms in the years of austerity after growing faster than in Germany and Italy before.

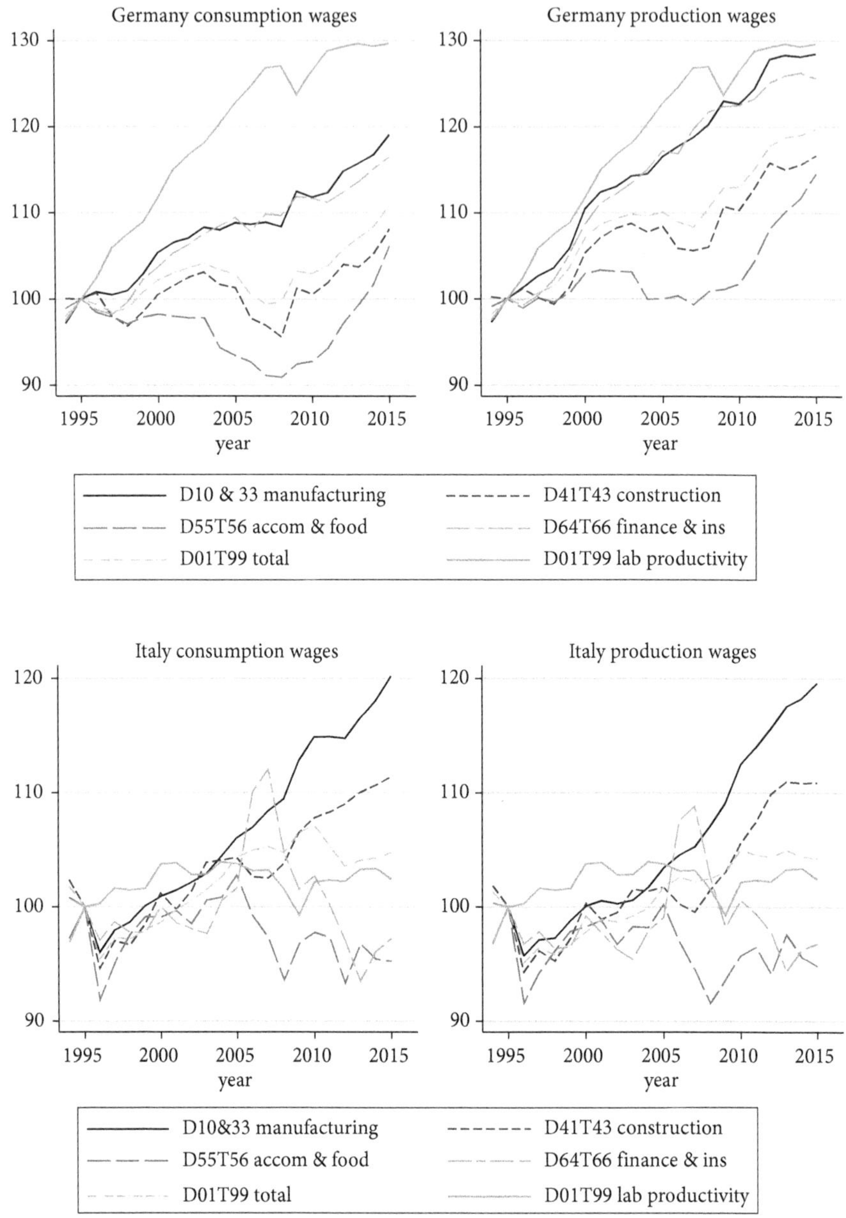

Figure 3.13 Real wages and labor productivity, 1994–2015

Source: OECD STAN Database.

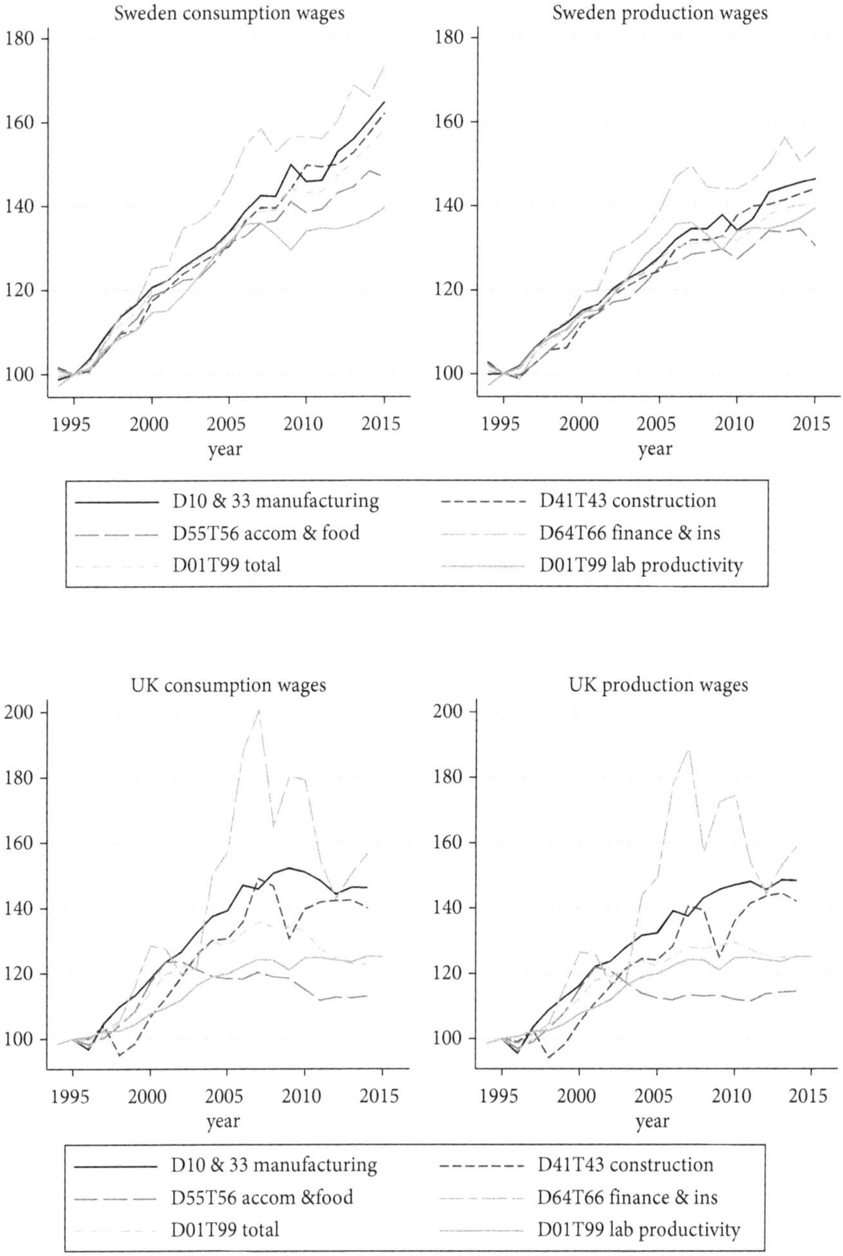

Figure 3.13 Continued

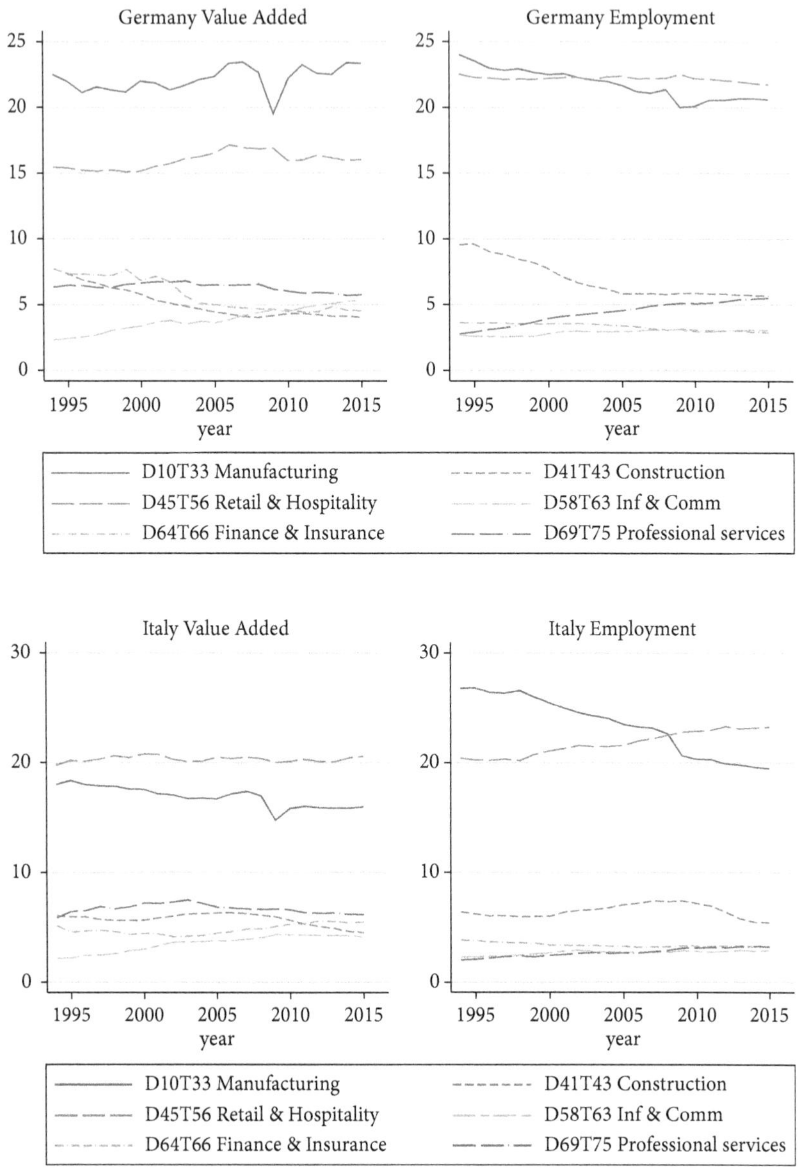

Figure 3.14 Value-added and employment shares of sectors, 1994–2015

Source: OECD STAN Database.

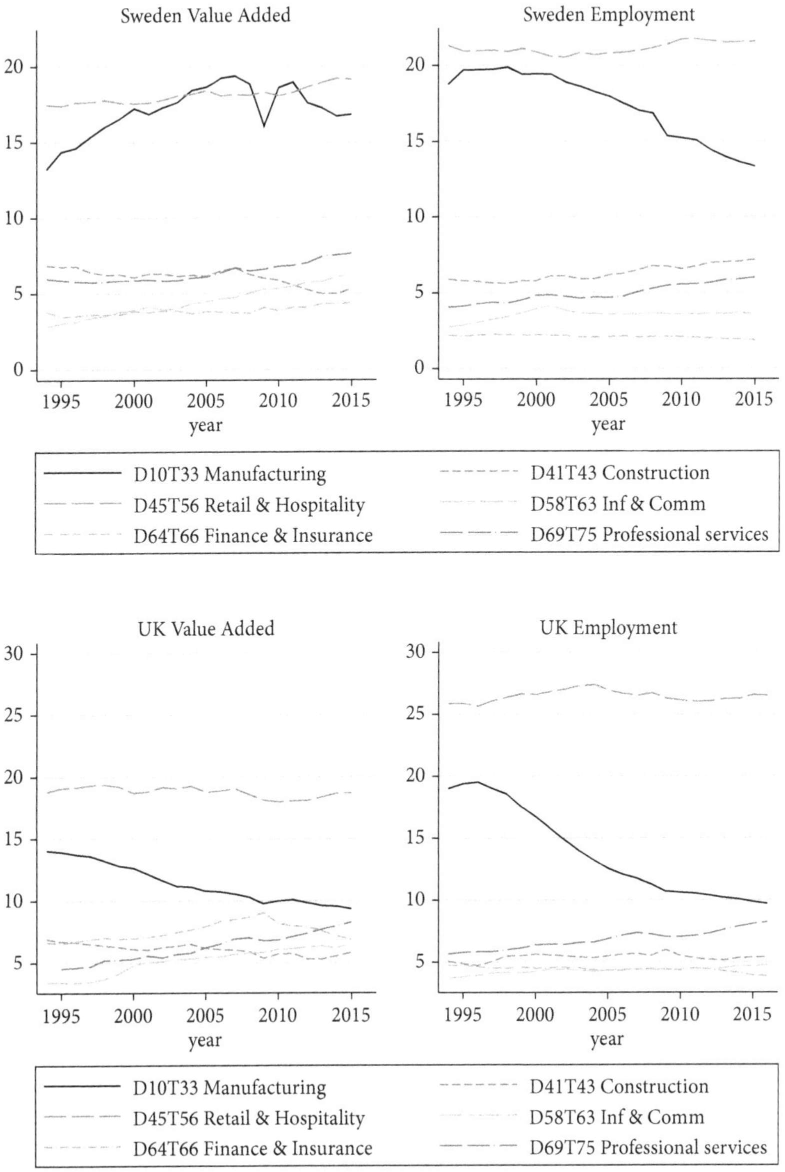

Figure 3.14 Continued

The same phenomenon of stagnating labor productivity is even more clearly visible in the Italian case, where labor productivity has been practically flat for the past twenty years. Italy's manufacturing productivity growth has been much more disappointing than Germany, the UK, and especially Sweden's. The productivity performance of business services has been particularly disappointing. With very limited productivity growth, real wage growth (both consumption and production-based) has remained subdued in Italy. Italian manufacturing wages have grown faster than national productivity, but in line with sectoral productivity (not shown). As in Germany, the intersectoral distribution has been fanning out, with workers in the business service sector experiencing negative real wage increases (not shown). However, the decline of business service productivity has been even greater than the decline of real wages. It is not clear what explains the stagnation of productivity. Several authors point to the combination of demand stagnation and labor market liberalization as the culprit (Daveri and Parisi 2015; Jona Lasinio and Vallanti 2013; Tridico and Pariboni 2018; Tronti 2009).

Different growth models rest on different dominant sectors (Baccaro and Pontusson 2016). It is therefore helpful to examine how the sectoral composition of GDP has changed before and after the crisis. Based again on OECD STAN data, Figure 3.14 examines the distribution of value-added (VA) (share at constant prices) and employment (share of hours worked) shares across the following sectors between 1994 and 2015: manufacturing, construction, retail and hospitality, information and communication, finance and insurance, and professional, business, and technical services.

In Germany, manufacturing is larger than in the other countries. In fact, it has a higher share of value-added than retail and hospitality. This share has remained constant throughout the period, unlike in the other three countries where it has declined (in Sweden the decline has begun in the early 2010s). The German manufacturing share of employment, instead, has declined a bit, but remains around 20%, slightly below the employment share of the retail and hospitality sector. Overall, the German economy has remained firmly centered on manufacturing. Interestingly, the German construction sector has shrunk between the mid-1990s and the mid-2000s.

The Swedish trajectory is *sui generis* and confirms that a structural shift may be occurring in Sweden in the post-crisis period. The Swedish manufacturing sector has been declining in importance, certainly in terms of employment share and, since the early 2010s, in terms of value-added as well (after growing in the pre-crisis period). In 2015 the Swedish manufacturing sector had a share of working hours of around 14% of the total, while the share of the retail and hospitality sector was more than 20%. The information and communication sector and the professional services sector have been expanding their shares of value-added, and, albeit to a more limited extent, their employment shares, too. Overall, the Swedish economy seems to be less centered on manufacturing and more on high-value added services than the German economy.

Manufacturing employment has been declining in Italy throughout the period, and the crisis seems to have accelerated the decline. However, with an employment share of just below 20%, the manufacturing sector remains an important employer in Italy. The decline of manufacturing has not been compensated by the expansion of high-value added service sectors like information and communication, professional services, and finance and insurance.

This type of substitution is instead present in the UK, where the manufacturing sector has been declining dramatically to less than 10% of both VA and employment in 2015. The high-value added services have been growing in the same periods, and together represent a greater share of the British economy than manufacturing.

7. Some Final Remarks

In this paper, we have sought to extend the analysis of post-Fordist growth models in Baccaro and Pontusson (2016) to the post-crisis period as well. Germany has emerged as an export-led economy which has been enabled by institutionalized wage moderation, specifically in the low-skilled service sectors, and an inflexible nominal exchange rate. Exports are the most important growth driver, and being more price-sensitive than in other countries, and possibly more price-sensitive than in the past (Baccaro and Benassi 2017), wage moderation and the ensuing real exchange rate devaluation are of utmost importance. Politically, the manufacturing sector is the dominant sector and has probably increased its influence on policy over time.

Our interpretation of the Swedish growth model in the 15 years before the crisis is that, differently from Germany, it was based on an increase the non-cost competitiveness of Swedish exports. This enabled a growth model in which there was no pressing need for wage and demand repression for export stimulation. In fact, the evidence has shown that, in comparison with the German model, the Swedish growth model is characterized by greater household consumption, faster and more equitable wage growth, and a tendency for real exchange rate appreciation.

The British growth model appears the mirror image of the German model: household consumption is the sole driver of growth, supported not just by household debt but also by real wages (which grew at a healthy pace at least until 2007), even though the growth is unequally distributed across sector. In addition, there is a tendency for competitiveness to deteriorate and for the current account to show persistent deficits. The latter did not precipitate any rebalancing because, at least until the crisis, the rest of the world was willing to finance the British current account by purchasing British assets.

The Italian case stands out for its inability to find a viable growth driver in the post-Fordist period. Consumption growth has been limited due to meagre wage growth and restrictive fiscal policies for most of the period. The export sector is too small and price sensitive to play the role of growth driver. Two factors feature prominently in the Italian stagnation: the inability to stimulate external demand through an exchange rate devaluation, which is precluded by membership in the Eurozone, and the dismal performance of labor productivity, whose roots are not clear, but may be associated to the combination of insufficient demand and labor market liberalization.

To what extent have the growth models change in response to the crisis? In Germany, the UK, and Sweden, domestic consumption stimulated by fiscal means played an important role in cushioning the impact of the contraction of world trade in 2008–9. The massive stimulus undertaken by the British Labour government is exactly what we would expect from a government managing a consumption-led economy. It must be noted, however, that the export of financial services was an important component of the British growth model in the pre-2007 period. While international finance arguably became even more important once the real-estate bubble burst and households had to reduce their indebtedness, the currency depreciation generated by expansionary government policies posed a major threat to Britain's comparative advantage in this sector. The reorientation of fiscal policy by the first Cameron government can thus be seen as an effort to rebalance the British growth model by scaling back its dependence on household consumption and relying more on high-end service exports. This effort appears to have backfired. In fact, wage and consumption stagnation has limited the growth performance of the British economy in the post-crisis period.

While household consumption has contributed more to German economic growth in recent years than it did in the decade leading up to the Great Recession, there can be little doubt that German economic policies have been geared towards restoring the primacy of manufacturing exports within the German growth model. The crisis appears to have strengthened rather than fractured the dominant social coalition in Germany, centered on the export-oriented manufacturing sector. However, our analysis suggests that the viability the Germany's export-led model depends on factors the policy-making elite does not directly control, such as continuation of the international free trade regime and the continued existence of the euro in its current form.

Sweden is arguably the country whose growth model has been most affected by the crisis. One might have expected that the crisis would have tipped the balance between consumption-led and export-led growth in favor of the latter, but the opposite seems to have happened. It is striking that Sweden's REER appreciated sharply while Germany's REER declined over the recovery of 2010–14 (see Figure 3.11). Not surprisingly, Sweden's trade surplus turned negative while the German trade surplus recovered. As suggested above, Sweden's increased dependence on the domestic components of aggregate demand has been promoted by expansionary or, at least, relatively lax monetary and fiscal policies, combined with a quite dramatic retreat from redistribution ("bourgeois Keynesianism"). The continued rise of household indebtedness, signs of another real-estate bubble, and the deterioration of the trade balance raises questions about the economic rationale of this policy orientation.

Domestic politics shed at least some light on the policy choices of Swedish governments in 2010–14. Headed by Fredrik Reinfeldt, the bourgeois coalition that came to power in 2006 included four parties with divergent priorities and lost its parliamentary majority in the election of 2010. While the Social Democrats lost more votes than the Alliance parties, the right-wing populists gained parliamentary representation for the first time in 2010. As a result, the government parties held only 173 out of 349 seats in the parliament of 2010–14. By contrast, David Cameron and Angela Merkel both had comfortable majorities with one coalition partner and, at least in the German case, the opposition was quite supportive of the turn to austerity. In other words, the Swedish government had strong political-electoral reasons to avoid the "tough decisions" that would have been required to pursue export-led growth. Our analysis suggests that the Swedish economy may be undergoing a structural shift away from manufacturing and towards a greater importance of services.

The Italian case serves as a reminder that "government weakness" does not necessarily lead to expansionary macroeconomic policies. The Italian story is first and foremost a story of government policy being severely constrained by the combination of public debt and Eurozone membership, with disastrous consequences for economic growth. The contraction of domestic consumption appears to have contributed to some improvement in export competitiveness as well as a decline in imports, but the Italian export sector is simply too small to act as growth driver for the economy. Burdened by an exchange rate which is too strong for its needs, highly price-sensitive Italian exports would need a more dramatic reduction of domestic wages and prices relative to competitors than has been achieved in the post-crisis years. However, it is difficult to imagine Italian citizens putting up with another decade of austerity.

We close with the following paradox. Of the four countries discussed in this paper Germany has clearly fared best since the onset of the Great Recession in terms of growth and employment. Not surprisingly, its growth model and dominant social coalition remain intact. When all is said, however, it could be that the crisis will prove, for "external" reasons, to have been the beginning of the end of the export-led model that Germany adopted in the second half of the 1990s. Again, the long-term viability of this model would seem to depend critically on keeping peripheral economies in the Eurozone. As we are reminded daily, the crisis of the Eurozone periphery is far from over.

References

Akerlof, George A. 1982. "Labor Contracts as Partial Gift Exchange." *The Quarterly Journal of Economics* 97(4): 543–69.

Armingeon, Klaus and Lucio Baccaro. 2012. "Political Economy of the Sovereign Debt Crisis: The Limits of Internal Devaluation." *Industrial Law Journal* 41(3): 254–75.

Auboin, Marc and Floriana Borino. 2017. "The Falling Elasticity of Global Trade to Economic Activity: Testing the Demand Channel." *WTO Staff Working Papers ERSD-2017-09.*

Baccaro, Lucio and Chiara Benassi. 2017. "Throwing out the Ballast: Growth Models and the Liberalization of German Industrial Relatioins." *Socio-Economic Review* 15(1): 85–115.

Baccaro, Lucio and Jonas Pontusson. 2016. "Rethinking Comparative Political Economy: The Growth Model Perspective." *Politics & Society* 44(2): 175–207.

Baccaro, Lucio and Jonas Pontusson. 2020. "Operationalizing Growth Models." Unpublished draft.

Bhaduri, Amit and Stephen A. Marglin. 1990. "Unemployment and the Real Wage: The Economic Basis for Contesting Political Ideologies." *Cambridge Journal of Economics* 14: 375–93.

Boyer, Robert. 1990. *The Regulation School: A Critical Introduction.* Translated by C. Charney. New York: Columbia University Press.

Boyer, Robert. 2015. *Economie Politique Des Capitalismes.* Paris: La Découverte.

Bussière, Matthieu, Giovanni Callegari, Fabio Ghironi, Giulia Sestieri and Norihiko Yamano. 2013. "Estimating Trade Elasticities: Demand Composition and the Trade Collapse of 2008–2009." *American Economic Journal: Macroeconomics* 5(3): 118–51.

Carlin, Wendy and David Soskice. 2015. *Macroeconomics.* Oxford: Oxford University Press.

Chwieroth, Jeffrey M. 2010. *Capital Ideas: The IMF and the Rise of Financial Liberalization.* Princeton, NJ: Princeton University Press.

Daveri, Francesco and Maria Laura Parisi. 2015. "Experience, Innovation, and Productivity: Empirical Evidence from Italy's Slowdown." *Industrial & Labor Relations Review* 68(4): 889–15.

Dornbusch, Rudi. 1996. "The Effectiveness of Exchange-Rate Changes." *Oxford Review of Economic Policy* 12(3): 26–38.

Faini, Riccardo and Andre' Sapir. 2005. "Un Modello Obsoleto? Crescita E Specializzazione Dell'economia Italiana." In *Oltre Il Declino*, edited by T. Boeri, R. Faini, A. Ichino, G. Pisauro and C. Scarpa. Bologna: Il Mulino, 19–65.

Frieden, Jeffry A. 2006. *Global Capitalism: Its Fall and Rise in the Twentieth Centur.* New York: Norton.

Goodfriend, Marvin. 2007. "How the World Achieved Consensus on Monetary Policy." *Journal of Economic Perspectives* 21(4): 47–68.

Holmes, Douglas R. 2019. "A Tractable Future: Central Bankers and Their Publics." In *Uncertain Futures: Imaginaries, Narratives, and Calculation in the Economy*, edited by J. Beckert and R. Bronk. New York: Cambridge University Press.

Iversen, Torben and David Soskice. 2012. "Modern Capitalism and the Advanced Nation State: Understanding the Causes of the Crisis." In *Coping with Crisis:*

Government Responses to the Great Recession, edited by N. Bermeo and J. Pontusson. New York: Russell Sage.

Johnston, Alison, Bob Hancké, and Suman Pant. 2014. "Comparative Institutional Advantage in the European Sovereign Debt Crisis." *Comparative Political Studies* 47(13): 1771–800.

Jona Lasinio, Cecilia and Giovanna Vallanti. 2013. "Reforms, Labour Market Functioning and Productivity Dynamics: A Sectoral Analysis for Italy." *MEF Working Paper Series, Italian Ministry of Economy and Finance: Italian Ministry of Economy and Finance.*

Lavoie, Marc and Engelbert Stockhammer. 2013. *Wage-Led Growth*. London: Palgrave.

Lavoie, Marc. 2014. *Post-Keynesian Economics: New Foundations*. Cheltenham, UK: Edward Elgar.

MacKenzie, Donald Angus, Fabian Muniesa and Lucia Siu. 2007. *Do Economists Make Markets? On the Performativity of Economics*. Princeton, NJ: Princeton University Press.

Martin, Cathie Jo and Kathleen Thelen. 2007. "The State and Coordinated Capitalism: Contributions of the Public Sector to Social Solidarity in Postindustrial Societies." *World Politics* 60: 1–36.

Onaran, Ozlem and Thomas Obst. 2015. "Wage-Led Growth in the Eu15 Member States: The Effects of Income Distribution on Growth, Investment, Trade Balance, and Inflation." *Greenwich Papers in Political Economy, University of Greenwich, #GPERC28.*

Onaran, Özlem and Giorgos Galanis. 2014. "Income Distribution and Growth: A Global Model." *Environment and Planning* A 46(10): 2489–13.

Pontusson, Jonas. 2013. "Unionization, Inequality and Redistribution." *British Journal of Industrial Relations* 51(4): 797–825.

Pontusson, Jonas and Lucio Baccaro. 2020. "Comparative Political Economy and Varieties of Macroeconomics." *Oxford Research Encyclopedia of Politics*. Oxford University Press, doi: https://10.1093/acrefore/9780190228637.013.161

Pontusson, Jonas and Damian Raess. 2012. "How (and Why) Is This Time Different? The Politics of Economic Crisis in Western Europe and the United States." *Annual Review of Political Science* 15(1): 13–33.

Pontusson, Jonas and David Weisstanner. 2018. "Macroeconomic Conditions, Inequality Shocks and the Politics of Redistribution, 1990–2013," *Journal of European Public Policy* 25(1): 31–58.

Raess, Damian and Jonas Pontusson. 2015. "The Politics of Fiscal Policy during Economic Downturns, 1981–2010." *European Journal of Political Research* 54(1): 1–22.

Scharpf, Fritz W. 1991. *Crisis and Choice in European Social Democracy*. Ithaca, N.Y.: Cornell University Press.

Shapiro, Carl and Joseph E. Stiglitz. 1984. "Equilibrium Unemployment as a Worker Discipline Device." *The American Economic Review* 74(3): 433–44.

Storm, Servaas and C.W.M. Naastepad. 2012. *Macroeconomics Beyond the Nairu*. Cambridge, MA: Harvard University Press.

Streeck, Wolfgang. 1994. "Pay Restraint without Incomes Policy: Institutionalized Monetarism and Industrial Unionism in Germany." In *The Return of Incomes Policy*, edited by R. Dore, R. Boyer and Z. Mars. London: Pinter, 118–40.

Temin, Peter and David Vines. 2014. *Keynes*. Cambridge, MA: MIT University Press.

Tridico, Pasquale and Riccardo Pariboni. 2018. "Inequality, Financialization, and Economic Decline." *Journal of Post Keynesian Economics* 41(2): 236–59.

Tronti, Leonello. 2009. "La Crisi Di Produttività Dell'economia Italiana: Scambio Politico Ed Estensione Del Mercato." *Economia e Lavoro* XLIII(2): 139–57.

Woodford, Michael D. 2003. *Interest & Prices*. Princeton, NJ: Princeton University Press.

4

Cross-National Variation in Growth Models: Three Sources of Extra Demand

Georg Picot

1. Introduction

The global financial crisis of 2008–9 has drawn attention to the economic growth regimes that contributed to causing the crisis. The subprime lending practices in the US and the wider financialization of the US economy have received particular attention. Also, the trajectories of other countries, such as Greece and Spain, have been widely discussed. Yet, public debate and academic scholarship have not sufficiently appreciated the variety of growth regimes before and after the crisis. Only recently has research in comparative political economy started to account for different models (e.g. Baccaro and Pontusson 2016). Yet, this literature prevailingly analyzes only a couple of exemplary countries empirically—often a selection of "usual suspects" that are frequently subject to case studies. This chapter has two main objectives. First, it proposes an innovative and parsimonious framework of categorizing growth models. Second, it maps the variety of growth models across developed countries. The introductory chapter by Hassel and Palier in this volume also analyzes a large set of countries rather than a few usual suspects. While Hassel and Palier focus on growth regimes, i.e. on institutional, policy, and organizational frameworks, I focus on growth models, i.e. sources of demand that result from growth regimes.

The conceptual framework presented in this paper makes use of a spending-based decomposition of GDP and focuses on three broad, potential sources of additional economic demand: public deficits, private deficits, and trade surpluses. These are ways of generating extra demand by borrowing (domestic deficits)[1] or lending (external surplus), which I will call "demand boosters." The empirical analysis identifies the combination of these demand boosters across twenty-eight OECD countries and over three sub-periods between 1995 and 2016 by conducting a fuzzy-set ideal type analysis.

[1] In this chapter, "domestic deficits" refers to public and private deficits.

Georg Picot, *Cross-National Variation in Growth Models: Three Sources of Extra Demand* In: *Growth and Welfare in Advanced Capitalist Economies: How Have Growth Regimes Evolved?* Edited by: Anke Hassel and Bruno Palier, Oxford University Press (2021). © Oxford University Press. DOI: 10.1093/oso/9780198866176.003.0004

The next section will draw on existing literature and develop the theoretical framework. The third section describes the method and data used. This is followed by an analysis of growth models as well as a preliminary review of differences in economic outcomes between the models. Finally, I will conclude and indicate some implications.

2. A new taxonomy of economic growth models

2.1 Motivation

Since the Fordist period of relatively abundant growth after World War II ended, we see more imbalanced ways of fostering growth. Krippner (2011) has convincingly shown for the United States how policymakers' ad hoc responses to low economic growth have brought about financialization of the economy including high levels of private debt, which ultimately led to the financial crisis of 2008. Similarly, Streeck (2011) observes a sequence of economic imbalances in advanced democratic capitalist countries since the 1970s, from inflation to public deficits to private deficits, intended to cushion the conflict between democracy and capitalism that opens up as growth declines (see also Streeck 2014).

While examining common trends is useful, it is vital not to lose sight of cross-national diversity. In this chapter, I accept the premise by Krippner (2011), Streeck (2011), and others that low growth has led to deficit-driven growth strategies. However, a rich tradition of comparative political economy (CPE) (see Hassel and Palier, this volume) has shown that advanced capitalist economies can be organized in substantially different ways. In line with this tradition, my chapter finds clear cross-national differences in growth models. It is well known that welfare state institutions and industrial relations vary substantially across states (e.g. Hall and Soskice 2001; Esping-Andersen 1990; Arts and Gelissen 2010; Crouch 1993). Moreover, social and economic institutions are often interlinked and complementary in such a way that they form distinct "models," "varieties," or "regimes." The welfare state is a vital part of growth regimes, by propping up economic demand, providing and shaping investment in labor force skills, and affecting labor costs (Hassel and Palier, this volume).

Less recognized in the CPE literature is the international interdependence between political economies. Arguably, the specific imbalances in different national economies have reinforced each other through international trade and capital flows in the run-up to the 2008 financial crisis. If so, the differences between them were crucial for inflating the financial bubble that burst in 2008 (Iversen and Soskice 2012; Hall 2014).

At the same time, much of the literature on growth models analyzes just a few exemplary cases and does not provide a comprehensive account of cross-national variation. This entails two problems: (1) that usual suspects, such as Germany and the US, are taken as representative for groups of countries (such as Coordinated Market Economies and Liberal Market Economies) without further empirical evidence; (2) that the diversity of growth regimes beyond two or three theoretically identified models is being underestimated. Indeed, when considering more countries, Hassel and Palier in this volume find five different growth regimes. To make up for the two mentioned problems, this chapter provides a systematic empirical account of growth models in twenty-eight developed economies since 1995.

2.2 The Conceptual Framework

In the long term and in a closed economy—or on the global scale—economic output can increase as a result of population growth or as a result of higher productivity (output per person; Piketty 2014: Ch. 2).[2] From a normative perspective, an increase in output due to population growth is not particularly interesting as it does not increase the material resources per person. Hence, for increasing growth in the long term, raising productivity is vital.

Productivity can be increased by various capital investments (including investments in "human capital") and by reorganizing production processes. Productivity investments can focus on specific or general skills, on incremental or radical innovation, and be publicly or privately funded. According to the CPE literature, private funding would be expected to play a major role in Liberal Market Economies (LMEs), both by private firms spending on research and development for radical innovations and by private funding of education (Hall and Soskice 2001). In Coordinated Market Economies (CMEs), firms more commonly pursue incremental innovation, which is often linked to their investments in vocational training. In these economies, we can expect more state support for innovation and education than in LMEs. Nordic countries have generally been good at building social policies in line with the idea of social investment (Morel et al. 2012), such as upskilling Active Labor Market Policies and high-quality public education, including childcare, helping them to adapt the workforce to technological progress. In Southern Europe, fragmented industrial relations and lower state capacities constrain public support for productivity investments. For a more detailed discussion of the role of education and training in growth regimes, see Hassel and Palier as well as Chevalier in this volume. I will briefly return to investments in productivity toward the end of the chapter, to see whether

[2] More precisely, rather than population size the number of people in employment is decisive. This is targeted by the common supply-side strategy of labor market activation (cf. Eichhorst et al. 2008; Clasen and Clegg 2011; Bonoli 2013).

the growth models identified in this chapter are associated with different levels of investment in education.

My main analysis, however, will adopt a more short-term and demand-side perspective. In the short term, open economies have many more options of boosting growth than in the long term. I will mostly take a demand-side perspective, hence focusing on growth models, for three reasons: (1) examining spending is appropriate for studying economic imbalances of the kind suggested by the literature (e.g. Krippner 2011; Streeck 2014); (2) a demand-side analysis helps to consider economic interdependence between countries; and (3) even nominally supply-side strategies often have important implications for demand, for example when financial deregulation facilitates consumer credit and thus spending (Crouch 2009).

The framework I propose for conceptualizing different short-term ways of boosting economic growth starts from the expenditure-based decomposition of the Gross Domestic Product (GDP):

$$Y = C + I + G + (X - M)$$

Economic output (Y) can be divided into private consumption spending (C), private investments (I), government spending (G), and the balance between exports (X) and imports (M). Each of these elements can be the source of extra demand. If spending by households, firms, or government exceeds their revenue, consumption, investments, and government spending respectively are higher than they otherwise would be, thus increasing domestic demand. If exports exceed imports, the economy benefits from more foreign demand than it would if exports were equal to imports.

If we drop the distinction between private consumption and private investments,[3] we can simplify the scheme and identify three ways to boost demand: private deficits, government deficits, and trade surpluses. The first two enhance domestic demand, the third exploits foreign demand. Note that not only the third demand booster relies on international transactions. Private and government deficits by themselves can be financed through domestic as well as foreign credit. If both the private and the public sector run deficits, as was the case, for example, in the United States in 2005–7, they actually have to be funded from abroad,[4] which ultimately means from countries with current account surpluses. By the same token, an economy cannot "run" all three demand boosters at the same time. Domestic deficits (both private and public) cannot go along with a current account surplus because a current account surplus implies that more values flow

[3] The distinction would matter from a supply-side or productivity perspective, but it is not relevant for the demand-side perspective adopted in the present analysis.

[4] In theory, domestic deficits (i.e. *flows*) can be paid out of domestic saving *stocks*. Yet, these stocks would inevitably be used up soon.

out of the country than in. Further, there is of course no necessity for an economy to run deficits or surpluses at all. In principle, private and public actors can balance their books and, in this case, the current account will be balanced as well.

The mentioned deficits and surpluses can of course fluctuate over time. They may be affected by exogenous economic shifts or they may change due to short-term government policies, such as mere countercyclical use of public deficits. By contrast, this chapter traces where and when these deficits or surpluses have occurred persistently over time. In such cases, we can interpret them as a consequence of growth regimes. They occur with certain continuity because they are facilitated by institutions and long-term policies, in particular: the financial system, corporate governance structures, product market regulations, wage-setting institutions, labor market regulation, the education and training system, and social protection policies (see Hassel and Palier in this volume). In my framework, a specific combination of the three demand boosters lasting over several years (e.g. over a business cycle) is a specific type of growth model. Growth models are then persistent spending patterns that are an intermediate outcome of growth regimes and strategies, intermediate in the sense of being a link between the growth regime and the actual economic growth outcome.

Note, therefore, that governments cannot directly choose a growth model. Their growth strategy may aim at a certain growth model. However, to work towards it, they have to adapt the growth regime, where they are confronted with institutional path dependencies. Moreover, the effects of the growth regime depend on exogenous economic fluctuations. Even public deficits, the demand booster most closely connected to government, are affected by economic shocks, demographic trends, and past financial commitments, rather than being the direct result of a precise spending strategy. I do argue, however, that the size of demand boosters in cross-national comparison and over a multi-year period reflects the growth regimes, which in turn can be transformed by growth strategies.

Further, I use the term "growth models" independently of success in actually generating growth. Demand boosters are by themselves suited to increase economic output, but actual growth depends on a wider range of factors. Similarly, the spending patterns that underlie demand boosters not only affect growth but are also themselves affected by it. For example, a recession (possibly caused by an exogenous shock) leads almost automatically to government overspending. Nevertheless, recession-induced overspending can be seen as maintaining demand under the given circumstances, rather than cutting spending or raising taxes.

My approach has some similarities with the one by Baccaro and Pontusson (2016; see also their chapter in this volume). Like them, I investigate growth models in the post-Fordist, low-growth era from a demand-side perspective and with an interest in different potential drivers of demand. Both approaches are sensitive to cross-national diversity, possibly diverging from the political-economic models established in the literature. Also the periodization is similar by analyzing separately the build-up to the financial crisis as well as on the changes after the crisis. The main difference is that I use decomposition of GDP to analyze three demand boosters, which together encompass the spending side of the economy. Thus, the three constituent parts of my growth models are more comprehensive, but the analysis is less detailed and less sensitive to the composition of demand in terms of sectors and income distribution. Baccaro and Pontusson (2016) make a strong argument that the price-sensitivity of exports can be used to distinguish among export-oriented models (see Hassel and Palier in this volume for a similar distinction), which is beyond the scope of my analysis. Somewhat puzzling, however, is that government spending is missing from their account. Finally, although not directly implied by my taxonomy of growth models in terms of three demand boosters, my argument remains more open to the relevance of supply-side institutions—in this respect consistent with Hassel and Palier's approach to growth regimes in this volume.

2.3 The Range of Growth Models

Various authors have pointed out how different political-economic models are associated with the domestic deficits or external surpluses of interest in this chapter (see also Hassel and Palier in this volume). From a Varieties of Capitalism perspective, vocational training, wage moderation as well as fiscal and monetary restraint in CMEs favor the export sector, while weak collective bargaining, financial deregulation, and more growth-oriented fiscal and monetary policy sustain domestic demand in LMEs (Iversen and Soskice 2012). Iversen and Soskice (2012) have further pointed out that the imbalances of LMEs and CMEs have reinforced each other before the crisis, as the external surpluses by CMEs helped to satisfy the need for credit in LMEs. The way financial deregulation has facilitated private-deficit-driven economic demand in LMEs by giving people on low income access to credit has been widely recognized (see e.g. Crouch's 2009 notion of "privatized Keynesianism"). However, growth models based on domestic demand (private or public) can be found also in Southern Europe, where lacking wage coordination and expansionary fiscal policy have contributed to domestic demand, while European Economic and Monetary Union (EMU) amplified diverging price dynamics between Northern and Southern Europe and facilitated cheap credits flowing from Northern to Southern Europe (Hall, 2014). Also scholars from the Regulation School have highlighted differences between growth models before the Great Recession. They have extended this perspective to Central and Eastern Europe (CEE) where they distinguish between dependent industrialization (e.g. Poland, Slovak Republic, and Czech Republic) and dependent financialization (e.g. the Baltic states; Becker and Jäger 2010; Bieling 2012; Avlijaš et al. in this volume).

The three demand boosters, private deficits, public deficits, and external surpluses, can be combined in seven ways (mathematically eight, but one is economically impossible). Using this taxonomy of growth models, the chapter contributes to one of the aims of this volume, which is to distinguish growth models beyond the broad distinction of export-led and domestic demand-led (see Hassel and Palier, this volume). In the following, I go through the possible combinations and indicate, based on the literature, which cases can be expected to display each of these growth models (see Table 4.1). The first growth model builds exclusively on continuous trade surpluses. This is the "export-led growth model." As mentioned, this does not mean that such economies run no private or public deficits at all, but only that they are moderate in size or not frequent. This model can be expected in CMEs, in particular Continental and Nordic Europe. The main strength of Continental European economies is in export of high-quality manufacturing, while Nordic economies are more successful in exporting high-end, ICT-intensive services (see Hassel and Palier, and Thelen, this volume). Also in East Asia, an export-led growth model is likely due to CME-similar institutions supportive of exports. As highlighted by Iversen and Soskice (2012), but following also from general theory of international trade, we would not expect CMEs to combine trade surpluses with private or public deficits due to restrictive monetary and fiscal policies that seek to contain inflation and real exchange rates. Japan, as is widely known, has extraordinarily high public debt and has had high public deficits since the early 1990s. Hence, we know empirically that Japan does not fit this expectation and combines

Table 4.1 A new taxonomy of growth models

Growth model	Private deficit	Public deficit	Current account surplus	Expected cases
Export-led	0	0	1	Continental, Nordic, (East Asia, esp. South Korea)
Finance-led	1	0	0	Baltic, (English-speaking)
State-led	0	1	0	Visegrád
Domestic-led	1	1	0	Southern Europe post-EMU, (English-speaking, esp. US)
Mixed export-state	0	1	1	Southern Europe pre-EMU, (East Asia, esp. Japan)
Mixed export-private	1	0	1	
Balanced	0	0	0	
[impossible]	1	1	1	

Note: "1" indicates presence and "0" absence of a deficit/surplus (understood as sustained and sizable deficit/surplus); in the column with expected cases, ambiguous cases are in brackets.

trade surpluses with public deficits even if we lack a consistent theoretical explanation.[5]

Growth models that foster domestic demand can make use of private or public deficits. Large and continuous private deficits would be expected in highly financialized economies, such as English-speaking countries and the Baltic states.[6] In LMEs there is no contradiction between private deficits and loose fiscal policy (Iversen and Soskice 2012), even if the latter is more likely a consequence of low taxes than of high spending. Hence, in these countries domestic demand may well be propped up by government deficits, in addition to the lavish use of private debt, which is in line with the fact that the US, as is widely known, has had high public deficits in many years. In Australia and Canada, abundant natural resources may contribute to more balanced or even positive external accounts in spite of liberal institutional incentives. Growth models where private deficits dominate will be called "finance-led."

Public deficits have been widespread in many developed countries in recent decades. Yet, only in some would they be expected to play a dominant role compared to the other two demand boosters. This will be called the state-led growth model. Although CEE countries tend to have high export shares, many of them, in particular the so-called Visegrád group (Poland, Hungary, Czech Republic, and Slovak Republic), are characterized as "dependently industrialized" (Bieling 2012), "Dependent Market Economies" (Nölke and Vliegenthart 2009), or "FDI-led growth models" (Bohle and Regan 2019) because many export firms are foreign-owned and exports are tied into the production chain of foreign companies. Although high export shares make these economies export-oriented (Bohle and Regan 2019; Palier and Hassel, this volume), exports are to a high degree balanced by imports (for example, when components are imported and the assembled product exported; Bohle and Regan 2019: 9). Therefore, the Visegrád countries do not gain a lot of extra demand from exports. By contrast, public deficits are likely to be high in these countries for a variety of reasons: (1) up to the late 1990s, the continued costs and fiscal imbalances of the economic transition; (2) investment incentives and favorable tax rules to attract foreign direct investments (Bohle and Regan 2019); (3) in some countries, such as Poland and Hungary, a turn towards state-led developmentalism after the global financial crisis (Toplišek 2020; Naczyk 2019). Therefore, we can expect public deficits to be the most consistent demand booster in the Visegrád countries.

[5] An important driver of public deficits in Japan is of course demographic ageing, which is more pronounced than in other developed economies. A reason why governments do not manage to adjust fiscal dynamics is suggested by Estevez-Abe (2008: 98–100). She explains that changes in the electoral system in the early 1990s made it electorally more risky for governments to impose new financial burdens on the majority of voters.

[6] On financialization in the Baltic states as well as Bulgaria and Romania, see Becker and Jäger (2010: 13–16).

High public deficits are also likely to have played a leading role in Southern Europe before EMU when they were frequently supplemented by trade surpluses with the help of strategic currency devaluations, implying a mixed export-state model (Ferrera 2010). Under EMU, national currency devaluations were no longer possible and the scope of public deficits was constrained. Instead, these countries received easy access to foreign credit. This may have led to private deficits as an important demand booster, but may also have induced looser public spending and, thus, public deficits in spite of EMU. This growth model can be called "domestic-led" as it combines private and public deficits. Yet, it has widely been acknowledged that Spain relied more strongly on private than public deficits. Perez and Rhodes (2015: 193–4) trace the distinct fiscal policy in Spain back to how Spain reacted to the crisis of the European Exchange Rate Mechanism in the early 1990s. As mentioned above, it is possible that some English-speaking countries also combine private and public deficits.

The logically possible combinations in this taxonomy include two growth models that would mix a current account surplus with either public deficits or private deficits. As mentioned above, pursuing external surpluses while boosting internal demand is economically contradictory (unless, as Baccaro and Pontusson 2016 argue, if exports are price-insensitive). These are therefore unlikely growth models. The combination of external surplus and public deficit may nevertheless be found in Southern Europe prior to EMU when these two factors were reconciled through strategic exchange rate devaluations. As mentioned above, we know empirically that this combination is also expected in Japan. By contrast, it is impossible for a country to run an external surplus and domestic deficits in both private and public sector at the same time. Finally, it would be possible that an economy does not strongly use any of the three demand boosters. Such a "balanced growth model" (see Table 4.1) would have to rely on productivity increase and mere short-term occurrence of domestic deficits or external surpluses.[7]

3. Data and Method

The main empirical task of this chapter is to map the variety of growth models across developed countries by applying the taxonomy developed above. The analysis covers as many developed capitalist democracies as possible across Europe, North America, East Asia, and the Antipodes, while excluding the OECD members Turkey, Israel, Chile, and Mexico. States that are not OECD members could not be covered due to data limitations. Also for Luxembourg and Iceland, crucial data was not available. Consequently, the dataset comprises

[7] My notion of "balanced growth model" differs from Baccaro and Pontusson (this volume). They use the term for the combination of demand from household consumption as well as exports.

twenty-eight developed capitalist democracies (for a list see Table 4.2 further below). This is far more comprehensive than most studies on this topic.

Although the main interest of the chapter is in cross-sectional variation, I will also trace changes in growth models over time. This will enable me to look into both the conditions that led up to the global financial and economic crisis as well as its consequences. The data reaches back to 1995. For earlier years, there was not sufficient data available. However, the middle of the 1990s makes for a good starting point as many governments embarked on substantial welfare state reforms at that time (Palier 2010; see also the chapter by Hall in this volume). Moreover, by this time the most tumultuous phase of post-socialist transition in Eastern Europe was over. At the other end, the period of analysis dates until 2016, the last year with almost complete data available.

I have divided the overall period of analysis (1995–2016) into three economically distinct phases. The first period, 1995–2000, covers a time of relatively sustained growth, finishing with the peak of the "dot-com bubble" (see Figure 4.1); it also includes the crucial years of the run-up to EMU when many European states were making an effort to fulfill the convergence criteria.[8] The second period, 2001–7, exactly extends over one business cycle, from the bursting of the Dot-com bubble to the year before the global financial and economic crisis erupted. Hence, this period captures the growth models that were part of the global economic constellation leading to the crisis. Next, I have deliberately omitted the trough years of the crisis 2008–9, as the circumstances were exceptional and characterized by emergency measures rather than growth models in any meaningful sense. Consequently, the third period is 2010–16 and comprises the rather slow and varied economic recovery. In fact, several European states fell back into recession in 2012.

As the taxonomy of growth models in this chapter starts from a decomposition of GDP, the measures of the three demand boosters are deliberately comprehensive. High reliance on exports is operationalized by a current account surplus as percentage of GDP. The current account consists of the trade balance as well as international primary income (from investments or remittances) and net cash transfers (such as donations or international aid). The main interest in this chapter is of course in the trade balance. I use the current account balance anyway in order to maintain the comprehensiveness of the taxonomy. In any case, the trade balance is the principal component of the current account balance and the two are highly correlated.

Public deficit is measured as general government net borrowing as a share of GDP. This is the standard measure used for comparing public budget balances. For instance, it is the basis for the European Commission's assessment of the

[8] The EMU convergence criteria were adopted in the Maastricht Treaty in 1992; the initial Eurozone member states were decided in May 1998; and the euro came into force in January 1999.

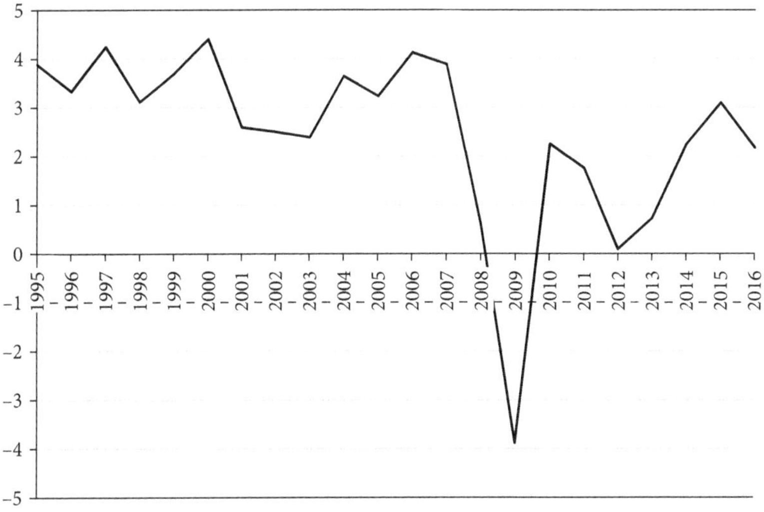

Figure 4.1 Economic growth rates 1995–2016, average of 28 OECD countries
Source: OECD.

Maastricht criterion on public deficits. It covers all levels of government as well as social security funds. A drawback is that it includes payments of interest on debt, which are driven by the historical record of debt accumulation and do not directly contribute to demand. There are three reasons why this is nevertheless the best indicator for the purposes of this chapter. First, although interest payments do not themselves generate economic demand, they constitute income for other actors who may use it for consumption or investment. Although for national GDP this income is "lost" if it is paid to foreign investors in government bonds, in this case it is reflected in the current account balance. Second, for a government that faces high deficits partly due to interest payments, the alternative would be to lower spending or to increase taxes. Both would have a negative effect on economic demand. Hence, although a high public deficit with high interest payments does not fully contribute to demand it is still a sign of upholding demand in spite of high public debt. Third, to be consistent with the GDP-decomposition approach of the theoretical framework, it is necessary to choose a comprehensive measure rather than one that excludes interest payments. If interest payments were deducted from public deficit figures, they would have to be excluded as well from private deficit and current account figures. This would defeat the comprehensive conceptual framework and entail an infeasible accountancy exercise.

The measure of private deficits is equivalent to the one for public deficits, i.e. net borrowing by the private sector as share of GDP. This comprises net borrowing by households and corporations. The concept of "privatized Keynesianism"

(Crouch 2009) mostly focuses on household deficits under financialized capitalism. Yet, it is important to include spending by corporations, which contributes to economic demand as well.

The use of broad measures may handicap interpretation in some cases. However, their use is consistent with the theoretical framework of this chapter, and interpretation can be aided if necessary by additional, more specific statistics. Moreover, the use of comprehensive indicators allows exploiting accountancy identities in the data: private and public deficits add up to the current account deficit; and it is impossible for a country to use all three demand boosters concurrently.

For determining which combination of the three demand boosters are deployed across developed countries, I use fuzzy-set ideal type analysis (Kvist 2007). This method is designed to flexibly analyze combinations of empirical conditions. It uses the value of one for indicating full presence of a certain condition (here, full use of a demand booster) and the value zero for full absence. At the same time, the method allows for gradual values between zero and one, where all values above 0.5 mean that the condition is more present than absent and vice versa below 0.5. In a process called calibration, the indicators listed above are used to assign to each case a gradual membership score. Using Boolean algebra, the conjunction of values for all three demand boosters will yield membership scores for each logically possible combination, i.e. each of the hypothesized growth models above, but cases will have a score above 0.5 in only one of the seven models. Fuzzy-set ideal type analysis is an efficient way to summarize a large amount of data in a systematic and transparent way. It allows for case-oriented analysis even when the number of cases is large.

4. Mapping the Growth Models

Table 4.2 presents the descriptive data of the three main measures, private deficits, public deficits, and current account surpluses. As is customary for surplus/deficit data, it presents the balances, which means that deficits are negative and surpluses positive. The table shows the averages over the period of analysis (1995–2016) excluding the slump years 2008–9.

The accountancy identity of private and public deficits adding up to current account deficits can be recognized well in the table. That they rarely add up exactly can be attributed to this highly aggregated data often not being entirely precise, as well as to small incongruences in the dataset (regarding source of data and years available, as documented in the table's note). The main point to note from the table is the overall distribution of the three demand boosters. While cross-national variation of current accounts spreads relatively evenly around a midpoint of approximately zero, the other two indicators do not. As is well known,

Table 4.2 Averages of demand boosters 1995–2016 (excluding 2008–9), percentage of GDP

	Private surplus (+)/deficit (–)	Public surplus (+)/deficit (–)	Current account surplus (+)/deficit (–)
Australia	-3.51	-0.86	-4.38
Austria	3.30	-2.62	0.78
Belgium	5.12	-1.99	2.52
Canada	-0.08	-0.57	-0.60
Czech Republic	0.92	-3.53	-2.86
Denmark	3.90	0.14	3.86
Estonia	-5.69	0.58	-5.90
Finland	2.73	0.45	3.03
France	3.27	-3.53	0.46
Germany	5.56	-2.11	3.43
Greece	1.66	-6.96	-6.04
Hungary	2.55	-5.19	-3.32
Ireland	2.00	-2.49	0.24
Italy	3.73	-3.41	0.38
Japan	8.58	-5.67	2.65
Korea	0.56	1.89	2.73
Netherlands	8.24	-1.82	6.44
New Zealand	-4.53	1.06	-3.81
Norway	0.07	9.96	10.28
Poland	2.00	-4.07	-3.40
Portugal	0.33	-4.96	-5.91
Slovak Republic	0.72	-4.91	-4.90
Slovenia	3.28	-3.77	0.18
Spain	0.53	-3.50	-2.86
Sweden	5.18	-0.16	5.06
Switzerland	10.13	-0.48	10.41
United Kingdom	1.24	-3.43	-2.68
United States	1.54	-4.36	-3.25
Median	*2.00*	*-2.55*	*0.21*
Standard deviation	*3.50*	*3.18*	*4.47*

Note: Where OECD data for current account balances was missing (some countries at the beginning of the period), they were supplemented with UNCTAD data. A few country averages of private deficits are based on fewer years owing to data availability: Hungary (only 2016 missing), New Zealand (1995–97 and 2016 missing), and Spain (1995–98 missing). Public deficit data for Japan was missing for 1995–2004 and was imputed, using the accountancy identity: public net lending = current account balance – private net lending.

Source: OECD.

governments overwhelmingly ran deficits in recent decades: hence the median of –2.55. This is in line with the literature that highlights a common tendency of political economies to counter the era of low growth by overspending. By contrast, private actors in advanced capitalist economies have a tendency to save (median 2.00). This suggests that the narrative of financialization leading to "privatized Keynesianism" cannot easily be generalized. The standard deviation in the bottom row of the table shows that variation around the midpoints is substantial, which supports the motivation of this chapter to explore cross-national diversity of growth models.

Calibration is crucial in fuzzy-set analysis. The calibration thresholds for this analysis were decided on the basis of the average data from Table 4.2 over the entire period, instead of each subperiod. This conforms to Kvist (2007) and makes it possible to consistently track changes in growth models between the three subperiods. Calibration of the current account balance is straightforward. The target set is defined as economies with a lasting and large current account surplus. The crossover threshold between membership or not is set at 0, when exports equal imports. Full members of the set are countries with a surplus of 4 or more percent GDP. Fully out of the set are countries with a deficit of at least –4 (see Table 4.3).[9]

Calibration of private and public deficits faces the difficulty that, as shown above, neither distribution is centered on zero. In most countries, private actors run surpluses and governments run deficits. In fuzzy-set analysis it is recommended to use theoretical and substantive considerations in calibrating membership scores (Schneider and Wagemann 2012). Regarding the public budget, small deficits are widely seen as normal and unproblematic. In Europe, the euro convergence criteria have established –3% as a widely acknowledged threshold.

Table 4.3 Calibration of set membership scores

Original data	Set for fuzzy-set analysis	Lower bound (for membership scores of 0)	Crossover point (distinguishing between above and below 0.5)	Upper bound (for membership scores of 1)
Current account surplus (+)/deficit (–), % GDP	Economies with lasting and large current account surplus	–4	0	4
Public surplus (+)/deficit (–), % GDP	Economies with lasting and large public deficit	1	–3	–5
Private surplus (+)/deficit (–), % GDP	Economies with lasting and large private deficit	4	0	–4

[9] Using the defined thresholds, the raw data is transformed into fuzzy-set scores by a logistic function using the fsQCA software (www.fsqca.com).

The calibration of this demand booster accepts this value as the crossover point. Therefore, the fuzzy-set results will only identify countries with large deficits as part of the group of countries that use public deficits to boost economic demand. This is a conservative measurement that factors in how widespread small government deficits are. Countries are considered full members of this set only if their deficit is –5% or more. They are scored as fully out of the set if they regularly run surpluses of 1% or more.

Regarding private net borrowing, there is neither a widely shared judgement on the size of these deficits nor an established institutional threshold. It is striking that according to Table 4.2 even the US and UK ran on average slight private surpluses over this period even though they are widely regarded as typical cases of growth models driven by private credit. Yet, recent scholarship has cast doubts on the robustness of this characterization (Baccaro and Pontusson 2016; Barnes 2016). Therefore, the assignment of these cases should not guide the calibration. A calibration that takes into account the center of gravity of the distribution (median: 2.00) and specific cases, such as US and UK, would have to choose a surplus value as crossover point. However, in contrast to the choice for public deficits above, this would be a lenient rather than a conservative adjustment, i.e. it would run the risk of categorizing too many cases as running private deficits, even some that have slight surpluses. Therefore, I accept zero as the most straightforward crossover point for this calibration. Full membership in the set of countries with repeated and big private deficits occurs when the average deficit is –4% or more. Countries are fully out of the set if they run surpluses of 4% or above.

Table 4.4 provides an overview of the incidence of the various growth models that the fuzzy-set ideal type analysis identified. There are four points to take away from the table. First, it confirms that advanced capitalist countries generally responded to the era of low growth by trying to gain extra demand from either internal deficits or external surpluses. In only five of overall eighty-four country-periods (twenty-eight countries over three subperiods) did economies not resort to the marked use of any of the three demand boosters (balanced model). Second,

Table 4.4 Incidence of growth models over time, twenty-eight OECD countries

Growth model	1995–2000	2001–7	2010–13
Export-led	8	11	9
Finance-led	4	6	3
State-led	8	3	9
Domestic-led	2	5	0
Mixed export-state	2	1	5
Mixed export-private	2	1	0
Balanced	2	1	2

Table 4.4 shows that, at the same time, there is substantial diversity in the use of demand boosters. Counter to literature that suggests common trends (Streeck 2011), developed economies have very different modes of tackling the low-growth era.[10] Third, the table supports the notion from economics of international trade as well as Varieties of Capitalism that growth models tend to have a certain internal consistency (Iversen and Soskice 2012). Few economies mix sustained current account surpluses with large deficits in either the private or the public domestic sector: four in 1995–2000, only two in 2001–7, and five in 2010–16. In the latter period, all five mix export with public deficits, for which it certainly mattered that public deficits were generally high in the aftermath of the crisis.

Fourth, while there was no notable tendency of developed countries to move towards a common growth model over these three periods, we can observe a few more subtle shifts. The "purity" of the growth models was somewhat higher in the run-up to the crisis (2001–7). More countries than in the other two subperiods pursued export-led, finance-led, and domestic-led growth, while less countries had growth models that mixed external surplus with internal deficits. Moreover, the state-led growth model was less common than in the other two subperiods. Hence, growth was more strongly driven by external demand and internally by private deficits. This "purity" of the growth models made it possible that they mutually reinforced each other through international financial flows (Iversen and Soskice 2012; Hall 2014). After the crisis (here, 2010–16), we see the state-led model rising again as well as the mixed export-state model, which, as mentioned, is a direct consequence of the crisis. It reflects the financial commitments governments incurred by bailing out banks, providing unemployment benefits, and stimulating the economy, as well as decreased public revenues due to low growth. However, yearly data show that in many countries public deficits declined over the period and economies reverted to their pre-crisis growth models. Similarly, the yearly data show that immediately after the financial crisis, private deficits disappeared as private actors had no longer the same easy access to credit and postponed spending due to the uncertain economic environment and low inflation. In many countries private deficits picked up again during 2010–16.

Table 4.5 lists the more detailed findings by country, grouped into the clusters commonly identified by the literature. The table also reports to what degree cases fulfill the respective model. Fuzzy-set scores close to one mean that the model is almost perfectly represented, while values close to 0.5 mean that the fit is very loose. To start with, the table highlights nicely how dominant the export-led growth model is in Continental Europe. In 2001–7 this was indeed the only growth model among the Continental European countries in the sample. In the

[10] As found in Table 4.2, moderate overspending by governments is in fact a common feature in advanced economies. This is explicitly omitted from the calibration of the public deficits for the fuzzy-set analysis. Growth models are nevertheless distinct beyond this moderate commonality.

Table 4.5 Growth models 1995–2016

Country	1995–2000	2001–7	2010–16
Continental			
Austria	State-led (0.67)	Export-led (0.65)	Export-led (0.62)
Belgium	Export-led (0.68)	Export-led (0.86)	State-led (0.52)
France	Export-led (0.51)	Export-led (0.51)	State-led (0.66)
Germany	State-led (0.58)	Export-led (0.53)	Export-led (0.87)
Netherlands	Export-led (0.73)	Export-led (0.82)	Export-led (0.55)
Switzerland	Export-led (0.76)	Export-led (0.88)	Export-led (0.92)
Nordic			
Denmark	Export-led (0.66)	Export-led (0.61)	Export-led (0.76)
Finland	Export-led (0.9)	Export-led (0.81)	Balanced (0.63)
Norway	Mixed export-private (0.66)	Export-led (0.67)	Export-led (0.51)
Sweden	Export-led (0.8)	Export-led (0.95)	Export-led (0.88)
East Asia			
Japan	Mixed export-state (0.85)	Mixed export-state (0.93)	Mixed export-state (0.84)
Korea	Mixed export-private (0.66)	Mixed export-private (0.66)	Export-led (0.96)
Southern Europe			
Greece	State-led (0.88)	Domestic-led (0.87)	State-led (0.96)
Italy	Mixed export-state (0.82)	State-led (0.57)	Mixed export-state (0.51)
Portugal	Domestic-led (0.65)	Domestic-led (0.92)	State-led (0.84)
Spain	Domestic-led (0.72)	Finance-led (0.94)	State-led (0.54)
Central and Eastern Europe			
Czech Republic	State-led (0.72)	State-led (0.52)	Balanced (0.65)
Hungary	State-led (0.56)	Domestic-led (0.56)	Mixed export-state (0.51)
Poland	State-led (0.68)	State-led (0.65)	State-led (0.84)
Slovak Republic	State-led (0.79)	Domestic-led (0.82)	State-led (0.72)
Slovenia	State-led (0.65)	Finance-led (0.57)	Mixed export-state (0.92)
Estonia	Finance-led (0.89)	Finance-led (0.97)	Export-led (0.65)
English-speaking			
United States	Finance-led (0.66)	Domestic-led (0.55)	State-led (0.86)
Australia	Finance-led (0.88)	Finance-led (0.95)	Finance-led (0.51)
New Zealand	Finance-led (0.95)	Finance-led (0.97)	Finance-led (0.58)
Canada	Balanced (0.52)	Export-led (0.64)	Finance-led (0.69)
United Kingdom	Balanced (0.58)	Balanced (0.6)	State-led (0.87)
Ireland	Export-led (0.55)	Finance-led (0.84)	Mixed export-state (0.78)

Note: The names of the growth models are defined in Table 4.1 above. The numbers in brackets are fuzzy-set scores. As explained in the text, the years 2008 and 2009 are omitted deliberately.

phases before and after, four out of six countries had export-led models, the other two state-led. As expected, the export-led model is dominant in the Nordic countries as well. Sweden and Denmark had export-led economies in all three sub-periods. Norway complemented its export-led growth with private deficits in 1995–2000. Finland can be considered a balanced growth model in the post-crisis period as it had on average a moderate public deficit (–2.3% of GDP), a small private surplus (1.3) and a slight current account deficit (–1). Also in East Asia, the strong contribution of current account surpluses can be observed as hypothesized. In Japan, it was combined in all three phases with high public deficits. In South Korea, it went along with private deficits in the two subperiods before the crisis.

The picture in Southern Europe is a bit heterogeneous but broadly consistent with the expectations from the literature. Domestic deficits, in particular public deficits, prevail as demand boosters. Italy mixed public deficits with an external surplus in the run-up to EMU and managed to return to an external surplus in 2013 while also public deficits have declined (narrowly a mixed export-state model in 2010–16, with a fuzzy-set score of only 0.51). In the pre-crisis period after EMU (2001–7), domestic deficit-driven growth occurred in all four South European countries. The two countries, Greece and Portugal, in which both the private and the public sector contributed to boosting demand, were also the two South European countries that were bailed out by European and international institutions after 2010. In Italy government deficits prevailed, and in Spain private deficits, reflecting the housing bubble that built up in Spain in that period. Thus, the taxonomy of this contribution captures the commonality as well as the diversity of the South European political economies in this period (cf. Perez and Rhodes 2015).

In 1995–2000, all growth models in Central and Eastern Europe, except Estonia, were state-led as expected. In 2001–7, Hungary and the Slovak Republic supplemented public deficits with private deficits, while Slovenia shifted to a finance-led model. After the crisis, the picture is much more heterogeneous, with Hungary and Slovenia achieving external surpluses in addition to public deficits. Estonia, the only Baltic country in the sample, had a clearly articulated finance-led growth model in both subperiods before the crisis, as expected. It transformed to an export-led model afterwards, probably due to its severe internal devaluation program ahead of joining the Eurozone in 2011.

Finally, in English-speaking countries the dominant contribution of private deficits to boosting economic demand is broadly confirmed, especially in Australia and New Zealand, but with variations in the other cases. In the US, the emphasis on boosting private demand in 1995–2000 was in 2001–7 accompanied by large public deficits, as result of G.W. Bush's tax cuts, and in 2010–16 became an only state-led model. Canada had a balanced model in 1995–2000 and a current account surplus as main demand booster in 2001–7, based on export of minerals and energy. Somewhat surprisingly, the analysis identifies Britain as a balanced growth model in both pre-crisis periods. This runs counter to its widespread characterization as a liberal, debt-driven economy (e.g. Crouch 2009). In the seven years before the financial crash, the private sector in Britain was on average slightly in surplus (0.57% of GDP), the government deficit was a moderate –2.3%, and the current account was in deficit by –2.5%. This finding supports the call for a more nuanced understanding of the British political economy (Baccaro and Pontusson 2016; Barnes 2016). One reason for the low current account deficit is certainly that the City of London exports many financial services. Ireland also diverges from the typical pattern of English-speaking countries by having had high external surpluses in 1995–2000 and in 2010–16 combined with public deficits. The government facilitated this through tax incentives for multinational corporations. In contrast to the Visegrád countries, these multinationals are more strongly involved in services, hence generating fewer imports to counterbalance the exports.

If we zoom out from the more differentiated country-by-country consideration, we can summarize that in Continental and Nordic Europe as well as in East Asia current account surpluses are the main way of boosting economic growth by profiting from demand abroad. By contrast, Southern and Eastern Europe as well as English-speaking countries tend to boost economic demand through domestic deficits, in Southern and Eastern Europe more strongly through public deficits and in English-speaking countries more strongly through private deficits. In spite of these patterns at the group-level, the analysis has also found notable diversity within each cluster, which is not always adequately accounted for by current CPE theory. While some countries have changed their growth models after the global financial and economic crisis, the mentioned pattern holds by and large both before and after the crisis. The economic recovery is therefore built on an international configuration of growth models that resembles the one that led to the crisis. This supports the path dependency suggested by Hassel and Palier (this volume) as governments' growth strategies are conditioned by the existing growth regime.

5. The Performance of Growth Models

In this section, I consider how the identified growth models performed in actually achieving growth as well as in terms of employment and investment in education. This is only a first cut, using simple descriptive statistics to examine the association of various growth models with the mentioned economic outcomes. For the interpretation, it is important to keep in mind that some of the growth models comprise institutionally diverse economies and that the outcomes in question are of course affected by a wide range of factors beyond the three demand boosters this chapter focuses on.

Growth rates of economic output are the most obvious outcome of interest in the context of this chapter. In addition, employment rates are generally seen as macro-economically the most important labor market outcome.[11] The theoretical section pointed out that productivity can be regarded as crucial for growth in the medium- to long-term. Accordingly, this section looks at the extent to which various growth models are associated with investment in productivity. For simplicity, I focus on investment in education (public and private spending on education as percentage of GDP), which can be seen as the most important productivity investment in knowledge economies. I have averaged the outcome indicators for each country over the respective subperiod and aggregated these further into averages of the countries belonging to each growth model. While I report all results in Table 4.6, the interpretation focuses on the growth models with most country cases and hence less noise in the data.

The finance-led model generated the highest rates of economic growth in all three subperiods—apart from the mixed export-private model, the figures for which are based solely on Norway (1995–2000) and South Korea (1995–2000 and 2001–7). The lowest growth rates were associated with the state-led model in 1995–2000 and 2010–16. However, it is likely that some of the causation runs the other way, as low growth leads to higher public deficits. Indeed, in 2010–16, many countries were still affected by the global financial and economic crisis, and Greece and Portugal (among the state-led economies of the period) had negative average growth. In the pre-crisis years 2001–7, export-led countries had on average the lowest growth rates. This reason may be that much growth in those years was driven by heavy domestic borrowing in other countries. Although the export-led model benefits from the demand generated in other countries, it is plausible that the mediated growth effect is weaker. The standard deviations of economic growth rates were very low for the finance-led and the export-led model (except the latter in 1995–2000), which suggests some homogeneity of countries belonging to the models.

The finance-led model was associated with the highest employment rates in 1995–2000, whereas in the other periods the export-led model was leading in this regard. In the finance-led economies, this was presumably facilitated by deregulated service employment. Among the states with export-led growth the result is driven by the Nordic countries. As is well known, high employment in the Nordic countries is to a large extent the result of public employment and care services that facilitate female employment (Mandel and Semyonov 2006). The high-quality export sector benefits from these public services (through education, family-work reconciliation, and lower wage pressure) and contributes to the tax basis for them.

[11] The employment rate, measured as share of working-age (15–64) population in civilian employment, is preferred to unemployment, as the unemployment rate is measured in relation to the labor force and hence strongly affected by labor market participation.

Table 4.6 Performance of growth models

1995–2000	ec. growth			employment	
	N	mean	SD	mean	SD
Export-led	8	4.09	2.33	66.97	7.56
Finance-led	4	4.27	1.15	68.84	3.94
State-led	8	3.40	1.15	61.27	5.43
Domestic-led	2	3.99	0.17	58.58	9.05
Mixed export-state	2	1.77	0.54	60.76	12.12
Mixed export-private	2	5.01	1.83	69.27	10.47
Balanced	2	3.63	0.24	69.79	1.43
All cases	28	3.78	1.57	64.93	7.06

2001–7	ec. growth			employment	
	N	mean	SD	mean	SD
Export-led	11	2.24	0.53	70.61	5.68
Finance-led	6	4.72	1.62	67.59	4.15
State-led	3	3.28	1.85	58.46	6.10
Domestic-led	5	3.55	1.93	62.70	6.75
Mixed export-state	1	1.28		69.14	
Mixed export-private	1	4.91		63.47	
Balanced	1	2.75		72.61	
All cases	28	3.20	1.60	67.01	6.58

2010–16	ec. growth			employment		govt educ. exp.		priv. educ. exp.	
	N	mean	SD	mean	SD	mean	SD	mean	SD
Export-led	9	2.11	0.94	72.58	4.10	5.85	1.30	0.67	0.64
Finance-led	3	2.54	0.35	71.11	2.99	4.94	0.64	1.96	0.13
State-led	9	1.04	2.04	62.35	5.54	5.07	0.78	0.98	0.67
Domestic-led	0								
Mixed export-state	5	2.13	2.54	62.99	5.84	4.40	0.67	0.76	0.51
Mixed export-private	0								
Balanced	2	1.33	0.80	68.51	0.69	5.47	1.83	0.39	0.24
All cases	28	1.76	1.68	67.29	6.58	5.23	1.12	0.87	0.65

Note: "ec. growth" are annual rates of economic growth averaged over the period and across countries; SD are standard deviations and measure the variation of period averages across countries; "employment" are employment rates as percentage of population aged 15–64; "govt educ. exp." is general government spending on all public and private education institutions covering all International Standard Classification of Education levels as percentage of GDP; "priv. educ. exp." is the same spending but from the non-educational private sector (i.e., households and private organizations that are not themselves educational institutions). The education spending data is available only for limited years. The data reported here is based on 2013 and 2014, for some countries also 2010–12. No education spending data was available for Canada and Greece; for Denmark only 2012 public spending; for Switzerland only public spending; and for the US only 2010 and 2011. The countries belonging to each growth model can be found in Table 4.5.

Source: OECD.

That Nordic countries and consequently export-led countries were not leading in employment levels in 1995–2000 has to do with the fact that in the late 1990s they still recovered from their own domestic crises. In all three subperiods, employment was lowest in countries with state-led growth models. Again, this can of course be affected by reverse causality as low employment puts pressure on fiscal budgets. The standard deviations in employment rates of the countries with finance-led growth models are the lowest in all periods (aside from the balanced model in 2010–16 with only two cases), pointing again to congruence within this model.

Turning to investment in education, the highest public spending on education can be found in export-led economies. The result is once more driven by the Nordic countries, while the high standard deviation indicates that the Continental European states that make up most of the other countries in this group spend considerably less. Private spending on education is unsurprisingly highest in countries with finance-led growth models. This spending is itself often funded through loans (i.e. private deficits). Standard deviations in education expenditures are again lowest within the finance-led model.

Overall, we can say that the finance-led growth model fares best in terms of economic growth and has the highest private spending on education. The export-led model is strongest in employment and public investment in education, on both counts mostly driven by the Nordic countries. The state-led model tends to deliver the lowest growth and lowest employment. Yet, we need to keep in mind that these are often economies in particular distress, where high public deficits are the result of economic difficulties rather than their causes.

6. Conclusion

In line with the literature on the low-growth era of democratic capitalism (e.g. Streeck 2011), I have shown that most of the covered twenty-eight OECD member states rely on what can be called deficit-driven growth models. However, that literature neglected the cross-national diversity of growth models. Institutionalist scholars, on the other hand, point out cross-national variation in economic models including the growth regimes that underlie the various deficit-driven growth models (e.g. Iversen and Soskice 2012; Hall 2014). Yet, the institutionalist literature often relies on a limited number of exemplary cases. This contribution, by contrast, is the first to provide a systematic and encompassing account of cross-national variation of growth models. To this end, I have developed a new, parsimonious taxonomy that rests on the possible combinations of three ways of boosting demand: private deficits, public deficits, and external surpluses.

The findings confirm that cross-national variation of growth models, and therefore growth regimes, is substantial. It is also broadly consistent with our knowledge of institutional configurations in various clusters of political economies. An export-led model prevailed in Continental Europe, the Nordic countries, and, to some extent, East Asia. Growth in Southern Europe was mostly propped up by domestic deficits, especially public but often mixed with private deficits. The pattern in Eastern Europe is more mixed, but state spending played an important role in most cases. Finance-led growth, i.e. with large private deficits, prevailed in English-speaking countries, with the notable exception of the United Kingdom. While each cluster displays the main demand booster as expected, the analysis found also non-negligible within-cluster variation that needs further attention by CPE research.

The identified cross-national variation supports the notion that the different growth models reinforce each other as current account surpluses of the Northern European and East Asian export-led economies feed into domestic deficits in Southern Europe, Eastern Europe, and English-speaking countries. This interdependence is an important challenge for CPE, which by design starts from a focus on national cases, and calls for a more vibrant dialogue between CPE and International Political Economy (IPE). The demand-side GDP-decomposition approach of this chapter can help to integrate the external economic dimension into an analysis of national growth models.

Apart from attending to within-cluster variation and dialogue with IPE, future research should build on the analysis in this chapter in three ways, as some of the chapters in this volume do already. First, scholars should examine more closely the growth regimes that underlie the identified growth models. This is particularly desirable as different institutional configurations can generate the same growth model, for example an export-led model. Second, more research should be conducted on the growth strategies and politics that reproduce growth regimes. I have pointed to institutional path dependencies, but analyzing political power and economic ideas is similarly pertinent in this regard (Hall, this volume). Third, the composition of demand and exports should be analyzed more closely. For example, Baccaro and Pontusson (2016; and in this volume) as well as Hassel and Palier in this volume show that the different composition of the respective export sectors can shed light on differences between the growth models in Nordic Europe and Continental Europe. This is not picked up by my analysis because it only looks at the general account balance.

From a normative perspective, we can draw three lessons from this chapter. First, given the diversity of growth models, there can be no one-size-fits-all policy recommendations. In particular, economies relying mostly on external demand and those relying mostly on domestic demand differ fundamentally in their economic mechanics and underlying growth regimes. Beyond this broad distinction, this chapter has theoretically and empirically identified seven different growth models, thus recognizing further diversity. Second, it is unreasonable when national leaders in states with export-led growth models point the finger at countries with high domestic deficits. Export-led economies benefit from and fund the demand generated by those domestic deficits. Their account surpluses would be indeed impossible without other countries' account deficits. Besides, continuously lending abroad has its own downsides as the home population basically consumes less than it produces. Third, after the global financial and economic crisis, most countries have reverted to the same growth models that led up to the crisis. Such a pattern is not sustainable in the long run and may well lead to the next major crisis. Counterbalancing this trend will not be easy, as national growth models are based on growth regimes that have emerged over decades and are hard to change. Nevertheless, welfare state reforms can contribute to more domestic spending in export-led countries and lower deficits in the finance-led and state-led growth models, as well as to more sustainable long-term growth through investment in social care and education.[12]

References

Arts, W.A., and J. Gelissen. 2010. "Models of the Welfare State." In *The Oxford Handbook of the Welfare State*, edited by Francis G. Castles, Stephan Leibfried, Jane Lewis, Herbert Obinger and Christopher Pierson. Oxford: Oxford University Press, 569–83.

Baccaro, L., and J. Pontusson. 2016. "Rethinking Comparative Political Economy: The Growth Model Perspective." *Politics & Society* 44: 175–207.

Barnes, L. 2016. "Private Debt and the Anglo-Liberal Growth Model." *Government and Opposition* 51: 529–52.

Becker, J., and J. Jäger. 2010. "Development Trajectories in the Crisis in Europe." *Debatte. Journal of Contemporary Central and Eastern Europe* 18: 5–27.

Bieling, H.-J. 2012. "EU Facing the Crisis: Social and Employment Policies in Times of Tight Budgets." *Transfer: European Review of Labour and Research* 18: 255–271.

Bohle, D., and A. Regan. 2019. "Business Power, Growth Models, and Politics of Comparative Capitalism: Explaining the Continuity of FDI-Led Growth in Ireland and Hungary." unpublished manuscript.

Bonoli, G. 2013. *The Origins of Active Social Policy: Labour Market and Childcare Policies in a Comparative Perspective*. Oxford: Oxford University Press.

Clasen, J., and D. Clegg. 2011. *Regulating the Risk of Unemployment: National Adaptations to Post-Industrial Labour Markets in Europe*. Oxford: Oxford University Press.

Crouch, C. 1993. *Industrial Relations and European State Traditions*. Oxford: Clarendon Press.

Crouch, C. 2009. "Privatised Keynesianism: An Unacknowledged Policy Regime." *The British Journal of Politics & International Relations* 11: 382–99.

[12] Many ideas in this chapter have originally emerged from discussions with Lucy Barnes and Marek Naczyk. I am grateful to Anke Hassel, Anna Klabunde, Deborah Mabbett, Bruno Palier, and two anonymous reviewers for their comments. This was the last academic paper that my father, Arnold Picot, read and commented on. It is therefore dedicated to him.

Eichhorst, W., O. Kaufmann, and R. Konle-Seidl (eds.). 2008. *Bringing the Jobless into Work? Experiences with Activation Schemes in Europe and the US*. Berlin & Heidelberg: Springer.

Esping-Andersen, G. 1990. *The Three Worlds of Welfare Capitalism*. Cambridge: Polity Press.

Estévez-Abe, M. 2008. *Welfare and Capitalism in Postwar Japan*. Cambridge: Cambridge University Press.

Ferrera, M. 2010. "The South European Countries." In *The Oxford Handbook of the Welfare State*, edited by Francis G. Castles, Stephan Leibfried, Jane Lewis, Herbert Obinger and Christopher Pierson, Oxford Handbooks in Politics & International Relations. Oxford: Oxford University Press, 616–29.

Hall, P.A. 2014. "Varieties of Capitalism and the Euro Crisis." *West European Politics* 37: 1223–43.

Hall, P.A., and D. Soskice (eds.). 2001. *Varieties of Capitalism: The Institutional Foundations of Comparative Advantage*. Oxford: Oxford University Press.

Iversen, T., and D. Soskice. 2012. "Modern Capitalism and the Advanced Nation State: Understanding the Causes of the Crisis." In *Coping with Crisis: Government Reactions to the Great Recession*, edited by Nancy Bermeo and Jonas Pontusson. New York: Russell Sage Foundation, 35–64.

Krippner, G.R. 2011. *Capitalizing on Crisis: The Political Origins of the Rise of Finance*. Cambridge MA: Harvard University Press.

Kvist, J. 2007. "Fuzzy Set Ideal Type Analysis." *Journal of Business Research* 60: 474–81.

Mandel, H., and M. Semyonov. 2006. "A Welfare State Paradox: State Interventions and Women's Employment Opportunities in 22 Countries." *American Journal of Sociology* 111: 1910–49.

Morel, N., B. Palier, and J. Palme, eds). 2012. *Towards a Social Investment Welfare State? Ideas, Policies and Challenges*. Bristol: Policy Press.

Naczyk, M. 2019. "Taking Back Control: Indigenous Managerial Elites' Push for State-Led Developmentalism in Poland's Dependent Market Economy." Paper presented at the 31st Annual EAEPE Conference, Warsaw, 12–15 September 2019.

Nölke, A., and A. Vliegenthart. 2009. "Enlarging the Varieties of Capitalism: The Emergence of Dependent Market Economies in East Central Europe." *World Politics* 61: 670–702.

Palier, B., ed. 2010. *A Long Goodbye to Bismarck? The Politics of Welfare Reforms in Continental Europe*. Amsterdam: Amsterdam University Press.

Perez, Sofia A., and Martin Rhodes. 2015. "The evolution and crises of the social models in Italy and Spain." In *European Social Models from Crisis to Crisis: Employment and Inequality in the Era of Monetary Integration*, edited by Jon Erik Dølvik and Andrew Martin. Oxford: Oxford University Press, 177–213.

Piketty, T. 2014. *Capital in the Twenty-First Century*. Cambridge MA: Harvard University Press.

Schneider, C.Q., and C. Wagemann. 2012. *Set-Theoretic Methods for the Social Sciences: A Guide to Qualitative Comparative Analysis*. Cambridge: Cambridge University Press.

Streeck, W. 2014. *Buying Time: The Delayed Crisis of Democratic Capitalism*. London: Verso.

Streeck, W. 2011. "The Crises of Democratic Capitalism." *New Left Review* 71: 5–29.

Toplišek, A. 2020. "The Political Economy of Populist Rule in Post-Crisis Europe: Hungary and Poland." *New Political Economy* 25: 388–403.

5

Forced Structural Convergence in the Eurozone

Fritz W. Scharpf

1. Introduction: Multilevel European Government in Comparative Policy Research

The present volume is systematically assessing the mutual effects of various types of demand-driven "growth models" and welfare state reforms under the impact of global capitalism. Given its comparative perspective, the focus is on national responses that must accommodate economic as well as social concerns, and the implicit assumption is that even after the end of the period of post-war "embedded liberalism" (Ruggie 1982), nation states have retained sufficient governing capacities to arrive at diverse but overall viable solutions. With this I generally agree (Scharpf 1991; Scharpf and Schmidt 2000).

In my more recent work, however, I have come to focus increasingly on the asymmetric impact of European legal and institutional integration on member states with different socio-economic traditions, institutions, political priorities and practices. One example is the liberalizing and deregulatory impact of the expansionary judicial interpretation of "negative integration" and the "liberties" ensuring the free movement of goods, services, establishments, capital, and persons. It hardly affects the status quo of "liberal market economies," but may destroy critical institutions, policy legacies, and practices of "coordinated market economies" (Scharpf 2010). My present contribution focuses on the asymmetric impact of the European Monetary Union and of the regime that was established in response to the euro crisis of 2010. The effect is acknowledged in the editors' introductory framework referring to Southern Europe's change from a "domestic-demand strategy" to a strategy of "competitive impoverishment" after the euro crisis of 2010. What my chapter may add to the framework is a more explicit focus on the causal importance of two specific aspects of multilevel government in the Eurozone.

The first aspect relates to a distinction in democratic theory between external constraints of the action space of democratic self-government, and external interventions violating its "non-domination" precondition (Pettit 1997; Eriksen 2018). Democracy does of course not presuppose omnipotence, and self-government

Fritz W. Scharpf, *Forced Structural Convergence in the Eurozone* In: *Growth and Welfare in Advanced Capitalist Economies: How Have Growth Regimes Evolved?* Edited by: Anke Hassel and Bruno Palier, Oxford University Press (2021).
 DOI: 10.1093/oso/9780198866176.003.0005

is not denied by having to cope even with brutal external challenges (think of Britain after Dunkirk) or with severely constrained action spaces. But self-government is incompatible with *Fremdherrschaft*—that is, with having to obey a "foreign" governing power that is not authorized by the democratic processes of the community that is governed. Below, I will try to show that the rules imposed by the post-2010 euro regime are disabling self-government in Southern, but not in Northern European polities, and that their asymmetric impact cannot be democratically legitimated on the European level.

Though legitimacy issues need not necessarily matter in a framework for empirical policy studies, it should be of interest that multilevel euro government will also affect policy outcomes in asymmetric ways. The editors' introductory framework implicitly assumes that growth strategies and welfare state reforms are interdependent, and that governments and national politics must necessarily seek solutions that accommodate economic as well as social policy concerns. But these entirely plausible background assumptions do not hold for member states under the euro regime. The regime's multilevel constitution is that of a "government of governments." All relevant governing competences and resources remain on the national level, where they are to be exercised by democratically accountable governments. But their exercise is constrained by euro rules, and it may be preempted by the hierarchical intervention of Eurozone authorities that, in attempting to stabilize the Monetary Union, are exclusively concerned with monetary and economic purposes. Since these interventions may be enforced by severe sanctions or the threat of immediate state insolvency, their impact will asymmetrically affect the balance between economic policy and welfare state reforms in ways that could not be explained by reference to economic factors and political forces operating on the national level.

Thirty years ago, the famous Cecchini Report on the "Costs of Non-Europe" (Cecchini et al. 1988) tried to assess the benefits that Europe would lose if it failed to complete the single market program by 1992. The Delors Commission presenting the report was enthusiastic about the "permanent boost to the prosperity of the people of Europe" that the Single Market would bring about (SEC (88) 524 final). Only two years later, in its own report "One Market—One Money," the Commission (1990) was equally certain of the additional economic benefits that the single currency would generate. In the meantime, we know that the EU members of 1992 have been trailing the OECD in cumulative economic growth and that since 1999 growth in the euro area (EA) has been weaker than in the rest of the EU.[1] From an economic perspective, therefore, two of the great triumphs of

[1] Cumulative economic growth 1992–2015: EU 12, 40 percent vs OECD, 49 percent; 1999–2015: EA 11, 22 percent vs EU, 26 percent (World Bank data).

Moreover, as John Weeks (2018) has recently shown, for all nineteen EA economies, extra-EU exports have risen faster than intra-EU exports between 2001 and 2017. In other words, monetary integration seems actually to have depressed internal EU trade in comparison to worldwide trade.

European integration do not appear to have been particularly successful in comparative terms.[2] But that is not my present concern.

Whereas Cecchini had looked at the potential economic costs of non-integration, I will be looking at the real politico-economic and democratic costs imposed by the monetary over-integration of structurally heterogeneous "Northern" and "Southern" political economies. Unlike its more flexible predecessor regime, the European Monetary System (EMS) of 1979, the European Monetary Union (EMU) explicitly removed or rigidly constrained national problem-solving capacities without, however, creating European capacities that could address the diversity of national economic conditions. The result was, first, a dramatic failure of economic governance resulting in the euro crisis and, then, the creation of a new euro regime which, through centralized controls over national policy choices, is meant to save the common currency by enforcing the structural convergence of EMU member states on the "Northern model." In this chapter, I will reconstruct the economic logic supporting the present asymmetric regime, highlight its extremely unequal impact, and explain the reasons for its incompatibility with democratic legitimacy on national and European levels.

2. The Monetary Union: Failure of an Asymmetric Regime

Capitalist economies are inherently unstable. But after the catastrophe of the Great Depression and World War II, capitalist states developed demand-oriented tools for macroeconomic stabilization. Even though their effectiveness had been challenged in the 1970s by the oil price and stagflation crises following the demise of the Bretton Woods regime of stabilized exchange rates (Scharpf 1991), the instruments of monetary, fiscal, and exchange rate policy were still employed by European states before they joined the EMU in 1999. In order to manage the ups and downs of national economies, governments could employ restrictive monetary policy and fiscal restraint to dampen inflationary booms; they could support economic recovery through fiscal reflation and an accommodating monetary policy; and they could also combine monetary and fiscal adjustment with changes of the exchange rate in order to correct external imbalances. None of these interventions worked perfectly, but they did allow democratically accountable governments to exercise significant influence over the economic fate of their countries.

[2] Undeterred by past performance, in 2014 the "Cecchini Revisited" report commissioned by the European Parliament promised additional economic growth of 5–8.63 percent if the remaining obstacles to market integration in the EU were to be removed (Pataki 2014).

Moreover, from 1979 to 1999, the EMS had been designed to deal with external imbalances and exchange rate fluctuations between hard- and soft-currency economies. It was meant to protect member state currencies against speculative attacks in international capital markets but also allowed agreed-upon currency realignments to correct persistent external imbalances. By and large, and until it was upset in 1992–93 by the monetary shocks following German unification (Higgins 1993; Padoa-Schioppa 1994; Marsh 2009), the EMS worked reasonably well (Artis and Taylor 1993; Helleiner 1994; Höpner and Spielau 2017). However, exchange rate realignments were politically controversial, and since the Bundesbank was exclusively focusing on price stability in Germany, other governments resented its dominance in monetary coordination—which, together with political concerns raised by German unification, provided a window of opportunity for the "integrationist" Delors Commission and its neoliberal or monetarist economic advisors to mobilize political support for its "One Market—One Money" program (McNamara 1998; Dyson and Featherstone 1999).

2.1 The EMU Destroys Existing Governing Capacities

The Monetary Union removed not only the option of currency realignment but also the capacity to influence the course of the national economy through national monetary policy. Moreover, the capacity for national fiscal expansion was practically eliminated by the Stability Pact. At the same time, however, member states were also freed from the discipline of international currency markets and the threat of balance-of-payments crises. Exchange rate and monetary policy became exclusive competences of the European Central Bank (ECB), whose institutionally protected independence was thought to be justified by its unequivocal mandate to preserve price stability in the Eurozone (Dyson 2000). This loss of national problem-solving capacity was not compensated by functionally equivalent European governing powers.

The EMU had no budget of its own and thus no capacity for countercyclical fiscal intervention. Whereas the ECB's centralized monetary policy was able to stabilize average inflation rates in the Eurozone, its "one-size-fits-all" policy instruments could not respond to structural divergence and the non-synchronized ups and downs and "asymmetric shocks" of the former hard- and soft-currency member economies. Hence, its uniform interest rates were too low for economies with higher rates of growth and inflation and too high for economies in a recession with low rates of inflation—and real interest rates diverged even more. Instead of stabilizing Eurozone economies, it deepened the recession of 2002 in low-inflation Germany and fueled credit-financed booms of consumer spending and real estate bubbles in Greece, Ireland, and Spain.

The result was a dynamic divergence of external balances in the Eurozone, where the rising current account deficits and capital imports of booming economies corresponded to the rising export surpluses and capital outflows of stagnant economies like Germany. When interbank lending came to a "sudden stop" in the International Financial Crisis of 2008/9, credit-dependent Southern economies suffered, banks faltered, and state deficits escalated as governments came to the rescue of overextended banks. In early 2010, finally, when capital markets challenged the solvency of the Greek state and seemed to threaten others, state credit crises were interpreted as a euro crisis that might ultimately endanger the European Union itself.

All this is now common knowledge (Jones et al. 2016). It is also understood that blaming the crisis on the fiscal irresponsibility of debtor governments was, at best, a half-truth for Greece and totally wrong for Ireland and Spain, where fiscal performance from 1999 to 2008 had been exemplary—and far better than in Germany. Nevertheless, the fiscal blaming frame prevailed in May of 2010, when Germany and other surplus governments (fearing the impact of Greek insolvency on their own banks and economies) decided to ignore the no bail-out rules of the Maastricht Treaty. They reluctantly provided intergovernmental rescue loans for Greece, then for Ireland and Portugal, and later for other states as well. In all these cases, loans were linked to strict "conditionalities" requiring drastic cutbacks in public expenditure—ostensibly to reduce state deficits and debt and thus the danger of future financial challenges and potential euro crises—all of which seems well explained by the constellation of national economic interests, actor perceptions, and the bargaining powers prevailing at the time (Iversen et al. 2016; Schimmelfennig 2015).

In addition to their insistence on fiscal retrenchment, the Commission (2010) and the ECOFIN Council also began to focus on the external balances of debtor states and on the role that current account deficits might have played in the crises. As these "imbalances" were reflected in greatly overvalued real effective exchange rates, their proximate cause was assumed to be a loss of international "competitiveness" generated by above-average increases of unit labor costs.[3] As a consequence, the "structural reforms" imposed on debtor states also included requirements without immediate fiscal effect, the purpose of which was to reduce unit labor costs (amounting to an "internal devaluation") through "supply-side" measures such as the liberalization of services, the deregulation of employment protection rules, the reduction of minimum and replacement wages, and the institutional weakening of unions and collective bargaining (Tsoukalis 2016).

[3] It has been shown that this supply-side explanation does not generally fit the facts (Wyplosz 2013; Sanchez and Varoudakis 2013; Jones 2016; Storm and Naastepad 2016).

2.2 The New Euro Regime: Convergence through Austerity and Supply-Side Reforms

The basic logic of the initial euro-rescuing policies, which combined financial support to avert acute state-credit crises with conditionalities imposing fiscal austerity and supply-side reforms, is maintained and generalized in the permanent euro regime that has been installed in all Eurozone states since 2011. It includes the intergovernmental European Stability Mechanism (ESM) as a permanent source of conditional emergency credits, the European Semester, the "Six Pack" and "Two Pack" legislation, the Fiscal Compact and elements of a future Banking Union. Apart from the latter, however, there is no outright creation of European capacities and governing resources that could substitute for the national macro-economic competences that were lost in the EMU.

Instead, the present euro regime must assume that the euro crisis should and could have been averted by member states using their remaining national competences—that is, without being able to correct the destabilizing impulses of uniform ECB monetary policy and without the option of currency realignment. Retrospectively and counterfactually, that implies that by practicing fiscal restraint and supply-side reforms in the years before 2008, Southern governments would have avoided credit-financed booms and the rise of external imbalances, which subsequently produced state-credit crises. Prospectively, moreover, the belief that fiscal austerity and internal devaluation would also ensure recovery from the "Great Recession" also seems to have benefited from a stylized model of recent German performance: After initially violating the deficit rule of the Stability Pact in a deep recession, the government had resorted to fiscal retrenchment, cutbacks on unemployment support, and flexible employment rules—which, in combination with union wage restraint, were believed to have soon brought about an export-led recovery (Scharpf 2018a). In other words, the new euro regime relied not only on controversial supply-side economic theory but also seemed to have some real-world plausibility.

In any case, the crisis seemed to have demonstrated that at least some Eurozone governments acting on their own could not be trusted to use their available competences in ways that were compatible with the overall stability of the Monetary Union. If the Maastricht Treaty's no bail-out clause had been applied, of course, the Greek insolvency might have provided powerful incentives for good behavior in the future (Sandbu 2015). Since the clause was ignored, and with the permanent European Stability Mechanism (ESM) in place, creditor governments and Eurozone authorities saw reason to worry about moral-hazard problems.

As enforceable "conditionalities" and Troika controls could only be imposed when a government had actually applied for rescue loans, the new regime was designed to create a system of "precautionary conditionalities." Under the "Excessive Deficit Procedure" (EDP) and the "Macroeconomic Imbalances

Procedure" (MIP), therefore, the Commission will annually assess the economic and fiscal performance of member states and issue annual country-specific recommendations that will prescribe not only national fiscal policies but may also—over the full range of member state competences—specify national action which, in its view, could help avoid the rise of external and internal imbalances in a particular economy. These recommendations, relying on persuasion and public naming and shaming in the context of the European Semester, may also be hardened into binding requirements that may ultimately be enforced through severe financial sanctions that the Council could avert only through a "reverse qualified majority" vote (Degryse 2012; Bauer and Becker 2014; Seikel 2016).

If this regime had been in place and had been rigorously enforced between 1999 and 2008, it might indeed have prevented economic overheating and the rise of external deficits in Greece, Ireland, and Spain. After 2010, however, the requirements of fiscal austerity and wage-reducing reforms were imposed on economies struggling with a deep crisis, a huge output gap, and exorbitant rates of unemployment. Why such a regime should have been politically accepted appears puzzling. Since Germany is presently doing well under these rules, it may be expected to defend the regime (Iversen et al. 2016); and since Germany and other creditor states have greater bargaining power in the informal decision processes of the ECOFIN Council's Eurogroup (Varoufakis 2015, 2017), power asymmetries are sometimes seen as a sufficient explanation (Marsh 2013; Kundnani 2014; Story 2014; Tsoukalis 2016; Steinberg and Vermeiren 2016). Even authors who put more of the blame on the misguided macroeconomic theory of the present regime and on the ill-designed institutions of the Monetary Union will trace these back to the influence of German ordo-liberalism and the long shadow of the Bundesbank (De Grauwe 2012; De Grauwe and Ji 2013; Blyth 2013; Young 2014; Stiglitz 2016; Brunnermeier et al. 2016).

That may be so, more or less.[4] What I find interesting, however, is that the EMU was not created at the demand of Germany, but by some of the best and the brightest non-German European monetary economists, such as Tommaso

[4] In fact, the French–German division of mainstream economics recorded by Brunnermeier et al. (2016) may suggest the opportunity for a fascinating sociology-of-knowledge study: Assume a structural difference between hard-currency economies cum export-led "growth models" and soft-currency economies depending on domestic-demand led growth (Baccaro and Pontusson 2016 and in this volume). And assume also that the policy recommendations of neoliberal-monetarist economics will prioritize price stability and favor supply-side structural reforms, whereas (neo- and post-) Keynesian economics favoring full employment will support demand reflating monetary, fiscal, and wage policies. Should one then be surprised that the mainstream of academic economists in Germany and its hard-currency allies in Northern and Eastern Europe is supporting austerity and supply-side rules for the EMU, whereas the academic critics of the euro regime are mainly working in Anglo-Saxon and Southern-European soft-currency countries? And if you then add the fact that the euro was to be rescued through intergovernmental credits, and the asymmetric bargaining power of creditor over debtor states, one may be less puzzled by the dominance of neoliberal ideas in the government of the Eurozone (Schmidt and Thatcher 2014a; 2014b).

Padoa-Schioppa (1994/2003), along with the Delors Commission and the governments of all countries that later joined the single currency. The present regime, moreover, is defended and justified not only by Germany and its Northern allies, but it was proposed, designed, justified, and elaborated by the Commission. It is fully supported by the ECB and has not yet been rejected even by the governments of countries suffering most under its strictures. One may surmise, therefore, that arguments supporting it may appeal not only to German economists, lawyers, central bankers, and ministers. And the catchword in those arguments appears to be "convergence."

For the "Five Presidents" of the European Union, "*the notion of convergence is at the heart of our Economic Union*"—and it has been so from the beginning (Five Presidents' Report 2015: 7). When (mainly American) economists had initially warned that Europe with its diverging economic structures was not an "optimal currency area" (e.g., Eichengreen 1990, 1992; Feldstein 1997), their empirical assessment had not been in dispute. Under the EMS, governments had been painfully aware of the divergence between hard- and soft-currency economies and the political costs of currency realignments (Höpner and Spielau 2017), while the central bankers of soft-currency economies had resented having to accommodate inflationary pressures. The Commission (1990), however, had promised that the Monetary Union itself, through greater capital mobility and more intense market competition, would soon generate the structural convergence that was indeed considered essential for the proper functioning of the common currency.

After that expectation was dramatically refuted in the first decade of the EMU,[5] the Commission (2010), the Council, and the ECB concluded that since convergence had not come about through market forces, it had to be brought about through state action. And since member states could not be trusted to take necessary action, the required measures had to be defined and enforced by a European regime. In a most remarkable document (Five Presidents' Report 2015), the presidents of the European Commission, the European Council, the European Parliament, the European Central Bank, and the Eurogroup jointly asserted that the EMU cannot reach its goals as long as the *structural* and *cyclical* divergence among Eurozone economies persists. At the same time, they implicitly acknowledged that divergent economic cycles and asymmetric shocks would indeed require some loosening of fiscal austerity at the national level and also "a mechanism of fiscal stabilization for the euro area as a whole." Nevertheless, such concessions to the need for targeted macroeconomic intervention should only be considered "*in the medium term, as economic structures converge towards the best standards in Europe*" (Five Presidents' Report 2015: 4).

[5] The "one-price" argument did more or less hold for export industries. What had been ignored was the fact that external competition would not correct the divergence of wages and prices in the large domestic sectors of Southern economies.

In the Presidents' view, therefore, the present euro regime was not designed to promote the rapid recovery of crisis economies, for which the pro-cyclical enforcement of fiscal austerity was implicitly conceded to be counterproductive. Instead, structural convergence must have priority. Hence, the present regime of fiscal austerity and wage-reducing reforms must not only be maintained; it must be reinforced and extended through an additional system of national "Competitiveness Authorities" and through an even "stronger Macroeconomic Imbalances Procedure" with legally binding "high-level standards defined in EU legislation."

2.3 Structural Differences of Northern and Southern Political Economies

In order to assess the implications of enforced structural convergence, one first ought to have a clear understanding of the type of structural differences that may affect the macroeconomic performance of Eurozone economies. Before they joined the Monetary Union, the member states of the EMS had been described as either hard- or soft-currency economies whose different inflation dynamics had resulted in periodic revaluations or devaluations of national currencies. These differences are represented by cumulative exchange rate adjustments vis-à-vis the deutsche mark (DM) in the decade before the EMS was shaken in the turbulences following German unification (Table 5.1). At that time, the hard-currency group had included Austria, Germany, the Netherlands, and Finland, whereas Greece, Portugal, Spain, and Italy appeared as the core members of a soft-currency "club med," which to a somewhat lesser extent also included France, Ireland, and Belgium.

After the Maastricht commitment to create the EMU, these differences were reduced under the influence of the accession requirements. These had specified upper limits on public sector deficits and debt, which governments might perhaps

Table 5.1 National exchange rates vs Deutschmark: Changes 1979–89 in percent

Austria	3.62
Germany	0.00
Netherlands	–2.98
Finland	–7.06
Belgium	–23.68
Ireland	–29.12
France	–31.58
Italy	–37.89
Spain	–41.87
Portugal	–68.24
Greece	–69.30

Source: Bundesbank, Fxtop, own calculations.

meet by creative budgeting. Beyond that, they required convergence to low inflation rates—whose divergence had been the proximate cause of the need for currency realignments under the EMS regime. In the end, and contrary to many expectations, all soft-currency economies were also able to meet the inflation criteria—through severely restrictive monetary policies and through the heroic efforts of governments and unions to suppress the rise of unit labor costs from the mid-1990s onward (Ferrera and Gualmini 2000, 2004; Hassel 2003). However, once accession had been achieved, national central banks lost control. Nor were the exceptional efforts to suppress inflation through social pacts maintained by governments and unions. Hence the original differences between hard- and soft-currency economies reasserted themselves.

Unlike the EMS, the EMU had no instruments that could deal with these differences. The Stability Pact provided only (weak) controls over public sector deficits but was not concerned with divergent rates of inflation. While the ECB was able to control average inflation in the Eurozone, its uniform policies could not be targeted at individual national economies—where they instead tended to generate destabilizing and divergence-enhancing pro-cyclical effects (Enderlein 2005; Enderlein et al. 2012; Geiger and Spahn 2007; but see Issing 2005). In any case, differences in national inflation rates persisted and even increased during the first decade of the EMU (Table 5.2).

At the same time, the single currency had freed EMU states from the discipline of having to defend their balance of payments. It had thereby also cut the linkage between national imports and exports which, before 1999, had generally prevented imports from running far ahead of exports, whereas runaway exports would be reined in by rising exchange rates. In the Monetary Union, by contrast, there were no automatic correctives that would prevent a persistent divergence of national imports and exports. Thus, in effect, exports tended to increase

Table 5.2 Changes of consumer price index 1999–2008 in percent

Germany	16.71
Finland	18.30
France	18.56
Austria	21.08
Netherlands	21.89
Belgium	23.31
Italy	24.17
Portugal	30.25
Spain	34.21
Greece	34.80
Ireland	42.38

Source: World Bank, own calculations.

more than imports in former hard-currency economies, whereas in former soft-currency economies the rise of imports generally exceeded that of exports (Table 5.3). The resulting rise of current account deficits in former soft-currency economies is by now considered as the root cause of the state finance crises that culminated in the euro crisis of 2010.

Under the EMS, the discussion of differences between hard- and soft-currency economies had mainly focused on government fiscal policies and accommodating or non-accommodating national monetary policies. Since monetary choices were eliminated in the EMU, the Stability Pact had focused on preventing "loose" fiscal policies alone. Hence, when the euro crisis happened nevertheless, it was quasi-automatically attributed to the "fiscal irresponsibility" of debtor states—an explanation which, though it was patently absurd for Ireland and Spain, still plays a pernicious role in justifications of the present euro regime. At around the same time, however, the Commission (2010) had more plausibly begun to focus on external imbalances and the excessive dependence of deficit economies on capital inflows as a proximate cause of the euro crisis. In its view, external deficits were the symptom of a loss in international competitiveness that had been caused by excessive increases of unit labor costs. Indeed, current accounts and unit labor costs had diverged between 1999 and 2008, and they appear to be strongly related (Figure 5.1).

Since the realignment of nominal exchange rates was no longer available, external imbalances would now have to be corrected through internal adjustment. Assuming a causal chain that started with excessive wage increases affecting domestic inflation and export prices and then current accounts, the

Table 5.3 Imports and exports in percentage of GDP (1999 and 2008)

	Imports			**Exports**		
	1999	**2008**	**Change in percent**	**1999**	**2008**	**Change in percent**
Germany	26.41	37.73	42.86	26.96	43.80	62.46
France	23.68	29.28	23.62	26.08	28.12	7.83
Italy	21.42	27.63	28.99	23.20	26.86	15.78
Ireland	73.54	75.51	2.68	86.61	84.11	-2.88
Belgium	60.61	80.21	32.34	64.56	80.88	25.27
Netherlands	54.50	61.27	12.42	59.91	69.79	16.51
Austria	38.90	48.82	25.50	39.36	53.25	35.30
Finland	28.64	41.28	44.17	37.60	44.90	19.40
Portugal	36.83	40.81	10.81	26.48	31.26	18.05
Spain	28.28	30.36	7.33	26.35	25.62	-2.76
Greece	28.12	35.97	27.90	19.26	23.36	21.32

Source: OECD National Accounts Statistics, own calculations.

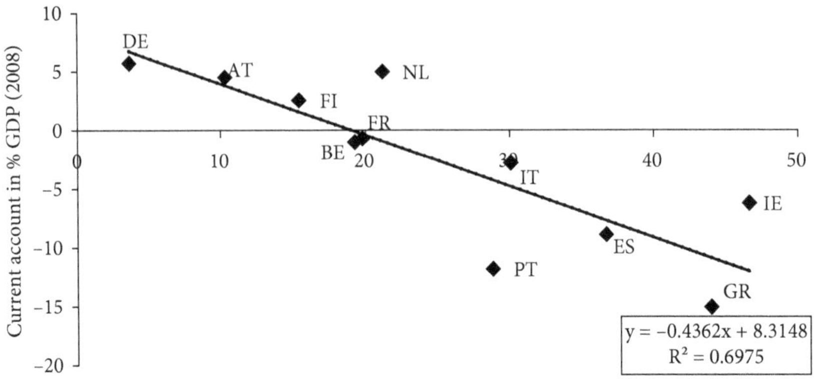

Figure 5.1 Cumulative growth of unit labor costs (1999–2008) vs current account in 2008

Source: OECD, own calculations.

Commission was quick to invoke neoliberal supply-side explanations:[6] it must be institutional "rigidities" of labor and product markets that explain the failure to reach balanced external accounts. Hence what is needed are "structural reforms" that would increase price and wage flexibility. Moreover, since current account deficits (rather than surpluses) were seen as the proximate causes of the crisis (Commission 2012a), such reforms had to be targeted at factors causing above-average increases of unit labor costs in deficit economies, rather than at the below-average increases in surplus countries like Germany. In other words, the purpose of reforms had to be "internal devaluation" and structural reforms reducing wage pressures in deficit economies.

The Commission's supply-side emphasis is also shared by a less dogmatic theoretical and empirical literature focusing on the influence of wage-setting institutions on macroeconomic performance. Calmfors and Driffil (1988; Calmfors 1993) had proposed a simple hump-shaped relationship between real-wage increases and the centralization of wage negotiations. Wage rises are expected to be comparatively low in decentralized (firm-level) bargaining, where unions cannot exercise market power.[7] And they are also expected to be comparatively low in highly centralized (economy-wide) bargaining systems, where economically rational union leaders are assumed to "internalize" the effects of wage increases on inflation and (anticipating the effect of monetary and fiscal

[6] There is also a more recent literature promoting a demand-side explanation of the euro crisis (Wyplosz 2013; Jones 2016) which, however, never gained influence on Eurozone policies.

[7] That is not generally plausible. In decentralized bargaining, wage-setting is likely to be highly volatile, with rapid rises during an upswing and rapid declines during a downswing of the economy, and it will be highly unequal, with steep rises in regions, sectors, and skill groups where demand is high. This, apparently, is the ideal pursued by "structural reforms" imposed by the Commission and the Troika on the labor markets of crisis economies.

restraint) on unemployment. By contrast, wage-push inflation is expected from an intermediate level of centralization, where union leaders exercising bargaining power in smaller units are assumed to ignore the external effects of wage settlements on the rest of the economy.

The model is useful because it attempts to explain macroeconomic differences as the outcome of strategic choices by rational and self-interested collective actors (union leaders, in this case) under the influence of nationally differing institutional settings.[8] In other words, it tries to explain the presence or absence of a national *capacity*[9] *for voluntary wage restraint.*[10] In its original form, however, the model is incomplete in two regards: it does not explicitly model the dual and potentially conflicting utility functions of union leaders—who must try to raise the incomes but also protect the existing jobs of their members—and its implicit focus is on expanding economies, where jobs are not directly threatened. In such cases, the rise of inflation may indeed be treated as a "collective bad" whose avoidance presupposes a centralized capacity to overcome collective-action problems among a plurality of bargaining units. In a declining economy with rising unemployment, however, the threat of job losses will be experienced as a "private bad" by individual workers—which should induce unions to accept wage concessions regardless of the degree of centralization (Scharpf 1991).[11] This latter omission may also explain the model's lack of attention to the crucial difference of union responses in the exposed (traded) or sheltered (non-traded) sectors of the economy.

In the sheltered sector, where goods and services are locally produced and locally consumed, wages affect the costs of production as well as household incomes and potential domestic demand. To some extent, therefore, rising unit labor costs may result in price increases that can be passed on to consumers without endangering profits and employment. In the exposed sector (and under fixed exchange rates), however, price increases are constrained by international competition. Hence, increases of unit labor costs above the international level are likely to entail job losses, either because of a loss of export sales or, if prices are maintained, because of a loss of profitability. Regardless of the size of bargaining units, rational unions in the exposed sector are therefore always bargaining in the shadow of international competition and of potential job losses. They should

[8] It should go without saying that all rational-choice models of collective bargaining are associated with huge *ceteris paribus* clauses. They can help to formulate and criticize expectations about general tendencies, but they cannot predict, or be "tested" by, the outcomes of specific interactions under historically contingent conditions (Scharpf 1997).

[9] Whether an existing capacity is actually exercised depends also on the political context. As long as governments were thought to prioritize and protect full employment, the interest in real wage increases shaped union strategies even in the highly centralized Swedish system of the 1970s (Scharpf 1991: ch. 6).

[10] Compulsory wage controls were tried and failed in the 1960s and 1970s (Scharpf 1991: ch. 5).

[11] With Keynesian beliefs, a centralized union may in fact try to dampen the macroeconomic decline by stabilizing wage incomes and domestic demand, whereas decentralized bargaining units would deepen the recession through downward wage competition.

thus be expected to be generally more cautious in their wage demands than sheltered-sector unions that have less reason to fear the loss of existing jobs.

Since all economies include both sectors, mere differences in the relative sizes of their exposed and sheltered sectors should thus have an effect on the general propensity to generate wage-push inflation. Moreover, rational unions in a fully centralized system would not merely attempt to dampen the rise of inflation in the domestic economy; they would also have to balance the benefits of general wage increases against the possibility of job losses in the exposed sector. By contrast, in a decentralized system of wage-setting with smaller bargaining units, unions in the sheltered sector should generally be expected to seek higher wage increases than unions in export industries. But since intersectoral spillovers might affect export prices, export-sector unions should also have an interest in formal or informal wage coordination across sectors (Driffil 2006; Hancké 2013).

This suggests that any model trying to explain the persistence of above-average and below-average increases of unit labor costs by reference to national wage-setting structures should include two dimensions: institutional differences in the capacity of unions to achieve voluntary wage restraint, and differences in the relative size of the exposed and the sheltered sectors.

With regard to the first dimension, several decades of comparative research in the neocorporatist and the varieties-of-capitalism frameworks have provided a rich source of theory and evidence that enables one to assess the capacity for either centralized or coordinated strategic wage-setting in the industrial-relations systems of Eurozone economies (Scharpf 1991; Hall and Soskice 2001; Hancké 2013; Höpner and Lutter 2018; Nölke 2016). The potential for centralized wage-setting used to be highest in Scandinavian political economies and in Austria, whereas Belgium, the Netherlands, and Germany were generally regarded as systems with a potential capacity for inter-sectoral wage coordination.[12] While union density has gone down everywhere, export-sector unions continue to be relatively strong. In Anglo-Saxon economies, by contrast, coordination is impeded by competition between small unions, and in Southern political economies, unions tend to be divided by political affiliation, and union density and politicization tend to be greatest in the public sector. Hence, political inter-union conflicts will stand in the way of voluntary wage coordination—except that the extreme weakness of export-sector unions in France does facilitate a stronger role of the state in wage-setting.

The second dimension is implied in recent work on the difference between export-led and domestic-demand-led national "growth models" (Hall 2014; Johnston and Regan 2016; Baccaro and Pontusson 2016; Hope and Soskice 2016). What matters most in the present context is the pragmatic implication that the economic effect of export-led growth depends critically on the relative size

[12] But as Donato Di Carlo (2018) is showing, that does not apply to Germany after the 1990s, when public sector wages actually lagged behind industrial wage increases.

of the export sector.[13] If it is large, wage restraint and the rise of exports may indeed pull the economy out of a recession, whereas the increase of exports alone may not do much for an economy that depends on growth in a large sheltered sector (see Johnston in this volume).

Taking the share of exports in GDP in 1989 and 1999 as a proxy measure,[14] one finds that the relative sizes of the exposed and sheltered sectors varied greatly in Western Europe. Among the smaller Eurozone economies, there is a striking difference between Belgium, the Netherlands, and Ireland with very large export sectors, Austria and Finland with relatively large export sectors, and Greece, Spain, and Portugal, where the export sectors are quite small.[15] Larger economies have generally smaller shares of exports and imports than do small economies, but Germany was moving ahead of France and Italy in the 1980s (Table 5.4).

In combination, these dimensions suggest a fourfold table with clear implications for wage-driven inflation dynamics: economies with a large exposed sector and wage-setting institutions that allow voluntary wage restraint should be expected

Table 5.4 Exports in percentage of GDP (1979, 1989, 1999)

	1979	1989	1999
Germany	25.19	31.51	26.96
France	20.72	21.66	26.08
Italy	22.39	18.52	23.20
Ireland	44.46	58.86	86.61
Belgium	49.92	63.57	64.56
Netherlands	47.86	55.03	59.91
Austria	30.88	35.02	39.36
Finland	29.58	23.02	37.60
Portugal	21.20	29.47	26.48
Spain	13.70	16.60	26.35
Greece	15.17	15.95	19.26

Source: Ameco, World Bank.

[13] To be clear: both economies with large and small exposed sectors may be equally viable internationally, as long as export incomes are sufficient to pay for the country's imports. But in a recession, only countries with a large export sector can hope to achieve economic *recovery* through strategies favoring export-led *growth*.

[14] The proxy is incomplete, since the definition of the exposed or traded sector refers to production not only for export but also for domestic consumption in competition with imports. In effect, therefore, the relative size of the exposed sector is larger than the export share of GDP.

[15] The question, which I will not pursue here, is what may explain the initial differences among economies of similar size. In Southern Europe, a potential influence may be the long shadow of fascist (and protectionist) "state corporatism" (Schmitter 1974). By contrast, the rise and persistence of export-led growth in the "small open economies" (Katzenstein 1985) of Northern Europe probably started from an initial endowment in goods and services with a large international market (timber and pulp, iron ore, steel and shipbuilding, trading and shipping, etc.) and a subsequent emphasis on high value-added portfolios that were internationally attractive but also vulnerable to changes in external markets (Wierts et al. 2013; Storm 2016).

	Large export sector	Large domestic sector
Wage coordination possible	(1) Northern	(2) Germany
Voluntary Wage Coordination	(4) Ireland	(3) Southern

Figure 5.2 Characteristics of Northern and Southern political economies

to avoid inflationary wage push (Figure 5.2). By contrast, economies with a large sheltered sector and with fragmented or competing unions should tend to generate above-average increases of unit labor costs. With this classification, two of the fields correspond roughly to the earlier distinction between hard- and soft-currency economies, which in the present discussion are also described as Northern and Southern political economies.

In Field (1) we find former hard-currency economies that had large export sectors and coordinated wage-setting in the decades before 1999. That clearly includes the Netherlands, Belgium, Austria, and Finland. By contrast, Field (3) describes economies with a relatively small export sector and relatively high wage pressures, including Greece, Spain, Portugal, as well as Italy and France, countries that had also been members of the former soft-currency group. But there are two countries that do not seem to fit the pattern: Ireland and Germany.

Structurally, Ireland should be located in Field (4), combining a very large export sector (due to its position as the gateway to Europe for US multinationals) with British-style decentralized and inflation-prone industrial relations. In the run-up to the Monetary Union, wage pressures had been dampened by temporary "social pacts" and costly government policy concessions (Hassel 2003; Regan 2011). After accession, social pacts ended and wage push was further stimulated by an unimpeded boom in the real estate and construction industries. Once the bubble burst and employment collapsed in the crisis, the decentralized wage-setting system also facilitated a dramatic fall of unit labor costs—which in the meantime has in fact contributed to export-led recovery of the Irish economy.

More interesting for theory and more important in practice is the German case. In line with other large economies, which generally have less trade than smaller ones, the relative size of the German export sector was quite moderate until the mid-1980s, at about the same level as that of the UK and not much higher than in France, and Italy. By reference to its economic structure, it should thus also have pursued a domestic demand-led growth strategy. If it nevertheless appears as the extreme case of a hard-currency economy, this cannot be explained by its industrial-relations system—where wage-setting is not centralized but determined at the sectoral level and where public sector unions have at times launched very aggressive wage campaigns (Scharpf 1991). What has mattered consistently, however, is the stability orientation of the independent Bundesbank which responded with rigorous monetary restraint to all inflationary impulses, whether originating from wage increases in the exposed or sheltered sectors, from public sector deficits, or from oil price hikes—with no regard to its impact on economic growth or unemployment. In effect, the wage-setting practices of German unions were thus forced to resemble those appropriate to export-led growth strategies—except that expected growth effects were constrained by dramatic DM revaluation in the 1970s and by EMS currency realignments in the 1980s. In the end, Germany had the hardest currency but experienced neither export-led nor domestic-demand led economic growth in the seventies and the eighties (Scharpf 2018a).

But why did the German hard-currency wage-setting practices continue when the Bundesbank finally lost its punitive power after the country entered into the Monetary Union? There is a long answer to this question (Scharpf 2018a). The short one is, simply, that for the first time since the end of the Bretton Woods regime, these practices were rewarded by the EMU, rather than frustrated by currency realignments. Thus, the exceptional rise of German exports which had begun in the mid-1990s[16] was not dampened, and imports were not stimulated, by a rise of the exchange rate. Hence the Monetary Union had the effect of transforming the sectoral structure of the German economy from one with the appropriately small export sector of a large European economy to a different one where the share of the domestic sector has shrunk and where the export sector has increased to a size that used to be characteristic of small open economies (Figure 5.3).

Since Germany has now also come to fit the pattern defined in Field (1) of Figure 5.2, Eurozone economies can be described by one of two structural patterns: Northern economies, structurally defined by the combination of a large export sector with an institutional capacity for wage restraint, include Germany, Austria, the Netherlands, Belgium, Finland, and presently Ireland as well, whereas Southern economies, which combine a large domestic sector with industrial relations systems that tend to generate wage-push inflation, include not only Greece, Spain, and Portugal but also Italy and France. In the literature, this

[16] The rise of the German export share starting in the mid-1990s is best explained by the expansion of international demand for German investment goods after the fall of the Berlin Wall and by the opportunities to outsource the production of components to low-wage regions with skilled industrial work forces in Central and Eastern Europe (Marin 2006; Geishecker 2006; Dustmann et al. 2014). Both of these factors also benefited Austria, but they could not be exploited to the same extent by the UK, France, and Italy.

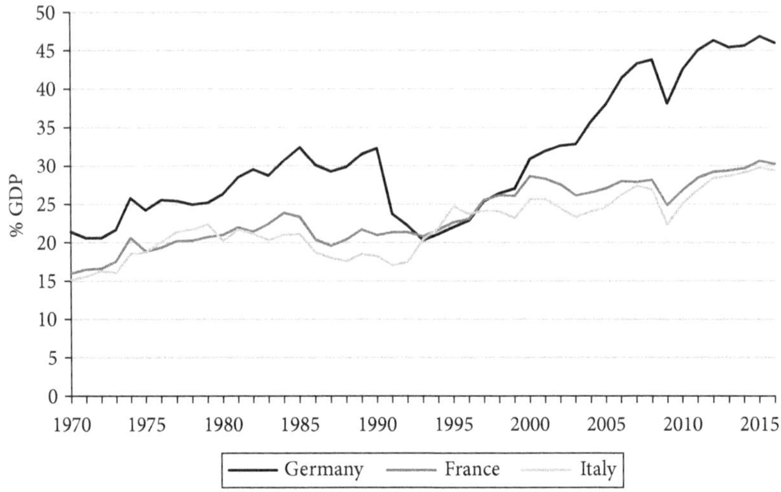

Figure 5.3 Exports in percentage of GDP for Germany, France, Italy (1970–2016)
Source: Ameco, World Bank, own calculations.

division is sometimes associated with deep cultural differences between a "Germanic" and a "Latin" Europe (Agamben 2013), but the "North–South" distinction is also used without cultural connotations by political economists like Torben Iversen and his colleagues (Iversen et al. 2016).

At this point, and with a better understanding of the nature and the hardness of structural (sectoral and institutional) differences among Eurozone economies, we return to the question raised at the end of the last section. After 1999, the impact of the uniform regime of the original Monetary Union on member states with persistent structural differences caused the dramatic economic divergence that culminated in the euro crisis of 2010. Since the new euro regime, which was put in place after 2011 to stabilize the EMU, is once more imposing uniform rules on Eurozone economies that continue to be structurally different, its immediate impact will again be asymmetric. The question is therefore whether it will also founder on the hard rock of these structural differences, or whether it will ultimately achieve the structural convergence on which not only the report of the Five Presidents but all "integrationist" manifestos and plans must place their hope.

3. The Asymmetric Impact of the Present Euro Regime

Since the euro crisis started as a state solvency crisis, it was perhaps inevitable that initial responses, and the conditionalities attached to bail-out loans, emphasized fiscal retrenchment. And since the crises occurred in economies whose current account deficits had made them vulnerable to external financial challenges, it seemed also plausible to impose structural reforms intended to achieve "internal devaluation" by reducing unit labor costs (Schimmelfennig 2015). But it is much less plausible that the Commission, the ECB, and Eurozone governments—in their search for a long-term regime that would attain "*what EMU was to be: a place of prosperity based on balanced economic growth and price stability, a competitive social market economy, aiming at full employment and social progress*" (Five Presidents 2015: 4)—should simply have generalized the immediate crisis responses of fiscal restraint and supply-side reforms without systematically considering their impact on structurally heterogeneous Eurozone economies. It appears, however, that they have done just that.

Apart from the banking union, the new regime has not yet created any additional European capacities for macroeconomic management. The Excessive Deficit Procedure and the Fiscal Compact have tightened the rules limiting public sectors deficits and debt, they have greatly extended the Commission's supervisory, preventive, and corrective authority to intervene in national policy choices, and they have strengthened its independence from the Council when enforcing its recommendations through severe financial sanctions. The common thrust of these rules is on fiscal restraint. There is no recognition, in other words, that a fiscal stimulus might be required in a recession. Similarly, the Commission's (2012b) "Scoreboard" for the Macroeconomic Imbalances Procedure defines limits for external deficits more restrictively (at 4 percent of GDP) than for external surpluses (at 6 percent of GDP). And it only defines upper limits for private sector credit and debt, house prices, and changes of unit labor cost, but is not concerned with the possibly deflationary effects of public and private sector savings, declining property values, or the possibility of excessive wage restraint. The main emphasis is on reducing unit labor costs in order to improve international competitiveness—and thus to achieve export-led economic growth (Commission 2012c).[17]

These policies had highly asymmetric impacts on Northern and Southern economies that were struggling to recover from the "Great Recession" of 2009/10 under the constraints of a single currency. Their combination of fiscal consolidation and wage restraint did support the "flight into exports" through which Northern countries with large export sectors and with a capacity for voluntary wage restraint have tended to respond to economic downturns or even deep crises like those in Sweden in the early 1990s or in Germany in the early 2000s. But their immediate economic effects were catastrophic in Southern economies whose export sectors were too small to generate much economic growth, whereas their

[17] In the frame of supply-side economics, one might also hope to achieve a profit-led rise of investments in the sheltered sector of the economy—an argument, however, that is not explicitly invoked by the Commission or the Five Presidents in their justification of the euro regime.

large domestic sector was pushed even deeper into recession by the combination of fiscal austerity and wage depression.

Policy response to a recession	North (Export/domestic sector: 70:30)		South (Export/domestic sector: 25:75)	
	Export Sector	Domestic Sector	Export Sector	Domestic Sector
Fiscal & wage reflation	Large Losses	Small Gains	Small Losses	Large Gains
Fiscal & wage restraint	Large Gains	Small Losses	Small Gains	Large Losses

Figure 5.4 Divergent North/South impacts of expansionary and restrictive policies

The asymmetry is illustrated in Figure 5.4 by reference to ideal-type Northern and Southern economies (resembling the Netherlands and Spain, respectively, in 2008). It assumes that in response to the "Great Recession" both countries could have chosen one of two responses—either to reflate domestic demand in order to generate growth in the domestic sector or to reduce prices and wages to increase external competitiveness and exports. In the Netherlands, demand reflation would have had little effect on the small domestic sector,[18] whereas a decline of international competitiveness might have damaged the large export sector. In Spain, by contrast, the large domestic sector would have benefited from demand reflation, whereas fiscal austerity and wage depression would have deepened the domestic recession without generating much export-led growth.

If both types of member states had been able to enact their nationally preferred policies after the immediate euro crisis was resolved, however, economic divergence in the Eurozone would have escalated once more, and the next crisis might well have destroyed the Monetary Union.[19] Instead of seeking a compromise solution (which was probably not available), the new euro regime took sides: its rules imposing fiscal austerity and supply-side reforms on all Eurozone economies are those that Northern governments would have chosen for themselves in light of the structural opportunities and constraints of their own political economies. At the same time, they are also the rules which no autonomous and politically accountable Southern government should have chosen in response to a deep

[18] Fiscal reflation, in particular, would be inefficient for small open economies, as most of the deficit spending would spill out into increasing imports, rather than boosting the domestic economy.

[19] That caveat also applies to suggestions that the euro crisis should have been averted by the ECB acting as a lender of last resort (De Grauwe 2013), and to proposals for risk-sharing solutions to deal with "asymmetric shocks" affecting individual Eurozone economies (Schelkle 2017)—which have been accorded political priority in the Commission's (2017) *Reflection Paper on the Deepening of the Economic and Monetary Union* and in present policy debates. These proposals might suffice to avert acute crises of state finance. But if structural divergence should persist, the governments of soft-currency economies would still need to be prevented from adopting the reflationary fiscal policies that would be most appropriate for their type of economic structures.

economic crisis and in light of the structural constraints of its political economy. In short, the economic impact of the present euro regime is fundamentally asymmetric. It fits the structural preconditions and economic interests of Northern economies, and it conflicts with the structural conditions of Southern political economies—which it condemns to long periods of economic decline, stagnation, or low growth.

Eight years after the beginning of the euro crisis, the euro regime has in fact succeeded in eliminating the current account deficits, and it could also take credit for dampening the rise of unit labor costs in Southern economies (Table 5.5). As a consequence, export shares of GDP have risen, but while Ireland, with its very large export sector, seems to be on the road to export-led recovery, GDP in Southern economies has hardly risen above, or is still lower than the pre-crisis level of 2008. In any case, employment rates have declined significantly, and unemployment is still excessively high in Greece and Spain. Moreover, fiscal austerity has reduced domestic demand and economic activity in the domestic sector to such an extent that public sector debt was not reduced but actually continued to increase in all Southern states after 2010.

By contrast, Northern economies and Germany in particular seem to have done much better under the post-crisis regime.[20] In international debates, the asymmetric impact of the present euro regime is increasingly recognized, and many critics are quick to explain it as a consequence of hardball bargaining by Germany and its Northern allies. As I suggested above, that may explain responses at the onset of the euro crisis, but not necessarily the design of the subsequent euro regime. In any case, the asymmetric distribution of bargaining power would have changed if Southern governments, individually or as a group, had been willing to question their membership in the Monetary Union—which would have threatened not only some big French and German banks but also the advantages which export-dependent Northern economies have been deriving from the single currency (Scharpf 2014).

In actual fact, however, not only Northern governments, but all European authorities—the Commission, the ECB, and the European Parliament—and also all Southern governments and their parliaments were and still are committed to maintain the Monetary Union. This suggests that the regime is still seen as serving the overriding purpose of defending the common currency and preventing another euro crisis. From that perspective, however, the initial asymmetry of euro-rescuing policies may well have been inevitable. Putting it bluntly, the proximate cause of the euro crisis was not current account surpluses, but the vulnerability of externally over-indebted economies to financial challenges

[20] The relatively weak performance of the Dutch economy was due to the collapse of a housing boom, and Finland suffered from weak Russian demand and from the failure of Nokia, which was a major part of its export sector.

Table 5.5 Economic performance (2008–18)

	Current account in % GDP		Employment rate	Public debt in % GDP	Exports in % GDP	Cumulative GDP growth	Cumulative growth of ULC
	2008	2018	Changes 2008–2018 in percent				
Germany	5.69	7.35	8.27	−0.24	8.26	14.99	25.45
Netherlands	4.98	10.84	3.04	4.40	20.82	11.71	14.99
Austria	4.49	2.33	3.11	21.06	4.71	12.28	25.87
Finland	2.55	−1.37	1.44	81.20	−14.12	3.20	21.82
France	−0.70	−0.64	0.65	48.02	11.44	9.88	16.30
Belgium	−1.01	−0.99	3.29	15.32	2.10	13.40	18.21
Italy	−2.81	2.60	−0.21	30.82	17.09	−4.26	16.02
Ireland	−6.24	8.95	−1.44	58.49	45.43	55.05	−25.94
Spain	−8.90	1.94	−3.22	140.59	37.05	5.38	1.33
Portugal	−11.83	0.40	2.46	63.54	39.22	2.54	4.43
Greece	−15.11	−2.83	−10.62	64.26	54.65	−23.89	0.74

Source: OECD, World Bank, own calculations.

(Council of Europe 2011, §4). Since these were arising in Southern member states, the measures were targeted at the manifest deficiencies in their performance.

And once the initial requirements of fiscal retrenchment and supply-side wage compression for the crisis states were in place, the subsequent euro regime was largely shaped by path-dependence. Changing the rules to allow fiscal reflation in unreformed Southern states would again have increased public sector deficits and the risk spreads of their state bonds. And even if expansion were to be financed through Eurobonds, rising domestic demand would again increase imports, current account deficits, and the dependence on sustained capital inflows. At the same time, relaxing the downward pressures on unit labor costs would have prevented the intended improvements of export competitiveness. In other words, changing the original approach would have counteracted the program that had just been imposed on crisis countries and, perhaps even more important, would have meant having to deny the economic assumptions and expectations on which these conditionalities had been based.

So, if the Monetary Union was to be maintained, and if both the structural divergence of Northern and Southern economies and the starting date of the euro crisis in 2010[21] are taken as givens, the asymmetric direction of the initial euro rescuing policies and their continuation in the present euro regime appear to have been pretty much inevitable. But that will, of course, not ensure the regime's economic and political sustainability over the longer term.

4. The Political Economy of Forced Convergence

Under the present regime, the prospects for Southern economies, societies, and polities are dismal indeed. Whereas Ireland, with its large export sector, is recovering from the crisis and Spain is benefiting from the decline of other Mediterranean tourist regions, even rigorous demand and wage depression allowed at best slow economic and employment gains in other economies that continue to depend primarily on a large domestic sector. In other words, almost a decade after the beginning of the crisis, economic stagnation and underemployment in the South are still continuing. But what about the longer term?

[21] If the structural divergence of Northern and Southern economies had not been ignored in the original design of the Monetary Union, a euro regime with a starting date of 1999 might have been more symmetrical. Instead of budget deficits, it could have taken inflation differentials as its target variable. And as national fiscal and wage policies were the only remaining instruments for the macroeconomic management on the national level, low-inflation member states in a recession like Germany might have been allowed, or even required, to reflate fiscally, whereas high-growth Ireland and Spain would have had to practice fiscal austerity and wage restraint even though their budgets were in surplus. Whether such a differentiating and flexible regime would have been politically feasible before, and economically sustainable after 1999 is, of course, uncertain. It seems obvious, however, that it could not have been introduced as a response to the crisis of 2010.

4.1 Forced Convergence May Work

The Five Presidents' Report (2015) insisted that a viable Monetary Union presupposes structural convergence among Eurozone economies, and it appeared to assume that the consistent and persistent enforcement of the present euro regime will in fact achieve it. By implication, this belief is also shared by Southern governments, all of whom—with the possible exception of the Italian coalition in government between Spring 2018 and summer 2019—remain committed to the Monetary Union, regardless of the economic and social damages imposed by the euro regime. They might prefer more flexible and symmetric enforcement, but since the Northern economies seem to be doing well under the EMU, whereas Southern economies are slow in recovering, the direction of the structural change seems not in question. In that sense, Agamben (2013) is right: the present euro regime must indeed be seen as an effort to impose a "Germanic" socioeconomic model on "Latin" societies.[22] And the rules and precepts imposed by the present regime appear to be designed for this purpose.

That is obviously the function of past and present requirements for structural reforms intended to inhibit the rise of unit labor costs[23] and thus to increase export competitiveness through "internal devaluation." What is less obvious, however, is the crucial role of fiscal austerity in the structural transformation of Southern economies. It is often condemned for its negative impact on domestic economies (De Grauwe and Ji 2013; Blyth 2013; Stiglitz 2016), or considered economically irrational since it did not even succeed in reducing public sector debt (Krugman 2012, 2013). Paradoxically, however, it is precisely this apparent failure that points to austerity's most effective contribution to structural convergence: by reducing domestic demand, fiscal retrenchment has not only helped cut imports and thus current account deficits, but it is actually shrinking the size of the domestic sector. Capacities that are underemployed will disappear as firms go bankrupt and skilled workers are laid off. Thus, even if exports would not be increased much by wage depression, the *relative* size of the export sector will increase as the domestic sector is reduced through the continuing decline or stagnation of domestic demand. This effect is most obvious in Greece, where GDP declined by 23.9 percent between 2008 and 2018, whereas the share of exports in GDP increased by 54.7 percent (Table 5.5 above).

[22] This is not necessarily a concern of Northern governments. Germany had originally envisaged a smaller and structurally more coherent Monetary Union (Schäuble and Lamers 1994) and might still prefer it today if the transition could be managed in an orderly way. But the defense of inclusive membership appears to be a crucial concern of Eurozone authorities and of modernizing elites in the South who—ever since Mitterrand's conversion to *franc-fort* policies after 1983—seem to have resented the soft-currency character of their own political economies.

[23] From what has been explained above, however, it follows that "reforms" meant to reduce union power and to increase wage competition can, at best, bring about more wage flexibility but not the capacity for wage restraint that is characteristic of Northern political economies.

If fiscal austerity and the downward pressure on unit labor costs are maintained and if the relative size of the domestic sector is shrinking, this also implies that the economic basis of the characteristic Southern "growth model" is eroding. Moreover, as the relative and absolute size of the exposed sector increases, so will the share of the total labor force whose jobs are directly affected by international competition. Even if wage-setting institutions should not change, the generally lower wage pressures in the exposed sector are thus likely to dampen average wage-push inflation in the economy at large. By the same token, the rising share of workers and firms with an interest in export-led economic growth is also likely to have an effect on the politics of industrial policy. In other words, under the impact of the euro regime, Southern political economies should gradually come to approximate the structural characteristics of the Northern model—with a relatively large sector that is exposed to international competition and with wage-setting practices that are less prone to generating wage-push inflation.

In purely economic terms, therefore, enforced structural convergence does not appear impossible in principle. It may succeed in the long run if the present regime is enforced long enough and if it is not derailed through another crisis in the Eurozone or in the global economy. In that sense, the present euro regime should be seen as a technocratic gamble with huge economic uncertainties—on which I will not speculate here. But it seems interesting to question the attractiveness of the goal if it could be approximated.

4.2 Is the Prize Worth Winning?

Critics of the present euro regime often suggest that the target of convergence on the Northern model is self-contradictory for the Eurozone as a whole. Not all economies could aspire to be like Germany because not all could run current account surpluses at the same time (e.g., Krugman 2012). Now it is true enough that any trade surplus must be matched by a deficit somewhere else in the world. But if convergence were achieved, the Eurozone itself would operate as a large integrated economy whose exchanges with the rest of the world are moderated by an exchange rate. And if we then assume that it will continue to be governed by the present precepts of fiscal restraint and wage restraint, it would operate like the German economy did during the period of flexible exchange rates from the end of the Bretton Woods regime in the early 1970s to the run-up to the Monetary Union in the early 1990s. During that period, Germany was, only exceeded by Switzerland, the paradigmatic hard-currency and low-inflation economy. Nevertheless, German current accounts, though generally in surplus, were rarely rising significantly faster than imports between 1970 and 1999 (Figure 5.5), and the German export share of GDP rose only slowly and roughly in parallel to other European economies of similar size (Figure 5.3 above).

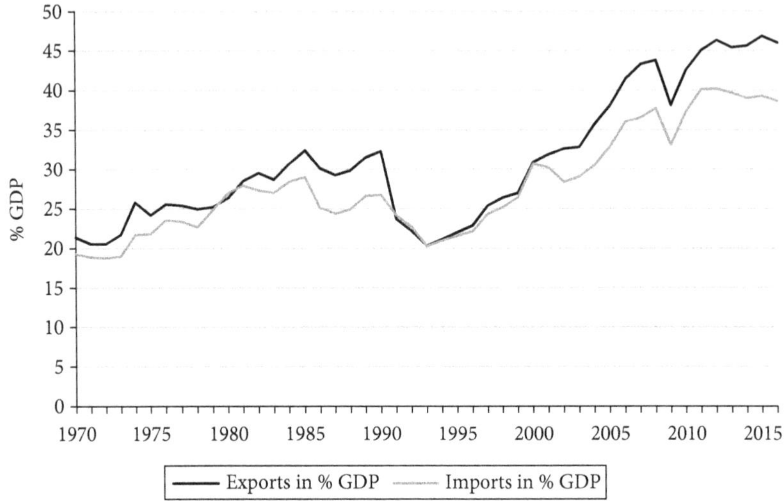

Figure 5.5 Exports and imports in percentage of GDP for Germany (1970–2016)
Note: Up to 1990 data refer to West Germany.
Source: Ameco, own calculations.

In other words, hard-currency policies will be able to increase competitiveness (and have the effect of beggar-thy-neighbor practices) only under conditions where exchange rate adjustments are delayed or totally ruled out among the members of a monetary union. For Germany in the 1970s and early 1980s, however, the competitive advantages that unions might have expected to achieve through wage restraint were neutralized through automatic or agreed-upon exchange rate realignments. Hence, unless the ECB would be willing and able to intervene in international currency markets to achieve a significant and sustained undervaluation of the euro, any advantages which a convergent Eurozone might expect from emulating Germany would also be neutralized by changes of the euro exchange rate.

What would be different if structural convergence were achieved is the wider range of options available to EMU-wide macroeconomic policy. In Germany, the Bundesbank's uncompromising commitment to price stability did not only constrain union wage policy and government fiscal policy (Scharpf 1991: ch. 7) but also meant that it was slow in fighting recessions and quick in capping recovery (Schettkat and Sun 2009). Thus it not only constrained the rise of domestic demand but also imposed a stop–go pattern on domestic investments that limited the expansion of productive capacity. In effect, what Germany gained from its stability policies was only price stability—combined with the pride of having a hard currency and cheap vacations abroad. But in comparison to its less rigid European neighbors, it paid for it with lower economic growth (Figure 5.6 below; Scharpf 2018a).

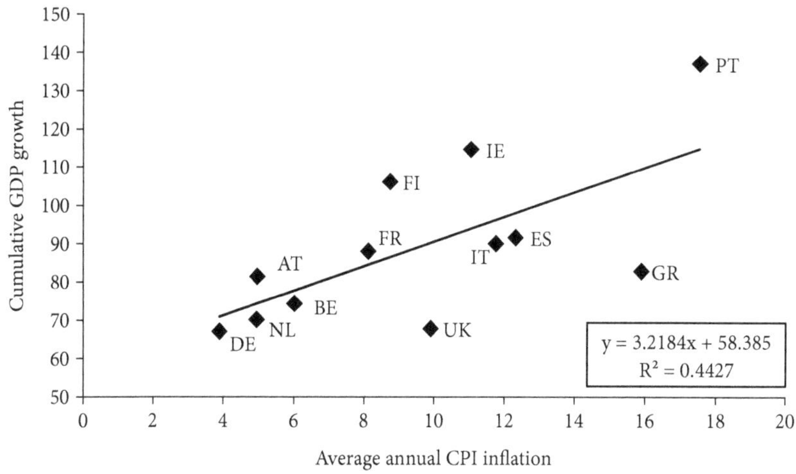

Figure 5.6 Inflation vs cumulative GDP growth, EA11 and UK, 1970–89
Source: World Bank, OECD, own calculations.

In the present context, these reminiscences have two implications. If the Monetary Union were to achieve structural convergence on the Northern model and if the present euro regime were to continue unchanged, then the economic course of the Eurozone as a whole should resemble the German performance in the 1970s and 1980s. The effects of price stability and wage restraint on international competitiveness would be neutralized by a rising euro exchange rate, and the present headline promise of export-led economic growth would be frustrated. But as the euro would then be a hard currency, its stability in international financial markets should be secure.

However, as a very large and structurally more coherent economy that is linked to its international environment through flexible exchange rates, the Eurozone would not *have to* repeat the German experience of the 1970s and 1980s. A future euro regime might instead aim at somewhat less price stability and more economic growth, perhaps approximating the position of France in Figure 5.6. This had been Mitterrand's hope when he insisted on the Monetary Union. Although the hope was unrealistic for the heterogeneous Eurozone of 1999, it might be realized after structural convergence—just as the Five Presidents (2015) had envisaged countercyclical national and European fiscal policies after convergence.

To conclude, the present euro regime amounts to an attempt to enforce the structural convergence of Eurozone economies based on the Northern model. In purely economic terms, this may not be strictly impossible. If convergence should be achieved, it would not only stabilize the common currency but might also allow more attractive macroeconomic options to be realized in the Eurozone. In contrast to some of their critics, such as Paul Krugman (2012), Marc Blyth (2013), or Joseph Stiglitz (2016), I thus do not consider the promoters and defenders of the present euro regime to be either ignorant or dogmatically blindfolded. They should at least be given credit for constructing a gigantic, and indeed hubristic, experiment in technocratic social engineering whose visionary goal is the creation of an integrated European economy that is fit for competition in the ever more contested global markets.

5. A Disaster of Political Legitimacy

But if the present euro regime could be considered as an economic gamble that might succeed if it is not busted by another crisis, it must also be seen as an equally uncertain political gamble whose failure might destroy the Monetary Union. The political risk arises from the extremely unequal distribution of the economic, social, and moral costs of structural convergence. Whereas the perceived financial risks of rescue credits were (reluctantly) legitimated in creditor states, the burdens of Southern adjustment were not freely chosen by democratically accountable national governments, and the European-level governmnt that imposed them was and is immunized against the risks of democratic accountability.

5.1 Legitimacy on the National Level

The fundamental legitimacy problem of the present euro regime is the asymmetry of its impact. In Northern member states, export-led models of economic growth are profiting from fixed exchange rates in the EMU, and the rules of the euro regime are generally compatible with the preferences of dominant national interests, including unions in export industries. As there is no shared sense of economic and social decline ascribed to the EMU, its *output legitimacy* is not in question. Since the euro regime is compatible with the existing institutions and practices of hard-currency political economies, there is also no sense of a manifest external interference with the autonomy of national self-government (Walter 2016). That does not rule out dissatisfaction with the ECB's low-interest policy and worries about the anticipated liability for bail-out loans, which may be politically exploited by protest parties. And even if left-wing political parties are blaming the rise of domestic social inequality on fiscal austerity and supply-side reforms, these are challenged and publicly defended as contestable policy choices of politically accountable national governments. Hence they will not disrupt the *input-oriented* legitimating mechanisms of representative democracy on the national level.

In Southern political economies, by contrast, any claims to *output-oriented* legitimacy were undermined by the fact that the euro regime was interfering with their institutionally entrenched growth models. Since they were prevented from reflating domestic demand, the impact on their large domestic sectors was entirely negative, with unemployment—and in particular youth unemployment—rising to record levels. Under these conditions, output-oriented legitimating arguments might either rely on counterfactual comparisons with the presumed catastrophe of exit from the Monetary Union, or on the uncertain promise of a better future after structural convergence has been achieved. The appeal of the latter argument would be limited, however, since it would also highlight the purposeful destruction of cultural and institutional traditions and practices considered part of the collective identity of "Latin" societies.

In the *input-dimension*, political dissatisfaction, opposition, and protests have escalated in Southern polities as the misery of economic decline, mass unemployment, and the loss of welfare-state support continued to take its toll, and as the unequal impact of the regime on Northern and Southern countries became ever more obvious. It was not even expected, therefore, that the requirements of Commission-defined "Memoranda of Understanding" would be autonomously chosen and implemented through national political processes. Instead, they were enforced by the threat of immediate state insolvency that was maintained, step-by-step, by partitioning agreed-upon rescue loans into smaller tranches that would be withheld until the Troika of inspectors from the Commission, the ECB, and the IMF had certified perfect compliance. It did not matter, therefore, that governments under Troika control were not reelected. And since neither the outcome of elections nor national referenda made a difference, public support for democracy itself has dramatically declined in "program countries" (Armingeon et al. 2016).

For the same reasons, the general euro regime adopted after 2011 is based on the presumption that politically accountable national governments will be tempted to resist fiscal-austerity and supply-side recommendations. In the European Semester, therefore, budget proposals must be submitted to the Commission before they are introduced in parliament; and under the Excessive Deficits and Imbalances procedures, country-specific recommendations may ultimately be enforced by severe financial sanctions. In any case, autonomous national policy choices are only acceptable if they conform to the functional imperatives that are considered necessary for achieving structural convergence. And since there is reason to think that constituency interests and preferences in Southern political economies are likely to conflict with these imperatives, the euro regime must seek to constrain, and if necessary disable, the democratic responsiveness of Southern governments and hence the *input-oriented* democratic legitimacy of Southern polities.

5.2 Legitimacy on the European Level

On the European level, arguments asserting *output-oriented* legitimacy tend to begin by hailing the Monetary Union as the crowning achievement of economic integration whose collapse would strike a fatal blow to the common commitment to European integration. And in spite of the huge economic and social transition costs and risks implied by the present regime, that commitment still seems to prevail. In any case, European authorities and the governing majorities of all Eurozone states as well as the pro-European mainstream of elites in business, labor, the media, and academia appear to believe that maintaining the Monetary Union is serving the European public good. In normative terms, however, the appeal to a postulated common interest is undermined by the distributive inequality of the euro regime's impact on Northern and Southern economies (Tsoukalis 2016).

The objection may be clarified by comparison with another monetary union: On July 1, 1990, the currency of the German Democratic Republic was integrated with the deutsche mark of the Federal Republic of Germany at an extremely overvalued (but politically unavoidable) exchange rate whose economic impact on East and West Germany was extremely unequal. In the historically integrated German political community, however, the support for monetary integration could not override political and moral concerns over its distributive injustice. Even though the extremely expensive German "transfer union" (Streeck and Elsässer 2016) was highly inefficient in economic terms (Sinn and Sinn 1994), both parts of the country have treated it as a self-evident moral obligation under the normative criteria of distributive justice and equality in the reunited nation state.

Now, obviously, the Eurozone is neither a politically integrated state nor a morally integrated political community where appeals to culturally entrenched obligations of redistributive solidarity and burden sharing are politically compelling. By reverse implication, however, the appeal to a common economic self-interest in maintaining the Monetary Union also cannot justify severe sacrifices imposed on some member states, but not on others. As a consequence, the euro regime's claim to *output-oriented legitimacy* is undermined by the fact that the apparent injustice of its unequal impact can neither be politically resolved on the European level, nor can it be plausibly declared to be normatively irrelevant.

On the European level, *input-oriented legitimacy* of the euro regime is ruled out by the present institutional set-up. The initial response to the threat of the euro crisis, and essentially all subsequent policy choices as well, have been taken on the Summit level and in the Eurogroup of the ECOFIN Council by the heads and finance ministers of Eurozone governments operating in the mode of intergovernmental negotiations. Assuming that these are accountable to their national parliaments and electorates, it is often argued that Council decisions adopted by consensus are also supported by a chain of input-oriented legitimation. But the validity of this argument is limited in two ways.

National heads of government and ministers may each be nationally authorized to agree to general rules and also to specific sacrifices applying to their own state—but national accountability cannot legitimate them to impose specific sacrifices on another state. By implication, the input legitimacy of negotiated agreements imposing specific sacrifices on a particular member state depends entirely on the legitimating chain in that state. And that chain may be broken when agreements must be accepted under an extremely unequal distribution of bargaining power, or under duress—which was approximated when the recipients of rescue credits and then the governments of program countries had to accept Commission-defined conditionalities under the threat of immediate state insolvency.

The second limit of input-legitimated intergovernmental rule-making arises even if asymmetric bargaining powers had played no role in the original agreement. But if circumstances or political preferences are changing, these rules may no longer reflect a present political consensus. Under consensual decision rules, however, intergovernmental agreements will remain legally binding unless a new consensus may be achieved for their abolition or amendment. Intergovernmental rule-making, in other words, may initially reflect an input-oriented convergence of national interests and preferences. But it will also create a system of extremely asymmetric institutional bargaining power under which the promoters of change will be blocked by the vetoes of the beneficiaries and defenders of previously agreed-upon rules. Hence, as Varoufakis (2015, 2017) found out to his surprise, in deliberations of the Eurogroup at the height of another Greek crisis, the only acceptable topic for discussion was compliance with previously agreed-upon rules (Tsebelis 2016).

If the intergovernmental Council cannot link the present euro regime to input-oriented democratic legitimacy on the national level, none of the supranational actors involved in Eurozone policy choices—the ECB, the Commission, and the European Court of Justice —would even claim to be democratically accountable to the citizens and voters that are suffering under the policies imposed by the regime. Where they play an active role, as the ECB definitely does, their claim to authority is based on a combination of technocratic expertise with the assertion of implicit emergency powers to do "whatever it takes" to save the Monetary Union, rather than on democratic legitimacy or the strict construction of Treaty law (White 2015; Kreuder-Sonnen 2016; Menéndez 2017). On the European level, in short, the euro regime is defined by the asymmetric bargaining power of Northern governments and by technocratic authorities, none of which have reason to fear the electoral responses of the constituencies whose interests and life chances are most directly affected.

5.3 The Specter of Politicization

If the Eurozone government, based on asymmetric intergovernmental power and technocratic authority, appears institutionally designed to rule out democratic responsiveness, it also has the effect of suppressing the manifestation of the fundamental North–South conflict on the European level. It is pushed back into national containers, where frustration, resentment, and recriminations are articulated in the media, mass demonstrations, strikes, and violent protests—without affecting policy choices that had been settled on the European level. In order to appreciate the importance of these conditions, let us consider counterfactual conditions in which Eurozone policies had to be adopted by democratically accountable actors in European politics.

Let us assume that a Eurozone parliament with broad competences did exist—shaped, perhaps, by the "T-Dem Treaty for the Democratization of the Governance of the Euro Area" proposed by Thomas Piketty and colleagues (Hennette et al. 2017a, 2017b). Assume further European media providing credible information and a forum for transnational discussions on issues on the Eurozone agenda, as well as national media covering the politics and public debates of other EU member states. And finally, assume a system of political accountability in which European policy-makers are made to depend on citizens, mediated through politically responsive political parties and a more representative and effective European Parliament (Warren 2018) whose members must actively compete in local constituencies.[24]

It seems obvious that, with these conditions in place, a more democratic Eurozone government could not continue to ignore the fundamental distributive conflict between Northern and Southern Eurozone societies, and it could not prevent its politicization in Europe-wide and national media and public debates. Political parties could no longer avoid addressing it in their campaign manifestos; and individual candidates would have to take a stand in their local constituencies. As a consequence, a Euro-level parliament with full legislative powers (including the power of legislative initiative) could not avoid putting the present euro regime and its continuation on the European political agenda.

But what would be the substance of politicized debates on the euro regime in public and among representatives who are responsive to the interests, perceptions and preferences of their constituents? Southern speakers would point to the regime's dismal economic and social effects, to the destruction of culturally salient institutions and practices, and to the morally unjustifiable asymmetry of the euro

[24] These requirements do not presuppose first-past-the-post elections in single-member districts. They can also be met in systems of proportional elections where the total number of seats won by a party depends on its share of total votes, but where all candidates must stand locally and must succeed on their local votes.

regime. They would also emphasize how the regime is serving Northern economic interests, and that it was established and continues to be defended by the exercise of German power—which even rejects all demands for compensatory transfer programs. From a Northern perspective, by contrast, the issue would be stabilizing the Monetary Union, rather than distributive justice. Southern troubles were brought about by incompetent governments, corrupt bureaucracies, and unrealistic popular expectations; and public protests are expressions of anti-German resentment and of a lack of gratitude for generous rescue loans. In any case, however, they are symptoms of an irrational resistance against necessary structural changes—which also implies that the present euro regime must be protected against moral hazard through even tighter rules, more controls, and more severe sanctions.

If these conflicting interests, preferences and world-views were to clash in public and parliamentary debate on the European level, it seems clear that the present euro regime could not be reaffirmed in broad political consensus. And even if an ideal solution (which would need to stabilize the euro while satisfying both Northern and Southern economic and moral interests) could be imagined,[25] it could not possibly be invented and consensually adopted in the context of politicized confrontation, and of the hostile "interaction orientations" (Scharpf 1997: 84–9) and the mutual distrust that has been brought about by the Monetary Union (Streeck 2015). Moreover, as I have argued in another paper (Scharpf 2017), under the *no-demos* conditions prevailing in the European polity, politicized conflicts over fundamental interests, values, and identities cannot be legitimately resolved by majority rule. Hence if a new euro regime cannot be adopted in consensus, any attempt to impose one or the other solution by parliamentary majority is more likely to destroy the EMU than to settle the issues.

To conclude: If Eurozone policies had to be determined in politicized public and parliamentary debates, the Monetary Union in its present shape could not survive, but neither could an alternative euro regime be created with input-oriented democratic legitimacy. At present, the Monetary Union depends upon a depoliticized technocratic form of government that is supported by asymmetric intergovernmental bargaining power and the force of previously agreed-upon European law. It would be undermined by serious efforts to democratize the

[25] Present proposals and academic discussions suggest that future state finance crises should be averted through the completion of the banking union, the creation of fiscal capacities for anti-cyclical intervention and the explicit acceptance of the ECB's role of lender of last resort (Commission 2017). But though the need for structural convergence is downplayed, there is no suggestion that fiscal constraints and requirements of structural reform could be relaxed. In other words, Southern economies could not be allowed to return to the expansionary fiscal and wage practices on which the success of their domestic-demand led growth models had depended.

government of the Eurozone. This also suggests that aspirations toward Eurozone democracy must either envisage a politically integrated federal state[26] or a reduced and more flexible form of monetary integration (Scharpf 2018b).

References

Agamben, Giorgio. 2013. "The 'Latin Empire' Should Strike Back." Voxeurop, March 26, 2013. www.voxeurop.eu/en/content/article/3593961-latin-empire-should-strike-back

Armingeon, Klaus, Kai Guthmann, and David Weisthanner. 2016. "How the Euro Divides the Union: The Effect of Economic Adjustment on Support for Democracy in Europe." *Socio-Economic Review* 14(1): 1–26.

Artis, Michael J. and Mark P. Taylor. 1993. *The Stabilizing Effect of the ERM on Exchange Rates and Interest Rates: An Empirical Investigation.* IMF Working Paper 94/29. Washington, DC: International Monetary Fund.

Baccaro, Lucio and Jonas Pontusson. 2016. "Rethinking Comparative Political Economy." *Politics and Society* 44(2): 1–33.

Bauer, Michael W. and Stefan Becker. 2014. "The Unexpected Winner of the Crisis: The European Commission's Strengthened Role in Economic Governance." *Journal of European Integration* 36(3): 213–29.

Blyth, Marc. 2013. *Austerity: The History of a Dangerous Idea.* Oxford: Oxford University Press.

Brunnermeier, Markus K., Harold James, and Jean-Pierre Landau. 2016. *The Euro and the Battle of Ideas.* Princeton: Princeton University Press.

Calmfors, Lars. 1993. "Centralization of Wage Bargaining and Macroeconomic Performance: A Survey." *OECD Economic Studies* No. 21 (Winter 1993): 161–91.

Calmfors, Lars and John Driffil. 1988. "Bargaining Structure, Corporatism and Macroeconomic Performance." *Economic Policy* 3(6): 13–61.

Cecchini Report. 1988. *Europe 1992: The Overall Challenge.* SEC (88) 524 final. April 13, 1988. Brussels: Commission of the European Communities. http://aei.pitt.edu/3813

Cecchini, Paolo, Michael Catenat, and Alexis Jaquemin. 1988. *The European Challenge 1992: The Benefits of the Single Market.* Aldershot: Wildwood House.

Council of Europe. 2011. *Council Conclusions on an Early Warning Scoreboard for the Surveillance of Macroeconomic Imbalances.* November 8, 2011. www.consilium.europa.eu/uedocs/cms_data/docs/pressdata/en/ecofin/125974.pdf

[26] That implies the creation of large and effective governing and problem-solving capacities on the European level. There is no existing federal state that must exercise its governing responsibilities by directing and controlling the exercise of governing functions that are formally assigned to its member states, and for whose exercise member state governments are democratically accountable. In that sense, the construction of the EMU must also be considered a constitutional abomination.

De Grauwe, Paul. 2012. *Economics of Monetary Union*. Ninth edition. Oxford: Oxford University Press.

De Grauwe, Paul. 2013. "The European Central Bank as Lender of Last Resort in the Government Bond Markets." *CESifo Economic Studies* 59(3): 520–35.

De Grauwe, Paul and Yuemei Ji. 2013. *The Legacy of Austerity in the Eurozone*. CEPS Commentary, October 4, 2013. Brussels: Centre for European Policy Studies. https://www.ceps.eu/publications/legacy-austerity-eurozone

Degryse, Christophe. 2012. *The New European Economic Governance*. ETUI Working Paper 2012/14. Brussels: European Trade Union Institute.

Di Carlo, Donato. 2018. *Does Pattern Bargaining Explain Wage Restraint in the German Public Sector?* MPIfG Discussion Paper 18/3. Cologne: Max Planck Institute for the Study of Societies.

Driffil, John. 2006. "The Centralization of Wage Bargaining Revisited." *Journal of Common Market Studies* 44(4): 731–56.

Dustmann, Christian, Bernd Fitzenberger, Uta Schönberg, and Alexandra Spitz-Oener. 2014. "From Sick Man of Europe to Economic Superstar: Germany's Resurgent Economy." *Journal of Economic Perspectives* 28(1): 167–88.

Dyson, Kenneth. 2000. *The Politics of the Eurozone: Stability or Breakdown?* Oxford: Oxford University Press.

Dyson, Kenneth and Kevin Featherstone. 1999. *The Road to Maastricht: Negotiating Economic and Monetary Union*. Oxford: Oxford University Press.

Eichengreen, Barry. 1990. *Is Europe an Optimal Currency Area?* CEPR Discussion Paper 478. London: Center for Economic Policy Research.

Eichengreen, Barry. 1992. *Should the Maastricht Treaty Be Saved?* Princeton Studies in International Finance No. 74. Princeton: Princeton University Press.

Enderlein, Henrik. 2005. "One Size Fits None." *Central Banking Journal* 16(1): 24–8.

Enderlein, Henrik et al. 2012. *Completing the Euro: A Roadmap towards Fiscal Union in Europe. Report of the "Tommaso Padoa-Schioppa Group."* Studies and Reports 92. Paris: Notre Europe.

Eriksen, Erik O. 2018. "Political Integration and the Problem of Dominance." *European Journal of Political Research* (January). https://onlinelibrary.wiley.com/doi/abs/10.1111/1475-6765.12263

European Commission. 1990. *One Market, One Money: An Evaluation of the Potential Benefits and Costs of Forming an Economic and Monetary Union*. Brussels: European Commission, Directorate General for Economic and Financial Affairs.

European Commission. 2010. *Surveillance of Intra-Euro-Area: Competitiveness and Imbalances*. European Economy 1/2010. Brussels: European Commission, Directorate-General for Economic and Financial Affairs.

European Commission. 2012a. *Current Account Surpluses in the EU*. European Economy 9/2012. Brussels: European Commission, Directorate-General for Economic and Financial Affairs.

European Commission. 2012b. *Scoreboard for the Surveillance of Macroeconomic Imbalances.* European Economy Occasional Papers 92. Brussels: European Commission, Directorate-General for Economic and Financial Affairs.

European Commission. 2012c. *Labour Market Developments in Europe 2012.* European Economy 5/2012. Brussels: European Commission, Directorate-General for Economic and Financial Affairs.

European Commission. 2017. *Paper on the Deepening of the Economic and Monetary Union.* https://ec.europa.eu/commission/sites/beta-political/files/reflection-paper-emu_en.pdf

Feldstein, Martin. 1997. *The Political Economy of the European Economic and Monetary Union: Political Sources of an Economic Liability.* NBER Working Paper 6150. Cambridge, MA: National Bureau of Economic Research.

Ferrera, Maurizio and Elisabetta Gualmini. 2000. "Italy: Rescue from Without?" In *Work and Welfare in the Open Economy*, Vol. 2: *Diverse Responses to Common Challenges*, edited by Fritz W. Scharpf and Vivien A. Schmidt. Oxford: Oxford University Press, 351–98.

Ferrera, Maurizio and Eilisabetta Gualmini. 2004. *Rescued by Europe? Social and Labour Market Reforms in Italy from Maastricht to Berlusconi.* Amsterdam: Amsterdam University Press.

Five Presidents' Report. 2015. *Completing Europe's Economic and Monetary Union.* Report by Jean-Claude Juncker in close cooperation with Donald Tusk, Jeroen Dijsselbloem, Mario Draghi and Martin Schulz. Brussels: European Commission.

Geiger, Felix and Heinz-Peter Spahn. 2007. "One Size Fits None? Common Monetary Policy and Inflation Differentials in EMU." In *European Integration in Crisis*, edited by Eckhard Hein, Jan Priewe, and Achim Truger. Marburg: Metropolis, 281–300.

Geishecker, Ingo 2006. "Does Outsourcing to Central and Eastern Europe Really Threaten Manual Workers' Jobs in Germany?" *World Economy* 29(5): 559–83.

Hall, Peter. 2014. "Varieties of Capitalism and the Euro Crisis." *West European Politics* 37(6): 1223–43.

Hall, Peter and David Soskice (eds.). 2001. *Varieties of Capitalism: The Institutional Foundations of Comparative Advantage.* Oxford: Oxford University Press.

Hancké, Bob, 2013. *Unions, Central Banks, and EMU: Labor Market Institutions and Monetary Integration in Europe.* Oxford: Oxford University Press.

Hassel, Anke, 2003. "The Politics of Social Pacts." *British Journal of International Relations* 41(4): 707–26.

Helleiner, Eric. 1994. *States and the Reemergence of Global Finance: From Bretton Woods to the 1990s.* Ithaca: Cornell University Press.

Hennette, Stéphanie, Thomas Piketty, Guilleaume Sacriste, and Antoine Vauchez. 2017a: *Pour un traité de democratization de L'Europe.* Paris: Éditions du Seuil.

Hennette, Stéphanie et al. 2017b. "For a Treaty Democratizing Euro Area Governance—(T-Dem)." *Social Europe*, April 27, 2017. https://www.socialeurope.eu/treaty-democratizing-euro-area-governance-t-dem

Higgins, Bryon. 1993. "Was the ERM Crisis Inevitable?" *Federal Reserve Bank of Kansas City Economic Review* (Fourth Quarter): 27–40. www.kansascityfed.org/Publicat/Econrev/EconRevArchive/1993/4q93HIGG.pdf

Hope, David and David Soskice. 2016. "Growth Models, Varieties of Capitalism, and Macroeconomics." *Politics and Society* 44(2): 209–26.

Höpner, Martin and Alexander Spielau. 2017. "Better than the Euro? The European Monetary System (1979–1998)." *New Political Economy* 23 (1): 160–73.

Höpner, Martin and Mark Lutter. 2018. "The Diversity of Wage Regimes: Why the Eurozone Is Too Heterogeneous for the Euro." *European Political Science Review* 18(1): 71–96.

Issing, Otmar. 2005. *One Size Fits All! A Single Monetary Policy for the Euro Area.* Speech by Otmar Issing, Member of the Executive Board of the ECB. International Research Forum, Frankfurt am Main, May 20, 2005. www.ecb.europa.eu/press/key/date/2005/html/sp050520.en.html

Iversen, Torben, David Soskice, and David Hope. 2016. "The Eurozone and Political Economic Institutions." *Annual Review of Political Science* 19: 163–83.

Johnston, Alison and Aidan Regan. 2016. "European Monetary Integration and the Incompatibility of National Varieties of Capitalism." *Journal of Common Market Studies* 54(2): 318–336.

Jones, Erik. 2016. "Competitiveness and the European Financial Crisis." In *The Political and Economic Dynamics of the Eurozone Crisis*, edited by James A. Caporaso and Martin Rhodes. New York: Oxford University Press, 79–99.

Jones, Erik, Daniel Kelemen, and Sophie Meunier. 2016. "Failing Forward? The Euro Crisis and the Incomplete Nature of European Integration." *Comparative Political Studies* 49(7): 841–73.

Katzenstein, Peter. 1985. *Small States in World Markets: Industrial Policy in Europe.* Ithaca: Cornell University Press.

Kreuder-Sonnen, Christian. 2016. "Beyond Integration Theory: The (Anti-) Constitutional Dimension of European Crisis Governance." *Journal of Common Market Studies* 2016(6): 1350–66.

Krugman, Paul. 2012. "Germans and Aliens." *New York Times*, January 9, 2012. http://krugman.blogs.nytimes.com/2012/01/09/germans-and-aliens/?_r=0

Krugman, Paul, 2013. "The Harm Germany Does. The Conscience of a Liberal." *New York Times*, November 1, 2013. https://krugman.blogs.nytimes.com/2013/11/01/the-harm-germany-does/

Kundnani, Hans. 2014. *The Paradox of German Power*. London: Hurst.

Marin, Dalia. 2006. "A New International Division of Labor in Europe: Outsourcing and Offshoring to Eastern Europe." *Journal of the European Economic Association* 4(2/3): 612–22.

Marsh, David. 2009. *The Euro: The Politics of the New Global Currency.* New Haven: Yale University Press.

Marsh, David. 2013. *Europe's Deadlock: How the Euro Crisis Could Be Solved—and Why It Won't Happen.* New Haven: Yale University Press.

McNamara, Kathleen R. 1998. *The Currency of Ideas: Monetary Politics in the European Union.* Ithaca: Cornell University Press.

Menéndez, Agustin J. 2017. "The Crisis of Law and the European Crisis: From the Social and Democratic Rechtsstaat to the Consolidating State of (Pseudo-)technocratic Governance." *Journal of Law and Society* 44(1): 56–78.

Nölke, Andreas. 2016. "Economic Causes of the Eurozone Crisis: The Analytical Contribution of Comparative Capitalism." *Socio-Economic Review* 14(1): 141–61.

Padoa-Schioppa, Tommaso. [1994]2000. *The Road to Monetary Union in Europe: The Emperor, the Kings, and the Genies.* Oxford: Oxford University Press.

Pataki, Zsolt. 2014. *The Cost of Non-Europe in the Single Market: "Cecchini Revisited." An Overview of the Potential Economic Gains from Further Completion of the European Single Market.* CoNE 1/2014. PE 510.981. Brussels: European Added Value Unit of the Directorate for Impact Assessment and European Added Value; Directorate-General for Parliamentary Research Services (DG EPRS) of the European Parliament.

Pettit, Philip. 1997. *Republicanism: Theory of Freedom and Government.* Oxford: Clarendon Press.

Regan, Aidan. 2011. "The Political Economy of Social Pacts in the EMU: Irish Liberal Market Corporatism in Crisis." *New Political Economy* 17(4): 465–91.

Ruggie, John Gerard. 1982. "International Regimes, Transactions, and Change: Embedded Liberalism in the Postwar Economic Order." *International Organization* 36(2): 379–415.

Sanchez, Jose Luis Diaz and Aristomene Varoudakis. 2013. *Growth and Competitiveness as Factors in Eurozone External Imbalances: Evidence and Policy Implications.* Policy Research Working Paper 6732. Washington, DC: The World Bank.

Sandbu, Martin. 2015. *Europe's Orphan: The Future of the Euro and the Politics of Debt.* Princeton: Princeton University Press.

Scharpf, Fritz W. 1991. *Crisis and Choice in European Social Democracy.* Ithaca: Cornell University Press.

Scharpf, Fritz W. 1997. *Games Real Actors Play: Actor-Centered Institutionalism in Policy Research.* Boulder: Westview.

Scharpf, Fritz W. 2010. "The Double Asymmetry of European Integration or why the EU Cannot Be a Social Market Economy." *Socio-Economic Review* 8(2): 211–50.

Scharpf, Fritz W. 2014. "No Exit from the Euro-Rescuing Trap?" In *Complex Democracy: Varieties, Crises, and Transformations*, edited by Volker Schneider and Burkard Eberlein. Wiesbaden: Springer, 135–54.

Scharpf, Fritz W. 2017. "De-Constitutionalization and Majority Rule: A Democratic Vision for Europe." *European Law Journal* 23(5), 315–34.

Scharpf, Fritz W. 2018a. *International Monetary Regimes and the German Model.* MPIfG Discussion Paper 18/1. Cologne: Max Planck Institute for the Study of Societies.

Scharpf, Fritz W. 2018b. *There Is an Alternative: A Two-tier European Currency Community.* MPIfG Discussion Paper 18/7. Cologne: Max Planck Institute for the Study of Societies.

Schäuble, Wolfgang and Karl Lamers. 1994. *Überlegungen zur europäischen Politik.* CDU/CSU-Fraktion im Bundestag. September 1, 1994. www.cducsu.de/upload/schaeublelamers94.pdf

Schelkle, Waltraud. 2017. *The Political Economy of Monetary Solidarity: Understanding the Euro Experiment.* Oxford: Oxford University Press.

Schettkat, Ronald and Rongrong Sun. 2009. "Monetary Policy and European Unemployment." *Oxford Review of Economic Policy* 25(1): 94–108.

Schimmelfennig, Frank. 2015. "Liberal Intergovernmentalism and the Euro Area Crisis." *Journal of European Public Policy* 22(2): 177–95.

Schmidt, Vivien A. and Mark Thatcher (eds.). 2014a. *Resilient Liberalism in Europe's Political Economy.* Cambridge: Cambridge University Press.

Schmidt, Vivien A. and Mark Thatcher. 2014b: "Why Are Neoliberal Ideas so Resilient in Europe's Political Economy?" *Critical Policy Studies* 8(3): 340–7.

Schmitter, Philippe C. 1974. "Still the Century of Corporatism?" *Review of Politics* 36(1): 85–131.

Seikel, Daniel. 2016. "Flexible Austerity and Supranational Autonomy: The Reformed Excessive Deficit Procedure and the Asymmetry between Liberalization and Social Regulation in the EU." *Journal of Common Market Studies* 54(6): 1398–416.

Sinn, Gerlinde and Hans-Werner Sinn. 1994. *Jumpstart: The Economic Unification of Germany.* Cambridge, MA: MIT Press.

Steinberg, Federico and Mattias Vermeiren. 2016. "Germany's Institutional Power and the EMU Regime after the Crisis: Towards a Germanized Euro Area?" *Journal of Common Market Studies* 54(2): 388–407.

Stiglitz, Joseph E. 2016. *The Euro and Its Threat to the Future of Europe.* London: Allen Lane.

Storm, Servaas. 2016. *German Wage Moderation and the Eurozone Crisis: A Critical Analysis.* Blog entry on: *Perspectives,* January 8, 2016. New York: Institute for New Economic Thinking. https://www.ineteconomics.org/perspectives/blog/german-wage-moderation-and-the-eurozone-crisis-a-critical-analysis

Storm, Servaas and C.W.M. Naastepad. 2016. "Myths, Mix-ups, and Mishandlings: Understanding the Eurozone Crisis." *International Journal of Political Economy* 45(1): 46–71.

Story, Jonathan. 2014. "The Euro Crisis and German Primacy." In *The Eurozone Crisis and the Future of Europe: The Political Economy of Further Integration and*

Governance, edited by Daniel Dăianu, Giorgio Basevi, Carlo D'Adda, and Rajeesh Kumar. Basingstoke: Palgrave Macmillan, 109–25.

Streeck, Wolfgang. 2015. "Why the Euro Divides Europe." *New Left Review* 95: 5–26. https://newleftreview.org/article/download_pdf?id=3142

Streeck, Wolfgang and Lea Elsässer. 2016. "Monetary Disunion: The Domestic Politics of Euroland." *Journal of European Public Policy* 23(1): 1–24.

Tsebelis, George. 2016. "Lessons from the Greek Crisis." *Journal of European Public Policy* 23(1): 25–41.

Tsoukalis, Loukas. 2016. *In Defence of Europe: Can the European Project Be Saved?* Oxford: Oxford University Press.

Varoufakis, Yanis. 2015. *As It Happened: Yanis Varoufakis' Intervention during the 27th June Eurogroup Meeting.* Blog entry on: *Yanis Varoufakis: Thoughts for the Post-2008 World*, June 28, 2015. https://yanisvaroufakis.eu/2015/06/28/as-it-happened-yanis-varoufakis-intervention-during-the–27th-june–2015-eurogroup-meeting/

Varoufakis, Yanis. 2017. *Adults in the Room: My Battle with Europe's Deep Establishment.* London: The Bodley Head.

Walter, Stefanie. 2016. "Crisis Politics in Europe: Why Austerity Is Easier to Implement in Some Countries Than in Others." *Comparative Political Studies* 49(7): 841–73.

Warren, Thomas. 2018. "The European Parliament and the Eurozone Crisis: An Exceptional Actor?" *British Journal of Politics and International Relations*, May 2, 2018. http://journals.sagepub.com/doi/abs/10.1177/1369148118768141

Weeks, John. 2018. "Trade Performance in EU Internal Market in Euro Area." *Social Europe* Blog, July 9, 2018. https://www.socialeurope.eu/trade-performance-in-eu-internal-market-in-euro-era

White, Jonathan. 2015. "Emergency Europe." *Political Studies* 63: 300–18.

Wierts, Peter, Henk van Kerkhoff, and Jakob de Haan. 2013. "Composition of Exports and Export Performance of Eurozone Countries." *Journal of Common Market Studies* 52(4): 928–41.

Wyplosz, Charles. 2013. *Eurozone Crisis: It's about Demand, Not Competitiveness.* Unpublished manuscript. Geneva: The Graduate Institute.

Young, Brigitte. 2014. "The Power of Ordoliberalism in the Eurozone Crisis Management." In *The Eurozone Crisis and the Future of Europe: The Political Economy of Further Integration and Governance*, edited by Daniel Dăianu, Giorgio Basevi, Carlo D'Adda, and Rajeesh Kumar. Basingstoke: Palgrave Macmillan, 126–37.

PART II

THE POLITICS OF GROWTH STRATEGIES

6

Transitions to the Knowledge Economy in Germany, Sweden, and the Netherlands

Kathleen Thelen

1. Introduction

The "digital revolution" that began in the late 1960s has transformed product markets and production processes in rich democracies. As underlined by Hassel and Palier in the first chapter of this volume, observers depict the changes underway as a transition from the Fordist industrial economy to a new "knowledge economy," characterized by rapid technological innovation and associated with a heightened premium on higher education (Iversen and Soskice 2015; Hall, this volume). Although the challenges of this transition are broadly similar across the rich democracies, individual countries have navigated the course differently.

This chapter compares three countries that exhibit different trajectories of change: Germany, Sweden, and the Netherlands. Unlike their liberal counterparts (including the United States and the United Kingdom), all three countries feature strong social partnership between unions and organized employers, and they are all considered examples of coordinated market economies in the literature on varieties of capitalism. However, despite these similarities, each has adapted differently to the challenges and opportunities of the new knowledge economy. Germany has vigorously defended its strength in high-quality manufacturing through the digital transformation of products and production within the traditional industrial core. Sweden, by contrast, has moved more strongly to compete directly in high-tech sectors, especially information and communications technologies (ICT). Finally, the Dutch have increasingly turned to high-end business services, deploying new technologies to return to the country's historic strengths in trade and finance.

What accounts for these divergent trajectories? I argue that differences in the structure of organized labor and business interests, and in the institutions that structure their interactions with each other and with the state, produced different coalitional alignments that have led these countries onto divergent paths toward the knowledge economy today. In Germany, unions and employers are organized along industrial lines, and manufacturing interests dominate the producer-group

Kathleen Thelen, *Transitions to the Knowledge Economy in Germany, Sweden, and the Netherlands* In: *Growth and Welfare in Advanced Capitalist Economies: How Have Growth Regimes Evolved?* Edited by: Anke Hassel and Bruno Palier,
Oxford University Press (2021). © Oxford University Press. DOI: 10.1093/oso/9780198866176.003.0006

landscape on both sides of the class divide. Market pressures since the 1970s have inspired intense cross-class cooperation within the industrial sector and forged a formidable political alliance focused on defending areas of traditional strength. State policy reflects and reinforces the dominance of manufacturing interests through partnerships with industries that promote knowledge-intensive innovation within the industrial core. Sweden's producer-group landscape, by contrast, features more encompassing, sector-spanning interests, a constellation that blocks strategies focused on defending particular sectors. However, the division of blue- and white-collar interests into competing union confederations and the growing power of salaried interests within the labor movement have allowed the state to play a more constitutive role through policies that facilitated the consolidation of a new coalition of white-collar unions and innovation-intensive sectors. Finally, in the Netherlands, where national-level corporatist institutions had originally been devised to promote industry, the collapse of traditional manufacturing in the 1970s created an organizational vacuum. This vacuum allowed the state to actively engineer a more fundamental shift in the dominant growth regime with policies that cemented an unlikely alliance between blue-collar unions and high-end business services in support of the financialization of the Dutch political economy. In short, differences in the interest-group landscape produced different patterns of interaction between states and organized interests from which three different growth strategies emerged: supportive of a dominant coalition in Germany, enabling of an emerging coalition in Sweden, and transformative of a new coalition in the Netherlands.

2. Diverging Political-Economic Profiles

The divergent trajectories of change in these three countries cannot be captured by any single indicator. However, looking at relative changes in value-added in manufacturing as a share of GDP offers a start. As Figure 6.1 shows, manufacturing declined in all three countries in the 1970s and 1980s but leveled off in Germany and recovered to previous levels after the 2007–8 crisis. In the Netherlands, by contrast, manufacturing dropped sharply in the 1970s and continued to decline after that. The trend for Sweden lies in between: after a significant drop in 1990, Swedish manufacturing rebounded, but experienced more of a decline than in Germany after 2008.

Behind these broad trends lie significant differences in the export profiles of the three countries. The German export economy today is dominated by the very same sectors that we have long associated with that country's economic model. Cars continue to play an outsized role, leading the top ten exports (volume in billions of USD) by a wide margin, while closely related products, including

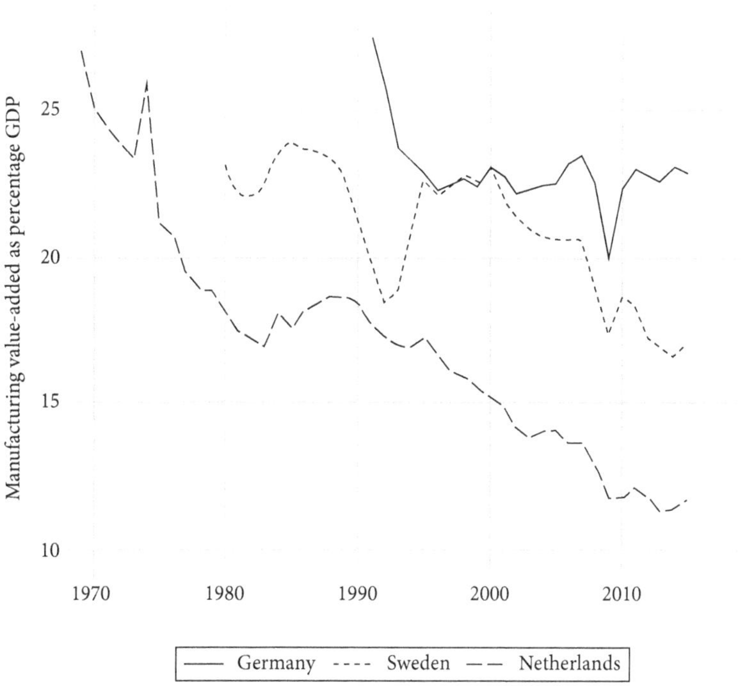

Figure 6.1 Manufacturing value-added as percentage of GDP

Source: World Bank National Accounts data and OECD National Accounts Data Files, 1969–2015. https://data.worldbank.org/indicator/NV.IND.MANF.ZS.

vehicle parts, engine parts, and machinery, also count among the country's top ten exports.[1]

Sweden presents a more differentiated export profile. The country combines significant exports in areas of traditional strength (cars and vehicle parts, but also raw materials such as wood) with a strong presence in ICT-related exports such as telecommunications and broadcasting equipment, which continue to play a significant role in the political economy even after the bursting of the dot com bubble.[2] The country's well-known move into ICT is reflected as well in a sharp rise in employment in ICT manufacturing and services in the 1990s, unmatched by Germany, where employment in these areas remained flat.[3] As Figure 6.2 shows, Sweden leads all other European countries save Finland in the number of ICT specialists employed throughout the economy.

[1] For the full export profile, see OEC (2016a).

[2] For the full export profile, see OEC (2016b).

[3] OECD STAN indicators (2011), at: https://stats.oecd.org/Index.aspx?DataSetCode=STAN INDICATORS.

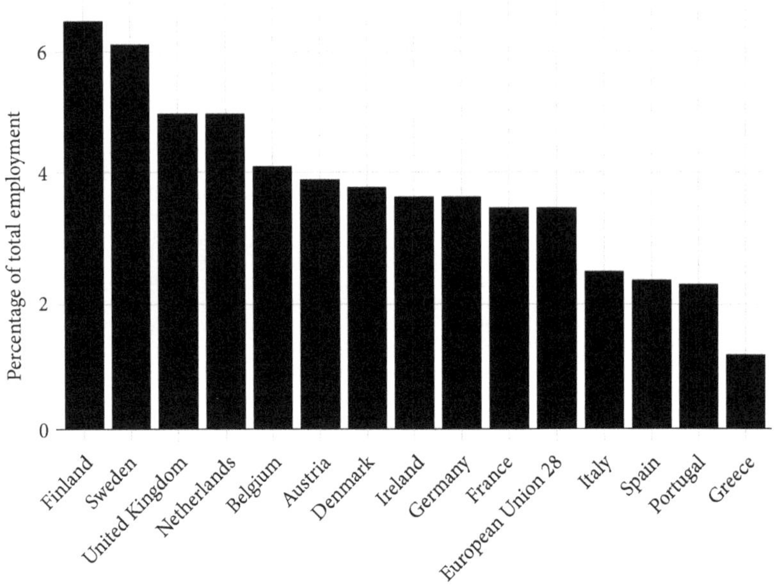

Figure 6.2 ICT specialists as share of total employment

Source: European Commission Digital Single Market Digital Scoreboard, "DESI by components: 2b1 ICT Specialists," 2017. https://digital-agenda-data.eu/charts/desi-components#chart={"indicator":" DESI_2B1_ICTSPEC,""breakdown-group":"total,""unit-measure":"pc_ind_emp,""time-period":"2017"}.

The Netherlands presents yet a different picture. The Dutch also experienced an increase in employment in ICT-related areas in the 1990s, and after the 1970s what has remained of Dutch industry is very high-end—computers, telecoms, broadcasting, and photo lab equipment are among the top ten exports.[4] More importantly, however, as Figure 6.3 shows, employment in business services rose steadily and rather sharply through the 1980s and 1990s, and by 1998 came to account for over 50 percent of total employment. Employment in FIRE industries (finance, insurance, and real estate) alone accounted for 28 percent of total employment in 2015.[5]

In sum, important differences in the dominant growth regimes emerged across the three countries in the 1980s and 1990s: Germany stayed within traditional areas of competitive advantage, continuing to move further upmarket in the same sectors that have anchored the economy for decades. Sweden and the Netherlands, by contrast, show much more movement—Sweden into higher-technology (IT) manufacturing and services, and the Netherlands into high-end business services.

[4] For the full export profile, see OEC (2016c).

[5] OECD STAN indicators (2011).

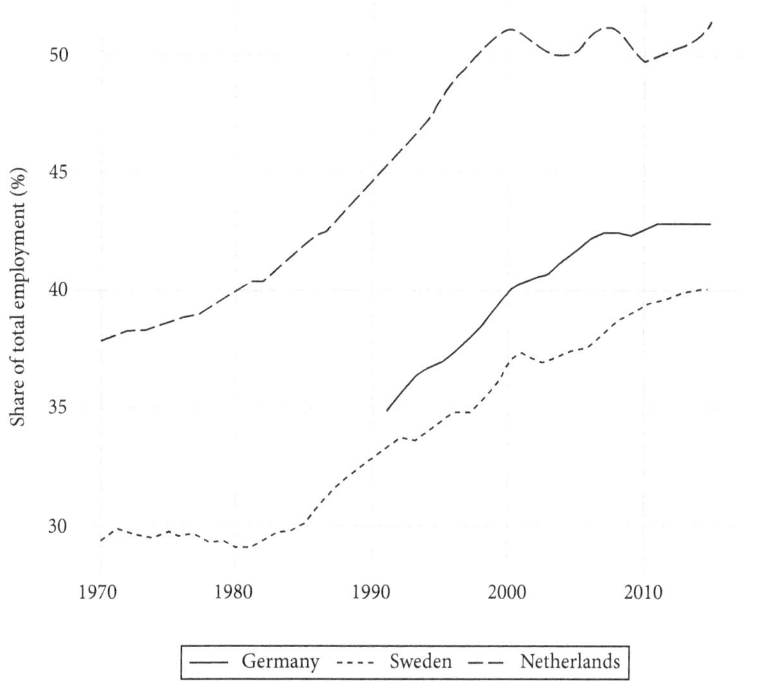

Figure 6.3 Employment share business service sector

Source: OECD STAN indicators, 1970–2015. https://stats.oecd.org/Index.aspx?DataSetCode=STANINDICATORS.

3. Explaining Divergent Trajectories

The dominant perspective in the literature on the comparative political economy of the rich democracies remains the influential Varieties of Capitalism (VoC) framework (Hall and Soskice 2001). This work distinguishes between liberal market economies (LMEs) of the Anglo-Saxon world and the coordinated market economies (CMEs) of Europe. It expects both types of political economies to adapt to changing market conditions by building on previous sources of institutional advantage, reinforcing differences between LMEs and CMEs. As such, nothing in the VoC literature could have predicted the evolution of two of these CMEs in an apparently liberal direction, as both Sweden's move into ICT and the Netherlands' move into business services are areas of economic activity closely associated with the liberal model.

An alternative perspective highlights the role of partisan politics in the evolution of advanced economies, locating the drivers of change in the voting public and the representatives they elect to office. The most important recent work in this vein, by Beramendi and colleagues, identifies four clusters corresponding to the social democratic, Christian democratic, liberal, and Southern European models (Beramendi et al. 2015). While illuminating the changing electoral foundations of social policy in these countries, their work does not explain the outcomes of interest in this chapter. For example, Germany and the Netherlands are both examples of what Beramendi et al. call "status oriented capitalism." (Beramendi et al. 2015:39). Yet the trajectories of change in the two countries' production profiles could hardly be more different.

Other lines of research are aimed at explaining the kinds of sectoral changes of interest here. Schneider and Paunescu (2012) demonstrate that the production profiles of some CMEs (including the Netherlands and Sweden) have shifted toward high-tech sectors typically associated with the liberal model. However, they do not pair this important observation with an explanation of the politics behind those changes. Ornston (2018), by contrast, does provide such an explanation, at least for the Nordic economies. Channeling insights from the corporatism literature, he suggests that the move into high-innovation sectors depends on corporatist consensus-building supported by state policy. The emphasis on the structure of organized interests and the role of the state is valuable, but this account obscures the intense contestation across and within sectors that often accompany these moves. Variation in the depth and character of that contestation, not consensus, is what gives the state an opening to steer outcomes in new directions.

Finally, Baccaro and Pontusson's (2016) analysis of growth models challenges consensus-based models and, like mine, draws attention to the distributive struggles that shape adjustment strategies. They draw a broad distinction between consumption-led growth and export-led growth, characterizing Germany as an example of export-led growth underwritten by suppression of wages (and consumption) and Sweden as a more "balanced" growth model that combines robust domestic consumption with strong exports. Although their outcome variable (growth) is different from mine (production profiles), their analysis is relevant because they argue that Sweden's more balanced model "critically depended on" the shift into ICT-related manufacturing and services (Baccaro and Pontusson 2016: 192). But how exactly did Sweden make the move into ICT? On that question, Baccaro and Pontusson's analysis is silent, though they do suggest that to answer it, it would be necessary to identify the specific "social blocs" that underpin different growth models. They further suggest that such an analysis would require attention paid to both the demand-side factors they emphasize and supply-side institutions such as education and national innovation policy. I agree; this is exactly the approach that is proposed by Hassel and Palier (this volume) and that I take in the analysis that follows.

The explanation offered here thus shares with Ornston (2018) an emphasis on the structure and strategies of organized interests and their interactions with the state. However, it embraces Baccaro and Pontusson's emphasis on distributive struggles both between labor and capital and within each bloc, while taking up their invitation to identify more precisely the specific social coalitions that lie behind divergent growth trajectories. My analysis shows how the trajectories of change we observe were shaped by the producer-group landscape and how state policy reinforced enduring or, in some cases, emerging coalitional alignments to set these three countries on different paths to the knowledge economy.

4. The German Growth Strategy: Doubling Down

Germany has long served as the exemplar of successful high-quality manufacturing targeting the upper end of traditional markets such as automobiles and capital goods. Debates over economic policy there center entirely on how best to defend and promote Germany as an attractive platform for high-end (now "advanced") manufacturing. In comparative perspective, the most remarkable feature of the German political economy is how little the country's product profile has changed over the post-war period.

Maintaining its commanding position in sectors like automobiles and machine tools is by no means a matter of inertia; this is an outcome that has to be actively defended and that has involved weathering a tremendous onslaught from both lower-cost producers and new entrants into the high-end markets that German producers have dominated for decades. Yet the German export machine has rarely looked stronger or more dominant. Exports make up a huge share of GDP, and Germany runs large trade surpluses year after year.[6]

The successful defense of the traditional core of German manufacturing is largely the work of a cross-class coalition within industry that is ideally configured and situated to defend and enhance these areas of strength. Both German unions and German employers are organized along sectoral lines, with weak overarching institutions and no serious crosscutting cleavages. On the union side, organization levels in manufacturing far outstrip those in services, and the metalworkers union (IG Metall) is by far the dominant actor. The largest of Germany's eight unions, it has never faced an effective counterweight; the overarching trade union confederation has no influence over the constituent unions. Public sector unions are formidable players in many advanced industrial countries, but the public sector in Germany is small by European standards (OECD 2015: 85, Tables 3.1 and 3.2). Finally, blue- and white-collar employees within a sector are organized into the same union, their fates jointly tied together and to the success of that sector.

The organization of German business mirrors that of unions. The employer associations that negotiate with labor are industry-based, and sectoral trade

[6] Spiegel Online (2018).

associations represent their interests politically. Moreover, unlike their conglomerate counterparts in Sweden, large German firms tend to be anchored in particular sectors (think of Daimler, VW, or BMW).[7] The same is true for Germany's powerful *Mittelstand* (small- and medium-sized companies), which is composed of firms whose fortunes are usually tied to particular industries (and sometimes, as suppliers, even to particular clients).

In short, manufacturing interests in Germany are tightly organized within particular industries and sectors. They are neither embedded in more encompassing associations nor forced to share power with similarly influential actors in other sectors. As the economy's unrivaled growth engine, industry enjoys outsized influence not just in the economy but in policy-making circles as well. These arrangements have helped forge an ironclad alliance in defense of long-standing sectoral strengths through both aggressive cost cutting and active adaptation of traditional institutional arrangements to new product markets and production technologies. The key developments in industrial relations, labor market policy, education/training, and innovation policy are outlined below.

In industrial relations, cross-class cooperation within the manufacturing core has intensified since the 1980s in response to heightened market pressures. Powerful works councils and managers have worked together over the past decades to control costs, outsourcing low-skill services previously performed in-house, and deploying temps and fixed-term workers to cover short-term cycles (Palier and Thelen 2010). Manufacturing unions and employers stood together to defend the principle of collective bargaining autonomy (i.e., non-state involvement) despite union weakness outside of manufacturing and the massive growth of low-wage work in the 2000s (Eichhorst and Marx 2009). It is an open secret that Germany's industrial unions were initially reluctant to support the introduction of a statutory minimum wage, fearing that this would produce downward pressure in their own wage negotiations.

Government policy reflects and reinforces the dominance of manufacturing interests. Labor market policies since the 1990s have stabilized employment for skilled manufacturing employees, even as they made work outside the protected core more flexible. The Hartz reforms of the early 2000s liberalized labor markets by slashing unemployment benefits and loosening restrictions on various forms of atypical work. However, even as government policy liberalized atypical employment, other measures specifically shielded skilled industrial workers from the vicissitudes of the market. In the turbulent years of 2008–9, the government passed three successive bills to extend the length and generosity of subsidies to firms wishing to avoid laying off their skilled workers (*Kurzarbeit*). Although employment in industry has fallen to about 20 percent of total employment in

[7] There are exceptions, of course, such as Siemens.

Germany, 80 percent of these subsidies went to workers in the manufacturing core. The metalworking sector collected the lion's share, and funds flowed disproportionately to two states (Baden-Württemberg and Bavaria) that lie at the heart of the German industrial export regime (Bundesagentur für Arbeit 2009). The government's "cash for clunkers" program (*Abwrackprämie*) sent a special lifeline to the car industry, causing a mini-boom for German automakers in the midst of the global crisis.[8]

Cost control strategies have been important in adjusting to a knowledge economy, but it would be a mistake to attribute the continued success of German industry solely, or even primarily, to wage suppression (Hope and Soskice 2016). Instead, continued success has involved the ongoing active adaptation of traditional political-economic arrangements to a rapidly evolving market context. In a period of explosive technological change, this especially applies to education and training. Governments in most other countries have responded to the increasing importance of high-end (especially engineering) skills by promoting higher education. However, in Germany, high-quality manufacturing has always relied heavily on firm-based vocational training, so employers and unions have worked together to upgrade the quality of such training as production becomes ever more knowledge-intensive (Thelen 2014: 86–93).

However, advanced manufacturing increasingly requires theoretical skills that firms themselves cannot provide efficiently. Thus, a further challenge has been to continue to attract the brightest students into industry while forestalling the drift toward what German employers consider "overly academic" training. The solution manufacturers have hit upon is to pursue partnerships with regional universities of applied sciences (*Fachhochschulen*) to create new and more demanding (also more theoretical) apprenticeships that confer, simultaneously, vocational certificates and bachelors' degrees. Top students are indeed drawn to these "dual study" programs, not just for the double certification but also because unlike "regular" university students they receive a wage (as apprentices) during their studies.[9] Crucially, access to these highly prized dual-study programs runs exclusively through companies; youth cannot apply directly but instead must be hired as apprentices by participating firms. Thus, rather than softening the line between vocational and university tracks as is occurring in most other countries, developments in Germany instead subsume part of the higher education system to the firm-dominated logic of the traditional vocational system (Thelen 2014: 89–90; Graf 2018; Chevalier, this volume).

The continued draw of the vocational system explains why academic higher education remains so dramatically underdeveloped in Germany. Figure 6.4 compares

[8] Ewing (2009).

[9] One study in Baden-Württemberg, for example, found that the students who were opting for such programs had higher Abitur scores than those who were going on to university. See Wiarda 2011.

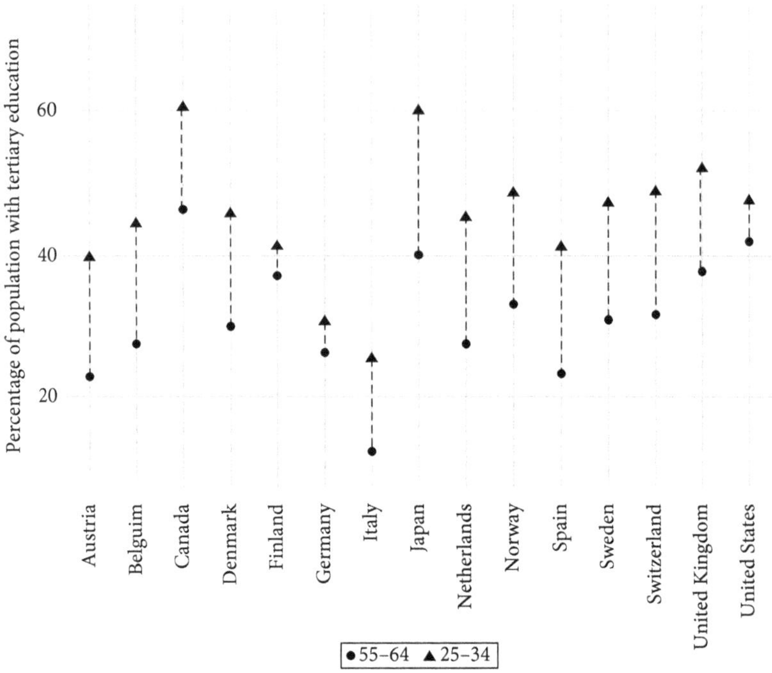

Figure 6.4 Population with tertiary education, 2016
Source: OECD Data, "Population with tertiary education," 2016. https://data.oecd.org/eduatt/population-with-tertiary-education.htm.

university completion rates for two generations. While most of the other rich democracies record large increases in tertiary completion rates among the younger cohort, Germany shows very modest movement.

Finally, the continued domination of manufacturing interests is on display in Germany's innovation policy. A national-level tripartite "Alliance for the Future of Industry" includes policy-makers and representatives of all the main manufacturing interests. The express goal is to defend Germany's position as an industrial power (*Industrie Standort Deutschland*) and to secure the competitiveness of German manufacturing in the digital era.[10] At the center of German innovation policy is an ambitious strategic initiative, *Industrie 4.0* (signaling the fourth industrial revolution), that involves major investments in research by government, universities, and companies. As a result of ongoing innovation within the industrial core, Germany has become a world leader in "internet of things" (IoT) and machine-to-machine (M2M) communication.[11] Although Industrie 4.0 is one of several "future projects" in Germany's "High Tech 2020" strategy, it is clearly the

[10] Bundesministerium für Wirtschaft und Energie (2020).

[11] See, for example, Chang 2016.

most important, receiving the lion's share of resources and attracting the greatest attention. For present purposes, what is as striking as the futuristic ambitions of this project is the cast of characters charged with implementing it, which reads like a who's who of the oldest and most influential actors in German economic history. The steering committee includes such nineteenth-century power brokers as the Trade Association for Mechanical Engineering (VDMA), the Federation of German Industry (BDI), the Manufacturers' Association for the Electrical Industry (ZVEI), the German Association of the Automotive Industry (VDA), and of course the IG Metall.

In sum, Germany's transition to the knowledge economy has not represented a sharp departure from traditional strengths, but instead a (so far extremely successful) doubling down on strategies supporting ever higher quality and increasingly digitized manufacturing. The developments outlined above reinforce the continued dominance of industrial interests in the German political economy, placing them at the center of the country's growth strategy for the knowledge economy.

5. The Swedish Growth Strategy: Branching Out

Sweden's post-war growth regime centered on many of the same export industries as Germany. However, manufacturing interests in Sweden compete for influence within a much denser organizational space where the relevant producer groups span sectors in ways that complicated the defense of particular firms and industries.

On the labor side, union density far exceeds that of Germany; Swedish unions have a stronger presence among both low-skill service workers and high-skill salaried employees. Manufacturing interests are powerful, but they are imbricated in associations that are both encompassing and crosscutting. Thus unlike its German counterpart, Sweden's main manufacturing union IF Metall is part of a broader blue-collar confederation that includes workers in other sectors, including low-skill services. IF Metall must also coordinate with white-collar unions in manufacturing that are themselves part of separate confederations of salaried employees, which have grown in size and strength with the shift in employment to services.

On the employer side, Swedish business interests are more concentrated and more diversified than in Germany. They are more concentrated because Sweden lacks an equivalent to Germany's politically influential *Mittelstand*. Instead, the economy historically has been dominated by a handful of large business groups, among them the vast Wallenberg dynasty, whose companies accounted for 10 percent of all private sector employment in Sweden in the 1970s (Lindgren 2002;

Larsson and Petersson 2013).[12] Today, the holdings of the top fifteen families in Sweden comprise 70 percent of the Stockholm exchange, and Sweden's two biggest business groups together hold controlling shares in thirteen of the country's twenty-five largest companies (Larsson and Petersson 2013: 6).[13]

Swedish business interests are also more diversified than their German counterparts, which, as we saw, tend to be rooted in particular industries. By contrast, Sweden's business groups have a presence across a wide range of sectors, spanning manufacturing and services and even export and domestic markets. For example, the Wallenbergs have major holdings in traditional manufacturing (e.g., ball bearings and appliances), but also in banking and ICT, and even education and healthcare. The country's second largest business group, Handelsbanken, has a similarly broad portfolio (Larsson and Petersson 2013: 6). Some prominent firms whose operations span different sectors have dual memberships in separate employer associations for industry and for services. For example, Ericsson is the largest member of the ICT group in the service employers' association Almega, but also belongs to the industry association Verkstadsföreningen. Other crossover companies include Kinnevik (telecommunications with roots in paper mills) and Industrivärden (active in banking, but also manufacturing, paper, and forest products, plus domestic and tradable services).

The very different producer-group landscape in Sweden supported a pattern of adjustment quite different from that of Germany. Stronger union presence outside manufacturing blocked German-style dualization, and indeed white-collar membership grew to outnumber blue-collar with the long-term shift in employment toward services. Sweden's business groups responded to market pressures by reshuffling their portfolios, exiting sectors such as automobiles, and moving upmarket into more knowledge-intensive manufacturing and services.[14] In the 1990s, Saab and Volvo passed into foreign hands, moves that in Germany surely would have triggered a spirited cross-class defense of treasured national symbols. However, in Sweden these events occurred without much drama, as business groups shifted resources into growth fields and the center of gravity in the labor movement began to tilt toward white-collar interests.

The move into ICT was led by a few key firms, most notably Ericsson, which wielded outsized influence both in the market and in politics.[15] The conservative

[12] Today, the Wallenbergs hold controlling shares in companies that together account for a third of those listed on the Swedish stock exchange, down from previous heights of over 50 percent (see Milne 2015; *The Economist* 2006: 73–4).

[13] Forsberg (2013).

[14] The philosophy of the Wallenberg business group, featured on its brochures, quotes a 1946 letter from Marcus Wallenberg to his brother Jacob: "to move from the old, to what is about to come, is the only tradition worth keeping." See, for example, https://www.wallenberg.com/en/family

[15] It is difficult to overstate the role that Ericsson (which occupies a prominent place in the portfolios of both of Sweden's two largest business groups) played in the ICT boom in Sweden. The company's export shares rose steadily in the late 1990s, and by 2000 accounted for almost 20 percent of total exports (Erixon 2011: 72.) But Ericsson was not alone. The country's fifth largest family-owned

government of 1990–94 strongly supported the move into high-technology markets through supply-side interventions—especially in education and innovation policy—and found ready allies both in Sweden's most influential business groups and in the expanding white-collar unions. The following paragraphs sketch out the relevant developments in four key arenas.

Major changes in industrial relations began in 1983 with the collapse of peak-level wage negotiations, a move that reflected the waning leadership of the blue-collar trade union confederation (LO). Wage decentralization in Sweden went beyond the widely known move from national-level to industry-level bargaining, allowing more room for local wage-setting. Employers sought such decentralized bargaining for the wage flexibility it offered, but unions of salaried professionals also favored local wage formation to address their members' demand for pay that reflected their investments in education and skills (Thelen 2014: 183; Ibsen and Thelen 2017: 423).

Wage decentralization exacerbated tensions between Sweden's blue- and white-collar confederations, and it also inspired competition between the two white-collar confederations whose members compete for status and jobs. Members of the academic/professional unions within the smaller Confederation of Professional Associations (SACO) are already university graduates. However, the same is not true for members of the larger Confederation of Salaried Employees (TCO), which, since the 1990s, has made increased access to higher education its number one priority. Merit- and education-based wage differentiation thus heightened demand for changes in state education policy. German-style (firm-based) apprenticeship had been eliminated decades before, but two-year vocational tracks continued to exist alongside three-year academic tracks in Swedish high schools. In 1991, the government passed a major reform, implemented over the next few years, that eliminated the two-year track and opened the path to university studies to all (Halldén 2008: 256; Chevalier, this volume). The government also increased spending on education from 5.3 percent of GDP in 1990 to 7.4 percent by 2000, and doubled spending on higher education specifically (from 1 percent of GDP to 2 percent in this period) (Steinmo 2010: 71, Table 2.11). As Figure 6.4 indicated, Sweden registered a very large increase in completion of tertiary education, and surpassed the United States by 2009.

Unlike in Germany, Sweden's labor market policy focused on easing the transition away from the traditional manufacturing core rather than on preserving it. During the 1980s, Swedish labor market policies had drifted toward defensive job-preserving measures (Pontusson 1992, 138), but the conservative government of the early 1990s answered a sharp and unprecedented rise in unemployment with a massive expansion of active labor market policies. Spending on ALMP rose

business group (Stenbeck) also moved aggressively out of traditional manufacturing and into IT sectors, especially media and entertainment, in the 1990s.

from 1.7 to 2.6 percent of GDP, and by the time the conservatives left office in 1994, fully 7.3 percent of the total labor force was engaged in ALMP programs. The subsequent social democratic government continued these policies. Over the entire 1992–97 period, ALMP expenditures as a share of total public expenditure and GDP was higher in Sweden than in any other OECD country, especially after adjusting for the rate of unemployment (Thelen 2014: 114, Fig. 4.1).

While labor market policies eased the transition out of traditional manufacturing, state innovation policy actively promoted the move into ICT. Prime Minister Carl Bildt, an early advocate (and well-known "computer freak") convened a government commission in 1993 that laid out a comprehensive plan for Sweden to become a leading player in the IT sector.[16] However, in a feature that is hard to square with Ornston's (2018) picture of consensus-based change, the commission did not include a single representative of Sweden's producer groups. It was instead composed of top executives from six firms that were all active in the telecommunications or computer software industries (including notably Ericsson's CEO), alongside experts from academia (Swedish Government 1994: 48). Sweden's innovation policy, unlike that of Germany, focused on infrastructure and especially users of IT rather than manufacturers (Fogelberg 2011: 15–16; Augustsson 2005: ch. 5). The commission's report, with the evocative title "Wings to Human Ability," recommended introducing computers into classrooms across Sweden, educating teachers in technology, and encouraging the integration of IT into instruction at all levels (Swedish Government 1994: 118).[17] The government financed these efforts by redirecting the defunct wage earner funds that had originally been intended to achieve collective ownership (Augustsson 2005: 89, n.37).

Swedish unions got on board after the conservative government left office and played a key role in disseminating IT technology and skills. Recognizing that computer literacy would be crucial to their members' employment prospects, the LO and TCO began to negotiate steep volume discounts from PC suppliers that they passed on to their members (Fogelberg 2011: 34). A large number of Swedish employees acquired their first home computer in this way.[18] The Swedish employee PC purchase schemes were wildly popular, and in 1997 political parties from both the right and left supported a measure to make these purchases tax-free. Thus developed "a three-party collaboration between the state, employers and unions" that resulted in a dramatic expansion of the number of Swedish households with a computer and internet access (Fogelberg 2011: 34). The biggest

[16] Author interview with Anders Hektor, senior member of the IT policy unit, Swedish Ministry for Enterprise and Innovation, Stockholm, May 2017.

[17] On the "IT in Schools" program (ITiS), see especially, Augustsson (2005: 88–9).

[18] Author interview with Mats Essemyr, Confederation of Salaried Employees (TCO), 2017.

increase occurred between 1996 and 2000, and by 2006, almost 1.6 million of Sweden's 4.3 million households had taken advantage of the Home PC program.[19] The program is now "considered a major reason for the rapid and, in an international comparison, early diffusion of PCs among Swedish households," and credited with having played an important role in Sweden's ICT transformation by providing a "great lift in digital literacy" (Fogelberg 2011: 34).[20]

The Social Democratic government of the late 1990s complemented these initiatives with policies to expand ICT skills within the general population (i.e., beyond the constituencies served by the union-based initiatives). The "Knowledge Lift" (KL) program of 1997–2002 offered training at existing adult education centers, and computer science was an especially popular subject in each of the five years the program ran. A separate program from 1998 to 2000, "Swedish Information and Technology" (SWIT), promoted IT skills specifically (Thelen 2014: 189).

These supply-side developments are crucial to explaining the Swedish ICT boom. Not only does Sweden feature an exceptionally large number of ICT specialists; the digital skills of the country's population as a whole are at or near the top of all EU countries.[21] The success of the Swedish gaming industry, as well as firms such as Skype and Spotify, are partly a function of the fact that the country has a population that consists of very sophisticated consumers (as well as producers) of ICT (Pontusson 2009: 108).

In sum, while Germany was doubling down in its traditional areas of manufacturing strength, Sweden moved into higher technology manufacturing and services. State policy played a key role in promoting ICT, but the producer-group landscape was critically important in facilitating a shift in Sweden's growth regime. The crosscutting interests of key producer group actors in Sweden prevented the emergence of a sector-based cross-class alliance of the sort that dominates the German political economy. Diversified business groups faced strong incentives to shift resources into more knowledge-intensive activities, and Ericsson played a central role, functioning "as an organizational and technological hub both within the ICT sector and between new and traditional industries in Sweden" (Erixon 2011: 71). State policy actively promoted the move upmarket through policies that also reinforced the shift in the balance of power within the labor movement away from the blue-collar LO and toward white-collar unions.

[19] The rapid diffusion of internet, broadband, and computers in the late 1990s (and beyond) is documented in Svenskarna och Internet (https://svenskarnaochinternet.se/rapporter/svenskarna-och-internet-2019/allmant-om-internetutvecklingen/).

[20] Hektor interview, 2017; See note 17.

[21] See the European Commission Digital Scoreboard (2020).

6. The Dutch Growth Strategy: Transitioning Back

Meanwhile, of the three countries considered here, the Netherlands has shifted the furthest, at least from its goals of the immediate post-war period. The institutions of Dutch corporatism had been expressly created in the 1940s to promote manufacturing to transform the country "from an agricultural into an industrial economy" (Bouwens and Dankers 2010: 753). However, industrial development in the 1950s and 1960s was premised on low-cost strategies that became unsustainable in the 1970s when revenues from natural resources caused a steep appreciation of the Dutch currency. The collapse of Dutch manufacturing created an organizational vacuum within the institutions of Dutch corporatism, allowing the state to engineer a more dramatic reconfiguration of the country's growth regime, one that has come to be premised on a new "owner-worker" alliance (Engelen, Konings, and Fernandez 2008: 629).

Producer groups in the Netherlands in the immediate post-war period closely resembled those in Germany in the 1950s and 1960s, with unions dominated by blue-collar workers and manufacturing interests enjoying privileged access to government. Unlike in Germany, however, Dutch social partnership relied more heavily on direct state support through the government's regular use of extension clauses to massively amplify the reach of union contracts (Hemerijck 1995: 201).

The institutions of corporatism that had been created to promote manufacturing survived its collapse. However, the goals and functions of the heralded Polder model were transformed in the 1980s as the government turned toward services and as social partnership came to revolve around negotiating an orderly retreat from manufacturing, especially via early retirement. Unions are full partners in the joint management of occupational pension funds, which grew over the 1990s from "sleepy bureaucratic" investors into "prominent financial institutions in their own right" (Dixon 2008: 265). These developments transformed union interests, paving the way for the consolidation of a new worker–owner alliance around finance and international business services. Again, I review the most significant changes in industrial relations, labor market policy, education, and innovation policy.

Industrial relations in the 1970s and 1980s were still dominated by manufacturing interests and were largely devoted to negotiating the terms on which industrial downsizing would occur. In Germany, the adjustments of the 1970s and early 1980s had left manufacturing leaner but also more competitive, while in the Netherlands manufacturing continued its decline. Membership in Dutch unions plummeted to below 20 percent, and the country's leading firms (including Philips, Shell, and Unilever) turned toward global expansion and diversification. With collective bargaining centered on industrial retrenchment and downsizing, supplemental "second-tier" (collectively bargained) pensions became a major theme in industrial relations. Thanks to a 1949 law that allowed the Ministry of

Social Affairs to declare occupational pensions negotiated at the industry level compulsory for all firms in the sector, 90 percent of Dutch wage earners participate in industry-wide funds co-managed by the social partners (Anderson 2012: 208).

On the employer side, the collapse of the heavily subsidized Rijn-Schelde-Verolme shipyards in 1983 spelled "an end to the old industry policy" (Velzing 2013: 218). The Ministry of Economic Affairs, which had previously interacted directly with leading manufacturers, now distanced itself and downgraded its Department of Industry. Within top government circles, new voices emphatically argued against intervening on behalf of industry and advocated a turn toward services.[22] The Dutch insurance industry (comprising ABN, Rabo, ING, and Aegon) became increasingly influential in this period, and the Dutch temporary agency firm Randstad grew mightily to become the second largest player in the industry worldwide.[23]

Labor market policy in these years began to reflect and reinforce the changed economic landscape as the government retreated from policies aimed at preserving manufacturing and promoted service employment instead. In part prompted by EU mandates, the government encouraged the entry of women into the labor market by removing some of the discriminatory policies (e.g., in the tax code) that had traditionally discouraged female employment—changes that coincided with a reduction in benefits for their under- or unemployed husbands (Watson et al. 1999: 26). Within a single generation the Netherlands experienced a very significant increase in female labor market participation (Thelen 2014: 164–5). Dutch women who had not expected to enter the paid workforce had mostly opted for the general rather than vocational track in upper secondary school, and thus entered the labor market with exactly the kind of skills (e.g., foreign languages) that service firms sought. The lack of public day care in this Christian Democratic country meant that most women worked part-time, but this did not pose a problem for the service industries they entered, where scheduling was anyway more fluid than in traditional manufacturing sectors.

Unions, initially skeptical about the rise in part-time employment, changed their tune in the early 1990s as growing levels of household debt rendered many families dependent on that second income to make their mortgage payments (Schwartz and Seabrooke 2008: 258). This shift brought their interests into alignment with those of service firms who valued the flexibility of part-time work. A major corporatist bargain in 1993 resulted in legislation upgrading the status and benefits of part-time work by prohibiting discrimination on the basis of working hours and ensuring equal treatment in wages, overtime pay, holidays, bonuses, occupational pensions, and training (Thelen 2014: 168).

[22] Author interview with a senior civil servant who was active at that time in the technology policy unit at the Economics Ministry, The Hague, June 2015.

[23] Author interview with Ad Kolnaar, former crown member of the Social-Economic Council, 2010.

The government's innovation policy further reflected and reinforced the growing influence of business services. A 1996 government report advocated using resources from the "old economy" (i.e., the exploitation of natural gas), to support the transition toward the "knowledge economy" (Vermeulen 2015: 36). Marja Wagenaar, social democratic MP from 1997 to 2002, emphasized "huge demand" on the part of the country's internationally oriented industry and finance sectors to use the gas revenues to develop a high-quality glass-fiber ICT network.[24] So, at about the same time that the Swedes were investing in the dissemination of IT skills, the Dutch focused on IT infrastructure beginning with the construction of a vast IT network (1996–1998), continuing with policies promoting the widespread use of ICT (1998–2001), and finally extending its application (beginning in 2001) (Jordi Molas-Gallart et al. 2003). The Netherlands emerged from these initiatives as a leader in e-health, e-education, and e-government. By 2013 it also led all other EU countries in the number of households with access to the internet at home, as well as in usage rates among its citizens.[25]

The move into knowledge-intensive business services was also accompanied and supported by important reforms to the education system. While Germany was avoiding a break with traditional firm-based VET, the Dutch state was engaged in reforms that promoted the kind of general skills that most observers see as central to the development of services, especially high-end services (Anderson and Hassel 2013: 187–8; Wren, this volume). While Germany continues to valorize practical training and discourage overly "bookish" studies, the Dutch government began favoring general education, arguing that while "practical skills can be relatively easily acquired" during an employee's working life, "gaps in basic knowledge are difficult to make up later" (SCP 2006: 269).

Thus, and again unlike in Germany, there has been a very significant increase in university attendance in the Netherlands, which over the past generation has nearly caught up to the United States. As Figure 6.4 showed, the trend in tertiary educational attainment in the Netherlands tracks rather closely with developments in Sweden, with large increases beginning in the 1990s. Changes in education in turn fueled steep increases in employment across a range of professional services between 1994 and 2008 as employment in lower-skill jobs shrank (Gielen and Schils 2014: 6).

Dutch unions continue to over-represent male manufacturing workers, but the transition out of manufacturing itself tied them closer to services and ultimately to financial services. One contributing factor, already noted, is the widespread dependence of households on 1.5 incomes (thus also women's employment) in a country characterized by extremely high consumer debt (Afonso and Visser 2015: 242). However, the bigger part of the story is the pension funds that are co-

[24] Author interview, Halfweg (Netherlands), June 2015.

[25] See European Commission Digital Scoreboard (2020).

managed by the unions. Dutch pension funds are truly massive, amounting in 2012 to 160 percent of the country's GDP (compared to German and Swedish pension funds, which account for a mere 6.3 percent and 9.2 percent of GDP, respectively) (OECD 2013: 11).

As Dutch pension funds grew to become large institutional investors operating on a global scale, unions became reliable allies in the financialization of the Dutch economy (Van der Zwan 2014: 118). A senior policy officer within the Dutch Social-Economic Council (SER) emphasizes the way in which joint pension management stabilizes Dutch corporatism: "The joint management of sector-wide pension funds is an important foundation of the institutional strength of Dutch unions."[26] He notes that their shared stake in the health of the second-tier pensions means that the social partners work together in this area "on an intense and ongoing basis."

These dynamics explain the very different reactions of the Germans and Dutch to the financial crisis of the late 2000s. In Germany the crisis mobilized a cross-class coalition of corporate insiders (managers and unions) against (financial) outsiders, while in the Netherlands, an alternative "worker–owner" coalition (unions + financial interests) dampened pressure for stricter regulation, not as a matter of regulatory capture but instead of "consensual politics" (Engelen, Konings, and Fernandez 2008: 621–2).

The transition into knowledge-intensive business services and finance represents, thus, a significant change in the Dutch political economy, especially when compared to the low-cost industrial strategies the country was pursuing in the 1950s and 1960s. In a phrase that no German policy-maker would ever utter, a representative of the Dutch Education Ministry says: "We think of ourselves as a service economy—finance and services."[27] The collapse of Dutch manufacturing in the 1970s had dramatically altered the producer-group landscape even as the path out of manufacturing laid the groundwork for a new cross-class coalition by transforming Dutch workers into owners (Engelen, Konings, and Fernandez 2010: 68–9). The venerable Polder model did not break down, but it was significantly reconfigured and came increasingly to serve FIRE industries.

7. Conclusion

This chapter has documented the political underpinnings of three quite different pathways toward a knowledge economy. The German case stands out for the remarkable continuity in the composition of economic activity, even as traditional products and production processes are being revolutionized by digital

[26] Author interview with Bart van Riel, 2015.
[27] Author interview with a senior official in the Dutch Ministry of Education, 2015.

technologies. In this case, a powerful and resilient cross-class coalition in manufacturing, supported and reinforced by state policy, is presiding over the transition to the knowledge economy.

Sweden has seen a series of subtler changes as many of the same business conglomerates that dominated the post-war growth regime have transitioned into different types of economic activity. Encompassing unions and crosscutting cleavages mitigated German-style dualism, facilitating a shift in resources into higher value-added markets in both manufacturing and services. Here state policy served as a midwife, assisting the move upmarket through innovation and education policies that created the infrastructure within which knowledge-intensive firms could thrive, while further enhancing the already-growing size and power of salaried employees within the labor movement.

The Netherlands, finally, has witnessed a more profound shift, as the collapse of the original low-cost manufacturing strategy paved the way for a more significant coalitional realignment to occur within the traditional institutions of social partnership. In this case, active government support for the transition to services and the evolution of organized labor's interests laid the foundation for a redirection of the Dutch political economy back to its historic strengths in trade and finance, though now in a decidedly higher-tech direction.

The three trajectories of change outlined here do not exhaust all possible routes toward a knowledge economy transition; other countries may chart different courses depending on the political dynamics and coalitions, as analyzed in other chapters in this volume. Moreover, all three of the pathways documented here appear to be economically viable in sense of producing growth, at least in medium run. However, each is vulnerable to somewhat different pathologies and associated with different distributional outcomes. Germany's manufacturing-based export-led growth is wildly successful in international markets. However, the continued emphasis on traditional sectors like automobiles still leaves German producers exposed to relentless cost pressures that are unlikely to let up, and that have already contributed to a growing divide between labor market insiders and outsiders. Thus, despite its enviable trade surplus, the German political economy has also seen higher levels of low-wage work and poverty.

The Swedish growth regime is more complex and to some observers more balanced (Baccaro and Pontusson 2016, and this volume). While it is true that the economy is performing well on many levels, the changes described above have set in motion potentially unsettling dynamics. High union coverage among low-skill workers has placed a more solid floor on downward wage pressures, but inequality in Sweden at the upper end of the income spectrum has risen as white collar interests have grown in size and strength. Employers have seized on these developments, attempting to sideline the LO entirely, which, if successful, would have a profound effect on Sweden's hitherto relatively egalitarian model of capitalism.

Finally, the Dutch growth regime also has its strengths, including, among other things, vastly improved levels of female labor market participation in a country that was once a spectacular laggard on this score. At the same time, however, the growing role of finance renders the Dutch political economy vulnerable to some of the pathologies that we have traditionally associated with liberal market economies such as the United States, including boom-bust-bubble dynamics and a further weakening and fragmentation of unions. As Engelen et al. have pointed out, the Netherlands is an extreme outlier in the context of the Varieties of Capitalism literature, combining as it does high coordination with high financialization (Engelen et al. 2010: 61). It remains to be seen how stable that combination will prove over the longer run.

Stepping back from the three countries explored in this chapter, two further overarching conclusions come into view. The first, wholly consistent with one of the core messages of the original Varieties of Capitalism framework, is that the shared pressures of technological change are unlikely to result in convergence on a single dominant model of capitalism. Second, the distinct trajectories that we have observed across these three coordinated market economies—including in some cases moves into areas of strength we have traditionally associated with the liberal model—suggest limits to the capacity of the VoC framework as originally conceived to capture current developments. My analysis suggests that a more dynamic understanding of political-economic resilience and change requires a shift in attention from the specific arrangements that support different models of capitalism to the changing political coalitions on which these models rest.[28]

References

Afonso, A. and Visser, J. 2015. "The Liberal Road to High Employment and Low Inequality?." In *European Social Models from Crisis to Crisis*, edited by Jon Erik Dølvik and Andrew Martin. Oxford: Oxford University Press, 214–45.

Anderson, K. M. 2012. "The Netherlands: Reconciling Labour Market Flexicurity with Security in Old Age." In *Labour Market Flexibility and Pension Reform*, edited by Karl Hinrichs and Matteo Jessoula. Basingstoke: Palgrave, 203–30.

[28] This chapter has first been published as "Transitions to the knowledge economy in Germany, Sweden, and the Netherlands." *Comparative Politics* 51(2): 295–15. I would like to thank *Comparative Politics* for permission to reprint this article, and to the conveners of the original "Growth Regimes" project, Bruno Palier and Anke Hassel. My thanks as well to Lucio Baccaro, Marius Busemeyer, Jan-Erik Dølvik, Anton Hemerijck, Martin Höpner, Daniel Mügge, Darius Ornston, Jonas Pontusson, Wiemer Salverda, Waltraud Schelke, Ben Schneider, Herman Schwartz, Jason Spicer, John Stephens, Ernst-Jan Velzing, and Jelle Visser for valuable input on the original article. I am grateful to Elizabeth Dekeyser, and especially to Olivia Bergman and Andreas Wiedemann, who provided expert research assistance.

Anderson, K. M. and Hassel, A. 2013. "Pathways of Change in CMEs: Training Regimes in Germany and the Netherlands." In *The Political Economy of the Service Transition*, edited by Anne Wren. Oxford: Oxford University Press, 171–94.

Augustsson, F. 2005. *They Did IT: The Formation and Organisation of Interactive Media Production in Sweden*. Stockholm: National Institute for Working Life.

Baccaro, L. and Pontusson, J. 2016. "Rethinking Comparative Political Economy: The Growth Model Perspective." *Politics & Society* 44 (June): 175–207.

Beramendi, P., Häusermann, S., Kitschelt, H. and Kriesi, H. 2015. "Introduction." In *The Politics of Advanced Capitalism*, edited by Pablo Beramendi, Silja Hausermann, Herbert Kitschelt and Hanspeter Kriesi. New York: Cambridge University Press, 1–64.

Bouwens, B. and Dankers, J. 2010. "The Invisible Handshake: Cartelization in the Netherlands, 1930–2000." *Business History Review* 84(4) (Winter): 751–71.

Bundesagentur für Arbeit. 2009. *Der Arbeitsmarkt in Deutschland: Kurzarbeit, Aktuelle Entwicklungen*. Berlin: Bundesagentur für Arbeit, 11–13.

Bundesministerium für Wirtschaft und Energie. 2020. "Gemeinsam die Industrie stärken." https://www.bmwi.de/Redaktion/DE/Dossier/buendnis-zukunft-industrie.html (accessed February 3, 2020).

Chang, L. 2016. "When It Comes to the IoT, Germany is Beating the U.S." *Digital Trends* (June).

Dixon, A. 2008. "The Rise of Pension Fund Capitalism in Europe." *New Political Economy* 13 (September): 257–8.

Eichhorst, W. and Marx, P. 2009. "Reforming German Labor Market Institutions: A Dual Path to Flexibility." *IZA Discussion Paper* 4100 (March 2009). Bonn: Forschungsinstitut zur Zukunft der Arbeit.

Engelen, E., Konings, M. and Fernandez, R. 2008. "The Rise of Activist Investors and Patterns of Political Responses." *Socio-Economic Review* 6(4) (October): 611–36.

Engelen, E., Konings, M. and Fernandez, R. 2010. "Geographies of Financialization in Disarray: The Dutch Case in Comparative Perspective." *Economic Geography* 86(1) (January): 53–73.

Erixon, L. 2011. "Under the Influence of Traumatic Events, New Ideas, Economic Experts and the ICT Revolution: The Economic Policy and Macroecnomic Performance of Sweden in the 1990s and 2000s." *Comparative Social Research* 28(1) (October): 265–330.

European Commission Digital Scoreboard. 2020. https://ec.europa.eu/digital-single-market/en/scoreboard/sweden (accessed February 4, 2020).

Ewing, J. 2009. "Car-Scrapping Plans—Germany's Lessons." *Der Spiegel*, May 7, 2009.

Fogelberg, H. 2011. "Research on IT Use and Users in Sweden, with Particular Focus on 1990–2010." *Working Paper of the Division of History of Science and Technology*, [TRITA/HST/2011/1], 15–16.

Forsberg, B. 2013. "De 15 nya familjerna." *Affärsvärlden*, June 25, 2013.

Gielen, A. and Schils, T. 2014. "Non-Standard Employment Patterns in the Netherlands." *IZA Policy Paper* 77 (January 2014).

Graf, L. 2018. "Combined Modes of Gradual Change." *Socio-Economic Review* 16 (2018): 185–205.

Halldén, K., 2008. "The Swedish Educational System and Classifying Education Using The ISCED-97." In *International Standard Classification of Education (ISCED-97)*, edited by Silke L. Schneider. Mannheim: MZES, 253–67.

Hall, P. and Soskice, D. 2001. *Varieties of Capitalism*, Oxford: Oxford University Press.

Hemerijck, A., 1995. "Corporatist Immobility in the Netherlands." In *Organized Industrial Relations in Europe: What Future?*, edited by Colin Crouch and Franz Traxler. Aldershot: Avebury, 183–226.

Hope, D. and Soskice, D. 2016. "Growth Models, Varieties of Capitalism, and Macroeconomics." *Politics & Society* 44 (June): 209–26.

Ibsen, C. L. and Thelen, K. 2017. "Diverging Solidarity: Labor Strategies in the New Knowledge Economy." *World Politics* 69(3) (July): 409–47.

Iversen, T. and Soskice, D. 2015. "Democratic Limits to Redistribution: Inclusionary versus Exclusionary Coalitions in the Knowledge Economy." *World Politics* 67 (April): 185–225.

Larsson, M. and Petersson, T. 2013. "Tradition and Renewal—Business Groups in Sweden from the late 19th Century to the Present Day." Paper presented at the European Business History Association, Uppsala, August 2013.

Lindgren, H. 2002. "Succession Strategies in a Large Family Business Group: The Case of the Swedish Wallenberg Family." Paper prepared for the 6th European Business History Association Congress, Helsinki, August 22–4.

Milne, R. 2015. "Meet the Wallenbergs." *Financial Times*, June 5, 2015.

Molas-Gallart, J., Tang, P., Flowers, S., Hulsink, W., Davies, A., Gooijer, W. and Spaapen, J. 2003. "A Review of the ICT Policy in the Netherlands and the UK." *Swedish Institute for Growth Policy Report* A2003:015. Stockholm: Swedish Institute for Growth Policy Studies.

OEC. 2016a. "What Does Germany Export? (2016)." http://atlas.media.mit.edu/en/visualize/tree_map/hs92/export/deu/all/show/2016/ (accessed February 3, 2020).

OEC. 2016b. "What does Sweden export? (2016)." https://oec.world/en/visualize/tree_map/hs92/export/swe/all/show/2016/ (accessed February 3, 2020).

OEC. 2016c. "What Does the Netherlands Export? (2016)." http://atlas.media.mit.edu/en/visualize/tree_map/hs92/export/nld/all/show/2016/ (accessed February 3, 2020).

OECD STAN indicators. 2011. "Employment Share in ICT Manufacturing and Service Activities." OECD STAN indicators, 1970–2014. https://stats.oecd.org/Index.aspx?DataSetCode=STANINDICATORS (accessed February 3, 2020).

OECD. 2015. *Government at a Glance 2015*. Paris: OECD Publishing.

OECD. 2013. *Pension Markets in Focus*. Paris: OECD.

Ornston, D. 2018. *Good Governance Gone Bad: How Nordic Adaptability Leads to Excess*. Ithaca, NY: Cornell University Press.

Palier, B. and Thelen, K. 2010. "Institutionalizing Dualism: Complementarities and Change in France and Germany." *Politics & Society* 38 (March): 119–48.

Pontusson, J. 1992. *The Limits of Social Democracy*. Ithaca: Cornell University Press.

Pontusson, J. 2009. "Once Again a Model: Nordic Social Democracy in a Globalized World." In *Futures of the Left*, edited by George Ross, James Shoch and James Cronin. Durham: Duke University Press.

Schneider, M. and Paunescu, M. 2012. "Changing Varieties of Capitalism and Revealed Comparative Advantages from 1990 to 2005." *Socio-Economic Review* 10 (October): 731–53.

Schwartz, H. and Seabrooke, L. 2008. "Varieties of Residential Capitalism in the International Political Economy." *Comparative European Politics* 6(3) (September): 237–61.

SCP (Dutch Office of Social and Cultural Planning). 2006. *Duaal Als Ideaal?* The Netherlands: The Hague.

Spiegel Online. 2018. "Deutschland erzielt weltweit größte Überschuss." *Der Spiegel*, August 20, 2018.

Steinmo, S. 2010. *The Evolution of Modern States*. New York: Cambridge University Press.

The Economist. 2006. "Sweden's Enduring Business Dynasty." *The Economist*, October 14, 2006, 73–4.

Swedish Government. 1994. *Vingar åt människans förmåga*. Stockholm: Statens offentliga utredninngar, 118.

Thelen, K. 2014. *Varieties of Liberalization*. New York: Cambridge University Press.

Thelen, K. 2017. "Diverging Solidarity: Labor Strategies in the New Knowledge Economy." *World Politics* 69 (July): 409–47.

Van der Zwan, N. 2014. "Making Sense of Financialization." *Socio-Economic Review* 12(1) (January): 99–129.

Velzing, E.-J. 2013. "Innovatiepolitiek: Een reconstructie van het innovatiebeleid van het miniterie van Economische Zaken van 1976 tot en met 2010." PhD Thesis, Amsterdam School of Economics Research Institute.

Vermeulen, N. 2015. "From Virus to Vaccine: Projectification of Science in the VIRGO Consortium." In *Collaboration Across Health Research and Medical Care: Healthy Collaboration*, edited by Bart Penders, Niki Vermuelen and John N. Parker. Surry, England: Ashgate Publishing, 31–58.

Watson, M., Bakker, B. B., Martijn, J. K. and Halikias, I. 1999. *The Netherlands: Transforming A Market Economy*. Washington DC: International Monetary Fund.

Wiarda, J. M. 2011. "Dual an der Spitze." *Die Zeit*, July 21, 2011. http://www.zeit.de/2011/30/C-Dual (accessed February 4, 2020).

7

Growth Strategies and Employers' Coalitions: Renewing Welfare States

Cathie Jo Martin

1. Introduction

The Danish Ministry of Energy, Utilities and Climate was established in 2015 to help this small, Nordic country gain independence from fossil fuels, embrace energy efficiencies, and establish new green technologies (State of Green n.d.). Many Danish employers see the green transition as a great opportunity to export cutting-edge technologies to world markets, while advancing a socially responsible agenda (Danish Energy Agency n.d.). In sharp contrast, the Environmental Protection Agency under President Trump embarked on a campaign of regulatory rollback, spurred on by industry groups with vested interests in weakening environmental standards. How can we make sense of these sharply divergent policy agendas and the preferences of employers who join in these campaigns?

The short answer is that Denmark and the United States have chosen different growth strategies. As shown by Hassel and Palier in Chapter 1 of this volume, different growth strategies are related to different growth regimes, embodied in the network of institutions and organizations that shape the economic, social, and environmental preferences of firms, workers, and consumers. Diverse growth regimes elicit distinctive choices of social and labor market policies, because modes of economic governance make different demands for the skills and productivity of workers.

Periodically, governments alter their growth strategies in response to exogenous stresses; their new goals and proposed policies to meet these goals may succeed in altering the growth regimes of their countries. The choice of new growth strategies at critical junctures is a dynamic process, fraught with conflict and sometimes tempered by compromise. Countries with similar past growth regimes may vary in their development of new growth strategies; indeed, the diversity of growth strategies after the global economic crisis resulted in a proliferation of hybrid growth regimes in the post-crisis, post-industrial economy (Picot, this volume) that shifted the boundaries of the welfare state (Avlijaš, Hassel, and Palier, this volume). Dominant producer groups are often crucial participants in post-crisis efforts to articulate new growth strategies. Yet the state

Cathie Jo Martin, *Growth Strategies and Employers' Coalitions: Renewing Welfare States* In: *Growth and Welfare in Advanced Capitalist Economies: How Have Growth Regimes Evolved?* Edited by: Anke Hassel and Bruno Palier,
Oxford University Press (2021). © Oxford University Press. DOI: 10.1093/oso/9780198866176.003.0007

must build coalitions with influential employers and organized interests to forge these new growth strategies (and changing social reform packages), and the process is neither automatic nor functionalist.

This chapter explores how employers choose to participate in the coalitions constructed around shifting growth strategies. Dominant producer groups' social preferences should be in accordance with countries' growth models articulated in earlier chapters. These include growth through the exports of manufacturing good, growth through exports of dynamic services, demand-led growth relying on public Keynesian fiscal policies, and demand-led growth relying on private Keynesian policies to foster easy credit and household debt. Thus, in countries that produce economic growth largely through exports, dominant producer groups should prefer social policies designed to sustain an export strategy.

Yet industrial relations institutions are also crucial to how dominant producer groups join with the state and other social actors to conceptualize their economic and social preferences, and to participate collectively in efforts to forge new growth regimes. Particularly in countries with macro-corporatist institutions, employers negotiate collective positions that sustain a high level of social provision conforming to economic growth. Macro-corporatist peak business associations expose employers to arguments about social contributions to economic growth, overcome limits to collective action, enforce compliance to negotiated regulations, and accord to business significant influence on policy outcomes. Most importantly, high levels of coordination augment capacities for economic correction at points in which older growth strategies become less viable.

The following pages set forth the expected welfare state preferences of dominant producer groups who pursue the alternative avenues for growth. I then explore how industrial relations organizations contribute to firms' preferences, willingness to enter into public–private coalitions, and capacities for economic adjustment. For example, in the wake of the global financial crisis, the Danish government articulated a new "green" growth strategy and worked with well-organized employers to expand the country's shrinking manufacturing sector with a vibrant renewable energy sector. Denmark's capacity for economic renewal and support from the social partners allows for continuing high levels of social provision.

2. Growth Strategies and Social Policies

During the post-war golden age of economic prosperity, industrial societies used social protection schemes to attain high levels of economic growth (Shonfield 1965). Yet economic transformations in the past few decades have, to varying degrees, reshaped the boundaries of welfare states. Deindustrialization sets limits on national capacities to pay for systems of social protections, because productivity growth rates are lower in many service sectors than in manufacturing

(Iversen and Wren 1998). The global financial crisis and subsequent Great Recession wreaked havoc on growth rates and eroded national capacities to offer social protections against growing economic risks. Policy-makers in many countries espoused the new economic wisdom of debt reduction and structural reforms to improve competitiveness (Lehndorff 2015: 13). In this vein, the EU 2020 strategy for economic competitiveness asked countries to combine growth-inducing economic policies with structural reforms of the welfare state (European Commission 2010; Hassel and Palier in this volume).

Countries have exhibited varying capacities to maintain social protections in the new age of austerity, in part due to their dominant growth regimes (Wren; Hassel and Palier, this volume). Countries may seek economic expansion with a flourishing export market, in which producers export high-quality manufacturing goods or dynamic services. Alternatively, countries may grow primarily by stimulating domestic consumption with the use of Keynesian government interventions (tax cuts or spending) or with private Keynesianism policies to spur household consumption (easy credit) (Baccaro and Pontusson 2016 and this volume; Hassel and Palier; and Picot, this volume).

Diverse growth regimes require different government growth strategies for intervening in economic and social policy areas, and there is a correspondence between national growth regimes and national welfare regimes. Countries that attain growth primarily through exports of manufactured goods or dynamic services for high value-added markets typically require high levels of workforce skills; and these are provided with supply-side investments in human capital (Wren in this volume). In these countries, we find public spending policies supporting high levels of skills training and active labor market policies. Other countries use demand-side policies to promote household consumption with public or private Keynesian interventions. Countries that stimulate growth through consumption may use Keynesian expansionist government fiscal policies (taxing and spending) or social benefits to spur household consumption (Hall and Soskice 2001; Iversen and Soskice 2001; Hassel and Palier, this volume). Countries espousing a financialization growth strategy also stimulate household consumption, but do so with policies that deregulate credit and real estate markets. These countries have low savings rates, housing price inflation, and high shares of pension funds (Hassel and Palier, this volume); this private Keynesianism (Crouch 2009) or commercial Keynesianism (Collins 1981; Martin 1991) growth strategy is most frequently found in liberal market economies.

In the early period of deindustrialization, countries tended to choose between export-led and consumption led growth with Germany and Britain offering obvious counterparts (Hassel and Palier, this volume; Hassel 2014); yet, since the crisis, these ideal types have morphed into a number of hybrid models, as national growth regimes may utilize a combination of growth strategies (Picot, this volume). Broadly speaking, the Continental and Nordic countries have high levels of export growth, in contrast to the low levels experienced by the liberal and Mediterranean countries. The Nordic countries also have high levels of demand-led growth (Baccaro and Pontusson; Hassel and Palier, this volume).

3. Growth Strategies, Producer Interests, and Welfare State Preferences

Governments develop strategies to promote economic accumulation and welfare state provisions that bolster economic growth, and they work with coalitions of core producers, workers, and consumers to accomplish these goals. Producer interests are particularly important to these coalitions, as they are most directly involved in the engine of growth. Industrial sector analysis allows us to identify diverse business sectors' preferences for social protections (Milner 1988; Salamon and Siegfried 1974; Jacobs 1988; Martin 1991; Mitchell et al. 1997; Martin and Thelen 2007; Palier and Thelen 2010; Martin 2016; Hassel and Palier in this volume; Thelen 2014, and in this volume). Producer interests are divided along several fault lines. The first fault line is whether firms produce manufactured goods or services. A second fault line is whether firms produce for export or domestic markets. Another cleavage separates firms with high-skill versus those with low-skill workers. These fault lines have bearing on producer groups' own production choices (competition on price versus quality), support for government growth strategies (export-led versus demand-led growth), and social preferences.

These cleavages lead to several types of producer groups. We identify six of these and present them successively. The first type of producer group consists of **export-oriented manufacturing sectors**. Although the production of services swamps manufacturing everywhere in Europe today, some countries have retained a larger share of manufacturing production than others and these industrial sectors may be particularly influential agents of export growth. (Manufacturing may also be returning to advanced industrial countries in the wake of the crisis.) Manufacturing companies producing for export markets (particularly in coordinated market economies) produce quality manufactures for high-end niches and require a workforce with high specific skills; in contrast, employers in services sectors tend to prefer programs to cultivate general skills. Manufacturers' needs for a skilled and stable workforce make them more supportive of social protections than their counterparts in liberal market economies which compete on price rather than quality and use workers with fewer skills (Lipietz 1987; Hall and Soskice 2001; Streeck 1992). These firms have high levels of collective bargaining, that (with solidaristic wages) both slightly depress the wages of high-end workers but enhance employers' commitment to productivity-enhancing social investments. Therefore, manufacturing firms producing for export markets should support higher levels of human capital investment (e.g. in vocational education and training (VET) and active labor market programs (ALMP)) to foster specific skills. They prefer social programs that enable moving less productive workers out of firms (Mares 2003).

Export-producing manufacturers may be less enthusiastic proponents of fiscal and social policies that stimulate demand, although as is discussed below, their support for passive social protections for marginal groups (which increase demand) partially depends on how employers are organized. Manufacturers producing for export markets may be wary of demand-led policies that threaten to inflate prices; moreover, they should oppose wage increases in domestic service sectors that do not reflect productivity growth. These employers should be more sensitive to inflation than to the unemployment of those outside of the core export sectors. Whereas they support social reforms to expand skills of core manufacturing workers, they may oppose passive benefits for low-skill and unemployed workers. They might prefer expansive vocational training programs for high-end blue collar workers, but they might demand high standards that constitute barriers to low-skilled youth, young service sector workers, and immigrants (Busemeyer 2014; Martin and Knudsen 2010). Thus, French and German export manufacturing companies have urged the state to protect the productivity of core sectors, to the neglect of other marginal workers, and this dualism has been apparent in the rise of firm-level bargaining over non-wage issues and atypical employment contracts. Incentives for the social partners to protect older insiders against younger outsiders bring some strong industrial relations organizations to deviate from prior broadly solidaristic social pacts reforms (Palier and Thelen 2010).

Countries with powerful manufacturers producing for export markets have fared well in the wake of the financial crisis, because their growth model did not rely on asset bubbles. This has allowed these countries to maintain relatively high levels of social protection (Wren 2013). Moreover, countries with manufacturing enterprises utilizing high and median technologies may have an easier time sustaining high levels of social spending and avoiding dualism than those with manufacturing firms relying on less developed technologies, due to the higher productivity growth rates in high tech firms (Schnyder 2012; Thelen, this volume; Wren, this volume).

The second type of producer group consists of **manufacturing firms using less highly skilled workers and producing for domestic markets**. For example, Hall and Soskice (2001) suggest that manufacturers in liberal market economies are less likely to compete in high-skill niches and more likely to rely on Fordist manufacturing processes than their counterparts in coordinated market economies. This makes these companies less willing to fund human capital investment than manufacturing companies in coordinated countries. Yet evidence suggests that these firms may support social spending more than low-skill service-sector companies. These manufacturers are often capital-intensive and, as such, will feel the impacts on profits of marginal wage increases less acutely than will labor-intensive companies. Large companies have more organizational slack than small companies and this increases their capacities to provide in-house or to pay for social protections for their workers. Thus, in a random sample of American companies, firm size mattered significantly to companies' support for national health reform, in part because larger companies were more likely already to provide health insurance for their workers (Martin 2000). Business organization may help to aggregate employers' interests around collective goals and manufacturing firms are generally more likely to belong to encompassing employers' associations even in less coordinated countries. For example in a 2011 survey, 27 percent of French manufacturing firms belonged to the two largest employers' associations (MEDEF and CGPME), whereas only 5 percent of French financial companies belonged to MEDEF and none belonged to CGPME (European Observatory of Working Life 2015b).

Manufacturers for domestic markets may have lower productivity rates that increase their aversion to passive social spending, but they are also less price-sensitive to wage inflation from demand-led policies than manufacturers of exports. Thus, domestic manufacturers may support stimulus policies to sustain high levels of consumption for their products. Today, advanced industrial countries have few firms in this segment of capital; yet historical evidence offers confirmation of domestic manufacturers' interest in stimulus policies. American manufacturers widely supported the debt-creating Kennedy tax cuts in the 1960s as a mechanism for stimulating growth. Concerns about the impact of tax cuts on balance of payment deficits, financial interests were less enthusiastic about the tax measure (Martin 1991).

Our third producer group consists of firms providing **domestic services in the private sector with low-skill workers**. These companies are likely to be the most resistant to all forms of social spending: they have limited incentives to invest in their low-wage workers, they are often small (although companies such as the US Walmart and the French Carrefour provide notable exceptions), they have low levels of productivity and they compete on price rather than quality. Although firms producing for domestic markets generally have incentives to support policies stimulating demand-led growth, these low-wage companies are very sensitive to policies that increase labor costs. As shown by the British Minimum Wage Commission in 2015, minimum wage jobs made up a very large percentage of British workers in low-skill sectors such as cleaning (31 percent), hairdressing (29 percent), and hospitality (25 percent). These are often small firms with lower levels of organization slack; for example, 12.2 percent of the workforce in companies with fewer than ten employees received minimum wage, compared to 7.8 percent for other small companies and 3.5 percent for large companies (Low Pay Commission 2015: 38–9). In a survey of 1,000 British companies, the Chartered Institute of Personnel and Development (CIPD) found that only 10 percent of firms with over 250 employees anticipated raising prices to respond to the government's National Living Wage, whereas 24 percent of those with under 250 employees) expected to increase prices (Chartered Institute of Personnel and Development 2016: 6). France has a higher minimum wage than the United States or Britain and this lifts retail workers, for example, above the low-wage threshold (Carre and Tilly 2017). Yet France suffers from low rates of employment and, even so, low-skill jobs are expected to constitute nearly 20 percent of employment by 2022 (France Strategie 2017: 4).

A fourth type of producer group includes **firms producing domestic services in public sectors**. Producers of public services should prefer investments to develop general skills through education programs rather than spending on specific skills development in vocational training programs. In this vein, Dutch employers have been shown to prefer public health graduates to have generic as opposed to field-specific competencies (Biesma-Blanco et al. 2007). Public sector service firms producing public sector services should particularly favor high levels of government spending to protect jobs. State employers have an obvious interest in expanding the skills and productivity of low-wage workers, particularly under conditions of austerity (Martin and Thelen 2007; Martin and Swank 2012). Countries with large public sectors may use the multiplier effect of government spending to boost aggregate consumption, increase real wage share, enhance demand-led growth, and implement redistribution. For example, the annual growth rate in Sweden (relying on a mix of exports and household consumption) between 1994 and 2006 was almost twice that of Germany (relying only on exports) (See Baccaro and Pontusson in this volume).

After the financial crisis, countries with a high tax base and robust public sector were better situated than countries with budget deficits, low taxes, and limited social spending to implement stabilization policies and continuing welfare state effort. In countries without large public sectors and high levels of public investment, core producers were more likely to demand that all fiscal and monetary policy be designed to support real exchange rates and protect exports (Cameron 2012). In this vein, Sweden's chief economist identified municipal investments as a crucial economic stimulant after the crisis, which was particularly important because the Swedish export economy is so vulnerable to international markets. Local governments managed to engage in economic stabilization policies without excessive deficits, so that only 26 of the 290 municipalities produced deficits for 2009 (Chefekonomens blogg 2010). At the same time, Thelen (in this volume) emphasizes the negative impact of growing private-sector provision of social benefits on support for robust state services in Sweden (see also Svallfors 2016).

Our fifth type of producer group comprises firms producing **dynamic services using highly skilled workers** producing for **export markets**. These include, most prominently, international business, financial services, and communications that have been greatly enhanced over the last two decades by advances in ICT. Export-led growth through high-end, knowledge- intensive business services has been made possible with investments in information technologies permitting high levels of productivity growth (Wren; Hassel and Palier in this volume, Breznitz and Zysman 2013). High-skill service sector companies that produce for export markets have a predilection for investments in general education systems because they hire few low-skill workers, make limited use of vocational training programs, and seek investments to cultivate strong general skills through tertiary education programs (Hall and Soskice 2001). Yet, firms in these sectors generally provide high levels of in-house training or seek state support for training of their own skilled workers. The European Working Conditions Survey found that financial workers (44 percent) were much more likely to have access to training paid for by the employer than workers in either manufacturing sectors (24 percent) or those in low-end service jobs such as hotels and restaurants (12.3 percent), or wholesale/retail (23.5 percent). Also receiving high levels of training were workers in public and social services, including public administration workers (44 percent), education (42 percent), and health (42 percent). Whereas only 16 percent of unskilled workers and 17 percent of machine operators receive training, 44 percent of professionals and 50 percent of senior managers receive training (Eurofound 2007: 50). Employees also felt much more involved in their organizations in financial and educational enterprises (over 40 percent) than in manufacturing, commerce, or hospitality enterprises (just over 20 percent) (Eurofound 2014: 8).

Companies producing traded services have reason for concern about price inflation and, therefore, should resist policies to stimulate domestic demand. But these firms also have strong productivity growth rates that enable countries with strong export service sectors to sustain higher levels of social protection and equality. The Netherlands—with its limited manufacturing base—has cultivated a vibrant traded business services sector since the 1990s, and the proportion of total employment claimed by high-skill jobs has expanded accordingly. The shift into more dynamic service sectors in Sweden has also contributed to continuing support for redistribution and equality (Wren; Thelen in this volume).

Our sixth type of producer group represents firms producing **services** utilizing **highly skilled workers** for **private domestic markets.** Service sector firms producing for domestic markets should be less concerned about price inflation than firms producing for traded business services. Financial, real estate, and other high-skill service sector firms have been the primary beneficiaries of a *financial growth model.* These firms support the growth of household consumption through easy access to credit, real estate bubbles, and expanded household debt rather than through direct government fiscal policies (Wren in this volume; Hassel and Palier in this volume). In Britain, for example, finance capital drove growth through successive assets bubbles—in shares, housing, and commodities such as oil—facilitated by an expansion of credit, decline of savings ratio and conspicuous consumption (Gamble 2009: 7–15; Wren 2013). Thus, although the financial sector was historically found to resist inflationary public policies (Salamon and

Siegfried 1974; Jacobs 1988; Collins 1981; Martin 1991), the growth in products enabling easy credit with financial deregulation has produced financial self-interests in a growth strategy that is arguably against the collective interests of a sound financial system (Warwick Commission 2009).

The different perspectives of manufacturing sector and high-skill financial sector employers are apparent in two Confederation of British Industry (CBI) surveys. In a June 2014 survey, financial firms identified the main factors limiting growth as excessive regulation (70 percent) and an insufficient level of demand (62 percent) (Confederation of British Industries 2014). British manufacturing companies presented a very different perspective in the CBI's Industrial Survey of 350 firms. The manufacturers worried that the British growth model relied too much on consumer debt, and advocated for an expanded industrial policy to spur manufacturing growth (Confederation of British Industries 2013). John Cridland (CBI Director-General) shared the manufacturers' perspective: "We are starting to see signs of the right kind of growth. In our view this is not a debt-fueled, housing bubble-led recovery—our forecast shows encouraging signs that business investment and net trade are starting to play their part" (Cadman 2014).

Countries relying on financialization experienced greater difficulty recovering from the Great Recession, as the financial crisis wiped out much of the ephemeral gains from the growth-propelling assets bubbles. Britain initially experimented with stimulus policy, but the crisis quickly became defined as a crisis of debt rather than of growth, perhaps in response to the country's powerful banking interests (Hay and Smith 2013: 302). Prime Minister David Cameron's structural social reforms accordingly emphasized austerity, deregulation, privatization, erosion of labor market cooperation, free trade, and education geared for economic competition (Department for Business, Innovation and Skills 2011: 3–6). When the Tories regained control of government in Britain, Cameron sought to expand social spending on new apprenticeships for young people; yet he simultaneously announced 25 percent cutbacks from the national education budget (Payne and Keep 2011). The fiscal legacy of the bursting bubbles and the new climate of austerity left Britain public finances significantly less prepared to take on brave new training initiatives.

Table 7.1 demonstrates the connection between countries' growth strategies and dominant producer coalitions. Each of the four quadrants contains a prototypical country. For each country, we may observe the share of real GDP growth on average from 1994 to 2007 offered by exports and by private final consumption expenditure (drivers of growth), and the percentage of value-added generated by diverse producer groups such as high- and medium-tech manufacturing, public sector employment, and the financial/real estate sector. First, the upper left quadrant represents countries (such as Sweden) that have high levels of growth in both exports and domestic consumption. These countries have a high proportion of export-oriented manufacturing firms and domestic service companies, and

Table 7.1 Growth strategies, producer coalitions, and social policies, sample countries

Demand-led growth	**High demand-led growth** *Public Keynesian policies—deficit fiscal policies, public debt* *Private Keynesian policies—credit deregulation & private debt*	**Low demand-led growth** *Tight fiscal policies* *Restrictive credit policies*
Export-led growth **High levels of export growth** *Human capital investment policies or HCI (VET & ALMP) in addition to general education*	**High export growth** **Low demand-led** Sweden: 7.8% exports 2.8% demand-led Swedish firms' share of value-added Man/high-med: 16.8/7.9% Pub Employ: 26.0% Finance/Real Estate: 28.1%	**High Export growth** **Low Demand-led** Germany: 7.9% exports 0.97% demand-led German firms' share of value-added Man/high-med tech firms: 22.6/13.2% Pub Employ: 10.6% Finance/Real Estate: 30.1%
Low levels of export growth *Lower HCI investment & greater reliance on general education*	**Low export growth** **High demand-led** UK: 5.4% export growth 3.4% demand-led British firms' share of value-added Man/high-med man: 12.4/5.2% Pub Employ: 18.3% Finance/Real Estate: 28.1%	**Low export** **Low demand-led** Italy: 4.6% export growth 1.6 demand-led Italian firms' share of value-added Man/high-med man: 16.0/6.0% Pub Employ: 13.7% Finance/Real Estate: 31.0%

Source: Components of real growth rates on average from 1994 to 2007, taken from OECD Quarterly National Accounts. Public sector employment data are taken from OECD. 2015. *Government at a Glance* (2015). Paris: OECD Publishing, https://doi.org/10.1787/gov_glance-2015-en. Figure 3.1. Data on industrial composition of economies taken from OECD, STAN Database (2011) https://stats.oecd.org/Index.aspx?DataSetCode=STAN08BIS.

we anticipate that these countries will pursue social policies that foster both supply-side human capital investment and demand-side public Keynesian policies. This is the classic Nordic model. Second, the upper right quadrant represents countries (such as Germany) that embrace export-led growth but that do not develop a demand-led growth strategy. These countries should have a high proportion of manufacturing firms and a small proportion of public sector employees. We expect these countries to develop high levels of spending on VET and social protections for specific skilled workers but to rely less on Keynesian demand-side interventions. Third, the lower left quadrant includes countries (such as the United Kingdom) relying on demand-led growth strategies (with private Keynesian policies). We expect that these liberal countries will have small manufacturing sectors but a high number of firms in finance services who favor private Keynesian policies over policies for export-led growth. Finally, the lower right quadrant contains countries (such as Italy) that have historically been on the periphery of Europe and have had low levels of growth in both exports and domestic consumption. We expect these Mediterranean countries to have both small manufacturing and small public service sectors. In this table, we present sectoral data from 2011, when countries were struggling to emerge from the financial crisis.

The prototypical country cases in Table 7.1 confirm our predictions about the relationship between producer coalitions and growth strategies. Thus in Sweden, a high proportion of real GDP growth on average from 1994 to 2007 happens through exports (7.8 percent), and Germany presents a similar pattern with 7.9 percent of real GDP growth on average during this period occurring through export-led growth. Yet Sweden (with 2.8 percent) and Germany (with 0.97 percent) have very different levels of demand-led growth as a percent of total real GDP growth during this period (see Table 7.1). The two countries' industry profiles in 2011 line up with this division in growth strategies. In Sweden, manufacturing firms with high and medium technology contribute about 16.8 and 7.9 percent respectively to value-added; and public sector firms contribute 26 percent. In Germany, manufacturing firms account for an even higher proportion (22.6/13.2 percent respectively); however, firms in public employment account for only 10.6 percent of all value-added in 2011. Finally, growth strategies seem to correspond to the countries' social provision profiles. Social democratic countries utilize both Keynesian fiscal policies and social investment interventions to protect against social risks, whereas corporatist-continental welfare regimes such as Germany have more restrained universal expenditures and lower levels of redistribution, even while they make significant human capital investments with excellent vocational training programs for their industrial workers (Martin and Swank 2012; Thelen 2014).

4. Refining our Conceptions of Producer Preferences

Our model suggests that dominant producer groups are associated with specific growth strategies and their attendant social policy profiles; however, Table 7.2 suggests that countries with similar welfare state regimes have somewhat different industry configurations and sources of growth. Countries with similar sources of growth and distributions of producer interests, in some cases, have different welfare regimes. Moreover, countries had different capacities to sustain challenges to their welfare states during the financial crisis and to renew their economies in the aftermath of the crisis. The second and third column of Table 7.2 show relative rankings on redistribution, with the Gini coefficient and the 90/10 disposable income ratio. We then see countries' comparative reliance on export-led growth

Table 7.2 Industrial sector composition of national economies (2011 and 2016) by welfare state regime and growth strategy

Country	Gini Coef	P90/10 dispos. income decile ratio	Export-led growth avg 1994–2007 =>2011–18 **Demand 1994–2007 =>2011–18**	Total industry 2016	Manunfac-turing 2011	Manufac-turing 2016	Total service 2016	Business service 2011	Business service 2016	'Finance/ real estate 2011	'Finance/ real estate 2016
Social Dem Denmark	251	2.9	5.7=>3.5% 2.3=>1.4%	18.8	10.8	15.5	75.3	45.5	49.4	29.9	25.5
Finland	0.260	3	8.4=>2 3.5=>1.3	20.3	17.2	16.9	70.2	44.9	45.8	27.6	24.2
Sweden	0.274	3.3	7.8=>3.4 2.8=>2.1	18.6	16.8	15.3	74.2	47.1	49.6	28.1	24.3
Christ Dem Austria	0.276	3.5	7=>3.5 1.9=>0.8	21.4	18.7	18.2	71	48.9	50.5	26.5	23.8
Netherlands	0.278	3.4	6.4=>4.3 2.5=>0.7	15.2	12.9	12.1	78.2	48.9	54.1	30.2	28.1
Germany	0.289	3.8	7.9=>4 0.97=>1.5	25.7	22.6	22.9	68.9	46.1	46.7	30.1	25.9
Switzerland (2008)	0.285	3.6 (15)	5.1=>3.3 1.5=>1.5	20.3	20.1	18.4	73.5	51.7	51.6	29.5	27.2
France	0.306	3.4	6.0=>3.5 2.3=>0.9	14.1	10.0	11.4	78.8	53.5	53.1	34.9	30.3
Southern Italy	0.327	4.5	4.6=>3 1.6=>–0.1	19.1	16.0	16.3	74	52.7	53.3	31.9	28.9
Spain (2009)	0.335	5.3	7.5=>0.5 3.3=>0.4	17.8	12.7	14.2	73.8	48.2	51	23.6	23.2
Liberal Australia	0.326	4.3	4.9=>5 4.2=>2.5	16.8	11.2	6.2	72.2	50.4	51.4	29.6	30.9
UK	0.351	4.2	5.4=>3 3.4=>2.1	14	12.4	10.1	79.2	52.7	57.3	28.1	32.8
US	0.390	6.3	6.0=>3.2 3.6=>2.5	15.1	11.7	12	79.5	54.6	54.8	36.5	31.9

Source: Data on Gini and Poverty Rate after taxes and transfers set at 50 percent from OECD Stats, Income Distribution and Poverty, 2012. Data on 90/10 ratio taken from OECD income distribution database. P90/P10 disposable income decile ratio. https://stats.oecd.org/viewhtml.aspx?datasetcode=IDD&lang=en# Data on export-led and demand-led growth taken from Quarterly National Accounts. P.6. Export of Goods and Services and P31S14_S15 Private Final Consumption Expenditure. https://stats.oecd.org/Index.aspx?DataSetCode=QNA%20#. Data on industrial composition of economies taken from OECD, STAN Database (2011). https://stats.oecd.org/Index.aspx?DataSetCode=STAN08BIS STAN Database (2016). https://stats.oecd.org/Index.aspx?DataSetCode=STANI4_2016#.

and demand-led growth. The final columns present the sectoral composition (total industry, manufacturing and services) of economies.

Several revelations merit our attention. First, service growth swamps manufacturing growth in virtually all core industrial countries, and manufacturing—or even industry including energy—as a percentage of total value-added is generally quite small. The value-added contribution of industry (including energy) as a percentage of all value-added in 2016 is highest at 25.7 percent in Germany. If export-oriented manufacturers have somewhat similar concerns across countries, it remains unclear why their (minority) voices would be heard more closely in some countries than others. This may well be due to their organizational strength, as I argue below. In addition, the economic share of finance and real estate is fairly similar across countries in 2011: in this year, the finance/real estate sector's share in Germany and the Netherlands is 30 percent, compared to 28 percent in the UK and Sweden. By 2016, however, the Nordic and Continental countries have scaled back their finance/real estate sectors; whereas, these sectors have grown in Australia and the United Kingdom (see Table 7.2).

Second, countries with quite similar welfare states have somewhat different economies in 2011, although again they have reset to be more similar by 2016. Thus, manufacturing contributes 16.8 percent of total value-added in Sweden, but only 10.8 percent in Denmark in 2011; by 2016, however, the countries show corresponding figures of 15.3 and 15.5 percent respectively. That these diverse economies produced such similar welfare profiles prompts further investigation (see Table 7.2).

Third, countries with similar economic compositions sometimes have different welfare states, and the hybrid nature of growth regimes poses problems for moving from an easily identifiable dominant sector to social policy change. Whereas Denmark is the most equitable country and the United Kingdom is the most inequitable European country on Table 7.1, their industrial, total services, manufacturing, and financial/real estate sectors make similar contributions to total value-added in 2011. In the first decade of the new century, Denmark adopted many of the problematic policies of the Anglo growth regime, by deregulating housing policies and spurring growth. Yet it has sustained high levels of social provision (if not high levels of growth), particularly in the areas in which the social partners exert considerable control (such as in vocational training, ALMP, and fully funded pension schemes arrived at through collective bargaining). Moreover, by 2016, the Danish manufacturing sector had experienced a resurgence, taking the country further away from the British model. See Figure 7.1.

Fourth, the countries' economic compositions did not immediately suggest who will be winners and who will be losers after the financial crisis. The Netherlands and Italy look very similar in their value-added contribution of industry, total services, and finance/real estate, and Italy leads Britain in business services and manufacturing. See Figure 7.2.

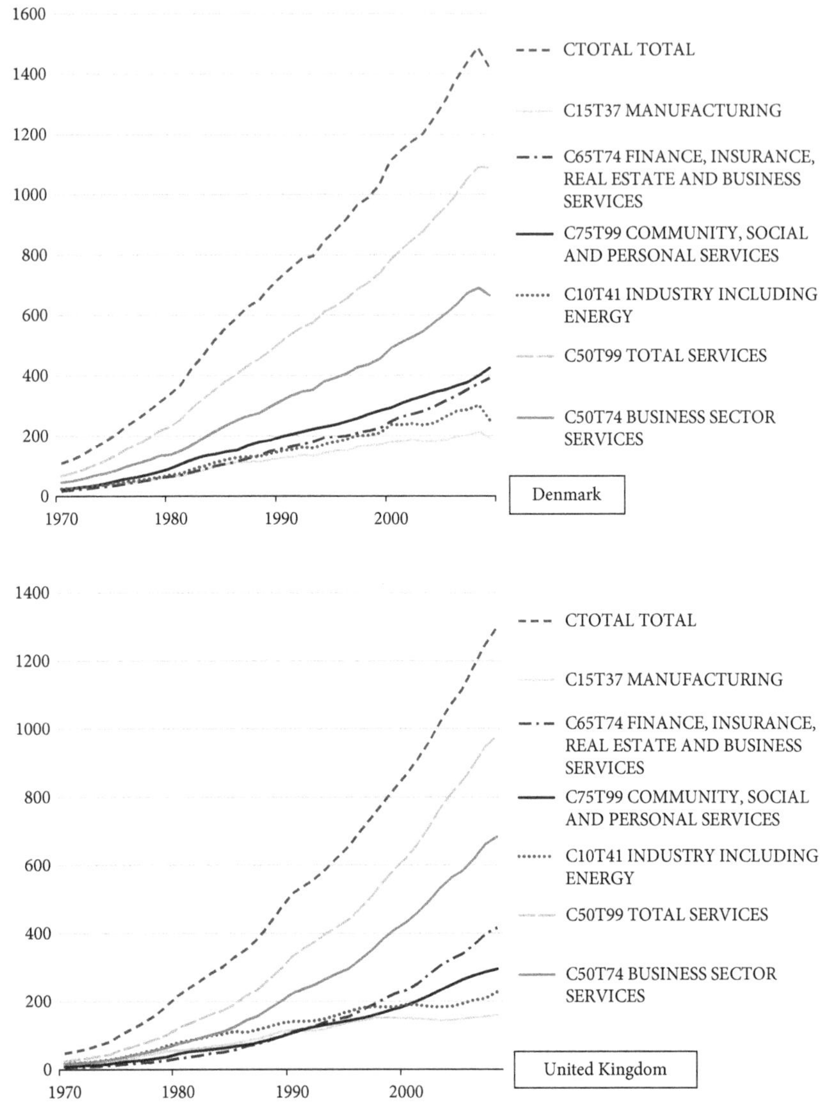

Figure 7.1 Growth of value-added in billions in Denmark and the United Kingdom

Source: Data on industrial composition of economies in national currency (and then euros) taken from OECD (2011), "STAN indicators ISIC Rev. 3 (Edition 2011)", *STAN: OECD Structural Analysis Statistics* (database), https://doi.org/10.1787/data-00561-en (accessed 10 August 2020).

To some extent, countries' choices of adjustment strategies in responding to the financial crisis reflected the pressures from global capital. Supranational organizations and foreign business—EU, NGOs, and financial investors—forced some countries to adopt policies at odds with their pre-crisis growth strategies. Erik

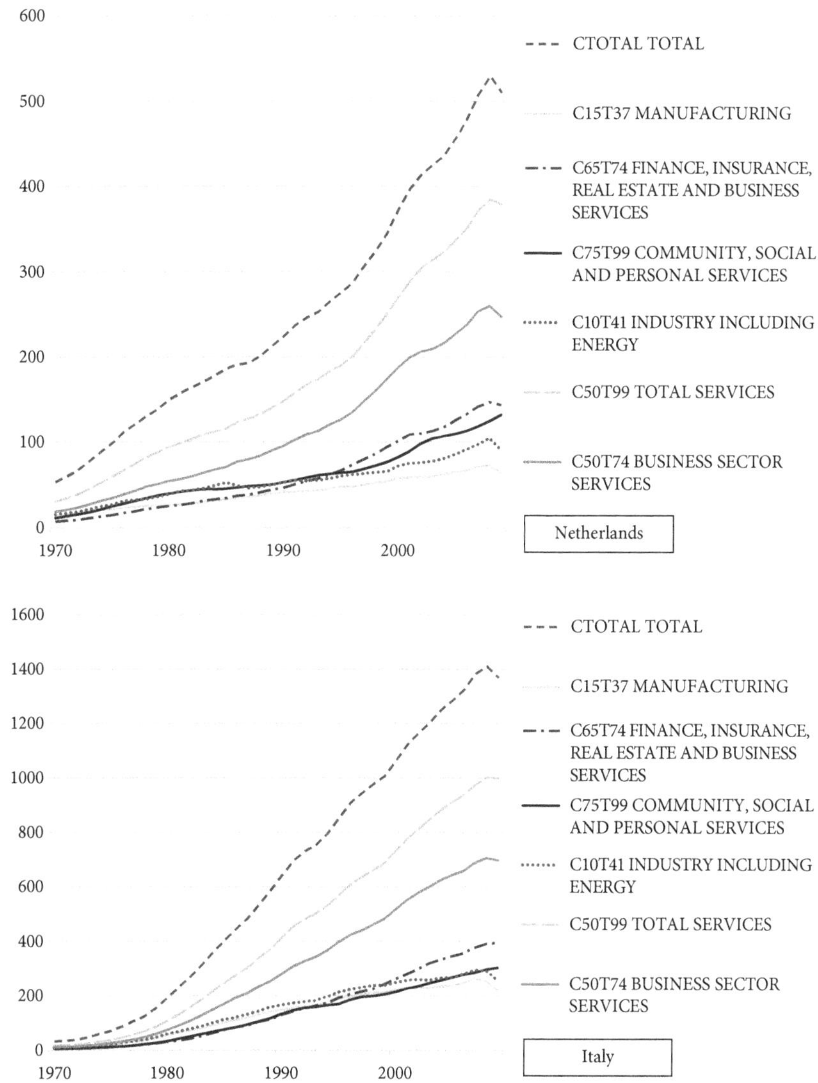

Figure 7.2 Growth of value-added in billions in the Netherlands and Italy

Source: Data on industrial composition of economies in national currency (and then euros) taken from OECD (2011), "STAN indicators ISIC Rev. 3 (Edition 2011)", *STAN: OECD Structural Analysis Statistics* (database), https://doi.org/10.1787/data-00561-en (accessed 10 August 2020).

Jones links cross-national differences in national austerity reforms post-crisis to the confidence of foreign financial investors (or the "sudden stop"). This confidence was only marginally related to the strength of export sectors, pre-crisis public and private debt levels, and level of competitiveness. Italy had a strong manufacturing export market before the crisis and its current account was rising before its balance of payments crisis in 2011; however, it was forced to adopt austerity measures (Jones 2015: 8–9). Spain faced a similar problem. Before the crisis, its export sector competed on quality; it had higher levels of labor productivity than Finland; its VET system was been praised by German multinationals; its institutions for coordination permitted rapid wage adjustments; and it met the EMU stability criteria. Indeed, from 1999 to 2007, Greece, Ireland, Italy, Portugal, and Spain lost less export market share than the United Kingdom, Switzerland, Denmark, Norway, and Sweden (all countries outside of the Eurozone). Denmark and the Netherlands (both highly deindustrialized) had the highest household debt ratios in Europe, yet these countries were able to assure foreign investors of their financial solvency (Jones 2015: 8–13). The differences in these cases had less to do with dominant producer groups, than with pre-existing budgetary surpluses and countries' capacities to assuage the fears of international capital. Thus, Jones suggests that after the crisis, countries could choose from two broad strategies: to embrace austerity and restrain (public and private) debt or to grow out of the crisis with stimulus policies and to build the confidence of foreign market investors without draining national economic resources. Choosing or being forced to consolidate public and private debt in a way that detracts from national economic growth is counterproductive (Jones 2015: 16, Johnston; Scharpf, this volume).

Finally, trajectories from 2011 to 2016 demonstrate countries' diverse capacities to forge new directions in the wake of the financial crisis. Thus, Denmark's manufacturing sector went from 10.8 percent of total value-added in 2011 to 15.5 percent in 2016. The Nordic countries all reduced their financial/real estate sectors' contribution of value-added during this period, but increased other types of business services. The Continental countries also either maintained or scaled back their financial/real estate sectors' contribution of value-added from 2011 to 2016, and Liberal countries had the highest share devoted to finance and real estate in 2016 (see Table 7.2).

These anomalies do not suggest abandoning our study of growth regimes and strategies: as countries' economic profiles certainly constrain their policy options, but more importantly, the choice of a new growth strategy and the capacity of governments to strike deals with influential producer, labor, and consumer groups is essential to economic renewal. Producer-group coalitions matter to how welfare states evolve (Martin 2000; Palier and Thelen 2010). Although the Mediterranean countries had few choices after the sovereign debt crisis (Baccaro and Armingeon 2012); political openings allowed other countries to choose how to meet the contingencies of the new economic climate. A range of strategic choices may be chosen by the dominant producer. Thus, we must think about how dominant producers (and other social actors) form their preferences for social policy options, forge coalitions, and in some cases help to redirect the trajectory of economic growth.

5. Labor Market Organization and Policy Coalitions

Industrial relations organizations of employers (and workers) matter to the preferences articulated by firms or sectors and to states' capacities to bring employers into coalitions supporting growth strategies. Business organizations shape both the expressions of corporate preferences and the types of coalitions that may develop among diverse sectors. Systems of industrial relations—macro-corporatism, sector coordination, and pluralism—have differing capacities to aggregate labor market partners.

Macro-corporatist systems organize employers into hierarchically ordered groups with centralized and encompassing peak associations at the top of the pyramid. Peak associations negotiate broad political agreements with the state and/or labor through collective bargaining and tripartite policy-making committees. This system of interest intermediation works in several ways to expand support for social provision. Highly organized employer (and labor) associations foster centralization and coordination in collective bargaining, and consequent wage compression motivates employers to eliminate low-skilled jobs and to support social programs that build human capital. Participation in macro-corporatist groups helps employers to overcome the limits to collective action. For instance, corporatist groups enhance the provision of skills, which is inadequate when left up to private firms fearing free-riding behavior by others. These groups bind firms to negotiated decisions and enhance the likelihood that employers with pay short-term costs for longer-term goals. Corporatist business associations have cognitive impacts on members, in educating employers about the benefits of social policies and bringing managers into contact with policy experts from government and organized labor; and these cognitive effects are particularly important to companies' support for social investments in marginal workers, where there is a less direct tie-in to productivity (Martin and Swank 2012).

Perhaps most importantly, macro-corporatist industrial relations systems allow business and labor to retain control over industrial and social policies. Because they participate extensively in the design of the policies, the social partners have a high level of satisfaction with and commitment to social and labor market programs. For example, the Danish state has periodically attempted to intrude in the jurisdictional control of the social partners over industrial policies and has been met with a united front by business and labor. In this vein, LO, DA, and other groups expressed outrage with the idea of a statutory minimum wage in Denmark. In a joint letter to the newspaper, Berlingske, the social partners said "No thanks" (Nej tak), writing that the proposal would do irreparable damage to the Danish model that has delivered one of the most flexible and well-functioning labor markets in Europe. The Danish model relies on the fact that the participating partners must take responsibility for their deals; moreover, control over wage-setting gives workers incentives to join a unions and employers an incentive to negotiate with unions. A statutory minimum wage would undermine these arrangements (Jensen et al. 2014).

In sharp contrast, *pluralist* systems of interest representation organize employers into a panoply of conflicting groups, with many purporting to aggregate business interests and with none having state-sanctioned, policy-making authority. This system of fragmented, decentralized and competing groups brings employers to look less favorably on government social policies. Pluralist systems have limited collective bargaining and few incentives for wage compression and skills enhancement. Competing encompassing associations compete for members and this reduces their capacities for collective action. These groups are not given access to participation in the tripartite forums that bring employers elsewhere into routinized dialogue with labor and government. Policy-making is generally limited to legislative forums, where business input is received without reciprocal demands for compliance.

Employers and labor unions in pluralist countries have far less policy-making authority than their counterparts in macro-corporatist countries and this also contributes to business mistrust of government. Whereas the Danish social partners were able to defend their authority against a statutory minimum wage, the French Macron Law in August 2015 increased the role of lay judges in labor disputes. Influenced by the Danish concept of "flexicurity," however, Macron subsequently passed ordinances that allowed for greater flexibility to determine agreements outside of the courts (Bellahouel 2018).

Countries with *sector coordination* organize employers at the industry level but have weaker peak associations that bring together diverse sectors across the economy and very limited if any involvement by the state in business–labor negotiations. This system is likely to foster deals between business and labor at the industrial sector level that do not extend across the economy. These deals typically offer core workers ample social protections but they neglect the interests of labor market outsiders, as labor market insiders have few incentives to fund programs for marginal workers (Palier and Thelen 2010; Hicks and Kenworthy 1998; Martin and Swank 2012; Martin and Thelen 2007). Moreover, organized labor tends to be much stronger in macro-corporatist industrial relations systems; unions both constrain employers' power (Huber and Stephens 2001; Korpi and Palme 1998) and educate business about their social interests.

These industrial relations systems have varying implications for state capacities to forge policy coalitions among diverse interests. Macro-corporatist industrial organizations enable the state to build bridges among export manufacturing sectors, traded high-skill service sectors, and public sector employers/workers who are more sympathetic to the interests of marginal workers. More encompassing associations tend to produce more comprehensive social pacts and may include policies that benefit the long-term unemployed, immigrants, and youth. High levels of coordination also have an impact on governments' capacities to sell their growth strategies to mobile capital and to prevent disinvestment.

For example in prior work, I demonstrated the importance of macro-corporatist associations as a source of policy information in a study of 107 randomly selected firms in Denmark and Great Britain. The Danish macro-corporatist groups were significantly more important to business support for active labor market policies than the British pluralist groups. Danish firms participated more in the programs than British firms and a much larger percentage of Danish firms identified their employer organization as their most important source of information about social policies. Membership in the employers' association was a significant determinant of positive participation by Danish employers but not British ones. Whereas Danish firms participated to gain access to a new labor pool, British firms largely participated for political reasons (such as selling to the public sector) and for access to cheap labor. Quantitative, cross-national analyses also find countries with macro-corporatist industrial relations to be significantly more likely to fund social programs than countries without such industrial institutions. Highly organized business is also a significant determinant of redistribution, when controlling for the partisan composition of government, party structure, and union organization (Martin and Swank 2012).

Granted, deindustrialization has been associated with some pressures on high levels of coordination, such as declining union density, particularly in manufacturing sectors. Swedish union density declined 10 percent between 2003 and 2013, particularly within the blue collar LO (European Observatory of Working Life 2015a). Yet Denmark and the Netherlands have sustained their high levels of coordination. Thus, Madsen (2015) suggests that the Danish flexicurity model, which relies on employer support for high levels of social investment, persists despite the slower growth after the global financial crisis. Touwen (2014) suggests that the hybrid nature of the Dutch economy has been a great strength in coping with post-crisis economic and political pressures. The Netherlands, somewhat paradoxically, used coordination to support openness, believing that globalization did not require deregulation. Dutch policy-makers compartmentalized policy changes, so that necessary adjustments to coordination in some domains did not require alterations in other areas. These insights help to explain why Denmark and the Netherlands have been able to achieve non-incremental policy adjustments even while preserving coordination in the new age of austerity, even while other countries have been less successful at defending their welfare states (See also Martin and Swank 2012; Thelen 2014, and in this volume).

6. Coordination and Adjustment to the Financial Crisis

High levels of employer coordination contributed to countries' capacities to respond to the financial crisis. The Swedish case was somewhat easy, as financial deregulation was more muted before the 2008 crisis. Sweden experienced a crisis in the early 1990s, after its deregulation of the financial sector in the 1980s. The reduction of lending ceilings and government bond requirements caused a rapid decline in asset values in the early 1990s, when large banks could not meet their regulatory capital requirements, and a liquidity crisis ensued. Sweden rather dramatically interrupted its trajectory of financial deregulation after this banking crisis and brought together a group of financial experts and major stakeholders across the political spectrum to put into place a new regulatory system. These consensual negotiations—with broad societal support—permitted a very rapid response in which the needs of the banking system were placed above the interests of bankers and shareholders, and transparent rules were implemented to protect against future financial instability (Bayram et al. 2014). After the 2008 crisis, the Swedish state assumed control over banks, in exchange for an influx of emergency cash, and then sold off its holdings after the crisis had passed (Jackson 2008), and later implemented a bank "stability" fee to help banks manage their own recovery (Saltmarsh 2010).

Macro-corporatist arrangements also helped Denmark to recover, after the country's disastrous experimentation with housing mortgage deregulation in the first decade of the twenty- first century. Denmark was the first country to guarantee all of its deposits and liabilities in sound banks, and despite an initial run on the kroner, it successfully defended the currency. Parties joined forces to approve of the plan, something Carter Dougherty in the *New York Times* (2008) attributed to Denmark's being "a well-governed nation." The Danish bailout plan won high praise from the EU, as the Danish government promised to guarantee all deposits, and Denmark repaid much of its foreign debt (EIU Views Wire 2009). The Lausanne's Institute for Management Development ranked Denmark number 1 in response to the crisis (Financial Times 2009).

The passage of the Danish budget law of 2012 also demonstrates the importance of coordination for economic management in the wake of the crisis. The budget law passed with overwhelming support from a broad coalition of social partners and parties (led by the minority government coalition of Social Democrats, Social Liberal, and Socialist People's Party and joined by the bourgeois opposition parties, the Liberals, and the Conservatives). The EU Fiscal Compact inspired the law, but citizens, social partners, and party leaders alike were fearful of the crisis and acted to forgo short-term self-interests for long-term collective benefits. This broad coalition put in place long-term controls over public spending (particularly at the municipal level) to "lash politicians to the mast" so that these could not easily be undone in the future (Suenson et al. 2016: 16).

Denmark also used the financial crisis as an opportunity to move into new green technologies and to rebuild its declining manufacturing sector. Already a leader in wind power technology, policy-makers determined that Denmark could make green technology a growth industry. Energy exports grew 29 percent between 2010 and 2016. Energy exports were 11.8 percent of all exports by 2016, and over 60 percent of green energy jobs are in industry and manufacturing.

This sector has also been a magnet for jobs. In 2016, job growth in the green energy sector was six times as high as job growth over the economy in general. Thus while renewable energy was 40 percent in 2012, it rose to 44 percent by 2017 (Danish Ministry of Energy, Utilities and Climate 2018: 23–4, 7). This helps to explain how the manufacturing share of total value-added in Denmark move from 11 percent manufacturing in 2011 to 15.5 percent in 2016 (see Table 7.2).

7. Employers' Coordinating Capacities and Investment in Skills

A high level of industrial organization also contributed to the Danish and Dutch capacities to sustain high levels of social investment in skills, despite the small industrial sectors of these economies. Over the past few decades, the Netherlands relied on high levels of coordination to pursue selective liberalization while maintaining high levels of social solidarity. Macro-corporatist institutions in the Dutch "polder" model allowed the Netherlands to use coordination to support the openness necessary to the prosperity of traded service sectors. The processes meant that Dutch policy-makers could compartmentalize policy change, so that adjustments to coordination in some domains did not require alterations in other areas. Dutch citizens did not view the deliberative process in the system of consultation as harming entrepreneurship or determining outcomes, because negotiators could embrace market discipline in some areas and social protections in others. Thus, the model of coordination helped to protect areas of social protection, even while targeted liberalization fostered the emergent growth strategy. This "compartmentalized liberalism" hybrid model permitted the evolution of its competitive traded business services sector (Touwen 2014). Today, Dutch employers have grown in confidence, due to favorable forecasts in exports, consumption, and investment (VNONCW 2015).

The advantages of macro-corporatist over pluralist industrial relations organizations are also apparent in a comparison of recent vocational training reforms in Denmark and Britain. Danish vocational education reform demonstrates the strength of coordination among the social partners. In the autumn of 2012, the Danish government set up a vocational education committee that included representatives from the Confederation of Danish Business (DA), the Confederation of Labor (LO), the organization representing municipalities (KL), and the major parties. The committee was charged with making recommendations for substantial changes to VET, in order to improve the quality and attractiveness of VET, to limit the number of young people dropping out of education, and to provide labor for a resurrected manufacturing sector (another goal of Danish policy-makers). The VET reforms were to meet the needs of both high-skilled technology workers and most marginal students. According to a respondent at the Confederation of

Danish Employers (DA), the business and labor participants on the committee were very much on the same wavelength on the reform. The social partners advocated for a pragmatic system, demanded that graduates have requisite skills, and sought to sustain their significant control over the content and substance of vocational training. They lobbied hard for a tenth year of study in the lower-secondary schools, so that late bloomers could develop requisite math and language skills for entering the VET programs (Interview with DA, June 14, 2015).

In contrast, British reforms for skills development were less successful, in part, due to the weak organization of the social partners. There was bipartisan and cross-class support for skills development, and Britain's small manufacturing sector sought enhanced workforce skills. Qualifications have grown, with an estimated 26 percent of jobs requiring college degrees by 2012 (up from 9 percent in 1986) and only 23 percent of jobs require no qualifications (down from 38 percent in 1986) (Adam 2014: 3). Government reports by both parties repeatedly recommend devoting substantial resources to apprenticeships and creating stronger employers' organizations to link education to the labor market (e.g. Wolf 2011: 10–12). Indeed, at the time, skills seemed to have become the panacea to all British ills (Keep and Mayhew 2010), and reforms have given employers too large a role in educational and vocational training with too little accountability (Gleeson and Keep 2004: 37). The Labour government's UK Commission for Employment and Skills (UKCES) received praise from both employers and labor, and some manufacturing sectors successfully launched coordinated efforts for skills development through the program (Interviews with CBI and TUC, March 2015).

Yet Britain's austerity regime had limited resources to devote to skills expansion, and the social partners lacked the requisite organization to obtain their policy goals for investment in human capital. The coalition government greatly reduced funding for the UKCES, replacing existing apprenticeships with "employer-designed Apprenticeship standards" (Department for Business, Innovation and Skills 2014: 9). A CBI representative explained that the coalition government's "answer to everything is apprenticeships" and that it pays too little attention to the need for real skills and for training that will be widely embraced by parents and children. A TUC representative expressed frustration with "the push for a change that accompanies every new government. David Blunkett established the Learning Skills Councils, and now the new government wants to establish its mark, and has a sought to overturn the old" (Interview with TUC, March 17, 2015). A CBI representative agreed that "The government's actions are primary driven by headlines . . . It would be best to get the government out of training and leave the system in place for a while" (Interview with CBI, March 26, 2015). The constant flip-flops create fragile public support for government initiatives, even when there is considerable consensus on the need for such reforms.

8. Conclusion

Countries with strong export-led growth regimes typically rely on different social policies than those with consumption-led growth, because growth regimes are broadly consistent with the preferences of dominant producer coalitions. Yet at moments of exogenous change, governments often adopt new growth strategies to revitalize their economies. In recent decades, governments have responded to challenges of deindustrialization and recovery from the financial crisis with shifting growth strategies, and dominant producer groups have been part of the coalitional bases of political support for these new initiatives.

Yet the role of employers is not automatic. Even in countries with export-led growth regimes, manufacturers constitute only a small part of the business community, as virtually all of the advanced, industrialized countries are swamped by services production today. Moreover, countries with rather different welfare states have similar economic profiles, and ones with quite similar welfare states have quite different economies. Thus, I suggest that the manner in which employers (often together with their labor counterparts) are organized contributes to governments' capacities to forge new growth strategies.

Strongly organized social partners in policy-making processes may help to nurture higher levels of commitment to social protections and to build broad cross-class coalitions around negotiated policy goals. Of course, one option for business and labor insiders is simply to protect their core interests against the demands of outsiders. Yet in countries with the most encompassing industrial relations, strong social partners have also helped to bolster the welfare state against attack by austerity-driven center-right governments. The capacities to strike encompassing pacts to meet social and economic goals may also serve to assuage the fears of foreign investors, by offering a sense of confidence and control in responding to new challenges. This may contribute to why countries such as the Netherlands and Denmark avoided suffering from their high debt:equity ratios in the early days of the financial crisis.

An essential question is whether the post-industrial economy and consequent shifts in national growth strategies demand particular forms of social reform, or conversely, whether variations in the institutions and rules structuring collective political engagement may facilitate both distinctive forms of social innovation and strategies for economic renewal. The organization of employers and workers may have bearing on national capacities to embrace future growth strategies. Just as the organization of the social partners influenced the development of coordinated market economies in the past (Martin and Swank 2012), capacities for labor market coordination may help countries to defend against erosion of welfare states in the new age of austerity.

References

Adam, Duncan. 2014. "United Kingdom: Trends in skills requirements and work-related issues." Eurofound, 26 January. https://www.eurofound.europa.eu/publications/article/2014/united-kingdom-trends-in-skills-requirements-and-work-related-issues (accessed February 20, 2020).

Avlijaš, Sonja, Anke Hassel and Bruno Palier. 2020. "Growth Strategies and Welfare Reforms in Europe." In *Growth and Welfare in Advanced Capitalist Economies. How Have Growth Regimes Evolved?*, edited by Anke Hassel and Bruno Palier. Oxford: Oxford University Press.

Baccaro, Lucio and Jonas Pontusson. 2016. "Rethinking Comparative Political Economy: The Growth Models Perspective." *Politics & Society* 44 (2): 175–207.

Baccaro, Lucio and Klaus Armingeon. 2012. "The Sorrows of the Young Euro." In *Coping with Crisis*, edited by Nancy Bermeo and Jonas Pontusson. New York: Russell Sage Foundation, 162–97.

Bayram, Ismail; DeWit, Andrew and Sven Steinmo. 2014. "The Bumble Bee and the Chrysanthemum: Comparing Sweden and Japan's Responses to Financial Crisis." *The Asia-Pacific Journal* 12 (16): 1–13.

Bellahouel, Sara. 2018. "The Macron Ordinances also aim at reducing the number of employer-employee disputes brought to court." Soulier Avocast, March 30, 2018. https://www.soulier-avocats.com/en/the-macron-ordinances-also-aim-at-reducing-the-number-of-employer-employee-disputes-brought-to-court/ (accessed February 26, 2020).

Biesma-Blanco, Regien; Pavlova, Milena; Van Merode, Frits and Wim Groot. 2007. "Using conjoint analysis to estimate employers preferences for key competencies of master level Dutch graduates entering the public health field." *Economics of Education Review* 26: 375–86.

Breznitz, Dan and John Zysman. 2013. "Introduction: Facing the double blind." In *The Third Globalization: Can Wealthy Nations Stay Rich in the Twenty-First Century?*, edited by Dan Breznitz and John Zysman. Oxford/New York: Oxford University Press, 1–28.

Busemeyer, Marius. 2014. *Skills and Inequality: Political Parties and the Political Economy of Education Reforms in Western European Countries*. Cambridge: Cambridge University Press.

Cadman, Emily. 2014. "CBI sees signs of 'right kind of growth.'" *Financial Times*, February 10, 2014. https://www.ft.com/content/7d1da2c2-926f-11e3-8018-00144feab7de (accessed February 20, 2020).

Gamble, Andrew. 2009. *The Spectre at the Feast*. New York: Palgrave Macmillan.

Cameron, David. 2012. "European Financial Responses to the Great Recession." In *Coping with Crisis*, edited by Nancy Bermeo and Jonas Pontusson. New York: Russell Sage Foundation, 91–129.

Carre, Francoise and Chris Tilly. 2017. *Where Bad Jobs are Better: Retail Jobs across Countries and Companies*. New York: Russell Sage Foundation.

Confederation of British Industries. 2013. "Growth in Manufacturing Output Strongest Since 1995." https://www.converternews.com/cbi-says-growth-in-manufacturing-output-strongest-since-1995/ (accessed February 26, 2020).

Confederation of British Industries. 2014. "Financial Services Firms See Fastest Growth Since 2007." https://insurancenewsnet.com/oarticle/Financial-Services-Firms-See-Fastest-Growth-Since-2007-a-563627

Chartered Institute of Personnel and Development. 2016. "Weighing up the wage floor." CIPD (February). https://www.cipd.co.uk/Images/weighing-up-the-wage-floor_2016-employer-responses-national-living-wage_tcm18-10963.pdf (accessed February 26, 2020).

Collins, Robert. 1981. *The Business Response to Keynes*. New York: Columbia University Press.

Crouch, Colin. 2009. "Privatised Keynesianism: An unacknowledged policy regime." *The British Journal of Politics and International Relations* 11(3): 382–99.

Danish Energy Agency. n.d. "Green Growth in Denmark." https://ens.dk/en/our-responsibilities/energy-climate-politics/green-growth-denmark (accessed February 26, 2020).

Danish Ministry of Energy, Utilities and Climate. 2018. "Denmark: Energy and climate pioneer." (April). https://en.efkm.dk/media/12032/denmark_energy_and_climate_pioneer_pdfa.pdf (accessed February 26, 2020).

Department for Business, Innovation and Skills. 2011. "Plan for Growth." https://assets.publishing.service.gov.uk/government/uploads/system/uploads/attachment_data/file/221514/2011budget_growth.pdf (accessed February 26, 2020).

Department for Business, Innovation and Skills. 2014. "Getting the Job Done: the Government's Reform Plan for Vocational Qualifications." (March 2014).

Dougherty, Carter. 2008. "No quick solution to financial crisis, Denmark shows." *New York Times*, October 27, 2008.

EIU Views Wire. 2009. "Denmark economy: Outlook—Dealing with the financial crisis." Economist Intelligence Unit, March 12, 2009. http://search.eiu.com/default.aspx?sText=%E2%80%9CDenmark%20economy:%20Outlook%20%20%20Dealing%20with%20the%20financial%20crisis.%E2%80%9D (accessed February 26, 2020).

European Commission. 2010. "Europe 2020: A strategy for smart, sustainable and inclusive growth." Brussels: European Commission (March 3), https://ec.europa.eu/eu2020/pdf/COMPLET%20EN%20BARROSO%20%20%20007%20-%20Europe%202020%20-%20EN%20version.pdf (accessed February 26, 2020).

Eurofound. 2007. *Fourth European Working Conditions Survey*. Luxembourg: Office for Official Publications of the European Communities.

Eurofound. 2014. "First findings." *Sixth European Working Conditions Survey*. Luxembourg: Office for Official Publications of the European Communities.

European Observatory of Working Life. 2015a. "Sweden: Fall in Union Density." August 31, 2015. http://www.eurofound.europa.eu/observatories/eurwork/articles/industrial-relations/sweden-fall-in-union-density (accessed February 20, 2020).

European Observatory of Working Life. 2015b. "France: New study sheds light on membership of employers organisations." November 24, 2015. https://www.eurofound.europa.eu/publications/article/2015/france-new-study-sheds-light-on-membership-of-employers-organisations (accessed February 26, 2020).

Financial Times. 2009. "Denmark plans tax cuts to spur spending." *Financial Times*, February 25, 2009.

France Strategie. 2017. "Boosting Employment in France." https://www.strategie.gouv.fr/sites/strategie.gouv.fr/files/atoms/files/17-27_boosting_employment.pdf (accessed February 27, 2020).

Gleeson, Denis and Ewart Keep. 2004. "Voice Without Accountability." *Oxford Review of Education* 30 (1 March): 37–63.

Hall, Peter and David Soskice. 2001. *Varieties of Capitalism*. Oxford: Oxford University Press.

Hassel, Anke. 2014. "The Paradox of Liberalization—Understanding Dualism and the Recovery of the German Political Economy." *British Journal of Industrial Relations* 52(1): 57–81.

Hassel, Anke and Bruno Palier. 2020. "Tracking the Transformation of Growth Regimes in Advanced Capitalist Economies." In *Growth and Welfare in Advanced Capitalist Economies. How Have Growth Regimes Evolved?*, edited by Anke Hassel and Bruno Palier. Oxford: Oxford University Press.

Hay, Colin and Nicola Smith. 2013. "The Resilience of Anglo-liberalism in the absence of growth." In *Resilient Liberalism*, edited by Vivien Schmidt and Mark Thatcher. New York: Oxford University Press, 289–312.

Hicks, Alex and Lane Kenworthy. 1998. "Cooperation and Political Economic Performance in Affluent Democratic Capitalism." *American Journal of Sociology* 6 (May): 1631–72.

Huber, Evelyn and John Stephens. 2001. *Development and Crisis of the Welfare State*. Chicago: University of Chicago Press.

Iversen, Torben and Anne Wren. 1998. "Equality, employment, and budgetary restraint: the trilemma of the service economy." *World Politics* 50(4): 507–46.

Iversen, Torben and David Soskice. 2001. "An Asset Theory of Social Policy Preferences." *American Political Science Review* 95 (4 Dec): 875–93.

Jackson, James. 2008. "The U.S. Financial Crisis: Lessons From Sweden." *CRS Report for Congress* Order Code RS22962 (29 September, 2008). http://fpc.state.gov/documents/organization/110770.pdf.

Jacobs, Dave. 1988. "Corporate Economic Power and the State." *American Journal of Sociology* 93 (4 Jan): 852–81.

Jensen, Claus, Mads Andersen, Karsten Dybvad and Kim Grauggard. 2014. "Lovbestemt mindsteloen—nej tak!" *Berlingske*, September 18, 2014. https://www.berlingske.dk/laesere/lovbestemt-mindsteloen-nej-tak (accessed February 26, 2020).

Jones, Erik. 2015. "Getting the Story Right: How You Should Choose Between Different Interpretations of the European Crisis (and Why You Should Care)." European Investment Bank Institute, *Europe Debates* (No. 5 January).

Keep, Ewart and Ken Mayhew. 2010. "Moving beyond skills as a social and economic panacea." *Work, Employment and Society* 24(3): 565–77.

Korpi, Walter and Joachim Palme. 1998. "The Paradox of Redistribution and Strategies of Equality." *American Sociological Review* 63 (September): 661–87.

Lehndorff, Steffen. 2015. *Divisive integration*. Brussels: European Trade Union Institute.

Lipietz, Alain. 1987. *Mirages and Miracles*. New York: Verso.

Low Pay Commission. 2015. "National Minimum Wage. Low Pay Commission Report. Presented to Parliament by the Secretary of State for Business, Innovation and Skills." https://assets.publishing.service.gov.uk/government/uploads/system/uploads/attachment_data/file/520052/National_Minimum_Wage_LPC_report_2015.pdf (accessed February 26, 2020).

Madsen, Per Kongshøj. 2015. "Er Dansk Flexicurity noget særligt?" In *Dansk flexicurity—fleksibilitet og sikkerhed på arbejdsmarkedet*, edited by Thomas Bredgaard and Per Kongshøj Madsen. København: Hans Reitzels Forlag, 3–74.

Mares, Isabela. 2003. *The Politics of Social Risk*. Cambridge: Cambridge University Press.

Martin, Cathie Jo. 1991. *Shifting the Burden: the Struggle Over Growth and Corporate Taxation*. Chicago: University of Chicago Press.

Martin, Cathie Jo. 2000. *Stuck in Neutral*. Princeton: Princeton University Press.

Martin, Cathie Jo. 2016. "Economic Prosperity is in High Demand: Commentary on Baccaro and Pontusson." *Politics & Society* 44(2): 227–35.

Martin, Cathie Jo and Duane Swank. 2012. *The Political Construction of Business Interests: Coordination, Growth and Equality*. New York: Cambridge University Press.

Martin, Cathie Jo and Kathleen Thelen. 2007. "The State and Coordinated Capitalism." *World Politics* 60(1) (October 2007): 1–36.

Martin, Cathie Jo and Jette Steen Knudsen. 2010. "Scenes from a Mall: Retail Training and the Social Exclusion of Low-Skilled Workers." *Regulation & Governance* 4(3) (September): 345–64.

Milner, Helen. 1988. *Resisting Protectionism: Global Industries and the Politics of International Trade*. Princeton: Princeton University Press.

Mitchell, Neil, Wendy Hansen and Eric Jepsen. 1997. "The Determinants of Domestic and Foreign Corporate Political Activity." *Journal of Politics* 59 (4 November): 1096–113.

Palier, Bruno and Kathleen Thelen. 2010. "Institutionalizing dualism: Complementarities and change in France and Germany." *Politics & Society* 38(1): 119–48.

Payne, Jonathan and Ewart Keep. 2011. "One Step Forward, Two Steps Back? Skills Policy in England under the Coalition Government." *SKOPE Research Paper* 102 (July), http://www.skope.ox.ac.uk/?person=one-step-forward-two-steps-back-skills-policy-in-england-under-the-coalition-government (accessed February 26, 2020).

Salamon, Lester and John Siegfried. 1974. "Economic Power and Political Influence: the Impact of Industry Structure on Public Policy." *American Political Science Review* 71 (4 Dec): 1026–43.

Saltmarsh, Matthew. 2010. "Swedish Bank Fee Sets Example for America." *New York Times*, January 21, 2010.

Schnyder, Gerhard. 2012. "Like a Phoenix from the Ashes? Reassessing the Transformation of the Swedish Political Economy since the 1970s." *Journal of European Public Policy* 19(8): 1126–45.

Shonfield, Andrew. 1965. *Modern Capitalism: The Changing Balance of Public and Private Power.* Oxford: Oxford University Press.

State of Green. n.d. https://stateofgreen.com/en/partners/danish-ministry-of-energy-utilities-and-climate/ (accessed February 26, 2020).

Streeck, Wolfgang. 1992. *Social Institutions and Economic Performance.* Beverly Hills: Sage.

Suenson, Emil Lobe; Nedergaard, Peter and Peter Munk Christiansen. 2016. "Why Lash Yourself to the Mast? The Case of the Danish 'Budget Law.'" *Public Budgeting & Finance* 36(1): 3–21.

Svallfors, Stefan. 2016. "Politics as organized combat." *New Political Economy* 21(6): 505–19.

Thelen, Kathleen. 2014. *Varieties of Liberalization and the New Politics of Social Solidarity.* New York: Cambridge University Press.

Touwen, Jeroen. 2014. "The Hybrid Variety. Lessons In Non-Market Coordination from the Business System in the Netherlands, 1950–2010." *Enterprise and Society* 15(4): 849–84. https://www.gov.uk/government/uploads/system/uploads/attachment_data/file/247695/0197.pdf (accessed February 26, 2020).

VNONCW. 2015. "COEN-enquête: Herstel Nederland zet door." https://www.vno-ncw.nl/forum/coen-enqu%C3%AAte-herstel-nederland-zet-door (accessed February 26, 2020).

Warwick Commission. 2009. "The Warwick Commission on International Financial Reform: In Praise of Unlevel Playing Fields." https://warwick.ac.uk/research/warwickcommission/financialreform/report/ (accessed February 26, 2020).

Wolf, Allison. 2011. *Review of Vocational Education: The Wolf Report.* London, HMSO.

Wren, Anne. 2013. *The Political Economy of the Service Transition.* Oxford: Oxford University Press.

8

Strategies for Growth and Employment Creation in a Services-Based Economy: Skill Formation, Equality, and the Welfare State

Anne Wren

1. Introduction

In this chapter, I argue that the institutions of skill formation, wage-setting, and public service provision in particular have an important role to play in the formulation of strategies for growth and employment creation in the new post-industrial, digitized, economic environment that Hassel and Palier describe in the first chapter. I analyze the evolution of labor market distributional outcomes associated with the challenges of deindustrialization and the revolution in ICT in three countries—the UK, Sweden, and Germany—that have varied historically in terms of their underlying welfare-regime structure (Esping-Andersen (1990); Hall and Soskice (2001)). In line with Hassel and Palier's introductory arguments, I suggest that cross-national variations in responses to these challenges, and in the economic and distributional outcomes with which they are associated, stem in part from the structure of existing institutional capacities at the national level, but that the adaptation of underlying growth models to the new environment can also create pressure for institutional reform.

In the chapter, I develop this argument as follows. In section 2, I describe how services sectors vary in terms of their production characteristics, their capacity for international trade, and the way in which they are impacted by the spread of ICT. *Non-Dynamic services* sectors (like childcare and a range of other personal services) are characterized by low rates of productivity growth, ICT intensity, and international trade. *Dynamic services* sectors (finance, communications, computer, and business services), in contrast, are increasingly characterized by relatively high levels of productivity growth, ICT intensity, and trade. *Welfare services* (public administration, education, and health) share some features of the other two categories but differ in that they are publicly provided to varying degrees across countries.

In sections 3, 4, and 5, I identify a set of links between welfare state institutions and capacities for growth and employment expansion across these different types

Anne Wren, *Strategies for Growth and Employment Creation in a Services-Based Economy: Skill Formation, Equality, and the Welfare State* In: *Growth and Welfare in Advanced Capitalist Economies: How Have Growth Regimes Evolved?*
Edited by: Anke Hassel and Bruno Palier, Oxford University Press (2021).
DOI: 10.1093/oso/9780198866176.003.0008

of services sector. I examine the economic and distributional outcomes associated with variations in these institutions in the three countries under investigation in the changing economic environment. My analysis focuses on the period of transition from the early days of the ICT revolution to the onset of the financial crisis in 2007–8. The argument in this chapter has parallels with that of Baccaro and Pontusson (2016 and this volume), but differs from those authors in its greater emphasis (shared with Hassel and Palier in their Introduction) on interactions between the supply and demand sides of the economy. In particular, I highlight the role played by skills policy in shaping patterns of specialization in high productivity, traded sectors, which are important engines of growth even in "consumption-led" regimes. Section 6 concludes.

2. The New Economic Environment

2.1 Deindustrialization and the ICT Revolution

As Hassel and Palier describe in their introductory chapter to this volume, over the past thirty years the wealthiest OECD economies—in Europe, North America, and Australasia—have experienced rapid deindustrialization. A range of factors have contributed to this process: some, like technological change and changes in the characteristics of consumer demand, are internal to the development process in the economies themselves; others, like increased competition from developing countries in the market for manufactured goods, are external. There is some debate as to the relative importance of these factors (although the evidence thus far appears to weigh in favor of domestic factors stemming from long run processes of economic development as the more dominant) (see, for example, Rowthorn and Ramaswamy 1999; Rowthorn and Coutts 2004, 2013). Critically though, there is little to suggest that any of the processes that have generated deindustrialization are likely to be reversed, implying that the challenge of adapting growth strategies towards successful competition in services-based markets will remain a critical one for governments. The impact of deindustrialization on national economies and labor markets has been profound: as can be seen from Table 8.1, in a range of OECD economies, manufacturing sectors accounted for less than a quarter (and in most cases less than one fifth) of total value-added, and provided employment for less than 15 percent of the working age population by the turn of the century. Thus, it is no surprise that the task of adapting national growth models to the new services-based context has been a key one for governments (see also Wren 2013).

The transition towards services has also coincided, however, with a technological revolution that has significantly impacted the services production process itself. In the past, the element of human interaction required for service provision

Table 8.1 Manufacturing sector share of employment (percentage of working age population) and value-added (average, 2000–5)

	Employment	Value-added
US	8.7	17.4
UK	9.1	15.4
Netherlands	8.7	14.5
Belgium	8.9	18.1
France	8.8	14.8
Spain	9.8	17.5
Portugal	13.2	16.3
Germany	13.8	22.6
Austria	11.3	19.9
Italy	10.9	19.6
Finland	12.4	24.9
Sweden	12.4	20.4
Denmark	11.5	15.3
Japan	12.5	20.9
Average	**10.9**	**18.4**

Source: EU-KELMS. http://www.euklems.net/.

placed limits on the capacity for productivity growth and international trade in services (as detailed most famously by Baumol 1967). The revolution in information and communications technologies (ICT) that has occurred over the last quarter century, however, has reduced or removed these constraints in some, but not all, services sectors, allowing for the possibility of the pursuit of high productivity growth models that are services sector-led. At the same time, the spread of the new technologies has shifted the relative demand for different types of skills with implications for welfare state and labor market policies. Before describing these changes, it is helpful to describe how the characteristics of production and trade vary across different types of service sector.

2.2 Variations in the Characteristics of Service Production

In earlier work I have distinguished between three different types of service sector, which I labelled "non-dynamic," "dynamic," and "welfare" service sectors (Wren 2013). These categorizations are not intended to be absolute, but they provide broad brush strokes for understanding variations in the characteristics of production between different types of services.

Non-Dynamic Service Sectors are those sectors which are most prone to the constraints on productivity growth identified by Baumol (1967). Good examples to think through here are waitressing, or childcare provision: it might be possible to increase the number of children supervised by one carer, or the number of tables served by one waiter, and so on, but in the process the quality of care and service will almost certainly decline. As a result, rates of productivity growth in these sectors remain low. For related reasons, these types of services remain significantly less impacted by the revolution in ICT that has occurred over the past twenty-five years. The new technology cannot substitute for those aspects of service provision that require face to face interpersonal interaction (cutting someone's hair, feeding a child, dressing a wound, for example). And, as a result, in areas in which this kind of human interaction is an important component of service provision, the diffusion of ICT, and its ability to enhance productivity, is limited in relative terms. For the same set of reasons these sectors are subject to significant natural barriers to trade, and remain largely untraded internationally. These characteristics apply to a range of social and personal and consumer services.

In contrast, in *dynamic service sectors*, like finance, business services, and communications, productivity and trade have been greatly enhanced over the last two decades by advances in ICT. It is well established that the new technology has significantly impacted on productivity growth in those sectors in which its diffusion has been most marked (Stiroh 2002; Triplett and Bosworth 2004; Jorgenson, Ho, and Stiroh 2008; Bosworth and Triplett 2007; Corrado et al. 2007), and, as the data in Table 8.2 indicates, knowledge-intensive service sectors have been at the forefront of this process. From the Table we can see that the contribution of ICT capital to the growth of value-added in business services, financial intermediation, and post and telecommunications over the past three decades has been highly significant when compared to its contribution in a range of services in which the face to face component of provision is more important (for example, hotels and restaurants, retail trade, public administration, education, and health and social work and other community social and personal services), and in most traditional manufacturing sectors (with the exceptions on the manufacturing side of electrical and optical equipment, and printing and publishing).

Table 8.3, meanwhile indicates that these patterns correspond with higher rates of productivity growth in the ICT-intensive services group (finance, computer and related business services, and post and telecommunications) than in their less ICT-intensive service sector counterparts (although the issue of the measurement of productivity in services, of course, remains controversial—see Triplett and Bosworth (2004) for a comprehensive review of the issues involved here).

Critically, also, the digitization of information and the ability to instantaneously transmit it across the globe, has significantly reduced the barriers to trade in more knowledge-intensive service sectors where face to face interpersonal interaction is a less important component of service provision, and these sectors have witnessed a significant expansion in levels of trade in recent decades (see Figure 8.1) (Sauve 2001; Freund and Weinhold 2002; Levy and Murnane 2005; Blinder 2007).

Table 8.2 Contribution of ICT capital to value-added growth by sector (percent)

	Level 1981*	Average 1981–2007**
Agriculture		
Agriculture, forestry, and fishing	0.025	0.059
Manufacturing sectors		
Food products, beverages, and tobacco	0.203	0.283
Textiles, leather, and footwear	0.057	0.129
Wood and wood products	0.146	0.185
Paper, paper products, printing, and publishing	0.445	0.607
Chemicals, chemical products	0.182	0.357
Rubber, plastics	0.194	0.237
Basic metals, fabricated metal products	0.175	0.238
Electrical, optical equipment	0.487	0.608
Transport equipment	0.255	0.298
Other manufacturing	−0.027	0.199
Service sectors		
Wholesale trade	0.578	0.675
Retail trade	0.342	0.410
Transport and storage	0.245	0.429
Post and telecommunications	**2.297**	**1.974**
Real estate	0.373	0.539
Other business activities (including renting of machinery and equipment)	**0.799**	**1.049**
Construction	0.076	0.156
Hotels and restaurants	−0.094	0.263
Financial intermediation	**1.366**	**1.477**
Public administration and defense	0.354	0.400
Education	0.146	0.220
Health and social work	0.131	0.201
Other community, social, and personal services	0.416	0.502

Note: Data for all countries in the EU-KLEMS database, except for Canada, Cyprus, Korea, Estonia, Greece, Latvia, Lithuania, Malta, Poland, Portugal, and Slovakia, where data was unavailable.

*Except for Sweden (1994), Germany (1992), Australia (1983), Czech Republic (1996), Hungary (1996), Ireland (1989), Slovenia (1996).

** Except for Japan (2006), France (2006), Belgium (2006), Slovenia (2006).

Source: EU-KLEMS. http://www.euklems.net/.

Thus, dynamic service sectors are more ICT intensive, more heavily traded internationally, and have a greater capacity for productivity growth than their non-dynamic counterparts, and this has important implications for employment creation strategies. Before considering these implications, however, I will outline how the characteristics of a third category of service sectors differ from these two.

Welfare Service Sectors—like government, education and health—are primarily distinguished from the other two sectors in that they are often publicly provided. In the aggregate these sectors share some of the characteristics of non-dynamic sectors described earlier. They are considerably less ICT intensive, display lower

Table 8.3 Rates of productivity growth, services and manufacturing, 2000–7 (Euro 15)

Sector	Productivity Growth (Average, 2000–7)
Manufacturing	3.74%
Hotels and restaurants	-0.58%
Other community and social services	-0.69%
Real estate activities	-0.82%
Wholesale and retail trade	1.83%
Education	-0.86%
Health	0.74%
Public administration and defense	1.37%
Post and telecommunications	10.75%
Financial intermediation	4.71%
Computer and related business activities	2.11%
Whole economy	1.45%

Note: Rates of Productivity Growth is measured as average annual percentage growth in labor productivity measured in terms of gross value-added per hour worked.

Source: EU-KLEMS. http://www.euklems.net/

rates of productivity growth, and are traded at lower levels than dynamic service sectors (see Tables 8.2 and 8.3). Of course, these aggregate sectoral patterns mask differences at the subsectoral level. Within the health sector, for example, some services, such as nursing, clearly possess the characteristics of the non-dynamic services group (nurses cannot tend to more patients without a decline in the quality of the service, for example, nor can ICT facilitate the provision of caring services at long distance), while in other areas, like the interpretation of radiology

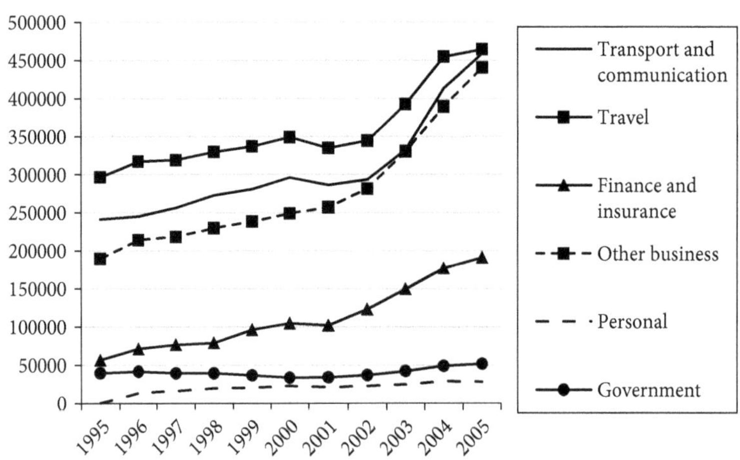

Figure 8.1 Cross-sectoral comparison of rates of expansion in service exports (total exports, OECD countries) 1994–2005 (modes 1 and 2, value in $US)

Source: OECD EBOPS Database.

scans, the diffusion of ICT can more easily facilitate productivity gains and international trade. Similarly, it might be argued, that while the scope for ICT to facilitate productivity gains and trade in the supervision and education of young children (where interpersonal interaction and student-teacher ratios are of critical importance to service provision), at higher educational levels, the potential for ICT to increase productivity and facilitate trade is greater.

Welfare state policies affect the capacity to create employment in all of these areas of service provision in important ways, although the key policies vary across sectors. Thus, the adaptation of growth and employment strategies to a post-industrial context can create pressure for welfare state reform. The nature of these relationships is detailed in the next three sections.

3. Supply- and Demand-Side Strategies for Employment Creation in Low Productivity Services Sectors

The decline in employment opportunities in manufacturing in recent decades has been compensated for in part by the expansion of less-skilled, and low-paid, private sector employment in non-dynamic service sectors (personal, consumer, and social services). Countries have varied in the extent to which they have relied on these sectors to fill the post-industrial employment gap, however, with Liberal regimes, like the UK and the US, to the forefront. As we can see from Figure 8.2, in the UK, the employment share of non-dynamic services sectors has expanded steadily since the start of the 1970s, so that they accounted for almost 30 percent of employment by 2005. In Sweden, in contrast, the figure was closer to one fifth, and there has been almost no expansion in the employment share of these sectors over the past thirty-five years. In Germany, unlike Sweden, non-dynamic service sectors have expanded steadily in importance in terms of employment creation since the start of the 1990s, although employment rates still fall significantly below those of the Liberal regimes.

In Liberal regimes, the expansion of employment in non-dynamic services sectors has been facilitated by institutions and policies on both the supply and the demand side. On the one hand, it has been heavily reliant on keeping *relative wages* in low-skilled service sectors low (Iversen and Wren 1998). The demand for personal and consumer services is very responsive to changes in prices (this is unsurprising when we consider their capacity for home production—think of catering and gardening services, for example). Given their low capacity for productivity growth, however, it becomes particularly important to keep relative wages low if this characteristic is to be exploited in order to facilitate an expansion in demand and employment. As a result it is harder to combine the expansion of lower-skilled service employment with equality than it was during the so-called "golden age" of manufacturing expansion in the 1950s and 1960s (when the

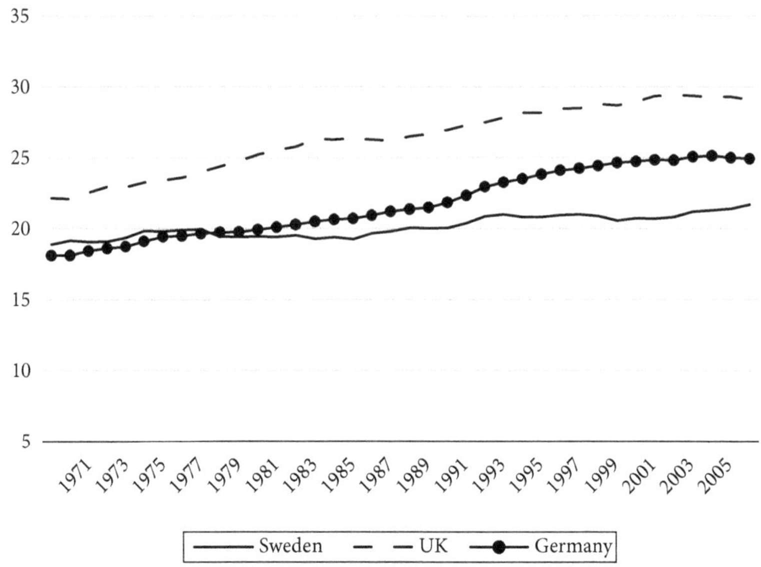

Figure 8.2 Employment in non-dynamic services sectors as percentage of total employment (1970–2005)

Note: Non-dynamic services are defined as hotels and restaurants, distribution, and other community, social, and personal services.

Source: EU-KLEMS. http://www.euklems.net/.

simultaneous occurrence of high demand elasticities for new consumer durables, and high rates of productivity growth in manufacturing sectors engendered by Fordist innovations in production processes, meant that relative prices could be kept low at the same time as real wage rates in these sectors were growing (Meidner 1974; Rehn 1985). An important component of the Liberal response to this trade-off between wage equality and employment creation in low-skilled, low productivity service sectors has been the removal or reduction of protections on the wages of low paid workers and attacks on the power of trades unions (Iversen and Wren 1998).

Figure 8.3 shows the evolution of wages in non-dynamic services sectors compared with the economy-wide (intersectoral) average wage from 1970–2005.[1] From Figure 8.3 we can clearly see the impact of the higher levels of wage protection enjoyed by low wage workers in the Swedish, and until more recently, the German economy compared with those in the UK. As early as the start of the 1970s the wages of workers in non-dynamic services sectors on average had fallen to 40 percent below those of the average UK worker: in Sweden and Germany they

[1] The figure shows the standard deviation of non-dynamic service sectors wages compared with the economy-wide mean, expressed as a percentage of the mean.

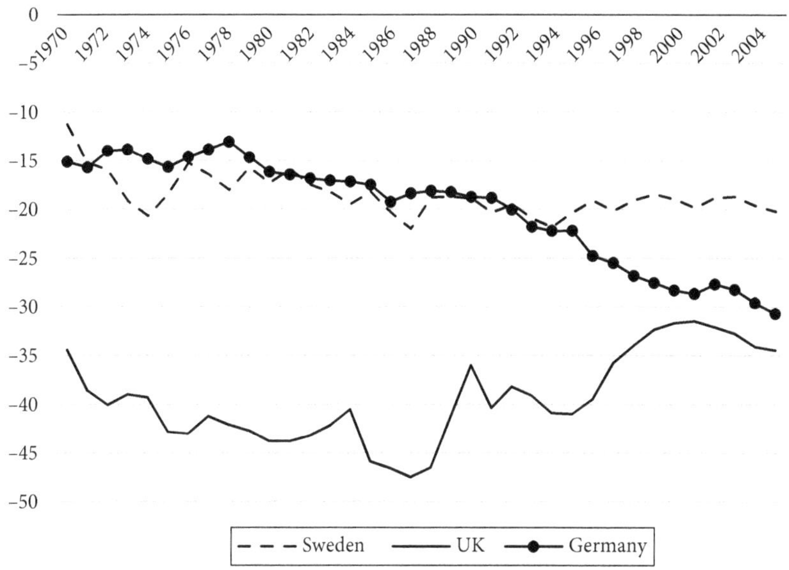

Figure 8.3 Non-dynamic service sector compensation compared with economy-wide average (1970–2005) (standard deviation as percentage economy-wide mean)

Notes: (1) Non-dynamic services are defined as hotels and restaurants, distribution, and other community, social, and personal services.

(2) Y-axis shows the standard deviation across non-dynamic service sectors expressed as a percentage of the economy-wide intersectoral mean.

Source: EU-KLEMS. http://www.euklems.net/.

were only 15 percent below. Under the Thatcher government, further attacks on collective bargaining rights and the removal of protections on the wages of the lowest paid workers caused this figure to fall further to nearly 50 percent. This trend was reversed slightly at the end of the 1980s, while the election of the Blair government on a mandate for the introduction of a minimum wage (and its subsequent introduction) at the end of the 1990s was associated with a more marked recovery of the relative wages of lowest paid services workers in the UK (albeit to significantly lower levels than those observed elsewhere). In Sweden, in contrast, the relative wages of workers in non-dynamic services sectors have remained protected compared with other countries, and relatively constant, hovering between 15 and 20 percent below the economy-wide average, since 1970.[2] In Germany, the effects of labor market dualization began to set in around the mid-1990s, in advance of the Hartz IV reforms, with the worsening labor

[2] It is important to emphasize that these figures refer to *wage* inequality. While ratios between wages in these low productivity services sectors and average wages in remained constant, *income* inequality did increase significantly in Sweden in this period (for example, the d5d1 ratio increased from 1.5 to 2

market position of less skilled and often insecure and un-unionized workers in low end services sectors, compared with the protected industrial core, reflected in declining relative wage rates (Gernandt and Pfeiffer 2006; Palier and Thelen 2010; Hassel 2014).

In addition to these supply-side factors, there has been a demand-side component to the expansion of employment in low-skilled service sectors. Some authors argue, for example, that an important factor was a structural shift in demand associated with a movement towards a new high participation equilibrium. Increases in family working hours raise the demand for services via a substitution effect (women working in the paid labor force purchasing childcare and catered food, for example), but also via an income effect (families that work more hours earn more money, and personal and consumer services are "luxury" items which occupy proportionately more of individual and household budgets as incomes rise). For the US case at least there is good evidence that the increase in demand for consumer and personal services was closely associated with increases in family working hours (as more women entered paid work, and more workers began to work longer hours) (see, for example, Freeman 2007; Gregory, Salverda and Schettkat 2007). However, the extent to which increased household working hours are an endogenous outcome of the removal of protections on low wages, and are thus related to supply-side interventions, has yet to be fully established.

Aside from this structural change, in the Liberal regimes, employment and output in low productivity services sectors has undoubtedly been buoyed by general demand conditions in this period. Baccaro and Pontusson (2016, and this volume) point to the growth of average real incomes in the UK from the mid-1990s to the onset of the crisis in 2007, and the increase in private sector debt in that country in the pre-crisis years has also been well documented (see for example Crouch 2009 and Barnes and Wren 2012). In the ten years preceding the onset of the financial crisis, private sector debt in the UK rose by nearly 60 percent of GDP[3] (from 99 percent in 1997 to 158 percent in 2007). Sweden also saw a (considerably smaller) rise in private sector debt in this period (from 92 to 107 percent of GDP), while in Germany levels of debt actually declined (from a high of 116 percent of GDP in 2000 to 97 percent of GDP by 2007) (Beck, Demirgüç-Kunt, and Levine 2008). Since the demand for a range of personal and consumer services is income elastic, rising real incomes should be associated with an expansion of demand in these kinds of sectors. It is reasonable to expect similar effects to arise from the expansion of the availability of cheap credit to the

between 1985 and 2010 (OECD 2018), largely as a result of changes in the tax and benefit regimes (OECD 2015)).

[3] Private sector credit by deposit money, banks, and other institutions to GDP. Source: Financial Structure Database (2018). https://www.worldbank.org/en/publication/gfdr/data/financial-structure-database

extent that it created the illusion of increased household wealth (both directly in providing consumers with credit lines for personal spending, and indirectly via its contribution to asset (and especially house price) inflation).

The relative weight of real income growth and the expansion of private sector debt in accounting for the expansion of demand in the UK in this period has yet to be fully assessed. Crouch (2009) and Barnes and Wren (2012), for example, emphasize the importance of debt driven demand, while Baccaro and Pontusson (this volume) emphasize the growth of real incomes. The accurate assessment of the relative weight of these effects in the pre-crisis period is an important empirical task—and beyond the scope of the current analysis. Rather, what I emphasize here is the following. For a domestic consumer demand driven strategy, like that described by Baccaro and Pontusson, and by Hassel and Palier in their first chapter, to be sustainable *over the long run*, without relying on either private sector or government debt, growing real incomes must be grounded in growth and productivity gains elsewhere in the economy. Thus, the supply-side institutions and policies that facilitate expansion in high productivity sectors are critical components in the development of *both* the consumer demand and export oriented strategies that these authors describe (on which more below).

If employment creation in non-dynamic services sectors has played an important role in compensating for the loss of industrial jobs in the UK over the last half century, in social democratic Sweden the pattern has been quite different. The employment share of these sectors has not shown much expansion since the start of the 1970s, and currently stands at roughly one fifth, compared with nearly a third in the UK, as shown in Figure 8.2.

Striking from Figure 8.4, on the other hand is the continued critical importance of the public sector to the Swedish labor market. In spite of retrenchment, nearly 30 percent of Swedish workers who were in employment in 2005 were directly employed by the government—compared with 11 percent in Germany and 19 percent in the UK. The significance of this factor in understanding the functioning of the Swedish post-industrial growth model cannot be overestimated. On the one hand, the public sector continues to act as a bulwark against the worst effects of deindustrialization by providing direct employment opportunities for workers at medium to low skill levels. On the other, the existence of a large core of workers in relatively well-paid and secure government jobs plays an important role in fuelling the domestic component of Swedish demand (as Hassel and Palier describe). Needless to say, this is a costly strategy in terms of government budgets, however, and thus the Swedish model also is ultimately reliant on the growth of productivity and incomes in dynamic economic sectors to keep the burden of taxation and/or public sector deficits associated with an expansive public sector in check.

In Germany, meanwhile, as argued in Iversen and Wren (1998), in the 1980s and 1990s, the emergence of a "trilemma" associated with attempts to create employment in non-dynamic services sectors, left governments caught

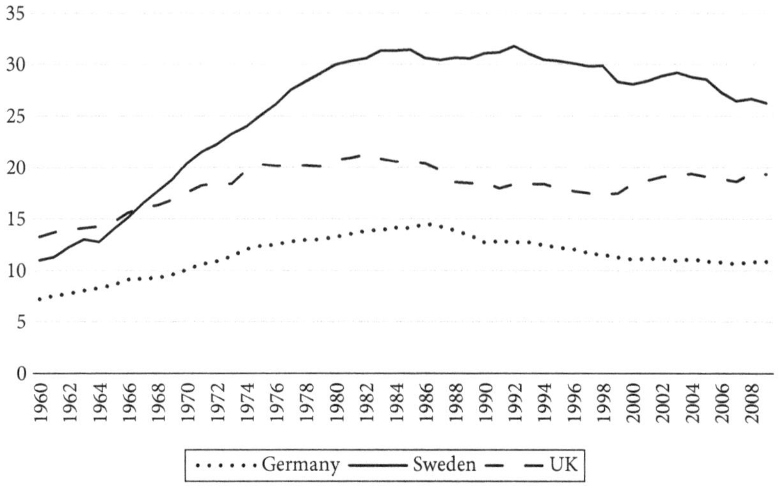

Figure 8.4 Civilian government employment as percentage of total employment
Source: Comparative Welfare States Database (Huber, Ragin, and Stephens 2014).

between the constraints of inherited political limitations on the size of the public sector (see, for example, Esping-Andersen 1990; Van Kersbergen 1995), and a network of institutions and policies that had the effect of sustaining high levels of wage equality (and strong protections on wages at the lower end of the earnings distribution) for labor market insiders in core sectors (both core elements of the German welfare-production regime (Hall and Soskice 2001). In this early period of deindustrialization, this policy combination was associated with low rates of service employment creation in Germany, compared with the UK and Sweden. However, the effects of this were dampened to some extent by the continued strength of the German industrial sector in relative terms, and by low rates of labor force participation associated with the single breadwinner model and generous early retirement programs.

The German economy has been far from immune to the effects of deindustrialization, however. In the thirty years from the start of the 1970s to the turn of the century in Germany, the proportions of employment and value-added in manufacturing sectors shrank from just over one third to approximately one fifth. The industrial core of the German economy has shrunk, therefore, as elsewhere, and, given the negative effects of the wage restraint required to sustain German manufacturing export performance on domestic demand (as described by Baccaro and Pontusson 2016, and this volume), the costs of a growth strategy centered on industrial exports in terms of the limits which it places on the capacity for employment creation elsewhere in the economy, arguably create considerable structural pressure for reform of the German model. Given low rates of income growth, and associated low levels of domestic demand, it is more difficult to exploit the income elasticity of demand for private personal and consumer services than in the UK. However, there remain considerable historical political obstacles to the expansion of public service provision and employment in Germany (again see Figure 8.4 for evidence on the continued divergence between Germany and Sweden (and to a lesser extent the UK) in terms of public employment). The shrinkage of the industrial core, meanwhile, has ultimately rendered the support of large numbers of labor market non-participants (early retirees and women working inside the home)—a safety valve for the German economy in the 1980s—harder to sustain.

In the face of these restrictions, successive German governments have tackled the issue of creating employment for less skilled workers in the only other manner available, that is through the dismantling of protections on the wages and employment of the lowest paid workers. This has served to exacerbate the dualization of the German labor market (Palier and Thelen 2010; Hassel 2014): for example, as we saw in Figure 8.3, it has resulted in significant reductions in the relative wages of workers in less productive services sectors, and these have fed into large increases in inequality at the lower end of the income distribution.[4] These changes, along with steadily increasing female labor force participation rates,[5] have been associated with the expansion of private sector employment in non-dynamic services sectors in this period, in a pattern which replicates that observed in Liberal regimes in the 1980s and early 1990s.

4. Strategies for Growth in a Digitized Post-Industrial Economy

The preceding discussion suggests that a focus on employment expansion in non-dynamic service sectors to compensate for the loss of manufacturing sector jobs raises the prospect of a rather unappealing set of political choices between employment creation, equality, taxation, and public and private sector indebtedness. It is important to emphasize also, however, that *none* of these strategies is, on its own, a sufficient long-term solution to the problem of deindustrialization. Rather, the development of sustainable post-industrial growth regimes requires strategies to facilitate expansion in high productivity sectors that can replace traditional manufacturing sectors as the dynamic drivers of growth.

[4] See Gernandt and Pfeiffer (2006); Fuchs-Schündeln, Krueger, and Sommer (2010) for more detail on increasing inequality in Germany.

[5] Between 1990 and 2015, labor force participation rates of women of working age (15–64) increased from 55 to 78 percent in Germany. In comparison, participation rates remained largely unchanged at between 80 and 85 percent in Sweden in this period, while in the UK the rate increased from 66 to 74 percent.

Table 8.4 Gross value-added (annual percentage change), manufacturing and market services

	Market services		Manufacturing	
	2002–7	2011–15	2002–7	2011–15
Germany	1.6	1.8	2.7	2.5
Sweden	4.1	2.9	5.5	–0.8
UK	4.0	3.0	0.3	0.5

Source: Van Ark and Jäger (2017), Data from EU-KLEMs (2017).

In the UK case, as can be seen from Table 8.4, the key drivers of the growth of value-added in recent times have been market services sectors (with post and telecommunications, financial intermediation, computers, and other business services, recording particularly strong growth[6]). Declining income from industrial exports has been partially compensated for by rapid increases in net export earnings from knowledge-intensive services (from 1.3 to 5.6 percent of GDP between 1991 and 2011).[7] And this expansion has been associated with increasing relative incomes in dynamic services sectors (see Figure 8.5).

While it is true, therefore, that the domestic component of demand is more important in relative terms in the UK than, for example, Germany, as Hassel and Palier and Baccaro and Pontusson emphasize, it is nonetheless important to recognize the role played by successful performance in dynamic service exports, and rising incomes in these sectors, in sustaining demand for income elastic consumer and personal services at the lower end of the UK market. This is a point which is somewhat underemphasized in accounts which characterize the UK model as purely "consumption-led." By the mid-2010s, the value of exports had risen to nearly 30 percent of GDP in the UK and, of these, more than 40 percent were exports of services (see Table 8.5). Without the contribution of these sectors, the high levels of domestic demand in the UK in this period could only have been sustained by even higher levels of debt.

In contrast with the UK, as is emphasized throughout this volume (see chapters by Baccaro and Pontusson, Hassel and Palier, and Thelen, among others), the German economic model remains heavily reliant on successful industrial export performance as the primary driver of GDP growth. German service sector exports

[6] EU-KLEMS. http://www.euklems.net/ (subsectoral breakdown figures available either directly from the EU-KLEMs website or from the author on request).

[7] In 2008, for example, the full breakdown of the components of services property and manufacturing income in UK balance of payments as a percentage of GDP in the UK in 2008 were as follows: Knowledge-intensive services (including finance, insurance, business services, computers, and information) +5.5; traditional services and transfers (including travel, transport, government, and transfers) –2.2; investment income, 2.3; manufactures –4.1; other goods (including food, energy, basic materials) –2.5; total current account balance –1.0. (Rowthorn and Coutts 2013).

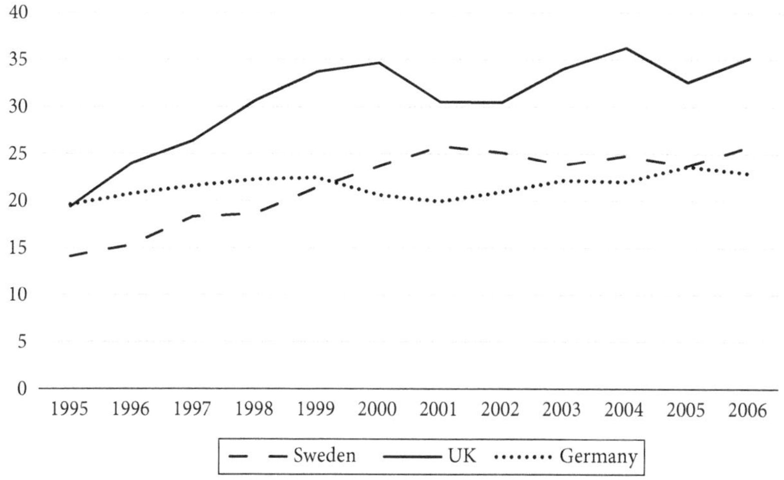

Figure 8.5 Average wages in dynamic services sectors compared with economy-wide average (1970–2005) (standard deviation as percentage economy-wide mean)

Notes: (1) Dynamic services sectors are defined as financial intermediation, post and telecommunications, computer and related service activities, R&D, and other business activities.

(2) Y-axis shows the standard deviation across dynamic service sectors expressed as a percentage of the economy-wide intersectoral mean.

Source: EU-KLEMS. http://www.euklems.net/.

Table 8.5 Export performance (1998–2015)

	Service exports (% total exports)			**Exports (goods and services) (% GDP)**		
	(1998–2000)	**(2005–7)**	**(2013–15)**	**(1998–2000)**	**(2005–7)**	**(2013–15)**
Germany	14.0	14.6	16.8	28.1	35.3	46.0
Sweden	16.4	21.2	30.4	42.1	43.5	44.8
UK	30.3	39.1	42.9	24.1	23.9	28.4

Source: World Bank. World Development Indicators. https://datacatalog.worldbank.org/dataset/world-development-indicators (accessed October 2018).

have yet to expand in the manner of those of Sweden or the UK (as shown in Table 8.5 services accounted for 17 percent of German exports in 2013–15, compared with 30 percent in Sweden and 43 percent in the UK), as have rates of growth of productivity and value-added in market services (see Table 8.4 and Van Ark, O'Mahoney, and Timmer 2008; Van Ark and Jaeger 2017). As emphasized earlier, however, strong manufacturing export performance has failed to render Germany immune to the effects of deindustrialization and the contribution of manufacturing to value-added and employment has shrunk in Germany, as elsewhere. Meanwhile the high levels of wage restraint on which

German industrial export sectors depend have had the effect of dampening domestic consumption demand (see also chapter by Baccaro and Pontusson). The response of successive German governments to the problem of employment creation in this context has been the dismantling of protections on the employment conditions of workers outside the industrial core, facilitating an expansion of output and employment in low productivity services sectors at relatively low wage rates.

Finally, to the extent that the Swedish welfare-intensive employment model has remained affordable, it has relied on successful export performance in ICT-intensive services and manufacturing sectors, as Baccaro and Pontusson (2016, this volume), Hassel and Palier (first chapter) and Thelen (this volume) argue (and see Table 8.5). As shown in Table 8.4, the growth of value-added in manufacturing was particularly strong in Sweden in the pre-crisis period, and this was fuelled largely by exponential growth in ICT-intensive sectors like electrical and optical equipment[8] (although the early evidence indicates that the Swedish manufacturing sector has been slower to recover from the effects of the global recession than that of Germany (see Table 8.4)). Export and value-added growth in dynamic services sectors have also been consistently strong in Sweden, however, with communications, computer, and business services amongst the strongest sectors in terms of value-added in the Swedish case.[9] The growth of value-added in this set of ICT-intensive sectors then has played an important role in financing demand, real wage growth, and public sector operating costs in Sweden in this period.

The key point here is that any sustainable strategy for employment growth must be reliant on the expansion of output and employment in high value-added sectors. In a context of deindustrialization, this means that facilitating successful performance in high productivity service sectors is increasingly important.[10] For this reason, analyzing the underpinnings of growth in these sectors is critical to our understanding of the functioning of post-industrial economic models. From a policy point of view there are many relevant factors here of course—including, but not limited to, investment in ICT, and the extent of regulatory barriers to services trade at both the domestic and international level (see, for example Van Ark and Jäger 2017). In the remainder of this chapter, however, I will focus on one area of *welfare state policy* that is of particular importance. It is well known that the institutions that shape the provision of education and skills are critical inputs in the process of enhancing productivity and generating economic growth (see, for example, Lucas 1988; Barro 1997, 2013; Soskice 1999; Hall and Soskice 2001; Carlin and Soskice 2015). Recent research indicates, however, that the

[8] EU-KLEMS. http://www.euklems.net/ (subsectoral breakdown figures available directly from the EU-KLEMs website, or from the author on request).

[9] EU-KLEMS. http://www.euklems.net/ (subsectoral breakdown figures available directly from the EU-KELMs website, or from the author on request).

[10] See also Van Ark, O'Mahoney, and Timmer (2008) and Van Ark and Jäger (2017).

development of the new information and communications technologies have shifted the demand for skills, or the composition of skills required for economic growth, in ways that may have important implications for existing educational models. These arguments are developed in more detail below.

5. Dynamic Service Expansion and the Institutions of Skill Formation

5.1 The ICT Revolution and the Demand for High-Skilled Labor

There are strong grounds to expect that the skill requirements of a growth model based on expansion in high productivity services sectors differ significantly from those of the manufacturing "golden age." As the data in Table 8.2 indicates, dynamic service sectors are the most ICT intensive of all economic sectors. This is significant for skills policy, since there is growing evidence that ICT and college-educated labor are complements in production (see, for example, Autor et al. 2003; Goos, Manning, and Solomons 2014; Michaels et al. 2014; Acemoglu and Autor 2011).

The key insights of this empirical literature are the following. First, the new technology is highly effective at performing routine tasks which can be specified by stored instructions—even where the required programs are highly complex (for example, bookkeeping or clerical work). As a result, it acts as a substitute for labor in performing these tasks. Since these tasks are typically carried out by workers at medium-skill levels (those with secondary, or some (but not complete) college education), therefore, the relative demand for labor at this skill level is reduced.

Second, and in contrast, the new technology is less effective at performing non-routine cognitive tasks requiring what Hall and Soskice would describe as high-end general skills "flexibility, creativity, generalized problem solving, and complex communications" (Autor, Levy, and Murnane 2003: 5). Instead it serves to complement the skills of the (typically college-educated) workers who perform those tasks: faster access to more complete market information, for example, may improve managerial decision-making, but it cannot yet substitute for that decision-making. Since technology is a complement to rather than a substitute for this type of human capital, investment in the new technology increases, rather than reduces the demand for college-educated labor. This implies that restrictions on the supply of college-educated labor may reduce the gains in productivity and output associated with investment in new technologies.

Finally, Autor et al. (2003) suggest that there exists a third category of tasks which they label as non-routine manual tasks. These tasks involve the kind of interpersonal interaction which, as I have already described, is inherent in many areas of service provision (cutting hair, caring for children, serving meals, etc.). In these areas, Autor et al. argue, the new technology is neither a substitute for nor a complement to labor input: where physical interpersonal interaction forms an important component of service provision, for example, it is more difficult to replace a worker with a computer; on the other hand, computing technology is also less effective, so far, at improving the productivity of labor in performing these tasks. As a result, the diffusion of the new technology has had, as yet, little significant implications for the demand for labor in these sectors. More generally, these sectors have not enjoyed the increases in productivity growth rates and international trade experienced in some other service sectors in part because they are less well placed to benefit from the effects of the ICT revolution. As a result, their expansion is more heavily reliant on factors such as the growth of income and wage and price flexibility in the domestic market, for the reasons previously discussed.

The key point here, however, is that ICT acts as a substitute for labor at medium skill levels, and complements the skills of workers with college level education. In this regard, the skill requirements of the current era of service expansion differ significantly from those of the era of industrial expansion which preceded it. In the 1950s and 1960s, Fordist industrial expansion was associated with an increased demand for labor at low to medium skill levels—and was particularly notable for the existence of complementarities in production between low and high-skilled industrial labor (see, for example, Wallerstein 1990). In contrast, successful expansion in high-end service sectors requires up-skilling, and increasing the numbers of workers receiving high quality tertiary education.

This underscores, of course, the importance of ensuring effective investment at the tertiary level, and also in facilitating tertiary enrolment and access. Recent research indicates, however, that it also implies a critical role for investment in schools-based learning beginning as early as the pre-primary level, since education at this level is increasingly regarded as a key determinant of tertiary outcomes—especially for children from lower-skilled households (see, for example, Cuhne and Heckman 2007; Heckman and Jacobs 2011).

5.2 Cross-National Variation in Skills Policy: Sweden, Germany, and the UK Compared

So how well equipped are existing welfare-production regimes to meet the skills demands of the service economy?[11] Liberal regimes have been relatively successful thus far at producing large numbers of high quality college graduates. However, the private sector route to tertiary investment pursued in the US, the UK, and

[11] See also Chevalier in this volume.

Table 8.6 Variations in educational investment strategies at the tertiary level

	Percentage age group with tertiary education (2017)		d9d5 Ratio		Public investment in tertiary education (% GDP) (2010)	Total investment in tertiary education (% GDP) (2010)
	55–64 Years	25–34 Years	Level 2005	Change 1995–2005		
Germany	26	31	1.70	-0.07	1.34	1.63
Sweden	31	47	1.65	+0.06	2.03	2.26
UK	37	52	1.98	+0.11	0.99	2.10

Source: OECD Education at a Glance (2018), OECD Statistics; on Public Investment in Education: Brady, Huber, and Stephens (2014).

elsewhere in recent decades has had negative consequences in terms both of equity and efficiency. First, it is reliant on high levels of wage inequality that incentivize individual investment in education (see Table 8.6 and Figure 8.5). Second, it has resulted in a rather unequal distribution of skills and, given the increasing cost of tertiary education, there is a risk that this distribution will be replicated across generations (Green, Green, and Pensiero 2014). Third, it has been associated with increasing levels of individual indebtedness in recent years (Stigliz 2012; Barrow, Brock, and Rouse 2013; Belfield, Farquharson, Sibieta 2018) which can constitute a barrier to tertiary enrolment for students from poorer backgrounds in particular.

Finally, and critically, there is some evidence to suggest that in spite of the incentives for private investment existing in these regimes, overall levels of educational investment have been insufficient. Goldin and Katz (2008), for example, cite a failure of the US education system to provide an adequate supply of college-educated workers to keep pace with technological change, as one of the primary causes of the increase in inequality in that country at the end of the last century.

The countries of central and Northern Europe face a different set of challenges as regards educational policy. Here high levels of coordination in wage bargaining ensure higher levels of wage equality. One effect of this though is to reduce the incentives for private individuals to invest in higher level skills—since the relative rewards to such investment are smaller. In these regimes, then, there is a risk of a shortage in the skills on which expansion in high-end knowledge-intensive services relies, unless the government steps in to subsidize them (see Iversen and Soskice 2010; Ansell and Gingrich 2013; Wren, Fodor, and Theodoropoulou 2013).

In the social democratic regimes of Scandinavia this is what governments have traditionally done—providing high levels of investment in school- and college-based education all the way from the pre-primary to the tertiary level, which have resulted in high levels of tertiary enrolment. Sweden, for example, spent more than twice as much of its GDP on public investment in tertiary education in 2010 than the UK. (see Table 8.5, and Wren 2013). This strategy has several potential advantages in terms of equity. It is less reliant on the existence of wage-premia for highly skilled workers to induce investment in higher level skills.[12] In addition, it can facilitate greater equity of access to tertiary education—in the first place, because that education is publicly financed, but also because the public financing of education for school-aged, and, even more critically pre-primary, children has knock-on effects on levels of equity in tertiary outcomes for children from different social backgrounds (see Heckman and Jacobs 2011). However, as with other components of the Swedish model, it is reliant on strong growth of value-added to finance the costs of the educational sector, as well as continued public support for high levels of educational spending.

In sharp contrast with Sweden, Germany has traditionally combined high levels of coordination in wage-setting with lower levels of public investment in tertiary and schools-based education, and levels of tertiary enrolment remain low in relative terms. The most recent OECD data, for example, shows that in 2017, just under a third of the German population between the ages of twenty-five and thirty-four had attained a tertiary education, compared with around half of UK and Swedish citizens in the same age group (see Table 8.6). Further, the German data shows that in spite of increased rates of enrolment in recent years, the rate of tertiary expansion in Germany has been considerably slower than elsewhere. Tertiary attainment rates amongst twenty-five- to thirty-four-year-olds are not much different from those observed amongst fifty-five- to sixty-four-year-olds in Germany: in the UK and Sweden in contrast, rates of attainment are significantly higher amongst the current cohort than their predecessors.

Traditionally, as Hall and Soskice (2001) have influentially argued, low rates of tertiary enrolment in Germany have been associated with the existence of a highly effective vocational training system. Large proportions of the workforce participated in apprenticeship-based training which equipped workers with strong firm and sector specific skills, and formed the basis for comparative advantage in core areas of industrial production (for example, capital goods). The question, however, is whether this strategy remains sustainable in an era in which employment expansion increasingly relies on exploiting the complementarities between ICT and college-educated labor.

[12] Although it should be noted that the wages of the most highly skilled workers in Sweden show some sign of having pulled away from those of their less skilled counterparts over the last couple of decades, albeit to a smaller degree than in the UK or the US (see Table 8.6 and Figure 8.5).

Table 8.7 Changes in wage bill share and hours worked, by skill level, all industries 1991–2005 (Germany, Sweden, and the UK)

		High-skilled	Medium-skilled	Low-skilled
Germany	Wage bill share	4.5(18.3)	–4.3(63.7)	–0.2(18)
	Share hours worked	1.8(9.5)	–2.8(62.1)	1.1(28.5)
UK	Wage bill share	10.5(27.9)	0.7(64.6)	–11.3(7.6)
	Share hours worked	9.4(18.9)	4.8(68.8)	–14.2(12.3)
Sweden	Wage bill share	9.9(26.8)	0.3(60.7)	–10.2(12.5)
	Share hours worked	8.5(19.9)	2.3(64.6)	–10.8(15.4)

Note: Wage bill share is the compensation of (wages earned by) workers in each skill category as percentage total labor compensation (total wages earned).

The first figure in each cell shows the change from 1991 to 2005. The bracketed figure shows the level in 2005.

Source: EUKLEMS. http://www.euklems.net/.

5.3 The Impact of Changes in Skills Demand on Labor Markets: Sweden, Germany, and the UK Compared

Table 8.7 provides some basic descriptive data to illustrate the impact of the developments described above on the Swedish, German and UK labor markets in the decades leading up to the financial crisis. The Table shows changes in the wage bill share[13] and the share of hours worked[14] at the high-, medium-, and low-skilled levels between 1991 and 2005[15] (in each cell the first figure shows the change over the entire period, and the bracketed figure shows the level in 2005).[16] The data in the Table is taken from the *EU KLEMS Growth and Productivity Accounts database (2008)*. In all three countries, the "high-skilled category" is restricted to those with a university degree. In the UK and Germany, "low-skilled" workers are those with no formal qualifications, and the "medium-skilled" category contains all those with intermediate level qualifications below those of a university degree. In Sweden, the "medium-skilled" category is explicitly restricted to those with higher and intermediate vocational training, while the "low-skilled" group includes those with intermediate general education along with those with no formal qualifications. Because of these slight variations in the definitions of

[13] Compensation of (wages earned by) workers in each skill category as percentage total labor compensation (total wages earned).

[14] Hours worked by workers in each skill category as percentage total hours worked.

[15] The period under investigation is restricted by the availability of labor input data in the EUKLEMS database.

[16] See Michaels, Natraj, and Van Reenan (2014) for a similar analysis aggregated across eleven OECD countries.

skill levels, some caution in terms of the cross-national comparison of levels, in particular, is warranted. Nevertheless, the data reveals some interesting and clear patterns of variation across skill levels and over time.

The first thing to note from the Table is that, as we would expect based on the preceding argument about the impact of ICT on the labor market, the demand for workers at the highest skill levels increased in all three countries in the period under investigation. The marked increase in the share of employment at this level cannot be accounted for by an increase in the supply of university graduates alone, since the wage share of this group has simultaneously increased.

The data does suggest that the re-orientation of labor markets towards the college-educated has so far been less marked in Germany: the increase in the wage and employment shares of the high-skilled are smaller in Germany than elsewhere. However, the fact that the wage bill share of the high-skilled has increased considerably more than their employment share indicates that demand for these workers outstripped supply in this period. Interestingly, Germany is also distinctive in that it is the only country of the three that displays evidence of a marked shift in demand *away* from workers with medium skill levels: the employment share of workers with formal qualifications at less than the university level declined by 2.8 percentage points, while the relative wages enjoyed by workers in this group declined even more (by 4.3 percentage points). In the UK and Sweden, workers with medium-level skills increased their share of employment, albeit without much change in their wage share.[17]

The evidence also suggests a movement away from employment at the lowest skill levels in both Sweden and the UK, while in Germany employment at the lowest skill levels has marginally increased. The latter effect is likely to be associated with the removal of protections on the wages of these workers and the dualization of the German labor market in this period, discussed in section 3: the declining wage share of low-skilled workers in the table, parallels the reduction in the relative wages of workers in non-dynamic services sectors in Germany visible in Figure 8.3.

In the aggregate then, the picture here is of a shift of demand towards the most highly skilled workers in all three countries, as hypothesized in the literature on skills biased technical change. Meanwhile it is in Germany that we see the greatest evidence of a hollowing out of labor market opportunities—with declining demand at the medium-skilled level, and an expansion of employment, albeit under worsening labor market conditions, at the low end.

[17] Although it should be noted that while the German and UK medium-skilled categories included workers with vocational and non-vocational qualifications, the Swedish category was restricted to those with vocational qualifications.

Table 8.8 Changes in wage bill share by industry and skill level, 1991–2005 (Germany)

	High-skilled	Medium-skilled	Low-skilled
Total manufacturing	5.1 (16.0)	0.4 (65.1)	-5.5 (18.9)
Electrical and optical	6.6 (23.3)	-1.3 (63.7)	-5.3 (13.0)
Construction	2.2 (8.6)	-6.0 (68.8)	3.8 (22.6)
Wholesale and retail, hotels, and restaurants	2.1 (8.1)	-8.1 (69.2)	5.9 (22.6)
Transport, storage, post, and communications	1.5 (7.1)	-7.4 (67.1)	5.9 (19.8)
Finance and insurance	5.4 (16.1)	-4.8 (76.8)	-0.6 (7.1)
Business Services and Real Estate	3.1 (28.9)	-8.5 (50.5)	5.5 (20.6)
Public administration, defense	1.1 (19.3)	2.4 (71.2)	-3.4 (9.4)
Education	4.3 (46.5)	-3.6 (45.4)	-0.6 (8.0)
Health and social work	-1.0 (18.8)	1.7 (69.1)	-0.7 (12.0)
Other community, social, and personal services	0.0 (22.5)	-2.2 (55.7)	2.2 (21.8)

Note: Wage bill share is the compensation of (wages earned by) workers in each skill category as percentage total labor compensation (total wages earned).

The first figure in each cell shows the change in the (within sector) wage bill share from 1991 to 2005. The bracketed figure shows the level in 2005. Slight variations in sub-sectoral breakdowns for services across Tables 8.8, 8.9, 8.10 reflect data availability

Source: EUKLEMS. http://www.euklems.net/.

The disaggregated data in Table 8.8 provide an even clearer picture of developments in Germany in this period.[18] The data indicates that the demand for labor with medium levels of skills has held up in manufacturing sectors:[19] the notable exception here is electrical and optical equipment, one of the most ICT intensive of the manufacturing sectors (see Table 8.2).[20] In contrast, all of the services sectors, with the exception of public administration and health and social work, show evidence of a sharp decline in the demand for medium-level skills, and in all sectors except finance and insurance and the three welfare sectors, this decline is associated with a marked expansion at the lowest level.

There is clear evidence here of the dualization of German labor markets. Whilst the core of medium-skilled workers in traditional industrial sectors remain in

[18] I have not included data on the shares of hours worked by skill level in Tables 8.8–8.10 for reasons of space and clarity. Note that in all instances these replicate the patterns in wage bill shares at the subsectoral level, except where reported in the text.

[19] I have not reported on the rest of manufacturing at the subsectoral level in the Table for reasons of space. Aside from electrical and optical equipment, all of the other subsectors of manufacturing show either no change or a marginally positive change in the wage bill share (and the share of hours worked) of workers with medium skills in this period (data available on request).

[20] This is the one subsector in Germany in which the direction of change in hours worked and the wage bill in this period are different. Thus the share of hours worked for workers with medium skill levels has increased, while their share of the wage bill has declined, indicating an over-supply of workers with medium-level skills.

Table 8.9 Changes in wage bill share by industry and skill level, 1991–2005 (Sweden)

	High-skilled	Medium-skilled	Low-skilled
Total manufacturing	9.2 (19.0)	5.8 (63.9)	-16.9 (17.0)
Electrical and optical	13.4 (35.5)	-3.5 (56.0)	-9.8 (8.4)
Construction	2.0 (5.0)	9.0 (74.8)	-11.0 (20.1)
Wholesale and retail	3.4 (11.1)	8.4 (70.5)	-11.9 (18.4)
Hotels and restaurants	2.1 (5.4)	7.6 (73.0)	-9.7 (21.6)
Transport, storage	5.0 (19.5)	4.1 (63.7)	-9.0 (16.9)
Post, communications	13.0 (19.1)	-13.3 (74.9)	0.2 (6.0)
Finance, insurance	18.2 (47.2)	-8.1 (50.8)	-10.1 (2.0)
Business Services and Real Estate	10.3 (38.8)	-1.5 (52.8)	-8.8 (8.4)
Education, public administration, defense	13.7 (39.8)	-7.9 (55.4)	-5.8 (4.7)
Health and social work	7.6 (41.2)	-6.0 (52.1)	-1.6 (6.7)
Other community, social, and personal services	9.5 (24.8)	3.5 (59.8)	-13.0 (15.4)

Note: Wage Bill Share is the compensation of (wages earned by) workers in each skill category as percentage total labor compensation (total wages earned).

The first figure in each cell shows the change in the (within sector) wage bill share from 1991 to 2005. The bracketed figure shows the level in 2005.

Source: EUKLEMS. http://www.euklems.net/.

relatively secure labor market positions, in services sectors the pattern is one of polarization, with expansions of demand at the lowest and highest end of the skills distribution and a hollowing out of middle. The evidence does not suggest that the mid-level skills which the German educational system provides (via vocational training or other means) are in high demand in relative terms in dynamic services sectors or in ICT-intensive manufacturing.

This contrasts with developments in Sweden and the UK (see Tables 8.9 and 8.10). These two countries have seen the wage and employment shares of the most skilled workers increase across all sectors to a far more marked degree than in Germany.[21] They have also experienced a sharp decline in the demand for workers with medium-level skills in ICT-intensive dynamic services sectors (like post and communications, finance and insurance, real estate and business services (in Sweden)), in ICT-intensive electrical and optical equipment in the Swedish case, and in education and health (the latter effect perhaps reflecting the high levels of ICT utilization in certain subcategories of the aggregated education and health sectors).

It is interesting to note, however, that in contrast with Germany, the wage bill share of workers with medium-level skills increases not just in traditional

[21] The only exception to this is real estate and business services in the UK, on which more later.

Table 8.10 Changes in wage bill share by industry and skill level, 1991–2005 (UK)

	High-skilled	Medium-skilled	Low-skilled
Total manufacturing	11.9 (21.2)	5.1 (67.4)	-17.1(11.4)
Electrical and optical	10.4 (20.5)	1.8 (69.7)	-12.2 (9.8)
Construction	4.5 (11.1)	5.2 (79.9)	-9.7 (9.0)
Wholesale, retail, hotels, and restaurants	7.5 (14.2)	7.3 (73.1)	-14.8 (12.7)
Transport, storage	3.9 (11.3)	5.1 (79.4)	-9.0 (9.3)
Post, communications	14.0 (19.2)	-1.0 (17.8)	-13.1 (10.0)
Finance, insurance	16.1 (41.9)	-12.3 (56.0)	-3.8 (2.2)
Business Services and Real Estate	-3.9 (32.6)	8.3 (62.2)	-4.5 (5.1)
Public administration, defense	13.3 (32.8)	-8.8 (64.2)	-4.5 (3.0)
Education	12.8 (65.4)	-9.8 (32.5)	-3.0 (2.1)
Health and social work	15.2 (35.0)	-2.0 (60.2)	-13.1 (4.8)
Other community, social, and personal services	11.7 (29.6)	-0.9 (62.8)	-10.8 (7.6)

Note: Wage Bill Share is the compensation of (wages earned by) workers in each skill category as percentage total labor compensation (total wages earned).

The first figure in each cell shows the change in the (within sector) wage bill share from 1991 to 2005. The bracketed figure shows the level in 2005.

Source: EUKLEMS. http://www.euklems.net/.

manufacturing sectors, but also in non-ICT-intensive, non-traded services—like construction, hotels and restaurants, and distribution (wholesale and retail trade).[22]

There are two possible explanations for this cross-national divergence in the demand for medium-level skills in non-dynamic services sectors. The first is that it is at least partially accounted for by cross-national differences in training regimes. In particular, the greater weight given to schools-based learning in both the UK and Sweden (the latter in part in the context of the vocational training system) may equip students better with a range of interpersonal skills that personal and consumer services demand (see, for example, Iversen (2005); Anderson and Hassel (2013)).

[22] There are differences across the two countries. In Sweden, the position of workers with medium-level skills has declined in the relatively ICT-intensive electrical and optical manufacturing sector (which was central to the growth of value added in Sweden in this period), while in the UK it has not. In the UK, meanwhile, the real estate and business services sector sees an apparent decline in demand at the highest skill levels, and an expansion in demand for medium-level skills. These differences may be due to differences in sectoral composition—there is significant variation across subsectors of real estate and other business services in terms of their skill composition, rates of productivity growth, and ICT intensity. Finally, in Sweden we see an expansion in the wage bill share of workers with medium-level skills in the non-traded and non-ICT-intensive other community, social, and personal services (OCSP) sector, compared with a decline in the comparable figure for the UK. This difference may be accounted for by higher levels of public sector employment in this sector in the Swedish case.

However, this argument on its own cannot explain why we see an expansion in the demand for low, rather than medium-skilled labor in the same sectors in Germany in this period. This pattern suggests rather that some of the interactions between supply and demand discussed in section 3 are likely to be relevant here. Specifically, the dismantling of the protections on the wages of workers outside the core of the German labor market has facilitated demand for these types of services based on low prices and wages paid to workers with very low levels of training (recall that the wage share of the low-skilled and the d1d5 ratio have both declined significantly at the same time as low-skilled employment in these sectors has increased). In other words, a classical "Liberal" response to the services economy "trilemma" (Iversen and Wren 1998).

The empirical assessment of these competing explanations is beyond the scope of this paper. What the preceding discussion and analysis does clearly suggest, however, is first, that the demand for highly skilled workers (with college degrees) has increased cross-nationally since the onset of the ICT revolution, especially in dynamic services sectors, but also in ICT-intensive manufacturing. This underscores the importance of supply-side policies aimed at providing these kinds of skills to facilitate growth in the new economic environment. Second, there is little evidence here that the German system of vocational training in its current form is providing the skills demanded by services sectors: rather the data on wage bill shares suggests a shift in the demand for labor in these sectors towards workers with the highest (tertiary) and lowest levels of skills, and a shift away from workers with medium-level skills.

6. Conclusions

In this chapter I have identified a set of links between welfare state policies and strategies for growth and employment creation in a post-industrial context. The relationship between the two works in both directions. The post-industrial growth models that countries pursue are shaped, in part, by the structure of existing welfare state institutions. However, the challenge of deindustrialization and the movement towards a more services oriented economy equally creates pressure for institutional reform. As discussed elsewhere in this volume, the direction that reform takes—and the choices that are available to governments—will depend in part on the existing institutional environment, and in part on the capacity to form political coalitions around strategic alternatives.

All countries have, to varying extents, relied on the expansion of employment in low productivity services sectors to compensate for the loss of industrial jobs. As evidenced by the three countries analyzed in this chapter, however, the method by which they have done this has varied—with different distributional consequences (on this, see also, Iversen and Wren (1998)). In the Liberal UK regime, an important component of the strategy pursued since Margaret Thatcher's reforms of the 1980s, has been to allow the relative wages of workers in low wage sectors to fall well below the average, facilitating the expansion of employment in a range of consumer and personal services, but at a substantial cost in terms of inequality. On the demand side also, relatively high levels of employment in these sectors in the UK have been sustained by increases in labor force participation (especially among women), rising incomes, and (in the pre-crisis period) by increasing private sector debt. During the period of recession and restricted credit that followed the crisis, however, the underlying skills-based and geography-based inequities associated with this strategy in the UK case became abundantly clear. In the North and West of the county, deindustrialization has been associated with the widespread loss of what had been relatively highly paid manufacturing jobs for less skilled workers, and an increasing concentration of less skilled employment in low paid and insecure services sector jobs. In contrast, highly paid jobs for university-educated workers in the new dynamic services sectors are heavily concentrated around London and surrounding areas. The political impact of this structural change in the UK economy is visible in the alignment of political cleavages on the issue of Brexit, and cuts across traditional party lines.

In social democratic Sweden, in contrast, the wages of workers in low productivity private services sectors have remained protected in relative terms since the mid-1970s, and these sectors remain considerably less important in terms of employment in Sweden than in the UK. In this country, however, the public sector has played a key role in employment creation since the early days of agricultural decline, and in the current context also it is welfare services sectors rather than low productivity private services sectors that dominate in terms of employment, at a cost in terms of government spending and taxation. In political and economic terms the sustainability of this model is dependent on continued strong growth in high value-added sectors to provide the tax revenues necessary to support an expansive welfare state. In periods of slow growth, political tensions over welfare state tax burdens and eligibility are more likely to emerge.

Finally, it is in Germany that we see most evidence of policy change in this area over the past two decades. Faced with the same sets of economic challenges stemming from long term trends towards deindustrialization and from the ICT revolution as other advanced economies, German governments have found themselves caught between historically inherited constraints on the extent of state service provision which limit the capacity for the expansion of public employment in welfare sectors; and an industrial policy which emphasizes protections on the relative wages of core industrial workers (to incentivize the long term relationships between firms and workers that facilitate the acquisition of high levels of firm specific skills), and economy-wide wage restraint (to facilitate international competitiveness in price-sensitive industrial sectors). In a context of deindustrialization, these constraints initially resulted in low levels of employment creation outside the shrinking industrial core in Germany, and growing rates of (costly) non-employment and unemployment. In response, successive German governments have pursued an essentially neoliberal route to the problem of low-skilled employment creation, dismantling protections on the wages of workers outside the industrial core, and the benefits available to labor market non participants, and facilitating a significant expansion of employment in low productivity services sectors, at a cost of increasing inequality.

As I have emphasized in the chapter, however, the strategies that countries have employed to generate employment in low productivity services sectors can only constitute a partial solution to the challenge of deindustrialization. More fundamentally, the development of sustainable strategies for growth and employment creation in a context of deindustrialization, and of revolutionary changes in information and communications technologies, relies on the creation of capacities to expand in ICT-intensive, high value-added sectors, and especially in dynamic services sectors. This is true not just for export-oriented economies, but also for those pursuing strategies that are more heavily "consumption-led," since sustainable demand expansions, be they publicly or privately financed, are ultimately reliant on income and productivity growth in dynamic sectors. In the Fordist era, productivity gains and expansion in traditional manufacturing sectors fuelled expansion and growth: similarly, in the current environment, ICT and knowledge-intensive services and manufacturing sectors have emerged as the new dynamic drivers of the economy.

Welfare state institutions also play an important supply-side role in facilitating expansion in these sectors, however. In this chapter I have highlighted in particular the significance of the institutions and policies that shape patterns of skill formation, since a growing body of evidence in the literature on labor economics suggests that the diffusion of ICT is associated with a marked shift in the relative demand for skills: most notably with an increased demand for college-educated labor, and with a reduction in the relative demand for those with mid-level skills (see Autor et al. (2003)). Variations in national educational regimes, therefore, have implications for countries' capacities to expand and compete in high value-added, ICT-intensive services sectors.

The three countries analyzed in this chapter vary significantly in terms of the structure of their educational systems (see Chevalier in this volume). And this has important implications both for their capacities to expand and compete in high value-added, ICT-intensive services sectors, and for the distributional outcomes with which this transition is associated. Thus, both Sweden and the UK have relatively high levels of tertiary enrolment, although their method of financing this enrolment varies. In the UK, levels of private individual investment in tertiary of education are high (and often debt financed), and are incentivized by high returns to educational investment in the form of skills-based intersectoral wage inequality. In Sweden, in contrast, stronger institutional constraints on relative wages mean that the rewards to skills are smaller in relative terms (although they are increasing also in the Swedish case), however the reduced incentives for individual investment in tertiary education are compensated for by high levels of public educational investment. In Germany in contrast, levels of tertiary enrolment remain relatively low by international standards, while large numbers of workers continue to participate in the apprenticeship-based vocational training regime which has long formed the basis for successful German industrial performance.

The evidence suggests that these inherited educational regimes have impacted on the development of post-industrial growth models. Of the three countries, it is Sweden and the UK (in which levels of tertiary enrolment are relatively high) that display more rapid rates of growth of value-added and greater export shares in ICT-intensive services sectors which demand higher level skills. Analysis of the structure of labor market demand based on data from EU-KLEMS meanwhile, confirms both the overall distributional impact of structural and technological change on the labor markets of these countries, and the way in which it has varied cross-nationally. Thus we can see that a generalized shift in demand towards university-educated workers has occurred in all three countries: and interestingly, also, that at least prior to the onset of the economic crisis, demand for university-educated workers outstripped supply by the greatest amount in Germany. At lower skill levels, meanwhile, the evidence suggests that while demand for the mid-level skills provided by the German vocational training regime was holding up in most manufacturing sectors, in services, and in more ICT-intensive manufacturing sectors, the pattern was one of "hollowing out." Wages and employment shares declined for those at medium skill levels, and expanded for those with the lowest and highest levels of skills. This suggests any strategic attempt to move the German growth model towards a greater emphasis on high productivity services rather than manufacturing is likely to require higher levels of investment in, and the expansion of, the German tertiary sector (see the chapter on Germany by Avlijaš et al. in this volume).

In general then, the evidence here suggests that the ways in which national growth strategies can be adapted to a post-industrial ICT-intensive environment, and the labor market and distributional outcomes associated with these changes, are shaped in part by the structure of existing educational regimes. This is another area, then, in which attempts to adapt to the new environment may create pressure for welfare state reforms, in instances where there is a mismatch between the supply of and demand for skills.

In their introductory chapter to this volume, however, Hassel and Palier remind us that it is critical to avoid functionalism in analyzing the potential links between national growth strategies and the trajectory of institutional change. Thus while it might be the case that we can draw links between skill formation strategies and the development of sustainable models for growth in a post-industrial context, this is far from implying that we can predict where reform will occur. Political coalitions in favor of high levels of public spending on education at the tertiary level, for example, are notoriously difficult to create (Ansell 2008) (especially in cases like that of Germany in which the existing tertiary sector is limited). Further, there is ample evidence that invested interests in institutions of education and training make them hard to change, once they are in place (see, for example, Thelen (2004); Iversen and Busemeyer (2014)). In Germany, for example, the interests of powerful producer groups in the existing system of vocational training makes the adaptation of these institutions difficult, and also potentially act as an additional obstacle to the formation of a coalition in favor of the expansion of the university sector (Thelen, this volume, and see also Martin (this volume) on producer-group politics and trajectories of change). In the UK, meanwhile, the heavy reliance on private sector investment in education creates important constituencies of voters who have made substantial personal investments in education, and hence may be less disposed to subsidize the educational investment of others. Under these circumstances, perhaps the greatest impetus for higher levels of public investment in the university sector in the UK case might come from producer groups reliant on the skills which the tertiary sector provides. There is important work to be done, then, in analyzing how pressures stemming from the adaptation of national growth strategies to a post-industrial context might impact on trajectories of educational reform.

References

Acemoglu, Daron and David H. Autor. 2011. "Skills, Tasks and Technologies: Implications for Employment and Earnings." In *Handbook of Labor Economics*, edited by O. Ashenfelter and D. Card. Amsterdam: Elsevier.

Anderson, Karen M. and Anke Hassel. 2013. "Pathways of Change in CMEs: Training Regimes in Germany and the Netherlands." In *The Political Economy of the Service Transition*, edited by Anne Wren. Oxford: Oxford University Press.

Ansell, Ben. 2008. "University Challenges: Explaining Institutional Change in Higher Education." *World Politics* 60(2): 189–230.

Ansell, Ben and Jane Gingrich. 2013. "A Tale of Two Trilemmas: Varieties of Higher Education and the Service Economy." In *The Political Economy of the Service Transition*, edited by Anne Wren. Oxford: Oxford University Press.

Autor, David H., Frank Levy, and Richard J. Murnane. 2003. "The Skill Content of Recent Technological Change: An Empirical Exploration." *Quarterly Journal of Economics* 118(4): 1279–333.

Baccaro, Lucio and Jonas Pontusson. 2016. "Rethinking Comparative Political Economy: The Growth Model Perspective." *Politics & Society* 44(2): 175–207.

Barnes, Lucy and Anne Wren. 2012. "The Liberal Model in (the) Crisis: Continuity and Change in Great Britain and Ireland." In *Coping with Crisis: Government Reactions to the Great Recession*, edited by Nancy Bermeo and Jonas Pontusson. New York: Russell Sage Foundation, 287–324.

Barro, Robert. 1997. *Determinants of Economic Growth: A Cross-Country Empirical Study*. Cambridge: MIT Press.

Barrow, Lisa, Thomas Brock, and Cecilia Elena Rouse. 2013. "Postsecondary Education in the United States: Introducing the Issue." *The Future of Children* 23(1): 3–16.

Baumol, William J. 1967. "Macroeconomics of unbalanced growth: the anatomy of urban crisis." *American Economic Review* 57(3): 415–26.

Beck, Thorsten, Aslı Demirgüç-Kunt, and Ross Levine. 2000. "A New Database on Financial Development and Structure." *World Bank Economic Review* 14: 597–605. (2018 Update).

Belfield, Chris, Christine Farquharson, and Luke Sibieta. 2018. *Annual Report on Education Spending in England*. London: Institute for Fiscal Studies.

Blinder, Alan. 2007. "How Many U.S. Jobs might be Offshorable?" *World Economics* 10(2), 41–78.

Bosworth, Barry P. and Jack E. Triplett. 2007. "The Early 21st Century U.S. Productivity Expansion is Still in Services," *International Productivity Monitor*, Centre for the Study of Living Standards 14 (Spring): 3–19.

Brady, David, Evelyne Huber, and John D. Stephens, Comparative Welfare States Data Set, University of North Carolina and WZB Berlin Social Science Center, 2020.

Carlin, Wendy and David Soskice. 2015. *Macroeconomics*. Oxford: Oxford University Press.

Corrado, Carol, Paul Lengerman, Eric J. Bartelsman, and J. Joseph Beaulieu. 2007. "Sectoral Productivity in the United States: Recent Developments and the Role of IT." *Finance and Economics Discussion Series*, Board of Governors of the Federal Reserve System (U.S), 24.

Crouch, C. 2009. "Privatised Keynesianism: An Unacknowledged Policy Regime." *The British Journal of Politics and International Relations* 11(3): 382–99.

Cuhne, Flavio and James J. Heckman. 2007. "The Technology of Skill Formation." *American Economic Review* 97(2): 31–47.

Esping-Andersen, G. 1990. *The Three Worlds of Welfare Capitalism*. Princeton, N.J: Princeton University Press.

Freeman, Richard B. 2007. "Can Marketization of Household Production Explain the Jobs Gap Puzzle?" In *Services and Employment: Explaining the U.S. European Gap*, edited by Mary Gregory, Wiemer Salverda, and Ronald Schettkat. Princeton and Oxford: Princeton University Press.

Freund, Caroline and Diana Weinhold. 2002. "The Internet and International Trade in Services." *American Economic Review* 92(2): 236–40.

Fuchs-Schündeln, Nicola, Dirk Krueger, and Mathias Sommer. 2010. "Inequality Trends for Germany in the Last Two Decades: A Tale of Two Countries." *Review of Economic Dynamics*, Elsevier for the Society for Economic Dynamics 13(1) (January): 103–32.

Gernandt, Johannes and Friedhelm Pfeiffer, "Rising Wage Inequality in Germany" (April 2006). *ZEW-Centre for European Economic Research Discussion Paper* No. 06–019; SOEP paper, No. 14.

Goldin, Claudia Dale and Lawrence F. Katz. 2008. *The Race between Education and Technology*. Boston: The Bellknap Press of Harvard University Press.

Goos, Maarten, Alan Manning, and Anna Salomons. 2014. "Explaining Job Polarization: Routine-Biased Technological Change and Offshoring." *American Economic Review* 104 (8): 2509–26.

Green Andy, Frances Green, and Nicola Pensiero. 2014. "Why are Literacy and Numeracy Skills in England so unequal?: Evidence from the OECD's Survey of Adult Skills and Other International Surveys." Centre for Learning and Life Chances in Knowledge Economies and Societies (LLAKES) Institute of Education, University of London.

Gregory, Mary, Wiemer Salverda, and Ronald Schettkat. 2007. *Services and Employment: Explaining the U.S. European Gap*. Princeton and Oxford: Princeton University Press.

Hall, Peter Anthony, and David Soskice (eds.). 2001. *Varieties Of Capitalism: The Institutional Foundations of Comparative Advantage*. Oxford; New York: Oxford University Press.

Hassel, Anke. 2014. "The Paradox of Liberalization—Understanding Dualism and the Recovery of the German Political Economy." *British Journal of Industrial Relations* 52(1): 57–81.

Heckman, James J. and Bas Jacobs. 2011. "Policies to Create and Destroy Human Capital in Europe." In *Perspectives on the Performance on the Continent's Economies*, edited by Edmund Phelps and Hans-Werner Sinn. Cambridge, MA: MIT Press, 253–323.

Iversen, Torben. 2005. *Capitalism, Democracy, and Welfare*. Cambridge; New York: Cambridge University Press.

Iversen, Torben and Marius Busemeyer. 2014. "The Politics of Opting Out: Explaining Educational Financing and Popular Support for Public Spending." *Socio-Economic Review* 12: 299–328.

Iversen, Torben and David Soskice. 2010. "Real Exchange Rates and Competitiveness: The Political Economy of Skill Formation, Wage Compression, and Electoral Systems." *American Political Science Review* (August): 1–23.

Iversen, Torben and Anne Wren. 1998. "Equality, Employment, and Budgetary Restraint: The Trilemma of the Service Economy." *World Politics* 50(4): 507–46.

Jorgenson, Dale, S., Mun S. Ho, and Kevin J. Stiroh. 2008. "A Retrospective Look at the U.S. Productivity Growth Resurgence," *Journal of Economic Perspectives*, American Economic Association 22(1) (Winter): 3–24.

Levy, Frank and Richard J. Murnane. 2005. *The New Division of Labor: How Computers are Creating the Next Job Market*. Princeton, NJ: Princeton University Press.

Lucas, Robert Jr., 1988. "On the Mechanics of Economic Development." *Journal of Monetary Economics* 22(1): 3–42.

Meidner, Rudolf. 1974. *Coordination and Solidarity: An Approach to Wages Policy*. Stockholm: Bokforlaget Prisma.

Michaels, Guy, Ashwini Natraj, and John Van Reenen. 2014. "Has ICT polarized skill demand? Evidence from eleven countries over 25 years." *Review of Economics and Statistics* 96(1): 60–77.

Palier, B. and Thelen, K. 2010. "Institutionalizing Dualism: Complementarities and Change in France and Germany." *Politics and Society* 38(1): 119–48.

Rehn, Gosta. 1985. "Swedish Active Labour Market Policy: Retrospect and Prospect." *Industrial Relations* 24(1): 62–89.

Rowthorn, Robert and Ken Coutts. 2004. "De-industrialization and the balance of payments in advanced economies." *Cambridge Journal of Economics* 28(5): 767–90.

Rowthorn, Robert and Ken Coutts. 2013. "De-industrialization and the Balance of Payments in Advanced Economies." *Future of Manufacturing Project: Evidence Paper 31*, Foresight, Government office for Science.

Robert Rowthorn and Ramana Ramaswamy. 1999. "Growth, Trade, and Deindustrialization." *International Monetary Fund Staff Papers* 46(1): 18–41.

Sauve, Pierre. 2001. "The Trade Policy Implications of the New Economy." OECD.

Soskice, David. 1999. "Divergent Production Regimes: Coordinated and Uncoordinated Market Economies in the 1980s and 1990s." In *Continuity and Change in Contemporary Capitalism*, edited by Herbert Kitschelt, Peter Lange, Gary Marks, and John Stephens. Cambridge; New York: Cambridge University Press.

Stiglitz, Joseph. 2012. *The Price of Inequality: How Today's Divided Society Endangers Our Future*. London: W.W. Norton & Company.

Stiroh, Kevin J. 2002. "Information Technology and the U.S. Productivity Revival: What Do the Industry Data Say?" *American Economic Review* 92(5): 1559–76.

Thelen, Kathleen. 2004. *How Institutions Evolve: The Political Economy of Skills in Germany, Britain, the United States, and Japan*. New York: Cambridge University Press.

Triplett, Jack E. and Barry P. Bosworth. 2004. *Productivity in the U.S. Services Sector: New Sources of Economic Growth*. Washington DC: Brookings Institution Press.

van Ark, Bart and Kirsten Jäger. 2017. "Recent Trends in Europe's Output and Productivity Growth Performance at the Sector Level, 2002–2015." *International Productivity Monitor*, Centre for the Study of Living Standards 33 (Fall): 8–23.

van Ark, Bart, Mary O'Mahoney, and Marcel P. Timmer. 2008. "The Productivity Gap between Europe and the United States: Trends and Causes." *Journal of Economic Perspectives* 22(1): 25–44.

Wallerstein, Michael. 1990. "Centralized Bargaining and Wage Restraint." *American Journal of Political Science* 33(4): 982–1004.

Wren, Anne. 2013. "Introduction: The Political Economy of Post-Industrial Societies." In *The Political Economy of the Service Transition*, edited by Anne Wren. Oxford: Oxford University Press, 1–99.

Wren, Anne, Mate Fodor, and Sotiria Theodoropoulou. 2013. "The Trilemma Revisited: Institutions, Inequality, and Employment Creation in an Era of ICT-Intensive Service Expansion." In *The Political Economy of the Service Transition*, edited by Anne Wren. Oxford: Oxford University Press.

PART III

GROWTH STRATEGIES AND WELFARE REFORMS

9

Always a Winning Strategy? Wage Moderation's Conditional Impact on Growth Outcomes

Alison Johnston

1. Introduction

Wages and wage-setting institutions are foundational components of comparative capitalism and growth model research. Wage-setting institutions directly link the organization of capitalism to the realms of social and welfare policy (Hassel and Palier this volume). Hall and Soskice's (2001) seminal volume demonstrates how the organization of the labor market impacts the types of skills that are promoted and fostered within a country's economy, which in turn influences the type of comparative advantage and product specializations that it has (see Hall and Soskice 2001 and Chevalier in this volume on skills and youth welfare programs). Labor market institutions also have important implications for wage outcomes, and in turn macroeconomic outcomes. In addition to works stemming from first- and second-"generation" comparative capitalism research (see Nölke 2016: 145–7, for a discussion on the evolution of the comparative capitalism literature), a robust (corporatist) literature in comparative political economy details how the scale of wage centralization and wage coordination impacts a country's capacity to deliver wage moderation,[1] which in turn impacts inflation, unemployment, growth, and even a country's external trade balances (see Cameron 1984; Bruno and Sachs 1985; Calmfors and Driffil 1988; Soskice 1990; Hall and Franzese 1998; Iversen 1999; Soskice and Iversen 2000; Johnston et al. 2014).

In a nutshell, the general argument advanced by these works is that countries with highly coordinated (or centralized) wage-setting have the ability to deliver comprehensive wage moderation, which lowers both inflation and unit labor costs, enabling employers to hire more workers (reducing unemployment) and expand production (boosting growth). Countries with moderately centralized and

[1] The terms "wage moderation" and "wage restraint" are used interchangeably in this chapter.

Alison Johnston, *Always a Winning Strategy? Wage Moderation's Conditional Impact on Growth Outcomes* In: *Growth and Welfare in Advanced Capitalist Economies: How Have Growth Regimes Evolved?* Edited by: Anke Hassel and Bruno Palier, Oxford University Press (2021). © Oxford University Press. DOI: 10.1093/oso/9780198866176.003.0009

coordinated labor markets, on the other hand, face collective action problems in the negotiation of wages—unions are powerful enough to push for higher wage settlements, but are not as encompassing enough to internalize the inflation externalities that come from their wage actions. While Calmfors and Driffill (1988) indicate that these inflationary outcomes wane under completely *decentralized* labor markets (as individualized bargaining keeps wage growth on par with productivity increases), Soskice (1990) argues that *uncoordinated* labor markets also fail to produce the comprehensive wage-moderation outcomes of highly coordinated wage-setting regimes, given the absence of actors that are able to coordinate and enforce moderated wage settlements across the entire labor market.

A standard assumption of the above works is that wage moderation is good for the economy, while wage inflation is not. It is easy to arrive at this conclusion if examining wage moderation from a supply-side perspective; employers respond *positively* to lower unit labor costs in their production decisions. However, these supply-side theories ignore the detrimental impact of wage moderation on the *consumer*; while lower wages *may* prompt firms to hire more workers, those workers may consume less than what they would otherwise with more buoyant wage growth. In other words, examining wage moderation from a demand-side perspective alludes to the fact that wage restraint can also produce detrimental economic effects by stifling workers' abilities to maintain a given level of consumption. These growth-reducing effects will be particularly pronounced if firms use cost savings from wage restraint to increase corporate savings and the accumulation of financial assets rather than to hire more workers.[2]

Baccaro and Pontusson's (2016), and the wider growth model literature's, primary innovation to comparative capitalism is to rethink the political organization of economies from a demand-side perspective, rather than a supply-side one. They argue that economies consist of two different components of aggregate demand, one revolving around exports (which, as Hassel and Palier outline in the introduction of this volume, can include the export of manufactured goods, as well as dynamic services), and another revolving around household domestic consumption. Wage moderation has different implications for these two drivers of demand. Particularly within monetary unions or hard currency pegs, comprehensive wage moderation benefits the export sector, because it produces lower inflation, which in turn enhances a country's real exchange rate and cost competitiveness (see Johnston and Regan 2016). However, comprehensive wage moderation also depresses domestic demand. Consequently, wage moderation has distributive consequences for different sectors; it helps the export sector at the expense of (sheltered) sectors that rely on robust domestic consumption. This

[2] Braun and Deeg (2018) provide convincing evidence that major German firms have been doing exactly this over the last two decades.

ultimately means that, from a growth model view, wage moderation's effect on the economy in aggregate depends upon the components of demand (exports or domestic consumption), which component dominates a country's economy, and the relative power of producer groups in export and sheltered sectors (on producers groups, see Thelen; Martin in this volume).

This chapter tests the empirical link between wage moderation/inflation, growth strategies, and the labor market institutions that underpin them, and real GDP growth. Employing a first-differenced, distributive lag panel analysis for eighteen OECD countries from 1970 to 2015, I use a two-pronged approach to examine when wage moderation produces beneficial growth outcomes. First, I empirically test the interaction effect between real wage inflation and the size of a country's export share on real GDP growth. Results indicate that while the presence of more intensified real wage *moderation* (when real wage growth undercuts labor productivity growth) is associated with higher GDP growth for countries with larger export shares, the presence of real wage *inflation* (when real wage growth overshoots labor productivity growth) does not yield differentiated growth outcomes for countries with large vs small export shares.

The second part of the empirical analysis tests the interaction effect between real wage inflation and the cohesiveness of a country's wage-setting institutions on real GDP growth. Cohesive, strongly coordinated wage-setting institutions are a common feature of countries that have championed export growth strategies (see Katzenstein 1985; Iversen and Soskice 2009). And yet, as I discuss below, wage moderation is not necessarily a foregone conclusion in coordinated wage-setting regimes. Over the past five decades, there has been a considerable degree of variation in the types of wage-setting regimes that produce the highest levels of real wage moderation throughout the OECD. Indeed, lesser coordinated wage-setting regimes outperformed their more coordinated counterparts in to some degree in the 1990s, 2000s, and especially in the 2010s with the rise of austerity. Because more coordinated wage-setting regimes tend to organize around the export sector, I hypothesize that these periodic mismatches between wage strategies and growth models are likely to produce detrimental macroeconomic outcomes for coordinated wage-setting regimes. My panel results reveal that real wage *moderation* corresponds to better growth outcomes for highly coordinated wage-setting regimes than it does for uncoordinated ones, while wage *inflation* corresponds to better growth outcomes in less coordinated wage-setting regimes than it does in coordinated ones. This result is highly robust and holds for alternative measures of wage-setting cohesion, as well as if unemployment rather than real GDP growth is used as the dependent variable.

The next section details how supply-side comparative capitalism theories have perceived the positive economic effects of wage moderation, in addition to providing a summary of wage moderation performance across different wage-setting regimes over the past five decades. Section 3 outlines how recent growth model theory has caused a rethink of the virtues of wage restraint, and the types of wage-setting institutions that underpin it. Section 4 discusses the sample, empirical estimator and model specifications that are used, while section 5 provides the results. Section 6 concludes with a discussion of the implications of my results for comparative capitalism research on the economic effects of comprehensive wage restraint, as well as how they can contribute to our understanding of current growth trajectories among Europe's diverse growth models during and after the sovereign debt crisis of the late 2000s.

2. Stylized Assumptions within Supply-Side Comparative Capitalism: The Link between Wage-Setting Institutions, Wage Moderation, and Macroeconomic Outcomes

Though wages and labor market institutions are central to the comparative capitalism literature, discussions about the macroeconomic implications of the organization of wage-setting well precede comparative capitalism research. Highlighted by Olson (1982), but also discussed and analyzed at length by other economists and political scientists (see Cameron 1984; Bruno and Sachs 1985; Nickell and Andrews 1983; Calmfors and Driffil 1988; Carlin and Soskice 1990, among many others), it was predicted that if labor unions were encompassing enough, "militant" wage settlements would transpire into higher national inflation, which in turn would erode the real wage that workers enjoyed. Wage militancy would also harm employment, by raising employers' unit labor costs. Consequently, this would incentivize encompassing labor movements to "internalize" externalities associated with wage-push, and negotiate more moderated wage settlements to temper inflation. Wage moderation, in turn, would yield lower inflation, lower unemployment, and higher growth. Variants of this story have evolved over the years. Calmfors and Driffil (1998), identified a humped-shaped, rather than linear, relationship between union organization and unemployment, arguing that decentralized labor markets accomplish similar inflation and unemployment outcomes as highly centralized labor markets that can coordinated nationwide wage moderation, because the market tempers wage growth. Soskice (1990) went on to argue that *coordinated* wage-setting should be treated differently from *centralized* wage-setting (although both types of labor market institutions are intricately connected in corporatist economies), and that wage coordination's impact on wage growth was curve-linear. Other political scientists argued that organized labor's impact on macroeconomic outcomes was contingent on the presence of other political variables and institutions; Lange and Garrett (1985) highlighted that only when left governments are in power do encompassing labor movements realize higher growth (because left governments are more likely to reward wage restraint from labor unions with welfare expansion), while Hall and Franzese (1998), Iversen (1999), and Soskice and Iversen (2000), outline that coordinated labor market institutions must also be paired with inflation-targeting, independent central banks in order for unemployment-reducing wage moderation to be realized. However, one important supposition united these (supply-side) works: nationwide wage moderation, delivered by cohesive labor market institutions, produced beneficial macroeconomic outcomes, while higher wage inflation led to greater inflation and unemployment.

While VoC later highlighted the importance of coordinated/centralized wage-setting institutions in upholding industry specific skills, the link between wage-setting institutions, wage moderation, and macroeconomic outcomes remained an important focal point, and indeed almost an explicit assumption, of comparative capitalism research. Enhancing wage coordination (in some cases through bi-partite and tri-partite social pacts) to deliver wage moderation was seen as a "winning strategy" to help countries with more dysfunctional wage-setting regimes meet the nominal convergence criteria[3] required to join the euro currency in 1999 (Hassel 2003; Hancké and Rhodes 2005). Moreover, though earlier (economic) theories on the link between labor market organization and macroeconomic outcomes largely rested on the assumption of a "closed economy" model (although Carlin and Soskice 1990 and Danthine and Hunt 1994 are notable exceptions), wage coordination implicitly became linked to external imbalances within "third-generation" comparative capitalism research that linked wage-setting institutions to macroeconomic outcomes under the euro currency (see Dullien 2003), as well as to national trajectories before and during the euro crisis (Hall 2014; Hancke 2013; Johnston et al. 2014; Johnston 2016; Iversen, Soskice, and Hope 2016; Höpner and Lutter 2018).[4]

In this third-generation comparative capitalism research, the link between coordinated wage-setting and low inflation became explicitly tied to *export-based growth strategies*. Coordinated (beggar-thy-neighbor) wage strategies that

[3] EMU's nominal convergence criteria required candidate countries to obtain low inflation, low nominal interest rates and maintain a fixed exchange rate with the European Currency Unit for two years.

[4] Central to this third generation of research was incorporating the link between wage coordination and low inflation into the economics of trade inside and outside monetary union. While low inflation is perceived to be economically desirable for (relative) closed economies, it can be particularly advantageous for open economies *under certain conditions*. The real exchange rate—an indicator of the "price competitiveness" of a country's exports—is composed of a country's nominal exchange rate multiplied by the ratio of the domestic inflation rate to the inflation rate of trading partners. Outside monetary union, countries with high inflation rates tend to have more depreciated nominal exchange rates than countries with lower inflation, because their currency was perceived as "less valuable" (Johnston and Regan 2016). Under monetary union, however, nominal exchange rates between countries that share the same currency disappear, causing the real exchange rate to be solely determined by a country's relative inflation rate. Ultimately, (corporatist) countries that could produce lower inflation rates realized more advantageous real exchange rates and in turn, trade surpluses under the common currency.

produced low inflation rates were also beneficial for trade, helping make countries' exports more price competitive in world markets. The assumption was that countries with coordinated wage-setting regimes were also those that were more likely to have growth models focused around the export sector (particularly the export of manufacturing goods), because cohesive collective bargaining regimes deliver nationwide wage restraint needed for maintaining cost competitiveness. Admittedly, the (political) linkage between coordinated labor markets and heavy exposure to trade was not new—Peter Katzenstein (1985), among many others, outlined that the success of small states in world markets could be attributed to cohesive collective bargaining institutions by which unions and employers could quickly adjust wages in the face of international economic shocks. Moreover, empirically, this link between coordinated wage-setting and the prominence of the export sector made sense. European economies with the largest export shares (the Nordic and Benelux countries as well as Germany and Austria) also had some of its most cohesive and organized wage-setting institutions. Hence, it could easily be assumed that the causal link between coordinated wage-setting institutions and large export shares operated through the former's capacity to deliver comprehensive wage moderation, which restrained growth in the real-exchange rate.

2.1 Wage Moderation Performance by Wage-Setting Regime: Do Coordinated Labor Markets Out-perform Non-coordinated Ones?

While the works above assume that highly coordinated labor markets are more capable of producing higher levels of wage moderation, empirically these wage-setting regimes did not always do so relative to their lesser coordinated counterparts over the past five decades. Figure 9.1 presents decade averages of real wage inflation (real wage growth minus labor productivity growth: positive values indicate that wage inflation is present, while negative values indicate that wage restraint is present[5]) across Kenworthy's (2001) five-point wage-coordination scale for the eighteen OECD countries included in this chapter's empirical sample in section 4.[6] A coordination index of one indicates that wage bargaining is fragmented and is largely confined to the plant or individual level. A coordination index value of two indicates the presence of mixed industry and firm-level bargaining with weak government coordination (through wage indexation or minimum wage-setting). A coordination index of three indicates that negotiated guidelines across sectors are based on centralized bargaining.

[5] Section 4 provides a fuller analysis of how wage inflation is constructed.

[6] These countries include Australia, Austria, Belgium, Denmark, Finland, France, Germany, Greece, Ireland, Italy, Japan, the Netherlands, Norway, Portugal, Spain, Sweden, the UK, and US.

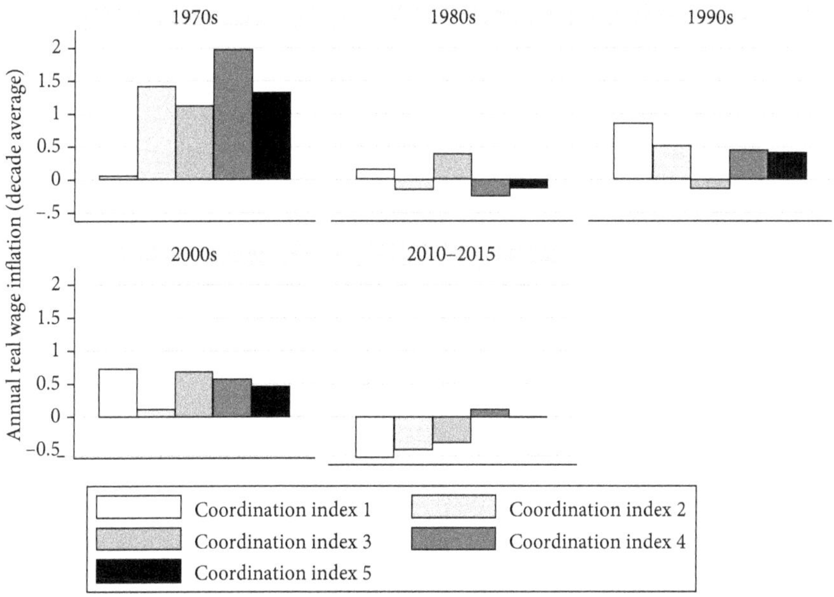

Figure 9.1 Wage inflation by wage coordination regimes (decade averages)

Wage inflation constructed from data from EU AMECO Database (2018). Wage coordination regime data taken from Visser (2016): lower codings indicate uncoordinated wage-setting, while higher codings indicate highly coordinated wage-setting.

A coordination index of four indicates that peak associations establish wage norms for the majority or entire economy (with or without the government's help), while an index of five indicates that both (nationwide) maximum and minimum wage rates are coordinated through centralized bargaining (see also Visser 2016, for formal definitions). With the exception of the US, there was a considerable degree of fluctuation in levels of wage coordination across the eighteen OECD countries during the last five decades, particularly during the 1990s amidst the drive to comply with the Maastricht nominal convergence criteria. Between 1970 and 2015, Austria and Japan saw a change in their wage-coordination index value once, the UK witnessed two changes, Australia and Germany observed three, Belgium, Denmark and France witnessed four, while the remaining countries (Greece, Ireland, Italy, the Netherlands, Norway, Portugal, Spain, and Sweden) witnessed more than five changes in wage-coordination index values (with Finland as many as fourteen changes—see Visser 2016).

During the 1970s, coordinated wage-setting regimes produced *higher* levels of wage inflation than completely uncoordinated regimes. This may have been driven in part by the fact that the inflationary effects of the OPEC oil shocks were more likely to be incorporated into wage settlements in more coordinated regimes—particularly those possessing wage indexation—than uncoordinated ones. During the 1980s, coordinated wage-setting regimes produced the levels of wage restraint (i.e., negative wage inflation) that they became known for—some of this is reflective of the political conflicts between organized labor and central banks in the transition towards a low inflation regime during the European Monetary System's first decade (see Scharpf 1991; Hancke 2013; Johnston 2016). Coordinated wage-setting regimes also produced lower levels of wage inflation than their uncoordinated counterparts in the 1990s, although moderately coordinated regimes (i.e., those in Southern Europe in the run up to the launch of the euro), witnessed the highest levels of wage restraint during this time. Highly coordinated regimes produced lower wage inflation during the 2000s than their lesser coordinated counterparts (although labor markets with mixed industry and firm level bargaining—coordination index of two—produced the lowest level of wage inflation during this decade). However, in the first half of the 2010s, wage restraint was far more intensified in wage-setting systems with low levels of coordination. This was largely driven by externally imposed austerity in the Eurozone South, whose labor markets were less coordinated before and during the crisis, as well as the self-imposed austerity seen in the UK, where wage-setting is completely uncoordinated.

How can the mixed empirical record of wage moderation in coordinated wage-setting regimes be reconciled with the implicit assumptions about the (labor market) institutional determinants of wage moderation made in earlier comparative capitalism literature? A power resource theorist would argue that if strong labor unions are pivotal in upholding highly coordinated wage-setting,[7] then higher levels of wage inflation in more coordinated wage-setting regimes should not be entirely surprising; after all, one of the central purposes of labor unions is to secure wage settlements that guarantee workers their fair share of the economic pie and boost the wage share. Answering this empirical conundrum is where insights from Baccaro and Pontusson's (2016) *demand-centered* growth model theory become especially helpful. Using a Kaleckian framework, Baccaro and Pontusson "treat distributive struggles as a key factor in the evolution of growth models" (181). In other words, while we cannot automatically assume that coordinated wage-setting will produce wage moderation *at all times*—given the inherent political struggles in the determination of wages in systems with strong and cohesive labor unions—we can suppose that wage inflation may have different macroeconomic implications for countries (and their wage-setting institutions) that organize around different sectors, based upon how they impact different components of aggregate demand.

[7] They are not in all cases: though some developed countries with highly coordinated wage-setting have low levels of trade union density, developed countries with high trade union density tend to have high levels of wage coordination.

3. The Conditioning Effect of Wage Moderation and Wage-Setting Institutions on Macroeconomic Outcomes: A Growth Model View

In contrast to earlier comparative capitalism literature, which is largely supply-side oriented, growth model theory approaches the organization of capitalism and the economy from a demand-side perspective. While this distinction may appear trivial, it has important implications for how wage inflation/moderation affects the economy at large. Central to the works highlighted in section 2, is the assumption that wage inflation is detrimental to the economy, and has the potential to produce higher inflation, higher unemployment and lower growth. From a supply-side perspective, this makes sense. Higher wages increase input costs for employers, which should cause them to shed labor in order to maintain their profit margins.

From a growth theory perspective, however, wage *inflation* can be beneficial for the economy because it boosts aggregate demand, which in turn drives growth. Baccaro and Pontusson (2016: 182) identify that two conditions must hold in order for a higher wage share (which would follow in the wake of *real* wage inflation) to increase consumption. First, the propensity to consume has to decline as income rises—in other words, for any given wage increase, the poor will consume a greater percentage of it than the rich, whose capacity to save is higher because their means of subsistence have been met. This is not an unreasonable assumption to make, and empirically, it has been well demonstrated that those with higher incomes have higher savings rates and marginal propensities to save (see Dynan et al. 2004 for an overview). Second, there has to be spare capacity for employers to respond to rising wages with rising output (rather than increasing prices). This assumption is more complicated, even for employers who have spare capacity. Menu costs may prohibit employers from immediately raising prices in the short run, and buoyant profit margins may also make it easier for employers to trade output increases for price increases. However, unless the marginal propensity to consume is zero (a highly unlikely scenario), an increase in wages will have a (greater than one) multiplier effect that will lead to increased spending, which will require firms to increase output in order to meet demand.

Wage rises do not benefit all parts of the economy however. Baccaro and Pontusson are quick to point out that rising wages will increase the trade deficit, as rising domestic prices (relative to foreign prices) will lead to (less competitive) exchange rate appreciations, assuming that the nominal exchange rate also does not fluctuate too strongly as a result of increased prices.[8] Hence, unlike their domestic sector counterparts, producers and workers in the export sector stand to

[8] This is more likely to be the case under hard pegs or monetary unions (see Johnston and Regan 2016).

lose from wage increases because a worsening of the real exchange rate will prompt a decrease in export demand. In other words, rising wages have different distributive effects across sectors; for sectors that are relatively sheltered from trade (and the countries in which these sectors dominate national output), rising wages have the potential to increase output and reduce reliance on credit to maintain a given level of consumption. In contrast, for sectors that are heavily exposed to trade (and the countries in which export sectors dominate national economic activity) rising wages has the potential to reduce output.

Whether rising wages are good or bad for the economy *as a whole* depends on an economy's sectoral composition, itself determined by the trajectory of a country's national growth strategy.[9] If the export sector holds a large share of national output (what Baccaro and Pontusson term export-led economies), then rising wages will be detrimental for *aggregate* employment and growth. However, if the domestic sector constitutes a larger share of national output, (as seen in domestic-demand or consumption-led growth models), rising wages will be beneficial for national employment and growth. This ultimately suggests that wage moderation is not always an optimal outcome that prior corporatist literature supposes—wage moderation may assist exports, but it depresses domestic demand, and for economies that rest upon domestic consumption-led growth strategies, wage restraint is self-defeating. These theoretical predictions establish my first set of testable hypotheses:

H_{1A}: *Wage inflation will lead to lower growth in countries with larger export sectors, but higher growth in countries with smaller export sectors.*

H_{1B}: *Wage restraint will lead to higher growth in countries with larger export sectors, but lower growth in countries with smaller export sectors.*

These hypotheses can also be extended to predicting how wage inflation's impact on growth interacts with national wage-setting institutions. Prior comparative capitalism (and comparative political economy) literature highlights that coordinated and highly centralized collective bargaining institutions are features of developed economies with robust export sectors and high trade shares (Katzenstein 1985; Iversen and Soskice 2009: 448; Johnston et al. 2014) because coordinated wage moderation helps maintain a competitive real exchange rate,

[9] Hassel and Palier in this volume explain that sectoral composition is not absolute, and that countries can favor multiple growth strategies at once. However, as long as different growth strategies rely on different wage dynamics (i.e., export growth strategies requiring nationwide wage moderation vs domestic consumption growth strategies requiring buoyant wage growth), sectoral conflicts in the determination of collective wage settlements remain embedded in countries' labor market institutions (see Brandl 2012; Johnston 2016).

even for liberal market economies with dynamic services sectors.[10] Coordinated wage-setting regimes produce particularly notable levels of wage moderation when the export sector is the "wage leader" or dominant producer group, and hence can place (or force) downward pressures on wages in the domestic (services) sector (i.e., Germany and Austria over the past three decades—see Johnston 2016).[11] However, Figure 9.1 demonstrates that highly coordinated regimes are capable of producing wage inflation on a temporal basis. These inconsistencies are empirically helpful, as they provide needed variation to determine whether the presence of wage inflation has similar effects on growth for coordinated and uncoordinated wage-setting regimes (in other words, our empirical sample is one that allows us to observe growth outcomes for coordinated bargaining regimes and uncoordinated bargaining regimes when they produce wage moderation *and* wage inflation). If coordinated wage-setting regimes help to uphold the status quo of export-led growth strategies, we should expect similar interactions between them and wage inflation when influencing growth. These predictions established the second set of testable hypotheses that are examined below.

H_{2A}: *Wage inflation will lead to lower growth in countries with highly coordinated labor market institutions, but higher growth in countries with less coordinated labor market institutions.*

H_{2B}: *Wage restraint will lead to higher growth in countries with highly coordinated labor market institutions, but lower growth in countries with less coordinated labor market institutions.*

4. The Empirical Relationship between Wage-Setting Institutions, Wage Inflation, and Growth: An Analysis of Eighteen OECD Countries

It goes without saying that any empirical analysis that uses real GDP growth as the dependent variable will be rife with endogeneity and simultaneity problems. Hence, I should emphasize that the following analysis is descriptive rather than causal, and seeks to determine whether wage restraint (or wage inflation) is associated with similar macroeconomic outcomes for (export-led) growth models that rest upon strongly coordinated wage bargaining and (consumption-led) growth models that rest upon weakly coordinated wage bargaining. In order to

[10] See Bacarro and Simoni (2007) for an account of Ireland's use of coordinated wage-setting to assist economic recovery in the 1980s.

[11] In the case of the Netherlands, wage moderation's (downward) impact on sheltered-sector wages led to an expansion in female part-time employment in the 1990s and 2000s, so households could compensate for stagnant wages. This expansion in employment, in turn, enhanced growth by increasing overall household incomes. I thank an anonymous reviewer for this point.

make an attempt to pacify simultaneity and reverse causality problems present in modeling real GDP growth, I utilize an ordinary least squares (OLS) distributive lag panel analysis for eighteen OECD countries[12] from 1970 to 2015, where all independent variables are modelled on a one-year lag. Moreover, with the exception of the wage-setting institutional variables and the size of the export share, all variables in the model are (first) differenced, rather than in levels, which are subject to greater simultaneity and endogeneity problems than first differences because level-based time series often suffers from non-stationarity.[13]

The two sets of hypotheses above are assessed via a two pronged estimation strategy. I run two distributive lag models that are similar in their specification, but differ in the interaction effect being examined. The baseline model to assess the validity of Hypotheses 1A and 1B can be summarized as follows.

$$\begin{aligned} y_{i,t} = {} & \alpha + \beta_1 Exports_{i,t-1} + \beta_2 WEU_{i,t-1} + \beta_3 Exports^{*}WEU_{i,t-1} \\ & + \beta_4 \sum \Delta X_{i,t-1} + \beta_5 \sum \Delta Y_{i,t-1} + \beta_6 \sum \Delta Z_{i,t-1} + \beta_7 \sum FE_i \\ & + \beta_8 \sum TE_t + \epsilon_{i,t} \end{aligned} \quad \text{[Eq.1]}$$

$y_{i,t}$ is the real GDP growth rate for country i at time t. $Exports_{i,t-1}$ is the size of country i's export sector at time t–1, measured as the export share (total exports to GDP). Data for real GDP growth was taken from the OECD (2018), while national export shares were computed from the EU's ECOFIN AMECO Database (2018). $WEU_{i,t-1}$ is a measure of wage inflation in country i at time t-1. Changes in nominal (or real) unit labor costs have been used as a measure of wage inflation/ moderation in empirical comparative capitalism research (see Höpner and Lutter 2018). However, this indicator poses a "kitchen sink" problem. Nominal/real unit labor costs capture labor's share in GDP, which can also be moved by variables that impact the use of capital (technological change, capital substitution, the price of capital, etc.). Selecting this as a measurement for wage restraint, therefore, is problematic for two reasons: one, it does not isolate for wage excess above productivity which is attributed *only* to labor, and; two, endogeneity problems arise because firms may decide to substitute away from labor towards capital if unit labor cost growth is attributed to excessive wage demands.

Similar to Baccaro and Simoni (2010), I select (Oliver Blanchard's) wages in efficiency units (WEU) to measure the degree of wage inflation (or moderation) within a country (Blanchard and Wolfers 2000; Blanchard 2006). Blanchard's WEU is equal to the annual percentage change in the *real* wage[14] minus the annual

[12] See footnote 6 for the list of these countries.

[13] Results from a Fisher-type (panel) unit root test indicate that real GDP growth fulfills the stationarity assumption required for time series. The dependent variable (real GDP growth) is not first differenced, because as a growth rate, it is automatically differenced.

[14] My measure of wage moderation/inflation uses real wage growth rather than nominal wage growth for two reasons: 1.) earlier works that empirically test the relationship between the organization of wage-setting and macroeconomic outcomes also use the real rather than nominal wage (see Calmfors and Driffill 1998; Soskice 1990); 2.) uunlike nominal wage moderation, real wage moderation

percentage change in labor productivity. Blanchard controls for changes in capital substitution/accumulation in his labor productivity measurement. Labor productivity is defined as the ratio of total factor productivity (TFP—the Solow residual) to labor's share in GDP; by dividing the log change in TFP by the log change in labor share, Blanchard includes a (rough) estimate of labor's contribution to productivity growth. Moreover, changes in the labor share will automatically account for changes in capital/labor substitution. If the efficiency wage unit is *positive*, this implies that *wage inflation exists* (in other words, annual real wage growth exceeds labor productivity growth in a given year). If the efficiency wage unit is *negative*, then *wage restraint is present* (annual real wage growth is lower than labor productivity growth in a given year). Real wage data (measured as real compensation per employee) and labor's contribution to TFP growth, are taken from ECOFIN's AMECO Database (2018). It should be emphasized that there is a high degree of correlation between Blanchard's constructed WEU and annual real unit labor cost growth—the pair-wise correlation coefficient between the two time-series within the sample is 0.941 (p-value = 0.000).

The baseline model to assess the validity of Hypotheses 2A and 2B is as follows:

$$\begin{aligned} y_{i,t} = \alpha &+ \beta_1 LMI_{i,t-1} + \beta_2 WEU_{i,t-1} + \beta_3 LMI^{*}WEU_{i,t-1} + \beta_4 \sum \Delta X_{i,t-1} \\ &+ \beta_5 \sum \Delta Y_{i,t-1} + \beta_6 \sum \Delta Z_{i,t-1} + \beta_7 \sum FE_i + \beta_8 \sum TE_t + \epsilon_{i,t} \end{aligned} \quad \text{[Eq.2]}$$

$LMI_{i,t-1}$ is the type of labor market institution present in country i at time t−1. Because major works in comparative capitalism emphasize the importance of *wage coordination* in describing the structure of labor market institutions (see Soskice 1990; Hall and Soskice 2001; Baccaro and Pontusson 2016), Table 9.2 prioritizes Kenworthy's (2001) five-point wage coordination index as the main measure of labor market institutions (values range from one, indicating no coordination, to five, indicating high coordination). However, Table 9.3 presents robustness checks for alternative measures of labor market institutions, which include wage-setting centralization (values range from zero, indicating that wage-setting is completely decentralized, to one, indicating that wage-setting is completely centralized[15]), trade union density, and more recent measures of export-sector dominance in wage-setting (see Traxler et al. 2001; Brandl 2012; Johnston 2016; Johnston and Regan 2017). Trade union density data was obtained from the

gauges the containment or growth of the wage share, which is a distributive measure because it indicates how much of domestic output goes to labor. I thank Lucio Baccaro for raising my attention to this point. Results on the interaction term in Tables 9.1 and 9.2 continue to hold, however, if nominal rather than real wages-in-efficiency units are used.

[15] This measure, taken from Visser (2016) is computed slightly differently than Iversen's (1998), but both are measures of the *level* at which wage bargaining takes place. More conveniently, Visser's (2016) index has more complete time-series for my 18 country sample.

OECD (2018), data for wage coordination and wage-setting centralization was taken from Visser (2016), and data for export-sector dominance in wage-setting was taken from Brandl (2012) and Johnston (2016).

While the independent effect of labor market institutions (and the export share) on real GDP growth is indeterminate (as the growth model and wider comparative capitalism literature highlight, different growth strategies, and the institutions that underpin them, can lead to similar macroeconomic outcomes[16]), it is anticipated that wage inflation on its own should boost real GDP growth, given its direct effect on enhancing *domestic* consumption. Hence, while β_1 in Equations 1 and 2 may lack significance, β_2 should be *positive* for both models (higher wage inflation leads to higher domestic consumption, which leads to higher growth). However, as theorized above, wage inflation is likely to have very different implications for a country whose growth strategy rests on boosting exports, than a country whose growth strategy rests on boosting domestic demand. For the former, wage inflation is detrimental to *exports* because it increases the national inflation rate, which causes the real exchange rate to worsen. For the latter, wage inflation enhances *domestic consumption*. The interaction term between a country's labor market institutions/ export share and degree of wage inflation ($Exports^{*}WEU_{i,t-1}$ *and* $LMI^{*}WEU_{i,t-1}$ in Equations 1 and 2, respectively) allows one to determine if wage inflation has beneficial effects for (domestic-led) growth model strategies that rest on uncoordinated labor markets and detrimental effects for (export-led) growth model strategies that rest on coordinated labor markets. Therefore, it is anticipated that β_3 should be *negative*—higher wage *inflation* in countries with highly coordinated labor markets and large export shares should reduce growth, but should enhance growth in countries with lowly coordinated labor markets and small export shares. Likewise, higher levels of wage *restraint* (negative WEUs), should enhance growth in coordinated labor markets and countries with large export shares, given its beneficial effects on export competitiveness, while wage restraint should be harmful to growth in less coordinated labor markets and countries with small export shares, given its damaging effects to domestic demand.

Rather than producing a model which incorporates every possible variable that impacts GDP growth, control variables are presented in (parsimonious) groups, in line with predictions from the growth model literature as well as major identities within macroeconomics. *Due to clear endogeneity and simultaneity problems, these sets of controls are presented in different models.* $\sum \Delta X_{i,t-1}$ is a vector that accounts for (lagged) first differences in the employment share of the four major sectors that growth model theory focuses on, as well as the lagged difference in the real

[16] Because the WEU variable controls for wage changes that stem from (among other things) the organization of wage-setting institutions, captures features of coordinated wage-setting that affect growth, but which are unrelated to wages (such as coordinated wage-setting's contribution to skill development within country i at time t−1). I thank Lucio Baccaro and Anke Hassel for this point.

interest rate (which is expected to have a dampening effect on growth—rising interest rates make servicing costs for investment, and consumption, more expensive). The growth model literature has identified four different "growth strategies" – growth driven by the export of dynamic services, the export of manufacturing goods, financially (debt) driven domestic consumption (common in economies with large low-wage services sectors), and wage-driven domestic consumption (see Hassel and Palier in this volume). The manufacturing sector's (International Standard Industrial Classification—ISIC—Category D) employment share (the percentage of a country's total employees that work in ISIC sector D) is used as a proxy for the prominence of exportable manufacturing goods in national employment. The employment share of post and telecommunications (ISIC Category 64), financial, insurance, real-estate and business services sectors (ISIC Categories JtK) within total employment, is used as a proxy for the prominence of exportable, dynamic services in national employment. Because wage-driven growth (for the purposes of domestic consumption) is most feasible within public services, given its comparative lack of cost-competitiveness constraints and a softer budget constraint (as governments can run annual deficits when costs of services exceed revenues to pay for them—see Johnston 2012), the employment share of the public administration and defense (ISIC Category L), education (ISIC Category M), and health and social work (ISIC Category N) sectors are used to proxy the prominence of the wage-driven domestic consumption growth strategy in a country's total employment. Finally, because debt-driven consumption growth arises when wages do not meet the consumption needs of workers, the employment share in the (low wage) sectors wholesale and retail trade (ISIC Category G) and hotels and restaurants (ISIC Category H), is taken as a proxy of the dominance of this particular growth strategy in a country's total employment. Data on the employment share is taken from the March 2011 release of the EU KLEMS dataset, because EU KLEMS releases after this time altered sectoral classifications, and do not contain sectoral data before the mid-1990s. Norway's sectoral employment data was taken from the OECD Structural Analysis Database (STAN, 2018).[17] Real interest rate data was taken from ECOFIN's AMECO Database (2018), except for Australia and Norway, whose more complete time-series data was taken from the OECD (2018).

$\sum \Delta X_{i,t-1}$ is a vector of (lagged, first-differenced) controls that belong to the Phillip's Curve identity—the unemployment rate and inflation rate. It is anticipated that (lagged) increases in the unemployment rate should be associated with weakened real GDP growth, while the effect of the (lagged first-differenced) inflation rate is indeterminate (given the fact that real GDP growth is already

[17] Norway is not included in the EU KLEMS dataset. While OECD STAN does have sectoral employment data for the other countries within the sample, it is subject to far greater gaps (particularly before the 1990s) than EU KLEMS; hence, EU KLEMS was given primacy for employment share data.

adjusted for inflation). Unemployment rate data is taken ECOFIN's AMECO Database (2018), while inflation data is taken from the OECD (2018). $\sum \Delta Z_{i,t-1}$ is a vector of the remaining components beyond consumption (which is accounted for in my wage inflation measure) that constitute a country's gross domestic product (embodied in the Y = C + I + (G−R) + (EX−IM) identity). These include the *lagged log change*[18] in real investment (proxied by gross fixed capital formation), real government spending, real government (taxation) revenues, real exports, and real imports. It is anticipated that increases in the (lagged log change) of real investment, real exports and real government expenditure should positively affect real GDP growth while increases in the (lagged log change) of real government revenues and real imports should reduce real GDP growth. Gross fixed capital formation spending data was taken from ECOFIN's AMECO Database (2018), while government expenditure, revenues, imports and exports data was taken from the OECD (2018).

$\sum FE_i$ is a vector of country fixed effects. In a first-differenced model, fixed effects account for country-specific growth trends (for example, catch-up growth in peripheral European countries during the 1970s, 1980s and 1990s would be captured by the use of fixed effects). However, the result for the interaction terms below are consistent if random effects are used (results provided in an online appendix[19]). $\sum TE_t$ is a vector of time effects that control for omitted variables that impact growth, which vary over time but impact countries similarly (such omitted variables would include global economic shocks like the OPEC oil crisis, the 2001 dot com bust, the 2008 Global Financial Crisis, etc.). Finally, in order to correct for downward bias in the error terms that stem from heteroscedasticity and serial correlation, panel corrected standard errors and a common autoregressive term were incorporated into the model (see Beck and Katz 1995).[20]

5. Results

5.1 The Export Share, Wage Inflation, and Growth

Results for Equation 1 are presented in Table 9.1. Model I presents the baseline model, which includes only (lagged) wage inflation, the (lagged) export share, and the (lagged) interaction between them, as well as fixed and time effects. As emphasized above, the different vectors of controls were not included in the

[18] These variables are measured in absolute amounts and not as a percentage of gross domestic product, as GDP growth would directly move the latter's denominator.

[19] Accessible at https://sites.google.com/site/dralisonljohnston/research

[20] An LR test for Model I in Tables 9.1 and 9.2 indicated that heteroscedasticity within panels was present. For Model I in Table 9.1, the chi-squared statistic was 311.75 (p-value = 0.000), while for Model I in Table 9.2, the chi-squared statistic was 222.40 (p-value = 0.000).

Table 9.1 Wage inflation, export shares, and growth

	Model I	Model II	Model III	Model IV
Wage inflation (t-1)	0.184**	0.119*	0.128*	0.000
	(0.013)	(0.069)	(0.078)	(0.999)
Export share (t-1)	0.046**	0.093***	0.034*	0.028
	(0.049)	(0.000)	(0.082)	(0.151)
Wage inflation (t-1)* Export share (t-1)	-0.008***	-0.004	-0.008***	-0.004
	(0.009)	(0.105)	(0.010)	(0.248)
Δ Manufacturing employment Share (t-1)		-0.236		
		(0.248)		
Δ Public services employment Share (t-1)		-0.336*		
		(0.096)		
Δ Dynamic services employment Share (t-1)		-0.702***		
		(0.006)		
Δ Low-wage services employment Share (t-1)		-0.295		
		(0.162)		
Δ Real interest rate (t-1)		-0.265***		
		(0.000)		
Δ Unemployment rate (t-1)			-0.421***	
			(0.000)	
Δ Inflation rate (t-1)			-0.125***	
			(0.001)	
Δ Gross fixed capital formation (t-1)				6.450***
				(0.002)
Δ Government expenditure (t-1)				2.814
				(0.452)
Δ Government revenue (t-1)				0.175
				(0.945)
Δ Exports (t-1)				1.369
				(0.437)
Δ Imports (t-1)				3.072*
				(0.057)
Constant	5.658***	4.590***	6.133***	5.808***
	(0.000)	(0.000)	(0.000)	(0.000)
Observations	781	607	775	666
R-squared	0.469	0.46	0.513	0.562
Chi-squared (p-value)	0.000	0.000	0.000	0.000

Note: Dependent variable is real GDP growth. Estimator used was an OLS model with panel-corrected standard errors and a common first-order auto-regressive term (p-values in parentheses). N-1 country dummies and time dummies included but not shown. *, **, and *** indicate significance on a 90%, 95%, and 99% confidence level, respectively.

same models given clear endogeneity and simultaneity problems (increases in gross fixed capital formation—in vector $\sum \Delta Z_{i,t-1}$—for example, will impact changes in unemployment—in vector $\sum \Delta Y_{i,t-1}$—and will be impacted by changes in the real interest rate—in vector $\sum \Delta X_{i,t-1}$). Model II adds the controls in vector $\sum \Delta X_{i,t-1}$ (lagged differences in employment shares across the four sectors that measure the prominence of different growth strategies, as well as the lagged difference in the real interest rate). Model III adds the controls in vector $\sum \Delta Y_{i,t-1}$ (the lagged difference in the unemployment and inflation rate). Finally, Model IV adds the controls in vector $\sum \Delta Z_{i,t-1}$ (the lagged log difference of real gross fixed capital formation, government expenditure, government revenues, exports and imports).

Results from Table 9.1 weakly support the first set of hypotheses. As expected, (lagged) wage inflation has a direct positive association with real GDP growth in three of the four models; from Models I-III in Table 9.1, for every 1 percentage point that real wage growth exceeds labor productivity growth in the previous year, real GDP growth will rise by .119 to .184 percentage points. However, this positive effect is dampened for countries with larger export shares: the beta coefficient on the interaction effect between a country's (lagged) export share and (lagged) wage inflation is negative. This interaction effect is only significant for two of the four models in Table 9.1, likely due to the fact that export share suffers from collinearity problems with the (first differences) in sectoral employment shares in Model II and, obviously, with the first differences of the logged value of total exports in Model IV.

Figure 9.2 demonstrates this interaction effect visually for two countries; one with an export share in the lowest decile of the sample (exports are 10% of

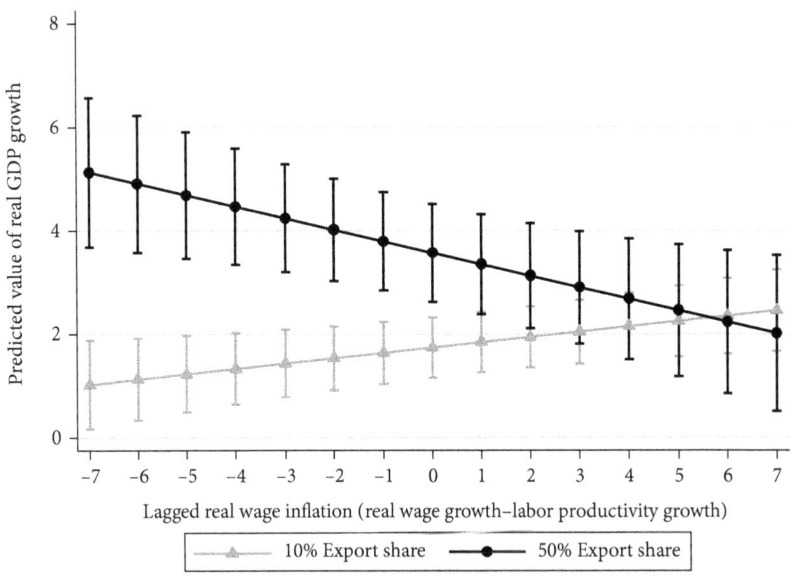

Figure 9.2 The interaction effect between the export share and wage inflation on predicted real GDP growth

Source: Graphic constructed from the output in Model I, Table 9.1. Predicted values presented with 90 percent confidence intervals.

GDP—documented by the gray line), and one with an export share in the highest decile of the sample (exports are 50% of GDP—documented by the black line). In the presence of higher (lagged) wage restraint (i.e., negative values of wage inflation), a country with a 50% export share has a higher (predicted) real GDP growth rate than a country with a 10% export share. On the other hand, higher levels of wage inflation lead to similar levels of growth between these two types of economies (because the confidence intervals of their predicted growth rates overlap). Hence, plotting the interaction effect between the export share and wage inflation demonstrates that Hypothesis 1B is substantiated (the economy which has an export share in the top tenth percentile has a higher growth rate than the country with an export share in the bottom tenth percentile when wage restraint is present), while Hypothesis 1A is not substantiated (in the presence of wage inflation, countries with both sizes of export sectors do not display significantly different GDP growth performance from each other).

5.2 Wage-Setting Institutions, Wage Inflation, and Growth

There is a significant degree of collinearity between a country's wage-setting institutions and the size of its export share within the panel sample; wage-setting coordination, bargaining centralization, trade union density and the presence of export-sector-favoring wage-coordination institutions share a 0.369 (p-value=0.000), 0.376 (p-value=0.000), 0.233 (p-value=0.000) and 0.168 (p-value=0.000) correlation coefficient with the export share, respectively. Consequently, we should expect the negative interaction term between wage coordination and wage inflation to demonstrate similar results as the interaction between the export share and wage inflation. Table 9.2 presents the results for Equation 2. As with Table 9.1, Model I provides the baseline model (only lagged wage inflation, wage-setting coordination, their interaction, and country and time effects are included as controls). Model II incorporates vector $\sum \Delta X_{i,t-1}$. Model III incorporates vector $\sum \Delta Y_{i,t-1}$, and Model IV incorporates vector $\sum \Delta Z_{i,t-1}$.

The results in Table 9.2 strongly support Hypotheses 2A and 2B, and their significance is stronger and more robust than those for the export share interaction models in Table 9.1. Similar to results in Table 9.1, (lagged) wage inflation is positively associated with growth in three of the four models: from Models I-III in Table 9.2, for every 1 percentage point that real wage growth exceeds labor productivity growth in the previous year, real GDP growth will rise by 0.19 to 0.28 percentage points. However, (lagged) wage inflation's positive association with real GDP growth is *dampened* for countries with *higher* levels of coordinated wage-setting; the interaction term (which is significantly negative for all four models in Table 9.2) cancels out the positive direct effect of wage inflation on growth. Figure 9.3 provides a visualization of this interaction, plotting the

Table 9.2 Wage inflation, wage coordination, and growth

	Model I	Model II	Model III	Model IV
Wage inflation (t–1)	0.282***	0.194**	0.224**	0.102
	(0.009)	(0.037)	(0.034)	(0.299)
Wage coordination (t–1)	–0.005	0.101	–0.032	–0.078
	(0.961)	(0.237)	(0.734)	(0.418)
Wage inflation (t–1)* Wage coordination (t–1)	–0.079***	–0.052**	–0.075***	–0.060**
	(0.004)	(0.025)	(0.006)	(0.018)
Δ Manufacturing employment Share (t–1)		–0.116		
		(0.589)		
Δ Public services employment Share (t–1)		–0.357*		
		(0.091)		
Δ Dynamic services employment Share (t–1)		–0.570**		
		(0.033)		
Δ Low-wage services employment Share (t–1)		–0.208		
		(0.382)		
Δ Real interest rate (t–1)		–0.262***		
		(0.000)		
Δ Unemployment rate (t–1)			–0.452***	
			(0.000)	
Δ Inflation rate (t–1)			–0.125***	
			(0.001)	
Δ Gross fixed capital formation (t–1)				5.372***
				(0.003)
Δ Government expenditure (t–1)				3.078
				(0.218)
Δ Government revenue (t–1)				–0.517
				(0.815)
Δ Exports (t–1)				0.079
				(0.963)
Δ Imports (t–1)				2.897*
				(0.058)
Constant	5.673***	4.856***	6.099***	5.788***
	(0.000)	(0.000)	(0.000)	(0.000)
Observations	767	607	761	659
R-squared	0.487	0.433	0.537	0.586
Chi-squared (p-value)	0.000	0.000	0.000	0.000

Note: Dependent variable is real GDP growth. Estimator used was an OLS model with panel-corrected standard errors and a common first-order auto-regressive term (p-values in parentheses). N–1 country dummies and time dummies included but not shown. *, **, and *** indicate significance on a 90%, 95%, and 99% confidence level, respectively.

association between (lagged) real wage inflation and real GDP growth for two different types of countries—one in which wage-setting is completely uncoordinated (in gray), and one in which wage-setting is completely coordinated (in black). In the presence of higher wage *restraint* (negative wage inflation), coordinated wage-setting regimes witness significantly higher real GDP growth than

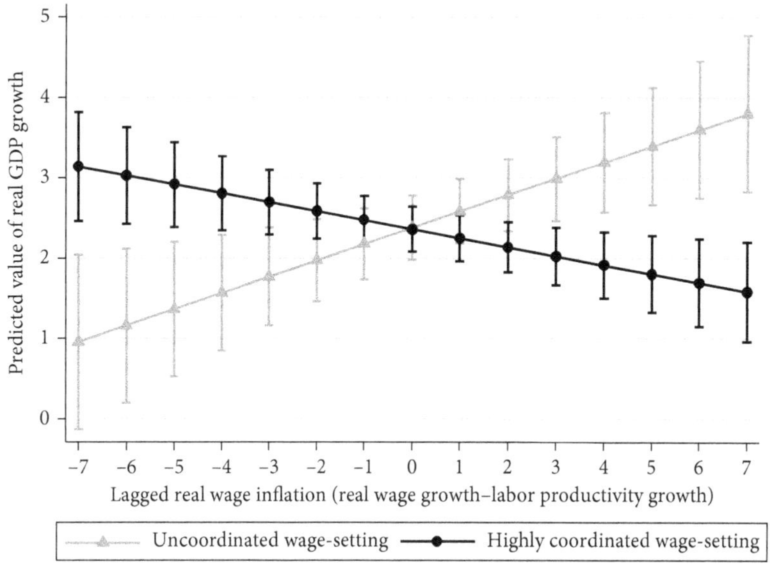

Figure 9.3 The interaction effect between wage coordination and wage inflation on predicted real GDP growth

Source: Graphic constructed from the output in Model I, Table 9.2. Predicted values presented with 90 percent confidence intervals. Uncoordinated wage-setting has a (Kenworthy) wage coordination index value of 1. Highly coordinated wage-setting has a (Kenworthy) wage coordination index value of 5.

uncoordinated wage-setting regimes. In contrast, uncoordinated wage-setting regimes witness significantly higher real GDP growth than coordinated ones in the presence of higher wage *inflation*. Hence, unlike results for the export share, both Hypotheses 2A and 2B are supported. The degree of wage coordination on its own (which captures wage-setting institutions' contributions to growth that are *independent* of their effect on wages) has no significant association with real GDP growth, as indicated by the variable's non-significant beta coefficients across all four models in Table 9.2. Rather, wage coordination's impact on growth is *conditioned* on the degree of wage inflation within an economy.

The negative interaction term between more cohesive wage-setting institutions and wage inflation also is present if other measures of labor market organization are used. Table 9.3 presents the results for when three alternative measures of wage-setting "cohesion" are used in place of wage coordination: wage centralization (Model I, Table 9.3), trade union density (Model II, Table 9.3), and the presence of bargaining regimes where unions in the export sector lead or control national wage-setting[21] (1 indicates they do, 0 indicates that they do not; Model

[21] Traxler et al. (2001), Brandl (2012), and Johnston (2016) identify four wage-coordination regimes where the export sector displays dominance over the sheltered sector in national wage-setting: pattern bargaining where export-sector-based unions (usually in manufacturing) establish their wage settlements

Table 9.3 Robustness checks for the link between wage-setting cohesion, wage inflation, and growth

	Model I	Model II	Model III
Wage inflation (t–1)	0.037	0.042	–0.056
	(0.631)	(0.592)	(0.321)
Wage centralization (t–1)	–3.187**		
	(0.016)		
Wage inflation (t–1)* Wage centralization (t–1)	–0.406***		
	(0.008)		
Trade union density (t–1)		0.005	
		(0.699)	
Wage inflation (t–1)* Trade union density (t–1)		–0.004***	
		(0.006)	
Export-favoring wage-setting coordination (t–1)			0.204
			(0.533)
Wage inflation (t–1)* Export-favoring wage-setting coordination (t–1)			–0.126*
			(0.061)
Observations	565	615	437
R-squared	0.625	0.619	0.523
Chi-squared (p-value)	0.000	0.000	0.000

Note: Dependent variable is real GDP growth. Estimator used was an OLS model with panel-corrected standard errors and a common first-order auto-regressive term (p-values in parentheses). Lagged logged differences in real gross fixed capital formation, government expenditure, government revenue, exports and imports, as well as N–1 country dummies, time dummies, and the constant term are included but not shown. *, **, and *** indicate significance on a 90%, 95%, and 99% confidence level, respectively.

III, Table 9.3). The specification for each model presented in Table 9.3 follows that from Model IV in Table 9.2, but for the sake of space, results for (lagged logged differences in) real gross fixed capital formation, government expenditure, government revenue, exports and imports are included but not shown in Table 9.3 (these results are available in an online appendix[22]). In contrast to results in

first, setting upper limits for bargaining in other sectors (as seen in Germany and Austria); state-imposed coordination where the state imposes an (upper limit) wage rule onto unions during wage negotiations (as seen in France and Belgium); peak bargaining, where union members in export sector unions outnumber their peers in sheltered-sector unions (as seen in Denmark), and; export-led wage pacts, where national wage pacts are initiated and drafted by export-sector unions, generally in times of economic crisis (as seen temporarily in the Netherlands). In contrast, they identify the following modes of wage coordination that lack export-sector leadership or agenda-setting: uncoordinated wage bargaining (as seen in the US and UK); peak bargaining, where union members in sheltered-sector unions outnumber their peers in export sector unions (Italy, Spain, and Portugal); and sheltered-sector wage pacts, where national wage pact agreements are initiated and drafted by unions in the sheltered (public) sector (as seen on a temporary basis in Ireland). Data on which countries lie in these different modes of wage-setting, and how their positions change over time, are taken from Brandl (2012) and Johnston (2016).

[22] Accessible at https://sites.google.com/site/dralisonljohnston/research.

Table 9.2, wage inflation on its own has no significant direct relationship with growth, although the beta coefficients do hold the expected positive sign. Rather, the association between wage inflation and growth is contingent on the type of bargaining regime in place. In the presence of wage *inflation*, real GDP growth is lower in: highly centralized bargaining regimes rather than less centralized ones (Model I, Table 9.3); in countries with higher rather than lower levels of trade union density (Model II, Table 9.3), and in countries with export-sector-dominated rather than sheltered-sector-dominated wage coordination (Model III, Table 9.3).

Finally, wage restraint's positive effect on growth in coordinated labor markets is also robust if unemployment is used as the dependent variable rather than real GDP growth.[23] Figure 9.4 provides the visualization of the interaction effect between wage inflation and the degree of wage coordination on unemployment (the model specification follows that of Model IV in Table 9.2; the full results for the empirical model are provided in an online appendix[24]). Figure 9.4 plots the

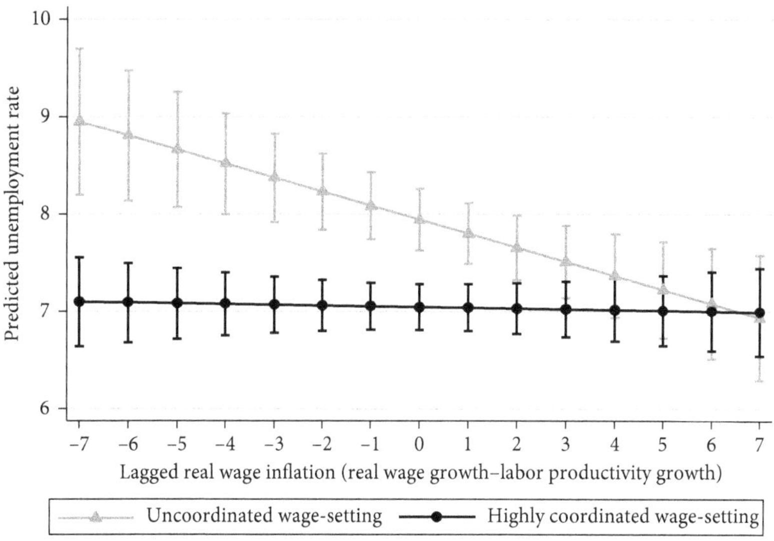

Figure 9.4 The interaction effect between wage coordination and wage inflation on the predicted unemployment rate

Source: Graphic constructed using the unemployment rate as the dependent variable, and the model specification in Model IV, Table 9.2 for the independent variables and error structure. Predicted values presented with 90 percent confidence intervals. Uncoordinated wage-setting has a (Kenworthy) wage coordination index value of 1. Highly coordinated wage-setting has a (Kenworthy) wage coordination index value of 5.

[23] The results for Table 9.1 demonstrated no significant interaction effect between the export share and wage inflation when unemployment was used as the dependent variable.

[24] Accessible at https://sites.google.com/site/dralisonljohnston/research.

association between (lagged) real wage inflation and unemployment for a country with completely uncoordinated wage-setting (index value of one, shown by the gray line), and a country with highly coordinated wage-setting (index value of five, shown by the black line). In the presence of wage inflation, there is no significant difference in unemployment rates between the two countries. However, in the presence of wage restraint, unemployment is higher in the country with uncoordinated wage-setting than it is in the country with highly coordinated wage-setting. Supporting the results above, this suggests that wage restraint is counterproductive in countries with uncoordinated labor markets, because it restricts demand and hence increases unemployment. In contrast, for countries with highly coordinated wage-setting, while wage restraint would stifle employment growth in domestic sectors, this effect appears to be countered by employment expansion in the export sector, given wage restraint's (competitiveness enhancing effects) on the real exchange rate.

Surprisingly, the results in Table 9.2 do not display any interactions with European Monetary Union. Several authors have highlighted how EMU provided coordinated market economies with a "comparative institutional advantage" to enhance their trade competitiveness via beggar-thy-neighbor wage strategies, which improved the competitiveness of their real exchange rate (Dullien 2003; Johnston et al. 2014). Not only do triple interaction terms between wage inflation, wage coordination, and EMU membership fail to display significant results, but additionally, when dividing the panel into two samples—one for countries not belonging to a monetary union, and another for countries that do—the interaction between wage inflation and wage coordination is only significant for the former group of countries, not the latter.

Finally, with regards to the results for other variables, (lagged) increases in the unemployment rate, real interest rate, and inflation rate are associated with lower GDP growth (as expected), while (lagged) increases in real gross-fixed capital formation is associated with higher real GDP growth (also as expected). Surprisingly, rises in (lagged) real imports are also associated with higher real GDP growth. This result may be spuriously driven by consumption's impact on growth and import demand that is not fully captured in wages—i.e., consumer demand that is driven by increases in consumer credit and debt. Rises in (lagged) public services and dynamic services employment are associated with lower real GDP growth. This relationship may be driven by the fact that services sectors realize lower productivity growth—which should transpire to lower real GDP growth—than goods-based sectors (see Baumol and Bowen 1965 on the "cost disease" phenomenon associated with services and the rise of its prominence in post-Fordist economies).

6. Conclusion

In addition to their implications for the literature, the results above, echoing Scharpf's contribution to this volume, can help explain macroeconomic outcomes in Europe during its current age of austerity, and why different countries were able to achieve different growth and unemployment outcomes with the delivery of prolonged wage moderation. Since the imposition of Greece's first bail-out program, the troika (the European Commission, European Central Bank and the International Monetary Fund (IMF)) advocated that cash-strapped, peripheral Eurozone economies which required financial assistance from the European Stability Mechanism and its predecessors had to implement comprehensive wage freezes in the public sector, among other reforms. Members of the troika presumed that not only would wage freezes reduce the public deficit, but they would also be deflationary and help restore competitiveness. *At the same time*, the troika also required peripheral economies to implement the type of market-friendly structural labor market reforms that would lower the degree of coordination and centralization in wage-setting. By advocating both of these strategies *simultaneously*, the European Commission, European Central Bank, and (to a lesser extent) the IMF,[25] have pushed peripheral Eurozone (bail-out) countries towards a low-growth, high unemployment equilibrium, as predicted from the results shown on the gray line in the left-hand side of Figures 9.3 and 9.4. Making this prescribed reform agenda even worse, the troika also required deep cuts to the welfare state, which effectively stunted the potential of a wage *and* welfare-based domestic demand growth strategy in the Eurozone's debtor economies (see Avlijaš, Hassel, and Palier in this volume).

While the economic outcomes of these policies seem obvious and counterproductive, they were heavily pushed in the European Council by Germany. However, Germany's eventual success with using prolonged wage moderation, transforming itself from the sick man of Europe to an export miracle, can also be explained by the results and conclusions drawn from the empirical analysis above. Due in part to its prolonged delivery of wage restraint, which was enabled by Germany's strongly coordinated labor market institutions, Germany realized prolific growth in its export share since reunification; between 1991 and 2015, Germany's export share as a percentage of GDP grew by almost 18 percentage points, the third highest level of growth in the Eurozone behind the Netherlands and Belgium (European Commission Directorate General for Economic and Financial Affairs 2018). The extensive series of "competitiveness-based" reforms that Germany's pursued after reunification, of which over a decade long of wage moderation was

[25] Clift (2018) presents an alternative narrative of the IMF's policy advice during the European debt crisis, highlighting that the institution was more in favor of demand stimulus and debt restructuring than other members in the troika.

an important component, caused the country to assume a "sinner/saint" mentality towards the perceived adjustment needed to be taken in the EMU South during the euro crisis (Newman 2015: 119). Germans perceived themselves as making notable and prolonged sacrifices that undercut their quality of life, and expected EMU "sinners" to do the same. However, this mentality ignores the fact that the structural features of the German labor market and the size of its export share enabled comprehensive wage moderation to eventually produce positive growth (and low unemployment) outcomes; Germany's growth and unemployment equilibrium in Figures 9.2, 9.3, and 9.4 lie not on the gray line but on the black one. In contrast, the average export share of Greece, Italy, Portugal and Spain at the onset of the crisis was only 15% of GDP, less than half that of Germany's, which limited the potential for any growth gains that could be had from nationwide wage restraint.

Finally, the results above suggest that, within comparative capitalism, a (demand-centered) rethink of wage restraint's effect on macroeconomic outcomes, along the lines of new growth model theory, is warranted. In contrast to the predictions of early comparative capitalism supply-side theories, wage restraint is not a winning strategy for all types of economies and growth strategies. Rather, wage moderation is associated with better growth (and unemployment) outcomes *only* for countries with larger export shares and more coordinated labor markets. For countries with smaller export shares and uncoordinated wage-setting, wage restraint is associated with (comparatively) lower growth and higher unemployment. In sum, growth model theory's demand-centered view of the organization of capitalist systems highlight that Europe's new era of wage stagnation will only witness further divergence in macroeconomic outcomes between economies whose wage-setting institutions and growth strategies are equipped to reap positive effects from wage moderation, and those whose economies and labor market institutions are not.

References

Baccaro, L. and Pontusson, J. 2016. "Rethinking Comparative Political Economy: the Growth Model Perspective." *Politics & Society* 44(2): 175–207.

Baccaro, L. and Simoni, M. 2007. "Centralized wage bargaining and the 'Celtic Tiger' phenomenon." *Industrial Relations: A Journal of Economy and Society* 46(3): 426–55.

Baccaro, L. and Simoni, M. 2010. Organizational determinants of wage moderation. *World Politics*, *62*(4), 594–635.

Baumol, W. and Bowen, W. 1965. "On the Performing Arts: The Anatomy of their Economic Problems." *American Economic Review* 55(1): 495–502.

Beck, N. and Katz, J. 1995. "What to do (and not to do) with time-series cross-section data." *American Political Science Review* 89(3): 634–47.

Blanchard, O. 2006. "European Unemployment: The Evolution of Facts and Ideas." *Economic Policy* 21: 5–59.

Blanchard, O. and Wolfers, J. 2000. "The Role of Shocks and Institutions in the Rise of European Unemployment: The Aggregate Evidence." *Economic Journal* 110(462): 1–33.

Brandl, B. 2012. "Successful Wage Concertation: The Economic Effects of Wage Pacts and their Alternatives." *British Journal of Industrial Relations* 50(3): 482–501.

Braun, B. and Deeg, R. 2018. "Investing in Exports: Finance and the German Growth Model." Conference Paper for the 2018 Council of European Studies annual conference, Chicago, USA, . March 28–30, 2018.

Bruno, M. and Sachs, J. 1985. *The Economics of Worldwide Stagflation*. Cambridge, MA: Harvard University Press.

Calmfors, L. and Driffill, J. 1988. "Bargaining structure, corporatism and macroeconomic performance". *Economic Policy* 3(6): 13–61.

Cameron, D. 1984. "Social Democracy, Corporatism, Labour Quiescence and the Representation of Economic Interest in Advanced Capitalist Society." In *Order and Conflict in Contemporary Capitalism*, edited by J. H. Goldthorpe. Oxford: Clarendon.

Carlin, W. and Soskice, D. 1990. *Macroeconomics and the Wage Bargain: A Modern Approach to Employment, Inflation and the Exchange Rate*. Oxford: Oxford University Press.

Clift, B. 2018. *The IMF and the Politics of Austerity in the Wake of the Global Financial Crisis*. Oxford: Oxford University Press.

Danthine, J. P. and Hunt, J. 1994. "Wage bargaining structure, employment and economic integration." 104(424): *The Economic Journal*: 528–41.

Dullien, S. 2003. "Is Small Really Beautiful? Explaining Different Unemployment Performances within the Euro-Zone." *European Political Economic Review* 1(2): 126–51.

Dynan, K. E., Skinner, J. and Zeldes, S. P. 2004. "Do the rich save more?" *Journal of Political Economy* 112(2): 397–444.

European Commission Directorate General for Economic and Financial Affairs. 2018. *Annual macro-economic database (AMECO)*. http://ec.europa.eu/economy_finance/ameco/user/serie/SelectSerie.cfm (accessed April–June 2018).

EU KLEMS. 2011. *Groningen Growth and Development Centre*. http://www.euklems.net. (accessed accessed April–June 2018).

Hall, P. A. 2014. "Varieties of capitalism and the Euro crisis." *West European Politics* 37(6): 1223–43.

Hall, P. A. and Franzese, R. J. 1998. "Mixed signals: central bank independence, coordinated wage bargaining, and European Monetary Union." *International organization* 52(3): 505–35.

Hall, P. and Soskice, D. 2001. "An introduction to the Varieties of Capitalism." in *Varieties of Capitalism: The Institutional Foundations of Comparative Advantage*. Oxford: Oxford University Press.

Hancké, B. 2013. *Unions, Central Banks, and EMU: Labour Market Institutions and Monetary Integration in Europe*. Oxford: Oxford University Press.

Hancké, B. and Rhodes, M. 2005. "EMU and labor market institutions in Europe: The rise and fall of national social pacts." *Work and Occupations* 32(2): 196–228.

Hassel, A. 2003. "The politics of social pacts." *British Journal of Industrial Relations* 41(4): 707–26.

Höpner, M. and Lutter, M. 2018. "The diversity of wage regimes: why the Eurozone is too heterogeneous for the Euro." *European Political Science Review* 10(1): 71–96.

Iversen, T. 1998. "Wage bargaining, hard money and economic performance: theory and evidence for organized market economies." *British Journal of Political Science* 28: 31–61.

Iversen, T. 1999. *Contested Economic Institutions: The Politics of Macroeconomics and Wage Bargaining in Advanced Democracies*. Cambridge: Cambridge University Press.

Iversen, T. and Soskice, S. 2009. "Distribution and redistribution: The shadow of the nineteenth century." *World Politics* 61(3): 438–86.

Iversen, T., Soskice, D., and Hope, D. 2016. "The Eurozone and political economic institutions." *Annual Review of Political Science* 19: 163–85.

Johnston, A. 2012. "European Economic and Monetary Union's perverse effects on sectoral wage inflation: Negative feedback effects from institutional change?" *European Union Politics* 13(3): 345–66.

Johnston, A. 2016. *From Convergence to Crisis: Labor Markets and the Instability of the Euro*. Ithaca, NY: Cornell University Press.

Johnston, A., Hancké, B., and Pant, S. 2014. "Comparative institutional advantage in the European sovereign debt crisis." *Comparative Political Studies* 47(13): 1771–800.

Johnston, A. and Regan, A. 2016. "European monetary integration and the incompatibility of national varieties of capitalism." *JCMS: Journal of Common Market Studies* 54(2): 318–36.

Johnston, A. and Regan, A. 2017. "Global finance, labor politics, and the political economy of housing prices." *Politics & Society* 45(3): 327–58.

Katzenstein, P. J. 1985. *Small States in World Markets: Industrial Policy in Europe*. Ithaca, NY: Cornell University Press.

Kenworthy, L. 2001. "Wage-Setting Institutions: A survey and assessment." *World Politics* 54 (October): 57–98.

Lange, P. and Garrett, G. 1985. "The politics of growth: Strategic interaction and economic performance in the advanced industrial democracies, 1974–1980." *The Journal of Politics* 47(3): 792–827.

Newman, A. 2015. "The Reluctant Leader: Germany's Euro Experience and the Long Shadow of Reunification." In *The Future of the Euro*, edited by Matthjis and Blyth. Oxford: Oxford University Press, 117–35.

Nickell, S. and Andrews, M. 1983. "Unions, real wages and employment in Britain 1951–79." *Oxford Economic Papers* 35: 183–206.

Nölke, A. 2016. "Economic causes of the Eurozone crisis: the analytical contribution of Comparative Capitalism." *Socio-Economic Review* 14(1): 141–61.

OECD Structural Analysis Database (STAN). 2018. http://www.oecd.org/sti/ind/stanstructuralanalysisdatabase.htm (accessed April–June 2018).

OECD. 2018. OECD.Stat. http://stats.oecd.org/ (accessed April–June 2018).

Olson, M. 1982. *The Rise and Decline of Nations*. New Haven, Connecticut: Yale University Press.

Scharpf, F. 1991. *Crisis and Choice in European Social Democracy*. Ithaca, New York: Cornell University Press.

Soskice, D. 1990. "Wage determination: the changing role of institutions in advanced industrialized countries." *Oxford Review of Economic Policy* 6(4): 36–61.

Soskice, D. and Iversen, T. 2000. "The non-neutrality of monetary policy with large price or wage setters." *The Quarterly Journal of Economics* 115(1): 265–84.

Traxler, F., Blaschke, S., and Kittel, B. 2001. *National Labour Relations in Internationalized Markets: A Comparative Study of Institutions, Change, and Performance*. Oxford: Oxford University Press.

Visser, J. 2016. ICTWSS Database. version 5.1. Amsterdam: Amsterdam Institute for Advanced Labour Studies (AIAS), University of Amsterdam.

10

Housing Finance Between Social Welfare and Growth Strategies

Alexander Reisenbichler

1. Introduction

Housing and mortgage markets sit at the intersection of growth regimes and the welfare state. These markets are not only important engines for economic growth, but they also increasingly fulfill social functions. In light of decades-long welfare state retrenchment, they help households obtain private social insurance through homeownership, yet also expose them to financial risk and growing levels of mortgage debt. While these broader trends have occurred in most advanced economies, there are significant differences in the interlinkages between housing finance, growth regimes, and the welfare state, as well as how these interlinkages have shaped growth strategies in the housing area.

Scholarship in comparative political economy rarely explores the deeper connections between housing finance, growth regimes, and welfare states. This is surprising given the sheer size of housing finance markets—amounting to US$11 trillion in mortgage debt in the United States and €7.3 trillion in the European Union in 2018 (EMF 2019; HFPC 2019)—linking financial markets to the real economy. Yet, the degree to which housing occupies a central position within growth regimes varies across countries. It is well known that housing and mortgage markets are engines of growth in the US economy, which helped produce a remarkable economic boom in the 1990s and early 2000s that came to a halt with the financial crash of 2008–9 (Schwartz 2009; Mian and Sufi 2014). But such dynamics are less common in other advanced economies. Where rising house prices are pronounced policy goals in the United States and the United Kingdom, partly to boost household wealth in lieu of traditional social programs (Rajan 2010; Crouch 2009; Hay 2009), the opposite is the case in Germany, where recent price increases in property markets have been met with hostility by much of the German electorate (roughly half of whom are renting their homes), the Bundesbank (having repeatedly sounded the alarm about overvalued housing markets that are considered sources of financial instability and asset bubbles), and policy-makers on the left and right. Linking the worlds of growth regimes and social welfare can shed light on these developments.

Alexander Reisenbichler, *Housing Finance Between Social Welfare and Growth Strategies* In: *Growth and Welfare in Advanced Capitalist Economies: How Have Growth Regimes Evolved?* Edited by: Anke Hassel and Bruno Palier, Oxford University Press (2021). © Oxford University Press. DOI: 10.1093/oso/9780198866176.003.0010

When advanced economies transitioned from what Hassel and Palier label the Fordist era to the knowledge economy, they adopted different growth strategies in housing finance. I show that demand-led economies relying on credit and consumption, such as the United States and the United Kingdom, are complementary to "financialized" growth strategies in housing finance. These include tax breaks and public guarantees of private mortgage debt to stimulate demand, credit, and consumption through the housing market. This growth strategy is also in line with the imperatives of an asset-based, privatized welfare state that promotes access to credit in lieu of traditional public welfare programs. In contrast, countries based on price-sensitive exports of manufactured goods, such as Germany, are complementary to conservative housing finance policies that limit housing consumption, domestic demand, and public deficits to secure cost competitiveness (Baccaro and Pontusson 2016, and in this volume). Finally, export-oriented economies specializing in high-tech manufacturing and dynamic services, such as the Nordic economies, might be characterized as intermediate cases, where dynamic housing markets neither reinforce nor contradict their growth regimes. As high-tech firms might be less concerned with securing cost competitiveness or restraining domestic demand, these countries can adopt "financialized" housing policies to boost private wealth and consumption.

To illustrate these arguments, this chapter discusses housing-related growth strategies in the United States and Germany since the 1970s.[1] In the United States, policy-makers adopted "financialized" growth strategies in housing finance—such as fiscal subsidies, off-budget government guarantees, and monetary stimulus—to stimulate housing credit, wealth, and consumption. In contrast, German politicians adopted conservative housing finance structures and structural reforms that scaled down already moderate public support for mortgage debt, such as tax subsidies for homeowners, with the goals of balancing budgets, reviving competitiveness, and reducing market distortions that channel investments away from production.

Growth strategies in housing finance have implications for how to think about inequality and the role of the state in advanced economies. First, while the literature in comparative political economy strongly emphasizes inequalities in wages and employment, such as labor market dualization, the focus on housing finance shifts our attention to equally important forms of inequality based on housing wealth and affordability. The second implication concerns the role of the state in capitalist diversity. Focusing on housing finance reveals that governments are often active drivers of growth in what they deem key sectors of their economies, an idea captured by the notion of growth strategy in this volume.

[1] On the politics of housing finance and the privatization of welfare in Eastern Europe, see Bohle (2014).

Finally, growth strategies are not preordained. Lawmakers can adopt policies that create frictions with growth regimes for ideological reasons or produce policy overshoot with unwanted economic outcomes.

2. Housing Finance and the Welfare State

What is the link between housing finance and the welfare state? Housing finance markets provide households access to mortgage debt, which enables them to accumulate private wealth in the form of homeownership. This allows households to save money they would otherwise spend on rent, sell their homes to cash in for their retirement, or pass property on to future generations—a "piggy bank" to hedge against risk: inflation, unemployment, or sickness (Crouch 2009; Ansell 2014). Households may also borrow money against their homes to pay for health care or their children's education. These privatized welfare functions are all the more important in an age of welfare retrenchment, when asset-based forms of social insurance have gained prominence (Mertens 2017). For these and other reasons, policies that subsidize mortgage debt are part of the so-called privatized welfare state, in which private markets help deliver social welfare with government support (Hacker 2002; Howard 1997). However, these policies also incentivize households to take on mortgage debt, which exposes them to financial risk, including bankruptcy, eviction, and foreclosure (Desmond 2016; Mian and Sufi 2014). In difficult times, homeowners cannot easily liquidate their housing assets—unlike selling stocks—and may be forced to sell their homes well below what they had paid for or pay underwater mortgages worth more than their homes.

Prior to the financial crisis of 2008–9, housing was not a priority in political science and welfare state research. Scholarship long prioritized other areas of social policy, such as pensions, employment, health care, or education. To the extent that scholars did focus on housing, they often analyzed public housing as a particularly vulnerable element of the welfare state, given the politically weak constituencies that benefit from it (Pierson 1994). One exception is the scholarship on the trade-off between homeownership and the welfare state. Figure 10.1 shows the variation in homeownership rates across a number of advanced economies, with the lowest rates found in Germany and Austria, the highest rates in Southern Europe (e.g., Italy and Spain), and in-between the Anglo-Saxon and Nordic countries. In a seminal study, Kemeny (1981) argued that high rates of homeownership translate into voter preferences for welfare state retrenchment, owing to the burden of ownership costs—i.e., mortgage interest and taxes—which would prevent voters from favoring higher taxes and redistribution. Along those lines, Castles (1998) suggested that high rates of homeownership would result in low voter favorability of generous public pensions, as the imputed income derived

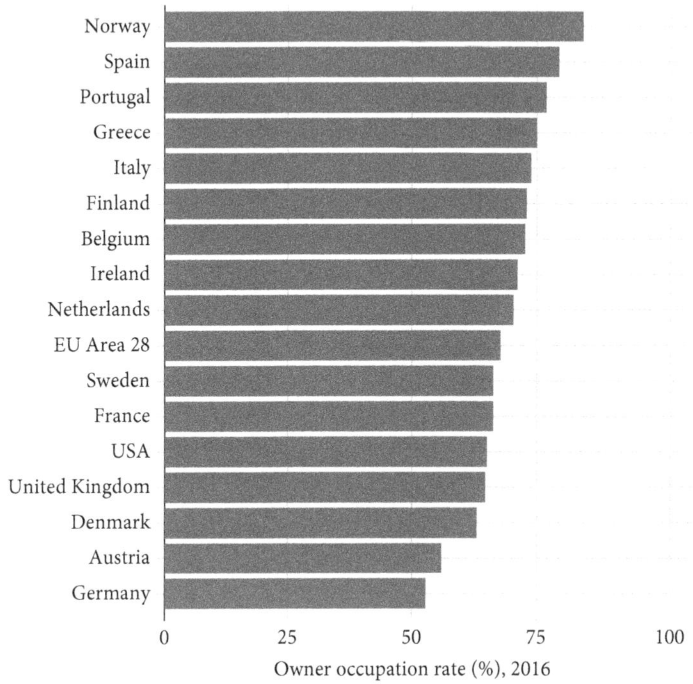

Figure 10.1 Homeownership rates in selected OECD countries in 2016

Note: Homeownership rates defined as distribution of population by tenure status. For the United States, it is the share of households living in owner-occupied homes.

Sources: EMF (2019); US Census Bureau. https://www.census.gov/housing/hvs/files/currenthvspress.pdf (last accessed January 24, 2020).

from homeownership can substitute for pensions.[2] These macro-level relationships between welfare states and housing are instructive, but we still know little about the precise political and historical forces driving these developments.

More recently, scholars advanced upon these insights and diagnosed trade-offs—as well as complementarities—between household debt and the welfare state. Figure 10.2 shows that high levels of mortgage debt, the largest component of household debt, can be found in Denmark, the Netherlands, and the United States, whereas debt levels are much lower in Austria and Germany.[3] Scholars in this camp suggest that, in an era of economic risk and retrenchment, households have taken on increasing levels of private debt, so as to obtain social insurance in private marketplaces (Conley and Gifford 2006; Crouch 2009; Rajan 2010;

[2] Van Gunten and Kohl (2020) updated and replicated these early studies, finding that these trade-offs were indeed present until the 1980s, but seemingly disappeared thereafter.

[3] Kohl (2018a) shows that higher levels of mortgage debt do not necessarily translate into higher rates of homeownership, speculating that low-income households and minorities do not enjoy equal access to credit markets.

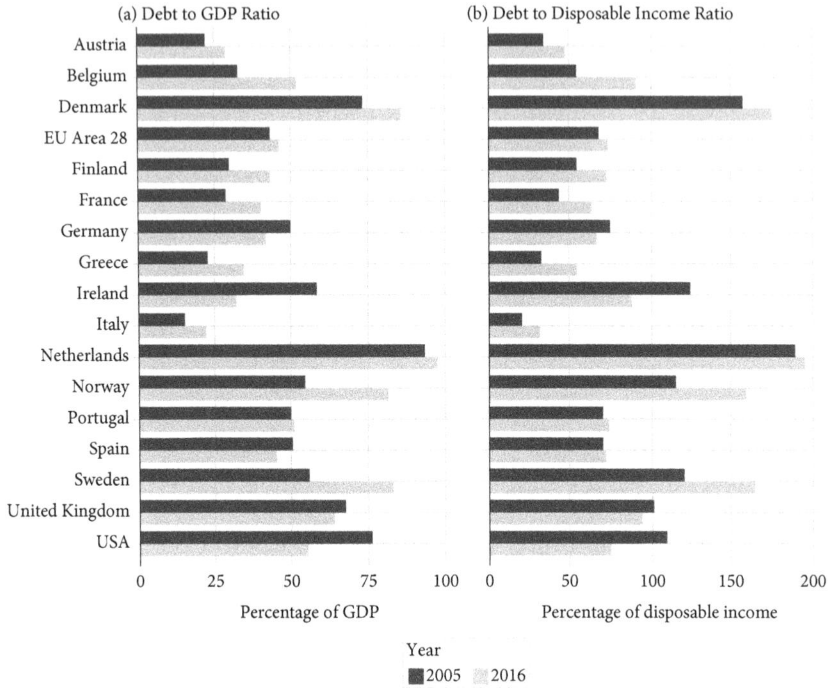

Figure 10.2 Mortgage debt in selected OECD countries in 2005 and 2016
Source: EMF (2017, 2019).

Schelkle 2012; Schwartz 2012; Trumbull 2014; Wiedemann forthcoming). Ahlquist and Ansell (2017) argue that this is especially the case in countries with high levels of inequality, which would induce households to increase private debt in order to maintain relative consumption. The Nordic countries, however, present a puzzle in that they have relatively low inequality *and* high mortgage debt (Anderson and Kurzer 2020). Here, Tranøy et al. (2020) suggest that precisely because households can rely on a well-developed social safety net, they are more willing to take on private debt (also see Van Gunten and Kohl 2020). In other words, household debt and strong welfare states might be more complementary than often assumed. Finally, Ansell (2014) shows that house prices affect voter preferences for welfare retrenchment. When voters experience house price appreciations, they are less likely to support redistribution, because they earn imputed income from their homes that can substitute for public social insurance. More generally, this line of scholarship focuses on a long-neglected and fundamental aspect of political economy—how housing and mortgage debt factor into the study of the welfare state, as both dependent and independent variables.

Scholars have also started to identify housing finance as an integral element of the public–private welfare state (Thurston 2018). This body of work demonstrates how certain social policies, such as tax breaks for homeowners, often grow undetected as part of the "hidden" welfare state and mostly benefit middle- and upper-income households (Howard 1997). Yet, others have argued that these policies are more visible than often assumed. Thurston's work convincingly shows that discriminatory US housing credit policies created political conflicts, as they disadvantaged racial minorities and women, who then successfully mobilized to expand the boundaries of these policies and the American public–private welfare state (Thurston 2018; Freund 2007). Some authors have also focused on how public polices mesh with private markets in the housing area (Fligstein and Goldstein 2012; Quinn 2019; Schwartz 2020). In the United States, housing finance policies are not merely subsidies; indeed, they constitute the very nature of US housing capitalism. Studying specific public policies in the housing area—and the political conflicts surrounding them—is a major contribution to our understanding of the public–private welfare state in the United States and beyond.

In sum, these authors successfully call our attention to studying the political causes and consequences of housing markets with respect to the welfare state. Yet, scholarship on the topic tends to overlook both the growth regime dimension within which these developments are taking place as well as the *politics* of credit policy in general and mortgage debt policy in particular.

3. Linking Growth and Welfare: Housing Finance Policy as Growth Strategies

Housing finance markets are important economic sectors in all growth regimes, given the large size of these asset markets as well as their social functions. The financial crisis of 2008–9 painfully demonstrated both points, as the collapsing US housing market almost brought the world economy to a standstill and wiped out the housing wealth of millions of households (McCarty, Poole, and Rosenthal 2013; Mian and Sufi 2014; Schwartz 2009). The reason why housing markets could do so much damage is that they are deeply embedded in domestic and global markets. Domestically, they are linked to important sectors, such as construction, banking, real estate, and retail. Globally, housing is one of the largest asset classes for investors, shaping global capital flows through markets for housing bonds, such as mortgage-backed securities or covered bonds (Ansell et al. 2018; Fuller 2019; Schwartz 2009). However, the extent to which housing is a key *engine* of economic growth differs in demand-led and export-oriented growth regimes, and policy-makers have therefore differed greatly in their desire to stimulate housing markets as growth strategies.

The comparative capitalism literature rarely explores the interlinkages between housing finance and the larger economy. As a result, prominent approaches, such as the varieties of capitalism (Hall and Soskice 2001), do not neatly map onto the world of housing finance. Startlingly, the United States, a quintessential liberal market economy, offers some of the most extensive public support for housing finance among advanced economies, whereas Germany, a coordinated market economy, has supported these markets much less (Reisenbichler 2020a). The work on the varieties of residential capitalism by Schwartz and Seabrooke (2008) provides a pioneering attempt at identifying the complementarities between housing and larger economic models, focusing on how corporatist structures, mortgage debt, and homeownership rates interact.[4] They group together liberal (high homeownership and mortgage debt), corporatist (low homeownership and high mortgage debt), familial (high homeownership and low mortgage debt), and statist (low homeownership and low mortgage debt) housing systems. While illuminating, this line of scholarship does not take into account the *politics* of housing finance policy that might explain this variation, including party and interest group politics or the growth regimes in which housing markets are embedded.[5]

This chapter concurs with the idea of complementarities between housing and the larger economy, but proposes a different way, in line with this volume's theoretical lens on growth regimes (see Chapter 1 in this volume). The central argument is that there is variation in the ways in which housing markets are embedded in growth regimes, and that this variation has political consequences for adopting housing finance policies as growth strategies[6]—that is, fiscal, monetary, and regulatory policy. While housing finance markets are often transmission belts for growth in credit-led, demand-driven growth regimes, they tend to be less central to export-oriented regimes with institutions that restrain consumption, credit, and wages. As a result, countries relying on credit and consumption have often adopted "financialized" housing policies to stimulate domestic demand, whereas countries based on manufacturing and price-sensitive exports have adopted solutions to restrain housing demand. As shown in Chapter 1, as well as in those by Thelen and Wren in this volume, the export-oriented Nordic economies specialized in price-insensitive high-tech exports and services might be characterized as intermediate cases, because financialized housing markets seem to neither reinforce nor contradict the Nordic growth regimes. In sum, the positioning of the housing sector within growth regimes matters for adopting growth strategies in the housing area.

In demand- and credit-led economies, such as the United States and the United Kingdom, housing markets are key engines for economic growth, as they link together households, financial markets, and domestic demand (Schwartz 2009,

[4] For a historical account of how these varieties developed, see Blackwell and Kohl (2018).

[5] On the connection between housing finance and party politics based on party manifesto data, see Kohl (2018b).

[6] For an extended version of this argument, see Reisenbichler (2020a).

2020; Fuller 2019; Hay 2009, 2013; Wood 2018; Oren and Blyth 2019). Owing to at least two channels, housing markets can be transmission belts for generating household consumption (Fuller 2019: ch. 3; Reisenbichler 2020b; Voigtländer 2014). First, the wealth channel posits that increasing house prices and wealth makes households feel richer, increasing their propensity to borrow and consume, such as through home equity withdrawal. Second, the credit channel suggests that rising house prices ease the credit constraints of households, where increasing housing wealth and collateral then drives households to borrow money against their homes to pay for health care and consumer goods or to start small businesses. As the housing sector is interest-rate sensitive—i.e., lowering mortgage rates tends to stimulate housing demand, while increasing rates does the opposite—policy-makers have incentives to lower the cost of mortgage debt, so as to unleash cascade effects of credit and consumption, particularly in contexts of well-developed, liquid housing finance regimes with liberal lending terms, low transaction costs, and various mortgage products (Wiedemann forthcoming; Schwartz and Seabrooke 2008).

To fuel these channels, lawmakers can deploy "financialized" housing policies as growth strategies.[7] The goal of these policies is to lower the cost of mortgage debt in order to stimulate housing demand, mortgage lending, and consumption. First, fiscal policy, such as mortgage tax breaks, lowers the cost of mortgage debt and consequently tends to stimulate housing demand, credit, prices, and consumption in the wider economy (Howard 1997; Schelkle 2012). Second, off-budget policies, such as public underwriting of private debt in the primary and secondary mortgage markets, reduce the risk for private lenders and the cost for borrowers, which then also stimulate mortgage lending, house prices, and domestic consumption (Thurston 2018; Quinn 2019). Finally, US central bankers long considered the housing market an important transmission channel for monetary policy. In its most basic version, the monetary transmission mechanism means that reducing interest rates lowers the cost of mortgages, which results in higher housing demand and house prices, stimulates bank lending, and generates household consumption. Central bankers can also achieve lower mortgage rates by stimulating housing directly through the purchase of mortgage debt and bonds in the open market (Reisenbichler 2020b). All these growth strategies are "privatized" welfare policies, as policy-makers subsidize and stimulate asset and housing markets as a form of private social insurance (Hacker 2002; Crouch 2009; Thurston 2018).

In export-oriented economies based on high-quality, price-sensitive manufacturing, such as Germany, housing is rarely an engine of growth. According to Baccaro and Pontusson (2016: 189–90, and in this volume), German manufacturing exports

[7] Schelkle (2012) calls such policies "market-creating," while Fuller (2015) characterizes them as "credit-encouraging."

are more price-sensitive than exports based on ICT, high-tech products, or services found in the Nordic countries. As a result, the German export-oriented regime prioritizes price stability and restraint in consumption, wages, and credit. These macroeconomic priorities ensure export and cost competitiveness through often-undervalued real exchange rates (Mertens 2015; Höpner 2019). Dynamic housing markets can create frictions with these priorities, as booming housing markets tend to channel investments away from the productive sector and stimulate unwanted domestic demand hurting export competiveness. As Muellbauer (1992: 547–8) notes, "increased housing demand has inflationary consequences," which directly contradicts the German growth regime's mantra of competitive disinflation (Höpner 2019).

Stimulating or financializing housing is therefore rarely a growth strategy in manufacturing-based growth regimes. Instead, the growth strategy is to promote policies that restrain housing markets and domestic demand. First, politicians have an incentive to adopt and retain restrictive mortgage finance systems (e.g., with high down payments) without public underwriting of mortgage debt in the primary and secondary market. This restrictive strategy induces households to save for down payments in a deposit-based mortgage system, coupled with a tightly regulated housing bond market, and discourages the withdrawal of home equity to finance household consumption (Voigtländer 2009; Mertens 2015). Restrictive mortgage systems then inhibit the wealth and credit channels, owing to high down payments and transactions costs, and the absence of equity release schemes (Voigtländer 2014). Second, fiscal subsidies on mortgage debt not only divert investments away from the productive sector but also tend to increase public deficits associated with current account deficits detrimental to exports (Manger and Sattler 2020). Third, German central bankers do not view housing as a core sector to transmit monetary policy, given that lowering interest rates in Germany's restrictive credit regimes does not fuel the wealth and credit channels to the same degree as in the permissive US credit regime (Reisenbichler 2020b). Instead, the uncompromising monetary priority is price and currency stability as well as market discipline to secure export competitiveness. The focus on price stability is reinforced by strong collective bargaining systems that produce wage restraint and thus suppress mortgage demand (Johnston and Regan 2017; Hall and Franzese 1998). Finally, large-scale social housing policies can support these regimes, as they tend to keep down housing costs, ensure adequate housing *supply*, and avoid wage-cost spirals.

Export-oriented economies specialized in less price-sensitive high-technology manufacturing and dynamic services, such as the Nordics (Baccaro and Pontusson 2016: 189–90), might be classified as intermediate cases and merit further investigation. While housing is not the core engine of growth in these economies, dynamic housing markets seem to neither reinforce nor contradict these growth regimes. They have instead shown a relatively high tolerance for expanding domestic demand, potentially owing to the nature of high-technology competition rooted in investment and innovation rather than cost competitiveness and the "balanced" nature of their growth model (Ornston 2018; Baccaro and Pontusson 2016). As a result, policy-makers can adopt "financialized" housing policies that produce sharp increases in house prices and mortgage debt. As Wood (2019: 834) argues in the case of Denmark, the liberalization of housing finance functioned as an expansionary equivalent to the "public Keynesian-style stimulus packages" of earlier decades and as a form of "privatized/house-price Keynesianism." Similarly, Anderson and Kurzer (2020) find that Denmark and Sweden (as well as the Netherlands) adopted policies to stimulate mortgage credit, so as to move away from publicly financed social housing and boost middle-class wealth. These developments tie in with what Ornston (2018) describes as a larger structural economic shift from exporting natural resources and low- and medium-tech manufacturing toward innovative high-tech industries and sophisticated services. Liberalizing financial markets facilitated this shift and accelerated "the redistribution of resources to new, growth-oriented enterprises" (Ornston 2018: 59; see also Chapter 1% by Hassel and Palier in this volume). In the absence of a German-style tradeoff between growing exports or domestic consumption (Baccaro and Pontusson 2016: 189), Nordic policy-makers might face fewer macroeconomic constraints when "financializing" housing markets and be willing to accept rising house prices, mortgage debt, and consumption (Wood 2019).

Finally, there is an important transnational dimension to housing finance markets and growth regimes. As export-oriented regimes tend to produce current account surpluses and demand-led regimes deficits, the excess savings of surplus countries are often channeled into the housing markets of deficit countries, such as through housing bond markets (i.e., for mortgage-backed securities in the United States or covered bonds in Europe) (Fuller, 2019; Ansell et al. 2018; Schwartz 2009). Ansell et al. (2018) show that deficit countries attract capital inflows from abroad, which tends to stimulate lending, domestic demand, and house prices in those countries and, in turn, decrease voter preferences for the welfare state. In the United States, in particular, the government-sponsored housing bond market attracted sizable capital inflows from abroad, because investments in US mortgage-backed securities were deemed safe and risk-free investments guaranteed by the US government. In sum, domestic housing finance systems are deeply integrated in global and regional markets, such as the European Union, and are thus influencing global capital flows.

4. Growth Strategies and Housing Finance in the United States and Germany

As advanced economies have transitioned to the knowledge economy since the late 1970s, moving away from Keynesian demand management and wage-led

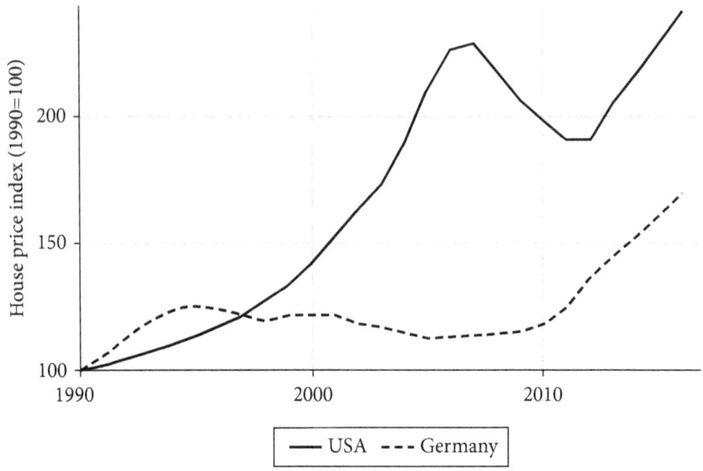

Figure 10.3 House prices in the United States and Germany
Source: Jordà, Schularick, and Taylor (2017).

growth, the United States and Germany readjusted their growth strategies to compensate for the drop in aggregate demand. While the United States pursued a strategy of financialization to support domestic demand, Germany doubled down on export-led growth based on cost competitiveness and high-quality manufacturing. These different trajectories are particularly discernible in housing finance. In the United States, policy-makers built an extensive infrastructure of policy support for housing finance, including generous tax breaks, government guarantees, and monetary stimulus, which some have labeled a strategy of "privatized" Keynesianism" (Crouch 2009) or "mortgage Keynesianism" (Prasad 2012). Germany avoided a path of housing financialization and instead retained conservative housing finance structures, while at the same time sacrificing moderate support for housing finance, such as tax breaks for homeowners, in the name of structural reform and fiscal consolidation.

Concomitantly, as Figure 10.3 shows, the United States not only experienced significant house price fluctuations tied to the business cycle, but also nominal house prices more than doubled from 1990 until the late 2010s. In Germany, house prices remained fairly stable until the late 2000s, but started rising in the 2010s as a result of ultra-low interest rates, a strong economy, supply restrictions, and demographic developments.

4.1 United States: Financializing Housing Markets

Responding to the tumultuous economic realities of the 1970s and 1980s, policymakers financialized the US economy to generate credit, consumption, and growth (Krippner 2011), including the country's housing market. As Jordà, Schularick, and Taylor (2016: 110) observe, "the growth of finance has been closely linked to an explosion of mortgage lending to households in the last quarter of the twentieth century." They find that mortgage lending as a share of total bank lending increased from 55% in 1970 to 70% in 2007 (p. 117), while mortgage debt as a percentage of GDP rose from 28% in 1970 to over 70% in 2004 (Green and Wachter 2007). Beneath these developments lurk important short-term and long-term growth strategies, such as fiscal policy (i.e., taxation), off-budget policy (i.e., underwriting mortgage debt), and monetary policy (i.e., quantitative easing), all of which tend to lower the cost mortgage debt, stimulate housing demand, credit, and prices, and generate consumption. These strategies provided a powerful cocktail of promoting consumption, growth, and privatized welfare, but they also contributed to instability during the financial crisis of 2008–9.

One important aspect of the financializing growth strategy was the creation and rise of mortgage securitization since the 1970s, often referred to as "housing finance revolution" (Green and Wachter 2007). Prior to securitization, the US housing finance system was based on deposits collected by the savings and loans (S+L) industry. When interest rates rose in the late 1960s, and investors and savers realized they could make more money elsewhere, the S+Ls started hurting, which resulted in illiquid mortgage markets.[8] Politicians of both parties then adopted a strategy of mortgage securitization in the late 1960s, which slowly shifted housing funding from the S+Ls to the capital market. In a series of reforms, successive administrations expanded the role of the government-sponsored enterprises (GSEs), Fannie Mae and Freddie Mac, in the secondary mortgage market (Fligstein and Goldstein 2012; Quinn 2019).[9] These privately operated, government-backed agencies would subsequently buy mortgages, pool them together into mortgage-backed securities, and sell them on to investors. Importantly, these institutions guaranteed investors the principal and interest payments of the underlying mortgages, which meant that the US government bore the risk of large-scale mortgage defaults. Through this off-budget government guarantee that reduced private market risk, the US government sought to generate new, stable, and liquid sources of mortgage finance that would lower the cost of mortgage debt, stimulate bank lending and consumption, and foster economic growth (Green and Wachter 2007). As the S+Ls did not recover from their industry-wide crisis in the late 1980s, the GSEs became the largest sources of

[8] As the S+Ls were limited in how much interest they could pay on deposits, and what investments they could undertake to compensate for dwindling deposits, which put them under pressure.

[9] Fannie had already existed as a government agency since the Great Depression, but was "privatized" in 1968, while retaining the full backing of the US government. Freddie, another for-profit and public–private enterprise, was created to compete with Fannie in 1970. Ginnie Mae was created as a fully public agency in 1968, offering insurance on mortgage-backed securities consisting of loans backed by the federal government.

mortgage funding, providing roughly 42% of all mortgage funding by the late 1990s (Fed 2019).[10] Given the publicly backed status of Fannie and Freddie, they crowded out private market competition within the securitization market, having originated more than 80% of mortgage-backed securities by the 1990s (HFPC 2019). The housing finance revolution was a key element of the financializing growth strategy.

Another housing-based growth strategy is the longstanding tax support for homeownership. Taxpayers had been able to deduct interest on consumer loans, including on mortgage interest, since the adoption of the US federal income tax in 1913. But these tax breaks were initially marginal given that most people did not pay income taxes before World War II (Howard 1997). The housing tax breaks started to increase in size and importance since the 1950s, when the tax base broadened and homeownership expanded. Since then, US governments offered a long list of tax advantages to homeowners—the mortgage interest deduction, property tax deduction, capital gains exclusion, and the foregone tax of imputed rent (i.e., a tax on the rental income one generates by living in one's own home). Yet it was not until the 1970s that tax expenditure on owner-occupied housing increased dramatically as a result of growing mortgage debt and homeownership. For instance, the mortgage interest deduction alone grew to $86 billion by 2009.[11] As tax breaks for homeowners have the effect of lowering the cost of mortgage debt, they blended in seamlessly with mortgage securitization in stimulating the American growth regime.

Despite the efforts of economists, bureaucrats, and rental housing advocates to eliminate the preferential tax treatment of homeowners, the subsidies survived major tax reforms, including the Tax Reform Act of 1986 and the Tax Cuts and Jobs Act of 2017. In the heated discussions leading up to the 1986 reform, the Reagan administration effectively declared the housing tax breaks off limits, considering them as tools to stimulate housing credit, wealth, and consumption in times of illiquid mortgage markets and high interest rates (Howard 1997). For the next thirty years, particularly the mortgage interest deduction had become a third-rail issue in US politics. However, Trump's 2017 tax reform included a temporary provision (until 2025) that capped the interest deduction for mortgages at $750,000 worth of principal (down from one million), a move considered to be an attack on coastal blue states with high house prices.[12] Even so, Slemrod (2018: 86) points out that the 2017 tax reform "did not directly address . . . the substantial income tax preference for owner-occupied housing arising from the

[10] In 1970, the S+Ls held a market share of 41% of total outstanding mortgage debt, which gradually decreased to 4% in 2010 (Fed 2019).

[11] Source: Joint Committee on Taxation, Congress of the United States. https://www.jct.gov/publications.html?func=startdown&id=3642 (accessed January 24, 2020).

[12] The tax reform increased the standard deduction, which encourages some homeowners to use the standard deduction over itemizing deductions, and capped the property tax deduction at $10,000.

complete exemption of the return (implicit rent) the asset provides." Homeowner tax breaks remain some of the most important—and regressive—subsidies in the income tax code. Together, they amounted to $83 billion in 2019.[13]

Until the early 2000s, the housing-based growth strategy seemed to work—but it eventually contributed to the financial crisis of 2008–9. The decade before the financial crisis saw unprecedented growth in house prices (see Figure 10.3), mortgage debt (see Figure 10.2), and mortgage securitization. As Schwartz (2009: xv) notes, "the US housing finance system gave the US economy above-average employment and GDP growth." Since the 1980s, successive administrations spurred these developments by introducing subprime mortgages to increase mortgage liquidity and extend mortgage credit to previously underserved parts of the population, such as low-income households and racial minorities (McCarty, Poole, and Rosenthal 2013). They also started relaxing the underwriting standards that defined what mortgages are eligible for Fannie and Freddie securitization. Armed with purportedly sophisticated financial instruments to manage risk, private banks viewed the growing subprime market as an investment opportunity, as the GSEs were limited to securitizing higher-quality mortgages (Goldstein and Fligstein 2012). Private banks increased their share of the securitization market to 20% in 2006 (HFPC 2019), mostly securitizing subprime mortgages, which resulted in excessive risk-taking, aggressive profit-seeking, and a full-blown house price bubble that led to the financial crisis of 2008–9 (Nelson and Katzenstein 2014).

Policy-makers then targeted the housing market to recover and revive the US economy since the Great Recession of 2008-9. When the housing bubble burst in 2008 and millions of homeowners started defaulting on their mortgages, Fannie and Freddie were exposed to financial losses and faced bankruptcy. Without hesitation, the Bush administration seized control of the two "too-big-to-fail" mortgage giants to protect the housing-based growth strategy, with the goals of retaining liquidity, restoring financial stability, and halting falling consumption (Thompson 2012; Reisenbichler 2020a). These actions also underline Fannie and Freddie's systemic importance for generating economic growth and privatized welfare. Economically, the two institutions are at the center of country's housing finance market deeply interconnected with other industries as well as investors at home and abroad. Socially, it is their mission to provide affordable mortgages to households as part of the privatized welfare state. By bailing out Fannie and Freddie, the US government quasi-nationalized the securitization market, where the two mortgage giants currently occupy a duopoly with virtually no private competition, underwriting $6.8 trillion in mortgage debt or 60% of the country's mortgage market in 2019 (HFPC 2019).

[13] Source: Joint Committee on Taxation. https://www.jct.gov/publications.html?func=startdown&id=5238 (accessed January 24, 2020).

More than ten years after the crisis, Fannie and Freddie have remained nationalized without being subject to comprehensive housing finance reform—a development President Obama's chief economist called the "key unfinished piece of business from the financial crisis" (Furman and Stock 2014). In general, Republicans and Democrats agree that the quasi-nationalization of Fannie and Freddie is undesirable, given that taxpayers are too exposed to the credit risk of mortgage securitization (Reisenbichler 2020a). Yet, when Congress, and the Obama and Trump administrations, discussed housing finance reform, they disagreed on the precise role of the US government in securitization. Reducing the role of the government, such as full-on privatization, would likely increase mortgage rates and could even threaten the liquidity of the beloved thirty-year, fixed-term mortgage, as private lenders would have to absorb credit risk on their own. This would have potentially detrimental effects on housing and consumption. These insights are not lost on politicians. There is a strong—and increasingly rare—bipartisan consensus on securing a strong role for the US government to bear *some* credit risk in mortgage securitization to secure low-cost mortgages. In 2019 and 2020, the Trump administration floated proposals to recapitalize and release Fannie and Freddie from government control, but they have not materialized.

Moreover, the Bush and Obama administrations adopted short-term fiscal and off-budget measures to revive housing and consumption during and after the crisis.[14] From 2007 to 2016, the Mortgage Forgiveness Debt Relief Act allowed homeowners to exempt from taxes income generated through debt forgiveness (or cancelled debt after foreclosure).[15] In 2009, the Obama administration launched the Making Home Affordable Program with $45.6 billion, which included two core components that concluded between 2017 and 2018: the Home Affordable Modification Program (HAMP) that restructured 1.7 million home loans (i.e., reducing interest and principal payments) and the Home Affordable Refinance Program (HARP) that allowed 3.5 million underwater homeowners to refinance mortgages at lower rates.[16] The rationale was that, if homeowners receive debt

[14] In 2012, the US government also negotiated $25 billion in settlements with five major banks as a consequence of their wrongdoing (i.e., the National Mortgage Settlement). These funds were used for forgiving homeowner debt and restructuring loans.

[15] The total cost of the tax break was roughly $1.4 billion from 2008 to 2017. Source: Joint Committee on Taxation. https://www.jct.gov/publications.html?func=startdown&id=1366 (accessed January 24, 2020).

[16] HAMP was financed by the Troubled Asset Relief Program (TARP), which was created by the Bush administration in 2008. The Making Home Affordable program also included the Home Affordable Foreclosure Alternative (HAFA) program, which facilitated the short sales or deeds-in-lieu of foreclosure for banks and troubled homeowners. Sources: US Treasury, Making Home Affordable Program Performance Reports. https://www.treasury.gov/initiatives/financial-stability/reports/Pages/Making-Home-Affordable-Program-Performance-Report.aspx (accessed January 24, 2020); Federal Housing Finance Agency, Refinance Reports. https://www.fhfa.gov/AboutUs/Reports/ReportDocuments/Refi_1Q2019.pdf (accessed January 24, 2020); US Treasury. https://www.treasury.gov/initiatives/financial-stability/TARP-Programs/housing/mha/Pages/default.aspx (accessed January 24, 2020).

forgiveness and refinancing help, this would prevent foreclosure and falling house prices, and instead stimulate aggregate demand. Although criticized for their miniscule size and messy rollout (Mian and Sufi 2014), these short-term measures offer additional evidence that policy-makers tried to stabilize house prices as well as reactivate credit lending and consumer spending.

Finally, it was not only elected officials targeting housing to recover growth. The Federal Reserve adopted large-scale monetary support for housing as part of its quantitative easing (QE) programs (Reisenbichler 2020b). From 2008 until 2018, the Fed has bought and held roughly $1.7 *trillion* in mortgage debt—that is, mortgage-backed securities issued or securitized by the GSEs—constituting roughly 40% of the Fed's balance sheet expansion since 2008. The goals of these actions were twofold: to help fix housing finance and stimulate growth through housing. The logic was to bring down the yields of mortgage bonds and raise asset prices. In less technical terms, the Fed sought to reduce mortgage rates, increase housing demand, credit, and prices, which would then stimulate consumption and growth.[17] In sum, the Fed identified housing as a key sector able to transmit monetary policy and stimulate growth.

Importantly, one third of the US population living in rental housing has not received much policy support as part of growth or welfare strategies. Many renters have struggled since the crisis, facing the prospects of eviction or increasingly unaffordable rental markets (Desmond 2016). Their struggles, however, have not translated into significant government action. The Housing and Economic Recovery Act of 2008 set up a National Housing Trust Fund to support affordable rental housing, especially for very low-income households, but the Fund has thus far only supported low income projects in the amounts of $174 million in 2016, $219 million in 2017, and $267 million in 2018.[18] It is also true that some states, such as California, recently legislated state-wide rent controls to mitigate growing affordability crises. While Democratic presidential nominee Joe Biden included affordable rental housing in his policy platform, the televised Democratic debates and media coverage in general rarely focused on the issue (Yentel 2019). Affordable rental housing remains secondary to homeownership, which is partly due to the centrality of homeownership finance for growth and welfare.

[17] This works through the portfolio rebalancing and signaling channels. The former means that housing bond purchases signal the commitment of the central bank to mortgage markets, which reduces the risk and yields of housing bonds. The latter is the portfolio-rebalancing channel, which means that housing bond purchases reduce the supply and increase the demand of these bonds, raising their prices and lowering their yields.

[18] The Fund was supposed to be financed through Fannie and Freddie starting in 2008, but these institutions were quasi-nationalized in the same year. The Federal Housing Finance Agency (FHFA), the new regulator of Fannie and Freddie, then temporarily suspended the Fund until 2016, which is when the program commenced. Source: National Low Income Housing Coalition. https://nlihc.org/explore-issues/projects-campaigns/national-housing-trust-fund (accessed January 25, 2020).

4.2 Germany: Reforming Housing Finance

When the miracle years of economic growth and welfare state expansion came to an end, the German economy experienced slowly rising deficits and unemployment from the late 1970s until the late 1980s. It adapted to these new macroeconomic realities by building on its existing strength in export-led growth. In contrast to the United States, German policy-makers have not chosen a path of financializing the German housing market (Cooper and Anderson 2020).[19] Mortgage lending as a share of total bank lending increased from 42% in 1970 to 51% in 2007, while mortgage debt as a percentage of GDP grew to 51% in 2005 and then fell to 42% in 2016 (Jordà, Schularick and Taylor 2016: 117; EMF 2017, 2019). However, these numbers are considerably lower than in the United States. Public policies in the housing area—that is, social housing policies, conservative mortgage market policies, and strict monetary policy—greatly contributed to a more restrained housing market. In response to structural economic problems in the early 2000s, the German state even eliminated longstanding tax subsidies for homeowners, as these policies produced unwanted domestic demand and contributed to a growing public finance crisis.

Instead of embarking on a path of dynamic mortgage securitization as a growth strategy, Germany developed a conservative mortgage market as part of what Mertens (2015) calls an "export-savings-regime." The traditional post-war export-savings model was based on channeling household savings into the capital market, so as to provide sources of long-term financing for export industries and housing (Logemann 2012).[20] While German savings rates decreased over time (Mertens 2017), savings remain an integral part of the German political economy in that deposits are the largest source of mortgage finance in the country. Covered bonds (backed by mortgages) are another source of mortgage finance, but only constitute roughly 16% of overall mortgage funding, amounting to €233 billion in 2018 (EMF 2019).[21] When it comes to lending, German banks require high down payments, high underwriting standards, and low loan-to-value-ratios of 78% (EMF 2019). German banks also rarely offer home equity loans or other financial products associated with stimulating consumer spending, nor is there a strong market for subprime mortgages (Mertens 2015: ch. 5). In addition, the federal government does not provide large-scale public underwriting of mortgages or

[19] It should be noted that Mertens (2017) and Wijburg and Aalbers (2017) find that Germany has indeed seen *some* financialization in housing, but much less so than in the United States.

[20] This strategy was supported by the Bundesbank's focus on internal price stability and external currency undervaluation (Höpner 2019).

[21] Covered bonds pool together mortgages and other loans. They are more conservative than mortgage-backed securities, as they stay on banks' balance sheets and cover only up to 60% of home values to absorb losses and protect investors from declining property prices.

mortgage bonds.[22] As these housing finance institutions and policies tend to restrain credit, domestic demand, and consumption, they work well in combination with the German growth regime.

Historically, social housing programs have similarly shown complementarities with the export regime. Adopted to counter the severe post-war housing shortages of more than 4.5 million homes, they offered large-scale support for the private housing market (i.e., subsidized loans or interest-rate subsidies on loans) to create affordable rental *and* owner-occupied housing for broad segments of the population, including the middle class (Voigtländer 2009: 357). These policies produced temporary synergies with the early export-led growth regime by increasing the *supply* of housing, which helped keep down house prices and living costs and avoid a wage-cost spiral. Indeed, housing shortages produced market rents that were well beyond the paying-power of many households in the early post-war years. At that time, the vast majority of new housing units was subsidized by social housing programs; yet, the share of subsidized units declined steadily to about one third of total new units once the housing crisis was over and the private capital market recovered. By 1970, the social housing programs had supported an astonishing number of 5.8 million new homes out of 11.4 million total new homes.[23] As builders received subsidies, they had to ensure long-term, below-market rents for these units, which contributed to securing price stability in property markets.

In the post-Keynesian era of welfare state retrenchment since the late 1970s, social housing programs were considered obsolete. Then Christian Democratic housing minister Oscar Schneider proclaimed that the country's rental housing market was in "excellent" condition, meaning that large parts of the population had access to affordable housing without major shortages (Egner 2014: 16). As a result, the federal government no longer viewed increasing the rental supply as a policy priority and scaled down social housing. Reunification led to a short-lived revival of social housing in the early 1990s, so as to modernize housing in the East and stimulate housing to cope with newcomers in the West. Yet, these and other subsidies contributed to an overheated housing market and construction sector in the East, producing housing vacancies of about one million units and ensuing demolitions funded by the federal government (Wijburg and Aalbers 2017; Michelsen and Weiß 2010). While social housing became a shadow of its former self by the late 1990s and early 2000s, these programs long reinforced the German growth regime, having subsidized 9 out of 24 million new homes between 1950

[22] The Kreditanstalt für Wiederaufbau (KfW), a government-owned development bank, extends small-scale subsidized loans to homeowners. Some *Länder* offer small-scale programs for homeowners, including subsidized loans.

[23] All social housing statistics are based on own calculations from *Bundesbaublatt* since 1952.

and 2000. In sum, social housing contributed to keeping rental and property market prices stable and addressing supply shortages.

Yet, not all housing policies produced complementarities with the German growth regime, such as generous tax support for homeowners. In the early post-war years, the German tax code subsidized the costs associated with owner-occupied housing through the *Eigenheimzulage* (i.e., homeownership tax allowance)[24] and savings contributions in building societies. While the former was adopted to encourage housing investment to overcome housing *supply* shortages, the latter was designed to rebuild the capital market by encouraging savings over consumption (Logemann 2012). By the 1970s, when housing and capital markets recovered, these tax breaks enjoyed little macroeconomic justification in times of sufficient housing supply. As a result, policy-makers scaled down tax subsidies for savings in building societies. Yet, the *Eigenheimzulage* grew into the country's largest tax subsidy, creating frictions with the growth regime by stimulating domestic demand, increasing fiscal deficits and public debt, and diverting investment away from the productive sector.

When Germany experienced structural economic problems and became the sick man of Europe in the late 1990s and early 2000s (Reisenbichler and Morgan 2012), policy-makers adopted structural reforms and austerity to revitalize export competitiveness, including the elimination of housing tax breaks (Reisenbichler 2020a). In addition to the Hartz labor and welfare reforms, they focused on the reform of subsidies (*Subventionsabbau*) and the tax system, so as to eliminate market distortions and reduce the deficit. As the single largest subsidy in the tax code, amounting to €11 billion in 2004, the popular *Eigenheimzulage* reflected the prevailing structural economic problems at the time.[25] The subsidy came under fire from the Social Democrats, who made its elimination a priority, as the subsidy strained the country's finances, channeled funds into unproductive areas of the economy, and mostly benefited rich over poor households, as well as richer Western states over poorer Eastern ones still reeling from a post-unification housing and construction boom and bust (Michelsen and Weiß 2010). In 2006, the Merkel grand coalition of Christian and Social Democrats eliminated the *Eigenheimzulage*. This was painful for the Christian Democrats, given their preference for conservative family life in single-family homes, a strong ownership ideology, and asset-based welfare priorities. Yet, the macroeconomic concerns of reducing public deficits and debt to reinvigorate the economy led the Christian Democrats to sacrifice homeownership support. In exchange for the tax subsidy, in 2008, the grand coalition adopted a subsidized homeownership pension savings

[24] The tax break was called "7b" from 1949 to 1986, "10e" from 1986 until 1996, and *Eigenheimzulage* from 1996 to 2006.

[25] Source: 20th Subsidy Report of the Federal Government. http://dip21.bundestag.de/dip21/btd/16/010/1601020.pdf (accessed January 24, 2020).

scheme (*Wohnriester*), in which savers could use subsidized pension savings for purchasing, constructing, or mortgage payments. This new policy is modest in size and constitutes a "nexus between debt-financed homeownership and private retirement provision" (Mertens 2017: 482). In sum, the frictions between homeowner tax subsidies and the growth regime made the homeownership subsidy vulnerable to reform.

In 2006, the grand coalition also eliminated federal social housing programs as part of its federalism reform to revive the economy (Reisenbichler 2016). The Merkel government agreed that country's complicated federalist setup needed overhaul, as it was holding back economic reforms. Social housing programs were an example par excellence of the complicated workings of federalism: concurrent jurisdiction, co-financing, and decisions at the state level that often did not match federal objectives. As housing markets were affordable and relatively well-functioning in the late 1990s and 2000s,[26] coupled with dim demographic projections, social housing programs were considered obsolete. The reform transferred the authority of social housing to the states and eliminated federal funding. Until 2019, the *Länder* received compensation (€518 million per year) for taking over social housing responsibilities, but the states could freely decide how to use these funds, including for the reduction of fiscal deficits.[27] In addition, as Wijburg and Aalbers (2017: 978) show, politicians sold off public housing associations to financial corporations, resulting in the privatization of 500,000 housing units between 1999 and 2006. Between 2002 and 2018, the social housing stock consequently halved from 2.5 to 1.2 million.[28]

One exception to these structural reforms and austerity measures was the reintroduction of a temporary and miniscule homeownership program between 2018 and 2020. After the German economy emerged as Europe's economic superstar from the Great Recession—with simultaneously rising property and rental prices in many metropolitan regions—the Merkel grand coalition adopted a temporary subsidy (*Baukindergeld*) limited to first-time buyers with children. According to the Bundesministerium des Innern, für Bau und Heimat/Federal Ministry of the Interior, Building and Community (2019), the ministry allocated a total of €9.9 billion for the temporary program from January 2018 until December 2020, a number much lower than the previous tax break (*Eigenheimzulage*).

[26] In 2003, only 32,000 units were subsidized through social housing.

[27] The federal government increased its social housing compensation payments to the federal states to €1 billion in 2016 and €1.5 billion from 2017 to 2019. From 2020 until 2024, the federal government allocated €1 billion each year to support the *Länder* for social housing initiatives. Source: Federal Ministry of the Interior, Building, and Community. https://www.bmi.bund.de/DE/themen/bauen-wohnen/stadt-wohnen/wohnraumfoerderung/soziale-wohnraumfoerderung/soziale-wohnraumfoerderung-node.html (accessed January 24, 2020).

[28] Federal Ministry of the Interior, Building, and Community. https://www.gruene-bundestag.de/fileadmin/media/gruenebundestag_de/themen_az/bauen/PDF/KA_Sozialwohnungen.pdf (accessed January 24, 2020).

However, the policy is hardly a growth strategy and better described as family and wealth policy to facilitate the longstanding Christian Democratic mainstay of homeownership.

In terms of monetary policy, the European Central Bank (ECB) has not stimulated the eurozone's housing market as a growth strategy since the Great Recession (Reisenbichler 2020b). While the ECB expanded its balance sheet to more than €4 trillion, its quantitative easing and bond-buying schemes have not targeted housing. The ECB's asset-buying scheme included housing-related covered bonds and asset-backed securities in the amount of only €290 billion by 2018 (i.e., amounting to only 6% of its balance sheet). The reason for the limited support of housing is that the eurozone comprises not only fragmented housing finance systems but also diverse national growth regimes—export-led in Northern Europe and consumption-led in Southern Europe. As a result, stimulating housing is not an overarching growth strategy in the eurozone. The German exchange-rate-sensitive growth regime is represented by the Bundesbank, which promoted a hawkish approach to quantitative easing to maintain market discipline, price stability, and financial stability. Relatedly, it sounded the alarm about an overheating property market in the country—property prices in the country (big cities) have increased 60% (100%) between 2010 and 2018—warning of asset price bubbles (Bundesbank 2018). German politicians on the left and right also criticized the ECB for ultra-low interest rates, which would squeeze the country's large savings constituency. German exporters similarly viewed loose monetary policy as a peril to currency stability and as market-distorting. When the ECB entered negative interest-rate territory in 2019, German tabloids portrayed Mario Draghi as Count Dracula ("Count Draghila"), sucking dry the savings accounts of Germans (Die Bild 2019). This reflects the larger frictions between ultra-loose monetary policy and the German export-savings model.

Since the financial crisis, housing affordability has become a major national debate again, underlining that rising rental and property prices are considered an economic problem (Cooper and Anderson 2020). Between 2010 and 2018, rental prices (of newly concluded rental contracts) have increased 37% in the country and up to 50% in big cities,[29] partly the result of the strong economy, demographic developments (e.g., net migration surpluses and population growth in many big cities), the status of German property as a safe asset, and insufficient housing supply and construction (Wijburg and Aalbers 2017). In 2015, the German government adopted a national, temporary "rental brake" (i.e., *Mietpreisbremse*), a measure that is supposed to control rent increases of new tenancies in expensive rental markets (i.e., the limit is 10% above the rental benchmark for a given area

[29] The rents of already existing tenancies increased by about 11%. Source: Bundesbank housing indices. https://www.bundesbank.de/resource/blob/615188/fd4c74c42ab45eaf1fb60a9b569b80c2/mL/indikatorensystem-zum-deutschen-wohnungsmarkt-data.pdf (accessed January 24, 2020).

and for a maximum of five years). Recent studies have found a moderate effect of the measure on limiting rent increases, but also that many landlords used loopholes to circumvent it (Michelsen and Mense 2018). As rental prices continue to increase in major cities, the city state of Berlin adopted a five-year-long rent freeze (i.e., *Mietendeckel*) in a political backlash against rising housing costs in early 2020, a measure currently reviewed by the Federal Constitutional Court. Some politicians on the left even supported campaigns to expropriate corporate landlords, such as Deutsche Wohnen and its 110,000 apartments in Berlin. Considering shortages of affordable housing a thing of the past was therefore premature. When eliminating federal social housing programs in 2006 – programs that previously contributed to price stability in the housing market – policymakers have been "overshooting" structural reforms and austerity.

Overall, German lawmakers rarely identify housing markets as vehicles for growth. To the contrary, when faced with structural economic problems, mortgage debt subsidies were sacrificed. Contrary to the United States, rising property prices—a source of stability in previous decades in the German context—are considered an economic problem and not part of solution for stimulating the economy.

5. Conclusion

Housing markets are integral components of advanced economies. Yet, their precise function for the welfare state and growth regimes varies across countries, which shapes the growth strategies available to policy-makers. While demand-led growth regimes are complementary to "financialized" housing policies that stimulate demand, credit, and growth, countries based on export-oriented manufacturing are complementary to conservative housing finance policies that limit housing and domestic demand. The former strategy is in line with promoting a privatized welfare state through access to credit, whereas the latter ties in with an approach limiting fiscal expenditure. Finally, in export-oriented economies specializing in high-tech manufacturing and dynamic services, "financialized" housing policies that boost private wealth and domestic consumption neither reinforce nor contradict these growth regimes. Empirically, this chapter has contrasted two out of the five possible growth strategies outlined in this volume—the financialized, domestic-demand strategy and the manufacturing-based, export-led growth strategy—by discussing housing finance developments in the United States and Germany.

The implications of growth strategies in housing finance are far-reaching, as they contribute to growing levels of wealth inequality in advanced economies. Particularly "financialized" housing policies favor those able and willing to climb the property ladder—by subsidizing mortgage debt that goes on to stimulate asset and house prices—but not those left behind in the increasingly unaffordable rental and property markets of metropolitan areas. As a result, these policies tend to reinforce housing wealth inequality, a dimension not often studied among comparative political economists who have emphasized inequalities in the labor market, such as dualization or wage inequalities (Palier and Thelen 2010). Yet, housing is an important driver of wealth inequality (Fuller et al. 2020; Fuller 2019) – particularly racial wealth inequality in the United States (Thurston 2018; Freund 2007)[30] – and a potential source of populism (Adler and Ansell 2020). It is therefore key to incorporate the politics of housing finance in studies of political economy.

Moreover, housing growth strategies are not preordained. One caveat is that policy-makers might very well adopt public policies that do *not* reinforce the growth regime. The German case, for instance, shows that the country had in place sizable tax subsidies for homeowners that stimulated private consumption and created frictions with the growth regime's imperative of restraining domestic demand and limiting fiscal deficits. Like other social policies, housing finance policies are multi-dimensional—spanning issues ranging from family values, redistribution, and wealth to urban development—such that elected officials might prioritize different dimensions across time and space. Another caveat is that, instead of producing efficient economic outcomes, growth strategies can lead to policy overshoot (Ornston 2018). Even if lawmakers identify growth strategies that are in line with the growth regime, they run the risk of overinvestment in and overreliance on certain sectors of the economy. The US housing finance market is an excellent example of overshoot, where politicians adopted generous fiscal, monetary, and off-budget subsidies that then partially fueled the housing bubble in the run up to the financial crash of 2008–9 (Calomiris and Haber 2014; McCarty, Poole, and Rosenthal 2013). Future research might profitably explore the degree to which the United States exhausted housing policies as an effective growth strategy in a post-crisis context, as households are facing the simultaneous developments of stagnating incomes and rising house prices, while lawmakers are facing the limits of how much more policy support they can offer.

Finally, the case of housing finance confirms that policy-makers in different growth regimes stimulate different sectors to generate growth. The growth regime perspective can explain why housing finance enjoys a privileged position in the demand-driven United States, a sector that received substantial government help as part of its "financialized" growth strategy. It can also explain why politicians

[30] In the United States, the homeownership gap between black and white households is currently at its highest rate in 50 years, as 71.9% of white households lived in owner-occupied homes but only 41.8% of black households in 2018. In addition to decades-long discrimination in federal housing policy and credit markets as well as lower household income, racial minorities were more likely to hold subprime mortgages and consequently experience financial hardship during and after the Great Recession. Source: Urban Institute. https://www.urban.org/urban-wire/breaking-down-black-white-homeownership-gap (accessed August 17, 2020).

rarely target housing finance to promote growth in export-oriented Germany. The state therefore becomes an active driver of growth in what political actors deem key sectors in advanced economies.

References

Adler, D. and Ansell, B. 2020. "Housing and Populism." *West European Politics* 43: 344–65.

Ahlquist, J. and Ansell, B. 2017. "Taking Credit: Redistribution and Borrowing in an Age of Economic Polarization." *World Politics* 69: 640–75.

Anderson, K. and Kurzer, P. 2020. "The Politics of Mortgage Credit Expansion in the Small Coordinated Market Economies." *West European Politics* 43: 366–89.

Ansell, B. 2014. "The Political Economy of Ownership: Housing Markets and the Welfare State." *American Political Science Review* 108: 383–402.

Ansell, B., Broz, L. and Flaherty, T. 2018. "Global Capital Markets, Housing Prices, and Partisan Fiscal Policies." *Economics & Politics* 30: 307–39.

Baccaro, L. and Pontusson, J. 2016. "Rethinking Comparative Political Economy: The Growth Model Perspective." *Politics & Society* 44: 175–207.

Blackwell, T. and Kohl, S. 2018. "The Origins of National Housing Finance Systems: A Comparative Investigation into Historical Variations in Mortgage Finance Regimes." *Review of International Political Economy* 25: 49–74.

Bohle, D. 2014. "Post-socialist Housing Meets Transnational Finance: Foreign Banks, Mortgage Lending, and the Privatization of Welfare in Hungary and Estonia." *Review of International Political Economy* 21: 913–48.

Bundesbank. 2018. "Monthly Report." vol. 70, no. 2, February.

Bundesministerium des Innern, für Bau und Heimat. 2019. "Pressemitteilung: Ein Jahr Baukindergeld." September.

Calomiris, C. and Haber, S. 2014. *Fragile by Design: The Political Origins of Banking Crises and Scarce Credit.* Princeton: Princeton University Press.

Castles, F. 1998. "The Really Big Trade-Off: Home Ownership and the Welfare State in the New World and the Old." *Acta Politica* 33: 5–19.

Conley, D. and Gifford, B. 2006. "Home Ownership, Social Insurance, and the Welfare State." *Sociological Forum* 21: 55–82.

Cooper, A. and Kurzer, P. 2020. "Similar Origins–Divergent Paths: The Politics of German and Dutch Housing Markets." *German Politics* (Early View).

Crouch, C. 2009. "Privatised Keynesianism: An Unacknowledged Policy Regime." *British Journal of Politics and International Relations* 11: 382–99.

Desmond, M. 2016. *Evicted: Poverty and Profit in the American City.* New York: Crown.

Die Bild. 2019. "So Saugt Graf Draghila Unsere Konten Leer." September 13.

Egner, B. 2014. "Wohnungspolitik seit 1945." *Aus Politik und Zeitgeschichte* 64: 13–19.

European Mortgage Federation (EMF). 2017. "Hypostat: A Review of Europe's Mortgage and Housing Markets." September.

EMF. 2019. "Hypostat: A Review of Europe's Mortgage and Housing Markets." September.

Federal Reserve System (Fed). 2019. "Federal Reserve Flow of Funds: Mortgage Debt Outstanding." December.

Fligstein, N. and Goldstein, A. 2012. "A Long Strange Trip: The State and Mortgage Securitization." In *The Oxford Handbook of the Sociology of Finance*, edited by K. Cetina and A. Preda. Oxford: Oxford University Press.

Freund, D. 2007. *Colored Property: State Policy and White Racial Politics in Suburban America.* Chicago: University of Chicago Press.

Fuller, G. 2015. "Who's Borrowing? Credit Encouragement vs. Credit Mitigation in National Financial Systems." *Politics & Society* 43: 241–68.

Fuller, G. 2019. *The Political Economy of Housing Financialization.* Newcastle: Agenda Publishing.

Fuller, G., Johnston, A. and Regan, A. 2020. "Housing Prices and Wealth Inequality in Western Europe." *West European Politics* 43: 297–20.

Furman, J. and Stock, J. 2014. "The Moment Is Right for Housing Reform." *Wall Street Journal* (April 10).

Green, R. and Wachter, S. 2007. "The Housing Finance Revolution." University of Pennsylvania, Institute for Law & Econ Research Paper 09.

Hacker, J. 2002. *The Divided Welfare State: The Battle Over Public and Private Social Benefits in the United States.* Cambridge: Cambridge University Press.

Hall, P. and Franzese, R. 1998. "Mixed Signals: Central Bank Independence, Coordinated Wage Bargaining, and European Monetary Union." *International Organization* 52: 505–35.

Hall, P. and Soskice, D. (eds.). 2001. *Varieties of Capitalism: The Institutional Foundations of Comparative Advantage.* Oxford: Oxford University Press.

Hay, C. 2009. "Good Inflation, Bad Inflation: The Housing Boom, Economic Growth and the Disaggregation of Inflationary Preferences in the UK and Ireland." *The British Journal of Politics and International Relations* 11: 461–78.

Hay, C. 2013. "Treating the Symptom not the Condition: Crisis Definition, Deficit Reduction and the Search for a new British Growth Model." *The British Journal of Politics and International Relations* 15: 23–37.

Höpner, M. 2019. "The German Undervaluation Regime under Bretton Woods: How Germany Became the Nightmare of the World Economy." MPIfG Discussion Paper 19/1.

Housing Finance Policy Center (HFPC). 2019. "Housing Finance at a Glance: A Monthly Chartbook." December.

Howard, C. 1997. *The Hidden Welfare State*. Princeton: Princeton University Press.

Johnston, A. and Regan, A. 2017. "Global Finance, Labor Politics, and the Political Economy of Housing Prices." *Politics & Society* 45: 327–58.

Jordà, Ò., Schularick, M. and Taylor, A. 2016. "The Great Mortgaging: Housing Finance, Crises and Business Cycles." *Economic Policy* 31: 107–52.

Jordà, Ò., Schularick, M. and Taylor, A. 2017. "Macrofinancial History and the New Business Cycle Facts." In *NBER Macroeconomics Annual 2016*, volume 31, edited by M. Eichenbaum and J.A. Parker. Chicago: University of Chicago Press, 213–63.

Kemeny, J. 1981. *The Myth of Home-Ownership: Private versus Public Choices in Housing Tenure*. New York: Routledge.

Kohl, S. 2018a. "More Mortgages, More Homes? The Effect of Housing Financialization on Homeownership in Historical Perspective." *Politics & Society* 46: 177–203.

Kohl, S. 2018b. "The Political Economy of Homeownership: A Comparative Analysis of Homeownership Ideology through Party Manifestos." *Socio-Economic Review* (early view).

Krippner, G. 2011. *Capitalizing on Crisis: The Political Origins of the Rise of Finance*. Cambridge: Harvard University Press.

Logemann, J. 2012. *Trams or Tailfins? Public and Private Prosperity in Postwar West Germany and the United States*. Chicago: University of Chicago Press.

Manger, M. and Sattler, T. 2020. "The Origins of Persistent Current Account Imbalances in the Post-Bretton Woods Era." *Comparative Political Studies* 53: 631–664.

McCarty, N., Poole, K. and Rosenthal, H. 2013. *Political Bubbles: Financial Crises and the Failure of American Democracy*. Princeton: Princeton University Press.

Mertens, D. 2015. *Erst Sparen, Dann Kaufen? Privatverschuldung in Deutschland*. Frankfurt: Campus.

Mertens, D. 2017. "Borrowing for Social Security? Credit, Asset-based Welfare and the Decline of the German Savings Regime." *Journal of European Social Policy* 27: 474–90.

Mian, A. and Sufi, A. 2014. *House of Debt: How They (and You) Caused the Great Recession, and How We Can Prevent It from Happening Again*. Chicago: University of Chicago Press.

Michelsen, C. and Mense, A. 2018. "Evaluierung der Mietpreisbremse." DIW Berlin, December.

Michelsen, C. and Weiß, D. 2010. "What Happened to the East German Housing Market? A Historical Perspective on the Role of Public Funding." *Post-Communist Economies* 22: 387–409.

Muellbauer, J. 1992. "Anglo-German Differences in Housing Market Dynamics: The Role of Institutions and Macroeconomic Policy." *European Economic Review* 36: 539–48.

Nelson, S. and Katzenstein, P. 2014. "Uncertainty, Risk, and the Financial Crisis of 2008." *International Organization* 68: 361–392.

Oren, T. and Blyth, M. 2019. "From Big Bang to Big Crash: The Early Origins of the UK's Finance-led Growth Model and the Persistence of Bad Policy Ideas." *New Political Economy* 24: 605–22.

Ornston, D. 2018. *Good Governance Gone Bad: When Adaptability Leads to Excess.* Ithaca: Cornell University Press.

Palier, B. and Thelen, K. 2010. "Institutionalizing Dualism: Complementarities and Change in France and Germany." *Politics & Society* 38: 119–48.

Pierson, P. 1994. *Dismantling the Welfare State? Reagan, Thatcher and the Politics of Retrenchment.* Cambridge: Cambridge University Press.

Prasad, M. 2012. *The Land of Too Much: American Abundance and the Paradox of Poverty.* Cambridge: Harvard University Press.

Quinn, S. 2019. *American Bonds: How Credit Markets Shaped a Nation.* Princeton: Princeton University Press.

Rajan, R. 2010. *Fault Lines: How Hidden Fractures Still Threaten the World Economy.* Princeton: Princeton University Press.

Reisenbichler, A. 2016. "A Rocky Path to Homeownership: Why Germany Eliminated Large-Scale Subsidies for Homeowners." *Cityscape* 18: 283–90.

Reisenbichler, A. 2020a. "Entrenchment or Retrenchment: The Political Economy of Mortgage Debt Subsidies in the United States and Germany." Unpublished ms.

Reisenbichler, A. 2020b. "The Politics of Quantitative Easing and Housing Stimulus by the Federal Reserve and European Central Bank, 2008–2018." *West European Politics* 43: 464–84.

Reisenbichler, A. and Morgan, K.J. 2012. "From Sick Man to Miracle: Explaining the Robustness of the German Labor Market During and After the Financial Crisis 2008–09." *Politics & Society* 40: 549–79.

Schelkle, W. 2012. "A Crisis of What? Mortgage Credit Markets and the Social Policy of Promoting Homeownership in the United States and in Europe." *Politics & Society* 40: 59–80.

Schwartz, H. 2009. *Subprime Nation: American Power, Global Capital, and the Housing Bubble.* Ithaca: Cornell University Press.

Schwartz, H. 2012. "Housing, the Welfare State, and the Global Financial Crisis: What is the Connection?" *Politics & Society* 40: 35–58.

Schwartz, H. 2020. "Covering the Private Parts: The (Re-)Nationalisation of Housing Finance." *West European Politics* 43: 485–508.

Schwartz, H. and Seabrooke, L. 2008. "Varieties of Residential Capitalism in the International Political Economy: Old Welfare States and the New Politics of Housing." *Comparative European Politics* 6: 237–61.

Slemrod, J. 2018. "Is This Tax Reform, or Just Confusion?" *Journal of Economic Perspectives* 32: 73–96.

Thompson, H. 2012. "The Limits of Blaming Neo-liberalism: Fannie Mae and Freddie Mac, the American State and the Financial Crisis." *New Political Economy* 17: 399–19.

Thurston, C. 2018. *At the Boundaries of Homeownership: Credit, Discrimination, and the American State*. New York: Cambridge University Press.

Tranøy, B.S., Stamsø, M.A. and Hjertaker, I. 2020. "Equality as a Driver of Inequality? Universalistic Welfare, Generalised Creditworthiness and Financialised Housing Markets." *West European Politics* 43: 390–11.

Trumbull, G. 2014. *Consumer Lending in France and America: Credit and Welfare*. New York: Cambridge University Press.

Van Gunten, T. and Kohl, S. 2020. "The Inversion of the 'Really Big Trade-Off': Homeownership and Pensions in Long-Run Perspective." *West European Politics* 43: 435–63.

Voigtländer, M. 2009. "Why Is the German Homeownership Rate So Low?" *Housing Studies* 24: 355–72.

Voigtländer, M. 2014. "The Stability of the German Housing Market." *Journal of Housing and the Built Environment* 29: 583–94.

Wiedemann, A. Forthcoming. *Indebted Societies: Credit and Welfare in Rich Democracies*. New York: Cambridge University Press.

Wijburg, G, and Aalbers, M. 2017. "The Alternative Financialization of the German Housing Market." *Housing Studies* 32: 968–89.

Wood, J. 2018. "The Integrating Role of Private Homeownership and Mortgage Credit in British Neoliberalism." *Housing Studies* 37: 993–1013.

Wood, J. 2019. "Mortgage Credit: Denmark's Financial Capacity Building Regime." *New Political Economy* 24: 833–50.

Yentel, D. 2019. "The Questions the Presidential Candidates Don't Get Asked." *Citylab*, September 13, 2019.

11
Fighting Youth Unemployment: Growth Strategies and Youth Welfare Citizenship

Tom Chevalier

1. Introduction

The welfare state matters for the life course. Although "social citizenship" (Marshall 1950) in general seems to make no distinction between citizens, in particular where age is concerned, welfare policies actually depend on one's situation in the life cycle. More generally, the state has a great impact on the life course (Mayer and Schoepflin 1989). Kohli (1986) has shown, for instance, how the life course has been institutionalized into three periods, which he has called the "tripartition of the life course." On the one hand, the rise of mass education systems at the end of the nineteenth century and the beginning of the twentieth century institutionalized the period of "childhood" (Heywood 2001). During this period, children are supposed to be in education and not work, while their family takes care of them. On the other hand, the rise of pension systems during the twentieth century also institutionalized the period of "old age," when people are supposed to retire after a life of work, while being supported by pensions (Guillemard 1986). In between these two periods, adulthood takes place, when people are meant to work and are entitled to social benefits.

The welfare state is crucial in several ways as regards this institutionalization of the life course (Leisering 2003). It separates and creates age periods: the implementation of a pension system is an example of this intervention by the welfare state, but it also shapes the transition from one status to another, from one period to another. Education is not only a way of institutionalizing childhood, but also an investment in human capital, which has enduring effects over the life course, as it determines, for instance, the kind of job one will get, and thus the pension one will receive. However, since the welfare state varies greatly from one country to another (Esping-Andersen 1990), the way it structures the life course also varies a lot. Julia Lynch (2006) has shown, for instance, to what extent the welfare state

Tom Chevalier, *Fighting Youth Unemployment: Growth Strategies and Youth Welfare Citizenship* In: *Growth and Welfare in Advanced Capitalist Economies: How Have Growth Regimes Evolved?* Edited by: Anke Hassel and Bruno Palier, Oxford University Press (2021). © Oxford University Press. DOI: 10.1093/oso/9780198866176.003.0011

can favor different age groups, being more child-oriented or more elderly oriented, while Birnbaum et al. (2017) have recently highlighted that the welfare state can be more or less "balanced" in terms of justice between the generations and age groups.

Through their effects on the welfare state, growth strategies also contribute to the structuration of the life course. For instance, reforms of pension systems have been brought about by the growth strategy fostered by the World Bank in 1994 with its report on "averting the old age crisis" (see Hassel and Palier, in this volume). The privatization of pension systems is indeed a way to fuel growth, through financialization, for example (see Hassel and Wiss 2019). Growth strategies have, therefore, had an effect, not only on old age but also on childhood. The rise of the "social investment welfare state" (Morel et al. 2012) means the expansion of education, and especially of higher education (HE), i.e., education for people over the age of eighteen, beyond the end of compulsory education (see also Wren, in this volume). What does that mean for the life course? Is it an extension of childhood? Is it the emergence of a new period in life? Is it an illustration of a blurring and decrease of the tripartition of the life course?

In this chapter, I will first stress that the transition to a post-industrial society has had consequences on the life course, and especially on the transition from childhood to adulthood, thereby creating "youth" as a new period in the life course. However, this transition varies a lot across countries, because of different institutional arrangements and public policies. Accordingly, I will describe these different arrangements of socio-economic institutions and policies, including education, the labor market, and welfare policies (with student support), by presenting the typology of "youth welfare citizenship regimes." I will then show that these regimes are congruent with specific growth strategies, i.e., the reforms implemented by governments in order to boost growth and job creation. In this case, specific policies in terms of skill formation, social protection for young people, and policies tackling youth unemployment. In the second part of the chapter, I will proceed to highlight four "typical" case studies (Seawright and Gerring 2008), showing how different growth strategies, presented by Hassel and Palier (in this volume), shape the youth welfare citizenship regimes of Sweden, Germany, the United Kingdom, and France. I will particularly analyze how growth strategies have been influencing the evolution of youth citizenship regimes, by looking at skill formation policies as well as the active labor market policies (ALMP) that aim to fight youth unemployment. The argument here is not causal, but rather contextual and systemic (Figure 11.1). The objective of the case studies will, therefore, be to present the congruence between a growth regime and the way socio-economic institutions structure the entry into adulthood, leading to a specific youth welfare citizenship regime, and how reforms, inspired by a specific growth strategy, contribute towards transforming that youth welfare regime.

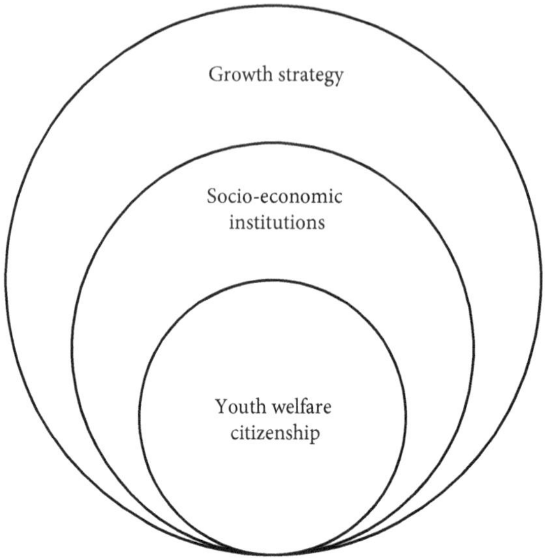

Figure 11.1 The logic of the argument

2. Theoretical Framework: The Transformation of the Transition to Adulthood, Youth Welfare Citizenship, and Growth Strategies

2.1 Youth Welfare Citizenship

The transformation of the life course in general, and of the transition to adulthood in particular, has led to the emergence of a new period of life between childhood and adulthood called "youth" (Billari, 2004; Walther, 2006). Young people can access adulthood and its related financial independence in two ways[1]: On the one hand, young people can access independence by entering employment via the labor market. This is the issue of "economic citizenship," structured by educational policy, labor market regulation, and employment policy. On the other hand, they can also access an income via public aid and social benefits delivered by the state, such as family benefits, tax relief for families, unemployment support, housing benefits, and student support (student grants and loans). This is the issue of "social citizenship."

With regard to social citizenship, two types of citizenship exist (Table 11.1). First, the social citizenship of young people can be "familialized." When access to social citizenship is familialized, youth is seen as an extension of childhood, and young people are treated institutionally as children. Parents are still supposed to take care of them, which means that benefits are mostly directed at them and not

[1] These youth regimes are discussed more at length in Chevalier (2016).

Table 11.1 The two types of youth social citizenship

	Familialization	Individualization
Maintenance obligations towards young adults	Yes	No
Age limits	High, around 25	Low, around 18
Status in social security	Dependent	Independent
Main source of student support	Family Policy	Grants and/or loans
Student grants and/or loans	Restricted and dependent on parental income	Extensive and independent of parental income

the young people, who thus remain as dependent children in social protection. Age limits for accessing social benefits are relatively high, usually well beyond the age of twenty, normally around twenty. In the situation where a child is expected to attend school, students are mainly supported by family policy (family allowances and tax relief for families) or student grants, depending on parental income. Illustrating the principle of subsidiarity, this familialized social citizenship is most often found in countries that have a Bismarckian welfare state, and where Catholicism is important (Chevalier 2018).

Second, in welfare states with a strong Protestant tradition (Manow and Van Kersbergen 2009), where rights are more individualized, the social citizenship of young people is also "individualized." Young people are thus considered to be adults and no longer children at the age that marks the end of compulsory schooling (usually around sixteen) or the acquisition of civil majority (eighteen). The age limits for accessing benefits are, therefore, relatively low, under the age of twenty, usually around eighteen, since young people are no longer considered to be children, even when they are pursuing studies. Family policy is not mobilized to support students, who receive extensive student support (grants and loans), independent of their parents' income.

Concerning economic citizenship, two strategies are also present (Table 11.2). The first is "inclusive," in the sense that education, central to the entry of young people into the labor market (Müller and Gangl 2003), is provided for all young people. The objective of this strategy is to provide them with skills. In order to ease the school-to-work transition, the emphasis is placed on education and training, in a "learn-first" perspective (OECD 2010). As a result, the education system is fostered and aims at low levels of dropouts. Active labor market policies invest in human capital (Bonoli 2010), especially concerning vocational education and training (VET) for low-skilled young people who find it difficult to enter into the labor market. An important aspect of this strategy is that second chances are available for low-skilled young people, for instance with "youth guarantee" programs. A strategy like this is followed when "macro-corporatism" (Martin and Swank 2012) is quite developed, leading to a specialization of the economy in high

Table 11.2 The two types of youth economic citizenship

	Inclusive strategy	**Selective strategy**
Objective of the strategy	Learn-first	Work-first
Skills distribution	For all Low educational inequalities High enrollment	For the best High educational inequalities Low enrollment
Target of intervention to fight youth unemployment	Supply of labor: low-skilled young people	Demand for labor: employers in the private sector, public sector
ALMP	Investment in human capital, VET	Subsidized jobs, reduction of youth labor costs

value-added sectors which require a highly skilled labor force. Subsequently, inclusive economic citizenship is usually found in "coordinated market economies" (Hall and Soskice 2001).

The second strategy is "selective," as the objective is not to provide skills for all, but only for the best. The education system is, therefore, quite elitist, producing important educational inequalities and high levels of dropouts. In this context, employment policies do not invest in human capital in order to boost young people's employability, but their main objective is to provide work for young people no matter what, illustrating a "work-first" perspective. It is, therefore, a policy focused on the demand for labor (in contrast to the inclusive strategy, which focuses on the supply of labor, i.e., young people). This fosters the development of low-skilled, low-quality jobs, either by lowering the cost of young people's labor, the flexibilization of the labor market, or subsidizing atypical jobs. One can find a strategy like this, when "macro-corporatism" is quite low in economies, which cannot specialize overall in high value-added sectors, but which polarize instead. This reflects the polarization of skills in the labor force (see Martin, in this volume).

Crossing these two dimensions of economic citizenship and social citizenship creates a typology of four youth welfare citizenship regimes (Table 11.3): the "monitored citizenship" (Germany being close to this type), the "enabling citizenship" (Sweden), the "denied citizenship" (France), and the "second-class citizenship" (UK).

Table 11.3 The regimes of youth welfare citizenship

	Familialization of social citizenship	**Individualization of social citizenship**
Inclusive economic citizenship	Monitored citizenship e.g. Germany	Enabling citizenship e.g. Sweden
Selective economic citizenship	Denied citizenship e.g. France	Second-class citizenship e.g. United Kingdom

2.2 The Effects of Growth Strategies

As mentioned by Hassel and Palier (in the first chapter of this volume), growth strategies rely on different education, employment, and social policies. These policies shape youth regimes through three channels: First, as far as aggregate demand is concerned, the overall level and distribution of skills in the population depend on whether growth is domestic, demand-led, or export-led. If it is export-led, firms ought to be highly competitive in global markets. As they would not be able to compete on a price basis with less-advanced countries in those markets, they must compete via the quality of production and the use of ICT. They thus specialize in high valued-added sectors, which rely on a highly skilled labor force. We should expect to find an inclusive, learn-first, economic citizenship in countries where growth is led by exports.

Second, supply is also of importance, as the Varieties of Capitalism (VoC) approach shows (Estevez-Abe et al. 2001; Hall and Soskice 2001; Iversen and Stephens 2008; Schmidt 2002). If the manufacturing industry is the engine of growth, then vocational training and apprenticeship should structure the skill formation system, while, if services are the engine of growth, school-based training should be pivotal. Furthermore, within services, if dynamic services are developing, investing in higher education (HE) also becomes more important (Ansell and Gingrich 2013; Durazzi 2019; Wren, in this volume). I sum up all these characteristics in Table 11.4.

Third, social citizenship is also affected by growth strategies, through its interconnection with economic citizenship. On the one hand, the expansion of HE, which is a crucial part of a growth strategy towards the knowledge economy, also depends on the development of student support, which is part of social citizenship. The individualization of student support allows the majority of students to access some support to pursue their studies, which is not the case if it is familialized (Garritzmann 2016). As a result, the development of dynamic services can put pressure on familialized social citizenship in order to allow for the development of high skills within the population.

On the other hand, unemployment support (i.e., unemployment insurance, unemployment assistance, and social assistance), which is part of youth social citizenship, can be shaped by a specific growth strategy. In fact, it is a component of ALMP, as "incentive reinforcement" is a type of policy that governments can adopt to fight (youth) unemployment, together with "occupation," "employment assistance," and "upskilling" (Bonoli 2010). However, the latter is more related to economic citizenship (see supra). As a result, when governments adopt a growth strategy in order to fight (youth) unemployment, they implement specific ALMP, which concern not only the economic citizenship of young people, but also their social citizenship.

Table 11.4 Growth strategies, socio-economic institutions, and youth welfare citizenship regimes

	The dynamic-services strategy	The high-quality, manufacturing-based strategy	The financialization-based strategy	The publicly supported strategy
Growth strategy characteristics				
Aggregate demand	Exports	Exports	Domestic demand: private debt	Domestic demand: wages
Main sector	Dynamic services	Manufacture	Finance	Manufacture
Skill content	General	Specific	General	Specific
Skill level	High	High/intermediate	Low/polarized	Low/polarized
VoC	CME	CME	LME	Statist
Socio-economic institutions underlying the strategies				
Industrial relations	High corporatism	High corporatism	Low corporatism	Low corporatism
Welfare regime	Social-democratic	Bismarckian	Liberal	Bismarckian
Skill formation system*	Statist skill formation system	Collective skill formation system	Liberal skill formation system	Statist skill formation system
Youth welfare citizenship				
	Enabling	Monitored	Second-class	Denied
Economic citizenship	Inclusive	Inclusive	Selective	Selective
Social citizenship	Individualized	Familialized	Individualized	Familialized
Countries	Sweden	Germany	UK	France

Note: *See Busemeyer, 2015

3. Growth Strategies, Youth Citizenship Regimes, and ALMP Reforms in Sweden, Germany, the UK, and France

In the following section, I will proceed to highlight four case studies, underlining the institutional complementarities between growth strategies and youth welfare citizenship regimes. For each case, I will illustrate the overall relationship between the youth regime and the adopted growth strategy. Then, focusing on recent reforms of ALMP targeted at young people, I will show how the distinct growth

Table 11.5 Economic citizenship of young people in France, Germany, the UK, and Sweden

	Sweden	Germany	UK	France
Early leavers* (18–24) who would like to work	2%	3.5%	3.2%	4.2%
Enrollment rate in education (20–9)	34.8%	34.2%	20.9%	21%
25–34 with tertiary education	46.4%	29.6%	49.9%	44.7%
Mean literacy score 16–24	278	279	266	275
Mean numeracy score 16–24	278	275	257	263
Main intervention in the labor market	VET and youth guarantee	VET and apprenticeship	Deregulation of the labor market and subsidized jobs	Subsidized jobs

*Early leavers: young people, whose highest level of attained education is ISCED level 0, 1, or 2.

N.B. OECD average for mean literacy and for mean numeracy: 275 and 267.

Source: Eurostat (2015); PIAAC (2015); OECD (2015) (online database).

strategies have shaped the responses of political parties to the increase in youth unemployment in the wake of the economic crisis.

As the data in Tables 11.5 and 11.6 show, the four countries under study (Sweden, Germany, the UK, and France) are close to the four "ideal-types," presented in the previous section, and will be treated as "typical" case studies (Seawright and Gerring 2008). The following case studies aim less at understanding the whole cases than to show the interconnectedness between a specific growth strategy and specific (skill formation and employment) policies towards young people. Following the insights of Vlandas (2013), I will, however, underline that the overall importance of growth strategies over the reforms of youth welfare citizenship does not mean that political parties do not matter at all: they are simply constrained by the economic and institutional context (see chapter by Avlijaš et al. in this volume).[2]

[2] I do not formulate any precise hypotheses about political parties' preferences in terms of ALMP reforms for two reasons: One, it can be argued that parties' preferences are somehow endogenous to the growth strategy and second, it is not the main point of my argument anyway, which is focused on growth strategies. I simply want to mention the role of party politics in order to avoid an over-deterministic lecture of my argument.

Table 11.6 Youth social citizenship in France, Germany, the UK, and Sweden

	Sweden	Germany	UK	France
Maintenance claims for adult young people	No	Yes	No	Yes
Age limits				
Family benefits for all children	16	18	16	20
Family benefits for young people still in education	It continues if still in compulsory education	25	20 (not for HE)	20
Social assistance*	Reflects maintenance claims	15 (25)	18	25
Student support				
Family benefits	No	Yes	No	Yes
Student grants/loans dependent on parental income	No	Yes	No	Yes
Access rate to grants and/or loans for full-time students	89%	25%	89.3%	39.2%
Tax relief for families with a child in HE	No	Yes	No	Yes

*RSA for France (both active and inactive population), ALGII (social assistance benefit) for Germany (only active population), income-based jobseeker's allowance (active population) and income support (inactive population) for the UK, and basic social assistance for Sweden (both active and inactive).

Source: MISSOC (2016) (online database); Eurydice (2017) (2016–17 for France and Germany; 2015–16 for Sweden and the UK). For maintenance claims: https://e-justice.europa.eu/content_maintenance_claims-47-en.do.

3.1 Sweden

Sweden has followed an export-of-dynamic-services strategy (see Hassel and Palier; and Thelen, in this volume).[3] The specific institutions prevailing in Sweden have allowed the country to adopt this specific growth strategy and its associated policies. After the crisis in the early 1990s, the government came back to (and renewed) the traditional Schumpeterian strategy of the "Rehn-Meidner" model and its focus on the export of quality goods, with a strong emphasis on high general skills. According to this strategy, a social investment strategy was needed with regards to both the skill formation regime and the welfare regime, in order to

[3] As shown elsewhere in this volume, Sweden is not focusing exclusively on export, since it is also balancing its growth model by supporting domestic demand (Baccaro and Pontusson, in this volume) and has developed privatized welfare services (Thelen, in this volume). For the sake of my "institutional complementarities" argument, I will focus here on the central role of dynamic services.

have a highly skilled labor force, upon which this strategy relies (Morel et al. 2012). Furthermore, following the Schumpeterian logic of a strategy like this, it was decided to invest in ICT in order to boost dynamic-services exports as well (Wren, in this volume). The corporatist institutions of Sweden have been able to coordinate with different actors in order to change the economic specialization towards these high-technology sectors, reflecting what has been called "creative corporatism" (Ornston 2013).

As a result, Sweden adopted an inclusive educational strategy, aimed at providing all young people with a set of skills. Sweden has a comprehensive and egalitarian educational system (Oftedal Telhaug et al. 2006), promoting general skills (Busemeyer 2009). This severely limits educational inequalities (Janmaat et al. 2013), keeps the share of early leavers, who have difficulty entering the labor market, low (only 2% of early leavers would like to work, see Table 11.5), and leads to a high enrollment rate in education (Table 11.5). The level of skills for the sixteen to twenty-four age group in 2015 was also quite high, in both literacy and numeracy (Table 11.5). More specifically, as the main sector for growth is dynamic services, which require high general skills (Wren, in this volume), HE has been put at the center of the strategy since the 1990s (see Table 11.5, as well as Ansell 2008; Anxo and Niklasson 2006).

The development of HE has been sustained by a widespread, universal, student support scheme (Ansell 2008; Garritzmann 2016), reflecting the general individualization of social citizenship. In fact, students can benefit from a scholarship and/or a loan, which does not depend on parental income, allowing the majority of students to access some kind of student support (89%, see Table 11.6). Young people, even when in higher education, between the ages of eighteen and twenty-nine (without children) can also claim for individualized housing benefit, if their own income does not exceed a certain amount.

Complementary to the educational system, training is also widely developed within the framework of ALMP. In fact, Sweden invested early on in these ALMP, which are part of the "Rehn-Meidner" model (Bonoli 2010), and young people have gradually formed an important part of those who benefit from it (Bourdet and Persson 1991). Low-skilled young people have received specific attention, leading to the creation of "youth guarantees." These ALMP are specifically aimed at low-skilled young people who have difficulty entering the labor market, and they guarantee them employment, education, or training, together with a social allowance. They were created in Sweden in the 1980s, and then spread over the Nordic countries in the 1990s (Hummeluhr 1997). The idea is both to give young people in difficulty a second chance and to invest in their human capital to produce a skilled workforce and bring them back to work, in the context of high youth unemployment.

In 2007, the official "Youth Job Guarantee" was adopted in Sweden by the right-wing government, which had been in office since 2006, unifying previous, different, existing programs for the sixteen to twenty-four year-olds. It was reformed in 2011, in the wake of the recession, by the same government, but with a stronger focus on job matching and work subsidies for employers instead of training schemes. This response to increasing youth unemployment by that government reveals two things coherent with our argument: First, growth strategies pave the way to welfare reforms in general, and ALMP reforms in particular. The focus of the government, when dealing with youth unemployment—the youth guarantee program—is on upskill-oriented ALMP, targeted at the supply of labor in line with the social investment/dynamic services, export-led growth strategy. Second, the right-wing government has developed demand-oriented schemes for the youth guarantee compared to training schemes, by introducing and expanding job matching and, since 2010, job subsidies for companies. This has more to do with a "selective" approach towards economic citizenship, like the other governmental reforms, aimed at reducing the cost of youth labor. Since 2008, employers hiring young people below the age of twenty-five have had their social contributions halved, and for those who hire young people who were previously unemployed for at least twelve months in the so-called "New Start Jobs" social contributions have been reduced.

The citizenship of young people in Sweden is therefore "enabling," insofar as young people are considered to be adults and the state sees them as a resource and, as a result, invests hugely in them through education and training. This investment is supposed to allow both greater autonomy, through their empowerment, and greater productivity, according to the growth strategy in place. However, within a strategy like this, some agency remains for political actors, as I show, regarding ALMP reforms since the beginning of the crisis.

3.2 Germany

In Germany, as shown by many chapters in this volume, an export-led strategy, relying on the manufacturing sector, has been pursued in the wake of the "Diversified Quality Production" that has long been the core of the German economy (Streeck 1991). This strategy requires a (mostly male) workforce with a set of specific skills for the manufacturing sector, leading to an inclusive economic citizenship of *learn-first*. However, in contrast with Sweden, specific skills at the intermediate level are more in demand than high general skills, especially since labor mobility, from declining sectors to dynamic ones, is not actively pursued as it is in Sweden. On the contrary: workers have been encouraged to stick to their traditional sectors (Estevez-Abe et al. 2001). However, the Hartz reforms have led to some changes in that regard, as all workers are no longer supposed to stay in their professions/sectors (see Wren, in this volume).

Despite the high stratification of a tripartite education system that selects and streams students into different academic tracks early on in their education, the objective of the skill formation system is still to deliver a minimal set of specific skills, which fit the needs of the industry (Estevez-Abe et al. 2001). The involvement of employers (Busemeyer 2009) in the system links it very closely to the labor market and allows for a very smooth and rather quick school-to-work transition.

Subsequently, it is not HE that is mainly developed, but vocational education and training. The HE system has, therefore, remained rather limited (Ansell, 2008), since only 29.6% of the twenty-five to thirty-four age group completed tertiary education in 2015 (Table 11.5). The dual system of apprenticeship has traditionally constituted the core of the German "high skill equilibrium" (Brown et al. 2001; Finegold 1999). All in all, there is a high rate of enrollment in German education, as well as high levels of skills, in both literacy and numeracy (Table 11.5).

The underdevelopment of HE is also coherent, with restricted support for students (Ansell 2008; Garritzmann 2016). In fact, BAföG (i.e., German student support: half-grant, half-loan) depends on parental income, university location, and whether the student still lives with his parents, which does not allow every student to receive it, like in Sweden. The level of access to this aid is thus relatively low (25%, see Table 11.6). This restriction is also a reflection of the familialization of social citizenship.

The important role of VET has kept youth unemployment at rather a low level. Furthermore, the German economy has been rather preserved from the crisis, compared to most countries. The government's actions with regard to youth unemployment have, therefore, differed since 2007 from those of other countries, since the issue of youth unemployment has been less prevalent. Reflecting the growth strategy, with its emphasis on manufacturing exports, most reforms have been following an inclusive approach of economic citizenship in two different ways.

On the one hand, the shift to a knowledge economy has meant that industry has been transformed with the expansion of advanced manufacturing. This has fostered new demands in terms of high skills, putting pressure on the university system and leading to the Higher Education Pact in 2007 (Durazzi and Benassi 2020; Durazzi 2019). This reform developed universities of applied sciences, especially in STEM disciplines. It illustrates both the investment in training and the importance of specific skills, pillars of a growth strategy led by exports in high-quality manufacturing.

On the other hand, since VET is still seen as the best way to promote youth employment in Germany (Thelen and Busemeyer 2012), ALMP have also been structured around this goal, by developing the so-called "transition system," which aims to prepare low-skilled young people to get back into the apprenticeship system, but without standardized certification (Kohlrausch 2009). This system has increased gradually up to the point, where about one third of total entries into VET are represented by young people (Kohlrausch 2009). This is consistent with the inclusive strategy, as ALMP are seen as complementary to the skill formation regime, by investing in young people's human capital through VET.[4]

The German growth strategy has, therefore, shaped governments' reactions in terms of skill formation and ALMP, by putting emphasis on vocational training, both at the high end (with the development of universities of applied sciences) and the low end (with the rise of the transition system). It is, however, difficult to glimpse any political agency in Germany for two reasons: Youth unemployment has remained very low compared to most countries, which has not made it a politically salient issue and there has not been an important change of government, as Merkel's Conservative Party has remained the first German political party (despite some changes in the composition of the governing coalition).

3.3 The United Kingdom

As amply shown in various chapters in this volume, the UK has followed a growth strategy directed towards financialization, based on three elements: growth has been domestic, demand-led; this demand has been fueled by private debt (Crouch 2009) and finance has been the main engine of growth. In terms of skills, this strategy has two consequences: the finance sector in particular, and dynamic services in general, rely on high general skills, and, as a result, wish HE to be expanded (Ansell and Gingrich 2013), and the overall economy is polarized between high-skill, high-wage jobs in the dynamic services and low-skill, low-wage jobs in the rest of the economy, especially in low-cost services (Green, 2001).

Hence, the youth economic citizenship appears to be selective, whilst HE is expanding (Table 11.5). In fact, the education system is very elitist and fragmented, and produces strong educational inequalities (Allmendinger and Leibfried 2003; Green et al. 2014; Janmaat et al. 2013), low enrollment in education, and a low level of skills (Table 11.5). This characteristic of the British skill formation system has been continuous, although education, and especially HE, was at the center of New Labour's agenda during the 2000s.

To allow for this expansion of HE, student support has been quite extensive. In the 1990s, a system of income-contingent repayment loans was implemented, in order to enable all undergraduate students to receive support so that more young

[4] Still, this system has been criticized because it does not seem that effective in promoting young people's employment, and, as a result, it would lead to a dualization of VET, with insiders going into the dual system and outsiders (usually male immigrants) stuck in this transition program (Busemeyer 2011; Kohlrausch 2009). It is possible to see that in the intermediate level of early leavers who would like to work (in Table 11.5).

people could pursue tertiary education (Garritzmann 2016; Harris 2000). When tuition fees were increased drastically, loans for tuition fees and maintenance for daily living expenses were designed as independent of parental income, which explains their importance (89.3% of students benefit from them, see Table 11.6). This extension of student support illustrates two important aspects.

First, the fact that student support has been extended exclusively through loans and not grants (unlike Sweden or Denmark, for instance, who use a combination of grants and loans) is consistent with the financialization strategy and its complementary welfare—the so-called "asset-based welfare state" (Hay 2013). This approach of the welfare state views the individual as a rational agent, who must invest in assets to ensure future welfare—which was exactly the idea with the expansion of HE and the extension of student loans: young people invest in their human capital, which will reward them with high-wage returns. As a result, it is logical that they would pay part of the investment, since the gains would be private.

Second, the extension of student support was possible because of the individualization of social citizenship of young people in the first place. Children can no longer claim maintenance from their parents when they reach the age of sixteen, or nineteen if still in education. Likewise, family benefits also have these age limits, which means that family policy does not play any role in student support (there is no tax relief for parents who have a child in higher education).

Concerning young people not in education, unemployment support (income-based jobseeker's allowance) and social assistance (income support) are available to them from the age of eighteen.[5] Those under twenty-five, however, receive benefits at a lower rate (Harris, 2000). This age limit of twenty-five does not illustrate the logic of familialization, but a fear of welfare dependency, typical of a liberal welfare regime and its targeted benefits. Young people are considered to be adults, but not entirely, as they are supposed to be more inclined to welfare dependency, an argument that justifies these lower rates in order to push them back to work. Accordingly, these benefits are activated, inasmuch as young people have had to participate in "welfare-to-work" programs.

Under New Labour governments, the "New Deal for Young People" (NDYP) was launched in 1998. The idea was to fight youth unemployment, by fighting both welfare dependency and investing in low-skilled young people's human capital. However, in practice, the training component of the program was rather weak, both because of decreased spending from the state and a low involvement from employers (Busemeyer 2015; Kohlrausch 2009), consistent with the low level of corporatism and employers' involvement in training in general (Martin and Swank 2004, 2012).

[5] The criteria of eligibility are the same as for Universal Credit, launched in 2019.

Although these ALMP seem to focus on low-skilled young people, echoing Nordic youth guarantees, they remain marginal in the overall employment policies implemented in the UK. In line with the selective strategy, public interventions focus mostly on the demand for work, through the deregulation of the labor market (Emmenegger 2009; Thelen 2014) and the lowering of youth labor costs, with the exclusion of young people under the age of twenty-one from the minimum wage decided by Wage Councils in 1986 (Jones and Wallace 1992) and, thereafter, the adoption of a reduced rate for young people of the national minimum wage in 1999, for instance. The main target of the employment policy has been the demand for work, and both the deregulation of the labor market and the decrease in labor costs for young workers (through job subsidies and a lower minimum wage) were at the core of state intervention.

After the 2008 crisis, reforms of ALMP have followed this strategy even more. The NDYP was replaced by the "Flexible New Deal," which itself was replaced by the "Work Programme" in 2011 by the Conservative government: young people under twenty-five, who have been benefiting from the jobseeker's allowance (JSA) for nine months, must participate in this program. In 2012, the "Youth Contract" was implemented, which included mostly work experience, apprenticeship grants for employers, or wage incentives for employers hiring young people (though this last scheme ended in 2014). A training component is also present, but is focused on the sixteen- to seventeen-year-olds. The same year, the Welfare Reform Act was adopted, in order to reduce welfare spending and strengthen welfare activation and conditionality and *ipso facto* recipients' welfare dependency on social benefits, by introducing Universal Credit instead of the main, means-tested benefits. Young people under twenty-five are still in receipt of lower rates and, since 2017, those under twenty-one now have to participate in the "Youth Obligation Support Programme" within the first six months of being unemployed. Before that, in 2015, employers' national insurance contributions for those under the age of twenty-one were also abolished.

As far as young people are concerned, the British growth strategy has, therefore, led to three main welfare reforms: First, the skill formation system has been transformed through the important development of HE in order to promote high general skills. Yet it remains very elitist, producing important educational inequalities, with many school dropouts and low-skilled young people, reflecting the overall polarization of the labor market. Second, the deregulation of the labor market, as well as the decrease in youth labor costs, is at the core of public intervention to fight youth unemployment. Third, the focus on welfare dependency as a determinant of youth unemployment translates into an increase in the activation of social benefits, together with a lowering of them for the unemployed, i.e., "incentives reinforcement"-oriented ALMP. Although New Labour tried to reorientate ALMP towards a more inclusive strategy with the NDYP, not only was it still suffering from a low level of human capital investment, but the return of a

Conservative government in 2010, in the wake of the crisis, has further reinforced the "selective"-orientation of ALMP reforms.

3.4 France

France relates more to the "publicly supported domestic demand" strategy of Southern Europe. As is shown in many chapters in this volume, French growth is led by domestic household consumption. The difference to the UK is that this demand is fueled by high social spending and relatively high wages, guaranteed by the presence of a high legal minimum wage (SMIC[6]) instead of private debt. However, the increase in wages was not in line with an increase in productivity (Askenazy et al. 2013). Subsequently, governments have been facing a dilemma: either increase investment in human capital to increase productivity (which only has long-term effects), or decrease labor costs to be in line with actual productivity (supposedly with an effect on employment in the short term), but possibly undermining consumption (Boyer 1995). The lack of coordination between economic and political actors has led to constant hesitation between the two strategies. Eventually policies leaned more towards the focus on labor costs—explaining the failed attempt to switch to an export-led regime (see Avlijaš et al. in this volume).

This is consistent with the skill formation system and the youth economic citizenship. In fact, the economy is dualized between a high-skill, high-wage sector, mostly represented by the former "champions nationaux" in industry (Palier and Thelen 2010), but also increasingly by dynamic services (Culpepper et al. 2006) and low-skill, low-wage jobs, mostly in services. Although the French skill formation system is "statist" (with low involvement from firms but high involvement from the state) as in Sweden, it is much more polarized, because of its "republican elitism" (Baudelot and Establet 2009). It produces high levels of inequalities in education, as well as a low enrollment rate in education and a lower level of skills (Table 11.5). These low-skilled young people are then in great difficulty in the labor market (4.2% of early leavers who would like to work, twice the Swedish rate; see Table 11.5), concentrating on low-quality jobs if they manage to access employment at all (Cahuc et al. 2011; Cahuc et al. 2013). This "selective" feature of youth economic citizenship eventually produces a structural high level of youth unemployment in France (Chevalier 2019).

Reflecting the growth strategy and its focus on labor costs, the intervention of the state to fight youth unemployment has focused on young people's labor costs. Since the Pacts for Employment ("Pactes pour l'Emploi") in 1977, the state has

[6] Salaire Minimum Intersectoriel de Croissance.

implemented many exemptions to social contributions for employers hiring low-skilled young people (Aeberhardt et al. 2011). The result has been to boost atypical employment for young people—the so-called "emplois aidés" (subsidized jobs), not only in the private sector, but also in the public sector, especially since the 1990s (Lefresne 2012). This intervention has, thus, focused on the demand for work.

Still, VET has been an important part of this employment policy (the so-called "politique d'insertion des jeunes"), in particular through the development of apprenticeship, but it has increasingly benefited not the low skilled, but young people in HE (Sanchez 2012). It reflects the overall elitist system that does not try to invest in the human capital of the low skilled, but, on the contrary, delivers skills to the already qualified, increasing skill inequalities.

Despite this selective economic citizenship that has produced important educational inequalities, HE has considerably expanded since the 1990s, partly because of the development of dynamic services. It appeared to be a strategy mainly to fight unemployment (young people going to universities were not counted as being unemployed), rather than a high-skill, dynamic service strategy, inasmuch as there was no parallel upgrade to the job structure, like there was in the growth strategy focused on quality exports in the Nordic countries (Ansell and Gingrich 2018). It is partly due to the low level of macro-corporatism, which, when it is present, allows economic actors to coordinate efficiently in order to specialize in high valued-added sectors. One subsequent consequence is the growing mismatch in skills and over-education among young people.

The youth social citizenship of young people is strongly familialized in France, as in most Continental countries with a Bismarckian welfare regime and a Catholic tradition (Chevalier 2018). As a result, this familialization also concerns student support. Not only is family policy crucial in supporting young people in HE (with family benefits and tax relief for families), but student grants also depend on parental income. This is why, unlike individualized student support, which benefits between 80 and 100% of full-time students, it applied to only 39.2% of students in France in 2016–17 (Table 11.6). [7]

How is it then possible to expand HE and restrict student support at the same time? At the beginning of the 1990s, i.e., at the same time the expansion of HE took place, housing benefits (ALS and APL) were opened up to young people not in paid employment, illustrating the French "publicly supported strategy" and expanding social spending. As an unintended consequence, this has allowed students to claim for this individualized benefit (Van de Velde 2008). In a familialized context, the individualization of student support, accompanying the expansion of HE, has taken

[7] During the mandate of François Hollande (2012–17), several reforms were passed concerning young people and education: one of them further extended the coverage of grants, from 30% to almost 40%, confirming Garritzmann's argument about the effect of left-wing parties on student finance (2016).

place at the margin, through a process of "conversion" (from housing policy to student support) (Chevalier 2012; Streeck and Thelen 2005).

In the wake of the crisis, governments have adopted reforms consistent with the growth strategy in place. Most of them have fostered atypical employment for young people in the context of high youth unemployment and a dualized labor market. However, one can still see some differences, depending on partisan politics. The right-wing government, in place when the crisis began, adopted welfare-to-work reforms: the means-tested benefit "revenu de solidarité active" (RSA) replaced the former "revenu minimum d'insertion" in 2008. Because of the familialization of social citizenship, young people below twenty-five cannot claim it. A "RSA jeune" was adopted in 2010. However, the conditions to access it (having worked two years over the last three) are so restrictive that very few can actually claim it (only 1,000 young people put in a claim in 2017).

In 2012, a left-wing government came to power, claiming to act for young people, unlike the previous government. Where youth unemployment was concerned, they implemented two opposing types of reforms: On the one hand, in line with Vlandas's findings (2013), they supported direct (atypical) job creation with the launch of a new type of subsidized job in 2014, the so-called "contrat d'avenir." On the other hand, they adopted a youth guarantee program ("garantie jeunes"), inspired by the Nordic countries and the EU, which was introduced experimentally in 2013 and then adopted in 2017.

This reform reflects a political move from the left, both in the direction of the individualization of social citizenship (young people aged eighteen to twenty-five can claim a benefit equivalent to the RSA) and of an inclusive economic citizenship, since its aim is to give low-skilled young people a second chance. Hence, political parties seem to have some agency over reforms. Nevertheless, two aspects limit this conclusion, reminding one of the structural effect of the growth strategy.

First, its implementation does not reflect the "learn-first" perspective of Nordic youth guarantees, but a "work-first" orientation: the objective remains to give young people a job as quickly as possible, rather than improving their skills. Second, the bulk of the government's intervention, in terms of spending, has mainly laid in its focus on the labor force in general with the "credit d'impôt pour la compétitivité et l'emploi" in 2014.

The French government's action to fight youth unemployment therefore reflects the growth strategy in place, by fostering atypical employment and reducing the cost of youth labor, although left-wing governments have tried to implement policies that echo the Nordic regime.

4. Conclusion

In this chapter, I have shown the complementarity between the growth strategies identified in this book, socio-economic institutions in general, and youth welfare citizenship in particular. Growth strategies are structured by, and in return shape, socio-economic institutions as well as youth welfare citizenship regimes. However, there is still some agency for political parties over youth-related issues, like ALMP reforms to reduce youth unemployment, though within the path traced by growth strategies. This result contributes to the literature in three ways.

First, this chapter validates the relevance of the growth strategy perspective adopted in this book. In fact, the two main sources of growth, i.e., the aggregate demand and the main economic sector, structure the content of skill (specific vs general, according to the sector) and its level and distribution (high and equal vs polarized, related to export performance). These have consequences, not only for the youth economic citizenship, but also for the youth social citizenship, through the importance of HE and, subsequently, the extension of student support (access to HE supposes some form of individualization of social rights). However, the source of domestic consumption is also important. If household consumption stems from private debt, then welfare becomes asset-based, which is consistent with the introduction of student loans in the UK. If household consumption depends on high wages, then the government is trapped in a dilemma: either it sustains wages (and therefore growth) but decreases the competitiveness of employers in the short-run at the expense of employment (supposedly at least); or it tries to decrease labor costs to boost competitiveness and subsequently foster employment. To solve this dilemma, I have shown that the French government has focused on the reduction of youth labor costs, in line with the dualization argument (Palier and Thelen 2010).

Second, it contributes to the social investment literature in two ways: On the one hand, the social investment literature has insisted on the importance of looking at the entire life course from a dynamic perspective, usually by emphasizing early childhood. I have shown here that the transition to adulthood has also been transformed, leading to the period of youth, and I have proposed a theoretical framework for understanding the way the welfare state can structure this transformed transition, articulating different policies that are not always analyzed together, i.e., education, ALMP, social policies, and student support. On the other hand, according to the general argument of the book, I have shown to what extent this social investment strategy (i.e., the "youth enabling citizenship" of the Nordic countries) depends on a specific growth strategy and not only on politics (Beramendi et al. 2015). If political parties do matter, they have a "conditional" effect, depending both on the party system (Manow et al. 2018) and the growth strategy. The policy implication is important, as it can be argued that adopting these social policies in a different economic context would either be impossible or would produce different effects.

Finally, it widens the literature on youth. In fact, youth studies and the sociology of youth transitions usually suffer from two limitations: They focus on young people and youth policies, without taking into account the overall economic and institutional context where youth transitions take place. As youth is conceptualized as a new stage of life, this sometimes justifies the idea that it is separated from the issues concerning the overall population. Here, I show that youth must be analyzed as a metonymy: it is indeed a specific part of the population and of the life course, but it represents what is happening more globally. As a result, to understand youth, one needs to look at the global picture of society. When scholars, working on young people, take the economy into account, they usually focus on common trends towards neoliberalization and what they mean for youth. Here, I show that the economy must indeed be taken in account, but that it is institutionally embedded (in line with the comparative political economy literature). This is why there is still high cross-national diversity instead of a "political economy of youth" (Côté 2014). I therefore argue more in favor of a "comparative political economy of youth transitions."

References

Aeberhardt, R., Crusson, L., and Pommier, P. 2011. "Les politiques d'accès à l'emploi en faveur des jeunes: qualifier et accompagner." In *France, portrait social.* Paris, INSEE: Insee Références, 153–72.

Allmendinger, J. and Leibfried, S. 2003. "Education and the welfare state: the four worlds of competence production." *Journal of European Social Policy* 13(1): 63–81.

Ansell, B. W. 2008. "University challenges: explaining institutional change in higher education." *World Politics* 60(2): 189–30.

Ansell, B. W. and Gingrich, J. 2013. "A tale of two trilemmas: Varieties of higher education and the service economy." In *The Political Economy of the Service Transition*, edited by Anne Wren. Oxford: Oxford University Press, 195–24.

Ansell, B. W. and Gingrich, J. 2018. "Skill in Demand? Higher Education and Social Investment in Europe". In *Welfare Democracies and Party Politics. Explaining Electoral Dynamics in Times of Changing Welfare Capitalism*, edited by Philipp Manow, Bruno Palier, and Hanna Schwander. Oxford: Oxford University Press, 225–53.

Anxo, D. and Niklasson, H. 2006. "The Swedish model in turbulent times: Decline or renaissance?" *International Labour Review* 145(4): 339–71.

Askenazy, P., Bozio, A., and García-Peñalosa, C. 2013. "Wage dynamics in times of crisis." *Notes du conseil d'analyse économique* (5): 1–12.

Baudelot, C. and Establet, R. 2009. *L'élitisme républicain : L'école française à l'épreuve des comparaisons internationales.* Paris: Seuil.

Beramendi, P., Häusermann, S., Kitschelt, H., and Kriesi, H. (eds.). 2015. *The Politics of Advanced Capitalism.* Cambridge: Cambridge University Press.

Billari, F. 2004. "Becoming an Adult in Europe: A Macro(/Micro)-Demographic Perspective." *Demographic Research* 3: 15–44.

Birnbaum, S., Ferrarini, T., Nelson, K., and Palme, J. 2017. *The Generational Welfare Contract: Justice, Institutions and Outcomes*. Cheltenham, UK; Northampton, MA: Edward Elgar Pub.

Bonoli, G. 2010. "The Political Economy of Active Labor-Market Policy." *Politics & Society* 38(4): 435–57.

Bourdet, Y. and Persson, I. 1991. "Politiques de l'emploi et durée du chômage: une comparaison franco-suédoise." *Observations et diagnostics économiques* 38: 65–92.

Boyer, R. 1995. "Wage austerity or/and an educational push: the French dilemma." *CEPREMAP Working Paper* no. 9516. Paper prepared for the 10th IIRA WORLD CONGRESS, Washington DC, May 31–June 4, 1995. http://www.cepremap.fr/depot/couv_orange/co9516.pdf

Brown, P., Green, A., and Lauder, H. 2001. *High Skills: Globalization, competitiveness, and skill formation*. Oxford: Oxford University Press.

Busemeyer, M. 2009. "Asset specificity, institutional complementarities and the variety of skill regimes in coordinated market economies." *Socio-Economic Review* 7(3): 375–406.

Busemeyer, M. 2011. "Varieties of cross-class coalitions in the politics of dualization: Insights from the case of vocational training in Germany." *MPIfG discussion paper* 11/13.

Busemeyer, M. 2015. *Skills and Inequality. Partisan politics and the political economy of education reforms in Western welfare states*. Cambridge: Cambridge University Press.

Cahuc, P., Carcillo, S., Galland, O., and Zylberberg, A. 2011. *La machine à trier: Comment la France divise sa jeunesse*. Paris: Eyrolles.

Cahuc, P., Carcillo, S., and Zimmermann, K. F. 2013. "The employment of the low-skilled youth in France." *IZA Policy Paper*, 64.

Chevalier, T. 2012. *L'Etat-providence et les jeunes*. Paris: L'Harmattan.

Chevalier, T. 2016. "Varieties of youth welfare citizenship. Towards a two-dimension typology." *Journal of European Social Policy* 26: 3–19.

Chevalier, T. 2018. "Social Citizenship of Young People in Europe: A Comparative Institutional Analysis." *Journal of Comparative Policy Analysis: Research and Practice* 20(3): 304–23.

Chevalier, T. 2019. "Pourquoi y a-t-il plus de jeunes au chômage en France qu'en Allemagne? Économie politique d'une citoyenneté économique." *Revue française de science politique*, 5(69): 793–20.

Côté, J. E. 2014. "Towards a new political economy of youth." *Journal of Youth Studies* 17(4): 527–43.

Crouch, C. 2009. "Privatised Keynesianism: An Unacknowledged Policy Regime." *British Journal of Politics & International Relations* 11(3): 382–99.

Culpepper, P. D., Hall, P. A., and Palier, B. (eds.). 2006. *La France en mutation. 1980–2005*. Paris: Presses de Sciences Po.

Durazzi, N. 2019. "The Political Economy of High Skills: Higher Education in Knowledge-Based Labour Markets." *Journal of European Public Policy* 26(12): 1799–817.

Durazzi, N. and Benassi, C. 2020. "Going Up-Skill: Exploring the Transformation of the German Skill Formation System." *German Politics* 29(3): 319–38.

Emmenegger, P. 2009. *Regulatory Social Policy: The Politics of Job Security Regulations*. Bern: Haupt Verlag AG.

Esping-Andersen, G. 1990. *The Three Worlds of Welfare Capitalism*. Princeton: Princeton University Press.

Estevez-Abe, M., Iversen, T., and Soskice, D. 2001. "Social Protection and the Formation of Skills: A Reinterpretation of the Welfare State." In *Varieties of Capitalism*, edited by Peter Hall and David Soskice. Oxford: Oxford University Press, 145–83.

Eurydice 2017. *National Student Fee and Support Systems in European Higher Education*. Luxembourg: Publications Office of the European Union.

Finegold, D. 1999. *The German Skills Machine: Sustaining comparative advantage in a global economy*. New York, Oxford: Berghahn Books.

Garritzmann, J. L. 2016. *The Political Economy of Higher Education Finance. The politics of tuition fees and subsidies in OECD countries, 1945–2015*. London: Palgrave Macmillan.

Green, A. 2001. "The United Kingdom—High skills/low skills model." In *High Skills. Globalization, competitiveness, and skill formation*, edited by P. Brown, A. Green, and H. Lauder. Oxford: Oxford University Press.

Green, A., Green, F., and Pensiero, N. 2014. "Why are literacy and numeracy skills in England so unequal? Evidence from OECD's Survey of Adult Skills and other international surveys." *LLAKES research paper*, 47.

Guillemard, A.-M. 1986. *Le Déclin du social : Formation et Crise des politiques de la vieillesse*. Paris: PUF.

Hall, P. A. and Soskice, D. (eds.). 2001. *Varieties of Capitalism: The Institutional Foundations of Comparative Advantage*. Oxford: Oxford University Press.

Hassel, A., Naczyck, M. and Wiss, T. 2019. "The Political Economy of Pension Financialisation: Public Policy Responses to the Crisis." *Journal of European Public Policy*: 26(4): 483–500.

Harris, N. S. 2000. "Social security and education." In *Social Security Law in Context*. Oxford: Oxford University Press, 327–61.

Hay, C. 2013. *The Failure of Anglo-liberal Capitalism*. Basingstoke: Palgrave Macmillan.

Heywood, C. 2001. *A History of Childhood: Children and Childhood in the West from Medieval to Modern Times*. Cambridge: Polity Press.

Hummeluhr, N. 1997. *Youth Guarantees in the Nordic Countries*. Paris: OECD Publishing.

Iversen, T. and Stephens, J. D. 2008. "Partisan politics, the welfare state, and three worlds of human capital formation." *Comparative Political Studies* 41(4–5): 600–37.

Janmaat, J. G., Duru-Bellat, M., Green, A., and Méhaut, P. (eds.). 2013. *The Dynamics and Social Outcomes of Education Systems*. Basingstoke: Macmillan.

Jones, G. and Wallace, C. 1992. *Youth, Family, and Citizenship*. Maidenhead: Open University Press.

Kohli, M. 1986. " The World We Forgot: A Historical Review of the Life Course." In *Later Life: The social psychology of ageing*, edited by V. W. Marshall. Beverly Hills: SAGE, 271–303.

Kohlrausch, B. 2009. *A Ticket to Work: Policies for the Young Unemployed in Britain and Germany*. Frankfurt: Campus Verlag.

Lefresne, F. 2012. "Trente-cinq ans de politique d'insertion professionnelle des jeunes: un bilan en demie-teinte." In *Politiques de jeunesse: le grand malentendu*, edited by Valérie Becquet, Patricia Loncle, and Cécile Van de Velde. Nîmes: Champ social, 106–25.

Leisering, L. 2003. "Government and the life course." In *Handbook of the Life Course*, edited by J. T. Mortimer and M. J. Shanahan. New York: Kluwer Academic Publishers, 205–25.

Lynch, J. 2006. *Age in the Welfare State: The Origins of Social Spending on Pensioners, Workers, and Children*. Cambridge: Cambridge University Press.

Manow, P., Palier, B., and Schwander, H. (eds.). 2018. *Welfare Democracies and Party Politics. Explaining Electoral Dynamics in Times of Changing Welfare Capitalism*. Oxford: Oxford University Press.

Manow, P. and Van Kersbergen, K. (eds.). 2009. *Religion, Class Coalitions, and Welfare States*. Cambridge: Cambridge University Press.

Marshall, T. H. 1950. *Citizenship and Social Class and Other Essays*. Cambridge: Cambridge University Press.

Martin, C. J. and Swank, D. 2004. "Does the organization of capital matter? Employers and active labor market policy at the national and firm levels." *American Political Science Review* 98(4): 593–611.

Martin, C. J. and Swank, D. 2012. *The Political Construction of Business Interests: Coordination, Growth, and Equality*. Cambridge: Cambridge University Press.

Mayer, K. U. and Schoepflin, U. 1989. "The state and the life course." *Annual review of sociology* 15: 187–209.

Morel, N., Palier, B., and Palme, J. (eds.). 2012. *Towards a Social Investment Welfare State?: Ideas, Polices and Challenges*. Bristol: The Policy Press.

Müller, W. and Gangl, M. 2003. *Transitions from Education to Work in Europe: The Integration of Youth into EU Labour Markets*. Oxford: Oxford University Press.

OECD. 2010. *Off to a Good Start? Jobs for Youth*. Paris: OECD Publishing.

Oftedal Telhaug, A., Asbjørn Mediås, O., and Aasen, P. 2006. "The Nordic Model in Education: Education as part of the political system in the last 50 years." *Scandinavian Journal of Educational Research* 50(3): 245–83.

Ornston, D. 2013. "Creative Corporatism. The Politics of High-Technology Competition in Nordic Europe." *Comparative Political Studies* 46(6): 702–29.

Palier, B. and Thelen, K. 2010. "Institutionalizing Dualism: Complementarities and Change in France and Germany." *Politics & Society* 38(1): 119–48.

Sanchez, R. 2012. "L'apprentissage en 2011." *DARES Analyses* 80: 1–8.

Schmidt, V. A. 2002. *The Futures of European Capitalism*, Oxford: Oxford University Press.

Seawright, J. and Gerring, J. 2008. "Case Selection Techniques in Case Study Research: A Menu of Qualitative and Quantitative Options." *Political Research Quarterly* 61(2): 294–308.

Streeck, W. 1991. "On the Institutional Conditions of Diversified Quality Production." In *Beyond Keynesianism.* Aldershot: Edward Elgar Publishing, 21–61.

Streeck, W. and Thelen, K. (eds.). 2005. *Beyond Continuity: Institutional Change in Advanced Political Economies.* Oxford: Oxford University Press.

Thelen, K. and Busemeyer, M. R. 2012. "Institutional Change in German Vocational Training: From Collectivism towards Segmentalism." In *The Comparative Political Economy of Collective Skills Systems*, edited by Marius Busemeyer and Christine Trampusch. Oxford: Oxford University Press, 68–100.

Thelen, K. 2014. *Varieties of Liberalization and the New Politics of Social Solidarity.* Cambridge: Cambridge University Press.

Van de Velde, C. 2008. *Devenir Adulte: Sociologie comparée de la jeunesse en Europe.* Paris: PUF.

Vlandas, T. 2013. "Mixing Apples with Oranges? Partisanship and Active Labour Market Policies in Europe." *Journal of European Social Policy* 23(1): 3–20.

Walther, A. 2006. "Regimes of youth transitions: Choice, flexibility and security in young people's experiences across different European contexts." *Young* 14(2): 119–39.

12
Growth Strategies and Welfare Reforms in Europe

Sonja Avlijaš, Anke Hassel, and Bruno Palier

1. Introduction

This chapter ends our journey exploring the role of growth strategies and associated welfare reforms in the evolution of advanced capitalist economies. Its key argument is that welfare reforms are institutionally and politically linked to countries' growth strategies, i.e. their adaptations to the new era of growth since the 1980s. Linkages between welfare systems and growth regimes (and economic activity more generally) are rarely made in the social policy literature. Usually, the main explanation for welfare state reforms refers to sociodemographic changes such as aging, entry of women into the labor market, and emergence of new social risks (Esping-Andersen 1999; Bonoli 2005; Hemerijck 2013). Recent research on the politics of the welfare state highlights the relevance of changes in citizen preferences for explaining welfare state reforms (e.g. Gingrich and Häusermann 2015). Here again, there is no link between welfare state reforms and national economic strategies. When welfare state reforms are linked to economic issues and policies, they are often portrayed as being imposed by generic global factors such as globalization, neoliberalism, and austerity, but not as mitigated by countries' institutional and political idiosyncrasies.

Yet, in practice, when welfare systems have changed (Hemerijck 2013; Palier and Hay 2017; Taylor-Gooby et al. 2017), their transformations have not been the same across all countries; they have not followed the same timing or the same logic, although the countries were exposed to the same exogenous, socio-demographic or economic forces of change. Why did the United Kingdom reform its pension system much earlier than Germany, despite the much stronger demographic pressure in Germany? Why did pension funds develop more in English-speaking and Nordic countries than in Continental and Southern Europe (Ebbinghaus 2011; Hassel et al. 2019)? Why did governments liberalize labor markets much sooner in English-speaking countries, and why did governments in Continental Europe only partially pursue this path, mostly affecting atypical employment (Emmenegger et al. 2012)? Why were social investment policies

Sonja Avlijaš, Anke Hassel, and Bruno Palier, *Growth Strategies and Welfare Reforms in Europe* In: *Growth and Welfare in Advanced Capitalist Economies: How Have Growth Regimes Evolved?* Edited by: Anke Hassel and Bruno Palier, Oxford University Press (2021). © Oxford University Press. DOI: 10.1093/oso/9780198866176.003.0012

(i.e. policies aimed at investing in and mobilizing human capital and capabilities) taken up more fully in Nordic countries than in Southern or Eastern Europe (Morel et al. 2012)?

This variety might simply be explained by welfare regime path dependence. But we see significant variation in how the countries' reforms correspond to national institutional contexts: while some reforms fit the country's institutional legacy (path-dependent reforms), others do not (path-breaking reforms), as Thelen shows in her chapter (this volume) with the cases of Sweden and the Netherlands. Moreover, even if path dependency plays a major role in shaping the trajectory taken by changing welfare states, it does not explain why there have been reforms in the first place, or the specific content and timing of these reforms. Adjustment to demographic and social changes or to changes in individuals' preferences cannot explain the differences in timing and content of the observed reforms.

In this final chapter, we build on previous chapters of this volume and on other research on welfare state transformation to demonstrate that referring to national growth strategies helps in understanding welfare reforms. Our key proposition is that welfare system reforms are part of a government's economic growth strategy. Economic growth and job creation are key concerns for governments, since these are two goals for which the government is most accountable to its electorate. As presented in Chapter 1, all the actions taken in order to boost growth and job creation comprise what we call growth strategies. We do not conceive of growth strategies as a strategic plan of action, premeditated by a specific government, but as a trajectory of reforms that emerges over time through a series of trials and errors and interactions between policy-makers and electoral and economic pressures (see Chapter 1 by Hassel and Palier, this volume). In that sense, growth strategies are not necessarily explicitly embedded in government policy discourse. Nevertheless, we argue that identifying and analyzing specific national growth strategies (as a pattern in a series of economic and social decisions) is necessary for understanding the content and timing of welfare state reforms. There are different ways to boost growth and jobs, and we contend that these national differences explain a substantial part of the welfare system reforms that have occurred since the 1980s.

In Chapter 1 of this volume, Hassel and Palier claim that five main growth regimes can be distinguished in contemporary advanced capitalist democracies. Working within these regimes (and sometimes in spite of them), governments in advanced industrialized European countries have pursued distinct strategies to generate growth in the post-Fordist era. In this chapter, we link these specific growth strategies to specific welfare state reforms:

- The high-quality manufacturing-based export-led strategy relies on wage moderation and on the protection of labor market insiders to maintain its international competitiveness, resulting in labor market and social protection dualization.

- The export of dynamic services strategy focuses on innovation and investment in a high-skill workforce to maintain product quality and develop new products and services. It requires financialization for promoting innovation capacity as well as social protection and social investment for developing a flexible but well-protected workforce.
- The FDI-financed export-led strategy attracts foreign investors with low corporate taxes and through specific social and educational policies that prepare the workforce for foreign investment. It relies on cost containment, but also on some compensation for the main "losers" of the strategy.
- The financialization strategy is related to the privatization and marketization of housing and pensions (but also education and other social services) to fuel the financial services industries.
- The publicly supported domestic demand-led strategy aims to stabilize employment and growth by keeping domestic demand steady through high minimum wages and social benefits.

Interactions between welfare system reforms and growth strategies are not automatic or purely functional. Reform attempts can have other goals (electoral, redistributive, coping with new social risks, and so on) and may create tensions between economic strategies, on the one hand, and social and political goals and interests, on the other. For the sake of our argument, the focus of this chapter is on the theoretically proposed complementarities between growth strategies and welfare system reforms. In reality, however, some of the "ideal typical" welfare reforms (which would be compatible with a country's growth strategy) may have been impeded in some cases, at least partially, due to electoral pressures, especially where the population has concerns about inequality or where the dynamics of electoral and party competition have trumped the economic growth agenda.

As we show in our empirical examples, there is no single mechanism connecting growth strategies and welfare reforms. The interaction between growth strategies and welfare system reforms can take place via at least three different mechanisms: i) the welfare system acts as an input for growth; ii) the existing welfare system is perceived as an obstacle to growth, so there is a need to reform, cut, or transform it to stimulate growth; and iii) growth takes place without positive redistributive impacts, so the welfare state is strengthened as a compensatory tool.

Evolving trajectories of growth and welfare regimes have made countries more distinct rather than similar over time. This becomes especially clear when we analyze the different mechanisms through which countries' growth strategies have shaped welfare reforms. We show that when seemingly similar reforms of the welfare system are driven by different growth strategies, the design and properties of these reforms differ, as do their implications for the country and its citizens.

This chapter is divided into four sections. Section 2 theoretically links the five stylized growth strategies to welfare system reforms. Section 3 traces the proposed linkages between growth strategies and welfare state reforms empirically by mapping key reforms of the welfare systems in several European countries. Section 4 brings the discussion back to the politics of growth and welfare in capitalist democracies.

2. Growth Strategies and Welfare State Reforms: The Theoretical Linkages

Several chapters in this volume have identified exports and domestic demand as the two key drivers of economic growth (especially Baccaro and Pontusson; Picot; Scharpf). Hassel and Palier (this volume) have shown in Chapter 1 that export-oriented economies rely on exporting high value-added services or manufacturing goods (of a greater or lesser quality), while domestic demand-driven ones can pursue stimulation of domestic demand via either private debt or wage and welfare benefits. All approaches have direct implications for welfare reforms. We start here by reviewing the basic connections between growth and welfare as they appear in various countries studied in previous chapters, before elaborating systematically the theoretical linkages between each growth strategy and the corresponding welfare state reforms.

When growth is driven by exports of high-quality manufactured goods, specialized skills of employees are a central element of the regime. For instance, it is well-known that in Germany these skills are provided by an efficient system of apprenticeship and vocational training, mainly financed and controlled by companies. Employers are dependent on the specific skills of their employees and have a keen interest in their willingness to participate in and support vocational training. Moreover, the employees' specialization is not easily transferable to other sectors, thus employers aim to ensure job security and social security for them.

As manufacturing exports are price-sensitive, wage moderation is important (see Baccaro and Pontusson, this volume). This is even more vital in cases of foreign direct investment (FDI)-dependent economies, such as the Visegrád countries in Eastern Europe. Here, the economy needs to attract foreign investment, upgrade production capacities, and protect the skills of the manufacturing workforce in order to guarantee productivity (but without spending too much so as not to deter FDI with higher labor costs). This leads to the maintenance of specific skill formation systems inherited from the socialist era and compensatory social protection for the losers of the restructuring of manufacturing industry, at the expense of female labor force participation as well as broader social investment. The FDI-led export growth strategy can, however, instead rely on dynamic services-oriented foreign investment, along with the dismantling of old socialist industries, as in the Baltic countries. The welfare reform then aims to develop general skills among the population and subsequently social investment, at the expense of compensatory social expenditure.

High-tech goods and services are less price-sensitive and require a highly skilled and flexible workforce (Wren, this volume). Firms need to be able to generate new innovative activities with high value-added, for instance in financial services (as in the United States or the UK) or new tech companies (the Nordic countries or California). In this instance, the stability of jobs and activities may not be as central as in the previous cases.

When domestic household consumption plays a stronger role in driving growth, two typical scenarios emerge. First, household consumption can be driven by private debt as in the US or the UK. In this case, the financial sector plays a vital role in economic growth. The privatization of education and social protection can contribute to this strategy by providing both market-based welfare to people and a growth opportunity for the financial sector. Second, wages and public benefits can support domestic demand (as in Southern European countries, including France). Here, compensatory social benefits (what Beramendi et al. 2015 call "social consumption") are key. In both these cases, the capacity to finance public debt and/or devalue the currency is crucial. Scharpf (this volume) shows how the Economic and Monetary Union (EMU) prevented the countries relying on domestic demand-led growth from devaluing their currency, leading to growing public debt. After the 2008 financial crisis, these countries have been under pressure to change their strategy and seek lower labor costs. Below, we call this the "competitive impoverishment" strategy, based on welfare state retrenchment and structural reforms.

Policy decisions are embedded in given economic structures and tend to buttress existing patterns of economic or sectoral specialization. However, they can also contribute to the transformation of growth regimes. For instance, financialization that sustains domestic demand can also contribute to the development of information and communications technology (ICT)-based sectors (Hassel and Palier, this volume), which in turn require an investment in higher skills (Wren, this volume). Thelen (this volume) shows how labor market reforms, as well as vocational training reforms, have accompanied the bifurcation of the Dutch growth regime and diversification of the Swedish one.

In the sub-sections that follow, we present in a stylized way the main mechanisms through which the different components of welfare system reforms interact with one another and with growth strategies. By analyzing ideal-typical cases, we spell out an institutional complementarities-based theoretical framework, which then explains (in section 3) how governments have used welfare reforms to (try to) stimulate growth.

We associate each of the five growth strategies with a typical set of changes in welfare policy that, combined, can be characterized as a more or less distinct type of welfare system reform. The five types of welfare state reforms are:

dualization of welfare, social investment, fiscal and social attractiveness, commodification of welfare, social protectionism. We focus here on the main welfare policy arenas: the labor market, wages, pensions, housing, education (social investment), and social benefits (social spending). In practice, the different types of welfare system reforms do not have to be mutually exclusive, but some policies are incompatible. As we show, for example, increasing wages and maintaining high social benefits might conflict with a policy that focuses on wage moderation in order to foster the export of manufacturing goods.

2.1 Manufacturing Export-Based Growth Strategy and the Dualization of Welfare

This growth strategy focuses on protecting traditional manufacturing industries in a context of globalization and deindustrialization, which requires maintaining the quality and productivity of the sector, while keeping prices low. The emphasis is on controlling labor costs via wage moderation (Johnston, this volume). As long as external demand compensates for the lack of domestic demand, wage moderation does not undermine growth.

Wage moderation and the preservation of quality in manufacturing labor is achieved through the protection of labor market insiders, close cooperation with manufacturing trade unions regarding investment and technology, and enhancement of skills through liaison with entities providing further or continuing education. Core workers in the manufacturing sector are promised employment protection in exchange for wage restraint and internal flexibility such as willingness to change jobs within the firm or variation in working time. As plant-level labor representatives prefer long-term investments and job security over short-term wage gains, local plant-level deals accumulate to shape sectoral policies of trade union wage restraint.

Since export capacity is key to this strategy, the real exchange rate is a central concern. Policies that might negatively affect the real exchange rate, such as accommodating fiscal or monetary policies and wage increases, are repressed institutionally and politically. These policy responses have repercussions not only for fiscal spending on education and childcare but also for labor market policies.

As demand stimulation is not an option, supply-side measures to reduce the reservation wage are introduced. The strategy also depends on the emergence of a cheap and flexible service sector, which makes domestic services affordable. Thus, dualization and supply-side labor market policies feed directly into the pattern of economic specialization (Palier and Thelen 2010; Hassel 2014). Companies use industrial restructuring to weed out less-productive service segments of the production processes from highly productive manufacturing ones. They thereby introduce an internal segmentation of their workforce and adopt changes in labor market rules that allow for a dualization of labor markets. The social partners, i.e. employers' and employees' representatives, tolerate the emergence of atypical employment and a low-pay segment in other sectors, including in services, in order to save the manufacturing industry (Palier and Thelen 2010).

Other welfare reforms aimed at securing cost competitiveness are complementary to the manufacturing export-based growth strategy. Pension and health reforms aim to limit the increase in social contributions to constrain non-wage labor costs. With regard to housing policy, Reisenbichler (this volume) shows that conservative housing finance policies are designed to restrain demand and dynamic housing markets in order to keep down the cost of living, wages, and inflation. Dynamic housing markets are not central in such a growth strategy also because wage moderation further depresses the demand for mortgages and because central banks in these economies are mostly preoccupied with low inflation, price stability, and market discipline.

2.2 Exports of Dynamic Services Growth Strategy and Social Investment

In the dynamic services-driven growth strategy, governments aim to boost the quality and innovation capacity of the business community in order to remain competitive in the knowledge economy. They invest in education and (re-)training of the workforce, as well as human capital more generally. A certain degree of labor force flexibility is required to adapt the economy to innovation and change, as well as to external competitive pressures. At the same time, workers need to be able to switch sectors, while preserving or renewing their skills. Since skill and social protection cannot be provided through employment security (which is associated with an economy that is too rigid and unable to innovate), protection and the formation and renewal of skills are provided to all by the (welfare) state. This allows workers to concurrently invest in their human capital through publicly financed education and training schemes while staying flexible in the labor market. Generous unemployment insurance also leads to a greater acceptance of risk, which enhances the workforce's capacity to cope with innovation (Boyer 2000: 6).

Therefore, social investment and social expenditure go hand in hand in this strategy, and they serve to boost labor productivity. Both factors, along with growing innovation, lead to wage expansion. Higher wages affect consumer behavior and stimulate domestic demand, which subsequently expands. Hence, this strategy allows for a combination of export-led and domestic demand-led growth.

This growth strategy requires that firms have access to venture capital which facilitates financialization. The welfare system can serve as a base for the expansion of finance, through pension funds or the development of private, social, and educational services. While a highly developed welfare state lowers the demand for market-based tools for risk diversification through private insurance, privatization of social services might be pursued as part of the expansion of dynamic services strategy.

Expanding financial markets help to facilitate innovation in the knowledge-based economy. While there are similarities between the dynamic services-based growth strategy and the financialization-based one described below, there is a key difference with regard to the role of the state. In the dynamic services-based growth strategy, the state foots the bill for education, social or health services, even though they can be provided by private firms, while financialization is pursued as a complementary strategy. Furthermore, despite the growing privatization and marketization of pensions, the state provides universal minimum pensions that reduce the individual market-based risk that citizens face vis-à-vis their retirement income, while social partners own the pension funds rather than private companies (Anderson 2019).

The aim of housing policy in this strategy is to provide universal access to housing for workers. It is a form of social investment, along with education and childcare, since its main policy aim is to improve workers' quality of life and thus boost their productivity. While private providers are included in service provision, the government regulates the market for all citizens and allows them access to social housing, rather than limiting its intervention only to those below a certain income threshold. In that sense, the role of the state in the housing market is strong, even when financial markets participate widely. As Reichenbichler (this volume) underlines, a dynamic market for housing finance is not an impediment to the dynamic services-based growth strategy. Wage growth and the expansion of domestic demand and credit underwrite a dynamic housing market. This is in contrast to the manufacturing export-based strategy, which is concerned with cost competitiveness of exports and therefore restraining wage growth.

2.3 FDI-Financed Export-Led Growth Strategy and Fiscal and Social Attractiveness

There is a third family of export-led growth regimes in which exports represent a significant share of GDP (see Table 1.2 in Hassel and Palier in this volume), and for which Foreign Direct Investment (FDI) is an important source of capital and innovation. These are "FDI-led growth regimes" (Nölke and Vliegenthart 2009; Bohle and Greskovits 2012; Bohle and Regan forthcoming). The growth strategy seeks to make the most of the position of specific national sectors in the global economy and find a niche in the global supply chains of multinational firms. Specific fiscal and social policies are developed in order to attract these FDIs.

In order to attract FDI, governments implement specific industrial polices including low corporate tax rates, but also tax incentives and subsidies targeting these specific sectors. Fiscal exemptions and cash subsidies complement low corporate taxation in order to target the investment to particular sectors of specialization. Some countries aim to attract multinational manufacturing firms (such as German or French automobile companies in Hungary) while others may want to attract American high-tech companies, for instance in Ireland (Bohle and Regan forthcoming).

Low labor costs are obtained through comparatively low levels of public social spending and non-wage labor costs. Policies thus focus on the liberalization of labor markets and social protection, welfare state retrenchment, and privatization in order to increase social attractiveness for foreign investors. When implemented, this growth strategy usually entails a deep transformation of the economy towards the sectors which attract FDI and may produce losers (such as domestic firm owners, workers from other non-favored sectors, or low-productivity workers in FDI sectors). In these cases, some social compensation mechanisms are introduced (e.g. severance pay, early retirement schemes), which ensures political stability that is also important for foreign investors. Fiscal capacities for social compensation are however limited because of the inability of these governments to raise taxes while at the same time maintaining their fiscal attractiveness for FDI.

Depending on which sectors attract high FDI, education and social policies may also be used to positively reinforce the strategy in favor of either (medium-skilled) manufacturing specialization or (more or less dynamic) services. If a government wants to support firms' comparative advantage in manufacturing, the maintenance of social insurance and a medium-skill educational system is necessary, and a compensatory welfare system (which also allows compensation for the losers of restructuring, for instance through early retirement) is favored over broader social investment. In contrast, if the government wants to provide foreign investors with a general-skilled workforce in order to develop ever more dynamic services, educational and social investment is supported (at the expense of compensatory social insurance).

2.4 Financialization-Based Growth Strategy and Commodification of Welfare

The financialization strategy uses the privatization and marketization of education and welfare (especially pensions and housing) to drive the overall financialization of the economy. This growth strategy relies on the residualization of public welfare and the rise of private social protection and education. Private welfare policies and access to mortgages encourage individuals to take responsibility for their own welfare through financial means. In the case of pensions, for example, privatization shifts the responsibility for provision to private actors, financial services, and employers, while marketization introduces market mechanisms into both public and private pension plans. Both reallocate retirement risks onto individuals and financialize their daily lives (Ebbinghaus 2015: 61; see also Engelen 2003; Hacker 2006; Langley 2008; Dixon and Sorsa 2009; Ebbinghaus 2011; Hassel et al. 2019).

In terms of housing, homeownership becomes the piggy bank of the middle classes as a form of additional retirement income (or savings). Furthermore, as Reisenbichler (this volume) explains, higher rates of homeownership may increase public support for welfare state retrenchment because expenses related to homeownership lower the incentives of voters to support public welfare expenditure, especially when it comes to pensions.

Also, financial centers provide well-paid jobs for some and attract investors. The growth of real incomes, in combination with a greater supply of financial instruments and a greater demand for housing, spurs both credit- and income-driven consumption and thus stimulates domestic demand. Rising house prices in a growing economy boost the wealth effect of financialization as they contribute to the wealth of the homeowners.

Greater financialization also drives technological innovation in dynamic services and greater demand for human capital investment. Innovation, particularly through ICT, is fostered by high levels of venture capital and general skills, but these are subordinated to the financial sector. The financial sector is important not only in terms of employment and added value, but also as a means for facilitating and shaping the real economy. Finance-driven economies offer particular services to international investors, particularly investment and mutual funds. The effects spill over onto the high street as well: the housing market keeps driving the wealth effect of financial growth, and house price inflation is not controlled (Reisenbichler, this volume).

Low wages in low-skill service sectors, a result of labor market liberalization and weakening trade union power, serve to stimulate domestic demand for personal and consumer services (Morel 2015; Wren, this volume). The significant wage discrepancy between high- and low-skill service jobs also boosts the demand for (higher) education. The financialization strategy relies on the growing demand for education as an opportunity to reduce state funding for education and enhance, via educational loans, market access to education. This further fuels the financialization-driven growth model and increases competition, especially in the higher education sector.

Because of comparatively high rates of growth and a dynamic labor market, people are not exposed to long spells of unemployment, hence there is less demand for social protection. The fact that only a minimal safety net against poverty is in place favors the existence of a low-wage labor market, which boosts the productivity of highly skilled workers, as they can outsource many of their non-work-related responsibilities to cheap service workers (Morel 2015). At the same time, given that domestic demand is the key driver of financialization, the state protects low-wage workers to a certain extent, for example, via income tax credits on earnings or a minimum wage, so that they do not end up having a negative effect on growth.

Therefore, financialization is fed through state retrenchment, privatization, and marketization of pensions, housing, and education, expansive wages, and the repression of social spending. These interactions create a cycle of economic growth and job creation, on the one hand, and a higher systemic risk from financial crises and growing wealth and income inequality, on the other.

2.5 Publicly Financed Domestic Demand-Based Growth Strategy and Social Protectionism

The basis of this growth strategy is government support for households and companies in order to maintain domestic demand. The nature of this strategy is thus embedded in state spending. It can be complemented by the financialization-driven strategy, which further boosts domestic demand. It may be more difficult to combine it with manufacturing exports, for reasons of labor cost.

In the ideal type of domestic demand-driven growth strategy, a generous national minimum wage and generous compensation through social benefits (especially pensions) feed household consumption, while companies are supported via state involvement, devaluation, and some protection against foreign trade and investment that reduces competitive pressure on firms (Molina and Rhodes 2007). Traditional firms benefit, as they are met with relatively low levels of product-market competition because of protectionist policies, which allow them to offer high employment protection to workers and face little pressure to boost competitiveness. In order to compensate for the lack of price competitiveness in international markets, the state ensures currency devaluation. Firms are also not constrained by short-term profits, because the financial system is centralized and bank-based rather than driven by financial investors, which further accommodates high employment protection. The state is, in turn, left with few resources to invest in innovation, but is also discouraged from investing, as its key focus is to protect the traditional sectors.

A low degree of financialization is reflected in the low penetration of private financial markets into pension and housing provision and in the reduced support for investment in innovation and the knowledge economy, which would be facilitated through a market for new financial products and services (Hassel and Palier, this volume). The absence of strong competitive pressure from global trade also discourages innovation, both at firm and state level, which exacerbates the vicious circle of pro-protectionist and anti-innovation policies (Capussela 2018).

The high level of employment protection, along with state protection of companies and their benefits, discourages workers from investing in their skills. This leads to low public demand for education, low enrollment rates in tertiary education, a weak and underfunded higher education system, weak vocational training, and no lifelong learning. A workforce with limited skills and education levels further limits the implementation of a high-skill and innovation-oriented industrial strategy. At the same time, an economy that is not based on knowledge and innovation does not demand these skills, which further undermines investment in human capital.

The decline of competitiveness leads to the shedding of labor in manufacturing and a further expansion of small firms in the service economy. Structural trends toward deindustrialization drive the dualization of the labor market. These structural pressures are reflected in the growing portion of labor market outsiders, i.e. flexible temporary and part-time contracts, which mostly affect new entrants into the labor market (younger workers). The growing precariousness of the labor force generates additional demand for non-employment-related social protection expenditures, while the public purse is being progressively depleted, as the country cannot find a sustainable engine for growth.

The publicly financed domestic demand-driven growth strategy is entrenched and reinforced politically. State spending is electorally constrained and geared towards protecting the vested interests of pensioners and the wealthy, as well as labor market insiders who benefit from social protection. These groups are favored over youth, who are consequently unable to access well-protected jobs and face a faltering economy that does not demand high skills. In this context, we see a political reinforcement of the economic division between pensioners and the wealthy, on the one hand, and youth and the poor, on the other.

Being caught in this vicious circle of low growth and high state expenditure, the publicly financed domestic demand-based growth strategy is least adapted to the new global drivers of growth (financialization and digitalization). For members of the Eurozone, export competitiveness is further undermined by the country's inability to devalue its exchange rate. Because of the Eurozone context, this growth strategy is also especially susceptible and non-resilient to systemic shocks such as financial crises, as well as to external pressures to maintain the stability of the EMU.

Within the Eurozone, these pressures have led to an externally imposed, austerity-based agenda of "competitive impoverishment" (see section 3.6). While the extent of the competitive impoverishment strategy has varied across countries, it is premised on the idea that the welfare state represents an impediment to growth and that internal devaluation of labor costs via deregulation of employment protection, reduction of minimum wages, and institutional weakening of unions and collective bargaining are necessary (see also Scharpf in this volume).

2.6 Overview of the Five Growth Strategies

Figure 12.1 summarizes the various components of the growth strategies and welfare system reforms that tend to be associated with them. Within each strategy, we emphasize the main engine for growth (export manufacturing sector, dynamic services, FDI, financial services, or wages and social benefits). We also highlight the main macroeconomic policies (in terms of budgetary and monetary policies) and the associated welfare policies i.e. labor market, education, and social policies.

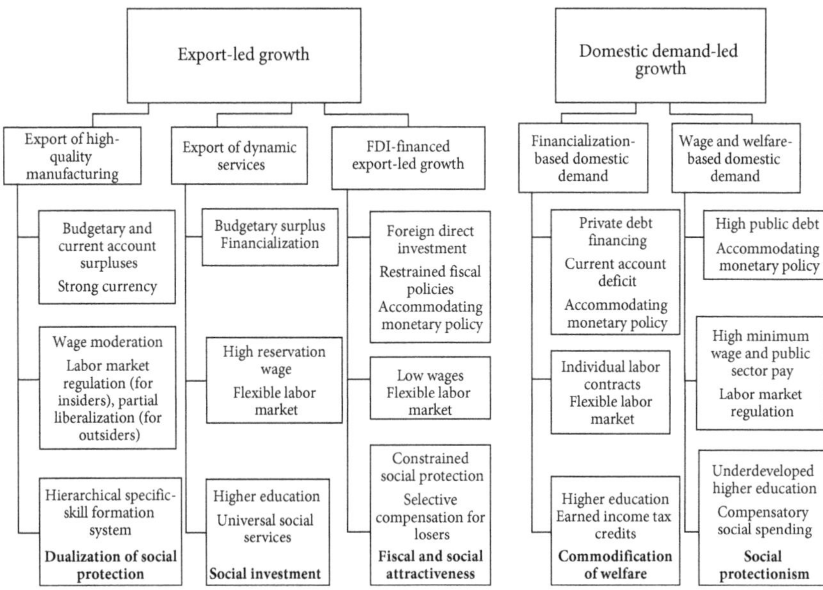

Figure 12.1 Welfare reforms in five distinct growth strategies

As a result, we show the relationship between the five different growth strategies and five main types of welfare state reforms:

(1) **Dualization of welfare.** Protecting medium and specialized skills, labor market regulation, and wage control, all policies favored by and favoring the manufacturing sector (to promote manufacturing exports as a driver of growth).
(2) **Social investment** and expansion of higher education (to promote economic specialization in innovation, the digital economy, and higher education as drivers of growth).
(3) **Fiscal and social attractiveness.** Attracting FDI through low corporate taxes and low labor costs, minimizing the cost of public welfare while compensating the main losers, promoting either medium-skilled (to attract

manufacturing FDI) or developing higher education (to attract high-tech FDI).

(4) **Commodification of welfare.** Asset-based social policy, access to credit to bolster demand and consumption, privatization of health insurance and pensions (to promote financial services as engine of growth).

(5) **Social protectionism.** Maintaining wage levels (minimum wages) and social spending despite deindustrialization to protect aggregate demand (to promote domestic demand as engine of growth). This strategy may be turned upside down to "competitive impoverishment" under external pressure (as has been the case in the Eurozone).

3. Tracing the Linkages through Country Cases

The empirical evidence presented in this section is mostly drawn from our own research, secondary sources, as well as other chapters in this volume. In the following case studies, we first examine the social policies adopted in Germany and how the dualization of the labor market occurred in support of export-oriented manufacturing. The analysis of the Nordic countries, specifically Sweden and Denmark, shows how they have combined social investment in human capital and education with innovation policies and financialization/privatization efforts. Then the cases of the Visegrád and Baltic countries are analyzed as (divergent) examples of how fiscal and social attractiveness policies that we associate with the FDI-led growth strategy have emerged and been implemented. Our survey of welfare system reforms in the UK serves as a case of commodification of welfare associated with the financialization growth strategy. Finally, we trace policies and reforms related to the domestic demand strategy in Southern Europe, especially in Italy and France.

3.1 Manufacturing Exports and Dualization of Welfare in Germany

Since the 1980s, the German political economy has increasingly specialized in high-quality manufacturing exports as a strategy for economic recovery and growth. Maintaining and strengthening the export-oriented manufacturing sector has involved maintenance of plant-level cooperation, facilitation of technological upgrading, and reduction of labor costs in order to keep the real exchange rate low. Such a growth strategy has turned out to be a mixed blessing. While it has preserved Germany's competitive edge vis-à-vis many other industrialized countries, it has also led to an increasing dependency on exports as the engine of growth. There has been no equally strong evolution of a domestic service economy beyond manufacturing-related services. By 2019, the share of exports in Germany's GDP was approaching 50%, while domestic demand has lagged behind other industrialized countries. Therefore, despite its size, Germany's growth strategy is that of a small open economy. This issue of export dependency has become increasingly important in light of the financial crisis of the late 2000s and global imbalances vis-à-vis Greece and the Eurozone, but also globally. At the same time, weak aggregate demand, which is an essential part of Germany's export-oriented growth strategy, both depresses domestic employment and endangers the still fragile construction of the Eurozone.

Export orientation during Fordism

Germany's economy already started to focus on exports in the 1950s. The key was long-term wage restraint on the part of trade unions in the manufacturing sector, a feature already emphasized by the first president of the German Central Bank, Wilhelm Vocke, when he highlighted the role of exports for Germany's success in 1951 (Höpner 2019). Restrictive monetary policy also became a central element of the German export model, in particular after the 1975 oil shock (Scharpf 1991). The German government was also highly active in replacing the Bretton Woods regime with a European currency regime (the European Monetary System (EMS) in 1979 and later the EMU in 1999) in order to stabilize exports (Hassel 2003, 99). The Deutschmark (D-mark) was deliberately undervalued and only reluctantly adjusted. Under the EMS, the D-mark appreciated eight times between 1979 and 1992 (Höpner and Spielau 2015). This indicates that Germany did not follow a "traditional" Fordist model of domestic consumption-led growth, but was instead characterized by an export-oriented growth model very early on during the post-war period.

Welfare expansion took place primarily through social insurance schemes which privileged those in secure employment in manufacturing rather than through universal schemes. In the 1980s, early retirement, status-maintaining unemployment benefits for the long-term unemployed, and strong employment protection for workers on permanent contracts provided a buffer for workers against economic restructuring. These schemes were paid for by higher insurance contributions and relatively low wage increases, both of which helped the government deal with the restructuring of the coal and steel industries and later with reunification. Sectoral real-wage restraint paid off for the individual worker in the long run, even if an economic downturn would force them out of the labor market (into either unemployment or early retirement). Employers benefitted from coordinated wage-setting and investments in productivity-improving technologies.

Some liberalization policies were introduced in the late 1980s. Public housing was gradually phased out through a change of law in 1989, which withdrew subsidies for social housing (Reisenbichler in this volume). The number of social housing units declined from almost four million subsidized flats in the 1980s to less than a million in 2020. A first step towards labor market liberalization was taken by deregulating temporary work agencies. In addition, pension reform was introduced, but was halted by the fall of the Berlin Wall.

The impact of reunification

Reunification in 1990 was the toughest challenge to the German growth regime since the oil crisis in the 1970s that prompted stronger wage restraint. As it required massive public spending on the Eastern Länder, reunification took a major toll on the German economy. During the first two decades of reunification, about 4% of GDP or seventy to eighty billion euros were transferred from West to East Germany annually (Ragnitz 2009), funded through higher taxes (the solidarity surcharge), social security contributions, and debt. The collapse of the East German labor market during the 1990s was buffered by generous early retirement schemes, retraining, and large-scale labor migration from East to West Germany. While the funding of reunification was, in fact, a major boost to domestic demand, the government responded to increasing public debt, high unemployment, and low employment rates by encouraging export-led growth. Throughout the 1990s, manufacturing companies restructured their business models in order to remain competitive. They engaged in plant-level concession bargaining, in which employment guarantees were used to achieve wage restraint (Hassel 2014; Palier and Thelen 2010). This strategy of plant-level cooperation, while the government continued high levels of social spending, particularly in East Germany, was characteristic of the Helmut Kohl (1982–98) government of the 1990s.

Liberalization and attempted financialization in the late 1990s

Economic pressure started to mount in the second half of the 1990s. The German export model was seen as exhausted. High social spending, low growth, and high unemployment dominated the public discourse. At the time, many policy-makers were actively considering a shift of the growth strategy towards a more liberal and Anglo-Saxon model. For instance, in the late 1990s, the Kohl government introduced several laws promoting capital markets. The government encouraged venture capital for new tech companies by establishing in 1997 a "new market," modelled on the US Nasdaq. In addition, privatization of pensions and public housing were put on the public agenda.

Pension privatization was driven by major concerns about the costs of aging and the impact of public pensions on labor costs. The Gerhard Schröder government (1998–2005) launched a new pension reform in 2001 that included both cuts to the public pension scheme and the possibility of compensation through subsidized private or occupational pension schemes (e.g. "Riester" pension) (Bonoli and Palier 2007; Naczyk and Hassel 2019). Reduced public spending on pensions would allow for stabilization of non-wage labor costs such as social insurance contributions, with a target of 20% of wages by 2020 and 22% by 2030. Publicly subsidized private pension schemes were introduced to compensate for cuts in public pensions, but they turned out to be a bad investment as returns were dismal. Only the occupational schemes that were negotiated by the social partners guaranteed top-up pensions; these were, however, only available in the manufacturing sectors and large firms. Consequently, pension privatization fed into the dualization mechanism—instead of financialization—and served mostly to compensate workers in the export sector for the public pension retrenchment, while the rest of the population received no compensation at all (Seeleib-Kaiser et al. 2012).

The most substantial policy reforms were the so-called Hartz reforms of 2003. Their aims were first, to lower the reservation wage in East Germany and, thereby, force the long-term unemployed to seek work; second, to cut the financial burden of high unemployment costs in both East and West Germany; and third, to increase the employment rate in general. The reforms cut the length of time a person could draw unemployment insurance benefits and introduced low means-tested benefits for the long-term unemployed. The line drawn between insurance-based benefits and means-tested benefits put manufacturing workers into the precarious position of looming poverty if they became long-term unemployed. As an effect, unions and works councils became even more focused on employment guarantees when negotiating with big manufacturing firms. The price for continued employment guarantees was an even stronger commitment to wage restraint (see Figure 12A.1 in the appendix, which shows the development of labor costs after 1997 and the massive restraint in wages). The Hartz reforms also included a number of other labor market liberalization measures, reinforcing insider and outsider divisions in the labor market by further facilitating temporary agencies, contract work, unprotected mini and midi jobs, and the like (Hassel 2014; Palier and Thelen 2010).

Renewed export strategy and the financial crisis

From the moment the Hartz reforms were adopted, the world economy picked up and moved into a long economic upswing. Exports started to boom and unemployment started to fall in both East and West Germany. Despite massive criticism of the Hartz reforms and the collapse of the Schröder government in 2005, the German economy's development overall was positive. As shown in Figure 12.2 total employment increased by 10%, and in particular part-time employment took off.

The development in the labor market reinforced the perception of almost all policy-makers that the export-based growth model was beneficial for all, in particular after the economy fared relatively well through the financial crisis of the late 2000s. Publicly subsidized short-shift working arrangements helped companies to weather the contraction of GDP in 2009, without shedding labor. Compared to the mid-1990s, the government's mood had completely changed by 2009. Since then export-led growth is well rooted in the policy community, despite

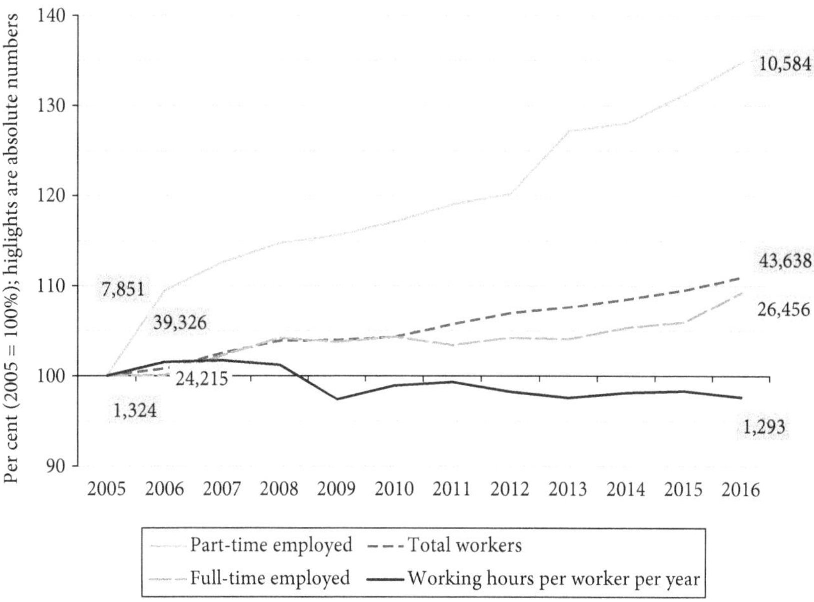

Figure 12.2 Employment and hours worked in Germany (2005–16)
Note: Indexed in 2005, employment in thousands.
Source: Schulze Buschoff and Hassel (2018).

the overall low wage growth and a large low-pay sector, which eventually led the government to adopt a minimum wage in 2015 from which point wages started to rise more in line with other countries in the Eurozone.

Digitalization and public investment

Since the financial crisis, the focus of policy-making has shifted towards re-regulation of the labor market, expansion of childcare, and transition to the knowledge economy. Growing employment in high-skilled services depends on investment in higher education and an expanding female labor force. Both are areas that the German welfare state has not been used to catering for. Rather the opposite, women's labor market participation in full-time equivalents remains comparatively low, and the share of the population with a tertiary education degree is among the lowest in the OECD, with 31% of twenty-five to thirty-four-year-olds having a tertiary degree, compared to 44% as an OECD average (OECD iLibrary 2019). However, public childcare for the under three-year-olds has doubled over the last fifteen years from 18% in 2005 to nearly 38% in 2017 (OECD Family Database).

The challenge of the transition to a knowledge economy is exacerbated by the demographic change that has kicked in forcefully since the financial crisis. It is estimated that Germany's workforce will shrink by 5–10% by 2060 (Destatis 2019), an estimate that includes the rising numbers of immigrants. The shrinking number of young people induces labor shortages, in particular at the high end of the scale of skill distribution. These demographic changes also underline the urgency of offering full-time careers for working mothers and addressing work–life issues.

Several developments since the financial crisis can be classified as a "conservative" social investment strategy of the German government. These include path-breaking measures in the field of gender policy (female quota on supervisory boards; pay transparency norms), universal provision of early childcare, and the expansion and increasing flexibility of the tertiary education system. With regard to the latter, vocational training has increasingly intertwined with higher education, as vocational training certificates are now accepted as a substitute for entry exams at many universities, and many "dual degree" programs that combine vocational or on-the-job training and college coursework have been set up (Eichhorst and Hassel 2018).

3.2 Export of Dynamic Services and Social Investment in Sweden and Denmark

Nordic countries are small, open economies, which were particularly affected by changes in the international economic environment of the 1970s and 1980s. During the 1990s, both Sweden and Denmark diversified their growth strategies towards innovative ICT-based services and privatized sheltered services. Denmark focused on environmental technologies, design, and pharmacy, while Sweden entered the ICT-based and high-end services sectors (Dølvik forthcoming). As demonstrated by Thelen (this volume), Sweden's business groups responded to market pressures not by defending traditional strengths but by shifting resources into new sectors. In order to support the shift towards highly skilled, dynamic services, governments cut some compensatory social protection in favor of social investment policies. According to Baccaro and Pontusson (this volume), one important reason for the Swedish switch in growth strategy towards innovation and dynamic services was the size of the country's welfare state. Because of the Swedish public sector's large size and the importance of domestic demand, wage repression to maintain international competitiveness, like in Germany, was not feasible. This approach has led to a smaller current account surplus and an increase in household debt since the late 1990s and to higher growth rates in Sweden than in Germany from 1997 to 2015. In the case of Denmark, the diversification of the growth regime was underpinned by a substantial liberalization of financial markets, especially the credit market, which stimulated private household debt (Ibsen and Knudsen 2019).

From retrenchment to social investment

During the 1980s, both Sweden and Denmark experienced high levels of unemployment and high interest rates. At first, these countries tried to maintain full employment by creating public jobs, but this led to increasing public debt, which was difficult to finance. By the end of the 1980s, unemployment rates were increasing rapidly. For the first time, there was a public debate about the potentially discouraging effects of welfare generosity. When conservative governments came to power (in 1982 in Denmark and 1991 in Sweden), budget cuts ensued, which were intended to reduce the generosity of social insurance and, specifically, unemployment compensation. According to Korpi and Palme (2003), expenditures on social insurance programs declined substantially in both Sweden and Denmark between 1975 and 1995. Spending on unemployment insurance declined by 24.5% in Denmark and by 7.3% in Sweden, sickness insurance by 21.4% and 13.8%, and work accident insurance by 21.4% and 21.8%, respectively (Korpi and Palme 2003: 435).

Spending cuts and lower public employment not only helped the countries to pay off their debts, but also enabled collective investments to restart growth driven by technological innovation and higher skills. Thelen (this volume) analyzes in detail the changes in the educational system in Sweden that eliminated the more vocational two-year track system, so that everyone would stay in school until the age of nineteen, thus opening the path to university education for all. As Thelen shows, the country also made huge investments in ICT training and household equipment, as well as in upskilling-focused labor market policies to help workers shift from manufacturing to ICT-based dynamic services.

Labor market policies were also redesigned in the early 1990s in both Sweden and Denmark. A clear trend can be traced towards "activation" through various social expenditure measures: for instance, reducing the length and generosity of unemployment insurance benefits (especially in Sweden), increasing pressure on the unemployed to work, and providing retraining opportunities for acquiring skills in order to find jobs in new sectors.

Parties of the right initiated these policies in both cases. However, when returning to power, the Social Democrats in neither country questioned the cuts made in welfare policies, nor the trend towards marketization and activation. Instead, they increased emphasis on the necessity to invest in general skills to prepare the population for the knowledge economy and to improve work–life balance for families. In Europe, this has later been labelled a "social investment" strategy (Morel et al. 2012).

Denmark created its own trademark in labor market policies by developing the "flexicurity model": "The model promotes high occupational and geographical labor mobility via low employment protection, compensated by generous unemployment benefits and ambitious active labor market policies aimed at skill improvement and activation for the unemployed" (Viebrock and Clasen 2009: 313). Among European countries, Denmark and Sweden spend the most on workers' training, public employment services, subsidies for private sector jobs, and the creation of government jobs. These expenditures amount to approximately 2% of GDP in both countries. They also include large-scale early childhood education and care programs and have the highest rates of childcare attendance for children between one and three (Palier and Hay 2017).

The aim is an early and continuous investment in human capital for everyone to further academic and professional success, to accompany professional transitions, to allow parents to combine family and work responsibilities, and to favor high rates of labor market participation. The provision of high-quality childcare for all children also creates quality jobs for workers in these sectors. Parental leave reforms have added a specific number of months for fathers with higher income replacement rates.

Therefore, the Nordic countries' adjustments to the welfare state went in the direction of boosting labor productivity in dynamic services via social investment policies and a reduction in the effect of moral hazards in social expenditures. While social spending in Nordic countries is still among the highest in the world, it has become more sustainable thanks to these reforms, as their social protection systems have managed to turn their social spending towards the education and mobilization of the workforce.

Steps to increase pension sustainability were also implemented early on, in 1991 in Denmark and in 1994 in Sweden, with the creation of a system of notional accounts in the latter. Furthermore, the countries have taken active measures to integrate growing numbers of immigrants into the labor force since the 1990s (Andersen et al. 2017: 96). These measures have indicated early efforts to tackle the adverse effects of aging, through pension reform, high net migration, and social investment (which focused on childcare and education). Nordic countries have some of the highest fertility rates in the European Union (EU) (between 1.7 and 1.9 children per woman).

Housing policy in the Nordic countries also illustrates a social investment-oriented approach, since housing is used to underpin and support worker productivity and decent living standards. Apart from public housing (some 20% of the total housing market), which is available to all citizens (in contrast to the UK, where eligibility is determined by means-testing), housing cooperatives have grown in importance (also around 20%). While the state regulates the entire housing market with some of the world's most pro-tenant rent control laws, public, cooperative, and private housing compete freely in the market, thus enabling consumer choice and increasing quality. The primary goal of housing provision is, therefore, not to feed the financial markets, as is the case in the UK, although financial markets are active participants in the marketplace (Terner Center 2017). The Swedish government also intervenes from the demand side by providing universal housing allowances at national and municipal levels. In that sense, there is no trade-off between household debt and welfare state expenditure in these Nordic countries, as is the case in the UK, because they complement one another. At the same time, and as Reisenbichler (this volume) points out, housing policies have served to boost private wealth in Nordic countries and thus have been some of the most important drivers of wealth inequality over the past few decades.

Privatization and financialization

As Thelen and Wren (both in this volume) emphasize, many of the adjustments made in the 1990s in the Nordic countries meant an exit from medium-high manufacturing sectors and move upmarket into ICT and knowledge-intensive manufacturing and services. However, restructuring also occurred through the privatization of previously sheltered service delivery (not financing, which remains public), especially in the educational and social services. This was also a way for the main Swedish business groups (like the Wallenbergs) to diversify their activities and for governments to address the demand for choice coming from the electorate since the 1980s (Blomqvist 2004). Privatization of service delivery went particularly far in Sweden. In the early 2010s, Swedish private schools enrolled almost a quarter of the total student body at upper secondary level (Erixon 2011: 15). Since the beginning of the 1990s, the share of for-profit schooling has increased from virtually zero to 18–19% in Sweden (and to around 5% in Denmark) (Szebehely and Meagher 2018). Private, for-profit provision of public services became a prominent feature of the Swedish new political economy, especially in the education and care sectors (healthcare, childcare, and care of the elderly). This became a source of new activity for many corporations, but also triggered an increase in inequality, since wages increased slowly in these sectors while they skyrocketed in the ICT sector.

While Nordic countries have followed the global trend of growing inequality, partly due to tax and benefit cuts in the 1990s, their Gini coefficients and poverty rates remain among the lowest in the OECD today (Andersen et al. 2017: 92). In effect, the wages of low-skill workers have fared relatively well in Sweden over this period, also due to a high demand for private services by middle- and high-income households and a broader union presence (see Wren and Thelen, both in this volume).

Nevertheless, while both countries have accommodated financial service providers in their economies, the state has acted as a strong regulator of private service providers in education, housing, and pensions especially in Sweden. Since the welfare state has served to feed dynamic services and innovation-oriented economies (see Baccaro and Pontusson, this volume), there was no dismantling of public financing of welfare services. Thus, although there has been a proliferation of private providers, the state continues to foot the bill and is supposed to ensure equality and universality in access to public and social goods and services. This makes the Nordic states rather distinct from the UK model, which has allowed a deterioration of public services along with a deregulation of pricing in private markets (Hood and Dixon 2015).

Both Sweden and Denmark have also liberalized their financial markets to support the financing of innovative start-ups and firms in the ICT sectors. Financialization in Denmark has been stronger, especially in pensions and housing. In fact, Denmark has the highest share of private pension contributions and benefits in Europe through a fully funded pension system governed by the social partners (Figure 12A.2 in the appendix). Denmark also relaxed constraints on the credit market, leading to a mortgage boom.

Reisenbichler (this volume) argues that Nordic countries adopted financialized housing policies as a way to liberalize financial markets and boost private wealth because firms were less concerned with wage restraint. There are, however, differences between Denmark, which allowed unsustainable levels of household debt to mount up during the 2000s, and Sweden, where the government has been more cautious concerning the accumulation of household debt. In 2010, the Swedish government capped mortgages at 85% of a property's value and introduced requirements to amortize on loans, while pursuing an expansionary monetary policy to boost consumption (Jansson 2013; also see Baccaro and Pontusson in this volume on the increasing role of domestic demand after the financial crisis in Sweden). Swedish policy-makers did not prioritize financial services' profits over macroeconomic stability and their accountability to voters. We argue that, in general, financialization is not a dominant strategy in the Nordic countries, but is complementary to the dynamic services strategy which emphasizes productivity and human capital formation.

After 2008, welfare reforms in Sweden and Denmark diverged. The Great Recession had a greater impact on Denmark, due to a self-inflicted financial crisis that led to seven years without economic growth. The main cause was the pegging of the Danish crown to the euro and the excessive liberalization of credit, which forced internal devaluations to manage demand shocks, and thus greater pressure on welfare and wage policies. By contrast, Sweden's growth rate after 2008 was among the highest in Europe (Andersen et al. 2017).

The situation in Denmark was aggravated by a stigmatization of recipients of social assistance linked to an increasingly anti-immigration discourse. Moreover, the low economic growth, provoked by too much liberalization, led to even more radical market-oriented solutions to fix the faltering economy (Andersen et al. 2017: 105). Denmark saw severe public spending cuts after 2010, although spending remained relatively high in comparison to other European economies. The country thus partly preserved its traditionally social democratic inclination despite significant cuts since it continued to have a high degree of inclusive and universal provision of state-financed welfare services and active support for the unemployed, along with an increasing emphasis on activation and some discrimination against migrants.

In the Nordic countries, there were considerable political and social conflicts related to immigration, and newly emerging political cleavages played a more important role in policy decisions than economic pressures did. For example, the 2011–16 reduction in public spending in Denmark would not have been politically imaginable only a few years before. In the Swedish context, public discontent over privatization of welfare services, their quality, and profits made by the private sector from taxpayers' money have been a source of vibrant national debate (Andersen et al. 2017: 95).

Given the stable macroeconomic environment and budgetary surpluses, some repairs to social protection have started in both countries. For example, Sweden raised the unemployment level of benefit ceiling significantly in 2015, while the Danish 2014 labor market reform relaxed eligibility conditions for unemployment benefits (Andersen et al. 2017: 106).

3.3 FDI-Led Export Growth and Fiscal and Social Attractiveness in Eastern Europe

One can distinguish between three types of countries in the EU which adhere to the FDI-led export growth strategy: Ireland, the Visegrád group (the Czech Republic, Hungary, Poland, and Slovakia), and the Baltic countries (Estonia, Latvia, and Lithuania). The Irish case has been extensively covered elsewhere (Regan 2012; Regan and Brazys 2018). In this section we focus on Eastern Europe. While there are several commonalities between the Visegrád and Baltic countries (low corporate tax, low labor costs, labor market flexibilization, and privatization to attract FDI), the two sets of countries also exhibit differences in labor market, educational, and welfare reforms which complement their specific drivers of export-led growth (manufacturing versus dynamic services). The FDI-led reindustrialization growth regime in the Visegrád countries relies on a Bismarckian type of welfare system, which predominantly consists of work-related compensation and cash benefits, while the Baltic trajectory of services liberalization and an ICT and knowledge-oriented growth regime pursues a social investment-oriented welfare state (Avlijaš 2020; Avlijaš forthcoming).

The foundation of the socialist growth model in Eastern Europe before 1989 was rapid industrialization underpinned by substantial welfare provisions for workers. Besides full employment and decent pensions in the context of centrally planned economies, Eastern European states provided universal healthcare and education, as well as subsidized housing. The region, therefore, experienced substantial socio-economic progress and welfare state development in the decades following World War II, amid authoritarianism and the absence of political competition. Following the economic and political crises since the 1970s and the demise of socialism in 1989, Eastern European countries embarked on the historically unprecedented transition to capitalism.

Along with the concurrent transition to democracy, major institutional reforms took place on the road to capitalism. Redistribution, which was a non-issue during socialism, began to dominate both the economic and political agenda in the context of privatization of publicly owned resources and new political competition. A new social contract had to be defined, which would affect both domestic and international stakeholders (e.g. foreign investors and the EU). The dominant perspective on welfare reforms during the early years of transition was mainly influenced by Janos Kornai's notion of the socialist state as a prematurely born welfare state (Szelenyi 2011). This approach implied that the purportedly overly generous welfare provisions from the socialist era needed to be reduced and possibly privatized in order to stimulate growth and allow Eastern European countries to recover from the transitional recessions that they were experiencing. Rapid liberalization was thus imposed from the onset of transition as an "obvious" solution to numerous practical economic challenges and employed as a tool for market-driven growth via privatization and trade openness.

Dramatic privatization of housing also took place across Eastern Europe in the context of the highly deregulated financial markets, the foreign takeover of the banking sector, and the massive inflow of credit to households. Domestic policy-makers supported these trends during the 2000s as part of their general growth strategies of attracting foreign capital, especially in the Baltic countries. The trend was further reinforced as a way to keep social peace by boosting household wealth in the context of worsening labor market conditions (Bohle 2013).

Amid these economic liberalization-driven processes, there was also a social countermovement at the domestic level (Bohle and Greskovits 2012). Pro-welfare state constituencies in Eastern Europe were stronger than in Western Europe, due to their welfare state legacy. The retrenching of existing social programs was politically difficult, and anti-reform voting emerged (Vanhuysse 2009: 56). An important question for policy-makers was how to ensure domestic political stability and reduce protest while implementing the liberalizing reforms imposed by the international discourses and pressures. The liberalization discourse and the domestic political conflicts over redistribution interacted in shaping the outcomes of welfare state reform in the region. These interactions produced a fiscally constrained, pro-social investment-oriented reform agenda in the Baltic and a fiscally constrained, pro-social compensation welfare state in the Visegrád region.

The literature has widely acknowledged that the Baltic and Visegrád countries have followed different trajectories of capitalist development since the early 1990s (Bohle and Greskovits 2012; Feldmann 2006; Nölke and Vliegenthart 2009). These different trajectories were path-dependent on the initial choices that the countries made, but they also reflected the ways in which foreign investors shaped economic developments in each of the regions.

The Visegrád FDI-financed manufacturing export growth strategy

The Visegrád countries (the Czech Republic, Hungary, Poland, and Slovakia) pursued reindustrialization, which was driven by FDI (coming mainly from Germany, Austria, France, and the UK) as the key source of capital and innovation. According to Bohle and Greskovits (2012), these four countries capitalized on their specialization in automobiles, machinery, and electronics industries during late socialism to transform their economies "into one of Europe's largest transborder clusters of complex-manufacturing export industries" (138). By offering subsidy packages and tax incentives to foreign investors and already removing market entry barriers during the early 1990s, these countries outcompeted the rest of Eastern Europe (the Baltic and South East Europe) in attracting most of the FDI. For this reason, Nölke and Vliegenthart (2009) refer to them as dependent market economies, ie economies that are dependent on FDI for sources of capital and innovation.

Since labor market attachment in the context of reindustrialization served as the primary basis for welfare eligibility, post-socialist Visegrád welfare states returned to their pre-1945 Bismarckian path (Vanhuysse 2009; Cerami 2010). The countries provided social compensation to the losers of economic restructuring in the form of unemployment benefits, pensions, and early retirement opportunities to ensure political support for their growth strategy. Cash benefits dominated the welfare state agenda in the Visegrád countries. However, while politically necessary, such large welfare state expenditures, along with generous subsidy packages to foreign investors, came at the cost of significant fiscal strains, especially in Hungary and Poland, which faced extreme early retirement booms (Bohle and Greskovits 2012; Vanhuysse 2009). The early retirement schemes resulted in strong pensioner constituencies that directed resources away from youth-oriented policies (Vanhuysse 2009: 59). The fiscal situation was further exacerbated by the recessions that the countries experienced during the initial transition, as well as by regional tax competition to attract FDI (and thus low tax revenue), and by the requirement of the EU's Stability and Growth Pact to maintain low budget deficits.

Due to rapid liberalization, trade openness, and a high dependency on foreign capital, export-oriented price competition became the basis of the growth strategy. However, given the relatively high educational attainment of the population that was inherited from socialism, reindustrialization was based on technological upgrading and middle- and high-skilled, rather than low-skilled jobs. Therefore, while the restructuring of the economy required a flexibilization of the labor market, the need to preserve workers' skills has led to the preservation of a certain level of employment protection, which is why there is no "race to the bottom" in employment relations despite strong competitive pressures.

While productivity gains were achieved through substantial labor-shedding, these "losers of transition" were protected with severance pay and early retirement packages, policies which, as noted earlier, put further pressure on the welfare state. This has also created a path dependency so that social protection expenditures on pensions have remained high and politically salient, making it difficult to redirect state resources into youth policy, social investment, and educational reform, as well as upgrading towards higher-quality products or switching to dynamic services. A market for private education has, however, emerged, since the relatively better-paid jobs in multinational firms have encouraged workers to invest in their skills, offsetting some of the negative effects of low state investment in education.

Financial markets have been dominated by foreign investors and predominantly focused on achieving short-term profits. This increases pressure on firms to shed labor and weaken employment protection to remain price competitive. At the same time, the financial sector offered market-based tools for risk diversification through private insurance, reducing the pressure for the state to increase its provision of social protection.

The FDI-financed dynamic service export-led growth strategy in the Baltic countries

The Baltic countries have built a different regime of foreign capital-dependent, post-socialist capitalism. Their strategy relied on rapid liberalization and macroeconomic stabilization to attract foreign capital into high-value service sectors, such as banking, telecommunications, and real estate. The strategy depends on both price and quality competitiveness and is centered not only on exports of high-value services, but also on substantial domestic consumption of telecommunications, finance, and retail.

As Bohle and Greskovits (2012) explain, just after the fall of their socialist regimes, the Baltic countries pursued an agenda of macroeconomic stabilization, extreme openness, and rapid liberalization of services, which resulted in a high influx of FDI in banking, logistic services, and real estate. Given that they pursued a concurrent agenda of nation-building following their secession from the Soviet Union, they also had a political interest in deindustrialization, as it served to weaken the position of ethnic Russian capital and labor, which had dominated Baltic industries at the onset of the transition (Avlijaš forthcoming). They also opted for the rapid introduction of national currencies and pursued national monetary independence.

This was done in a quest for international creditworthiness and legitimacy (Bohle and Greskovits 2012: 105). Alongside the liberalization of services, the Baltic countries also pursued an internationally competitive ICT and knowledge-oriented growth agenda, notably by using public procurement (Avlijaš 2020; Lumiste et al. 2008; Runnel et al. 2009). Low levels of employment protection and the increasing flexibilization of the workforce encouraged workers to invest in general skills that are easily transferable between firms and sectors of the economy rather than in specific skills. This state-led development of the highly dynamic service economy required the expansion of tertiary education. Educational expansion and reform, along with the digitalization of education and public services, were recognized as essential inputs for the Baltic growth model, and, between 1995 and 2015, the countries were among the highest spenders on education in the EU (Avlijaš 2020). Such an approach to economic development, most conspicuously in Estonia, resulted in the establishment of human capital-oriented social investment policies in the region.

Since the Baltics were as severely fiscally constrained as the Visegrád countries due to their initial transitional recessions and their strict adherence to macroeconomic stability, they redirected public resources away from direct cash compensation towards future-oriented social investment policies. This course was feasible since the high flexibility of the workforce, along with high employment rates and relatively high education levels, reduced the demand for social protection. Moreover, a foreign-owned financial sector with low ownership concentration offered market-based tools for risk diversification through private insurance. Also favoring this course was the political context in which the large Russian-speaking minority, the biggest "losers of transition," were effectively marginalized, and any political conflict surrounding reforms was transformed into an ethnic one (Bohle and Greskovits 2012; Avlijaš forthcoming). Thus, as the Baltic countries pursued their burgeoning social investment agendas, they were able to significantly cut social spending on cash benefits to compensate the losers of transition, which led to their characterization as "disembedded" neoliberal states (Bohle and Greskovits 2012).

Eastern European responses to the 2008 financial crisis

The 2008 crisis had an extremely negative impact on Eastern European GDPs, which dropped by up to 20% in some countries, due to their high exposure to international financial markets. The Baltic countries resorted to steep austerity measures, which severely impacted the less privileged parts of their populations, but allowed them to avoid external devaluation and preserve their middle-class and foreign business interests. For example, Estonia, which was among the worst hit countries by the 2008 crisis, avoided external devaluation, which would have burdened its indebted middle class and its transnational banks. Instead, the government resorted to severe austerity, with large wage cuts in the public and private sector, lay-offs, and further retrenchment of welfare programs, all of which disproportionately hit the lower-skilled and welfare-dependent parts of the population. The austerity program was effective within a year, allowing Estonia to join the euro in 2011, which enabled both its households and banks to restructure their debts under more favorable terms (Bohle 2013).

The Visegrád countries, in contrast, appear to have resorted to a mixture of political populism and economic policies that aimed to restore their national economic independence and a quiet continuation of subsidies for FDI in manufacturing, in tandem with the noisy politics of social compensation for pensioners and middle-class families (Bohle and Greskovits 2018). Using the example of Hungary, Bohle (2013) shows how the newly elected Hungarian Prime Minister, Viktor Orbán, committed to restoring the country's financial independence by introducing taxes on financial services and pushing costs onto banks and away from their customers, limiting housing repossessions by banks, renegotiating debt burdens for many debtors, and a series of other anti-financial, capital-oriented measures. But his government continued to support FDI in manufacturing industries (Bohle and Regan forthcoming). Thereby they averted evictions and a major mortgage crisis, but at the price of international reputational damage to the Hungarian government.

These trends indicate that neither of the two regions has made a U-turn in their dominant growth strategies since the 2008 crisis. If anything, the Visegrád countries have strengthened their focus on FDI-driven industrial upgrading by reducing government support to the FDI-driven development of finance and other dynamic services and entrenching the welfare agenda of social compensation at the expense of social investment. By contrast, the Baltic countries have increased their support for dynamic services and financialization-oriented economic activities, as well as their commitment to investment in human capital at the expense of social compensation for losers of these reforms.

3.4 Financialization and Commodification of Welfare in the United Kingdom

The UK was a leader among the advanced economies in adjusting to growing manufacturing competition from emerging countries by shifting to financial services as the new national engine of growth and swiftly shutting down extractive and manufacturing sectors of its economy. The conservative Thatcher and Major years (1979–97) were famously marked by a large-scale privatization of the British economy, including partial privatization of pension schemes (more general privatization was desired by the neoliberal governments, but it was not politically feasible, see Pierson 1994), as well as extensive privatization of social housing and deregulation of the housing market. The increasingly liberal and residual character of the British welfare state continued to be reinforced even after the end of the conservative era, since subsequent Labour governments continued to focus on reducing the cost of the welfare state and increasing its efficiency. Market mechanisms in social welfare provision continued to increase (especially in healthcare and pensions) and the selectivity of welfare policies grew, while the promotion of workfare measures accelerated, along with growing labor market flexibility (Palier and Hay 2017). This welfare state retrenchment trend has accelerated even further since the onset of the global economic crisis, following the austerity-driven agenda of the Tory government which came to office in 2010. While the general trend in UK welfare state reform since the 1980s has been towards reduction, some rebalancing of welfare state spending could be observed during the 2010s as the government attempted to mitigate the negative impact of the financialization-driven growth strategy on consumption capacities of low earners via, for example, income tax credits on earnings and basic pension.

Privatization of welfare

When it comes to specific welfare policy reforms that have been adopted since the 1980s, pension privatization is an important area. Conservative governments were unable to completely privatize the basic and complementary public pension systems during the 1980s (Pierson 1994). Instead they reformed public pensions by introducing price indexation of the basic pension level, reducing the guaranteed replacement rate of the public complementary pension, and favoring the expansion of private pension funds by proposing to those having a public complementary pension to "opt out" from public schemes and benefit from quite attractive fiscal exemptions if they did so (Bonoli and Palier 2000). As a result, the UK is among those countries with the highest private pension contributions and benefits in the OECD, together with other countries which have pursued the financialization growth strategy and those which have pursued the export of dynamic services growth strategy (Figure 12A.2 in the appendix).

The Thatcher government also eased access to credit for the middle classes during the 1980s and created a new constituency of homeowners by introducing a national "Right to Buy" (RTB) policy, which consisted of selling public housing to private tenants. The RTB policy was the largest single example of privatization in the UK in the period from 1980 to the mid-2000s (Disney and Luo 2017). This policy particularly benefitted low- and middle-income groups who purchased homes cheap and benefitted from the skyrocketing prices afterwards. Given the growing marketization of retirement schemes, housing served as an additional source of savings for retirement.

Housing privatization also went hand in hand with the deregulation of the UK housing finance market and opened the mortgage market up to much greater competition. This increased the supply of mortgages and reduced their price, which fueled the newly emerging appetite for house ownership among the British middle class and reinforced the country's growth model. As Reisenbichler (this volume) explains, the housing market has been an important transmission channel for monetary policy in the UK because lower mortgage rates lead to higher housing demand and house prices, which in turn stimulates bank lending and household consumption in the wider economy. The expanding housing market also fueled financial product innovation, which made access to mortgages easier for the poorer and less creditworthy households. Buy-to-let mortgages were one such innovative financial product that emerged in the financial services during the 1990s.

The significant wage discrepancy between high- and low-skill service jobs boosts the demand for (higher) education. Individual investment in human capital grew in importance, since it improves the potential for access to high-paying jobs in financial services, where decentralized wage-bargaining could not impose any collective levers on wage growth. In parallel, workfare measures were adopted for low-income groups. A continuous decline in the level of unemployment benefits went along with growing pressure on beneficiaries to return to the labor market. The unemployed lost the most from welfare state reforms during the Thatcher and Major eras (Bonoli and Palier 1998).

Targeted social investment and financialization of education under New Labour

The Blair government (1997–2007) did not stop the privatization and financialization trends of the previous neoliberal governments. Instead, it introduced mostly correctives and added a new component to it in the form of social investment. In other words, Blair's "Third Way" after 1997 continued to promote the highly financialized, dynamic services-driven model of growth for the UK, while directing a portion of its proceeds into social spending and social investment. According to Taylor-Gooby et al. (2017), New Labour started off with a "cautious expansion of state provision through social investment" (51), which included educational investment in low-performing regions, subsidized childcare, introduction of the national minimum wage (in 1998), and expansion of means-tested welfare and means-tested tax credits for those on low incomes.

In order to ensure that the unequal income and wealth effects of the financialization-driven economic growth would not start to impede growth via faltering domestic demand, working tax credits and other efforts to support the consumption of low earners were developed. The expansion of public social services also served to lift incomes of the bottom quintile of earners. The Blair and then Brown governments regularly increased and expanded income tax credits on earnings to boost the consumption capacities of the low earners.

Blair was very clear about the necessity of promoting investment in human capital, as it was deemed crucial for success in the new dynamic and financial services-driven economy. The chosen means to that end, however, continued to be market-based. The Blair era was thus characterized by a government-encouraged marketization and financialization of the higher education system. Following half a century of direct government funding for universities and direct student support via state maintenance grants, tuition fees were increased in 1998. Subsequent governments have further retrenched state funding, allowed the cap on fees to be raised, and removed restrictions on student numbers and the limit on fees for foreign students (Viña and Hale 2016). The retrenchment of state funding for education in a context of growing demand for education increases the marketization and financialization of access to education, especially via educational loans. This approach to the expansion of tertiary education is therefore different from the one in the Nordic countries, where private providers have also been introduced but the state has remained responsible for financing.

While New Labour did not dismantle the RTB housing policy, no new stocks of social housing were built, creating very long waiting lists. In the 2010s, the UK has the lowest level of peacetime house-building since the 1920s, and the chance of owning a home in the UK has more than halved in twenty years (Bennett 2017). The benefits of the RTB policy for homeowners have been further buttressed by an unregulated rental market with high prices. This has created a strong constituency of homeowners that is heavily and increasingly skewed against youth and towards older generations who purchased housing during the Thatcher era. The fact that no progressive land value tax has ever been introduced has further reinforced inequalities in the housing market and strengthened the wealth effect of housing for the older generations who accessed affordable housing during the Thatcher era at the expense of the young. Between 1995 and 2016, the average (median) ratio between the average house price in the region where a young adult lives and his/her annual net family income doubled, from 4 to 8 (Cribb et al. 2018). Affordability has thus become a growing problem over time.

The absence of new social housing has fueled the mortgage market and, along with growing salaries for some, has resulted in most of the new housing stock being bought from private owners at market prices. In summary, while the government initially encouraged homeownership through privatization of its stock of social housing, the construction of social housing was discontinued, while the demand for housing at market prices went up. This was fueled further by growing salaries and increased access to financial instruments such as mortgages to finance these purchases. Furthermore, the UK has seen a growing financialization of housing, whereby it is treated as a commodity to invest in and a means to accumulate and deposit wealth, rather than a place to live.

Further public retrenchment feeding private welfare since the 2008 crisis

A conservative turn in New Labour policies took place during the later 2000s, and their final years saw a partial loss of the social inclusion gains from the early 2000s, as the government failed to adjust the means-tested benefits to the cost of living after 2007 (Taylor-Gooby et al. 2017: 53), except for the pensioners. In 2010, in the wake of the financial crisis, the Tories came to power with an austerity-driven political platform aiming to balance the budget, reduce access to welfare, and activate those who were not participating in the labor market. Several benefit cuts and freezes have been introduced since 2010. The government raised the value-added tax, which affected the poorest the most, as they consume the highest portion of their income, and it raised income tax thresholds, which hit unemployed people and low-wage workers without children the hardest. While subsidized childcare for 15 hours per week was preserved, the overall costs of childcare skyrocketed between 2010 and 2015. Austerity measures also included significant cuts to the budgets of local councils, which are mostly responsible for providing social services (Taylor-Gooby et al. 2017: 56). The post-Blair years, therefore, saw a significant cut in social spending and, in that sense, a continuation and acceleration of the Tory policies from the Thatcher era. Given that these policies were administered in the wake of the 2008 economic crisis, the highly flexible UK labor market has seen a boom over the last few years in the most precarious forms of employment such as zero-hour contracts (contracts without guaranteed hours) and agency work. According to data from the UK Office for National Statistics,[1] zero-hour contracts peaked at 2.1 million in 2015, following which they saw a slight drop.

When it comes to housing, UK government measures in the aftermath of the 2008 crisis dampened the impact of the crash and recession on the housing market. The £15.5 billion worth of public schemes that were introduced in 2013 to support homeowners in the aftermath of the crisis (Jenkins 2013) indicates the growing importance of housing in the UK financial services-driven economy.

The Tory government also looked for ways to maintain the consumption capacity of low earners to stimulate domestic demand, but as cheaply as possible. The government thus argued that working tax credits, which were introduced as wage top-ups from public revenues, cost the state too much. Therefore, they tightened the eligibility criteria for tax credits in 2016 and increased income tax thresholds, while introducing a national living wage for those above 25 years of age, which is higher than the national minimum wage. They also banned employers from having an exclusivity clause in the zero-hour contracts, which likely explains why unit labor costs in the UK grew substantially less during the period 2009–17 than during 1997–2007 (see Figure 12A.1).

The Cameron government (2010–16) also implemented several changes in the pension system. Along with legislative provisions that have raised retirement age thresholds and that have encouraged employees to work past their retirement age, retirement saving requirements in employer-sponsored, private pension schemes were increased. In 2012, an "automatic enrolment" into pension funds was put in place for every salaried worker, in order to increase the number of people having a personal pension fund. In 2016, a flat-rate state pension was also

[1] https://www.ons.gov.uk/ (last accessed May 9, 2019).

introduced, that is aiming at merging the basic pension and the complementary public one to a flat rate basic state pension in the future. It will take decades to come into full effect, as current employees continue to benefit from the state scheme that they are already entitled to. These changes to the pension system have shifted a larger portion of the retirement burden onto employers and private pension providers. Pensioners' incomes rely more and more on private pension funds: while 44.5% of mean income of retired households came from private pensions and annuities in 1977, this share was 82.1% in 2017 (Office for National Statistics 2018: 15).

Due to uneven access to supplementary pensions that contributed to increase poverty amongst the elderly during the 1990s and early 2000s (Ebbinghaus 2019), governments have also made sure that the level of basic public pensions would be increased and sustained. The Blair government's decision to peg public pensions to earnings instead of inflation has been strengthen by the Brown government (with a mechanism of "triple lock" that guaranteed an increase of public pension of at least 2.5% per year) and maintained by the Tory governments. This has ensured the consumption capacities and political support of pensioners by enhancing their incomes, while concurrently benefits for the working-age population were cut.

The post-financial crisis years have also seen further cuts in public spending on higher education, which resulted in an unprecedented level of financialization in the higher education sector, as universities went to financial markets to obtain funding by issuing bonds. In fact, between 2010 and 2016, government grants to English universities halved from £8 billion to £4 billion per academic year, while income from tuition fees tripled between 2005 and 2015 (Viña and Hale 2016). In other words, weakening government support has pushed universities towards greater competition for students and towards international capital markets, which have an interest in them because they are deemed as rather safe investments. As Hale (2018) writes in the *Financial Times*, UK universities are a "popular target of investment for US pension and insurance money seeking long-term projects. Lloyds estimates that more than £3 billion has been borrowed by UK universities since 2016 on capital markets, with around half of that coming via private placements."

3.5 The Fate of Wage-Led Growth and Social Protectionism in Southern Europe: From Public Debt to "Competitive Impoverishment"

France and Italy were clear examples of wage demand-led growth regimes typical of Fordism (Boyer 1979 for France; Baccaro and Pontusson 2016 for Italy), despite the existence of some export sectors (such as French "champions" and Northern

Italian firms). Since the 1980s, these countries have been stuck in the Fordist growth model, being able to neither grow nor transform into new ones. Their "consumption-based welfare systems" (Beramendi et al. 2015) guaranteeing a high level of compensatory benefits, such as unemployment allowances and generous old-age pensions, are key to sustaining their domestic demand-led growth. Italy has been an example of "permanent stagnation" since the 1990s (Baccaro and Pontusson, this volume), while France has continuously failed to become an export-led economy (Culpepper et al. 2006). Before 2008, membership in the Eurozone secured relatively low interest rates that sustained a public debt-led growth. Since then, these two countries have pursued a competitive, low cost, and austerity strategy that only leads to poor growth (Johnston, this volume), further deindustrialization, difficulties in developing new, high-skilled dynamic services, massive unemployment (especially for youth), and low labor market participation. The other Southern European countries (Greece, Spain, and Portugal) benefitted greatly from EU accession in the 1980s, and then, like Italy and France, from the euro before the 2008 crisis. Since 2010, however, all of them have been deprived of the possibility of running a domestic demand, wage and welfare-led growth regime, after the EU imposed a more or less stringent "competitive impoverishment strategy," which we introduce at the end of this section.

Italy: permanent stagnation and the impossibility of reforming the welfare state

The Italian economy has been characterized by low expenditure on R&D, technological and organizational regress, and weak competition in domestic product markets (Capussela 2018). The large stock of public debt contributed to the country's inability to invest in new technologies and R&D. Italian firms have been growing more slowly and have been less innovative than those in other European economies. They have also declined in average size and productivity since the late 1980s. While none of these constraining factors on the economy are new in the Italian context, their importance has strengthened over time given the new global challenges that have emerged (Capussela 2018).

Italy has made repeated failed attempts to reform its model and boost its competitiveness since it prepared to join the euro in the mid-1990s (Hassel 2006). The contribution of net exports to growth was in fact negative from 1994 to 2007, and the share of ICT and services in exports declined. The decline of the wage share continued throughout the 1990s and the early 2000s (Baccaro and Pontusson 2016). As Italian exports are price-sensitive, these industries failed to make important gains in world markets. According to Baccaro and Pontusson (2016), this is due not only to Italy's specialization in labor-intensive manufacturing and the growing global competition in these industries, but also to the negative effect of Eurozone membership which further reduced the ability of Italian exporters to compete on price. At the same time, the growth of household consumption has been supported by a significant expansion of credit since the country adopted the euro, albeit starting at low levels (Baccaro and Pontusson 2016).

In the context of this low, and at times negative, growth, Italy has been stuck in a vicious cycle of having to control public debt and stimulate domestic demand with ever-scarcer resources. Due to the externally imposed fiscal constraints, first by the EMU and, after the financial crisis, by the ECB (Sacchi 2016), political conflict has revolved around the external push for fiscal cuts and domestic resistance to them. The Italian population refused to accept impoverishment because of international competitive pressure, and the Italian government did not accept to restrain domestic consumption.

Because neither side has pushed for it, Italy has not redirected any substantial social expenditures towards new social risks or social investment, except for some slight improvements in childcare policy (Kazepov and Ranci 2017). Spending on old-age and survivors' pensions as a percentage of GDP is the second highest (after Greece) in Europe,[2] while spending on family policy, education, and active labor market policy is much lower than in other EU countries. Some more recent efforts to boost female labor force participation and increase access to childcare, especially via the expansion of private childcare service providers, have partially fallen through, as their increased privatization had led to a deterioration in service quality (Kazepov and Ranci 2017).

Welfare reforms in a stalemate

In this context of push and pull factors for fiscal cuts in order to boost international competitiveness, we find a myriad of both passed but afterwards abandoned welfare state reforms in the spheres of pensions, labor markets, and education policy.

Already in the 1990s Italy tried to reform its pension system under fiscal pressure of the Maastricht criteria and implement a notional account system (as in Sweden). These reforms were delayed through very long phase-in periods (Ronchi and Vesan forthcoming). However, following the 2008 crisis, especially with the Fornero pension reform of 2011, the shift to defined contributions accelerated, along with the elimination of early pensions and further increases in the retirement age (Agostini and Natali 2016).

Comprehensive labor market reforms towards deregulation were adopted, first by the center-left government in 1997, then by the center-right in 2003 (Ronchi and Vesan forthcoming), and again in 2012 (Fornero labor market reforms). Their

[2] In 2015 this was 16.5% for Italy, 17.8% for Greece, and 15% for France, while the EU average is 12.8%. Eurostat data. https://ec.europa.eu/eurostat/statistics-explained/index.php/Social_protection_statistics_-_pension_expenditure_and_pension_beneficiaries (last accessed May 6, 2019).

goal was to diminish unemployment and labor market dualism by reducing protection against dismissal that permanent employees enjoyed (i.e. increasing flexibility) and promoting new types of labor contract (short term without justification, permanent contract with easier firing possibilities, etc.). Governments have also intervened with short-term policies to cushion the population from rising unemployment, such as expanding existing short-shift working arrangements after the 2008–9 shock (Vesan and Pavolini 2018). Yet, cuts to unemployment benefits and employment protection were more severe than efforts to prevent the rise in unemployment (Guillén and Pavolini 2015). Despite the professed intention of these reforms, the labor market has become increasingly dualized, particularly between age groups, where older workers still benefit from the more protected contracts, while young people are increasingly exposed to temporary contracts.

Consumption rather than investment

When it comes to education policy, Italy has lower tertiary educational attainment than most EU countries. Education policies were subject to retrenchment throughout the 2000s, in stark contrast with the general European trend. Most cuts came with the education reform adopted between 2008 and 2010 under the center-right Berlusconi government, which reduced expenditure for both compulsory and university education (Ronchi and Vesan forthcoming). Italy's underinvestment in education reflects the structure of its economy and labor market, which does not demand skilled labor and hardly invests in innovation and R&D (Kazepov and Ranci 2017). Because Italy has been going in the opposite direction from most other advanced economies where the demand for skilled labor has been growing, it has not prepared for the knowledge economy. Moreover, those with high skills have difficulties to find jobs, and economic returns to their skills are very low. This has further reduced incentives for both individuals and the state to invest in human capital (Kazepov and Ranci 2017).

We find no evidence that there has been a paradigmatic shift towards finding new sources of growth for the country. On the contrary, most of the few resources available for welfare expansion went to "short-term employment incentives, tax credits and, to a lesser extent, consumption-oriented benefits (unemployment benefits and, later on, the new residual minimum income scheme), which extended income support to categories that were previously left aside the Italian welfare system, such as young labor market entrants and the poor" (Ronchi and Vesan forthcoming: 10). These were all efforts by the government to maintain domestic demand via household consumption.

After seven years of stagnation, Italy returned to low growth (half of the Eurozone average) in 2014 with a supportive fiscal policy that "relied on waivers or flexible interpretations of EU rules" (Capussela 2018: 2). Following this long recession, average real disposable income is still a few points below its 1995 levels

(Capussela 2018: 2). Recent political developments in Italy (the domination of radical, anti-EU, and anti-migrant parties) illustrate the political danger of imposing austerity, welfare cuts, and wage moderation on a country that relies on domestic demand-led growth without organizing any transition to a different growth regime. In this volume, Johnston shows the negative results of wage moderation in this context, and Scharpf analyzes the political risks of such a strategy. At the time of writing, initiatives by the "populist coalition" government (2018–19) had been leaning towards income maintenance and compensatory welfare, such as the implementation of a minimum income scheme (the so called basic income promoted by the Five stars movement) and revalorization of pensions.

France: failed attempts to become an export-led growth economy

France is an interesting example of a failed attempt to switch to an export-led growth regime, while being restrained by the (institutional and political) legacy of the domestic demand-led one. The turning point starts in the 1980s, reinforced in the 1990s by several attempts at welfare retrenchment, and culminates in a series of policies to lower firms' labor costs. Lowering the cost of labor is still the cornerstone of French economic policies. Governments seek to enhance firms' external competitiveness via internal deflation, but without damaging domestic consumption (supported by a relatively high national minimum wage and generous social benefits). Most of the French growth strategy towards bolstering export capacity is thus based on cost reduction and is in reality a low-cost strategy that relies on dualizing welfare system reforms.

Trying to become an export-led growth economy without harming domestic demand

Traumatized by the double failure of Keynesian reflation plans (in 1974 and in 1981), French governments have changed their growth strategies to promote external "competitiveness" in the French economy. In 1982, the socialist government adopted a "policy of rigor" (austerity), especially by freezing welfare benefits (Palier 2005), and adopted a strong currency policy in 1983 (Culpepper et al. 2006). The 1980s were marked by industrial restructuring that was buffered by early retirement pension schemes and generous unemployment benefits as well as outsourcing and off-shoring (Palier and Thelen 2010). Reducing the size of the manufacturing workforce was meant to increase productivity and competitiveness. Compensatory measures were very costly and were financed by both an increase in social contributions and budget deficits. The looming of the euro, however, imposed limits on deficits and inflation. French governments have since then been trapped in a double bind: on the one hand, they try to follow the German path of rescuing the manufacturing sector via internal devaluation, but, on the other hand, they know that wage decreases or even stabilization and cuts in social benefits hurt growth and increase unemployment since the economy is mostly driven by domestic consumption.

Indeed, the French growth regime relies much less on exports than on domestic consumption, as is indicated by the almost permanent deficit of the current account[3] and by the low share of exports in GDP (around 30% of GDP in 2018, see Table 1.2 in Hassel and Palier, this volume). Household consumption is maintained by a relatively generous wage policy, in particular through the minimum wage. However, since the late 1980s, many economists and employers' representatives have complained about the cost of labor and have pushed governments to lower non-wage labor costs (Palier 2005, ch. 7; Carbonnier et al. 2016). Since net wage moderation risks stunting growth and triggers social unrest, non-wage labor costs have become the target of the economic strategy of French governments, implemented through incremental and partial welfare retrenchment and many exemptions to employers' social security contributions.

Ambivalences of the wage policy

In France, wages have continuously risen since the 1960s, in both exposed and sheltered, public and private sectors. The median net wage (gross wage minus social security contributions) of full-time, full-year, salaried male workers increased in real terms by about 15% from 1976 to 2010 in private and public firms. From the mid-1980s to 2007, individuals and households enjoyed gains in their disposable income of 30% and 23%, respectively (Askenazy and Palier 2018). Since 2008, wage increases in France have even been higher than productivity increases (Askenazy et al. 2013).

As analyzed by Höpner and Lutter (2018) and Scharpf (this volume), France (like other Southern European countries) lacks the capacity for wage coordination, which is instrumental for wage moderation. On the contrary, French industrial relations led to a wage push in all sectors, notably because unions are organized in national confederations and have their strongholds in the public sector. Wage rises in the private sector are supported by a relatively high national minimum wage that enjoys strong political support. Any attempt to reform it has led to strong social protest.[4] In France, the minimum wage is perceived as the best tool to limit an increase in inequality, and it has indeed been working (OECD 2015). The minimum wage usually rises faster than average and median net wages

[3] An exception is the 1990s, mostly explained by German reunification, when rising domestic demand in Germany boosted the French current account.

[4] Attempts to reform the minimum wage have always been strongly contested on the street, especially in 1994, when the government tried to create a specific (lower) minimum wage for youth, and in 2006 when a "Contrat Première embauche" would have allowed firms to hire new entrants to the labor market at a lower level than the minimum wage. Both attempts were abandoned due to massive demonstrations.

(Askenazy and Palier 2018). It is thus used as a tool to increase consumption, especially amongst low-income groups, and to limit wage inequalities in France.

However, French governments have tried to decouple minimum wage increase from inflation and limit the once traditional "coup de pouce" (push-up) aimed at boosting consumption. The last big push-up was in 1981 (a 10% increase of the minimum wage). However, there were also a number of minor "political" push-ups when new presidents and prime ministers took office (1995, 1997, 1998, 2001, and 2012). In the public sector, the evolution of wages is strongly contested. The "point system" (*point d'indice de la function publique*) that is used for calculating public servants' wages has hardly followed inflation and has been frozen for some years. However, wages in the public sector have, in reality, increased through the "normal" upgrades associated with career advancement (in terms of grade and age).

However, the rise of taxation over this period has eroded the purchasing power of wages incomes. Total taxation rose from 30% of GDP in 1960 to 45% in 2017 (Askenazy and Palier 2018). More than half (55%) of total taxation (including social contributions) goes to the social insurance system (of the rest, 30% go to the state budget and about 15% to local governments). While income tax is relatively limited in France (less than half of the households pay it, and it has been regularly reduced), there have been continuous increases in social contributions (paid by employees) and even more increases in local taxes (financing social assistance) and in consumption taxes, such as those on tobacco, alcohol, or soft drinks (earmarked to finance healthcare) and on gas and gas oil. The rise in the taxes on gas and gas oil in late 2018 triggered the *gilets jaune*—yellow vest mobilization.

Labor market and welfare reforms

France has gone through many labor market and welfare reforms since the 1990s (see e.g. Palier 2000, 2005, 2010; Hassenteufel and Palier 2016) aimed at reducing the overall cost of the welfare system, while protecting the core workers and activating those at the periphery of the labor market (Palier and Thelen 2010). Ultimately, these reforms have contributed to a dualization of the labor market and the welfare system (Palier and Thelen 2010; Seeleib-Kaiser et al. 2012).

As in Germany, during the late 1970s and the 1980s, France used insurance-financed welfare benefits to implement its first response to the end of Fordism, i.e. dealing with industrial restructuring via labor-shedding, generous unemployment allowances, and early exit policies (including putting the age of retirement at sixty in 1982). The aim was to save the industry by relieving it of part of its workforce. However, in the early 1990s, the EU context introduced new constraints. During the 1990s, all welfare reforms were made in the name of the introduction of the euro and the defense of French competitiveness in an open economy (Palier 2005, 2010). The goal was not to dismantle the welfare system but rather to rescue it through reforms. The logic of the reforms has always been the same: to reinforce the Bismarckian contributory mechanisms (one needs to pay more social contributions and for longer to be entitled to the same social insurance benefits) so that insiders bear less of the burden of the reforms than those who are unemployed or in atypical jobs. For outsiders a different welfare state has developed, consisting of means-tested benefits, income tax credits on earnings, and activation of unemployment insurances (Palier 2010).

These efforts at retrenchment have never been able to stop the growth of social expenditure, only to reduce its rate of increase. Despite dozens of reforms throughout the 1990s, 2000s, and 2010s, according to OECD SOCX data,[5] public social expenditure went from 24.3% of GDP in 1990 to a peak of 32.2% in 2014 (down to 31.2% in 2018). Since the 1990s, France has had the most expensive welfare state in the world, with expenditure being particularly high in old-age pensions (France has amongst the most generous pension system in the world),[6] healthcare,[7] and unemployment insurance. The French welfare system remains mostly a social consumption oriented one.

Not all workers can benefit from the generous welfare system, however, since changes in labor market policies have given a boost to atypical employment (Palier and Thelen 2010). Policies of labor market flexibility at the margins were aimed at developing low-paid jobs in the sheltered service sector and thus providing manufacturing and high-skill services with cheap outsourcing opportunities, a capacity to adjust the size of the workforce to economic conditions (with a rise in short-term contracts), and a relatively cheap domestic service environment. Since the 1990s, there has been a succession of changes in labor law including the Macron ordinance of "*loi travail*," adopted in 2018, that eased the use of atypical work contracts (Palier and Thelen 2010; Askenazy and Palier 2018). Trends at the end of the 2010s show an increase in very short-term contracts[8] and non-standard employment so that more than a third of the working population did not have a permanent work contract.

France has put in place a system that allows—and actually encourages—the development of low-paid jobs, while keeping the net hourly wages of these workers close to those of other workers. This occurs through the application of the minimum wage to all sectors (with only few exceptions), salary grids in industry agreements, which cover the vast majority of workers, an earned income

[5] https://stats.oecd.org/Index.aspx?datasetcode=SOCX_AGG (last accessed February 24, 2020).

[6] The standard of living for pensioners has continued to increase to an income of €2,049 per month in terms of per unit of consumption in 2013—almost equal to that of the working-age population (€2,062) and higher than the standard of living for the whole population (€1,946) and especially young people aged eighteen to twenty-four (€1,671) (COR 2015). It has remained above the standard of living of the active population since then.

[7] Health spending increased from 8% of GDP in 1990 to 11.5% in 2014, and has since remained at around this level.

[8] Since 2015, at least 4 million people are hired on a fixed-term contract of less than one month each quarter. About half are on contracts of less than one week (Askenazy and Palier 2018).

tax credits (*prime d'activité*), and specific social benefits for workers with very few hours of work (Askenazy and Palier 2018).

While these welfare and labor market reforms resemble those of Germany and were indeed inspired by the German example, which is prominent in the French economic debate, there are four main differences with Germany which are linked to the political priority to preserve French domestic consumption. First, in contrast to Germany, welfare expenditure has not diminished, and wages have increased during the 1990s and 2000s. Second, the reforms have been much less abrupt than the German ones (especially under Schröder); they have merely contributed to reducing the rate of increase of social expenditure, not shrinking it. Third, the rise in atypical jobs has not been accompanied by a sharp increase in working poverty as in Germany, thanks to a general minimum wage and specific subsidies. Fourth, the state spends much more money in France than in Germany to support the changes, especially to compensate for the general exemptions in social contributions and to finance low-paid job creation.

Lowering labor costs while maintaining consumption capacities

In order to protect businesses from carrying the burden of the expensive, consumption-oriented French welfare system, all governments since the early 1990s have continuously intervened to indirectly lower the cost of labor, i.e. to lower the level of social security contributions, especially for the low-paid (before exemptions, social contributions account for 60% of the firm's cost of labor). Both conservative and socialist governments have pursued this strategy (Askenazy 2011; Carbonnier et al. 2016). They first aimed to compensate for labor costs that minimum wages represent for firms employing people in low-skilled jobs. Over time, the social contribution exemptions have increasingly concerned higher wage levels, with the CICE (*credit d'impôt pour la compétitivité et l'emploi,* a tax credit for firms, calculated at a percentage of payroll, created in 2013 and worth €20 billion per year) reaching all wages up to 2.5 times the minimum wage. Institutionalized by Macron in 2019 as a permanent reduction in employers' social contribution, the very name of this measure (literally "tax credit for competitiveness and jobs") encapsulates the French growth strategy: reduction of labor cost to improve firms' competitiveness and boost job creation.

Not only French firms are able to benefit from these social contribution exemptions and tax credits, but private households are too, if they employ someone for domestic tasks like cleaning, home help, childcare, or elder care. France has created many (bad) jobs in these areas (around 1.23 million, according to Carbonnier and Morel (2018)), supported by many (inefficient) tax credits that are contributing to the further crowding out of French investment capacities.

This strategy of lowering labor costs is extremely costly for the public purse, since social contribution exemptions are compensated by the government budget (financed by other taxes). With an overall cost of around €50 billion per year

(Carbonnier et al. 2016), this tax and social contribution exemption strategy is increasing the public deficit and debt without triggering strong growth or the creation of good jobs. Yet, it continues to be the main economic instrument used by the government to boost firms' competitiveness. The French economic strategy is, thus, more a low-cost strategy than anything else.

A low-cost strategy

Despite governments' aim to support the competitiveness of manufacturing industrial sectors (and more recently the "French Tech"), there are few institutional changes that positively enhance such capacities. France has not been able to develop an efficient apprenticeship and vocational training system. It has also not developed a co-decision organization of corporate governance that would generate high-quality manufacturing, nor a wage coordination system that would allow for wage moderation, also indispensable for a manufacturing export-led strategy.

As for dynamic services, France is able to create good jobs in some sectors (banking, luxury) but lacks the basic institutions needed to pursue an inclusive social investment strategy. The number of children under three in formal childcare is now well below the German one (Collombet et al. 2017). Despite a will to "democratize universities" since the late 1990s, France still lacks an efficient university system that provides high general skills to all, since it remains strongly elitist (Chevalier, this volume). The distribution of literacy and numerical proficiency is among the most unequal in the OECD (close to Southern Europe, according to Programme for International Assessment of Adult Competencies PIAAC data).

The French case demonstrates the incompatibility between wage-led and manufacturing export-led strategies. Since its policies do not help to create enough good jobs or strong growth, France continues to finance its publicly subsidized, low-cost strategy through public debt. It is trapped in a low growth, low employment, low skill, high public expenditure, and high public deficit and debt circle, gradually getting closer to its Southern European neighbors. It has, however, been able to avoid a debt crisis and has, thus, eluded the drastic "competitive impoverishment" strategy that has been imposed by the EU on Portugal and Greece, and partly on Spain and Italy.

3.6 The EU-Imposed "Competitive Impoverishment" Strategy

As demonstrated by the study of Germany and France in this chapter, the wage and social benefits-based domestic demand-led growth regime is incompatible with a manufacturing export-led growth regime. As explained by Scharpf in this volume (see also Hassel 2014; Hall 2014; Höpner and Lutter 2018; Iversen and Soskice 2018; Johnston and Regan 2016), the differences between the two growth regimes are at the core of the explanation of the Eurozone crisis. Before the crisis, Southern European countries benefitted from low to negative real interest rates and from the credit ratings of the Eurozone as a whole, so that they could finance their domestic demand out of debt (more private in Portugal and Spain, more public in Italy, France, and Greece). However, inflation, wage increases, and the emerging credit bubbles led to a deterioration in competitiveness compared to their Northern counterparts, and, once the crisis struck, they had no instruments of their own (i.e. devaluation capacities) to deal with it. In parallel, Northern European Eurozone countries seemed to grow in the exact opposite direction: they organized low inflation and wage stagnation (and thus lower growth than in Southern Europe) during the first years of the Euro. They undertook major structural reforms of their labor markets and pension systems and managed to contain, and even decrease, their public expenditure from 2000 to 2007. They thus increased their competitive advantage in comparison to their Southern counterparts. With the euro, there is no exchange rate adjustment mechanism to counterbalance this advantage. What seemed at first glance to be an economic and social convergence between the core and periphery (the periphery, with higher growth, was catching up with the center) actually resulted in increased competitiveness in the Northern countries and diminished competitiveness in the Southern countries. Most Northern countries recovered quite rapidly from the crisis (already in 2010) and then were in the political position to impose their own views at the European level.

The new euro regime as an export-led growth regime

From 2010, the governance of the Eurozone started to change. Many decisions created a more coercive environment in the Eurozone: the adoption of the Six-Pack (in 2011), the fiscal compact (2012), and the Two-Pack (2013). National budgets, and thus details of welfare policy reforms, became the subject of scrutiny with strong potential for the EU to intervene (de la Porte and Heins 2016: 18–19).

The Six-Pack introduced the Macroeconomic Imbalance Procedure (MIP), which aims to monitor in detail the evolution of each EU economy. The fourteen "headline indicators" of the MIP reveal the kind of growth strategy the European Commission pursues,[9] which includes a balanced budget, low unemployment rates (including youth and long-term), and a high participation rate in the labor market. The MIP also observes the evolution of nominal labor costs, private sector debt, house price developments, financial sector liabilities, the current account balance, and the real effective exchange rate. Taken together, these indicators

[9] https://ec.europa.eu/info/business-economy-euro/economic-and-fiscal-policy-coordination/eu-economic-governance-monitoring-prevention-correction/macroeconomic-imbalance-procedure/scoreboard_en

reflect the "normal" situation of a manufacturing export-led growth regime (low public deficit and debt, limited increase in labor costs, potentially positive current accounts) more than anything else. In practice, the MIP represses instruments of domestic demand-based growth regimes, either through private debt, house price increases, and financialization, or through wage boosts and public deficits. Even though the Commission adopted a "social investment package" in 2013, there is little sign of active monitoring of the indicators proposed therein along the same lines as the MIP.

As Scharpf (this volume) demonstrates, the implementation of these economic control policies within the Eurozone aims at compelling the domestic demand-led growth regimes to become compatible with manufacturing export-led ones in a "forced convergence" process: "The main emphasis is on reducing unit labor costs in order to improve international competitiveness—and thus to achieve export-led economic growth." The goal however is not to help the Southern countries to become export-led growth countries themselves, i.e. to invest in specific skills or to develop wage coordination, but rather to make them abandon their previous practices which favor domestic-oriented sectors and domestic demand-driven growth. Southern European countries are expected to become cheap enough to become competitive (i.e. to sell cheap products abroad, attract foreigners with tourism, and attract FDI to develop some industrial activities). This entails a long phase of decline and impoverishment, hence our label: "competitive impoverishment" strategy. This is not a passive strategy (waiting to become poor to become competitive), but it supposes an active welfare state reform agenda to destroy the institutions and practices linked to a domestic demand-led growth regime.

Welfare retrenchment and structural reforms to implement the competitive impoverishment strategy

The reduction of unit labor costs to improve international competitiveness is at the core of the competitive impoverishment strategy. It implies both immediate cuts in public expenditure and more structural reforms to avoid any risk of an increase in unit labor costs in the future (Scharpf, this volume). Under the pressure of EU institutions, there have been waves of such reforms in Southern Europe since 2010. One channel was applied to all EU countries, namely the excessive deficit procedure (EDP). The other more stringent and intrusive channel was through Memoranda of Understanding (MOU) between the Troika (European Commission, European Central Bank, and International Monetary Fund) and the indebted countries that needed a bailout (such as Greece, Portugal, and partly Spain but also Cyprus, Hungary, Ireland, Latvia, and Romania). Italy also implemented some of these structural measures under the Monti government in the context of implicit conditionalities (Sacchi 2016).

As of mid-2011, twenty-four EU member states were subjected to the EDP. All countries had to control their budget deficit, inflation, and public expenditure.

However, the policies implemented in order to achieve this had a much stronger impact on Southern countries. In the first place, their deficits and debts were much higher (so they had to implement harsher adjustment plans). Second, implementing austerity measures on domestic demand-led growth regimes has a much harsher effect than applying them to an export-led growth one (where wage moderation and balanced budgets are already part of the strategy).

The measures adopted since 2010 by European Union governments have been mainly of three different types: wage-freezes for civil servants (and cutbacks in their numbers in MOU countries), privatization (especially in MOU countries), and social policy reforms. A number of countries reduced unemployment benefits (Portugal, Romania, Denmark, Ireland, the UK, Spain, and Greece) in an effort to activate the unemployed. Several countries also restricted unemployment claimants' rights to refuse an offer of employment (Spain and the UK), and several measures were adopted that increased labor market flexibility, notably affecting workers with open-ended contracts (Spain, Italy, Portugal, and Denmark). Some governments also reduced the public share of health expenditure, with such measures being imposed on Greece, Ireland, and Portugal as a condition for receiving aid within their MOUs. Budget consolidation plans also included pension/retirement reforms. Spanish and Greek reforms introduced cost-containing measures in a new calculation of their pension formulas as laid out in their MOUs. In Southern Europe (and the UK and Denmark), cuts have also been made in education and family policy expenditures (Palier et al. 2018).[10]

Whereas the impact of cuts has been limited in most Northern and Eastern European countries, Southern European countries suffered in many ways from such budgetary measures and structural reforms: Greece lost a quarter of its GDP between 2008 and 2016, Spain had no growth during the same period, Italy almost none, and Portugal only 3.39% (Scharpf, this volume). Moreover, while other countries rapidly recovered their capacity to invest in their own growth strategy, Southern European countries lost their capacity to boost growth and jobs through domestic demand, while not having the means to invest in any other strategies. There is growing divergence between Northern and Southern Europe in future oriented national social investment expenditure in the realms of health, education, family policies (like childcare), and (upskilling) active labor market policies (Palier et al. 2018). As a result, in Southern European countries, there are high levels of youth unemployment and a high number of Neets (neither in employment, education, or training), as well as a high number of well-educated youngsters leaving these countries (Lafleur and Stanek 2018).

[10] For an overview of the main decisions concerning welfare system reforms in Southern Europe see Guillén and Pavolini (2015, the whole special issue); Pavolini et al. (2016) for Italy and Spain; and Theodoropoulou (2016) for Portugal and Greece.

4. Conclusions: The Politics of Growth and Welfare Reform in Advanced Capitalist Countries

This chapter has illustrated how in European countries the dominant growth strategy has interacted with and shaped welfare state reforms. Analyzing the linkages between welfare states and growth strategies helps us to understand why welfare state reforms have been undertaken and their timing and content. While we do not pretend to provide a full explanation of welfare state reform trajectories, our account expands on the existing welfare state literature by answering why welfare state reform takes place even when it is politically costly.

We are now at the end of retracing the journey taken by capitalist growth regimes since the 1980s. The post-war era of welfare capitalism ended with the dissolution of the Bretton Woods system and the oil crisis of the mid-1970s. Since then advanced industrialized countries have undergone a constant process of economic restructuring. In line with other comparative political economy research (Crouch and Streeck 1997; Hall and Soskice 2001; Beramendi et al. 2015), we show that, despite common challenges, policy responses and reform trajectories have remained diverse.

With this volume we have taken a step towards understanding why these trajectories of change have varied across countries and which mechanisms and drivers have shaped them. To address these questions, some authors emphasize the electoral process, including the changing composition of the electorate and their policy preferences (Beramendi et al. 2015), while others focus on producer coalitions or social blocs and institutional legacies (Baccaro and Pontusson 2019). Some authors argue that there is a kind of division of labor here: electoral politics are dealing with very salient issues ("loud politics"), e.g. redistributive issues resulting from welfare state reforms, while business and producer groups deal with much less salient issues ("quiet politics"), such as economic policy issues (Culpepper 2010). By underlining the strong connections between welfare reforms and growth policies, we argue that one cannot just separate these two worlds of politics. There is a need to better understand how they interact. Like Hall (this volume), we argue that both processes work in tandem, or, as we illustrate below, in alternation.

To the current debate, we add the importance of governments' actions and their growth strategies. Policy-making by governments does not take place in a black box, automatically following demands of the electorate (through parties) or those of the dominant social blocs. In reality, governments are sandwiched between the demands of voters, on the one hand, and preferences of producer groups, on the other (see Figure 12.3). While these demands exert pressures which can even go in opposite directions, they also assign a pivotal role to governments in shaping the evolution of capitalist economies.

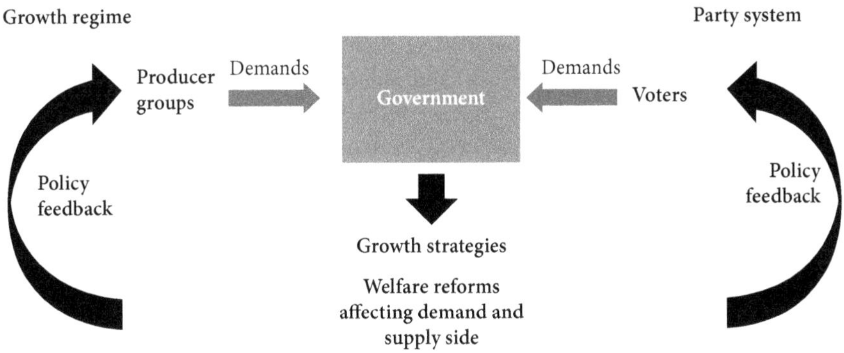

Figure 12.3 The politics of growth and welfare reforms

As this volume shows, governments' growth strategies are key to understanding how growth regimes evolve. We end this chapter by focusing on the politics of such strategies and propose a model which illustrates how both producer groups and electoral politics matter in shaping these strategies.

We start by emphasizing the key role of producer groups on growth strategies and, henceforth, on welfare state reforms, but then underline the political feedback (sometimes backlash) that these reforms may trigger, thus implying more noisy electoral politics into the process.

4.1 The Key Role of Existing Regimes and Producer Groups in Shaping Growth Strategies and Welfare Reforms

Government performance is measured against the country's economic growth and job creation. As the literature on economic voting has convincingly established, good economic performance contributes to the electoral success of incumbent politicians. A review of this literature by Lewis-Beck and Stegmaier (2015) established that governments are held accountable for economic performance in terms of outputs such as employment and income growth. Iversen and Soskice (2019: 164) maintain that the electorate, in particular the middle classes, expect and ensure that the governments they elect focus on prosperity and prompt governments to pursue an efficient growth strategy (in our terminology, not theirs).

As the economic vote is a key predictor for electoral success, it continues to guide policy-makers. However, different governments choose different roads to that end. Suitable policies are context-specific and not universal. Both Martin and Thelen (this volume) demonstrate that, when looking for clues as to which strategies are the most suitable for boosting growth and employment, governments take the interests of national producer groups into account. Producer groups with the most leverage tend to be firms and organized interests in the most productive or the most relevant parts of the economy. In manufacturing-based economies, such as Germany, they comprise business and labor communities in engineering, the car industry, and pharmaceutical industries. In finance-dominated economies, they are located in the major financial centers, as, for example, the City of London in the UK. In France, they represent the interest of French-based multinationals, such as the automobile industry, luxury groups, and supermarkets (Carrefour). In Southern Europe, the most relevant business communities might be state-run enterprises or those that are protected by the state.

Economic growth policies are confronted with the interests and power politics of the business community. Employment, innovation, and productivity take place overwhelmingly in private companies, in interaction with public research and innovation policies. The business community, therefore, has an important stake in how policies that affect them are implemented. There is a reciprocal and mutual dependency between business and state interests, but business elites pursue their own economic interests rather than that of the general public (Culpepper 2010; Hacker and Pierson 2010; Skocpol and Hertel-Fernandez 2016; Amable et al. 2019). Typically, producer groups exercise political influence quietly, away from the media (Culpepper 2010).

Martin chapter (this volume) underlines the variety of business interests depending on growth regimes. It also shows how the organization of business interests mediates and shapes the policy process regarding social and other policies. The degree of coordination, including macro-level concertation, and the degree to which the business community is able to communicate coherent preferences to governments have a key effect on policy outcomes. The business community's ability to forge alliances with trade unions and other civil society actors influences the framing of policy issues. Thelen (this volume) demonstrates the key role of producer groups in forging growth strategies.

While business groups in the dominant sector(s) tend to have privileged access to governments (and to media), we do not assume that they always have the upper hand. In fact, business interests and government priorities may not coincide. We do, however, expect government policy-making to take into account the demands of the dominant business community and their strategies of coping with economic and welfare restructuring.

Obviously, many other factors beyond the production regime and their representatives (producer groups) matter as well. Electoral rules, political institutions, political parties, and external events, as well as ideology and values, can lead policy-makers to adopt growth strategies that are not necessarily in line with the growth regime. In the medium to long run, however, we assume that the production regime will play an important role in influencing growth strategies, independent of the political configurations and institutions. The French case illustrates how much the legacy of an existing growth regimes weighs on the country's capacity to switch to another one.

The preference of the dominant sector informs policy-makers as to what the priorities of economic and social policies should be in order to protect, rescue or revive the existing growth regime (see also Iversen and Soskice 2018). As already demonstrated by Swenson (2002) and Mares (2003), and confirmed in this volume by Martin, these preferences do not always favor welfare retrenchment and liberalization. For example, in some contexts, social protection can serve as insurance for investment in skills, which business might support. In other contexts, business may favor public investment in higher education in order to develop general skills of the workforce. Martin (this volume) shows that the variation of business preferences for welfare reforms depend on the kind of business community that is dominant. In some cases, workers in key industries might support business preferences, especially since both typically benefit from the economic specialization process. Such cross-class coalitions are sector- (or country-) specific and largely focused on or coming from the dominant sector in the economy.

However, even within the context of a specific welfare and growth regime, the social policy response to promote growth that is in the interest of producer groups might trigger political contestation. Such was the case when, in 2003, the Schröder government in Germany introduced wide-ranging, business-friendly labor market and welfare reforms as a reaction to low growth and high levels of unemployment. While analysts continue to dispute the real effect of the reforms on growth and employment, labor market activation lowered the reservation wage and contributed to wage restraint, which in turn bolstered the export-oriented growth strategy and contributed to job creation in the service sector.[11] The reforms, however, also contributed to the development of low paid jobs and in-work poverty. In the end, Schröder's Social Democrat government was not rewarded for its reforms, and the party was punished badly in the polls for their choice. The example shows that growth strategies might be adopted in the interest of dominant producer groups or for electoral reasons (jump-starting growth and reducing unemployment). At the same time, the choice of reform is not obvious, nor is it clear that incumbent governments will benefit from undertaking welfare reforms in pursuit of their chosen growth strategies.

An even more telling example of political backlash to the implementation of a growth strategy is to be found, of course, in Southern Europe, where reforms implemented in the name of growth and EMU without voters' consent have led to electoral discontent. Governments that side with producer groups at the expense of important voter segments might be punished at the polls or experience fierce reactions. Governments are, therefore, pressured from both sides: producer groups and voters. The demands of the two sides might overlap (for instance a

[11] See Krebs and Scheffel (2013); Dustmann et al. (2014); and Bofinger (2017) for different assessments.

demand to protect key industries), but they might also clash. In the next subsection, we focus on how governments might respond to voters when adapting the country's growth regime.

4.2 The Electoral Challenge

Hall (this volume) points out that the most important feature of electoral politics is the structure of political cleavages. Cleavage refers to those issues that are the most salient to electoral politics and the alignment of social groups along them. "Cleavage structures evolve in response to changes in the size and socio-economic position of specific social groups, which are affected by economic developments, and in response to changes in the appeals mounted by political parties" (Hall, this volume).

Hall analyzes the rise of female employment as a key new political cleavage, as women's position in the labor market is determined in particular by family-friendly policies and childcare opportunities. While growth strategies during the era of liberalization beginning in the 1980s encouraged female employment, working women in turn started to demand better childcare (Hall, this volume). Morgan (2013) shows that since the late 1990s, important family policy reforms were introduced in Germany, the Netherlands, and the UK because party leaders needed new constituencies and thus feminized their party structures to attract female voters. Women working within the parties had played an important role in hatching or lobbying for these reforms. Such reforms were slow to materialize in Austria and Italy due to the absence of similar electoral dynamics. In a more general sense, as demonstrated by Beramendi et al. (2015), "investive" policies are demanded by service sector workers, who are often female. Low-skilled manufacturing workers, on the other hand, prefer "consumptive" social policies (Beramendi et al. 2015). Political parties regroup around these new cleavages and present their choices to the electorate in competition for votes.

How do these new cleavages influence growth strategies? The policy cleavage around investive versus consumptive social policies partly mirrors the five types of growth strategies and welfare state reforms identified in this chapter. When dynamic services are favored, social investment comes to the fore, and when manufacturing sectors are key, one is more likely to find a predominance of protective social policies that feed consumption.

In the context of financialization and very flexible labor markets, policies that allow or encourage an individual to invest in general skills is likely to be favored. Financialization leans more toward investive policies, as it gives access to credit to fund private education, including early childcare education. People investing in their own human capital through market mechanisms would likely prefer low social expenditure and easy access to credit and choice (through diversified private offers). These correspond to typical neoliberal proposals that New Labour kept on board to attract and keep upper middle-class voters. In the Nordic countries, the dynamic service strategy is directly related to investive policies in education and public educational spending. This strategy is very likely to be supported by the educated middle class. In the Nordic countries, educated people in interpersonal service occupations represent about a quarter of the workforce and therefore a good portion of the voting public, whereas the same group remains far below 10% in the Southern European countries (Beramendi et al. 2015).

The manufacturing export-led strategy pursues wage moderation and lower labor costs, while keeping labor market insiders protected. It is more related to consumptive policies, which on their own do not feed into a reduction of labor costs, but rather the opposite if they raise social contributions and the overall taxation of labor (the labor wedge). This is why dualization occurs, where only the most protected workers continue to have access to both public and private "consumptive" social insurance. Core workers in the manufacturing sector are promised employment protection in exchange for wage restraint and increased internal flexibility. Outsiders tend to work in low paid service jobs with low levels of protection (Emmenegger et al. 2012). Wage moderation and the preservation of quality in manufacturing labor is thus achieved through protection of labor market insiders, close cooperation with manufacturing trade unions on investment and technology, and enhancement of skills through liaisons with further education entities. Kazepov and Ranci (2017) have convincingly demonstrated that there is no political interest (nor actually any economic interest) in investive policies in Italy (and this could be generalized to other Southern European countries).

Overall, the electoral cleavage between the new (educated) middle class and the old middle class (routine-based jobs in both manufacturing and services) (Beramendi et al. 2015) also partially overlaps with the policies that are frequently employed in different growth strategies. The areas of overlap are particularly easy to detect in the strategy of dynamic service exports, which focuses on public investment in education. Here, a positive feedback process can be identified in which more employment in the services sector bolsters demand for social and educational services, which then promotes further investment in the knowledge economy. By contrast, the manufacturing export-led strategy, which tends to privilege the old middle class working in the favored industries, focuses on consumptive social policies and social protectionism and contributes to their self-reinforcement (sometimes up to the point of exhaustion, as in Southern Europe).

Electoral cleavages can reinforce growth strategies, but do not automatically do so. In the Nordic countries, pursuit of the chosen growth strategy and welfare policies has not been hampered by electoral cleavages since the preferences of producer groups and other voter groups tend to coincide. Yet, electoral cleavages might cancel each other out or conflict with each other, thwarting governments' efforts to introduce reforms. This is what took place in Italy, when both the Monti (2011–13) and the Renzi (2014–16) technocratic governments tried to promote social investment against the interests of producer groups and the majority of the electorate (Kazepov and Ranci 2017).

For us, however, the main electoral dimension of the process lies in the political feedback effects that growth strategies and their associated welfare reforms might trigger. Indeed, these feedback effects can reinforce electoral cleavages or even create new ones. Changes in welfare systems made in the name of growth strategies have left large groups of the electorate less protected than before and forced them into insecure jobs. More labor market insecurity and less social protection have in turn given rise to more demands for social protection. For example, unions pursued the introduction of a statutory minimum wage in Germany after labor market deregulation contributed to the rise of the low-wage sector and was met with criticism by the electorate. One could also interpret the emergence of UKIP in the UK, and henceforth Brexit, as well as populist movements in Southern and Eastern Europe, as a countermovement to the growth strategies that had been implemented before.

To recognize the two sides of the politics of growth—producer group preferences and electoral cleavages—can thus help to understand increasing levels of voter alienation with government policies. Many policies by the center-left governments of Tony Blair in the UK, Wim Kok in the Netherlands, and Gerhard Schröder in Germany during the 1990s and early 2000s were based on the belief that "good" welfare reform policy would serve the middle classes and generate growth and jobs. These policies included labor market liberalization, activation, and social investment. They were often accompanied by welfare cuts and the conditionality of transfer payments for the unemployed, which the more precarious parts of the electorate did not see as "good."

4.3 Political Salience as a Determinant of Path-Dependent versus Path-Breaking Reform Trajectories

Another important aspect of welfare reform is the salience and visibility of social policies. The dependence of large parts of the electorate on social policies and the importance of path-dependent developments in welfare reforms stand in contrast to many policies that interest the business community such as corporate governance reforms or the regulation of financial markets. As Culpepper (2010) has convincingly argued, the power of business varies between policy areas. The business community is particularly powerful with regard to economic policy issues that receive low media attention and are decided on in informal settings. The higher the salience of an issue and the more formal the institutional arena governing it, the greater the likelihood will be that business will have to build alliances with other actors. While the business community might be tempted to shift the arena from high to low salience and from formal to informal venues, other—civil society or party—actors will do the opposite. For these other actors, the framing of an issue as high salience and as governed by formal policy processes is advantageous for winning policy battles. The political battleground is, therefore, dependent on the framing of an issue and on defining the venue for its contestation.

The dynamics of policy-making when pursuing growth strategies can be illustrated with the example of German pension reform (see Naczyk and Hassel 2019). Before implementing the Riester pension reform, the Schröder government had envisaged opening up the German market for pension funds to bolster the private pension mechanism and to strengthen capital markets in Germany, thereby inducing financialization as a growth strategy. The government had prepared legislation to set up defined-contribution plans for private pensions with no guarantee of returns. This would have contributed to a more finance-led growth path in the German economy. The plan, however, failed as the government wanted to link the introduction of such plans to cuts in existing public pensions that allowed the opponents—mainly the insurance industry and some segments of organized labor—to thwart their introduction (Naczyk and Hassel 2019).

Naczyk and Hassel (2019) argue that pension reforms remained a technical issue as long as policy-makers kept the introduction of pure defined-contribution plans separate from cuts in public pensions. In an environment of "quiet politics," opposition to pension reform is harder to mobilize than it is for highly salient pension cuts. When—as in the German case—defined-contribution plans were presented in combination with retrenchment, the pension reform package became much more politicized. Arguments were heard in the public debate about threats to the actual pension payouts posed by the volatile portfolios of pure defined-contribution plans. The visibility and threat of pension cuts put strong pressure on politicians, compelling them to commit to safe and adequate pensions (Naczyk and Hassel 2019).

In other words, growth strategies that rely on welfare reforms are situated in the highly salient and contested arena of the politics of welfare reform, rather than in the hardly visible arena in which policies for business are determined. The stickiness of the welfare state also prompts strategies that correspond to the existing welfare and growth regime. Path-breaking reforms are much harder to achieve and sustain politically. We therefore argue that, in the context of long-established welfare and growth regimes, the dynamics of the policy process, situated between the quiet politics of business regulation and the noisy politics of welfare reform (and social policy preferences of changing electorates), largely determine the capacity of governments to effectively pursue their growth strategies. Governments have no choice but to mediate between quiet and noisy politics; policies will inevitably trigger responses and feedback loops from both producer groups and voters.

We finish this chapter by noting that, throughout our analyses of national growth strategies, we hardly came across the issue of climate change in the various growth strategies that we studied. In their search for growth, most governments have neglected the environmental issues that seem to contradict or hinder that quest. However, in a context of global warming and climate change, traditional patterns of growth will be increasingly questioned, and strategies for green growth are likely to be sought. The climate crisis will force governments to change course, either to control emissions or to cope with the effects of climate change. As climate change is bound to pose great costs on all governments (and the people they govern), growth strategies will have to adjust with regard to, at a minimum, transport and energy systems. Here, we expect to see a distributive impact across the board, with new, potentially quite noisy political dynamics emerging.

Appendix

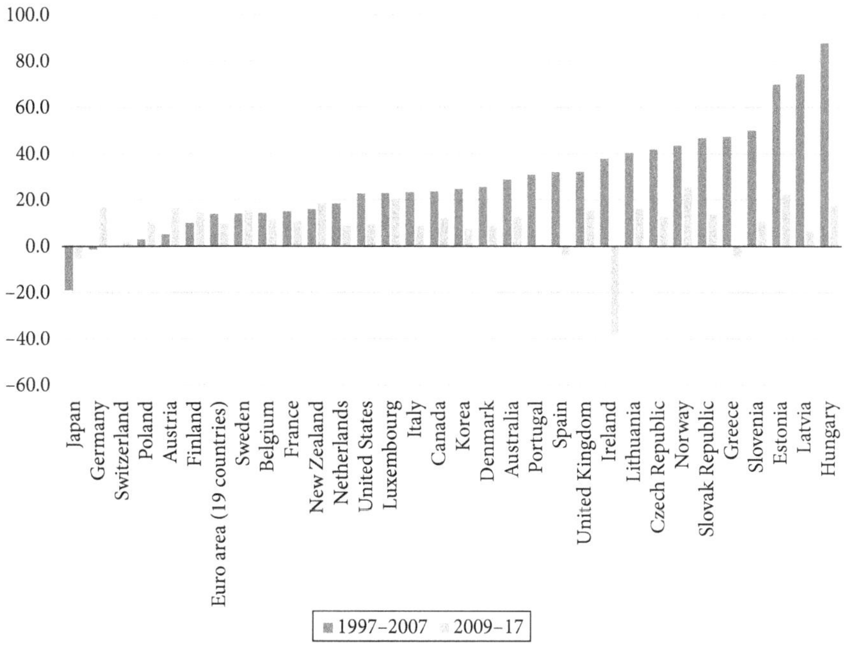

Figure 12A.1 Change in unit labor cost, selected OECD countries, 1997–2017

Source: OECD Dataset: Unit labor costs and labor productivity (employment-based), total economy; quarterly change. Data extracted on September 5, 2018, 07:12 UTC (GMT) from https://stats.oecd.org/

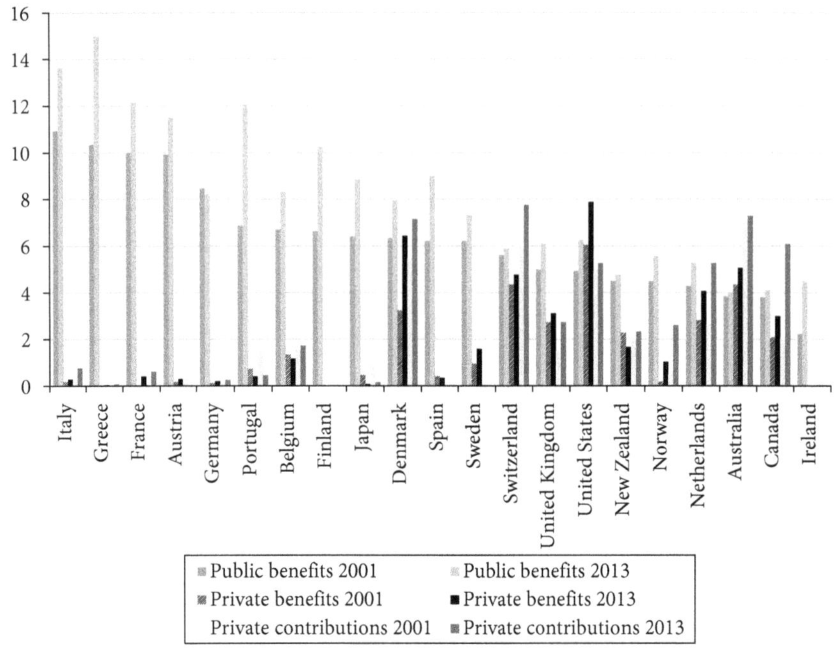

Figure 12A.2 Spending on public/private pensions and contributions to private pension plans as a percentage of GDP, 2001 and 2013

Notes: Data for private benefits in France (2001), Greece (2001), and Ireland (2001 and 2013) are missing; data for private contributions in France (2001), Ireland (2001 and 2013), Spain (2001 and 2013), and Sweden (2001 and 2013) are missing. For Sweden's private benefits, data were retrieved from https://data.oecd.org/ (2005 benefits for 2001).

Sources: Hassel et al. (2019). OECD SOCX; OECD Global Pension Statistics.

References

Agostini, C. and Natali, D. 2016. "Italian Welfare Reforms: Missed Opportunities for a Paradigmatic Change?" In *Challenges to European Welfare Systems*, edited by K. Schubert, P. de Villota, and J. Kuhlmann. Basel: Springer International Publishing, 395–418.

Amable, B., Regan, A., Avdagic, S., Baccaro, L., Pontusson, J. and Van der Zwan, N. 2019. "New approaches to political economy." *Socio-Economic Review* 17(2): 433–59. https://doi.org/10.1093/ser/mwz002

Anderson, K.M. 2019. "Financialisation meets collectivisation: occupational pensions in Denmark, the Netherlands and Sweden." *Journal of European Public Policy* 26(4): 617–36. DOI: 10.1080/13501763.2019.1574309

Andersen, J. G., Schoyen, M.A., and Hvinden, B. 2017. "Changing Scandinavian Welfare States: Which Way Forward?" In *After Austerity: Welfare State Transformation in Europe after the Great Recession*, edited by P. Taylor-Gooby, B. Leruth, and H. Chung. Oxford: Oxford University Press, 89–114.

Askenazy, P. 2011. *Les Décennies aveugles. Emploi et croissance (1970–2010).* Paris: Le Seuil, 140–2.

Askenazy, P., Diallo, R., Bonnand, G., Castel, R., Etienne, M., Palier, B., and Rivière, F. 2013. Face à la précarisation de l'emploi, construire des droits pour tous. Policy Note for Terra Nova.

Askenazy, P. and Palier, B. 2018. "Rising Precariousness Supported by the Welfare State." In *Inequality and Inclusive Growth in Rich Countries: Shared Challenges and Contrasting Fortunes*, edited by B. Nola. Oxford: Oxford University Press, 129–52.

Avlijaš, S. 2020. "Beyond neoliberalism? Revisiting the Welfare State in the Baltic States." *Europe-Asia Studies* 72(4): 614–43. https://doi.org/10.1080/09668136.2019.1709622

Avlijaš, S. Forthcoming. "Explaining the contrasting trajectories of Baltic and Visegrad countries." In *The World Politics of Social Investment (Volume II): The Politics of Varying Social Investment Strategies*, edited by J.L. Garritzmann, S. Häusermann, and B. Palier. Oxford: Oxford University Press.

Baccaro, L. and Pontusson, J. 2016. "Rethinking Comparative Political Economy The Growth Model Perspective." *Politics & Society* 44(2): 175–207. https://doi.org/10.1177/0032329216638053

Baccaro, L. and Pontusson, J. 2019. "Social Blocs and Growth Models: An Analytical Framework with Germany and Sweden as Illustrative Cases." In Unequal Democracies. Working Paper No. 7.

Bennett, O. 2017. "House Building Under The Tories Drops To Lowest Level Since The 1920s." *Huffington Post U.K. Edition*, May 9, 2017.

Beramendi, P., Häusermann, S., Kitschelt, H. and Kriesi, H. (eds.). 2015. *The Politics of Advanced Capitalism*. Cambridge, UK; New York: Cambridge University Press.

Blomqvist, P. 2004. "The choice revolution: Privatization of Swedish welfare services in the 1990s." *Social Policy Administration* 38(2): 139–55.

Bofinger, P. 2017. "Hartz IV: The Solution to the Unemployment Problems in the Eurozone?" *Intereconomics* 52: 353–57. DOI: 10.1007/s10272-017-0703-6

Bohle, D. 2013. "Post-socialist housing meets transnational finance: Foreign banks, mortgage lending, and the privatization of welfare in Hungary and Estonia." *Review of International Political Economy* 21(4): 913–48.

Bohle, D. and Greskovits, B. 2012. *Capitalist Diversity on Europe's Periphery.* Ithaca, NY: Cornell University Press.

Bohle, D. and Greskovits, B. 2018. "Politicising embedded neoliberalism: Continuity and change in Hungary's development model." *West European Politics* 42(5): 1069–93.

Bohle, D. and Regan, A. Forthcoming. "Business Power, Quiet Politics and State Elites. Explaining the Continuity of Foreign Direct Investment (FDI) Growth Models." Forthcoming in *Politics and Society.*

Bonoli, G. 2005. "The politics of the new social policies: providing coverage against new social risks in mature welfare states." *Policy & Politics* 33(3): 431–49.

Bonoli, G. and Palier, B. 1998. "Changing the politics of social programmes: innovative change in British and French welfare reforms." *Journal of European Social Policy* 8(4): 317–30.

Bonoli, G. and Palier, B. 2000. "From the cradle to ... where? Current pension policy trends in Western Europe." *Yearbook of European Administrative History* 12: 153–74.

Bonoli, G. and Palier, B. 2007. "When past reforms open new opportunities: Comparing old-age insurance reforms in Bismarckian welfare systems." *Social Policy & Administration* 41(6): 555–73.

Boyer, R. 1979. "Crise Actuelle (la): une mise en perspective historique. Quelques réflexions à partir d'une analyse du capitalisme Français en longue période." *Critiques de l'Économie Politique*, nouvelle série 7–8: 3–113.

Boyer, R. 2000. "Is a Finance-led growth regime a viable alternative to Fordism? A preliminary analysis." *Economy and Society* 29(1): 111–45. https://doi.org/10.1080/030851400360587

Capussela, A. L. 2018. *The Political Economy of Italy's Decline.* Oxford: Oxford University Press. http://www.oxfordscholarship.com/view/10.1093/oso/9780198796992.001.0001/oso-9780198796992-chapter-1

Carbonnier, C., Palier, B., and Zemmour. M. 2016. "Tax cuts or social investment? Evaluating the opportunity cost of French employment strategy." *Cambridge Journal of Economics* 40(6): 1687–705.

Carbonnier, C. and Morel, N. 2018. *Le retour des domestiques.* Paris: Le Seuil.

Cerami, A. 2010. "The politics of social security reforms in the Czech Republic, Hungary, Poland and Slovakia." In *A Long Goodbye to Bismarck?*, edited by B. Palier. Amsterdam: Amsterdam University Press, 233–53.

Collombet, C., Maigne, G., and Palier, B. 2017. Places en crèche: pourquoi l'Allemagne fait-elle mieux que la France depuis dix ans? Note de France Stratégie No. 56.

COR. 2015. *Évolutions et perspectives des retraites en France.* Rapport annuel du COR 2015. Paris: Conseil d'Orientation des Retraites. https://www.cor-retraites.fr/sites/default/files/2019-06/doc-3031.pdf

Cribb, J, Hood, A., and Hoyle, J. 2018. "The decline of homeownership among young adults." Institute for Fiscal Studies Briefing note BN224 (February 16). https://www.ifs.org.uk/publications/10505

Crouch, C. and Streeck, W. (eds.). 1997. *Political Economy of Modern Capitalism. Mapping Convergence and Diversity.* London: Sage.

Culpepper, P. D. 2010. *Quiet Politics and Business Power: Corporate control in Europe and Japan.* Cambridge: Cambridge University Press.

Culpepper, P., Hall, P., and Palier, B. (eds.). 2006. *Changing France: The politics that markets make.* London: Palgrave Macmillan.

de la Porte, C. and Heins, E. 2016. "A new era of European integration? Governance of labour market and social policy since the sovereign debt crisis." In *The Sovereign Debt Crisis, the EU and Welfare State Reform*, edited by C. De La Porte and E. Heins. London: Palgrave Macmillan, 15–41.

Destatis. 2019. Vorausberechneter Bevölkerungsstand. https://www-genesis.destatis.de/genesis/online?sequenz=tabelleErgebnis&selectionname=12421-0001

Disney, R. and Luo, G. 2017. "The right to buy public housing in Britain: A welfare analysis." *Journal of Housing Economics* 35: 51–68. https://doi.org/10.1016/j.jhe.2017.01.005

Dixon, A. D. and Sorsa, V. P. 2009. "Institutional change and the financialisation of pensions in Europe." *Competition & Change* 13(4): 347–67.

Dølvik, J. E. Forthcoming. *Welfare as a Productive Factor: Nordic approaches to growth and social policy reform.* Unpublished manuscript.

Dustmann, C., Fitzenberger, B., Schönberg, U. and SpitzOener, A. 2014. "From Sick Man of Europe to Economic Superstar: Germany's Resurgent Economy." *Economy Journal of Economic Perspectives* 28(1): 167–88.

Ebbinghaus, B. 2011. *The Varieties of Pension Governance: Pension Privatization in Europe.* Oxford: Oxford University Press.

Ebbinghaus, B. 2015. "The privatization and marketization of pensions in Europe: a double transformation facing the crisis." *European Policy Analysis* 1(1): 56–73.

Ebbinghaus, B. 2019. "Multipillarisation remodelled: the role of interest organizations in British and German pension reforms." *Journal of European Public Policy* 26(4): 521–39. DOI: 10.1080/13501763.2019.1574875

Eichhorst, W. and Hassel, A. 2018. "Are There Austerity-Related Policy Changes in Germany?" In *Labour Market Reforms in the Era of Pervasive Austerity: A European Perspective*, edited by S. Theodoropoulou. Bristol: Policy Press.

Emmenegger, P., Häusermann, S., Palier, B., and Seeleib-Kaiser, M. (eds.). 2012. *The Age of Dualization: The changing face of inequality in deindustrializing societies.* Oxford; New York: Oxford University Press.

Engelen, E. 2003. "The logic of funding European pension restructuring and the dangers of financialisation." *Environment and Planning A* 35(8): 1357–72.

Erixon, L. 2011. "Under the Influence of Traumatic Events, New Ideas, Economic Experts and the ICT Revolution: The Economic Policy and Macroeconomic Performance of Sweden in the 1990s and 2000s." In *The Nordic Varieties of Capitalism* (*Comparative Social Research, Vol. 28*), edited by L. Mjøset. Bingley: Emerald Group Publishing Limited, 265–330.

Esping-Andersen, G. 1999. *Social Foundations of Postindustrial Economies*. Oxford: Oxford University Press.

Feldmann, M. 2006. "Emerging Varieties of Capitalism in Transition Countries: Industrial Relations and Wage Bargaining in Estonia and Slovenia." *Comparative Political Studies*, 39(7): 829–54. https://doi.org/10.1177/0010414006288261

Gingrich, J. and S. Häusermann. 2015. "The decline of the working-class vote, the reconfiguration of the welfare support coalition and consequences for the welfare state." *Journal of European Social Policy* 25(1): 50–75.

Guillén, A. M. and Pavolini, E. 2015. "Welfare states under strain in Southern Europe." Special issue, *European Journal of Social Security* 17(2): 147–57.

Hacker, J. S. 2006. *The Great Risk Shift: The New Economic Insecurity and the Decline of the American Dream*. Oxford, New York: Oxford University Press.

Hacker, J. S. and Pierson, P. 2010. "Winner-Take-All Politics: Public Policy, Political Organization, and the Precipitous Rise of Top Incomes in the United States." *Politics & Society* 38(2): 152–204.

Hale, T. 2018. "Universities and the allure of capital markets." *The Financial Times*. http://ftalphaville.ft.com/2018/03/06/2199103/universities-and-the-allure-of-capital-markets/ (last accessed August 31, 2018).

Hall, P. A. 2014. "Varieties of Capitalism and the Euro Crisis." *West European Politics* 37: 1223–43.

Hall, P. A. and Soskice, D. (eds.). 2001. *Varieties of Capitalism: The Institutional Foundations of Comparative Advantage*. Oxford, New York: Oxford University Press.

Hassel, A. 2003. *Wage Setting, Social Pacts and the Euro. A New Role for the State*. Amsterdam: Amsterdam University Press.

Hassel, A. 2006. *Wage setting, social pacts and the euro*. Amsterdam: Amsterdam University Press.

Hassel, A. 2014. "The Paradox of Liberalization—Understanding Dualism and the Recovery of the German Political Economy." *British Journal of Industrial Relations* 52(1): 57–81. https://doi.org/10.1111/j.1467-8543.2012.00913.x

Hassel, A., Wiss, T. and Naczyk, M. 2019. "The political economy of pension financialisation: public policy responses to the crisis." *Journal of European Public Policy* 26(4): 483–500.

Hassenteufel, P. and B. Palier. 2016. "Still the sound of silence? Towards a new phase in the Europeanization of welfare state policies in France." In *The Sovereign Debt Crisis, the EU and Welfare State Reform*, edited by C. de la Porte and E. Heins. London: Palgrave Macmillan, 181–205.

Hemerijck, A. 2013. *Changing Welfare States.* Oxford: Oxford University Press.

Hood, C. and Dixon, R. 2015. *A Government that Worked Better and Cost Less? Evaluating Three Decades of Reform and Change in UK Central Government.* Oxford, New York: Oxford University Press.

Höpner, M. 2019. The German undervaluation regime under Bretton Woods: How Germany became the nightmare of the world economy. MPIfG Working Paper.

Höpner, M. and Lutter, M. 2018. "The diversity of wage regimes: Why the Eurozone is too heterogeneous for the Euro." *European Political Science Review* 10(1): 71–96.

Höpner, M. and Spielau, A. 2015. Diskretionäre Wechselkursregime, Erfahrungen aus dem Europäischen Währungssystem, 1979–1998. MPIfG Discussion Paper 15/11.

Ibsen, C. and Knudsen, J.S. 2019. Growth Strategies and Welfare Reforms in Denmark. Paper presented at the 2019 SASE Conference, New York City.

Iversen, T. and Soskice, D. 2009. "Distribution and Redistribution: The Shadow of the Nineteenth Century." *World Politics* 61(3): 438–86. https://doi.org/10.1017/S004388710900015X

Iversen, T. and Soskice, D. 2018. "A Structural-Institutional Explanation of the Eurozone crisis." In *Welfare Democracies and Party Politics: Explaining Electoral Dynamics in Times of Changing Welfare Capitalism*, edited by P. Manow, B. Palier, and H. Schwander. Oxford, New York: Oxford University Press

Iversen, T. and Soskice, D. 2019. *Democracy and Prosperity Reinventing Capitalism through a Turbulent Century.* Princeton: Princeton University Press.

Jansson, P. 2013. How Do We Stop the Trend in Household Debt? Work on several fronts, Speech by Mr Per Jansson, Deputy Governor of the Sveriges Riksbank, at the SvD Bank Summit, Stockholm, December 3, 2013. https://www.bis.org/review/r131203h.pdf (last accessed May 15, 2019).

Jenkins, P. 2013. "Fannie and Freddie no model for UK housing." *The Financial Times* https://www.ft.com/content/3b6e50f6-9545-11e2-a4fa-00144feabdc0 (last accessed February 13, 2020).

Johnston, A. and A. Regan. 2016. "European monetary integration and the incompatibility of national varieties of capitalism." *JCMS: Journal of Common Market Studies* 54(2): 318–36.

Kazepov, Y. and Ranci, C. 2017. "Is every country fit for social investment? Italy as an adverse case." *Journal of European Social Policy* 27(1): 90–104.

Krebs, T. and Scheffel, M. 2013. Macroeconomic Evaluation of Labor Market Reform in Germany. IMF Working Paper No.13/42. https://www.imf.org/en/Publications/WP/Issues/2016/12/31/Macroeconomic-Evaluation-of-Labor-Market-Reform-in-Germany-40318

Korpi, W. and J. Palme. 2003. “New Politics and Class Politics in the Context of Austerity and Globalization: Welfare State Regress in 18 Countries, 1975–95.” *The American Political Science Review* 97(3): 425–46. https://doi.org/10.1017/S0003055403000789

Lafleur, J. M. and Stanek, M. 2018. “Southern European Migration Towards Northern Europe.” *IEMed Mediterranean Yearbook 2018*, 325–28.

Langley, P. 2008. *The Everyday Life of Global Finance: Saving and Borrowing in Anglo-America*. Oxford, New York: Oxford University Press.

Lewis-Beck, M. S. and Stegmaier, M. 2015. “Economic Evaluations and Electoral Consequences.” In *International Encyclopedia of the Social and Behavioral Sciences*, 2nd edition, vol. 7, edited by J. D. Wright. Oxford: Elsevier, 26–32.

Lumiste, R., Pefferly, R., and A. Purju, A. 2008. *Estonia’s Economic Development: Trends, Practices, and Sources. A Case Study*. Washington, DC: World Bank Commission on Growth and Development. https://documents.worldbank.org/en/publication/documents-reports/documentdetail/280881468025510249/estonias-economic-development-trends-practices-and-sources

Mares, I. 2003. *The Politics of Social Risk. Business and Welfare State Development*. Cambridge: Cambridge University Press.

Molina, O. and Rhodes, M. 2007. “The Political Economy of Adjustment in Mixed Market Economies: A Study of Spain and Italy.” In *Beyond Varieties of Capitalism: Conflict, Contradictions, and Complementarities in the European Economy*, edited by B. Hancké, M. Rhodes, and M. Thatcher. Oxford: Oxford University Press.

Morel, N. 2015. “Servants for the knowledge-based economy? The political economy of domestic services in Europe.” *Social Politics: International Studies in Gender, State & Society* 22(2): 170–92.

Morel, N., Palier, B., and Palme, J. (eds.). 2012. *Towards a Social Investment Welfare State? Ideas, Policies and Challenges*. Bristol: Policy Press.

Morgan, K. J. 2013. “Path Shifting of the Welfare State: Electoral Competition and the Expansion of Work-Family Policies in Western Europe.” *World Politics* 65(01): 73–115.

Naczyk, M. and Hassel, A. 2019. “Insuring individuals . . . and politicians: Financial services providers, stock market risk and the politics of private pension guarantees in Germany.” *Journal of European Public Policy* 26(4): 579–98.

Nölke, A. and Vliegenthart, A. 2009. “Enlarging the Varieties of Capitalism: The Emergence of Dependent Market Economies in East Central Europe.” *World Politics* 61(4): 670. https://doi.org/10.1017/S0043887109990098

OECD Family Database. n.d. FP3.2 http://www.oecd.org/social/family/database.htm

OECD iLibrary. n.d. https://www.oecd-ilibrary.org/education/population-with-tertiary-education/indicator/english_0b8f90e9-en?parentId=http%3A%2F%2Finstance.metastore.ingenta.com%2Fcontent%2Fthematicgrouping%2F025421e5-en

OECD Publishing. 2015. *In It Together: Why less inequality benefits all*. OECD Publishing.

Office for National Statistics. 2018. "Household disposable income and inequality in the UK: financial year ending 2017." Statistical bulletin, January 10, p. 7.

Palier, B. 2000. "'Defrosting' the French welfare state." *West European Politics* 23(2): 113–36.

Palier, B. 2005. *Gouverner la sécurité sociale: les réformes du système français de protection sociale depuis 1945*. Paris: Presses universitaires de France.

Palier, B. 2010. "The Dualizations of the French Welfare System." In *A Long Goodbye to Bismarck*, edited by B. Palier. Amsterdam: Amsterdam University Press, 73–99.

Palier, B. and Hay, C. 2017. "The Reconfiguration of the Welfare State in Europe: Paying its Way in an Age of Austerity." In *Reconfiguring European States in Crisis*, edited by D. King and P. Le Galès. Oxford: Oxford University Press.

Palier, B., Rovny, A.E. and Rovny, J. 2018. "European Disunion? Social and Economic Divergence in Europe, and their Political Consequences." In *Welfare Democracies and Party Politics: Explaining Electoral Dynamics in Times of Changing Welfare Capitalism*, edited by P. Manow, B. Palier, and H. Schwander. Oxford: Oxford University Press, 281–97.

Palier, B. and Thelen, K. 2010. "Institutionalizing Dualism: Complementarities and Change in France and Germany." *Politics & Society* 38(1): 119–48.

Pavolini, E., León, M. Guillén, A.M., and Ascoli, U. 2016. "From Austerity to Permanent Strain? The European Union and Welfare State Reform in Italy and Spain." In *The Sovereign Debt Crisis, the EU and Welfare State Reform*, edited by C. de La Porte and E. Heins. London: Palgrave Macmillan, 131–57.

Pierson, P. 1994. *Dismantling the Welfare State? Reagan, Thatcher and the politics of retrenchment.* Cambridge: Cambridge University Press.

Ragnitz, J. 2009. East Germany today: Successes and Failures. CESifo DICE Report 4/2009.

Regan, A. 2012. "The political economy of social pacts in the EMU: Irish liberal market corporatism in crisis." *New Political Economy* 17(4): 465–91.

Regan, A. and Brazys, S. 2018. "Celtic phoenix or leprechaun economics? The politics of an FDI-led growth model in Europe." *New Political Economy* 23(2): 223–38.

Ronchi, S. and Vesan, P. Forthcoming. "Reforming without investing: explaining non-social investment strategies in Italy." In *The World Politics of Social Investment (Volume II): The Politics of Varying Social Investment Strategies*, edited by J. L. Garritzmann, S. Häusermann, and B. Palier. Oxford: Oxford University Press.

Runnel, P., Pruulmann-Vengerfeldt, P., and Reinsalu, K. 2009. "The Estonian Tiger Leap from Post-Communism to the Information Society: From Policy to Practice." *Journal of Baltic Studies* 40(1): 29–51. https://doi.org/10.1080/01629770902722245

Sacchi, S. 2016. "Conditionality by Other Means: European Union Involvement in Italy's Structural Reforms in the Sovereign Debt Crisis." In *The Sovereign Debt Crisis, the EU and Welfare State Reform*, edited by C. de la Porte and E. Heins. London: Palgrave Macmillan, 159–79.

Scharpf, F.W. 1991. *Crisis and Choice in European Social Democracy (Cornell Studies in Political Economy).* Ithaca, New York: Cornell University Press.

Schulze Buschoff, K. and Hassel, A. 2018. "Beschäftigungsrekorde bei zunehmender Ungleichheit auf dem Arbeitsmarkt. Arbeitsmarktentwicklung und -politik in der dritten Regierung Merkel (2013 bis 2017)." In *Zwischen Stillstand, Politikwandel und Krisenmanagement*, edited by R. Zohlnhöfer and T. Saalfeld. Berlin: Springer, 397–14.

Seeleib-Kaiser, M., Saunders, A., and Naczyk, M.P. 2012. "Shifting the public-private mix." In *The Age of Dualization: The changing face of inequality in deindustrializing societies*, edited by Emmenegger et al. Oxford: Oxford University Press, 151–75.

Skocpol, T. and A. Hertel-Fernandez. 2016. "The Koch Network and Republican Party Extremism." *Perspectives on Politics* 14(3): 681–99.

Swenson, P.A. 2002. *Capitalists against Markets. The Making of Labor Markets and Welfare States in the United States and Sweden.* Oxford: Oxford University Press.

Szebehely, M. and G. Meagher. 2018. "Nordic eldercare–weak universalism becoming weaker?" *Journal of European Social Policy* 28(3): 294–8.

Szelenyi, I. 2011. "Post-Communist Welfare Pathways: Theorizing Social Policy Transformations in Central and Eastern Europe." *Contemporary Sociology* 40(1): 19–20.

Taylor-Gooby, P., Leruth, B., and Chung, H. 2017. "Where Next for the UK Welfare State?" In *After Austerity: Welfare State Transformation in Europe after the Great Recession*, edited by P. Taylor-Gooby, B. Leruth, and H. Chung. Oxford: Oxford University Press.

Terner Center. 2017. *Housing in Sweden: An Overview.* Terner Center for Housing Innovation, University of California Berkeley, November. http://ternercenter.berkeley.edu/uploads/Swedish_Housing_System_Memo.pdf (last accessed May 9, 2019).

Theodoropoulou, S. 2016. "National Social and Labour Market Policy Reforms in the Shadow of EU Bailout Conditionality: The Cases of Greece and Portugal." In *The Sovereign Debt Crisis, the EU and Welfare State Reform*, edited by C. De La Porte and E. Heins. London: Palgrave Macmillan, 95–130.

Vanhuysse, P. 2009. "Power, Order and the Politics of Social Policy in Central and Eastern Europe." In *Post-Communist Welfare Pathways: Theorizing Social Policy Transformations in Central and Eastern Europe*, edited by P. Vanhuysse and A. Cerami. Basingstoke and New York: Palgrave Macmillan, 53–70.

Vesan, P. and Pavolini, P. 2018. "The Italian Labour Market Policy Reforms and the Economic Crisis: Toward the End of the Italian Exceptionalism?" In *Austerity Strategies and Welfare State in Europe*, edited by S. Theodoropoulou. Bruxelles: ETUI.

Viebrock, E. and Clasen, J. 2009. "Flexicurity and welfare reform: A review." *Socio-Economic Review* 7(2): 305–31.

Viña, G. and Hale, T. 2016. "University challenge: the race for money, students and status." *The Financial Times*, June 23, 2016. https://www.ft.com/content/c662168a-38c5-11e6-a780-b48ed7b6126f (last accessed August 31, 2018).

Name Index

Note: Figures and notes are indicated by an italic '*f*' and '*n*', respectively, following the page number.

Subject Index

Note: Tables, figures, and notes are indicated by an italic '*t*', '*f*', and '*n*', respectively, following the page number.

The manufacturer's authorised representative in the EU for product safety is Oxford University Press España S.A. of el Parque Empresarial San Fernando de Henares, Avenida de Castilla, 2 – 28830 Madrid (www.oup.es/en or product.safety@oup.com). OUP España S.A. also acts as importer into Spain of products made by the manufacturer.

www.ingramcontent.com/pod-product-compliance
Ingram Content Group UK Ltd.
Pitfield, Milton Keynes, MK11 3LW, UK
UKHW020842150926
475595UK00004B/130
* 9 7 8 0 1 9 8 8 6 6 1 7 6 *